THE LETTS COMPANION TO

ASIAN

FOOD & COOKING

THE LETTS COMPANION TO ASIAN FOOD & COOKING

Jacki Passmore

CHARLES · LETTS · FOUNDED 1796 · *Letts*

First published in 1991
by Charles Letts & Co. Ltd
Diary House, Borough Road,
London SE1 1DW
by arrangement with Weldon Russell Pty Ltd

Produced by Weldon Russell Pty Ltd
4/52 Ourimbah Road
Mosman NSW 2088, Australia
A member of the Weldon International Group of companies

British Library Cataloguing in Publication Data
Letts companion to Asian food and cooking.
    1. Food. Asian dishes. Recipes
    I. Passmore, Jacki
    641.595

    ISBN 1-85238-151-5

Publisher: Elaine Russell
Managing editor: Dawn Titmus
Coordinating editors: Ariana Klepac, Alice Scott, Jacquelin Hochmuth
Copy editors: Christine McKinnon, Robert Coupe, Mardee Haidin Regan
Macintosh operator: Rachel Smith
Illustrator: Jan Smith
Design concept: Warren Penney
Finished art: Kathie Baxter Smith
Production: Jane Hazell

Printed in Singapore by Kyodo Printing Co., Ltd

A KEVIN WELDON PRODUCTION

INTRODUCTION

For over two decades I have been professionally involved with Asian food as a writer, teacher, publicist, researcher, consultant and cook. In that time there have been many occasions to regret the lack of an in-depth reference book on Asian ingredients and cooking in my library. I was naturally delighted when my publishers proposed that we fill that gap.

Our objective was to produce an easy-to-use reference to all common, and many uncommon, Asian ingredients, their origins and how to recognize, store and use them. This would be supported by a guide to the cooking methods, preparation techniques and utensils used in each Asian country, with a short history of the cuisine of each country. Our territory ranged from India (including Kashmir), Pakistan and Sri Lanka on the western boundary; east through Nepal, Thailand, Cambodia, Laos and Vietnam; south to Malaysia and the neighboring islands of Indonesia; then northwards across the massive expanse of China, Taiwan, the islands of the Philippines, and on to northernmost Japan and Korea.

With the support of an enthusiastic team, I began the arduous task of sifting through a wealth of information culled from diverse sources. Months were spent poring over cooking, history and travel books, newspaper and magazine articles, encyclopedias and botanical references. Many hours were spent in conference with cooking, social history and linguistic experts, seeking those elusive gems of information that we hope make this book both informative and entertaining.

With the task of composing the entries underway, we turned to recipes. In all, the book includes almost 400 recipes, of which more than 300 are designed to illustrate the use of an ingredient, cooking method or particular style of cuisine. The remaining recipes cover techniques of making sauces, wrappings, pastries, doughs, dips, dressings, spreads and so on. All are essential to the use and understanding of the many different styles of cooking that have evolved throughout Asia.

In all, approximately 1000 cross-references, many in the language of their origin, link up the more than 1000 entries for further information or quick comparisons with other ingredients. Where possible, we have included ethnic names for ingredients relevant to the cuisine of each country. For Chinese ingredients, Cantonese (backed up by pinyin) has been used, and in the Indian entries the predominant language used is Hindi. In addition, there are pronunciation guides for all foreign head words and cross-references.

In endeavoring to make the cuisines of Asia more accessible, we hope we have been able to convey to the reader some of the essence and magic of the countries of their origin.

How to Use this Book

This encyclopedia is arranged in alphabetical order, using names in English and in their anglicized Asian where they are more commonly known by their original Asian name. In other instances, the Asian name, or names by which ingredients are familiar, will appear in alphabetical order as a cross-reference, directed to the entry where the item is described fully. There are more than 1000 such cross-references throughout the book. In addition there are pronunciation guides for all main entries and cross references.

Cooking methods, preparation techniques and a history of the cuisine of each country appear under the name of the country, and this introductory text also includes sample menus from that country with a listing of the appropriate recipes. To find where recipes appear, simply refer to the Recipe Index at the end of the book.

For expediency, certain ingredients of a similar nature have been grouped together under a collective heading, for example, all cabbage entries appear under the heading "Cabbage, Chinese." Bean Pastes and Sauces; Curry Pastes, Powders and Sauces; Flours and Thickeners; Melons and Gourds; Mushrooms and Edible Fungi; and Seaweed are all collective entries.

Beneath each entry is information labeled "also known as," which includes many of the Asian equivalents and other English names by which this item is otherwise known. Additionally, a further footnote, "see also," leads to other entries or recipes in which the item is used, to which it is related, or from which other relevant information can be obtained.

Recipe Index

In order to find the location of recipes mentioned in the text simply refer to the Recipe Index on page 319.

Measurements

The following measurement conversions have been used in this book:

1 tablespoon	=	(1/2 fl oz/15 ml)
1 cup	=	(8 fl oz/250 ml)
1 quart	=	(40 fl oz/1.14 l)

CONSULTANTS AND CONTRIBUTORS

The author and publisher wish to extend their thanks to the following contributors for their valuable assistance in the research, recipe testing, cross-referencing and compilation of the vast amount of material needed for the completion of this book: Ann Bradley, Carol Feuerriegel, Annette Grimsdale, Cindy Limque, Kris Riordan, Devon Roser.

Similar thanks are extended to the following consultants who reviewed parts of the manuscript relevant to their particular fields of expertise: Jennifer Fernandes, Sydney, Indian entries; Wendy Hutton, Singapore, Malaysian, Singaporean and Philippine entries; Bui Chanh Thoi, Brisbane, Vietnamese entries; Joyce Jue, San Francisco, Thai entries.

BIBLIOGRAPHY

Anwar, Zarinah, *The MPH Cookbook*, MPH Distributors, Singapore, 1978

Shatia, Savitri, *Shahi Tukre,* P. B. Roy, A. H. Wheeler & Co., India, 1975

Chang, Kwang-Chih (ed.), *Food in Chinese Culture*, Yale University Press, London, 1977

China Pictorial, *Secrets of the Master Chefs of China*, US China Pictorial (ed.) and Allen D. Bragdon Publishers, New York, 1983

Dalal, Tarla, *Indian Vegetarian Cookery,* Ebury Press, London, 1986

Davidson, Alan, *Seafood of South-East Asia*, Federal Publications, Singapore, 1974

DeWit, Antoinette, and Borghese, Anita, *The Complete Book of Indonesian Cooking,* The Bobbs-Merrill Company, New York, 1973

Doi, Masaru, *Cook Japanese,* Kodansha International, Japan, 1964

Douglas, James Sholto, *Alternative Foods,* Pelham Books, London, 1978

Dowell, Philip, and Bailey, Adrian, *The Book of Ingredients,* Michael Joseph, London, 1980

Fitzgibbon, Theodora, *The Food of the Western World,* Quadrangle/The New York Times Book Co., New York, 1976

Greenberg, Sheldon, and Ortiz, Elisabeth Lambert, *The Spice of Life,* Blackrod, New York, 1983

Huang, Su-Huei, *Chinese Cuisine, Wei-Chuan Cooking Book*, ROC Dept of Home Economics, Taiwan, 1974

Jaffrey, Madhur, *A Taste of India*, Pavilion Books, London, 1985

Kagawa, Dr Aya, *Japanese Cook Book*, Japan Travel Bureau, Japan, 1949

Keys, John D., *Japanese Cuisine: A Culinary Tour*, Charles E. Tuttle Co. Inc., Japan, 1966

Lee, Mrs Chin Koon, *Mrs Lee's Cookbook*, Lee Chin Koon, Singapore, 1974

Mark, Willy, *Chinese Cookery Masterclass* New Burlington Books, UK, 1984

Mehta, Jeroo, *101 Parsi Recipes*, G. H. Mehta for Vakils, Feffer and Simons Private Ltd, India, 1973

Ngo, Bach, and Zimmerman, Gloria, *The Classic Cuisine of Vietnam*, Barron's/
Woodbury, New York, 1979

Nicholson, B. E. (text S. G. Harrison, G. B. Masefield, M. Wallis), *The Oxford
Book of Food Plants*, Oxford University Press, 1969

Ochse, J. J., *Vegetables of the Dutch East Indies*, Australian National University
Press, Canberra, 1977

Pandya, Michael, *Complete Indian Cookbook*, Hamlyn, London, 1981

Passmore, Jacki, *All Asian Cookbook*, Ure Smith, Sydney, 1978

———— *Indian Cookery*, Eyre Methuen, London, 1980

———— *Asia the Beautiful Cookbook*, Child and Associates, Sydney, 1987

Passmore, Jacki and Reid, Daniel, P., *The Complete Chinese Cookbook*,
Lansdowne Press, Sydney, 1982

Pinsuvana, Malulee, *Thai*, Watana Panich Co. Ltd, Bangkok, 1986

Ranneft, *Indocooking: Introduction to the Indonesian Kitchen*, Garuda, Sydney,
1980

Sakamoto, Nobuko, *The People's Republic of China Cookbook*, Random House,
New York, 1977

Singh, Manju Shivraj, *Royal Indian Cooking*, Golden Press, Sydney, 1987

Skrobanek, Detlef, Charle, Suzanne and Gay, Gerald, *The New Art of Indonesian
Cooking*, Simon & Schuster, Sydney, 1988

Solomon, Charmaine, *The Complete Asian Cookbook*, Weldons, Sydney, 1990

Spayde, Jon, *Japanese Cookery*, Doubleday, Sydney, 1984

Stuart, Anh Thu, *Vietnamese Cooking*, Angus and Robertson, Sydney, 1986

Takahashi, Kuwako, *The Joy of Japanese Cooking*, Shufunotomo Co. Ltd, Japan,
1986

Tsuji, Shizuo, *Japanese Cooking: A Simple Art*, Kodansha International Ltd,
Japan, 1984

Veerasawmy, E. P., *Indian Cookery*, Arco Publications, Great Britain, 1968
(fourth edition)

Villacorta-Alvarez, Herminia, *Philippine Cookery and Household Hints*, Labrador
Publishing, Philippines, 1970

Vista Productions Ltd, *Favourite Malay Cooking*, Vista Productions Ltd, Singa
pore, 1977

Wilson, Marie M., *Siamese Cookery*, Charles E. Tuttle & Co. Inc., USA, 1972
(fourth printing)

Yee, Rhoda, *Dim Sum*, Taylor & Ng, USA, 1977

Zainu'ddin, A. G., *How to Cook Indonesian Food*, Australian Indonesian Associa
tion of Victoria, Australia, 1967

A

AAMCHUR: (India) A gray-brown seasoning used in Indian cooking to tenderize meats and for its tart flavor. It is made by grinding sun-dried, sliced, unripe mango to a fine powder. *Aamchur* quickly loses its fresh flavor so should be bought in small amounts and stored in a tightly capped spice jar. Lemon, lime and pomegranate juices, or tamarind water, are all acceptable substitutes for the sour flavor of *aamchur* in a recipe. For tenderizing, an effective substitute is two teaspoons of grated, unripe mango or papaya to replace half a teaspoon of *aamchur*.

Also known as *amchor* (India); dried green mango; dried mango powder; green mango powder

---

ABALONE IN OYSTER SAUCE
Serves 4–6

2¹/₂ cups (20 oz / 620 g) canned whole abalone, drained
2 tbsps minced scallions (spring / green onions)
1 tsp minced ginger
2¹/₂ tbsps vegetable oil
³/₄ cup (6 fl oz / 180 ml) chicken stock
1 tsp sugar
1 head lettuce, rinsed and separated
2¹/₂ tbsps oyster sauce
cornstarch (cornflour)
white pepper
1 tbsp finely minced ham

Cut abalone horizontally into thin slices. Stir-fry scallions and ginger in the oil for 1 minute; add abalone and stir-fry briefly. Add chicken stock and sugar and simmer for 5 minutes. Remove. Add lettuce and cook until limp, about 1 minute. Drain and arrange on platter. Add oyster sauce to pan and thicken sauce with a little cornstarch mixed with cold water to make a paste. Stir until thickened; return abalone to reheat. Add white pepper to taste and pour over lettuce. Sprinkle ham over finished dish.

See also: MANGO GREEN; TANDOORI CHICKEN TIKKAS (recipe)

ABALONE: (*Haliotis ruber* black lip, *H. laevigata* green lip) A mollusk inhabiting rocky coastal inlets which is harvested in Japan, Korea, Australia, Mexico and certain parts of China. It attaches itself firmly to rocks and ledges by its edible part, a muscle known as the "foot" or epipodium. The abalone foot is gray-brown in color, nestled in an oval-shaped, hard shell with an opalescent green lining. Japanese usually cook young abalone by a method known as *saka-mushi* (sake-steaming). Although abalone has a slightly chewy texture, it has a unique flavor. In China it is an expensive delicacy and the best-quality, fresh or dried abalone is usually affordable only on very

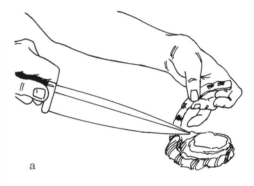

a

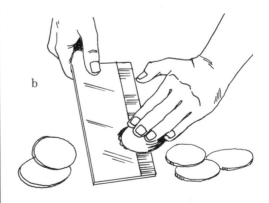

b

a. Trim ruff b. Slice horizontally

special occasions when it is served as one of the feature dishes in a banquet menu.

CANNED WHOLE OR SLICED ABALONE usually lacks the subtle flavor of fresh abalone and has a chewier texture, but is less expensive. In China, abalone is trimmed of its surrounding ruff and is used whole, or is sliced by pressing it firmly on top and slicing horizontally. It is cooked by simmer-stewing or braising and is most commonly served over braised lettuce in a sauce based on Chinese oyster sauce.

DRIED ABALONE: Like other dried seafoods, dried abalone is highly regarded by the Chinese, often in preference to the fresh product. They believe that eating it delays senility and increases fertility.

Soak dried abalone in cold water for six hours. Drain and scrub with brush. Cover with cold water, bring to a boil and simmer for four hours. Drain, rinse with cold water, trim off ruffled edge. Slice from top to bottom to give small, oval-shaped pieces, or slice horizontally. Whole abalone should be scored with the point of a sharp knife in a crosshatch pattern to tenderize and allow seasonings to penetrate.

FRESH ABALONE in its shell can be kept for several days in clean salt or fresh water, but change the water daily. A sharp, flexible knife is needed to remove it from its shell. The black, viscous coating should be scrubbed off with a brush, and the mouth, with its raspy radula, trimmed off. The frilled mantle or ruff around its edge can be left on or trimmed.

Also known as *bow yeu* (China); *awabi* (Japan)
See also: ABALONE IN OYSTER SAUCE (recipe); CHINA, CUTTING AND SLICING TECHNIQUES (HORIZONTAL SLICING)

ABALONE MUSHROOM: see MUSHROOMS AND EDIBLE FUNGI (OYSTER MUSHROOMS)

ABON: (*AH-BON*, Indonesia) see AGAR AGAR

ABURAGE: (*AH-BOU-RA-GUE*, Japan) see BEAN CURD (COTTON)

ACHUETE/ACHWETE: (*A-CHOO-UE-TE*, Philippines) see ANNATTO SEED

ADAS MANIS: (*AH-DOES MAH-NIECE*, Indonesia) see DILL

ADOBADO: (*A-DOE-BA-DOE*) see PHILIPPINES, COOKING METHODS

ADOBO: (*A-DOE-BO*) see PHILIPPINES, COOKING METHODS

ADOBO CHICKEN: (recipe) see CHICKEN

AEMONO: (*AH-E-MO-NO*, Japan) A Japanese term describing "dressed foods," which are salad-like dishes served chilled. *Aemono* dishes comprise one or several ingredients—usually chicken, seafood or vegetables—in a compatible dressing, which is made of a creamy to thick consistency by using puréed bean curd, ground sesame seeds or miso as the base. There are a number of classic *aemono* dressings, including a most delicious and unusual one which uses creamy sea urchin as its main ingredient. Like a salad, *aemono* dishes can be served at the beginning of a meal to replace an appetizer. They are also served at some meals towards the end, before the rice. An appealing tradition is the serving of a selection of small *aemono* dishes before dinner with hot *sake*. Another form of salad frequently served in Japan is *sunomono*, otherwise known as "vinegared food." They are small servings, like *aemono*, but dressed in tart vinegar dressings. A vinegar-dressed dish is served with most Japanese meals as a flavor highlighter, and particularly with fried foods to balance the oiliness.

Also known as "dressed foods;" *sakizuke*; *tsuki dashi*; *zenzai* (Japan)
See also: SUNOMONO

CRISP JELLO SWEETS
Serves 8–10

2 cups (16 fl oz / 500 ml) water
1 tbsp powdered agar agar
³/₄ cup (6 oz / 180 g) sugar
food coloring

Gently boil water with sugar and *agar agar* for 2 minutes. Divide mixture evenly among 4 bowls. Color each with a different food coloring. Pour into tiny wet molds and cool. Unmold. Serve as they are or floating in sweetened, thick coconut milk.

AGAR AGAR: (*Gelidium amansii*) A gelatin obtained from seaweed. Many types of red algae are now used to make *agar agar* particularly *Eucheuma* sp. and *Gelidium* sp. *Agar agar* has been used in China since AD 300. The method of extraction of the gelatinous properties of seaweed is thought to have been discovered only in the seventeenth century after a cook threw the remains of a seaweed jelly dish onto a snow-covered bush and later discovered that the water had run off leaving the jelly attached in strands. The cook was able to boil up the strands and use them again. The method of freezing and thawing to purify the gelatin is still used today in some commercial *agar agar* processing factories. *Agar agar* comes in powdered, strand and sheet forms and, unlike gelatin, is boiled for use. The many types of jellied sweets served in Thailand and the Philippines owe their firmness to *agar agar*, which is suited to hot, tropical climates. Once it sets, it does not melt, lose shape or stick to the molds. *Agar agar* has a melting point of 185°F (85°C) and gels at 110°F (43°C). Powdered *agar agar* is brought to a boil in water, and then simmered briefly; the filaments or sheets should be soaked to soften before boiling.

Also known as *kyauk kyaw* (Burma); *dai choy goh* (China); *abon* (Indonesia); *kanten* (Japan); *gulaman* (Philippines); *chun chow* (Sri Lanka); Ceylon moss; Chinese gelatin; grass jelly; heavenly grass; Japanese gelatin; seaweed gelatin; seaweed jelly

See also: CRISP JELLO SWEETS (recipe); SEAWEED

AGEDOFU: (Japan) see BEAN CURD (FRIED)

AGEMONO: (*AH-GUE-MO-NO*) see JAPAN, COOKING METHODS

AI GWA: (*NGAI-GWA*, China) see EGGPLANT (WHITE)

AJI NO MOTO: (*AH-JEE-NO-MO-TO*, Japan) see MONOSODIUM GLUTAMATE

AJI-SHIOYAKI: (*AH-JEE-SHI-O-YA-KEE*) see JAPAN, COOKING METHODS

AJOWAN: (*AJ-WAA-AN*, India) see AJWAIN

AJWAIN: (*AJ-WAA-AN*, India) *Carom ajowan* is a small, tear-shaped, ochre-colored seed spice from a shrub of the same family as cumin and parsley. It resembles lovage and is allied to licorice. The aroma of the crushed seeds is similar to the herb thyme. Although it has been used in India for centuries, it is little known in other parts of Asia. *Ajwain* is added

sparingly to curries and rice dishes and is used in pickle- and chutney-making as well as to flavor *papadams*. An infusion of *ajwain* may be taken as a medication for stomach ailments.

Also known as *ajowan, carom, omum* (India)
See also: TANDOORI BAKED POMFRET (recipe)

AKNI: (*AA-KH-NEE*, India) see GARHI YAKHNI
ALAMANG: (*A-LA-MANG*, Philippines) see SHRIMP PASTE

ALBACORE: (*Thunnis alalunga*) This long-finned tuna is common in the Pacific and Indian oceans and is fished by the Japanese who use its tender white to delicate rose-pink meat in *sushi* and as *sashimi*.
See also: SASHIMI; SUSHI

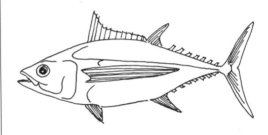

Albacore

ALMOND BEAN CURD: see BEAN CURD
ALMOND, BITTER: see APRICOT KERNEL

ALMOND JELLO WITH DICED FRUIT
Serves 6

1¹/2 tbsps unflavored gelatin
¹/2 cup (4 fl oz / 125 ml) water, boiling
1¹/2 cups (12 fl oz / 375 ml) lukewarm or almond milk
¹/2 cup (4 fl oz / 125 ml) light (whipping / single) cream
2 tsps almond essence (extract)
1¹/2 tbsps sugar
1¹/2 cups (10 oz / 300 g) diced fruit

Sprinkle gelatin over water, stand until softened then stir to dissolve. Add milk, cream, almond essence and sugar; mix well. Pour into a lightly oiled dish, cover and refrigerate until set. Cut into diamond-shaped pieces and divide between 6 dessert dishes, adding fruit.

ALUM: A colorless salt known as potassium alum—an ingredient in baking powder. In Asia it is used by Philippine, Thai and Vietnamese cooks to retain the crisp texture of fruit in desserts. Chinese cooks use it in vegetable pickles and as a preservative for such edible, peripheral parts of pork as ears and snouts. It is a white, crystalline substance resembling coarse salt and is sold in crumbled form or in larger pieces resembling Chinese rock sugar, although clearer in color.

Also known as *yaki myoban* (burnt alum) (Japan); *tawas* (Philippines); *poon dang* (Thailand); *phen* (Vietnam)

See also: LIME SOLUTION

AMARANTH: (*Amaranthus tricolor*) A relative of spinach and with a similar flavor, this leafy vegetable is an ancient food, being mentioned in early Chinese records, and is eaten throughout Asia. There are two types of amaranth in popular use. The green type closely resembles spinach and has a mild, watercress-like flavor, while the other has red stems with the red color spreading onto the leaves. Known in China as "red in snow," it grows in early spring while there is still snow on the ground. It is eaten fresh and is also salt-pickled. Generally the green one is preferred, although both are used extensively in vegetable dishes,

Amaranth

salads and sauces. It should be thoroughly rinsed and only very lightly cooked by steaming or stir-frying. Amaranth is highly nutritious and is believed to improve the functioning of kidneys, enhance breastfeeding and purify the blood. In Asia there are many different types of spinach-like vegetable including *kangkong*, otherwise known as water spinach, and the long-leafed, Japanese *horenzo*.

Also known as *een choy, hsien ts'ai, yin choy* (China); *chholai-ka-sag, saag* (India); *bajem* (Indonesia); *hiyu* (Japan); *bayam* (Malaysia); *kulitis* (Philippines); Chinese spinach; spineless amaranth

See also: KANGKONG; LAMB WITH CREAMED SPINACH SAUCE (recipe); SPINACH

AMCHOR: (*AM-CHOOR,* India) see AAMCHUR

AMCHUNDAN: (*UM-CHUN-DARN,* China) (quail) see EGG

AME: (*AH-ME,* Japan) A sweet jelly made from millet that is used in confectionery and also to flavor fish dishes. It is not to be confused with *an,* the sweet red-bean paste made from *azuki* beans.

AMORPHOPHALUS KONJAC: This perennial plant is known to have grown in the Chinese province of Sichuan for over 2000 years, and it has an equally long history in Japan. The tuber of the *amorphophalus konjac* is starchy and gray in color, similar to certain types of taro. Its unattractive appearance gave it its Chinese name *mo yu,* which translates as "devil's taro," and in Japan its popular name is "devil's tongue." It requires several different processes to make it palatable. In China "devil's taro" is peeled, pounded and boiled until the fibers break down, then solidified into a bean curd-like mass by adding a lime preparation. This is seasoned with five different flavors—salty, sweet, sour, tart and pungent—to make it into a tasty cake which is then known as "black bean curd" for its similarity in texture to bean curd. It is deep gray and has a soft and slippery feel in the mouth. Black bean curd is cut into strips, boiled briefly to remove any residue of lime, and added to braised dishes such as chicken, with broad bean paste and Sichuan peppercorns to season. "Snowed" black bean curd has been frozen, causing it to become porous and chewier in texture. It is usually cooked with tender meat like chicken for an interesting combination of textures.

KONNYAKU: "Devil's tongue" in Japan is an important ingredient which is known as *konnyaku*. It is made into unrefined (black) *konnyaku* by the same method as described for black bean curd, and refined (white) *konnyaku*, which has been filtered and bleached to a pale gray color. It is usually sold in small rectangular slabs that keep for some time. Fresh *konnyaku* may be bought, like bean curd, in tubs of water at Oriental food stores. *Konnyaku* is cut into strips to add to soups and braised dishes.

Also known as *ito konnyaku, konnyaku* (Japan); black bean curd; devil's taro; devil's tongue; "snowed" black bean curd

See also: BEAN CURD BY-PRODUCTS (BLACK); LIME SOLUTION; NOODLES (SHIRATAKI); SUKIYAKI (recipe)

AMYLE ESSENCE (EXTRACT): (*Amylacetate ester*) A clear, liquid, artificial banana-flavored essence used in Thai desserts.

Also known as *nam nomao* (Thailand)
See also: FLAVORINGS

AN: (*AH-NN*, Japan) see AZUKI BEAN; RED BEAN PASTE, SWEET

ANAGO: (*AH-NA-GO*, Japan) see EEL

ANCHOVY: (*Stolephorus heterolobus*) From the family Engraulidae, the long-jawed anchovy is extensively fished throughout Southeast Asia. Eaten fresh or marinated, salted and dried, it is one of the main fish used in fish sauce and other fermented fish products in Asia. The fry of anchovies is known in Southeast Asia as *ikan bilis* or *ikan teri* and is similar to whitebait. The tiny whole fish are generally salted, then sun-dried to use as a seasoning and condiment as well as to flavor soups and sauces. Dried *ikan bilis* is crisp-fried to serve as a snack or accompaniment to a curry meal. *Niboshi* is a similar fish used in Japan and Korea to make a fish-flavored broth and to fry as a side dish.

Also known as *nga-man-gyaung, yay-kyin-ngar,* (Burma)*; kung yue* (China)*; ikan bilis, ikan teri* (Indonesia)*; niboshi* (Japan)*; ikan bilis*

(Malaysia)*; dilis* (Philippines)*; pla bai pai, pla hua awn, pla katak* (Thailand)*; ca com* (Vietnam)
See also: BAGOONG; FISH; FISH, PRESERVED; FISH SAUCE; IKAN BILIS CRISPLY FRIED (recipe)

IKAN BILIS CRISPLY FRIED
Serves 8–10

8 oz (250 g) dried ikan bilis
1 large onion, chopped
2–3 green chilies, seeded
1½ tsp salt
1 tbsp sugar
2 tsps pepper
deep-frying oil
½ cup (4 oz / 120 g) shelled raw peanuts

Remove the heads from the *ikan bilis,* as they can be bitter when cooked. Rinse thoroughly in cold water and dry well. Grind onion and chilies to a paste, adding salt, sugar and pepper. Heat oil to smoking; reduce heat. Fry *ikan bilis* until lightly colored; drain. Fry onion paste separately in 2 tbsps oil for 3–4 minutes, until golden. Add *ikan bilis* and peanuts. Cook on high heat until crisp. Serve as a side dish.

ANCIENT EGG: see THOUSAND-YEAR EGG

ANDE: (*AN-DAA*, India) see EGG

ANGKAK: (*ANG-KAK,* Philippines) see FOOD COLORINGS

ANIS: (*AH-NIS*, Philippines) see ANISE, STAR; ANISEED

ANISEED (Anise): (*Pimpinella anisum*) A small brown, licorice-tasting seed from the anise plant. Known since early times in the Middle East and Asia, it is recorded that aniseed was known in Java (Indonesia) before AD 1200. The seed should be lightly roasted before use and can be used both whole and ground in marinades, pickles, chutneys and curried dishes. It is also used for its delicate licorice taste in liqueurs and sweets. In many countries it is an ingredient in digestive aids, while the whole seeds are also chewed to aid digestion and sweeten the breath. The flavor of anise and fennel is very similar, leading to a certain interchangeability of their Asian names,

many translating as "fennel" or "sweet fennel."
Also known as *pa chio* (China); *sonf* (India); *jintan manis* (Indonesia); *anis* (Philippines); *cay vi* (Vietnam)

ANISE, STAR: (*Illucium verum*) The seed pods of a tree of the Magnolia family. The tan-colored eight-pointed pods resemble stars, and when dried the segments split to reveal a shiny, flat, light brown seed in each point. Star anise has a pronounced licorice flavor. The ground spice is an essential ingredient in Chinese five-spice powder and whole or broken pods are frequently used in Chinese braised and stewed dishes. They are sometimes added to other smoke fuel for Chinese smoked fish and poultry. Star anise is frequently used in Vietnamese simmered dishes, but used to a lesser extent in other parts of Southeast Asia.

Whole star anise

Also known as *baht ghok* (Chinese); *bunga lawang* (Indonesia, Malaysia); *anis* (Philippines); *poy kak bua* (Thailand); *cay hoy* (Vietnam)
See also: FIVE-SPICE POWDER (recipe); HANOI BEEF SOUP (recipe); SPICED GROUND RICE (recipe)

ANITHI: (*ANEE-THEE*, India) see DILL

ANJAN: (*ANCHAN*, Thailand) The blue flower of a plant native to Thailand from which the color is extracted and used to dye foods, particularly jicama (yam bean) and water chestnuts used in desserts. The petals or whole flowers of the anjan plant are lightly crushed

in water to obtain the desired coloring.
See also: FOOD COLORING

ANNATTO SEED: (*Bixa orellana*) The red-brown, almost triangular small seeds from a small flowering tree native to tropical America, *annatto* seeds are used widely in Latin American cooking to impart a subtle but distinct flavor and red color. *Annatto* was introduced to the Philippines by Spanish traders where it found ready acceptance as a flavoring and coloring. The seeds are usually fried in oil or fat until they release their color and fragrance, then they are discarded and the oil used in a particular recipe. *Annatto* seeds are used by the Chinese to color foods such as roast pork and cold meats. The outer orange pulp surrounding the seeds is also used as a food dye.

ANNATTO LARD is used extensively in Philippine cooking. *Annatto* seeds are cooked in lard until the fat turns a bright red. It is then strained and the seeds discarded.
Also known as *achuete, achwete* (Philippines); *hot dieu mau* (Vietnam)
See also: FOOD COLORING; KARE-KARE (recipe); OILS AND FATS (LARD); ROAST PORK CANTONESE (recipe); VIETNAMESE-STYLE BEIJING DUCK (recipe)

AO-JISO: (*AH-O-JI-SO*, Japan) see BEEFSTEAK PLANT
AO-NEGI: (*AH-O-NE-GI*, Japan) see LEEK, ASIAN
AO-NORI: (*AH-O-NO-REE*, Japan) see SEAWEED
AO-TOGARASHI: (*AH-O-TOU-GA-RA-SHI*, Japan) see PEPPER

AO-YOSE: (*AH-O-YO-SE*, Japan) A natural green coloring obtained from the leaves of the spinach plant, that may be used to color various sweet and savory foods and confections. (Powdered green tea, *matcha*, is also used as a food coloring.)

To make 1 tablespoon of *ao-yose* grind 2 cups spinach leaves in a food processor with 1/2 cup water. Strain into saucepan and add another 1/2 cup water. Boil for 2 minutes. Place a piece of fine, clean cloth in a colander and pour in the liquid. Gently squeeze out the water leaving behind the bright green color.
See also: FOOD COLORING

APOG: (*A-POG*, Philippines) see LIME SOLUTION

APPA: (*AA-UP-PA*, Sri Lanka) Bowl-shaped, leavened rice pancakes eaten in Sri Lanka and throughout southern India as bread, usually at breakfast, often going by the name "hoppers." The dough, made from ground rice, rice flour and coconut milk, is leavened with a coconut toddy, the sap of the coconut palm, which causes it to ferment into a soft, spongy dough. *Appas* are cooked in a covered hemispherical pan resembling a miniature Chinese wok and known as a *cheena chatti*, literally "Chinese pan." When cooked they have a soft, spongy texture and appetizing yeasty taste. Another type of *appa* is formed from fine strings of dough, known as "string hopper." String hopper dough, cooked as a kind of lavish *pullao* (cooked rice dish) with hard-cooked eggs, nuts, peas and chili sauce, is served on festive occasions in Sri Lanka. *Appas* or string hoppers cooked with a whole egg broken into the center are known as *bittara appa*, a popular breakfast food. Yet another type of fermented dough breakfast bread is the *idli* or *iddi appa*, which is steamed in a special pan containing several recesses.
Also known as *appams, appe,* hoppers, *kallappams,* string hoppers, *wellayappams* (Sri Lanka)

APPA
Yields 10–12

*1 tsp active dry yeast
2 tsps sugar
2 tbsps warm water
1¼ cups (5 oz / 145 g) rice flour
1½ tsps salt
2 cups (16 fl oz / 500 ml) thick coconut milk*

Dissolve yeast with sugar and water. Set aside for 5 minutes. Sift flour and salt into a bowl, add coconut milk and yeast and mix to a smooth batter. Cover and leave overnight. Grease hopper pan (*cheena chatti*), place on moderate heat and pour in ⅓ cup batter. Tilt pan so batter forms a circle; cover and cook until firm and dryish. Ease hopper away from pan with a blunt knife. Cook remaining batter in the same way.

See also: BREAD, INDIAN; IDLIS; UTENSILS, BREAD AND PASTRY MAKING

BITTARA APPA

Prepare batter from Appa recipe. Heat the hopper pan, add ⅓ cup batter and tilt pan slightly. Crack an egg into pan taking care not to break yolk. Cover and cook over low heat until egg is cooked.

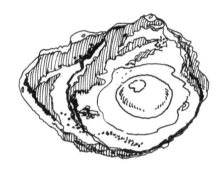

Bittara appa

APPAMS: (*UPPAM*, Sri Lanka) see APPA

APPE: (*AA-UP-PE*, Sri Lanka) see APPA

APRICOT KERNEL: (*Prunus armeniaca*) This small flat nut—the kernel removed from an apricot seed—has a distinct apricot aroma and a bitter flavor. It is used medicinally and is the source of the food flavoring known as almond essence. Although it looks like a small sweet almond, it is not at all related. The apricot, now grown all over the world, was originally native to China. The fruit's bitter kernel was used by the Chinese in medicines for respiratory ailments but in its raw state, it is toxic and must be treated before eating. The kernels are boiled briefly in water, then dried in a warm oven for at least 20 minutes to detoxify. Apricot kernels are used in some Chinese vegetarian dishes, but more often in desserts and are usually ground and mixed

15

with water to make a strong-tasting liquid which is served as a warm soup. As almond essence, it is used to flavor the sweet known as almond jello. Apricot kernels are sold by Chinese herbalists and in some Chinese food stores.
Also known as *p'ien t'ao jen* (China); bitter almond; Chinese almond
See also: ALMOND JELLO WITH DICED FRUIT (recipe)

ARAK: (*AR-RUCK*) see WINE, ASIAN

ARROWHEAD: (*Sagittaria sinensis*) A small, tuberous vegetable used in Japan and China, where it is grown extensively in Sichuan and Yunnan provinces. It resembles a lily bulb with smooth, beige skin and peeling, thin, brown, layered leaves. It has a bland, slightly sweet taste, and can be used in the same way as a potato.
Also known as *tsee goo* (China); *kuwai* (Japan)

Arrowhead tuber

ARROWROOT STARCH: see FLOURS AND THICKENERS

ARVI: (*ARE-VEE*, Indonesia) see YAM

ASADO: (*A-SA-DOE*) see PHILIPPINES, COOKING METHODS

ASAFOETIDA: (India) (*Ferula asafoetida*) A seasoning obtained from the milky resin of a plant of the Umbelliferae family, originally grown in Afghanistan and Iran. Today it is widely cultivated in the Middle East and used extensively in Indian cooking. It has an unpleasant, glue-like smell which is not transmitted to the food, and it is used in minute quantities to impart a subtle flavor. Its more important role is as an antiflatulent, and it comes in powdered form which can be added directly to a dish, or lump form—a piece the size of a pea, attached to the inside of a pan lid, is usually enough for one dish.
Also known as *sheingho* (Burma); *hing* (India); *perunkayan* (Sri Lanka)

ASAM/ASEM: (*AH-SUM*, Indonesia, Malaysia) see TAMARIND
ASAM GELUGOR: (*AH-SUM GE-LOO-GORE*, Malaysia) see TAMARIND
ASPARAGUS BEAN: see BLACK-EYED PEA (BEAN)
ASPARAGUS PEA: see WINGED BEAN
ATIS: (*A-TIS*, Philippines) see ROSE APPLE
ATSU-AGE: (*AH-TZU-AH-GUE*, Japan) see BEAN CURD (FRIED)
ATTA: (*AA-TAA*, India) see FLOURS AND THICKENERS
AWABI: (*AH-WA-BEE*, Japan) see ABALONE

AZUKI BEAN: (*Phaseolus angularis*) Small, dull, red-colored beans that grow on a plant native to China. They are recognizable by their almost square shape. The dried beans are used in China, Japan and Korea in many dessert dishes: a thick, sweetened paste of the beans is used to stuff sweet buns and pastries. In China, since the Han Dynasty (206 BC–AD 220), red beans have been used as food or offerings on festive occasions to invite prosperity and good luck. In some Asian households the dried beans are scattered around the house at New Year to ward off evil spirits. The whole, boiled beans are served over shaved ice as a summer dessert in Japan. In other parts of Asia they are boiled and seasoned like lentils to serve as a savory side dish. Dried *azuki* beans are sold by weight and can be kept in an airtight container for several years. They should be washed before use and cooked by boiling in lightly salted water. Puréed beans sold in cans are ideal for desserts and making ice cream, but they may be too moist to use as stuffing.

AN: (Japan) A sweetened paste of ground *azuki* beans which is available in smooth (*koshi-an*) and crunchy (*tsubushi-an*) forms.

SARASHI-AN: (Japan) A flour of ground *azuki* beans is made in Japan for use in desserts.
Also known as *hong dow* (China); *adzuki* beans; dried red beans; red beans; Tientsin red beans
See also: RED BEAN PASTE, SWEET

SWEET RED BEAN SOUP WITH MOCHI
Serves 6

3 cups (8 oz / 250 g) cooked azuki *beans*
2¹/2 cups (20 fl oz / 625 ml) water
1 cup (8 oz / 250 g) sugar
1–2 pieces mochi, *sliced*

In a large pan boil beans with water and sugar until thick but still liquid. Grill *mochi*, turning frequently until browned on the surface. Place *mochi* into deep dishes and pour on the red bean soup.

B

BABOY LETSONIN: (*BA-BOY LIT-SOO-NEEN*, Philippines) see PORK (SUCKLING PIG)

BABY CORN: see CORN (MINIATURE)

BACON, DRIED: see PORK, CURED

BACON, FRESH: see PORK (FRESH BACON)

BAECHU: (*BAE-CHOO*, Korea) see CABBAGE, CHINESE (NAPA)

BAGHAR: (*BA-GHAAR*, India) A mixture of ingredients fried in ghee, which is poured over a finished *dal* (lentil) dish. It is particularly popular in the state of Rajasthan. *Baghar* may include sliced onion, garlic and chilies with whole spices such as cumin, coriander or mustard seeds.
See also: INDIA, COOKING METHODS (CHAMAK); OILS, FLAVORED; SPICED RED LENTILS (recipe)

BAGOLAN: (*BAH-GO-LAN*, Philippines) see CUTTLEFISH

BAGOONG: (*BA-GO-ONG*, Philippines) *Bagoong* is the name given to salted and fermented shrimp (*alamang*) or small fish such as *dilis* (anchovies). They are packed in earthenware pots and cured for several weeks. *Bagoong* is used as a condiment or is cooked with other ingredients. The thin salty liquid that accumulates over the fish is drawn off and used separately as a condiment or seasoning sauce and is known as *patis*.
See also: ANCHOVY; FISH PASTE; FISH, PRESERVED (FERMENTED); PATIS

BAGOONG

1 part coarse salt
3 parts fresh dilis *or* alamang

Layer *dilis* or *alamang* in earthenware or glass jars, salting each layer generously. Cover and cure for 2 weeks for *dilis*, 3 weeks for *alamang*.

BAHT GHOK: (*BART KOK,* China) see ANISE, STAR

BAICAI: (*BAKCHOY,* China) see CABBAGE, CHINESE (BOK CHOY)

BAIGAN: (*BAIN-GAN,* India) see EGGPLANT

BAI HORAPA: (*BAI HORAPHAA,* Thailand) see BASIL (SWEET)

BAI KAREE: (*BAI KAREE,* Thailand) see CURRY LEAF

BAI KA-ROW: (*BAI KRA-PAO,* Thailand) see BASIL (PURPLE)

BAI TS'AI: (*BAK NGA-CHOY,* China) see CABBAGE, CHINESE (BOK CHOY)

BAJEM: (*BA-YEM,* Indonesia) see AMARANTH

BAKUDAI: (*BAH-KOO-DAH-I*) see JAPAN, GARNISHES

BALACHAUNG: (*BAR-LA-CHAUNG,* Burma) A strong-tasting side dish of fried, dried shrimp that accompanies most Burmese meals.

BALACHAUNG
Yields 2 cups (16 fl oz / 500 ml)

1 lb (500 g) dried shrimp
1 ³/₄ cups (14 fl oz / 430 ml) vegetable oil
3 tbsps minced garlic
2 tbsps minced scallions (spring / green onions)
1 tbsp minced ginger
1 tsp turmeric
1¹/₂ tbsps shrimp paste
salt

Grind shrimp to fine shreds in a food processor. Heat oil in a pan and fry garlic, scallions and ginger until lightly golden. Remove with a slotted spoon. Fry shrimp and turmeric until aromatic. Remove from the pan. Add shrimp paste to pan and mash until smooth. Return all ingredients to pan; add salt to taste. Cook together on medium heat until very aromatic. Cool. Store in a jar.

BALUT: (*BA-LOOT,* Philippines) The eating of *balut,* fertilized duck eggs, at the stage when the embryo has just turned into a chick, is a tradition peculiar to the Philippines. It is believed to increase masculine strength and potency.

BAMBOO LEAF: The long, narrow leaves of certain types of bamboo are used, like coconut leaves and strips of banana leaf, as wrappers for certain foods to be boiled, grilled or steamed. They are sold dried, in packs of about 30, and should be soaked in boiling water to soften before use. They impart a subtle and agreeable flavor to the food. Coconut leaves—individual leaf sections from the coconut palm frond—are used in the same way. Strips of banana leaf can be substituted.

See also: LEAVES USED AS FOOD CONTAINERS, PLATES, WRAPPERS

BAMBOO MUSTARD CABBAGE: see CABBAGE, CHINESE (CHUK GAAI CHOY)

BAMBOO SHOOT: (*Dendrocalamus asper*) The bamboo plant, native to Asia, makes an invaluable contribution to life in all Asian countries except India. Its stems and leaves are used in housing, its leaves in protective garments and food wrapping. It is made into cooking and eating utensils, astrological, religious and ceremonial paraphernalia, furniture, storage containers and luggage. Bamboo slips were used to document China's first recorded history. As if this indispensable plant was not already offering enough, its fresh young shoots were also discovered to be a food with a unique, sappy flavor and crunchy texture. Fresh bamboo shoots are easily recognizable—cylindrical shapes of overlaid, green-tinted, yellowish, papery leaves coming to a point at the top. The leaves must be removed to reveal the buff-colored shoot, which has a fibrous texture, and when cut in cross section shows an intricate pattern of overlapping layers that repeat the pattern of the external husk. Fresh bamboo shoots contain a toxin, hydrocyanic acid, that must be dispersed by parboiling. Slice off the leafy husk and base of the shoot. Cook whole or in chunks for at least five minutes or until the shoots no longer taste bitter. Drain, rinse and store in cold water. Unpeeled bamboo shoots can be kept in the refrigerator for at least a week. Peeled and parboiled, either prepared at home or purchased ready made from specialist Chinese markets, they will keep only one or two days in a plastic bag or up to five in a container of

18

water. They can be frozen, but the texture will become more fibrous. Canned bamboo shoot, once opened, should be transferred to a container of water and can be kept for up to six days if the water is changed daily. Sliced bamboo shoot, braised in soy sauce with spices, is also a readily available canned product that can be added as a strong-flavored seasoning vegetable to various dishes. There are hundreds of different types of bamboo and at least 10 have edible shoots. They broadly fall into two categories—spring and winter shoots.

DRIED BAMBOO SHOOTS are like hard slivers of wood and must be soaked, then slowly simmered to soften before cooking.

SALTED BAMBOO SHOOTS have a distinct flavor that enhances noodle dishes, soups and stews. They are often used in Vietnamese and Laotian cooking and are found also in some Malay-Chinese, northern and central Chinese recipes. Salted bamboo shoots are short, thin strips, thickly salt encrusted. They are soft and moist and should be thoroughly rinsed before use to remove excess salt, but do not require lengthy soaking.

SPRING BAMBOO SHOOTS are the type most usually found in the markets. They are about

10 in (25 cm) in length with a base measuring up to 5 in (12 cm) in diameter.

WINTER BAMBOO SHOOTS have a finer texture and a slightly more pronounced flavor. They are smaller and thinner and when peeled are a deeper shade of buff than spring shoots. Bamboo shoots are dried and salted as well as canned.

DRIED BAMBOO SHOOTS AND CHICKEN NOODLES IN SOUP
Serves 6

8 oz (250 g) sliced, dried bamboo shoots
8 oz (250 g) bun noodles
1¹/₂ lbs (750 g) chicken pieces
¹/₂ cup (4 oz / 120 g) sliced, canned bamboo shoots
fish sauce
fresh coriander (cilantro)
scallions (spring / green onions)

Soak dried bamboo shoots in water for 1 hour; drain. Place in a saucepan with cold water to cover. Bring to a boil, then drain. Cook noodles until tender, drain and set aside. Simmer chicken in 8 cups (2 qts/2 l) water for 20 minutes. Drain and shred. Flavor the stock with fish sauce and salt and return meat, dried bamboo and canned bamboo shoots. Bring to a boil; simmer briefly. Pour over noodles and garnish with chopped fresh coriander and scallions.

Also known as *wah-bho-hmyit* (Burma); *tumpaeng* (Cambodia); *chuk surn* (China); *rebury* (Indonesia, Malaysia); *takenoko* (Japan); *finlabong, labong* (Philippines); *naw mai, phai tong* (Thailand); *mang tre* (Vietnam)

See also: BAMBOO LEAF; BAMBOO SHOOT SALAD (recipe); KALE, BAMBOO SHOOTS AND CONPOY CRISP FRIED (recipe); CRABMEAT AND BAMBOO SHOOT OMELETTE (recipe); DRIED BAMBOO SHOOTS AND CHICKEN NOODLES IN SOUP (recipe); MUSHROOMS AND EDIBLE FUNGI; UTENSILS, BAMBOO

BAMBOO STEAMERS: see UTENSILS, STEAMERS

BAMBOO UTENSILS: see UTENSILS, BAMBOO

BAMBOO SHOOT SALAD
Serves 6

4 cups (2 lbs / 1 kg) sliced bamboo shoots
¹/₄ cup (2 fl oz / 60 ml) thick coconut milk
2 tbsps fish sauce
2¹/₂ tbsps lime juice
1 tbsp sugar
1 tbsp minced fresh red chili
1 tsp crushed garlic
2 tbsps finely chopped scallions (spring / green onions)
2 tbsps minced fresh herbs; such as basil, dill, coriander (cilantro)
3 shallots, thinly sliced

Blanch bamboo shoots; drain. Mix coconut milk, fish sauce, and lime juice with sugar, chili, garlic and scallions. Pour over bamboo shoots, mix and let stand for 30 minutes. Garnish with fresh herbs and shallots.

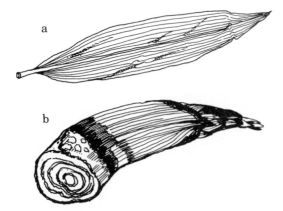

a

b

a. Dried bamboo leaf b. Fresh bamboo shoot

BANANA: (*Musa paradisiaca*) From the Musaceae family, the cultivated banana is a sterile hybrid which grows from a rhizome. It can grow to 30 ft (9 m) high. Many parts of the banana are used in cooking. The sweet banana is eaten ripe as a fruit and used green as a vegetable. Battered, fried or baked in their skins over hot coals, bananas are a popular Asian snack, while banana cooked with rice flour dough or glutinous rice and served with coconut cream is one of the most popular dessert combinations in many parts of Southeast Asia. Sliced, sun-dried banana is sold as a confection. The plantain banana has a lower sugar content and is used as a vegetable.

BANANA FLOWERS, which are the compact, deep purple, pointed heads at the tip end of a forming bunch of bananas, are used in Southeast Asian countries as a vegetable and garnish. In Indonesia they are mixed with pork and a hot *sambal*, cooked in a section of bamboo and served at festivals or wakes. In Laos, the national dish *khao phoune* would be incomplete without shredded banana flowers.

BANANA HEART is the tender core of the trunk, which is peeled and sliced to add to certain indigenous dishes such as Burmese *mohingha*. The sap from a banana trunk heart leaves an extremely strong stain that defies all efforts to remove it from clothes or hands. Always wear protective clothing and gloves when cutting or handling. The outer leaves must be peeled away first and the exposed core

cut crossways into thin slices that should be soaked in salted water for several hours. The sticky juice forms threads that can be easily pulled away.

Also known as banana trunk

BANANA LEAVES are large and pliable so are suitable for wrapping foods to be steamed or baked. In certain Indian communities, pieces of banana leaf are used as disposable plates and platters. In Vietnam they form the protective wrapping around pâtés and sausage-like processed meats, while in other regions they enclose glutinous rice and other snacks. They should be well rinsed before use, the central spine cut away and the leaf softened by holding over a flame or dipping into boiling water. It is preferable to choose leaves of a medium size for wrapping foods. Sometimes food wrapped in banana leaves acquires a delicate green color.

BANANA SHOOTS, which sprout near the base of the plant, are covered with a pot and left to grow without sunlight until they mature into long, thick, white spikes rather like gigantic white asparagus. In Indonesia they are cooked by roasting them in hot ashes.

BANANA CAKES
Yields 18

5 large bananas
²/₃ cup (3 oz/90 g) mung bean flour
¹/₃ cup (3 oz/90 g) crumbled palm sugar (or substitute brown sugar)
2¹/₂ cups (20 fl oz/625 ml) thin coconut milk
1¹/₄ cups (10 fl oz/375 ml) water
¹/₂ tsp salt
banana leaves or aluminum foil
vegetable oil

Steam unpeeled bananas for 10 minutes. Remove and cool. Peel and slice. Combine flour, sugar, coconut milk and water in a saucepan with the salt. Bring to a boil and cook, stirring, until the mixture is very thick. Cut foil or banana leaf into 6 in (15 cm) squares and brush with oil. Place a spoonful of dough and a slice of banana on each piece; fold into a square parcel. Secure with string or toothpicks, then chill until firm.

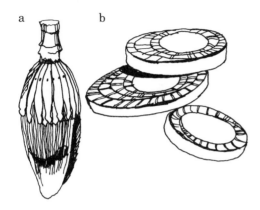

a b

a. Banana flower b. Sliced banana trunk heart

Also known as *kela* (India); *pisang, pisang raja* (large cooking bananas), *pisang susu* (Indonesia); *pisang, pisang kari* (large cooking bananas), *pisang kepok* (Malaysia); *saba, saging* (cooking banana), *puso no saging* (flowers) (Philippines); *kluay* (Thailand); *chuoi* (Vietnam)
See also: BANANA CAKES (recipe); MOHINGHA (recipe); STEAMED FISH IN BANANA LEAF CUPS (recipe)

BANDENG: (*BUN-DENG*, Indonesia) see BANGUS
BANGKWANG: (*BUNG-KWUNG*, Malaysia) see YAM BEAN

BANGUS: (*BA-NGOOS*, Philippines) (*Chanos chanos, C. salmoneus*) The large, greenish-gray milkfish, which grows up to 5 ft (1.5 m) in length, is one of the most popular eating fish in the Philippines and Indonesia, with more than 110,000 tons (100,000 tonnes) brought to

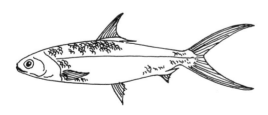

Bangus (milkfish)

the markets annually. They are hard to fish, ignoring bait and leaping out of nets, so the fry are gathered at sea and reared in fish ponds. Stuffed *bangus* is a popular dish, and the delicate meat also cooks well in a sour *sinigang*.
Also known as *bandeng* (Indonesia); *pisang-pisang* (Malaysia); *pla hai ling* (Thailand); *ca mang* (Vietnam); milkfish
See also: BANGUS STUFFED WITH VEGETABLES (recipe); SINIGANG (recipe)

BANGUS STUFFED WITH VEGETABLES
Serves 4–6

1¹/₂ lbs (750 g) whole bangus (milkfish) or sea perch
1 tbsp light soy sauce
1¹/₂ tbsps lemon juice
2 tbsps vegetable oil
1 onion, minced
4 cloves garlic, crushed
³/₄ cup (4 oz / 125 g) chopped green beans
2 tbsps chopped tomato
2 tbsps chopped parsley
1 egg
salt
pepper

Use kitchen shears to slit fish open. Clean thoroughly, wash and wipe dry, then carefully cut away backbone. Mix soy sauce with lemon juice and pour over the fish. Marinate for 1 hour. Heat 1 tbsp oil in a frying pan and sauté onion and garlic for 2 minutes. Add beans, cook for 2 minutes, remove from heat and stir in the tomato, parsley and beaten egg. Season with salt and pepper. Stuff into the cavity of the fish, close with wooden toothpicks. Heat 1 tbsp oil in a large pan and fry fish until golden brown. Turn and fry other side. Skin should be very crisp and meat cooked through but not dry.

BANH PHO: (*BEN FOR*, Vietnam) see NOODLES (RICE STICK)

BANH TRANG :(*BEN-TRAIN*, Vietnam) Round semitransparent, thin, hard and dry rice-paper crêpes that are used for wrapping Vietnamese spring rolls (*cha gio*) and a variety of grilled meats, with salad and herbs. A dough of finely ground rice, water and salt, with sometimes the addition of tapioca (cassava) flour as a strengthening agent, is passed through rollers and cut into circular shapes varying in size from 7 to 14 in (17.5 to 35 cm) in diameter. The damp rice papers are placed on bamboo mats to dry in the sun, imprinting a crosshatch pattern on them. *Banh trang* wrappers can be purchased from stores stocking Vietnamese or Thai ingredients and keep indefinitely in their dry state. To use they must be moistened by covering with a damp cloth until softened, or by dipping quickly into cold water. When making *cha gio* the wrappers can be brushed with a sugar-water solution, which results in a crisp, golden-brown surface when fried. Freshly made rice wrappers similar to fresh spring roll or egg roll wrappers are also made in Vietnam and are known as *banh uot*.

Also known as rice-paper wrappers; Vietnamese spring roll wrappers
See also: BANH UOT; CRABMEAT AND CHICKEN ROLLS (recipe); MEATBALLS OF PORK WITH SALAD GREENS (recipe); SPRING ROLL; TRIANGULAR ROLLS WITH WHOLE SHRIMP (recipe)

BANH UOT
Yields 24

1 cup (4 oz / 115 g) all-purpose (plain) flour
³/4 cup (3 oz / 90 g) tapioca starch (tapioca flour)
¹/2 cup (2 oz / 60 g) cornstarch (cornflour)
2¹/2 tbsps peanut oil
2¹/2–3 cups (20–24 fl oz / 625–750 ml) water

Combine all ingredients, mixing thoroughly. Heat a nonstick pan over medium heat. Pour in 2 tbsps of the batter, cover and cook for about 30 seconds. Check that bubbles have appeared and the pancake is dry on the underside. Remove and brush very lightly with oil. Stack cooked, oiled pancakes together when cool.

BANH UOT: (*BEN OUK,* Vietnam) These fresh rice papers are similar to freshly made spring roll or egg roll wrappers. They are used to wrap grilled or barbecued meat and salad. Substitute fresh spring roll, egg roll or lumpia wrappers or make them from the recipe. They can also replace the dried Vietnamese *banh trang* wrappers.
See also: BANH TRANG; LUMPIA WRAPPERS (recipe); SPRING ROLL

BAO: (*BO,* China) see CHINA COOKING METHODS (BLANCHING)

BARBECUED CHICKEN: (recipe) see CHICKEN

BARBECUED FISH BALLS ON SKEWERS: (recipe) see FISH

BARBECUED PORK CHINESE: see PORK, CHINESE ROAST

BARBECUES AND CHARCOAL COOKERS: see UTENSILS, BARBECUES AND CHARCOAL BURNERS

BARBECUE SAUCE: Several different sauces used in Asian cooking as seasonings or condiments come under the general classification of barbecue sauce. The Japanese commercial *tonkatsu* sauce is a classic, spicy, brown barbecue sauce. The Chinese have several: one is simply labeled "barbecue sauce" and is used principally as a seasoning for roasted and barbecued meats, particularly pork; *hoisin* is a

---

KOREAN BARBECUE SAUCE
Yields ¹/2 cup (4 fl oz / 120 ml)

¹/4 cup (2 fl oz / 60 ml) light soy sauce
1¹/2–2 tbsps water
1 tbsp yellow rice wine or black rice vinegar
1 tbsp minced scallions (spring / green onions)
¹/2 tsp minced garlic
gochujang or chili sauce
2 tsps ground toasted white sesame seeds

Mix soy sauce with water, rice wine or vinegar, scallions and garlic. Add *gochujang* or chili saucce to taste and the sesame seeds. Prepare 6–8 hours ahead.

sweet-flavored sauce that serves the same function as does *sha cha jiang*, another type based on ground peanuts. *Satay* sauce may also be included here as it accompanies barbecued meats. Made-up sauces accompany the table-top Korean barbecue and the Mongolian barbecue; and peanut sauce or a piquant sauce based on fish sauce and chili is served with Vietnamese barbecued foods.

See also: BEAN PASTES AND SAUCES (HOISIN); (SHA CHA JIANG); KOREAN BARBECUE SAUCE (recipe)

BASI : (*BA-SEE,* Philippines) see WINE, ASIAN

BASIL: (*Ocimum basilicum, Ocimum* spp.) This herb of the Labiatae or mint family has a large number of varieties, offering a wide range of flavors. Thought to be native to central–western China, records do not indicate the use of the herb in Chinese cooking, but it may have been used medicinally. Basil and many other fresh aromatic herbs are important ingredients in Thai, Laotian and Vietnamese cooking, being an essential element in their salads and raw vegetable platters as well as curried dishes. Basil is used to a small extent in Indonesia and Burma but rarely in other parts of Asia.

HAIRY BASIL has long, narrow pale green leaves. The sprigs culminate in a red-tinged cluster of seed pods which, when dried, are soaked for use in drinks and desserts. The leaves have a pronounced lemon scent and a peppery taste similar to Italian dwarf basil. It is known as *bai manglak* in Thailand where it is a salad ingredient and garnish. The seeds are used separately in a drink (see below).
Also known as (seeds) *tulsi* (India); *indring* (Indonesia); *luk manglak* (Thailand)

KERMANGI (Indonesia, Malaysia) is a type of basil native to these countries. It has a mild, although distinct flavor.

PURPLE BASIL has small, slightly tapering, round, mid-green leaves with a tinge of red-purple. The seed pods are spaced along a red-colored central stem. The flavor is indistinct when raw, becoming intense when cooked. In Thailand this variety of basil is known as *bai krapow / krapow.*

SELASIH (Indonesia) grows wild and is used frequently in curries. Its flavor is less agreeable than the other Indonesian basil, *kermangi.*

SWEET BASIL is the most common variety with green fleshy leaves, a strong flavor and is very aromatic. In Thailand it is known as *bai horapa / horabha* and is used to flavor curries and soups and is shredded in salads.

All varieties of basil are easily cultivated in warmer climates and grow prolifically. They can be propagated from slips placed in water until roots form, then transplanted into herb pots.
Also known as *rau que* (Vietnam)

SWEET BASIL SEEDS: The small black seeds of purple and hairy basil when soaked in water swell and become gelatinous. They are used in

SWEET BASIL SEEDS IN COCONUT MILK

1 tbsp sweet basil seeds
1 cup (8 fl oz / 250 ml) water
meat of 2 green coconuts, scraped from shell
3/4 cup (4 oz / 125 g) palm sugar (or substitute brown sugar)
2 cups (16 fl oz / 500 ml) coconut cream

Soak basil seeds in water for 10 minutes; drain. Spoon equal quantities of seeds into 6 bowls and add coconut meat. Mix palm sugar with coconut cream and taste for sweetness. Pour over, chill and serve.

Sweet basil

Indonesia and Thailand to make sweet drinks and desserts. Although they have no flavor the texture is interesting and they are thought to be cooling to the digestive system.
See also: MINT

BASKETS: see UTENSILS, STEAMERS

BATU GILING: (*BA-TOO GEAR-LING*, Indonesia) see UTENSILS, GRINDING

BAWANG: (*BAH-WUNG*, Malaysia) see ONION

BAYAM: (*BA-YUM*, Malaysia) see AMARANTH

BAY LEAF: see DAUN SALAM

BEANS: see BLACK-EYED PEA (BEAN); BROAD BEAN; LENTIL; LONG BEAN; SOYBEAN; WINGED BEAN

BEAN CURD: A soft, cream-colored gel made from dried soybeans. Originating in China it was discovered by an emperor in the Han Dynasty (206 BC–AD 220) who assembled a group of researchers to look for new medicines. In the course of their endeavors they discovered bean curd. It became known as "meat without bones" and is now made throughout Asia and in many other parts of the world. Nutritionists claim soybeans to be the only vegetable containing a complete protein and, as well, bean curd is very low in carbohydrates and cholesterol. The dried soybeans are soaked, puréed and boiled with water. The resulting milky liquid is strained and then mixed with a coagulant such as Epsom salts, vinegar, gypsum solution (hydrated calcium sulphate) or a natural solidifier such as sodium chloride (known as *nigiri* in Japan) which causes it to form curds. These are then transferred to cloth-lined wooden tubs and pressed with weights until compressed into bean curd. The formed fresh bean curd is cut into small squares and stored in cold water. Fresh bean curd readily absorbs the flavors from surrounding foods or sauces. It is inexpensive and nowadays easily obtained. Bean curd is sold by most Asian stores and can be refrigerated for about five days if covered with fresh water, changed daily. The bean solids left over from bean curd-making form a crumbly, moist white mass that is high in protein and is added to some dishes for bulk. In Japan, this is known as *okara*.

Also known as *dou-fu, dow foo* (China); *tahu* (Indonesia); *momen tofu, tofu* (Japan); *tahu, ta hua* (Malaysia); *tahure* (Philippines); *tauhu kao* (Thailand); *dau hu, dau hu chung* (Vietnam); bean custard; soybean cake

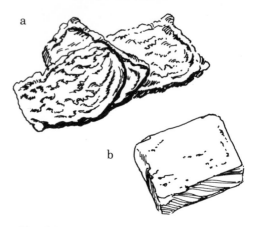

a. Fried bean curd   b. Pressed bean curd

ALMOND BEAN CURD: This is a misnomer. This popular Asian dessert is actually a sweetened almond milk jello, although it may also be made with soybean milk flavored with almond essence.
See also: ALMOND JELLO WITH DICED FRUIT (recipe)

BEAN CURD "BRAINS": Lightly coagulated bean curd has a soft, lumpy appearance and creamy/gray color resembling brains. It is used in vegetarian cooking, in stuffings and in braised dishes and soups.
Also known as *doufu nao* (China); *taho* (Philippines)

"COTTON" BEAN CURD: Japanese bean curd is generally softer, whiter and more delicately flavored than regular Chinese bean curd. "Cotton" bean curd, so named because it is strained through a semifine cloth, is smooth and slightly firm, having been pressed. Unless otherwise stated in recipes, this is the one to use. Chinese bean curd can be substituted. Sometimes squares of this type of bean curd are wrapped in fine cloth, giving the finished bean curd the appearance of small pillows. They are served cold with a dressing of soy sauce and chopped scallions with ginger.

Also known as *aburage, momen tofu* (Japan)

FREEZE-DRIED BEAN CURD: Sponge-like cakes of bean curd that have been freeze-dried. They are light in weight, yellow and expand to up to three times their size when soaked. The freezing process changes the texture, making it porous and firm, and these characteristics remain when the bean curd is rehydrated.

Also known as *koya tofu* (Japan)

FRIED BEAN CURD: Cubes of bean curd, about 1½ in (4 cm), are deep-fried until the surface is crisp and golden with little soft bean curd remaining inside. In Japan, one type of fried bean curd, *atsu-age* or *nama-age*, is cooked only for a short time leaving the outside golden while the inside is soft and white. Fried bean curd is used in vegetarian cooking and braised dishes and is cooked in its own right as a vegetable, usually with strongly flavored seasonings such as chili and black bean or oyster sauce. It can be stored for several weeks in an airtight container and must not be frozen as this will change its texture making it porous; nor should it be covered with water which will also spoil its texture.

Also known as *char doufu, doufu pok* (China); *agedofu, atsu-age, nama-age* (Japan); *tauhu tod* (Thailand); *dau hu chien* (Vietnam)

FRIED BEAN CURD POUCHES: When thin slices of bean curd are deep-fried they become crisp on the surface and dry out on the inside.

Fried bean curd pouch (aburage)

They can be cut along one edge and split open to form "pouches." Before use, the fried pouches should be steeped in boiling water to remove excess oil, then dried. In Japan, bean curd pouches are stuffed with vegetables, vinegar-seasoned rice and glutinous rice and are added whole or in shreds to soups, noodles and simmered dishes.

Also known as *aburage* ("golden purses"), *usu-age* (Japan)

GAN MODOKI: (Japan) These nutritious patties of mashed bean curd mixed with vegetables and spices are sold commercially as a vegetarian meal.

GRILLED BEAN CURD: Bean curd cakes are drained, pressed and dried on the surface, then lightly grilled until they are flecked with brown and the texture is firm. Grilled bean curd is usually cut into shreds for use in noodle dishes, vegetarian cooking and salads.

Also known as *doufu kan, gone* (China); *yakidofu* (Japan)

INSTANT BEAN CURD: A powdered form of bean curd sold in most Asian stores, it is easily made up by mixing the powder with water and the coagulant, over low heat. It is poured into a pan or mold to set. Usually bean curd made from instant mix does not taste as good as that produced commercially. When set, it should be covered with water and refrigerated and can be kept for several days if the water is changed daily.

OKARA: (Japan) The pulp or "lees" of ground soybeans which remains after the liquid has been drained off to make bean curd. It resembles moist, white paper pulp, is high in protein and provides fiber in a meal. It is used in soups, vegetable dishes and salads. In Japan it is sold where fresh bean curd is available.

PRESSED BEAN CURD: Weights are used to press out the excess water and compress the bean curd firmly. This may be done in large squares which are then cut into cakes, or into individual squares each wrapped in cloth. In certain instances, pressed bean curd may be painted on the surface with yellow food coloring, and is also sometimes lightly grilled or fried to give a toasted, brown appearance to the surface. Pressed bean curd is usually shredded and added to sautéed and braised dishes, or used raw, in stir-fries or in salads.

Also known as *doufu kan* (dry bean curd) (China); *taukwa, tauhu kuning* (yellow bean curd) (Indonesia, Malaysia); *agemono* (Japan); *tokwa* (Philippines); *tauhu leong* (Thailand); *dau hu ki* (Vietnam)

See also: LAKSA WITH CHICKEN AND COCONUT MILK (recipe); MEE SIAM (recipe)

SILK BEAN CURD: The name "silk bean curd" translates from its Japanese name *kinugoshi tofu*. In China its name translates as "water bean curd." It has a very smooth, delicate texture achieved by straining the coagulated liquid through fine mesh, then allowing the strained curds to settle without pressing. A similar process is used in the Philippines to make soft curd.

Also known as *shui doufu* (China); *kinugoshi tofu* (Japan); *taho* (Philippines)

See also: BEAN CURD (recipe); BEAN CURD CASSEROLE (recipe); BEAN CURD CUBES CRISP-FRIED (recipe); BEAN CURD SAUTE (recipe); "MA PO DOFU" (recipe); MISO SOUP (recipe)

BEAN CURD
Yields 2 large cakes

2 cups (1 lb / 500 g) soybeans
4^1/2 qts (4.5 l) water
1 tbsp Epsom salts
^{1}/3 cup (3 fl oz / 90 ml) boiling water

Soak soybeans overnight in ^{1}/3 of the water. Drain. Purée soybeans with remaining water, about 1 cup (8 fl oz/ 250 ml) at a time, until smooth. Bring to a boil stirring constantly over medium heat. Reduce heat and simmer 30 minutes. Stir frequently. Line a colander with clean cloth, pour in mixture and squeeze out as much liquid as possible. Mix Epsom salts with boiling water, pour into the liquid and mix sparingly. Pour into a cloth-lined box with drainage holes. Weight down and leave for 2–3 hours. Cut into squares and keep covered with cold water.

BEAN CURD CASSEROLE
Serves 8

^{1}/2 cup (2 oz / 60 g) sliced button mushrooms (champignons)
6 dried black mushrooms, soaked and halved
^{1}/2 cup (4 oz / 125 g) sliced, bamboo shoots
6 cubes fried bean curd, soaked, drained and halved
^{1}/2 cup (4 oz / 120 g) shredded ham
5 cups (40 fl oz / 1.25 l) chicken stock
2 tbsps shredded ginger
3 young Chinese white cabbages, halved
1 tbsp yellow rice wine
1^1/4 tsps salt
white pepper
4 cakes soft bean curd, cubed
1 tbsp rendered, chicken fat
2 tbsps sliced scallions (spring / green onions)

Place sliced button mushrooms, black mushrooms, bamboo shoots, fried bean curd, ham and chicken stock into a pan and simmer 10 minutes. Add ginger and cabbage; simmer 5 minutes. Add rice wine, salt, white pepper to taste, soft bean curd, chicken fat and scallions. Heat and serve.

BEAN CURD CUBES CRISP-FRIED
Serves 4

2 cakes "silk" bean curd, cubed
^{1}/2 cup (2 oz / 60 g) tapioca starch (kuzu starch)
3 cups (24 fl oz / 750 ml) vegetable oil
^{1}/2 cup (4 oz / 120 g) minced scallions (spring / green onions)
^{1}/3 cup (2 oz / 60 g) daikon oroshi
^{1}/4 cup (2 fl oz / 60 ml) mirin
1^1/4 cups (10 fl oz / 300 ml) dashi
2 tbsps light soy sauce

Coat bean curd lightly with tapioca starch. Heat oil. Carefully slide in bean curd and cook until surface is crisp and lightly golden. Drain and place in small dishes. Add scallions and *daikon oroshi*. Boil *mirin* for 30 seconds. Add *dashi* and soy sauce; heat through and pour over bean curd.

BEAN CURD SAUTE
Serves 4–6

6 cakes soft bean curd, cubed
3 cups (24 fl oz / 750 ml) peanut oil
8 oz (250 g) fresh bean sprouts, blanched
3/4 cup (4 oz / 120 g) chopped celery, with leaves
1/2 cup (2 oz / 55 g) shredded cabbage
light soy sauce
2 tbsps fried onion flakes
peanut sauce

Fry bean curd in oil until the surface is golden. Drain. Pour off all but 2 tbsps oil. Sauté vegetables 2–3 minutes; season with soy sauce. Place bean curd and vegetables in a serving dish; top with onion flakes which have been fried in oil over a medium heat until a rich brown. Serve with peanut sauce.

BEAN CURD BY-PRODUCTS: A variety of different by-products is made from bean curd for use as primary ingredients and seasonings.

BEAN CURD SKIN: When hot soybean milk is allowed to stand before the coagulant is added, a thick ochre-colored "skin" forms on the surface. This is lifted off and dried to become bean curd skin with a bland, creamy, nut-like flavor and a firm, chewy texture. The dried sheets are reconstituted to use as edible food wrappers for a variety of snack foods and dumplings, and are an ingredient in braised dishes and in vegetarian cooking. Bean curd skins are sold in most Asian food stores and will keep for many months in absolutely dry conditions. They come in large, flat sheets, which are fragile, but are the best way to buy the product for use as wrappers. Sticks or chips of the wrapper are suited for use in vegetarian cooking. Skins should be softened by covering them with a moist cloth before use. They do not require lengthy cooking so should be added in the final stages of cooking a braised dish or soup. Foods wrapped in bean curd skin may be deep-fried, braised or steamed.

BEAN CURD STICKS: These are sometimes called "bamboo" because of a resemblance to that plant. They are made in the same way as bean curd skins, but before drying are pleated and then hung on frames to dry in their characteristic stick-like shape. They should be softened by soaking before use and are usually cut into pieces and used in vegetarian dishes in place of meat—their texture being suitably chewy to be an acceptable substitute. Bean curd sticks are often deep-fried before use, making their surface crisp and bubbly.
Also known as *fu jook pin, gee jook,* (China); *yuba* (Japan); *forng ta ohu* (Thailand); rolled bean curd; second bamboo
See also: BEAN CURD; BEAN CURD CASSEROLE (recipe)

BLACK BEAN CURD: A gray-black, sponge-like curd similar in appearance to bean curd, but actually made from the root *Amorphophalus konjac.*
See also: AMORPHOPHALUS KONJAC

FERMENTED BEAN CURD: A seasoning ingredient made from fermented bean curd, red food coloring, and sometimes mixed with crushed rice or barley. Bean curd is fermented in jars either with brine, which gives it a strong and salty taste, or with Chinese rice wine, chilies and condiments, which makes it mildly pungent but less salty. It is popularly called "Chinese cheese" because of its similarity to a strong blue-vein cow's milk cheese. It may be served as a side dish sprinkled with oil or sugar to eat with rice, or cooked with vegetables as a seasoning. More often this fermented or "red" bean curd is served as a condiment, being mashed with a little of its liquid into a creamy paste. It gives a strong flavor accent to Chinese dishes such as rice *congee,* mutton or goatmeat casserole and other braised or stewed dishes.
Also known as *foo yu, fu-ru, narm yu* (China); *tahoe, tahu* (Indonesia, Malaysia); *tausi* (Philippines); bean curd cheese; Chinese cheese; pickled bean curd; red bean curd; soybean cheese
See also: BEAN CURD; BEAN PASTES AND SAUCES; GOAT CASSEROLE WITH FERMENTED BEAN CURD SAUCE (recipe)

MOLDY BEAN CURD: A type of rancid bean curd, overgrown with mold that is used occasionally in Chinese cooking for its unique pungent flavor. It is an acquired taste. Fermented bean curd is more commonly used.

BEAN CURD CHEESE: see BEAN CURD BY-PRODUCTS (FERMENTED)

BEAN JELLY: Jelly made from ground mung beans, powdered rice or buckwheat is a popular snack in the Sichuan province of China. Bite-size cubes dipped in spicy condiments are sold by street hawkers and in restaurants. One specialty of the province is crucian carp steamed in a sauce of chilies, fermented black beans, and garlic, with cubed, mung bean jelly added at the last moment. The texture is slightly rubbery; the flavor neutral, similar to bean curd, and it readily absorbs the accompanying seasonings.
See also: MUNG BEAN

BEAN PASTES AND SAUCES: Seasonings made from fermented soybeans are one of the oldest forms of food flavoring. Before 200 BC, the ancient Chinese used *shih* (a dark relish of salted and fermented soybeans) and *jiang* (fermented soybeans) in a thin, salty sauce. These were the precursors of the three main soybean seasonings used today: fermented black beans, soy sauce and bean paste.

To make all of these, yellow or black dried soybeans are partially decomposed by adding a mold culture, then they are salted, dried or mixed with brine. They are strongly flavored, salty and are used to enhance and intensify the taste of many Chinese dishes as well as foods from other Asian countries. Bean seasonings can be kept indefinitely in jars, except in hot and humid climates where they may require refrigeration to inhibit the growth of surface mold.

BEAN SAUCE follows the ancient recipe for *jiang* or pickled yellow soybeans in a salty liquid. It is essential to Sichuan and Hunan cooking and is also used extensively in Malaysian, Nonya and Singaporean cooking where it is known as *taucheo*. Bean sauce can be bought in cans and jars. Transfer canned sauce to a jar and store indefinitely in the refrigerator.
Also known as *mien see* (China); *tao co* (Indonesia); *taucheo, tau sa* (Malaysia, Singapore); *tuong ot* (Vietnam); bean paste; brown bean sauce; soybean condiment; yellow bean sauce

BLACK BEAN SAUCE is a recent addition to the variety of Chinese bean sauces. It contains puréed fermented black beans with a hint of garlic and star anise. Thin and salty, it is used over steamed meat or fish and occasionally as a dip or dressing for vegetables. For superior flavor it is best freshly made using fermented black beans.

CHILI BEAN PASTE is bean sauce with chopped dried chilies and sometimes also fermented black beans, garlic, and spices. It is this sauce that gives that special nutty, hot, salty taste to Sichuan and Hunan dishes, and is the same combination of ingredients that makes Korean *kochujang*. Intensity may vary from brand to brand as does its name.
Also known as *lat chu jeung, lat chu jeung yau* (garlic) (China); *kochujang* (Korea); bean paste with chili; hot bean paste; Sichuan hot bean paste

DHWEN-JANG (Korea) is a strongly flavored, salty form of bean paste, best substituted by red miso.
See also: MISO

HOISIN SAUCE (China) is a sweet-tasting, thick, reddish-brown sauce which is used as a condiment for roast pork and poultry, and to make a glaze for grilled meats. The red color comes from red rice which is colored with a natural food dye, usually *annatto* seeds. Ingredients in *hoisin* sauce are fermented soybean paste, sugar, garlic, and spices, which usually are Chinese five-spice or star anise and a hint of chili. A spicier version is known as *che hau* sauce and is used in the same way. A redder type of *hoisin* sauce may be called "barbecue sauce" and is used to glaze the skin of roasted meats, particularly pork and suckling pig, but is not to be confused with the Chinese barbecue sauce known as *sha cha jiang*.
Also known as *hoi sin cheung* (China); barbecue sauce; duck sauce

HOT BLACK BEAN SAUCE is a sauce of medium consistency, with a well-balanced combination of whole black beans, mashed chilies, Oriental sesame oil, garlic, and sugar. Sold in bottles, it can be added directly to stir-fried and steamed dishes. Fermented black beans with chopped chilies or hot bean paste can be substituted.

SHA CHA JIANG (China) is a tasty sauce with a slightly grainy texture, made from ground peanuts, dried fish, dried shrimp, chili, garlic, and spices which usually include coriander, Sichuan peppercorns, and star anise. Its flavor is similar to satay sauce which could, if necessary, be substituted. It is used mainly in Cantonese cooking, to glaze meats for grilling and can be used in stir-fries to give a mildly curried flavor. It is sold in bottles and can be kept indefinitely in the refrigerator.
Also known as *sha zha chiang* (China); barbecue sauce

SOYBEAN PASTE is a thick, dark brown, salty, seasoning paste of ground, fermented, black soybeans, with flour, salt, and water. It adds a strong, salty taste to Cantonese cooking and is also used in the northern and western parts of China, although there they are more inclined to use a hot bean paste. There are several types of dark soy pastes or sauces available from Chinese or Singaporean stores; some have a thinner consistency like that of cream.
Also known as *mean see jiang* (China)

SWEET BEAN PASTE in this context is not the sweet purée made from *azuki* beans, but a sweet, thick, dark brown sauce of ground, fermented soybeans and sugar. It gives a rich salty-sweet flavor useful in marinades and as a seasoning or condiment for roast meats. It is used in Taiwan more than in other parts of Asia.

BEAN PASTE DIP, SWEET
Yields 1 cup (8 fl oz / 250 ml)

1 tbsp Oriental sesame oil
2 tbsps sweet bean paste
2 tbsps sugar
1/2 cup (4 fl oz / 125 ml) water

Heat sesame oil in a small pan, then add the remaining ingredients and bring to a boil. Cook, stirring, until thickened. Cool before use. Refrigerate for 1–2 weeks. Serve with Chinese roast pork or poultry.

Also known as *tim mean jiang* (China)
See also: BEAN PASTE DIP, SWEET (recipe); DUCK SAUCE (recipe); FERMENTED BLACK BEAN; MISO; SOYBEAN; SOY SAUCE

BEAN PATTIES: (recipe) see LENTIL
BEAN SAUCE: see BEAN PASTES AND SAUCES
BEAN SHOOT: see BEAN SPROUT

BEAN SPROUT: (*Phaseolus aureus* Roxb., *Glycine max* L.) Sprouted beans are a nutritious, easily digested vegetable popular in most parts of Asia. In all Asian countries except India, it is the green mung bean and the yellow soybean which are sprouted. Indians prefer sprouting some of their many different types of lentil, although they, too, occasionally sprout mung beans. Sprouting is simply achieved by spreading dried beans on trays and applying controlled amounts of moisture over a three- or four-day period. Bean sprouts can be kept fresh in airtight plastic containers for up to one week, but are at their best when very fresh. Rinse thoroughly and cook only briefly, or blanch in boiling water for a few seconds to remove any surface bacteria, then refresh in icy cold water to use in salads. Canned sprouts are not particularly successful as they lose their appealing crunch and much of their taste. Drained, canned sprouts are slightly improved by soaking in iced water.

MUNG BEAN SPROUTS are about 2 in (5 cm) long, silvery in color and with a small, yellow-green pod on top. They have a delicate taste and are crisp but perishable. Use in salads or stir-fry as a vegetable. Excellent in soups and hotpots, they must be added at the very last minute to prevent overcooking.

SILVER SPROUTS are quite simply mung bean sprouts with roots and seed pods removed. These elegant little silvery slivers are used to garnish special dishes like braised shark's fin. The Cantonese stir-fry them with wide rice ribbon noodles.

SOYBEAN SPROUTS are large, up to 5 in (12.5 cm) in length, a deep, almost yellow color and strong in flavor. They are stir-fried as a vegetable, served under hot, sliced roast meats and are added to vegetarian dishes, braised and stewed dishes, and soups.

Also known as *daai dau nga choy* (soybean sprout), *ngunn nga choy* (silver sprouts), *nga choy*, *sai dau nga choy* (mung bean sprout) (China); *tauge* (Indonesia); *moyashi* (Japan); *kacang ijo, kacang djong, kacang padi* (Malaysia); *togue* (Philippines); *taun gawk* (Thailand); *gia* (Vietnam); bean shoots

See also: LENTIL; MUNG BEAN; SOYBEAN

BEAN SPROUTS STIR-FRIED WITH SHREDDED PORK
Serves 6

8 oz (250 g) lean pork, finely shredded
2 tsps light soy sauce
1 egg white, beaten
3 tsps cornstarch (cornflour)
8 oz (250 g) bean sprouts
3 tbsps (1¹/2 fl oz / 45 ml) vegetable oil
¹/2 tsp minced ginger
1¹/2 tsps minced scallions (spring / green onions)
1 tbsp (¹/2 fl oz / 15 ml) oyster sauce
1 tsp sugar
few drops Oriental sesame oil
¹/3 cup (3 fl oz / 90 ml) chicken stock

Marinade pork with light soy sauce, egg white and 2 tsps of the cornstarch for 20 minutes. Stir-fry sprouts in dry pan for 1 minute. Remove. Heat oil and stir-fry pork for 1–2 minutes. Add ginger, scallions and bean sprouts. Stir-fry briefly. Add oyster sauce, sugar and sesame oil. Mix chicken stock with remaining 1 tsp cornstarch. Add and stir until thickened.

BEAR'S PAW: In the central and northern provinces of China the paws of large black bears have been a banquet delicacy since the Han Dynasty (206 BC–AD 220). They are essentially a novelty item on a menu designed to impress. The paw has a soft-textured, gelatinous meat with a distinct gamey flavor that must be neutralized by maceration in lime solution and marination in strong seasonings. It is usually cooked by slow braising in a rich brown sauce.

Also known as bear's palm

BECHE DE MER: *(BESH DE MAIR)* see SEA SLUG

BEEF: Beef is a favored, although expensive, delicacy in Japan and Korea. In Japan a special type of beef cattle is reared for the famed *kobe* steaks. The cattle are hand-massaged and fed with beer and grain to produce rich tender meat well marbled with fat. For *sukiyaki* and the Korean hotpot *shinsulro*, prime steak is cut as thin as tissue so that it cooks within seconds.

Chinese cooks generally prefer beef thinly sliced in stir-fries and they marinate it with wine and seasonings to tenderize it before cooking. Beef is not widely eaten in India, where the cow is sacred for the predominant Hindu population, but it is enjoyed as an important meat in Indonesia, Malaysia, The Philippines, Thailand and Vietnam. In many instances it is actually buffalo meat that is used. Vietnamese cuisine features many different types of beef noodle dishes. In Thailand the meat is curried in rich sauces or shredded into tasty warm salads known as *laab*. Tart beef dishes are also an important aspect of the Thai cuisine, as are Spanish-inspired braised beef stews such as *estofado* in the Philippines. In Laos a creamy raw meat dish, *lap*, is made from beef, buffalo or deer meat.

BEEF AND NOODLES IN RICH BROTH
Serves 6–8

1¹/2 lbs (750 g) braising beef
1¹/2 lbs (750 g) beef shank with bone
6 thick slices fresh ginger
2 pieces dried tangerine peel
4 whole star anise
1 medium onion, halved
12 cups (3 qts / 3 l) water
salt and pepper
fish sauce
1¹/2 lbs (750 g) bun noodles
³/4 cup (1¹/2 oz / 45 g) chopped scallions (spring / green onions)
1¹/2 cups (2 oz / 60 g) fresh bean sprouts
fresh coriander (cilantro), chopped
nuoc cham sauce

(cont'd)

(Beef and Noodles in Rich Broth cont'd)

Cut meat into large pieces, place in a large pan with ginger, dried tangerine, star anise, onion and water. Bring to a boil, then simmer, skimming occasionally, for about 2¹/₂ hours. Season to taste with salt, pepper and fish sauce. Cook noodles in salted water until tender; drain. Divide among 6–8 large bowls. Pour on broth and chopped meat. Add scallions and bean sprouts. Garnish with chopped fresh coriander and serve with *nuoc cham* sauce.

BEEF TENDONS, extracted from shins, legs and the backbone of beef cattle, are enjoyed in the Chinese home or restaurant as a tender, bland-tasting meat. They are sold in fresh or dried form, the latter requiring extensive soaking to reconstitute before cooking. Like other cartilages such as shark's fin, beef tendon is eaten in the belief that it prevents bones becoming brittle with age.

BEEF BALLS
Serves 6

2 lbs (1 kg) beef round (round steak), cubed
¹/₂ cup (4 fl oz / 125 ml) fish sauce
2 tsps baking soda (bicarbonate of soda)
1 tbsp potato or tapioca starch (tapioca flour)
¹/₂ cup (1 oz / 30 g) chopped scallions (spring / green onions)
salt and black pepper
6 cups (1¹/₂ qts / 1.5 l) beef stock
chili sauce
Oriental sesame oil
12 banh trang *wrappers, each 6 in (15 cm)*
lettuce
1 cup (2 oz / 60 g) minced fresh herbs, such as basil, coriander (cilantro), mint

Mix beef with fish sauce, baking soda, flour, scallions, and generous amounts of salt and black pepper. Leave overnight then grind the meat to a smooth, thick paste. With oiled

(cont'd)

(Beef Balls cont'd)

hands, form into small balls. Poach meatballs in beef stock or water flavored with fish sauce, until they float to the surface. The meatballs can be served in soup bowls with a little of the stock, chopped scallions and chili sauce, or fry them in sesame oil and serve rolled in softened *banh trang* wrappers with lettuce and fresh herbs.

BEEF FONDUE WITH VINEGAR
Serves 6

1 lb (500 g) beef fillet (tenderloin / sirloin), thinly sliced
black pepper
1 large onion, sliced
³/₄ cup (6 fl oz / 180 ml) white vinegar
4 cups (1 qt / 1 l) water
1 tbsp plus ¹/₄ tsp minced garlic
1 tbsp plus 2 tsps sugar
2 cups (8 oz / 250 g) chopped tomatoes
1 tbsp minced red chili
1 tbsp shrimp (prawn) sauce
2 tbsps fish sauce
1 tbsp lime / lemon wedges
12 banh trang *wrappers*

Arrange beef on a platter and season generously with black pepper. Marinate onion in ¹/₄ cup vinegar. Bring water to a boil, add 1 tbsp garlic, 1 tbsp sugar, and tomatoes. Boil 15 minutes, then strain into a fondue pot and add remaining ¹/₂ cup vinegar. Heat to a simmer. Grind remaining ¹/₄ tsp garlic, chili, and shrimp sauce with remaining 2 tsps sugar, fish sauce, and lime/lemon juice to make a sauce, thinning with water as necessary. Cook beef by dipping briefly into the stock. Dip *banh trang* into water to soften; drain. To eat, wrap pieces of salad, cooked meat and onion slices in *banh trang* wrappers. Roll up and dip into the sauce.

BULGOGI BARBECUE
Serves 6–8

2 lbs (1 kg) lean beef fillet (tenderloin / sirloin)
1/2 cup (4 fl oz / 125 ml) light soy sauce
1/4 cup (2 fl oz / 60 ml) dark soy sauce
1/4 cup (2 oz / 60 g) finely chopped scallions
(spring / green onions)
2–3 tsps minced garlic
2 tsps minced ginger
2 tbsps ground toasted white sesame seeds
1/2 tsp black pepper
1 tbsp sugar
1 tbsp Oriental sesame oil
Korean Barbecue Sauce

Thinly slice beef across grain, then into narrow strips. Mix remaining ingredients with pepper, sugar, and sesame oil. Pour over beef, cover and marinate for at least 3 hours. Using chopsticks, lift the meat onto a heated tabletop griddle to cook. Dip into Korean Barbecue Sauce before eating.

CHINESE BEEF MARINADE

Use to flavor and tenderize sliced or shredded beef or Chinese stir-fries.

For 1 lb (500 g) beef:

2 tbsps light soy sauce
1 tsp dark soy sauce
3 tbsps vegetable oil
2 tbsps cold water
1 tbsp yellow rice wine
2 tsps sugar
1/2 tsp salt
1/4 tsp white pepper
2 tsps minced ginger

Optional additions:

1–2 tsps Oriental sesame oil
1–2 tsps minced garlic
1 tbsp cornstarch (cornflour)
1 tbsp dark soy sauce
1 egg white, well beaten

Mix the ingredients together in a glass or stainless-steel dish. Add beef cut into thin slices, strips or shreds. Mix well and marinate for 20 minutes. Drain before using.

DRY SPICED BEEF
Serves 6–10

1 1/2 lbs (750 g) beef steak
2 tbsps coriander seeds
1/2 tsp cumin seeds
1/4 cup (2 fl oz / 60 ml) clear honey
1/4 cup (2 fl oz / 60 ml) fish sauce
1/4 cup (2 fl oz / 60 ml) water
lettuce
lime sauce

Partially freeze beef, then cut into paper-thin slices. Roast the coriander and cumin seeds in a dry pan until very aromatic then grind to a powder. Mix with honey, fish sauce and cold water. Spread meat on baking trays, coat liberally with the sauce and place in a very low oven for about 10 hours until meat is dry but still flexible. Heat deep-frying oil in a pan. Fry beef over very high heat until browned. Serve on lettuce with lime sauce.

FRIKKADELS
Yields 24

1 lb (500 g) finely minced beef
1/2 cup (1 1/2 oz / 45 g) desiccated coconut
1/2 tsp minced garlic
2 tbsps minced onion
2 tsps chopped dill or mint
1 tbsp lemon juice
1/2 tsp salt
1/2 tsp pepper
1/2 egg, beaten
dry bread crumbs
ghee or vegetable oil

Mix together beef, coconut, garlic, onion, dill, lemon juice, salt and pepper. Knead to a smooth paste and form into 24 small balls. Coat each with beaten egg and bread crumbs and fry in ghee or oil until well browned. Drain. Serve as an appetizer with a hot chutney or sambal, or with *lampries*.

HANOI BEEF SOUP

2 lbs (1 kg) beef shank with bones
8 slices fresh ginger
4 shallots, peeled
2 star anise
1 piece cassia bark
8 cups (2½ qts/2.5 l) water
1 cup (8 oz/250 g) thinly sliced onion
12 oz (375 g) fresh bean sprouts, blanched
6 oz (200 g) beef fillet (tenderloin/sirloin),
thinly sliced
8 oz (250 g) banh pho rice noodles
salt
white pepper
fish sauce
lime juice
1 red chili, shredded
scallions (spring/green onions), minced
fresh coriander (cilantro)

Cut the meat into large pieces and place meat and bones in a large pan with ginger, shallots, anise and cassia. Add water and bring to a boil; skim, then simmer for 1½–1¾ hours. Arrange onion, bean sprouts and beef on a plate. Boil noodles in salted water until tender; drain and rinse with cold water. Remove meat from broth; cut into small pieces, discarding bones. Strain broth and season with salt, pepper, fish sauce and lime juice. Return meat and heat to boiling. Divide noodles among 6–8 bowls, pour on the hot broth and meat, garnish with chili, scallions and coriander and serve sliced onion, bean sprouts and raw beef separately to add to the soup as desired.

HOT RED CURRIED BEEF COUNTRY-STYLE
Serves 6

2 cups (16 fl oz/500 ml) thick coconut milk
2–3 tbsps red curry paste
2 lbs (1 kg) round steak (beef round), sliced
2 cups (16 fl oz/500 ml) thin coconut milk
2 kaffir lime leaves, shredded
2 red chilies, seeded and shredded

(cont'd)

(Hot Red Curried Beef Country-Style cont'd)

1 tsp salt
2 tbsps fish sauce
fresh coriander (cilantro) or basil leaves

Simmer thick coconut milk over low heat for about 10 minutes until it thickens and oil appears on the surface. Increase heat, add curry paste, cook for 5 minutes. Cut beef into narrow strips. Add to the pan along with thin coconut milk, lime leaves, chilies, salt and fish sauce. Bring to a boil and simmer until meat is tender. Garnish with coriander or basil leaves.

LAOTIAN TARTARE STEAK
Serves 8

3 medium eggplants (aubergines)
1½ tsps minced garlic
6 red chilies, seeded and chopped
1 tsp chopped greater galangal
2 tsps fennel seeds
1½ lbs (750 g) minced beef
1 cup (7 oz/200 g) ground rice, roasted
2 tbsps lemon juice
2 cups (16 fl oz/500 ml) beef stock
1½ cups (3 oz/90 g) minced scallions
(spring/green onions)
1 cup (2 oz/60 g) finely chopped fresh mint
fish sauce
fresh herbs, such as mint, dill, basil, fennel,
daun kesom
lettuce leaves

Grill unpeeled eggplants until blackened on the skin and soft inside. Peel under running water and dry. Grind garlic, chilies, greater galangal and fennel to a paste with a little water. Add eggplant and purée to a smooth paste. Blend meat, ground rice, lemon juice and beef stock to smooth cream. Mix with eggplant purée and add scallions, mint and fish sauce to taste, beating until mixture is creamy, and adding more stock if necessary. Serve with herbs and lettuce leaves.

"MA PO" DOFU

14 oz (400 g) lean minced beef
1 tbsp cornstarch (cornflour)
¹/₂ tsp salt
¹/₂ tsp pepper
2 tbsps light soy sauce
2 tbsps oil
1 tbsp fermented black beans, chopped
2 tsps hot bean paste
1 tsp minced garlic
2 tsps minced ginger
1 tsp minced chili
2 tbsps chopped scallions (spring / green onions)
1 tsp Sichuan peppercorns, crushed
2 tbsps yellow rice wine
2 tsps sugar
1 cup (8 fl oz / 250 ml) water or chicken stock
4 squares soft bean curd, cubed

Mix beef with cornstarch, salt and pepper, and 1 tbsp of the soy sauce. Stir-fry in oil until color changes. Add black beans, bean paste, garlic, ginger, chili, scallions and peppercorns to the pan and stir-fry for 2 minutes. Add the remaining 1 tbsp soy sauce, wine, sugar and water or stock and bring to a boil. Simmer until liquid is reduced; add the bean curd and simmer gently to heat through.

MUSAMAN CURRY
Serves 6–8

2 lbs (1 kg) braising beef, cubed
3¹/₂ cups (28 fl oz / 885 ml) thin coconut milk
1 cup (5 oz / 155 g) chopped roasted peanuts
1¹/₂ tbsps fish sauce
8 dried chilies
2 tbsps coriander seeds
1 tsp caraway seeds
1 tsp minced lemon grass
1 tbsp minced ginger
1 tsp salt
1 tsp black peppercorns
8 bay leaves

(cont'd)

(Musaman Curry cont'd)

¹/₂ tsp shrimp paste
vegetable oil
1 short stick cinnamon
3 green cardamom pods, peeled and seeds crushed
5 whole cloves
8 scallions (spring / green onions), minced
2 tsps minced garlic
¹/₄ cup (2 fl oz / 60 ml) tamarind water
palm sugar (or substitute brown sugar)

Place beef in a pan with the coconut milk and peanuts. Add fish sauce, bring to a boil, reduce heat and simmer for 1 hour. In a dry pan, roast chilies, coriander and caraway seeds until aromatic. Grind to a fine powder; then add lemon grass, ginger, salt, peppercorns, bay leaves and shrimp paste; grind together. Fry in 2 tbsps oil for 2–3 minutes. Add to the meat with the cinnamon, cardamom and cloves and cook until tender. Fry scallions and garlic in oil until crisp. Add to the pan and flavor sauce with tamarind water, sugar and additional fish sauce to taste.

TAPA
Serves 6–10

1 lb (500 g) beef steak
2 tbsps minced garlic
2 tsps minced ginger
1 cup (8 fl oz / 250 ml) white vinegar
1 tbsp black pepper
¹/₃ cup (3 oz / 90 g) sugar

Cut beef against the grain into paper-thin slices, then into narrow strips. Mix garlic with other ingredients, adding black pepper and sugar. Spread over meat. Cover and refrigerate overnight. Spread meat on oven racks. Warm in a very low oven for 5–6 hours until meat feels firm and dry. Fry on both sides until crisp before serving.

ASIAN

WARM MINCED BEEF SALAD
Serves 6

1 lb (500 g) lean minced beef
¼ cup (2 fl oz / 60 ml) fish sauce
½ cup (4 fl oz / 125 ml) lime juice
1 tsp sugar
1 tsp greater galangal, shredded
2 tbsps ground roasted rice
1 tsp ground roasted chili
1 cup (2 oz / 60 g) chopped scallions (spring / green onions)
½ cup (½ oz / 15 g) chopped mint leaves
lettuce
4 cups (1½ lbs / 750 g) sliced vegetables, such as broccoli, green beans, eggplant (aubergine), zucchini (courgettes)

Heat a wok and dry-fry ground beef until cooked. Mix fish sauce, lime juice, sugar, *greater galangal*, rice, chili, scallions and mint leaves, tossing lightly. Serve on lettuce with the sliced vegetables.

BEEF, SEVEN STYLES OF: (Vietnam) A tradition of serving seven different beef dishes at one meal became fashionable in Vietnam in prosperous times. *Bo bay mon*, or "beef in seven dishes," is still served in a few famous restaurants in Vietnam and always begins with beef fondue with vinegar. The meal concludes with a gruel of rice and diced meat with crisply fried noodles and peanuts known as *chao thit bo*. The intervening courses may comprise any of the many grilled, roasted or tabletop-cooked beef dishes, simmered beef or the popular soup noodle dishes featuring beef.
See also: BEEF FONDUE WITH VINEGAR (recipe)

BEEFSTEAK PLANT: (Japan) (*Perilla arguts*) A member of the mint family, this plant of the genus *Perilla* is native to China, Burma and the Himalayan mountains. For centuries the Japanese have cultivated both the green and red varieties of beefsteak (*shiso*) for its leaves which are both garnish and vegetable, and for its color of which the red is more important. The stems of the flowering seed pods and the sprouts are also used as a garnish. The fresh leaves are available in some specialist Asian greengroceries, but are not sold in dried or frozen form as these would be unsuitable for use. Salted or pickled *shiso* leaves are eaten as a pickle.

GREEN SHISO leaves with their wide, flat shape, deep green color, and serrated edges make an attractive garnish. They are also battered and fried as *tempura* and chopped to add to *sushi*. Mint or basil can be substituted as garnish.
Also known as *ao-jiso*

HANA HOJISO are the small stems of flowering seed pods of the *shiso* plant. They can be used as a garnish, particularly with *sashimi*. The seeds are scraped from the stem into the soy dip.

MEJISO are sprouts of the *shiso* seed that are crisped in cold water and used as a garnish.

RED SHISO leaves have their main use in the pickling industry, being added to *umeboshi* for their color and flavor. They are also used in the manufacture of some confectionery.
Also known as *perilla; shiso*
See also: SASHIMI WITH LEMON (recipe); TEMPURA

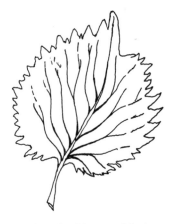

Beefsteak plant leaf (green shiso)

BEER, ASIAN: Beer consumption in Asia is high and there are several popular brands available throughout the area. China's *Tsingtao* (*Quingdao*) from Shandong province rules supreme in this expansive land. In Japan connoisseurs continually argue the comparative merits of *Kirin* and *Sapporo*; and the *San*

Miguel of the Philippines is considered one of the world's finest beers. *Kirin* beer was named after a legendary Chinese creature that was thought to exist more than 2500 years ago. **See also:** WINE, ASIAN; WINE, CHINESE

BEEHOON: (*BEE-HOON*, Malaysia) see NOODLES (RICE VERMICELLI)

Beijing duck

BEIJING DUCK: Over the centuries, the Chinese have bred a special duck for use in the famous dish, roast Beijing (Peking) duck. It has a meaty breast, and a layer of fat evenly spread between meat and skin so that the skin separates from the meat when cooked. Air is blown between the meat and fat to aid this purpose. The ducks are seasoned, hung to dry so the skin tightens, glazed with ingredients including maltose (malt sugar), then suspended in tall brick ovens to roast over charcoal or wood fires.

See also: DUCK SAUCE (recipe); MALTOSE; MANDARIN PANCAKES (recipe); VIETNAMESE-STYLE BEIJING DUCK (recipe)

DUCK SAUCE
Yields 1¹/₂ cups (13 fl oz / 400 ml)

To accompany Beijing duck, roast pork and crisp skin poultry.

2¹/₂ tbsps Oriental sesame oil
¹/₂ cup (4 oz / 120 g) sugar
¹/₂ cup (4 oz / 120 g) sweet bean paste
¹/₂ cup (4 fl oz / 125 ml) water

Heat sesame oil in wok, add other ingredients and mix. Simmer until thickened, about 2 minutes. Store in refrigerator for several weeks.

MANDARIN PANCAKES
Yields 12

2¹/₂ cups (10 oz / 300 g) all-purpose (plain) flour
1 cup (8 fl oz / 250 ml) water
Oriental sesame oil

Sift flour into bowl. Bring ³/₄ cup (6 fl oz/ 180 ml) water to a rolling boil and quickly stir into flour. Work to a soft dough. Add remaining ¹/₄ cup (2 fl oz/70 ml) water (cold) and knead until smooth on a lightly oiled board. Cut into 12 pieces. Brush one side of 2 pieces of dough with sesame oil. Press oiled sides together and roll out. Repeat with remaining dough. Heat a nonstick pan and wipe with sesame oil. Cook the pancakes in pairs until upper and lower sides are specked with brown. Remove from pan. Separate and fold into triangles to serve with slices of Beijing (Peking) duck.

VIETNAMESE-STYLE BEIJING DUCK
Serves 8

5 lbs (2 kgs) fresh duck
1 tbsp annatto seeds
1/2 cup (4 fl oz / 125 ml) sweet soy sauce (kecap manis)
3/4 tsp five-spice powder
1/4 cup (2 oz / 50 g) sugar
1/2 cup (1 oz / 30 g) sliced scallions (spring / green onions)
vegetable platter
rice vermicelli
nuoc cham sauce

Pour boiling water over duck; drain well. Crush *annatto* seeds and soak in 1/4 cup boiling water for 15 minutes. Strain, mixing with sweet soy sauce, five-spice powder and sugar. Place duck on a rack over a roasting pan. Pour some of the marinade into the cavity of the duck, put in the scallions. Close with a skewer. Brush remaining marinade over the skin. Roast in a preheated oven at 350°F (180°C) for 45 minutes. Brush again with marinade. Roast a further 45 minutes on 300°F (150°C). Paint with remaining marinade and finish cooking in a hot oven. Slice and serve with a vegetable platter, cooked rice vermicelli and *nuoc cham* sauce.

BELIMBING: (*BEH-LIM-BING*, Malaysia) (*Averrhoa bilimbi*) A relative of the carambola (star fruit), light green, acidic fruit is about 3 in (7.5 cm) in length, with a firm, slightly rough skin and looks like a small, underripe mango. It is used in Indonesia, Malaysia, the Philippines, and Thailand to impart a sour taste to foods. In Indonesia it is also used medicinally to induce profuse perspiration. The sour flavor may also be achieved by using citrus juices, tamarind, unripe (green) mango and certain types of eggplant.
Also known as *belimbing wuluh* (Indonesia); *kamias* (Philippines); *madun* (Thailand); cucumber tree, sour finger carambola
See also: STAR FRUIT

BELINJO: (*BEH-LEAN-JO*, Indonesia) see MELINJO

BENGAL GRAM: (*BAN-GAA-LEE GRAM*) see CHICK-PEA

BENGALI RICE: see RICE (NON-GLUTINOUS)

BENI SHOGA: (*BE-NEE SHOW-GA*, Japan) see JAPAN, GARNISHES; GINGER

BENITADE: (*BEE-NEE-TAH-DA*, Japan) see JAPAN, GARNISHES

BENTO: (*BEN-TO*, Japan) A lacquered box, which is divided into compartments, and used in Japan to serve an individual meal, usually lunch. It contains different types of food in each compartment. The *bento* is a popular meal for travelers, but is also enjoyed as a way of tasting new seasonal dishes or a selection of different dishes at one time.

Japanese restaurants in the West often offer a *bento* meal, sometimes comprising as many as eight different small dishes, as a means of sampling the various cooking styles and traditional seasonings and tastes.

Bento box

BESAN: (*BE-SAN*) see FLOURS AND THICKENERS

BETA-JIO: (*BE-TAH-GEE-OH*) see JAPAN, COOKING METHODS (SALTING)

BHAJIAS: (*BHA-JI-AA*, India) see PAKORA

BHARTA: (*BHUR-TAA*, India) see INDIA, COOKING METHODS

BHATURAS: (*BHA-TOO-RAA*, India) see BREAD, INDIAN

BHINDI:(*BHIN-DEE*,India)(*Hibiscus esculentus*) Also known as okra, *bhindi* is a plant of the cotton family. It grows extensively in India and bears edible, furry fruit pods which contain many small white seeds. *Bhindi* has a mucilaginous consistency. It is used as a vegetable, particularly by vegetarian Indians who usually cook it with spicy curry sauces to enliven its bland taste. It is not to be confused with the vegetable commonly known as Chinese okra which is the angled luffa (*Luffa acutangula*).
Also known as gumbo, lady's fingers, okra
See also: LUFFA, ANGLED

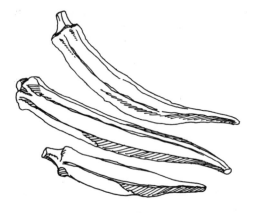

Fresh bhindi pods (okra)

BIBINGKA: (BEE-BING-KA, Philippines) see RICE DOUGH

BIHOON: (*BEE-HOON*, Philippines) see NOODLES (RICE VERMICELLI)

BIKO
Serves 6–8

1¹/₂ cups (12 oz / 350 g) malagkit *(sticky glutinous rice)*
1¹/₂ cups (12 fl oz / 375 ml) thick coconut milk
2 cups (16 fl oz / 500 ml) thin coconut milk
¹/₈ tsp ground aniseed
2 cups (14 oz / 400 g) sugar

Wash *malagkit* and drain. Place coconut milks and aniseed in a saucepan. Add *malagkit* and cook over low heat stirring occasionally. When liquid has been almost absorbed, add sugar and stir continuously until thick. Serve with *latik*.

BIKO: (*BEE-KOH*, Philippines) A dessert made from glutinous rice, coconut milk and sugar. It is poured into dishes or molds lined with banana leaves and served with *latik* (brown coconut milk curd).
See also: LATIK; STEAMED GLUTINOUS RICE IN COCONUT MILK (recipe)

BIN DOU: (*BIN DAU*, China) see BROAD BEAN
BIRD'S EYE CHILI: see CHILI (THAI)

BIRD'S NEST: The edible nest of a breed of swallow, the *Collocalia*—a cave swiftlet which inhabits caves, cliffs and islands off the coast of southern China, Thailand and Vietnam. The birds regurgitate bits of seaweed with their saliva and use it to make their nests which are usually located in almost inaccessible places. The reason for the extreme expense of the dried bird's nest is twofold. The Chinese regard bird's nest as beneficial to the toning of the blood, which in turn improves the complexion, therefore making it an important medicinal food. The methods employed to harvest them from the high cliffs and caves are extremely dangerous with frequent loss of life, and consequently wages for workers are high.

Dried bird's nest

Birds' nests are unimpressive in their dried state, being grayish lumps of a strand-like, plastic-looking substance which must be soaked, thoroughly rinsed, and picked over before cooking. They are cooked in a sweet or savory clear soup with little extraneous flavorings to mask their delicate taste. The bird's nests are packed in attractive paper boxes and are available, although expensive, at Chinese grocers and pharmacies.

Also known as *yan wo, yin wor* (China); *sarang burung* (Malaysia)

See also: BIRD'S NESTS IN SWEET SOUP (recipe)

BIRD'S NESTS IN SWEET SOUP
Serves 6

6 oz (185 g) dried bird's nests, soaked 5–6 hours
boiling water
1/3 cup (1 1/2 oz / 45 g) dried lotus seeds, soaked 3–4 hours
5 cups (1 1/4 qts / 1.25 l) water
1/4 cup (2 oz / 60 g) crushed rock candy sugar
1/2 cup (4 fl oz / 125 ml) thin coconut milk, optional

Pick out any impurities from nests, rinse well, drain and cover with boiling water. Cook for 1 hour. Drain lotus seeds, cover with boiling water. Cook until tender. Drain; remove seed cores. Bring water to a boil. Add sugar and stir to dissolve. Add bird's nests and lotus seeds and simmer 5–6 minutes. Stir in coconut milk, if using, and serve hot.

BIRIYANI OF RICE AND CHICKEN: (recipe) see CHICKEN

BISCOCHO: (*BEES-KO-CHO*, Philippines) Toast which is oven- or sun-dried and crumbled to use for thickening meat sauces like *lechon sarsa* (liver sauce).

See also: LIVER SAUCE (recipe)

BITTARA APPA: (*BITH-THARA AA-UP-PA,* Sri Lanka) see APPA

BITTER ALMOND: see APRICOT KERNEL

BITTER MELON: see MELONS AND GOURDS

BLACHAN: (*BE-LA-CHUN*, Malaysia) see SHRIMP PASTE

BLACK BEAN CURD: see AMORPHOPHALUS KONJAC

BLACK BEAN: see FERMENTED BLACK BEAN

BLACK BEAN SAUCE: see BEAN PASTES AND SAUCES; FERMENTED BLACK BEAN SAUCE (recipe)

BLACK CARP: see CARP

BLACK CHILI: see CHILI

BLACK CUMIN: see CUMIN; NIGELLA

BLACK-EYED PEA (BEAN): (India) (*Vigna catjang*) A bean of South American origin where it is known as the black-eyed pea. It has pods that grow up to 2 ft (60 cm) in length, and is closely related to the beans used throughout China and India known as long beans, snake beans or long-podded cow peas. The beans resemble kidney beans in size and shape, but are yellow-brown to red in color with a dark "eye." They are often referred to as asparagus beans, but are not to be confused with the asparagus pea or winged bean (*Psophocarpus tetra gonolobus*).

Also known as *lobhia, lobia* (India); *kajang merah, kajang panjang* (Indonesia)

See also: BLACK-EYED PEA (BEAN) SALAD (recipe); LONG BEAN; WINGED BEAN

BLACK-EYED PEA (BEAN) SALAD
Serves 6

1 cup (7 oz / 200 g) black-eyed peas (bean), soaked
1/2 cup (2 oz / 60 g) chopped tomato
1/2 cup (2 oz / 60 g) chopped onion
1 cup (4 oz / 125 g) chopped cooked spinach
1 fresh green chili, seeded and chopped
1 tbsp vegetable oil
1 tsp lemon juice
1 tsp sugar
1 tsp salt
fresh coriander (cilantro)
mint

Drain beans; cover with salted water and boil until cooked. Drain. Add the salad vegetables and chili. Toss well. Mix oil with lemon juice, sugar and salt and pour over the salad. Stir in herbs; chill before serving.

BLACK FUNGUS: see CLOUD EAR FUNGUS

BLACK LENTIL: see LENTIL

BLACK MOSS: see SEAWEED (HAIR VEGETA-
BLE)

BLACK MUSHROOM: see MUSHROOMS AND
EDIBLE FUNGI

BLACK SESAME SEED: see SESAME SEED

BLACK SOYBEAN: see SOYBEAN

BLACK TREE FUNGUS: see CLOUD EAR
FUNGUS

BLACK VINEGAR: see RICE VINEGAR

BLANCHED CHINESE CHIVES: see CHIVES,
CHINESE (YELLOW)

BOFU: (*BOO-WHO,* Japan) see JAPAN, GAR-
NISHES

BOG RHUBARB: see COLTSFOOT

BOK CHOY: (*BAK CHOY*) see CABBAGE,
CHINESE

BOMBAY DUCK:(India)(*Harpodon nehereus*)
The bummalow (bomeloe) or Bombay duck is
a predatory fish inhabiting the waters off the
west coast of India around the port city of
Bombay. It has a tapering body up to 16 in
(40 cm) long. It is an almost translucent
silver-beige color with a large head and has
hard, needle-like teeth. During the monsoon
season it preys on shoals of small fish and
shellfish brought to the surface by the disturbed waters. It is thought to have acquired
its popular name, Bombay duck, because it is
easily netted from the water's surface at this
time. As the flesh is perishable, the fish is only

a
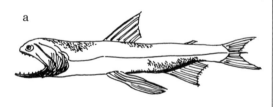

b

a. Fresh Bombay duck
b. Dried Bombay duck fillet

occasionally used fresh. It is processed by
salting and sun-drying and is sold whole, in
fillets or in broken pieces. Bombay duck is
fried or grilled to serve as a pungent, crisp
accompaniment to curries.
Also known as *nga hnap* (Burma); bomeloe,
boomla, bummalow (India); *lumi* (Malaysia);
pla pak khom (Thailand); *ca khoai* (Vietnam);
Maldive fish

BOMELOE: (*BAMM-A-LO,* India) see BOMBAY
DUCK

BONITO: (*Auxis thazard*) From the marine
family Scombridae, this fish plays a major role
in the cuisine of Japan. The bonito, or frigate
mackerel, has dark flesh which is of only moderate quality. It is not sought after for eating
fresh. However, in Japan the dried meat is
used as the base of all broths and stocks (*dashi*),
often being teamed with *kombu,* the giant sea
kelp, to give a flavor that is uniquely and
distinctly Japanese. When the meat is dried it
turns a gray-black with an ash-white coating
of mold (green mold means it retains moisture,
yellow indicates acidity). It is so hard that two
pieces hit together make a metallic sound.
Bonito must be shaved for use on a special
shaving apparatus known as a *katsuo-kezuri-
ki.* It is sold in these blocks as *katsuobushi* or
in ready shave form, either as *hana-katsuo* or
kezuri-bushi which are tissue-thin shavings,
buff in color. Bonito is also ground and made
into granules for use as instant *dashi.* Shaved
bonito is added to sauces for extra flavor. It is
removed before using the sauce and sometimes reserved for a second use. *Ito-kezuri-
katsuo* are fine, rosy pink, dried, thread-like
bonito shavings which appear frequently as a
fishy-tasting, unusually textured garnish,
particularly over fried dishes such as *agedashi
dofu* (fried bean curd) and *beinasu* (eggplant in
sauce). It may be sprinkled over rice dishes
such as scattered rice.
See also: BEAN CURD CUBES CRISP-FRIED (recipe);
DASHI; EGGPLANT IN SAUCE (recipe)

BOOMLA: (*BOOM-LAAH,* India) see BOMBAY
DUCK

BONNET GOURD: see LUFFA, ANGLED

BORECOLE: see CABBAGE, CHINESE (RAPE, SEEN CHOY)

BOTTLE GOURD: see MELONS AND GOURDS

BOW YEU: (*BAU YUE*, China) see ABALONE

BOXTHORN: (*Lycium chinese* Mill.) A member of the Solanaceae family which encompasses eggplants, tomatoes and bell peppers, it is a leaf vegetable growing on tall, straight, unbranching stems that are closely covered with small, deep-green, oval leaves. When they come to the market the stems are about 14 in (35 cm) long and some have strong thorns. Only the leaves are used and should be cooked quickly. Cantonese use them only in a soup, usually with pork liver.

Boxthorn

MATRIMONY VINE: A close cousin to the boxthorn, it is also used in Chinese cooking. It grows on a spiny shrub (not a vine) with its slightly longer leaves growing along the slender branches. The leaves, flowers, roots and seeds are all used medicinally and the leaves are cooked in a soup. The flavor is minty, so the leaves are also used to brew a tea which is thought to be good for kidney problems.

WOLFBERRIES: These are the seeds of the matrimony vine. They are important medicinally and when cooked with fungi are thought to be good for the lungs and kidneys. Tiny, pointed, slightly wrinkled-looking seeds that turn a bright red when cooked, they are sold alone or in packs with other herbs and ingre-

dients from which the Chinese make a tonic soup. Wolfberries make an attractive and healthy addition to braised dishes of pork, turtle and chicken.

Also known as *gau gei choy* (China)

BRAN MASH: see NUKA

BREAD, INDIAN: A wide variety of bread is made in India under the collective name *roti*, a word which, interestingly, equates with the French word for toast, *rotie*. In the major cities of India it is not unusual to see *tandoor waalas*: itinerant cooks with portable *tandoor* ovens, set up on street corners to cook bread for nearby households. Grains in the form of bread provide much of the carbohydrates consumed by the Indians and are considered to be as important as rice as a staple food. In the south bread is made from rice and lentils; in the north from wheat. Semolina and grains such as millet and maize are also used.

CHAPATIS are an unleavened, thin, flat, round bread made from finely milled wholemeal flour known as *atta*. They are cooked on a *tawa*, a heavy, very slightly curved pan, over a charcoal or wood-fired stove. *Chapatis* are served throughout India, and particularly in the central Indian states, often in preference to rice. They are also sometimes cooked with a filling, particularly spiced potato or cauliflower.

Also known as *phulkas*

See also: CHAPATIS (recipe)

KULCHAS are made of leavened white flour dough, pressed into rounds and deep-fried. They may have a filling of curd cheese or spiced vegetables added before cooking.

MAKKI KI ROTI: A finely ground cornmeal is used in the Punjab to make this thin, crisp-soft bread.

NAAN: A soft-textured bread made from white flour (*maida*) leavened with *khamir*, a natural yeast. Popular in northern India, the teardrop-shaped bread is baked by moistening one side and attaching it to the inside wall of a *tandoor* oven. The bread cooks in minutes and is retrieved by hooking it from the oven wall with a metal spike. *Naan* may be decorated with onion, poppy or sesame seeds, chopped garlic or smeared with food coloring. Stuffed *naans* are made by placing spicy fillings of chicken or *panir* cheese between two layers of dough before baking.

PARATHAS require perhaps the most skill to perfect. They are crisp, buttery, layered breads which are also served plain or stuffed.

PURIS: A number of other types of bread are cooked by deep- or shallow-frying, usually in ghee. *Puris* and *bhaturas* expand like small balloons in hot deep oil. They are served with vegetarian foods, particularly *dal* (lentil), potato and bean dishes. Cooked *puris* are stuffed, sandwich style, with hot curried fillings as a quick snack.

Puri (balloon bread)

ROOMALI ROTI is a delightful bread as thin as the scarf after which it is named. Its counterpart in the south is the wide, thin, crisp but pliant *dosa*, made from fermented lentils and rice, or from oats, coconut or semolina. Also from the south is the soft steamed *idli*, similar to the Sri Lankan *appa*.

See also: APPA; BITTARA APPA (recipe); CHAPATIS (recipe); FLOURS AND THICKENERS; FRIED BALLOON BREAD (recipe); KHAMIR; LAYERED BUTTERED BREAD (recipe); PAPPADAM; SOUTHERN INDIAN BREAKFAST BREAD (recipe); ROTI JALA (recipe); SRI LANKAN STYLE FLAT BREAD (recipe); TANDOOR; TANDOORI BAKED BREAD (recipe)

CHAPATIS
Yields 12

2 cups (8 oz / 250 g) maida flour
¹/₂–²/₃ cup (4–5 fl oz / 125–150 ml) warm water
ghee

Blend flour in a mixing bowl or food processor with water to make a slightly firm dough. Knead vigorously for about 8 minutes until the dough is an elastic ball. Wrap in a damp cloth and let stand for at least 1 hour. Divide into 12 pieces. Roll the *chapatis* into thin 4–5 in (10–12 cm) rounds on a lightly floured surface. Heat a flat iron griddle or *tawa* and rub vigorously with a ghee-moistened cloth. Cook the *chapatis* over medium heat until flecked with brown, then turn.

FRIED BALLOON BREAD
Yields 18

3 cups (12 oz / 360 g) atta flour
1¹/₄ tsps salt
1¹/₄ tbsps softened ghee
deep-frying oil and ghee

Combine flour and salt, add ghee and mix until crumb-like. Gradually add lukewarm water to make a dough firm enough to knead. Knead for 5–6 minutes, divide into 18 pieces and roll out. Deep-fry, one at a time, in 3 parts vegetable oil, 1 part ghee. Immediately push under oil and splash top of bread with oil to encourage it to puff out. Turn and cook other side briefly.

LAYERED BUTTERED BREAD
Yields 8

2 cups (8 oz / 250 g) atta flour
¹/₂–²/₃ cup (4–6 fl oz / 125–180 ml) warm water
1 tsp salt
melted ghee

(cont'd)

(Layered Buttered Bread cont'd)

Blend flour with water and salt to make a smooth, slightly firm dough. Knead for at least 8 minutes, until the dough is smooth and springs back when pressed with a finger. Divide into 8 pieces. Roll into 8 in (20 cm) rounds and brush tops generously with ghee. Fold in a pleated strip, twist into a curl and roll flat. Heat a *tawa* or griddle and oil with ghee. Cook the bread on both sides until crisp and golden, adding more ghee as needed.

Layered buttered bread (parathas)
a. Divide pastry into strips
b. Twist into strips
c. Roll out

ROTI JALA
Yields 18

4 cups (1 lb / 500 g) all-purpose (plain) flour
1¹/₂ tsps salt
2 eggs, beaten
4 cups (1 qt / 1 l) thin coconut milk
ghee

Sift flour into a bowl with salt. Add eggs, half the coconut milk, stir until smooth, add remaining coconut milk then strain. It should be the consistency of thick cream. Use a *roti jala* cup, or a can perforated at the bottom to pour the batter in a lacy pattern into a hot skillet, lightly greased with ghee. Cook on both sides, roll up and serve.

SOUTHERN INDIAN BREAKFAST BREAD
Yields 8

1¹/₃ cups (8 oz / 250 g) uncooked rice
¹/₃ cup (2 oz / 60 g) polished split black lentils (dal)
1 tsp salt
oil
Dal and Vegetable Sauce (see recipe)

Soak the rice and lentils separately in warm water for up to 6 hours. Drain, grind separately with salt, adding enough water to make a smooth paste. Mix together to make a creamy batter, adding more water as needed. Cover and leave to ferment overnight. Heat a griddle, *tawa* or heavy frying pan and grease lightly. Pour in batter to cover the base of the pan in a thin pancake. Brush oil around the edges of the pancake and cook on medium-low heat until crisped and golden underneath. Lift and turn carefully, cook briefly on other side. Serve with Dal and Vegetable Sauce.

SRI LANKAN-STYLE FLAT BREAD
Yields 12

2 cups (8 oz / 250 g) self-rising flour
¹/₂ cup (2 oz / 60 g) rice flour
¹/₂ cup (1¹/₂ oz / 45 g) finely ground fresh or desiccated flour
1 tsp salt
1–1¹/₄ cups (8–10 fl oz / 250–300 ml) cold water

In a mixing bowl combine flours with coconut, salt and cold water to make a soft dough. Knead for 5 minutes, wrap in plastic and set aside for at least 1 hour. Divide into 12 pieces and roll out into rounds about 5 in (13 cm) in diameter. Cook on a lightly oiled griddle, or *tawa*, on both sides until golden.

STEAMED BREAD DOUGH

$1/2$ cup (4 fl oz / 125 ml) milk, at room
temperature
$1/3$ cup (3 oz / 90 g) sugar
2 tsps active dry yeast
$1/2$ cup (4 fl oz / 125 ml) water, at room
temperature
$1/2$ tsp salt
$2^1/2$ cups (10 oz / 300 g) all-purpose (plain)
flour, sifted

Pour milk into a bowl, add 1 tbsp sugar
and the yeast. Let sit 10 minutes. Add
remaining sugar, water, salt and the
sifted flour. Knead for 5 minutes. Cover
with damp cloth. Let rise for 1 hour.
Punch down, knead lightly again. To
use, shape dough as desired, place on
paper in steamer and steam until
springy and dry to the touch.

BREAD CRUMBS: see PANKO

BREADFRUIT: (*Artocarpus communis*)
Breadfruit has a knobby green skin separated
into five-sided segments. The fibrous starchy
flesh tastes like yam or potato when cooked.
Breadfruit is not widely eaten in Asia but is
available in Indonesia and the Philippines. It
should be green and hard when cooked as a
roasted vegetable and yellow-brown and soft
when used for desserts. Cut the breadfruit in
half, scoop out the white pulpy flesh and remove the seeds. Boil the flesh and use in place
of potato or add sugar, spices and coconut milk
and serve as a dessert. The seeds may be
roasted like chestnuts.
See also: CHESTNUT; POTATO; YAM

BREADMAKING UTENSILS: see UTENSILS,
BREAD AND PASTRY MAKING

BREM BALI: (*BREM BA-LI,* Indonesia) see
WINE, ASIAN

BRINJAL: (*BRIN-JAL*, India) see EGGPLANT

BROAD BEAN: (*Vicia faba*) Broad beans are
an ancient vegetable known from the European Iron Age. In Asia broad beans are eaten
in India and in the eastern coastal Chinese
region around Shanghai where they are cooked,
skinned and served in an oil or brown-sauce
dressing. Dried broad beans are used extensively. They must be soaked overnight to
rehydrate and in China are steamed and served
cold in a sesame oil dressing as an appetizer. A
snack of crisp-fried, salted, or dry-roasted broad
beans is enjoyed in many parts of Asia. In
Sichuan province they are made into a pungent seasoning. The beans may be sprouted
and the resultant vegetable cooked as a stir-
fry or used in soups. Elsewhere in Southeast
Asia broad beans are replaced by the strong-
smelling *parkia,* which proliferate there. The
fava or horsebean is smaller in size, although
similar in taste, and is used to some extent
throughout the region.

BROAD BEAN PASTE is a strong seasoning
made from broad beans.

BROAD BEAN SAUCE: A thick, brown,
highly spiced sauce made from ground broad
beans seasoned with garlic and chili. It ranges
in taste from mild to strongly spiced and intensely hot. The best is made in Pixian, a city
in the Sichuan province, where it is used instead of soybean-based seasoning sauces.
Also known as *bin dou* (beans), *douban lajian,
doubjiang* (bean paste) (China); *soraname*
(Japan)

BROCCOLI WITH CRABMEAT SAUCE
Serves 4–6

1 lb (500 g) broccoli florets, rinsed
5 tsps vegetable oil
salt
white pepper
sugar
2 tbsps minced scallions (spring / green
onions)
1 tsp minced ginger
2 oz (60 g) flaked crabmeat
1 tbsp yellow rice wine
$3/4$ cup (6 fl oz / 180 ml) chicken stock
2 tsps cornstarch (cornflour)
2 egg whites, lightly beaten

Place broccoli in a dish, add 2 tsps
vegetable oil and a little salt, white

(cont'd)

(Broccoli with Crabmeat Sauce cont'd)

pepper and sugar. Steam over simmering water for 6 minutes. Drain. Heat remaining oil in a wok and stir-fry broccoli briefly. Fry scallions and ginger briefly, add crabmeat and rice wine. Cook for 20 seconds. Mix chicken stock with cornstarch. Pour into pan. Stir over medium heat and slowly add beaten egg whites. Simmer 1 minute; season to taste. Pour over broccoli.

BROWN BEAN SAUCE: see BEAN PASTES AND SAUCES

BROWN PEPPERCORN: see SICHUAN PEPPERCORN

BUAH KELOH: (*BOO-WAH KEH-LOCH,* Malaysia) see DRUMSTICK VEGETABLE

BUAH KERAS: (*BOO-WAH KEH-RUS,* Malaysia) see CANDLENUT

BUAH PELAGA: (*BOO-WAH PEH-LAH-GAR,* Malaysia) see CARDAMOM

BUCKWHEAT NOODLES: see NOODLES (SOBA)

BUFFALO: (*Bubalus bubalis*) The meat of the water buffalo, known commonly as *carabao* or *karabou,* and another species known as *tamarau,* is eaten in many parts of Southeast Asia instead of beef. Native to India and several other neighboring countries, the buffalo is an invaluable beast of burden on many Southeast Asian farms. Its meat is used in braised dishes and stews in Laos, Cambodia and Indonesia. In Laos it is puréed to make *lap,* a raw meat dish served on special occasions. The skin is boiled until tender and used as a meat. In Cambodia buffalo skin is dried and cooked until crisp, then added in strips to stews. In Java, Indonesia, it is usually cooked in a hot curry sauce. *Longsong* is the Laotian style of tabletop hotpot in which thin strips of buffalo meat or venison are cooked in a pot of simmering, herb-flavored stock and dipped into a rich, roasted peanut sauce. A similar dish is made in Cambodia using beef and vegetables and is known as *yao horn.* Buffalo meat is also eaten in Nepal, where it may be roasted or made into curries and *koftas* (meatballs).

Also known as *carabao, karabou, karibu,*

kerbau (Indonesia)*; rango ko masu* (Nepal)
See also: BUFFALO MEAT STEW (recipe)

BUFFALO MEAT STEW
Serves 6

1¹/₂ lbs (750 g) buffalo meat, cubed
2 medium eggplants (aubergines), sliced
8 oz (250 g) leafy vegetables, rinsed
1¹/₄ cups (6 oz / 185 g) long beans (green beans), sliced
1 cup (2 oz / 60 g) chopped cloud ear fungus, soaked
12 slices greater galangal
3–4 fresh red chilies, seeded and sliced
1¹/₂ tsps crushed fennel seeds
salt
pepper
¹/₂ cup (1 oz / 30 g) chopped scallions (spring / green onions)
¹/₄ cup chopped fresh herbs, such as mint, basil, chervil, watercress, daun kesom

Place meat and eggplants in a saucepan. Cover with water and cook until eggplants are tender. Remove eggplants, but simmer meat until tender. Peel and mash eggplants and return to pan with vegetables, beans, fungus, *greater galangal,* chilies and fennel. Boil uncovered until tender and sauce has thickened. Season with salt and pepper. Add scallions and fresh herbs.

BUKO: (*BOO-KOH,* Philippines) see COCONUT

BULB GARLIC: see GARLIC

BULGOGI: (*BUL-GO-GY,* Korea) see UTENSILS, HOTPLATES AND GRIDDLES; KOREA

BULGOGI BARBECUE: (recipe) see BEEF

BUMMALOW: (*BAMM-A-LO,* India) see BOMBAY DUCK

BUN: (*BOON-K,* Vietnam) see NOODLES (RICE STICK NOODLES)

BUNGA CINGKEH: (*BOONGA CHING-KEAH,* Malaysia) see CLOVES

BUNGA LAWANG: (*BOONGA LAH-WUNG,* Indonesia, Malaysia) see ANISE, STAR

BURDOCK ROOT: (*Arctium lappa*) The long, slender, irregularly shaped root of the burdock plant, an ancient vegetable of Eu-

rope that is cultivated for culinary use in Japan. It has a crunchy texture and although its own flavor is bland, it absorbs the flavors of the sauces and stocks in which it is cooked. The roots should be washed and pared before use. Often used in *nimono* (simmered) dishes.
Also known as *gobo* (Japan)
See also: JAPAN, COOKING METHODS

BURMA: Burma is sandwiched between Laos, India, China and Thailand and has a long seacoast offering an abundance of seafood. Its cooking is multifaceted. *Mohingha* is undeniably Burma's most common dish, and one of the tastiest imaginable. Rice vermicelli bathed in a creamy coconut seafood curry as thin as soup, it is accompanied by a multitude of side-dishes from wedges of hard-cooked eggs and limes, to fried garlic and scallions, roasted powdered chick-peas, sliced chilies, bite-size patties made from shrimp or mung beans, and slices of the tender heart of banana trunk. Curries form the heart of Burmese cooking and are usually powerfully flavored. Fresh turmeric, ginger and *greater galangal* root are indispensable seasonings. Equally important are the pungent fermented fish seasonings *pazun ngapi*, made from shrimp, *ngan pya ye*, fish sauce in the tradition of the Vietnamese *nuoc mam*, and *ngapi*, as well as dried shrimp ground to fluffy shreds or a fine floury powder. Burmese cooking has been influenced by ingredients from neighboring countries such as soy sauce and dried mushrooms from China, chick-pea flour for thickening and aromatic *garam masala* from India. Sesame seeds, coconut and palm sugar are used in many luscious desserts and sweet cakes, and the fruits of the sea make simple crisp-fried snacks, flavorsome soups and spicy hot curries. Rice is the mainstay of the Burmese diet and is brought piping hot to the table at every meal, even though the curries and other dishes may only be served at room temperature. Eating with the fingers is traditional (although many people now prefer using a spoon and fork) and is enjoyed most with a dish known as *htamin lethoke*—literally rice mixed with the fingers. Rice is cooked by the absorption method, using a carefully measured amount of water which is totally absorbed into the rice grains in cooking.

This method renders the rice moist, fluffy and just sticky enough to hold together when eating. Lemon grass and coconut milk are sometimes used for flavoring. *Balachaung* is a potent homemade condiment essential to the Burmese table. It is a paste of ground, dried shrimp, garlic, ginger, sesame oil, turmeric and shrimp paste. Its powerful odor may be offensive, but its intense flavor is a highlight not to be missed.

BURMA RECIPES

Appetizers
Bean Patties
Cellophane Noodle Soup
Twelve Parts Soup

Main Courses
Htamin Lethoke
Mohingha
Pork Curry in Burmese Style

Accompaniments
Vegetable Salad

Dessert
Semolina Cake

DINNER MENU
(see recipes)
Serves 6–8

Bean Patties

Pork Curry in Burmese Style
Vegetable Salad
White Rice

Semolina Cake

BURONG DALAG: (*BOO-WRONG DA-LAG*, Philippines) A mudfish considered a delicacy in central Luzon and Laguna. As with much of the seafood fished in the Philippines, it is preserved by pickling: layering in earthenware pots covered with salt, soft boiled rice,

and the coloring agent *angkak*. After several days' curing, the fish may be sautéed with tomatoes, onions and garlic.
See also: FOOD COLORING; FISH, PRESERVED

BUTTERBUR: see COLTSFOOT

BUTTERMILK: The liquid remaining after butter has been separated from cream is used in India to add richness to curries and as a beverage in the form of *lassi*, a salty or sweetened drink, although *lassi* is more commonly made with yogurt.
Also known as *chhas, lassi, matha* (India)
See also: BUTTERMILK CURRY (recipe); LASSI

BUTTERMILK CURRY
Serves 4–6

1 tbsp besan *flour, toasted*
1¹/₄ cups (10 fl oz / 300 ml) buttermilk
1¹/₂ tsps minced garlic
1¹/₂ tsps minced ginger
1 tsp cumin
1 tsp coriander seeds
3 fresh green chilies, seeded and slit
2 tbsps ghee
5 curry leaves
¹/₂ tsp mustard seeds
¹/₄ tsp asafoetida
1 tsp sugar
¹/₄ tsp turmeric
1¹/₄ tsps salt
fresh coriander (cilantro)

Mix *besan* flour and buttermilk to a smooth paste. Grind garlic, ginger, spices and chilies to a paste. Heat ghee and fry curry leaves, mustard seeds and *asafoetida*. When the seeds stop popping, add seasoning paste and fry briefly. Add sugar, turmeric, salt and the buttermilk paste. Bring slowly to a boil. Garnish with fresh coriander.

CABAI: (*CHA-BUY*, Indonesia) see CHILI
CABAI HIJAU: (*CHA-BUY HE JAU*, Indonesia) see CHILI
CABAI MERAH: (*CHA-BUY MAY-RAH*, Indonesia) see CHILI
CABAI RAWIT: (*CHA-BUY-RAW-WIT*, Indonesia) see CHILI

CABBAGE, CHINESE: The various edible plants of the family Brassicaceae have been an important foodstuff in China since ancient times. Several varieties have been cultivated for centuries, in particular *bok choy* (*pau ts'ai*) or Chinese white cabbage, *pe ts'ai* or napa (celery) cabbage, and *gai choy* (*gai ts'ai*) or mustard cabbage.

Various types of Chinese cabbage are also used in other parts of Asia, notably Korea where it is usually pickled with garlic and chili; and Japan, Singapore and Malaysia where it is eaten as a fresh vegetable or made into a pickle. Several types of Chinese cabbage may be pickled in brine, or sun-dried and salted for use out of season as a vegetable or as a flavoring ingredient in soups and in braised or stir-fried dishes. In northern China and Korea, and to a lesser extent in Japan, pickled cabbage is served as a side dish with meals.

Most types of Chinese cabbage are now readily available year-round in Oriental food stores and major supermarkets. When buying, choose vegetables with brightly colored, unmarked leaves and firm, crisp stems. Store in the vegetable compartment of the refrigerator for up to five days. Cook Chinese cabbage until crisp-tender when stir-frying. Both stems and leaves should turn a deep, bright green. Stem vegetables can be cut diagonally into 2 in (5 cm) pieces for use in mixed, stir-fried dishes and soups. When cooking as a vegetable or in braised dishes, they should be cut in half to give pieces of about 7 in (17 cm). Chinese celery cabbage can be cut into strips of about 1¹/₂ in (3 cm) or be shredded finely or coarsley according to the dish. The thicker stems should be cooked slightly longer than the tender, leafy tops.

See also: CABBAGE, PICKLED; PICKLED VEGETABLES (recipe)

BOK CHOY (*Brassica chinensis*) has long, thick, fleshy white stems with mid-green leaves similar in shape to spinach. Both stems and leaves are eaten, but the stems require more cooking. The cabbage is best picked young, at a height of about 7 in (17 cm) (known as baby *bok choy*) when it is very tender. Some *bok choy* varieties have a central stem with small yellow flowers similar in appearance to *choy sum*. *Bok choy*, with its delicate flavor, is used in stir-fried, braised or simmered dishes and in soups. The tender young hearts are particularly prized, and are usually cooked by poaching in flavored stock or salted water. They are often served with a creamy sauce. Substitute *choy sum* or *pe ts'ai*.

Also known as *baicai, bai ts'ai, ch'ing ts'ai, pak chai, pau ts'ai* (China); Chinese chard; Chinese white cabbage; white mustard cabbage

CHOY SUM (*Brassica chinensis* var. *parachinensis*) has pale green, long, medium-size stems with rounded, pale to mid-green leaves. It may show small yellow flowers at the tips of the inner stems. The name *choy sum* translates as "vegetable hearts." *Choy sum* cabbage closely resembles the central stems of *bok choy* (see above) and it is commonly believed that the two vegetables are closely related. The stems have a distinct flavor and slight bitterness and are always eaten, often in preference to the leaves. Thicker stems should be peeled, but the younger or thinner stems can be cut in half, making pieces of about 5 in (12 cm) in length. These may be steamed or poached in stock or water and are usually served with oyster sauce as a dressing. Substitute peeled common broccoli stems, *bok choy* or *gai larn*.

Also known as flowering white cabbage

CHUK GAAI CHOY (*Brassica juncea* var.) has thin, ribbed, mid-green stalks in a sparse bunch, with mid-green serrated leaves extending almost to the base. It grows to a height of about 12 in (30 cm). Some varieties form loosely packed heads. It has an unpleasantly strong flavor that diminishes after parboiling. It is usually chopped and added to soups as mustard greens, but the parboiled vegetable is also an agreeable addition to stir-fried dishes and goes particularly well with a garlic and black bean sauce.

Also known as bamboo mustard cabbage

DAAI GAAI CHOY (*Brassica juncea*) is a strong and bitter-tasting vegetable with a rounded head resembling a lettuce. It has thick, grooved, pale green stems and curly, textured, pale green leaves. When cooked fresh it has a slightly astringent taste that is best in braised and simmered dishes and in soups. It is more often used in its pickled or salted forms as a pungent vegetable or flavoring ingredient.

Also known as Swatow mustard cabbage
See also: CABBAGE, PICKLED

GAI LARN (*Brassica alboglabra*) closely resembles *choy sum*, the flowering white cabbage, but has small white flowers instead of yellow. It is somewhat similar in flavor to kale which can be substituted, although they are not recognized as being related. The grayish to mid-green stems are favored, and the tops are usually trimmed before boiling, steaming or stir-frying. The flavor is fresh but slightly bitter and, like *choy sum*, it is often served with oyster sauce. It is also used in many soup and noodle dishes and is at its best in winter.

Also known as *kai laarn* (China); Chinese broccoli; Chinese kale
See also: GAI LARN WITH OYSTER SAUCE (recipe)

JIU LA CHOY (*Brassica juncea* var.) has pale green to white, thickish stems with pointed, mid-green leaves. It grows to about 18 in (45 cm) making it one of the longest leafy vegetables. It is a variety of mustard cabbage, with the characteristic strong and slightly bitter flavor and is best as a vegetable dish. Chop leaves and stems crossways and parboil for 1–2 minutes before stir-frying. Substitute *bok choy* or *gai larn*.

Also known as Chinese green cabbage; sow cabbage

NAPA CABBAGE (WONG NGA BAAK) (*Brassica pekinensis*) is the pale green, large and tightly packed Tientsin (Beijing/Peking) cabbage which has a mild but distinct flavor. It is similar in appearance to Romaine (Cos) lettuce, and its length and tight-packed construction also give it the name celery cabbage. It is tender when cooked by stir-frying or simmering, and is often used in hotpot cooking. Much of the Tientsin cabbage grown in northern

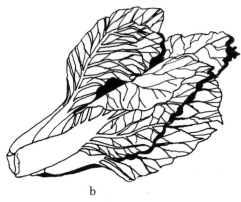

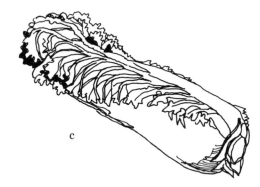

a. *Choy sum*
b. *Bok choy*
c. *Napa cabbage* (Wong nga baak)

China is pickled in salt with chilies for use as a side dish. It makes a good substitute for common cabbage in salads or coleslaw. (Because of its flavor and aroma, common cabbage is not suited to Chinese cooking.) To use, cut into crossways strips of about 1½ in (4 cm), or shred finely. The thicker stem ends should be cooked slightly longer than the tender, leafy tops. This cabbage is also grown in Korea and used to make their popular *kimchi* (salt and chili pickled cabbage). It is also used in Japan, particularly in one-pot dishes such as *sukiyaki*.
Also known as *pe ts'ai*, *wong bok* (China); *hakusai* (Japan); *baechu*, *kimchi* (Korea); *pechay* (Philippines); celery cabbage; Korean cabbage; napa cabbage; Tientsin (Beijing/Peking) cabbage
See also: KIMCHI (recipe); "LION'S HEAD" MEATBALLS (recipe)

RAPE (*Brassica napus*)**:** Rape has been known as a vegetable since ancient times. Broccoli rape, heart of rape and winter rape are each used extensively as a vegetable in northern China but in other parts of China *bok choy*, napa cabbage and spinach are usually substituted. Oil extracted from rape seeds was one of the earliest forms of cooking oil. It is still made today in a limited way. Like other Chinese cabbages, rape can be kept fresh for just a few days in the refrigerator, loosely wrapped in plastic.
Also known as *quinchoy* (winter rape) (China); *yu choy sin* (heart of rape); *yu choy, yu ts'ai* (broccoli rape); borecole; cole; coleweed

SEEN CHOY (*Brassica oleracea* spp.) is a midgreen, curly leafed vegetable, closely related to rape, with a distinct cabbage flavor that is used in stir-fried, vegetarian and braised dishes. Common cabbage can be substituted in the latter types of dishes and broccoli florets in the former. This vegetable may be dried for preservation and is then used in braised dishes, or may be deep-fried until very crisp.
Also known as *sien ts'ai* (China); borecole; curly kale; kale

TAAI GOO CHOY (*Brassica chinensis* Jus. var. *rosularis*) is otherwise known as flat cabbage for its low-growing widespread shape. It has the white stems of *bok choy* and small, rounded, deep-green leaves with white veins.

49

It grows well in the Shanghai district and is resistant to snow and frosts. It should be washed thoroughly and can be used in any recipe for *bok choy*.

Also known as Chinese flat cabbage; flat cabbage

GAI LARN WITH OYSTER SAUCE
Serves 4

4¹/2 cups (1 lb / 500 g) gai larn
2 tbsps vegetable oil
1 tbsp shredded ginger
³/4 tsp sugar
2¹/2 tbsps oyster sauce

Cut vegetable into 3 in (8 cm) lengths, drop into simmering water to cook 1¹/2 minutes. Remove and drain. Heat oil in a wok and stir-fry vegetable with ginger for 1 minute. Add sugar. Transfer to a serving dish and pour on oyster sauce.

LAOTIAN CABBAGE SOUP
Serves 6

1 small onion, chopped
³/4 tsp minced garlic
1 tsp minced greater galangal
2 tsps ground coriander
2 tbsps vegetable oil
4 ¹/2 cups (1 lb / 500 g) finely shredded cabbage
1 tsp white pepper
6 cups (1¹/2 qts / 1.5 l) beef stock
2 tbsps fish sauce
salt

Sauté onion, garlic, *greater galangal* and coriander in oil for 2 minutes, then add the cabbage and pepper and sauté for 2 minutes. Add beef stock, fish sauce, salt to taste and bring to a boil. Simmer for 10–12 minutes.

CABBAGE, PICKLED: Throughout Asia cabbage is a major garden crop, and in most countries it is preserved in some form for use year-round. In northern China the tightly packed, pale green napa cabbage is slightly pickled in vinegar with salt, sugar and chili to

---

PICKLED CABBAGE IN CHICKEN SOUP WITH HAM
Serves 6

6 cups (1¹/2 qts / 1.5 l) chicken stock
4 oz (125 g) Chinese ham, thinly sliced
2 oz (60 g) pickled mustard cabbage, shredded

Heat ingredients together for 5–6 minutes. Serve.

SICHUAN CABBAGE WITH PORK
Serves 6

1¹/2 lbs (750 g) boneless fresh ham, with rind
dark soy sauce
oil
12 oz (375 g) chopped pickled mustard cabbage (Sichuan preserved cabbage)
3 tbsps minced ginger
2 pickled red chilies, chopped
¹/2 cup (1 oz / 30 g) chopped scallions (spring / green onions)
1¹/2 tbsps fermented black beans, chopped
¹/3 cup (3 fl oz / 90 ml) light soy sauce
¹/4 cup (2 fl oz / 60 ml) yellow rice wine
1¹/2 tbsps crushed rock candy sugar

Place pork, skin upward, in a large pan and cover with cold water. Bring to a boil, then simmer for 2 hours. Drain, reserving 1 cup (8 fl oz/240 ml) of the liquid. Dry pork, rub with dark soy sauce, deep-fry in very hot oil to color the surface. Drain. Cut into thick slices and arrange in a heatproof dish. Cover with pickled cabbage, ginger, chilies, scallions and black beans. Add light soy sauce, wine and crushed rock sugar. Steam for about 1 hour.

---

serve as a side dish. A similar pickle is served in Malaysia and Singapore, though it is usually sweeter tasting and may contain ginger.

KIMCHI is a potent cabbage pickle favored in Korea which is mainly made from napa cabbage.

SICHUAN PICKLED MUSTARD, CABBAGE: In the central province of Sichuan, mustard cabbage is pickled with salt, chilies and garlic, and fermented in large pottery tubs to make a pungent pickle. On maturation it is used as a strongly flavored seasoning ingredient, which is added to stir-fried, simmered and braised dishes, and soups.

See also: CABBAGE, CHINESE; KIMCHI (recipe); PICKLED CABBAGE IN CHICKEN SOUP WITH HAM (recipe); SICHUAN CABBAGE WITH PORK (recipe)

CABE: (*CHA-BAY*, Indonesia) see CHILI

CA COM: (*CAR COM*, Vietnam) see ANCHOVY

CADJU: (*KA-JU*, Sri Lanka) see CASHEW NUT

CAKE-MAKING UTENSILS: see UTENSILS, CAKE AND DESSERT MAKING

CA KHOAI: (*CAR KWAI*, Vietnam) see BOMBAY DUCK

CALIFORNIA CHILI: see CHILI

CALIFORNIA ROLL: see SUSHI

CALROSE RICE: see RICE (NON-GLUTINOUS)

CA MANG: (*CAR MONK*, Vietnam) see BANGUS

CAMBODIA: Cambodia, with its narrow coastal strip fronting the Gulf of Thailand, enjoys a wealth of seafood which is prepared simply by grilling, or poaching in aromatic, herbaceous stock with tart ingredients such as vinegar, tarmarind or lime juice. Of these, the most popular is undoubtedly *samla mchou banle* with its aromatic lemon-scented citronella (lemon grass). Fish, squid and shrimp are fermented and processed into *tuk trey*, the ubiquitous fish sauce enjoyed in all Southeast Asian countries. A cook-at-the-table "steamboat" of seafoods, meatballs, vegetables and noodles is a popular eating style. Cambodians also enjoy grilled meats in the form of bitesize cubes of meat similar to *satay*, or tiny meatballs grilled over charcoal. Kebabs of cubed fish, or whole small fish and shellfish are also cooked in this way with a simple marinade or dressing to add flavor. Herbs such as fennel, dill, basil and mint, with garlic, ginger, lemon grass, *greater galangal* and chilies are added generously to many dishes. As in Vietnam, grilled foods may be wrapped with salad ingredients and dipped into a spicy sauce before eating.

See also: LAOS

CAMPHOR WOOD CHIPS: (*Cinnamomum camphora* L.) Chinese clothes storage trunks of aromatic camphor wood have been sold in Western countries for at least 100 years, so we are familiar with this uniquely fragrant wood. Wood chips left over from the trunk-making industry were found, when burnt, to give off a wonderfully aromatic smoke which chefs from Sichuan province in China used for their famed "camphor- and tea-smoked duck." Camphor wood is hard to find in Western countries, but a reasonably good effect can be achieved by smoking Chinese green tea leaves. Other smoke fuels used in China include pine needles, sugar, raw rice and jasmine tea.

Also known as *jern cha* (China)

See also: CAMPHOR- AND TEA-SMOKED DUCK (recipe)

CAMPHOR- AND TEA-SMOKED DUCK
Serves 8

6 lbs (2.5 kgs) fresh duck
salt
2 tbsps pepper
1 lb (500 g) camphor wood chips, or 1 small
bundle camphor tree leaves
1/2 cup Chinese green tea leaves
1–2 pieces dried orange peel
vegetable oil

Rinse duck and pour boiling water over skin and inside cavity. Drain thoroughly. Rub salt and pepper evenly over the duck, sprinkling a little inside. Wrap with plastic and refrigerate for 6–7 hours. Line a large wok with a double thickness of aluminum foil and place wood chips, tea leaves and orange peel in center. Heat until it begins to smoke, then reduce heat. Place duck, breast downwards, on a rack over smoke, cover and smoke for 10 minutes, turn and smoke other side for at least 8 minutes. Transfer duck to a steamer and steam for 1³/₄ hours. Pat skin dry, deep-fry in hot oil until crisp and deep brown.

CANDLENUT: (*Aleurites moluccana*) A hard, dry-textured nut, from a tree of the Euphorbiaceae family, which includes such diverse plants as the blackcurrant, poinsettia and cassava (manioc). Grown and used in Malaysia and Indonesia, originally the nuts were ground to a paste with copra and cotton and used to make candles (giving the nuts their popular name). This is still done in remote villages in Indonesia. The nuts were also used as pieces in a game and for gambling. The harvested nuts are roasted until the hard shell has nearly carbonized. They are then broken open and the kernel removed. The gray-to-cream colored nuts, not unlike a macadamia in shape but with a drier texture, are sold whole. They have a slightly bitter flavor and are not eaten raw as the oil is thought to be toxic. The kernels are ground and used as a binding and enriching ingredient in curries, and are added to hot and cold sauces and *sambals*.
Also known as *kyainthee* (Burma); *kemiri* (Indonesia); *buah keras* (Malaysia)
See also: CHICKEN LIVERS IN SPICY SAUCE (recipe); LAKSA WITH CHICKEN AND COCONUT MILK (recipe)

CANTALOUPE: see MELONS AND GOURDS

CAPSICUM: see PEPPER

CARABOU: (*KAH-REE-BOO*, Indonesia) see BUFFALO

CARAMBOLA: see STAR FRUIT

CARAMEL COLORING: A food coloring used in Chinese cooking, particularly in the region of Shanghai on the east coast, and also in Vietnam, to give a rich, dark gloss to gravies and sauces. It can be purchased commercially and looks like thick soy sauce. It has neither a sweet nor salty taste. At home it is made by cooking sugar with a small quantity of water until it turns dark brown and loses its sweetness. Sugar cooked in vegetable oil to a deep red-brown is another form of caramel used in Chinese and Indian cooking, and is used to make certain sweet and sour dishes. In Malaysia and Singapore a thick, sweet, dark soy sauce known as *timcheong* can be used for similar effect.
See also: NUOC MAU (recipe); SOY SAUCE, SWEET AND SALTY

CARAWAY MINT: see RAU LA TIA TO

CARAWAY SEED: (*Carum carvi*) The aniseed-flavored seed of a biennial plant which reaches a height of about 2½ ft (75 cm). The ripe seeds, which resemble aniseed, have a tendency to shatter when dry, so are harvested at night while moist with dew. In Asia caraway seeds are used primarily in India, Sri Lanka and Burma to flavor cakes, curries and pickles. They are highly regarded as a carminative and are included in medicinal preparations for stomach ailments. In Vietnam the leaves of the caraway plant are used as a herb.
Also known as *shah jeera* (India); *jemuju* (Malaysia)
See also: RAU LA TIA TO

CARDAMOM: (*Elettaria cardamomum*) A perennial, thin, willowy bush that grows to about 13 ft (3 m) high. It has seed pods which are picked for use as an aromatic spice. A native of India, it is the second most expensive spice in the world (the first is saffron) because each pod must be taken from the branch by hand. It is an ancient spice that has been used for centuries in the Middle East. Arabs chew the seeds as a confection and add it to their strong coffee to soften its bitterness. Indians use it extensively in their cooking, particularly in the northern states where it is a valued ingredient in *garam masala* and other spice mixtures. They also chew the seeds after a meal to refresh the mouth and aid digestion, and add it to a sweet aromatic tea that is traditionally made with boiled buffalo's milk. Cardamom grows wild in the lower hills of the Indonesian island of Java where it is now widely cultivated. Its tender young leaves are used in Indonesia and Thailand to flavor food and as a wrapper. It is also used to some extent in the cuisines of other parts of Asia. Cardamom has a delicate fragrance that is easily lost in the cooking process. Whole pods or seeds should be bought in preference to the powdered spice. Toast the seeds in a dry pan or hot oven for a few minutes before grinding for immediate use. Cardamom used in sweet dishes and drinks does not require toasting. There are two major types of cardamom in common use.

BROWN/BLACK CARDAMOMS are the larger type, with coarser, stringy pods and larger dull-black to gray seeds. They are used mainly in pickles and chutney.

GREEN CARDAMOMS have pale green, smooth pods that become buff- to white-colored with age, or after bleaching. They are a three-sided oval shape. Each pod contains numerous, shiny, gray-black seeds, which are used whole, lightly crushed or powdered in both sweet and savory dishes, and in pickles and chutney.
Also known as white cardamom

LEAVES of the cardamom plant resemble ginger or turmeric leaves—dark green, shiny and pointed. They have a subtle aroma of the spice and are added to some dishes for this flavor or used for wrapping foods.
Also known as *phalazee* (Burma); *sha jen* (China); *elaichi* (India); *kepillaga* (Indonesia); *buah pelaga* (Malaysia); *enasal* (Sri Lanka); *kraven, luk kraven* (Thailand)
See also: MASALA

CARIYA PATTA: (*CURRY PAT-TAA*, India) see CURRY LEAF
CAROM: (*CAR-ROM*, India) see AJWAIN

CARP: (*Cyprinus carpio*) An elegant, ornamental, freshwater fish which is eaten in China and Japan for its delicate flesh. Several species of carp are used in cooking.

BLACK CARP and **SILVER CARP** both grow to a very large size and their meat is usually prepared as thick steaks.

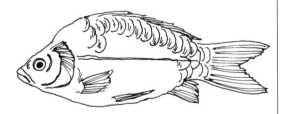

Black carp

CHUB is very large and dark-skinned with a head accounting for one-third of the total weight. It is a fleshy, fatty, tender and full-flavored meat. Braised chub's head in soups or stews is a popular dish in China and Japan.
CRUCIAN CARP is silver-colored and similar to bream in appearance.
GRASS CARP has a long, round body, not unlike a mullet.
ROCK CARP characterized by its head, thick body, small bones and rich meat and is considered one of the most delicious of the freshwater fish. Any fleshy white fish can be substituted.
Also known as *lei yu, li yu* (China)
See also: "WESTLAKE" FISH (recipe)

CARROT: (*Daucus carota*) The common carrot is used throughout Asia. In India it is made into a pungent pickle, used in vegetarian cooking and made into a delightful, creamy sweet pudding that is usually decorated with the beaten silver foil known as *varaq*. In China,

---

MARINATED CARROT (VIETNAM)
(Carat Ngam Dam)
Yields 1 cup

1 medium carrot
1½ tsps sugar
1 tsp salt
1 tsp white vinegar
¼ cup (2 fl oz / 60 ml) water

Peel carrot and cut into paper-thin strips, then shred very finely. Mix remaining ingredients with water, add carrots and knead with fingers to soften. Let stand 15 minutes; Drain. Use as a garnish or add to *nuoc cham* sauce.

---

carrots are carved into decorative garnishes for serving plates or intricately worked table centerpieces such as dragons and phoenixes for banquets. In Vietnamese restaurants, finely shredded carrot appears in many of the dipping sauces that accompany meals. In Vietnam, carrot should only be served in the classic *nuoc cham* sauces when it accompanies the small, crisp rolls known as *cha gio* It is an ingredient in salads throughout Southeast Asia, particularly Cambodia, Thailand and Vietnam.
Also known as *gajar* (India)
See also: NUOC CHAM; VARAQ (India)

CARVING VEGETABLES: see CHILI FLOWER; CHINA, GARNISHES; JAPAN, GARNISHES

CASHEW NUT: (*Anacardium occidentale*) The cashew tree is a tropical tree native to America and it grows readily in Peninsular Malaysia, Sri Lanka and Indonesia. The curved, ochre-colored nut protrudes from a purple-red pod known as the cashew apple which is eaten raw as a fruit or added to salads in Indonesia. Fresh raw cashews are used as a vegetable in curries, while roasted and dried nuts are added to stir-fries, rice and desserts.

CASHEW NUT CURRY
Serves 4–6

1 cup (8 oz / 250 g) raw cashew nuts
3 ¹/2 cups (28 fl oz / 885 ml) thin coconut milk
1 medium onion, finely sliced
3 fresh green chilies, seeded
¹/2 pandanas leaf
6 curry leaves
¹/2 tsp turmeric
1 cinnamon stick
1 tsp minced garlic
1 tsp minced ginger
salt
black pepper

In a nonaluminum pan simmer the first 6 ingredients together with turmeric, cinnamon stick, garlic and ginger, for 30 minutes. Season with salt and black pepper. Discard pandanus leaf and cinnamon stick before serving.

They are a common ingredient in Indian vegetarian cooking, and in ground form are used to thicken and enrich curries. The Javanese use the very young leaves to flavor rice. A potent liqueur known as *kaju* is made from the juice of the cashew apple. The shell contains an oil that is an irritant to the skin and is used commercially in waterproofing and preserving products.
Also known as *yao dou, yiu gor* (China); *kadju, kaju* (India); *kacang mete, kacang monyet* (Indonesia); *gajus* (Malaysia); *casoy* (Philippines); *cadju* (Sri Lanka)
See also: CASHEW NUT CURRY (recipe)

Cashew apples

CASOY: (*CA-SOY*, Philippines) see CASHEW NUTS
CASSAVA: see TAPIOCA
CASSAVA CHIPS: see KRUPUK

CASSIA: (*Cinnamomum zeylanicum, C. cassia*) Cassia has the aroma of cinnamon but it is coarser in texture and less subtle in taste. A native of Vietnam, it is now grown extensively in China, India, Indonesia and Burma. The reddish-brown quills are stripped from the branches, and the bark is dried and ground to a powder or cut into rectangular pieces. It is less expensive than Sri Lankan cinnamon, but offers a less subtle flavor. Cassia powder is one of the essential ingredients of Chinese five-spice powder.

CASSIA LEAVES and buds can be eaten fresh as a vegetable. Dried or fresh, they are used for flavoring foods as a substitute for curry leaves. In China during the Ming Dynasty, the flowers were used in preference to the bark as a seasoning.
Also known as *kuei* (China); *kashia keihi* (Japan); *ob choey* (Thailand)
See also: CINNAMON

CASSIA BLOSSOM WINE: see WINE, CHINESE

CAUL FAT: The lacy, transparent, fat membrane which covers the internal organs of a pig. It is used to wrap fragile foods before grilling, steaming or frying. In China it is used around whole fish, and in Vietnam it is used to encase minced meat for sausages and pâtés. It holds the food together and, as the fat melts, slowly imparts its own rich flavor to the food. Not often found fresh in butchers' stores, it can be bought frozen. Thaw and remove the layers needed, returning the remainder to the freezer. If unobtainable, food may be coated with cornstarch or wrapped in greased parchment (greaseproof) paper, depending on the cooking process.

Also known as *mong yau* (China); *entosensal* (Philippines); lard net
See also: LIVER AND PORK BALLS (recipe); PORK

CAULIFLOWER: (*Brassica oleracea*) Cauliflower is used frequently in Indian cooking as a vegetable. There is a popular recipe from northern India where the whole cauliflower is baked under a blanket of spices and yogurt. As a spicy filling for unleavened bread and crisp pastries, cauliflower is finely chopped, the water squeezed out and the pulp fried with spices. Elsewhere in Asia it is used less frequently, mostly as a substitute for Chinese broccoli (*gai larn*).

Also known as *yair choy far* (China); *phool gobhi* (India); *kubis bunga* (Indonesia, Malaysia)
See also: CABBAGE, CHINESE

CAVIAR: Various types of salted fresh roe or eggs (caviar) are used in Asia.

IKURA (Japan) are orange-red eggs of salmon which are most prized. Each fat, round capsule is about ¼ in (0.5 cm) in diameter, and when eaten, the firm skin pops to release the creamy textured, rich, concentrated fish-flavored oils within. *Ikura* is most frequently used as a topping for *sushi*. It is encased in a retaining border of *nori* seaweed.

Also known as caviar pearls; keta caviar; salmon caviar; salmon roe

NAMA-WUNI: (Japan) Sea urchin roe which is more creamy than *ikura* in texture and exceptionally rich in flavor. A bright orange-red color, it is used as a garnish for a variety of Japanese seafood dishes including raw sea urchin flesh served in its own shell.

SHRIMP (PRAWN) EGGS are minuscule orange-red eggs taken from female shrimp.

They are dried and salted which transforms them into tiny, red, hard grains. Used in northern and north-eastern Chinese cooking, their flavor is, like so many Chinese dried seafood ingredients, strongly fishy. Shrimp eggs are scattered over the surface of soups and vegetable dishes and are used to decorate the surface of some open types of *dim sum* dumplings, such as *siew mai* (meat dumplings). They are also used to garnish the stylized cold platters that precede an important Chinese banquet. A rare and expensive item, they are not usually available except from specialist Chinese stores. Chopped lobster liver, grated hard-cooked egg yolk or very finely chopped carrot serve the same decorative purpose. Store dried shrimp eggs in a tightly sealed glass jar in the refrigerator.

Also known as *har gee* (China)
See also: TOMALLEY

TARAKO: (Japan) Codfish roe is enjoyed in many parts of the world for its mildly fishy flavor and creamy-grainy texture. In Japan, salted codfish roe is used in some simmered dishes.

TOBIKO: (Japan) The roe of flying fish is orange-red and formed of small, firm grains that release only a hint of oil when chewed. The flavor is less pronounced than *ikura*, the texture crisp and has a pleasing crunch. Less expensive than most other types of caviar, it too is used as a topping for *sushi*, and is sometimes sprinkled as a garnish over vinegared salads or rice dishes.
See also: SUSHI (recipe); TOMALLEY

CAVIAR PEARLS: see CAVIAR (IKURA)
CAYENNE PEPPER: see CHILI
CAY HOI: (*KAY HOI*, VIETNAM) see ANISE STAR
CAY VI: (*KAY VEE*, VIETNAM) see ANISEED
CELERY CABBAGE: see CABBAGE, CHINESE (NAPA)

CELERY, CHINESE: (*Apium graveolens* var.) This vegetable resembles common celery, but has narrower, deeper green stems and a stronger flavor. It is mainly used in Chinese soups and braised dishes. The use of celery as

55

a food is recorded in the oldest Chinese documents, but these early references may have been to a type of water "dropwort" *ch'in (Oenanthe stolonifera)* which grows wild.

Also known as *kunchoi* (China); *kinchay* (Philippines); *ceun chai* (Thailand)

CELLOPHANE NOODLES: see NOODLES (BEANTHREAD VERMICELLI)

CELLOPHANE NOODLE SOUP: (recipe) see NOODLES

CENGKEH: (*CHEUNG-KEAH*, Indonesia) see CLOVES

CEUN CHAI: (*KHEUN CHAI*, Thailand) see CELERY, CHINESE

CEYLON MOSS: see AGAR AGAR

CHA (CHAI/CHAY): (*CHA*, China) see TEA

CHAAT: (*CHAAT*, India) A word describing a combination of diced fruit and vegetables, sometimes with meat or shrimp. It is tossed with a sharp dressing containing *aamchur* or tamarind and chili.
See also: AAMCHUR; MASALA

CHAAT MASALA: (*CHAAT MA-SAA-LAA*, India) see MASALA

CHAAT MURGH: (recipe) see CHICKEN

CHABAI: (*CHA-BUY*, Malaysia) see CHILI

CHADO: (*CHA-DOH*, Japan) see CHA NO YU

CHA DOUFU: (*JA DAU-FU*, China) see BEAN CURD (FRIED)

CHA GIO: (*CHA YOR*, Vietnam) see BANH TRANG

CHAMAK: (*CHA-MUK*, India) see INDIA, COOKING METHODS

CHAMPIGNON: see MUSHROOMS AND EDIBLE FUNGI

CHANE JOR GARAM: (*CHA-NAA JOR GA-RAM*, India) see CHICK-PEA

CHANNA/CHANNA KI DAL: (*CH-NAA / CHA-NAA KEE DAAL*, India) see CHICK-PEA

CHA NO YU: (*CHA-NO-YU*, Japan) The *cha no yu* or *chado* is the traditional Japanese tea ceremony, a tradition practised for many centuries.
See also: CHAWAN; TEA

Split bamboo tea whisk and bowl for use in the tea ceremony

CHAPATI: (*CHA-PAA-TEE*, India) see BREAD, INDIAN

CHARCOAL COOKING: see UTENSILS, BARBECUES AND CHARCOAL BURNERS

CHAROLI NUT: (*CHA-RO-LEE*, India) These small, round, subtly flavored nuts are used to garnish Indian sweetmeats. Melon seeds or pine nuts can be substituted.
Also known as *chironju* (India)

CHA SIEW: (*CHA SIL*, China) see PORK, CHINESE ROAST

CHA SIEW BOW: (*CHA SIL BO*, recipe) see PORK, CHINESE ROAST

CHA SIEW JEUNG: (*CHA SIL JEUNG*, China) see ROAST PORK SPICES

CHASNI: (*CHAA-SH-NEE*, India) A sweet syrup used in Indian cooking to glaze the surface of food to be grilled, or roasted over charcoal on a spit, or in a *tandoor* (clay oven). *Chasni* is usually applied to rich meats like duck and pork, with tart juices added to balance the flavor.
See also: INDIA, COOKING METHODS

CHASNIDARH: (*CHAA-SH-NEE-DAAR*, India) see INDIA, COOKING METHODS

CHATTI: (*CHATTEE*, Sri Lanka) An unglazed clay cooking pot used in Sri Lanka and India for cooking curries, rice and *dal* (lentils). Because of their porous surface, the pots develop a unique flavor from absorbing the aromatic oils of spices and other ingredients after frequent use. This in turn can help to develop the flavor of a dish. Where possible, cooks keep *chatties* for specific dishes; one for fish, one for chicken, one for vegetables and so on. The *chatti* is similar to the round-based, flared-necked *tasala* of Nepal and Kashmir, and to the clay pots used for cooking in the Philippines. Indian ice cream, *kulfi*, was traditionally made in a large, round-bottomed *chatti* which was rocked continually over a tub of saltpeter and small round pebbles. A chemical reaction caused the pebbles to chill, freezing the ice cream.

Also known as *tasala* (Nepal); *palayok* (Philippines)

See also: KULFI; UTENSILS, POTS AND PANS

CHAWAL: (*CHAA-VUL*, India) see RICE (GLUTINOUS)

CHAWAN: (*CHA-WAAN*, Japan) A small, round, porcelain or ceramic cup about 2 in (5 cm) in height and diameter, without a handle, used in Japan for drinking tea. A taller version of this cup, sometimes with a lid, is used as a cooking pot for the dish Egg Custard Steamed in a Teacup (*chawan mushi*).

See also: CHA NO YU; EGG CUSTARD STEAMED IN A TEACUP (recipe)

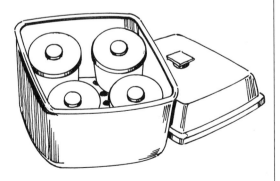

Chawan mushi cups in covered bain marie

CHAWARA: (*CHA-AA-RAA*, India) see DATES

CHAYOTE: see MELONS AND GOURDS

CHEEGAY: (*CHEE-GYE*, Korea) A thin stew midway between a stew and a soup, is a popular way of cooking many different types of ingredients in Korea. Crabs and fish, bean curd and *kimchi* are commonly served in this way.

CHEEGAY OF FISH
Serves 6–8

2 lbs (1 kg) cod or other firm white fish fillets
salt
white pepper
Oriental sesame oil
6 in (15 cm) piece dried kelp seaweed (muik)
1/2 cup (1 oz / 30 g) chopped scallions (spring / green onions)
6 dried black mushrooms, soaked
8 cups (2 qts / 2 l) water
12 clams, soaked and scrubbed
1 cup (4 oz / 125 g) young spinach
2 cups (8 oz / 250 g) chopped cabbage
1 tbsp dhwen-jang or red miso

Cut fish into large cubes, season with salt and pepper and sprinkle on a little sesame oil. Score the surface of the kelp, place in a pan with scallions and mushrooms and add the water. Bring to a boil, simmer 6–8 minutes, then add remaining ingredients, stirring to dissolve the bean paste. Season to taste with salt and pepper and simmer until fish and vegetables are tender. Sprinkle on a little sesame oil before serving.

CHEENA CHATTI: (*CHEENA CHATTI*, Sri Lanka) see UTENSILS, BREAD AND PASTRY MAKING

CHEESE, COTTAGE: see PANIR

CHE HAU SAUCE: (*CHE HOW*, China) see BEAN PASTES AND SAUCES (HOISIN)

CHENG MEIN: (*CHING MIN*, China) see FLOURS AND THICKENERS (WHEAT STARCH)

CHENNA: (*CHAI-NAA*, India) see PANIR

CHESTNUT: (*Castanea sativa*) Chestnuts have been uncovered from tombs dating back to the earliest part of China's recorded history.

These soft-textured nuts, with their smooth, hard, shiny, brown shells are used fresh and dried in China, and also in Japan. Chestnuts are mainly used in braised and simmered dishes in China, particularly with chicken or cabbage, and in a sweet soup. In Japan they are added to steamed, grilled and baked dishes. They are also mashed and sweetened to use in confectionery, sweet fillings and desserts.

CANDIED CHESTNUTS are popular in Japan where they are known as *kuri ama-ni*. Similar to *marrons glacés* they are sold whole or in broken pieces in cans, packed in syrup. They are used whole or mashed for desserts or confections.

DRIED CHESTNUTS must be soaked, then require lengthy cooking, so are usually used in slow-cooked or braised dishes. They are sold by weight and will keep indefinitely in dry conditions.

FRESH CHESTNUTS have to be removed from their hard shells, then the inner skin pared away. Soaking the nuts before attempting this usually makes it easier. In autumn, the incomparable aroma of charcoal-roasted chestnuts tempts pedestrians at many city street corners where vendors set up portable cookers laden with this favorite snack.
Also known as *lut tzee* (China); *kuri* (Japan)

CHHAS: (*CHAAS*, India) see BUTTERMILK

CHHOLAI-KA-SAG: (*CHO-LAA-EE-KAA-SAAG*, India) see AMARANTH

CHICKEN: Chicken accounts for a large percentage of the meat eaten in Asia, providing a good source of protein in the diets of both urban and country populations. Chickens have been domesticated in China for many centuries, and are used in cooking in thousands of different ways.
Also known as *chi*; *gai* (China); *murgh* (India); *ayem* (Indonesia); *ayam* (Malaysia); *kai* (Thailand)
See also: CRABMEAT AND CHICKEN ROLLS (recipe); OILS AND FATS (CHICKEN FAT); YAKITORI (recipe); YOGURT CHICKEN (recipe) *and recipes following*

CHICKEN BLOOD which has been set with a coagulating agent and then steamed, is used as an ingredient in soups and stewed dishes in certain parts of China. Pigs' blood may be treated in the same way. It is considered a warming food and usually served in winter. It may be omitted from a recipe, or replaced by bean curd.
Also known as *gai hoot* (China)

ADOBO CHICKEN
Serves 6–8

3 lbs (1.5 kgs) chicken pieces
2 tsps salt
1 tsp pepper
1 tbsp minced garlic
2 bay leaves
³/4 cup (6 fl oz / 180 ml) white vinegar
2 tsps sugar
2¹/2 cups (20 fl oz / 625 ml) vegetable oil
lettuce, shredded
tomato wedges
pineapple cubes

Cut chicken into serving pieces. Rub with salt, pepper and garlic and place in a dish with bay leaves. Sprinkle on vinegar and sugar to marinate. Cover and set aside for 2 hours. In a nonaluminum pan, simmer chicken in marinade, turning frequently until tender, and the liquid completely evaporates. Heat oil in another pan and fry chicken on both sides until well colored and crisp. Lift out, drain, and serve on a bed of shredded lettuce with tomato wedges and cubes of fresh pineapple.

CHICKEN FEET have a soft, gelatinous meat much appreciated by Chinese, who do not seem to be disturbed by the amount of chewing, nibbling on and spitting out of the many small bones. The feet should be dipped into boiling water to loosen the skin, then slowly braised with strong seasoning like soy sauce, fermented black beans, garlic and chilies, until tender. A popular *dim sum* dish.
Also known as *phong jau* (China)

CHICKEN LIVERS are enjoyed for their rich flavor and tender texture and are used throughout Asia. In India and the Southeast Asian countries they are curried and grilled on skewers; in Japan they are cooked as *teppan yaki* by grilling on a hotplate; and in China they are stir-fried or used in soup.

Also known as *jigan* (China)
See also: CHICKEN LIVERS IN SPICY SAUCE (recipe)

CHICKEN SKIN is treated as an ingredient in its own right. In Thailand it is shredded, crisp-fried and added to salads, while in China it is braised in a brown sauce with ingredients such as bamboo shoots and button mushrooms. Crisp skin chicken is enjoyed in Chinese and Vietnamese communities for its wonderful contrast of crisp, lightly spiced skin and tender, succulent meat.
See also: CHINA, COOKING METHODS; CRISP-FRIED CHICKEN (recipe)

CHICKEN STOCK is made by simmering chicken carcasses in water with onion and ginger. It is important in Chinese cooking as it is the base of most soups and cornstarch-thickened sauces. Concentrated chicken stock powders, cubes and extracts are added to many Chinese dishes to intensify flavor.
Also known as chicken broth
See also: CHICKEN STOCK (recipe)

BARBECUED CHICKEN
Serves 6

6 chicken Marylands (drumstick with thigh
attached)
2 tsps minced garlic
1 1/2 tsps minced ginger
4 oz (120 g) coriander (cilantro) roots, stems
2 tsps black pepper
1 1/2 tbsps sugar
2 tbsps dark soy sauce
vegetable oil

Prick chickens with the point of a skewer. Grind garlic, ginger, coriander and pepper together. Spread over the chicken and marinate for 2–4 hours. Mix sugar with soy sauce. Grill the chicken over charcoal, brushing with oil and the sweetened soy. Turn frequently until glazed on the surface and tender inside.

BIRIYANI OF RICE AND CHICKEN
Serves 6–8

2 lbs (1 kg) chicken, boned and cubed
1 1/2 cups (12 oz / 350 g) minced onion
2 tbsps minced garlic
2 tbsps ginger
2–3 green chilies, seeded and
chopped
1 tbsp chopped fresh coriander (cilantro)
2 1/2 cups (20 fl oz / 625 ml) plain
(natural) yogurt
1 3/4 cups (13 oz / 400 g) long
-grain rice
4 green cardamom pods, peeled
and seeds crushed
6 whole cloves
1 cinnamon stick
5 tbsps ghee
1 1/2 tsps salt
2 cups (16 fl oz / 500 ml) chicken stock
or water
1/2 tsp powdered saffron
2 tbsps milk, boiling
4 hard-cooked eggs, peeled and sliced
2 large onions, sliced and crisp-fried
3/4 cup (4 oz / 125 g) cooked green peas
toasted almonds
raisins fried in ghee

Marinate chicken with onion, garlic, ginger, chilies, coriander and yogurt for 3 hours. Wash rice and drain well; place in a heavy pan with cardamom, cloves, cinnamon stick and 2 tbsps ghee. Fry until rice is lightly colored. Add salt, chicken stock or water, cover and cook rice for 15 minutes. Mix saffron and boiling milk, pour evenly over rice and stir. Layer rice in a buttered ovenproof dish with the marinated chicken, sliced egg, fried onions and peas, ending with rice as the top layer. Add remaining 3 tbsps ghee cut into small pieces. Cover, place in a preheated oven at 250°F (120°C) and cook for about 40 minutes. Garnish with the almonds and fried raisins.

CHAAT MURGH
Serves 4

1 lettuce
2 medium tomatoes, sliced
2 hard-cooked eggs, sliced
1 onion, thinly sliced
2 green chilies, seeded and shredded
2 tbsps lemon juice
salt
sugar
1 tbsp chaat masala
8 oz (250 g) cooked chicken, shredded

Arrange lettuce in a serving dish and top with the salad ingredients. Mix lemon juice with salt and sugar to taste; add *chaat masala* and pour over the chicken. Leave to stand for 10 minutes before serving.

CHICKEN CURRY
Serves 6

3 tbsps ghee or vegetable oil
2½ lbs (1.25 kgs) chicken, boned and cubed
1½ cups (6 oz / 185 g) chopped onions
1½ tsps minced garlic
4 dried red chilies, soaked, drained and minced
1½ tsps minced ginger
6 curry leaves
1½ tbsps ground coriander
2 tsps ground cumin
1–3 tsps chili powder
1½ cups (6 oz / 185 g) chopped tomatoes
½ cup (4 fl oz / 125 ml) tamarind water
1 stalk lemon grass, split
1¼ cups (10 fl oz / 300 ml) thick coconut milk
salt
pepper

Heat ghee or oil in large pan and fry chicken until evenly colored; remove. Sauté onions, garlic, chilies, ginger and curry leaves in the pan for 3 minutes. Add spices and chili powder. Fry briefly. Add chopped tomatoes, tamarind water, lemon grass and coconut milk. Bring to a boil. Season with salt and pepper and simmer 5 minutes. Return chicken, cover and cook for about 30 minutes.

CHICKEN IN CREAMY SPICED SAUCE
Serves 6

6 tbsps (3 fl oz / 90 ml) peanut oil
3 lbs (1.5 kgs) chicken, quartered
1½ cups (6 oz / 185 g) chopped onions
1 tsp minced garlic
1 tbsp ground coriander
1 tsp ground cumin
2½ tsps chopped greater galangal
1 tsp mashed shrimp paste
¼ cup (2 fl oz / 60 ml) tamarind water
1½ tsps palm sugar (or substitute brown sugar)
4 candlenuts, ground
2 cups (16 fl oz / 500 ml) thick coconut milk
3 tbsps kecap manis
salt
chili flakes

Heat 4 tbsps (2 fl oz/60 ml) peanut oil in a large pan and fry the chicken until evenly colored; lift out. Sauté onions and garlic in 2 tbsps peanut oil to deep brown. Add spices, *galangal* and shrimp paste and cook briefly. Add tamarind water, sugar, candlenuts and coconut milk and bring almost to a boil, stirring constantly. Simmer for 4–5 minutes, stir in *kecap manis*, add the chicken pieces with salt and chili flakes to taste. Cover and simmer gently for about 1 hour, occasionally turning the chicken and basting with the sauce.

CHICKEN LIVERS IN SPICY SAUCE
Serves 4–6

1 lb (500 g) chicken livers
¼ cup (2 fl oz / 60 ml) vegetable oil
1 cup (4 oz / 185 g) chopped onions
1¼ tsps minced garlic
3–4 fresh red chilies, seeded and shredded
1 stalk lemon grass, slit
12 candlenuts, crushed

(cont'd)

(Chicken Livers in Spicy Sauce cont'd)

1½ cups (12 fl oz / 375 ml) thin coconut milk
salt
brown sugar
lemon juice
fried onion flakes

Rinse livers and dry. Cut into small pieces and fry in vegetable oil until no pink color shows; remove. Sauté onions and garlic until soft and golden. Add chilies, lemon grass, candlenuts and coconut milk. Return livers. Cook gently until tender. Add salt, brown sugar and lemon juice to taste. Garnish with onion flakes which have been fried in oil until they turn a golden brown.

CHICKEN RICE NOODLES WITH PORK
Serves 6

2 qts (2 l) water
1½ lbs (750 g) chicken thighs
½ lb (250 g) pork fillet (tenderloin)
2 tbsps fish sauce
salt
pepper
2 Chinese sausages (lap cheong), sliced
12 oz (350 g) bun noodles
2–3 eggs, beaten
2 tbsps chopped fresh coriander (cilantro)
2 tbsps minced scallions (spring/green onions)

Boil water in a saucepan; add chicken and pork and simmer 30 minutes. Remove meat and cut into small pieces. Return bones to pan with fish sauce; boil 10 minutes; then season with salt and pepper. Discard chicken bones; return meat and add sliced sausages. Boil noodles separately until tender; drain. Make thin omelettes wih eggs; cool and cut into fine shreds. To serve, divide noodles among 6 bowls, add egg shreds, coriander and scallions, then pour on the meat stock.

CHICKEN SALAD WITH MINT LEAVES
Serves 6

1 lb (500 g) cooked chicken meat, shredded
1 small onion, sliced
¼ cup (2 fl oz / 60 ml) white vinegar
¼ cup (½ oz / 15 g) chopped scallions (spring/green onions)
⅓ cup small mint leaves
chili flakes
salt
black pepper

Mix chicken with onions and vinegar. Marinate 15 minutes; drain. Add scallions, mint leaves, chili flakes, salt and black pepper to taste. Serve cold.

CHICKEN STOCK
Yields 1 qt (1 lb)

Bones and necks from 2 chickens
1 leek or 2 scallions (spring/green onions)
1 tbsp vegetable oil
4 slices fresh ginger, peeled
1½ tsps salt
2 qts (2 l) water

Rinse chicken bones and drain. Chop leeks or scallions and sauté in oil to lightly color. Add bones, ginger, salt and water. Bring to a boil and simmer, uncovered, over low heat for 1½ hours, skimming surface occasionally. Cool and strain. Refrigerate for 3–4 days, or freeze.

CRISP-FRIED CHICKEN
Serves 4

3 lbs (1.5 kgs) chicken pieces
1 tsp five-spice powder
2 tbsps light soy sauce
1 tbsp yellow rice wine
1 tbsp cornstarch (cornflour)
½ cup (4 fl oz / 125 ml) water
1 tbsp salt
1 tbsp sugar
vegetable oil

(cont'd)

(Crisp-fried Chicken cont'd)

Cut chicken into serving pieces. Mix five-spice, soy sauce and wine, adding cornstarch, water, salt and sugar. Pour over chicken and marinate for 3–4 hours, turning frequently. Drain and coat lightly with extra cornstarch. Deep-fry in moderately hot oil until golden and cooked through.

DRUNKEN CHICKEN
Serves 6

2 lbs (1 kg) chicken pieces
1¼ cups (10 fl oz / 300 ml) yellow rice wine
1 tsp salt
2½ tsps sugar
fresh coriander (cilantro)

Rinse chicken, cover with water and bring to a boil. Reduce heat and simmer, tightly covered, for about 20 minutes. Drain, place chicken in a deep dish. Mix wine with salt and sugar; pour over the chicken. Cover with plastic wrap and leave overnight to marinate. Drain, garnish with coriander and serve cold.

EIGHT TREASURE CHICKEN
Serves 6

3½ lbs (1.75 kgs) chicken
¼ cup (2 oz / 60 ml) glutinous (sticky) rice, soaked
20 dried lotus seeds, soaked
6 dried black mushrooms, soaked and diced
1 pork kidney, diced and soaked
2 tbsps dried shrimp, soaked
1 lap cheong sausage, sliced
2 tbsps dried bamboo shoots
¼ cup (2 oz / 60 g) green peas, parboiled
2 tbsps vegetable oil
1 tsp salt
3¼ cups (26 fl oz / 810 ml) chicken stock
2 tbsps yellow rice wine
1 tsp Sichuan peppercorns

(cont'd)

(Eight Treasure Chicken cont'd)

½ cup (1 oz / 30 g) diced scallions (spring / green onions)
1 tsp minced ginger
2 tbsps dark soy sauce
oil for deep-frying

Debone whole chicken; season wih salt and wine. Steam rice and lotus seeds until tender. Stir-fry mushrooms, drained kidney and shrimp, sausage, bamboo shoots and peas in the oil for 2 minutes. Add rice and lotus seeds, salt and ¼ cup chicken stock. Stuff into the chicken and close the opening with skewers or string. Place in a deep dish and add remaining 3 cups chicken, stock or water, rice wine, peppercorns, scallions and ginger. Cover and simmer-stew for 1¾ hours, until tender. Remove, drain and dry the skin. Rub with dark soy sauce and deep-fry until golden brown.

RENDANG CHICKEN
Serves 4–6

3 lbs (1.5 kgs) chicken pieces
salt
black pepper
vegetable oil
1 cup (2 oz / 60 g) minced scallions (spring / green onions)
1 tbsp minced garlic
4–8 fresh red chilies, seeded and minced
1 stalk lemon grass, halved lengthways
1 tbsp turmeric
1½ cups (12 fl oz / 375 ml) thick coconut milk
½ tsp tamarind concentrate
1½ tbsps lime juice
2–3 lime leaves

Cut chicken into serving pieces; season with salt and pepper. Brown in oil until evenly colored. Grind scallions, garlic and chilies to a paste with 2 tbsps oil. Fry until browned, add lemon grass, turmeric, coconut milk and tamarind. Simmer 5 minutes. Add chicken with lime juice and leaves. Simmer until tender.

SALT-BAKED CHICKEN

2¹/₂ lbs (1.25 kgs) chicken
¹/₂ tsp white pepper
1 tsp sugar
1 tbsp yellow rice wine
3 scallions (spring/green onions), chopped
2 tbsps shredded ginger
2 dried or fresh lotus leaves
vegetable oil
8 lbs (4 kgs) coarse salt

Rinse the chicken; dry well. Rub skin with a mixture of pepper, sugar and wine. Place scallions and ginger in the cavity. Leave for 2 hours. Soften lotus leaves in boiling water. Drain, dry and brush with oil. Wrap around the chicken. Heat salt in a large, heavy wok for about 12 minutes. Make a depression in the center, put in the chicken and cover with salt. Cover the wok and cook on moderate heat for 25 minutes. Lift out chicken, turn, re-cover with salt and cook a further 25–30 minutes, until pink and tender. Remove lotus leaves. Cut chicken into bite-size pieces to serve.

Salt-baked chicken ready to wrap in lotus leaves

THAI GINGER AND CHICKEN IN COCONUT SOUP
Serves 4–6

1 lb (500 g) dark chicken meat, cubed
2 cups (16 fl oz/500 ml) thick coconut milk
6 thick slices greater galangal
3 kaffir lime leaves
1¹/₂ cups (13 fl oz/400 ml) water
2 fresh red chilies, seeded and sliced
2 tbsps lime juice
2 tbsps fish sauce
coriander (cilantro) leaves

In a medium saucepan, mix chicken, coconut milk, *greater galangal*, lime leaves and water. Bring slowly to a boil. Add chilies, lime juice and fish sauce and simmer until chicken is tender, about 6 minutes. Add coriander leaves.

XACUTTI CHICKEN
Serves 4

2¹/₂ lbs (1.25 kgs) chicken pieces
¹/₃ cup (3 oz/90 g) ghee
1¹/₂ cups (12 oz/350 g) minced onions
2 tsps minced garlic
2 tsps minced ginger
1 recipe xacutti masala
¹/₂ tsp turmeric
6 whole cloves
2 cinnamon sticks
1 cup (8 fl oz/250 ml) thin coconut milk
salt
lemon juice
toasted desiccated coconut

Skin chicken and cut into 2 in (5 cm) pieces. Heat ghee and fry the onions, garlic and ginger for 5 minutes. Add *xacutti masala*, turmeric, cloves and cinnamon sticks. Fry for 5 minutes, adding a little water if the mixture dries. Add chicken and cook until evenly colored. Pour in coconut milk, cover and cook on low heat until the chicken is very tender. Season to taste with salt and lemon juice. Garnish with toasted coconut.

CHICK-PEA: (*Cicer arietinum*) Yellow chick-peas and the related brown *Bengal gram* of India, are an important staple in the Indian vegetarian diet. Known popularly as *channa*, most Hindus eat *channa* on Fridays as it is considered auspicious. Chick-peas originated in west Asia and grow extensively in India. They are cultivated only minimally elsewhere in Asia.

CHICK-PEAS BRAISED WITH SPICES

Serves 4

1¹/₂ cups (8 oz / 250 g) kabli channa (chick-peas)
2 tsps minced garlic
1¹/₄ cups (5 oz / 155 g) chopped onions
3 medium tomatoes, chopped
2 fresh green chilies, seeded and chopped
¹/₃ cup (3 oz / 90 g) ghee or vegetable oil
1 tbsp ground coriander
1 tbsp ground cumin
1¹/₂ tsps garam masala
³/₄ tsp turmeric
1¹/₂ tsps salt
¹/₂ tsp pepper
1 tbsp lemon juice
fresh coriander (cilantro)

Wash chick-peas; drain and soak in cold water overnight. Drain and boil in plenty of salted water with half the garlic until tender; drain. Sauté remaining 1 tsp garlic with onions and chilies in ghee or oil until onions are soft and lightly colored. Add spices, turmeric, salt, pepper and the tomatoes. Cook for 4 minutes. Add chick-peas and cook for 5–6 minutes. Stir in lemon juice and fresh coriander to taste.

BENGAL GRAM (*Dolichos biflorus*) are more wrinkled in appearance and of a brownish color, but can be used in any recipe for chick-peas. They are preferred in the Indian states of Rajasthan and Maharashtra, and are known affectionately as "horse gram" because horses are fond of them. A delightful snack comprises miniature fried *puris*, puffed like small balloons, which are split and filled with a spicy chick-pea curry. The flavors are highlighted with a dab of yogurt and a sweet ginger sauce known as *sonth*.

CHANNA KI DAL is a split, polished chick-pea used in Indian cooking as a *dal* or lentil.

HARE CHANNA are fresh or dried green chick-peas.

YELLOW CHICK-PEAS have hard, pea-sized, cream-colored seeds with a pleasant, nutty flavor. They are sometimes referred to as white chick-peas because of their pale color compared to *Bengal gram*. They are usually sold in dried form and require extensive cooking to soften. Chick-peas are cooked in many different curry styles, but perhaps their most complementary ingredients are ginger, tomatoes and *aamchur*. The yellow variety is known in India as *kabuli channa*. A finely milled flour known as *besan* is made from dried chick-peas. The sparse leaves contain oxalic acid and should not be eaten. *Chane jor garam* or *bhuje houey chane ki dal* are highly spiced, flattened, dry-roasted chick-peas seasoned with *aamchur*, chili and cumin. It is a popular snack sold in newspaper cones by streetside vendors.

See also: CHICK-PEAS BRAISED WITH SPICES (recipe); FLOURS AND THICKENERS (BESAN); LENTIL

CHIKU: (*CHEE-KOO*, Indonesia) see SAPODILLA
CHIKUWA: (*CHI-KOO-WA*, Japan) see KAMABOKO

CHILI: (*Capsicum annum, C. frutescens*) Archaeological records suggest that chilies were eaten in Mexico 9000 years ago and were cultivated 2000 years later. Introduced to Asia from the Americas, chili is used in all cuisines of the region. There are two distinct families: sweet or bell peppers (green peppers, capsicums) and hot peppers, otherwise known as chilies. The hot chili pepper is a perennial plant that thrives in hotter climates. There are many different types of hot chilies, varying in size and shape, as well as color and intensity of flavor. In Thailand there are more than 10 varieties of chilies which are described further under the Thai name *prik*. The large, deep-red chilies of Kashmir, known as

Kashmiri or *degi mirich* are used throughout India for color and flavor rather than piquancy. Chilies used in southern India and Sri Lanka, and similarly in Indonesia and Malaysia, are usually intensely hot. Chili is used in many forms. The whole fresh, green or red pods are added directly to dishes and are chopped and shredded to add to curries, soups and stir-fries, or mixed with soy sauce, vinegar or fish sauce to accompany dishes as dips. The dried pods are used whole, broken, desiccated or ground to a powder. They are also steeped in oil to make a clear, hot-flavored oil used extensively in Chinese cooking. Dried chilies are sometimes roasted in a hot oven or in a dry pan to increase their pungency and to add a rich, toasted flavor. The chili known as "goat pepper" is a small variety from Indonesia which is used for pickles and is dried and sold in whole, broken or desiccated form for export. In Thailand, and some other parts of Southeast Asia, roasted and ground chili is added to rice to use as a coating for fried foods, and as a thickener. Pulped fresh chili is made into many different types of sauce and seasoning paste of which the Indonesian *sambal ulek*, the Malaysian *rempah* and the Chinese chili bean pastes are the most extensively used. Chili is an important ingredient in pickle- and chutney-making, and is itself made into an extremely hot, pungent pickle. The fresh pods are carved into food decorations in Indonesia and Malaysia, and are finely shredded or sliced to be used as a garnish throughout Asia. In most instances, green chilies are milder in flavor than red. Deseeding chilies decreases their intensity. Dried chilies should be stored in dry conditions, preferably in an airtight container. The following are some commonly used chilies.

BLACK CHILIES are little known and similar in shape and size to *jalapenos*. A deep purple-black in color and mild in taste. When completely ripe they turn red.

CALIFORNIA OR ANAHEIM CHILIES are large, mild in flavor and a deep red color. They are similar in appearance, taste and intensity to the chilies grown in Kashmir known as *kashmiri* or *degi mirich*. They can be used fresh when a red color is required in a dish, but are often used in dried form. Roasting in a hot oven

or dry pan before use itensifies the flavor and marginally increases the hotness.

CAYENNE PEPPERS are about 3 in (8 cm) long and used fresh or dried for their hot flavor as well as to add a red color to a dish. They are often ground for use in cooking and as a condiment.
Also known as *prik chee far* (Thailand)

JALAPENO CHILIES are the popular Mexican chilies that are about 2½ in (6 cm) long, plump in shape and gently tapered. Picked when green, they have a full flavor and are used fresh in curries, or pickled as an accompaniment or ingredient in salads. Pickled *jalapeno* chilies can be eaten separately as a snack.

KASHMIRI CHILIES are long, and a deep red color, similar to California chilies. Mild in flavor they are used for their color.
Also known as *degi mirich*, *kashmiri mirich* (India)

NEW MEXICAN CHILIES are about 3 in (8 cm) long and ¼ in (0.5 cm) wide. They are harvested when red. Hot in flavor, they are used in curries, *nam prik*, *sambals* and other kinds of hot sauces, and are ground or desiccated.
Also known as *prik khee noo* (Thailand)

ORNAMENTAL CHILIES have multicolored fruits ranging from purple, through pink, yellow and green. They are very hot, but lack flavor and should be avoided in cooking as certain types are known to be toxic if eaten.

SERRANO CHILIES are perhaps the most widely available and are easy to grow at home. They are usually sold green, but are sometimes also available red. They are short and plump about 1½ in (4 cm) long and ½ in (1.25 cm) wide. The flavor is strong and rich.

THAI "BIRD'S EYE" CHILIES (*prik khee noo suan*) are the ones which give Thai food its reputation for hot tastes. They are tiny red or green chilies no more than ½ in (1.25 cm) in length and intensely hot. They may have been so named for their eye-like shape, or because mynah birds love to eat them and usually become very talkative afterwards.

TOGARASHI CHILIES are the tiny, intensely hot chilies used in Japanese cooking as a condiment and in the *shichimi* mixed condiment.

YELLOW CHILIES are a little larger than a *jalapeno* with a smooth, waxy skin that has earned them the name "yellow wax chilies." They are very hot in flavor and are not be confused with the Thai yellow chili known as *prik yuak* which is a pale, yellow-green color, has a very mild taste and is usually stuffed to serve as a snack.

Also known as *nga yut thee* (Burma); *degi mirich*, *kashmiri mirich* (Kashmiri chilies), *hara mirich* (green), *lal mirich* (red) (India); *cabe, cabai, cabai hijau* (green), *cabai merah* (red), *cabai rawit* (bird's eye) (Indonesia); *togarashi* (Japan); *chabai, cili padi* (bird's eye), *lada, lada hijau* (green), *lada merah* (red), (Malaysia); *rathu miris* (Sri Lanka); *prik, prik chee far, prik khee noo, prik khee noo kaset, prik khee noo suan, prik noom, prik yuak* (yellow) (Thailand)

See also: BEAN PASTES AND SAUCES; CHILI FLOWERS; CHILI SOY SAUCE (recipe); GREEN CURRY PASTE (recipe); NAM PRIK; ORANGE CURRY PASTE (recipe); PRIK; RED CURRY PASTE (recipe); REMPAH; SHICHIMI

CHILI BEAN PASTE: see BEAN PASTES AND SAUCES

CHILI, DRIED: Dried red chilies are used extensively in Asian cooking. Drying is done for practical purposes so that chili is always available, but the process also adds certain nuances and increases the intensity of flavor. There are chili-hot dishes in every Asian cuisine, with the exception of Japan where chili is used only as a condiment. In tropical Asia chili-hot foods are the focal part of the various cuisines. In Sri Lanka and southern India, Tamil cooks do not consider it extreme to add as many as 30 chilies to a single dish. In Sichuan, whole dried chilies are cooked in a dry pan until crisp, deep-brown and fiercely intensified in flavor. Drying strands of the large, mildly-flavored *Kashmiri mirich* decorate ceilings and rooftops in the northern Indian state of Kashmir during the summer months. The Korean seasoning and condiment *silgochu*, is finely shredded, dried chili. All

types of red chilies are sold in dried form. The Thai bird's eye chili and the slightly larger, slender and long Thai (*prik chee far*) and Japanese (*togarashi*) chilies are the hottest. In general, the larger chilies are milder in flavor, and the intensity can be further decreased by removing the seeds. To prevent loss of flavor dried chilies can be stored in a covered container in the refrigerator.

CHILI FLAKES: These are crushed, dried chilies, usually with their seeds, that are used in many recipes in preference to whole chilies or chili powder, the latter tending to give a sauce a slightly gritty feel.
See also: CHILI, DRIED

CHILI FLOWER: Chili flowers are used as a garnish in Southeast Asia. They are easily prepared, but must be made a few hours in advance and placed in ice water to encourage the "petals" to curl.

Use long, red or green chilies without imperfections. With a sharp knife slice the chilies lengthways into five to eight even segments

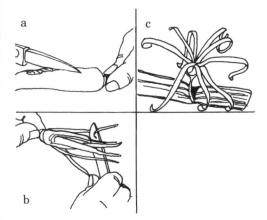

Chilli flower garnish
a. Slit open chili from stem to tip
b. Cut into long strips holding stem
c. Place in ice water to curl "petals"

(depending on the size of the chili) without disturbing the inner seed stamen. If the "petals" adhere to the stamen, release with the point of the knife. Place in ice water until segments have curled. They can be kept for up to three days in water in the refrigerator.

CHILI, GROUND ROASTED: This has a rich, nutty flavor and is intensely hot. Made by browning whole or broken dried chilies in a dry pan or hot oven, then grinding to a coarse powder in a mortar or spice grinder, it is added to ground rice as a strongly flavored thickener or coating for fried foods. It may also be sprinkled over foods as a condiment.

Also known as *nil thee* (Burma); *sabut lal mirich* (India); *lombok* (Indonesia); *ao-togarashi, togarashi* (Japan); *mak phet kunsi* (Laos); *cabai* (Malaysia); *siling labyo* (Philippines); *rathu miris* (Sri Lanka); *prik chee far* (Thailand)
See also: CHILI; CHILI PASTES, POWDERS AND SAUCES; PRIK; SILGOCHU

CHILI HANDLING: (*Oleoresin capsaicin*) The volatile oil that gives chili its hot taste can cause severe skin irritation. It retains its intensity in dried chilies. Play safe by wearing disposable gloves when working with chilies, and avoid rubbing the eyes or face. Handle the chili, and particularly the seeds, as little as possible, and wash hands, knife and work surface thoroughly with soap or detergent immediately after preparing chilies.
See also: CHILI; PRIK

CHILI OIL: (China) An intensely hot, clear red oil used as a condiment and to impart a sharp, hot flavor to cooked dishes. Made by infusing crushed, dried red chilies in hot oil. Readily available in small bottles from Chi-

---

CHILI OIL
Yields 1/2 cup (4 fl oz / 125 ml)

1/2 cup (4 fl oz / 125 ml) vegetable oil
2 1/2 tbsps dried red chili flakes

Heat vegetable oil to smoking point, reduce heat and allow to partially cool. Stir in chili and leave for 2–3 days, then filter into a bottle and seal. For a more fragrant oil use sesame oil instead of vegetable oil. Refrigerate to store for several months.

---

nese food stores, it should be kept in the refrigerator, tightly capped, to prevent loss of potency. It can be made at home.
Also known as *lat you* (China)
See also: CHILI; CHILI, DRIED; CHILI PASTES, POWDERS AND SAUCES; OILS, FLAVORED

CHILI PASTES, POWDERS AND SAUCES: Chilies impart a hot flavor to dishes. As an ingredient it comes in several forms, being either fresh or dried, whole or broken chilies, or further processed into pastes, powders and sauces to use as a seasoning or condiment.

CHILI PASTES: Hot seasoning pastes made from chilies are used in cooking in central-western China, Indonesia and Korea. Elsewhere chili pastes are more commonly used as a condiment. Their manufacture differs from country to country, but mostly comprises dried or fresh chilies ground to a thick paste and preserved with salt and sometimes vinegar or other acidulating agents such as tamarind. Some retain the fresh flavor of chilies, others are fermented to add a pungency to the naturally hot flavor. In China, chili is added to fermented soybeans to make a powerful seasoning known as chili bean paste, hot bean paste, or Sichuan chili sauce. Another full-flavored Chinese chili paste combines whole or ground garlic with chili and gives an intense flavor to dishes. The Vietnamese chili pastes are extremely hot and are used as a condiment. Chili mixed with garlic, ginger and cooked with vinegar form the base for the chili pastes from Malaysia, Sri Lanka and Singapore, which have a milder, sweeter flavor than the Chinese paste. In Indonesia, chili ground with salt and sometimes mixed with tamarind water is known as *sambal ulek* (*olek*), which is readily available and can be substituted for fresh chilies in most recipes. In Korea a similarly flavored sauce is known as *gochujang*. There are now several brands of puréed fresh chilies available, which spare the cook the hazards of dealing with fresh chilies.
Also known as *lat jiu din*, *lat jiu keung yau* (chili paste with garlic) (China); *sambal ulek* (Indonesia); *gochujang* (Korea); *prik bod* (Thailand)

CHILI POWDER is made by finely grinding dried red chilies. There are many different types of chili powder, ranging from mild to extremely hot, with some having a certain amount of cumin powder added to decrease the hotness and give more depth to the flavor. Of the various chili powders readily available, the brightest red colored and those from Japan and Thailand are generally the hottest. Cayenne pepper can be substituted. Chilies in flake form, made from dried chilies, can replace chili powder in a recipe.

Also known as *pisi hui lal mirich* (India); *togarashi* (Japan)

CHILI SAMBAL

3 green chilies, seeded and sliced
1/4 cup (2 fl oz / 60 ml) white vinegar
2 tsps salt
1–2 tsps sugar

Pour vinegar over chilies and add salt and sugar. Let stand for at least 3 hours.

CHILI SAUCE is like its counterpart, chili paste, in that there are myriad types ranging from innocent-looking, thin red sauces with fiery hot characteristics, to thick, granular sauces mixed with banana or sugar which can be quite sweet and mild. The standard Chinese chili sauce is medium to hot, an orange-red in color and reasonably thick. It is used mainly as a dip, particularly for fried foods and *dim sum*. Vietnamese chili sauces, like their pastes, have an intense, fiery flavor which should be treated with caution. The Thais have a fondness for excessively sweet chili sauces which are recognizable by their thin, clear, red base in which float fragments of chili and chili seeds. They usually look much hotter than they are. One particular Thai favorite is known as *siracha*. Thai chili sauces may be labeled simply "chicken," "fish" or "seafood" sauce and are intended as a dip with these foods when crisp-fried or grilled. Indian cooks prefer to add chilies direct to a dish in dried or fresh form and so rarely use chili sauces.

Also known as *lat jiu, lat jiu jiang* (China); *sos cihi* (Malaysia); *siracha, sos prik* (Thailand)

See also: BEAN PASTES AND SAUCES; CAMBODIAN SPICY PORK (recipe); CHILI; CHILI, DRIED; CHILI OIL; MEE SIAM (recipe); NAM PRIK PAO; PRIK

CHILI SOY SAUCE
Yields 1¹/₄ cups (10 fl oz / 300 ml)

¹/₂ cup (4 fl oz / 125 ml) chili sauce
¹/₂ cup (4 fl oz / 125 ml) light soy sauce
1¹/₂ tsps minced garlic
1 tbsp minced ginger
2–3 tsps sugar

Mix together, stirring to dissolve sugar.

CHILI POWDER/SAUCE: see CHILI PASTES, POWDERS AND SAUCES

CH'IN: (*CHIN*, China) see CELERY, CHINESE

CHINA: Chinese is the oldest and most well-documented cuisine in the world. History, geography, climate, and imagination have shaped it into the most extensive and creative of all cuisines. For the convenience of easy reference, Chinese cooking is generally classified into four major regional categories. Northern cuisine encompasses that of the capital city Beijing, and the old cuisine of Mongolia. Here wheat flour buns share top billing with rice and millet as the staple starch food. Lamb takes precedence over pork, and vegetables are few. Seasonings are subtle, with emphasis on the yeasty pungence of rice wine, vinegar and "wine lees." Roasting is a popular cooking method. The eastern-coastal regions, dominated by the major city of Shanghai, favor rich, brown sauces, braised and stewed dishes, thick "meaty" noodles of wheat flour, and both fresh and salt water seafood. The central-western regions prefer vibrant flavors achieved by the liberal use of chilies, garlic, ginger and fermented bean seasonings. Curing, pickling and marinating give added intensity to many dishes. By contrast, the cooking of the south and southern coast is bland and subtle. Pork is used extensively, as are chicken, shrimp, and fish, which are cooked by steaming or stir-frying.

The Chinese enjoy communal eating, using a small china rice bowl (*faarn woon*) and chopsticks (*fai chee*). Plates are set in the center of the table and people help themselves directly. With each meal, a staple of white rice, bread, buns or noodles is served. A meal generally comprises several dishes, usually including a soup that is eaten mid-meal. Green or black tea is drunk during the meal from tiny china (*cha buey*) tea cups. Rice wine at slightly above room temperature is served at banquets, although Cognac is now favored when affordable. Chinese banquet etiquette is complex and age-old. The seating arrangement, tableware, order of appearance of each type of dish on the menu, toasts and all other aspects of the banquet must adhere to traditional rules. The meal will begin with cold meats and appetizers, then the expensive and impressive dishes, such as shark's fin or abalone, followed by poultry, then seafood, and dishes containing vegetables. Noodles, rice, and soup are served towards the end of a banquet, either preceded or followed by a sweet dish. The Chinese breakfast is usually a simple meal such as *congee* or *juk* (a thin rice gruel). Mid-morning through midday is the time to enjoy *yum cha*: delicious tiny buns and tasty meats served with tea.

CHINA, COOKING METHODS: Although

it is now the technique most widely associated with Chinese cuisine, stir-frying is a relatively new cooking method in China. In many instances Chinese cooks use two, or even more, methods for cooking just one dish.

BLANCHING is a preparatory method which the Chinese call *bao*, usually used in conjunction with other processes. Vegetables are quickly parboiled in water or oil to intensify their color and to draw off acids. They are cooled in cold water and drained before cooking is finished by another method, usually stir-frying. Some seafoods to be served plain with sauce dips are cooked by blanching. *Ju* is a type of blanching or quick boiling for about five minutes in plain water, to release blood and fragments of bone. This is often done with meats before slow simmering.

BOILING has two methods: *Cuan* is meat or other ingredients cooked in simmering liquid, such as a hotpot or steamboat on the table.

Suan is plain boiling of large cuts of meat, to cook them prior to using other techniques for flavoring. Double boiling refers to meats first cooked by plain boiling in water, then cooked again in seasoned liquids. *Xiu* is a combination technique in which ingredients are first fried or steamed, then simmered, and lastly cooked over higher heat, uncovered, to concentrate the sauce. *Liu*, another combination technique, involves coating ingredients with cornstarch, frying or steaming, then simmering in a sauce. Cold mix or *liang-ban* is a method used often in China, particularly in the central and northern provinces, for the preparation of dishes at the beginning of a meal. The technique can be quite complex, calling for roasting, boiling, steaming or poaching of the main ingredients, followed by marinating or dressing in fragrant sauces and condiments.

DEEP-FRYING or *ja*, is done effectively in a Chinese wok. Its smoothly sloped sides and depth make it an ideal pan for this cooking method. Because the surface of the oil is wide and shallow at the edges, oil does not bubble dangerously over the sides. When deep-frying Chinese food, test the heat of the oil by dipping wooden chopsticks into the center. A small cloud of briskly moving, fine bubbles around the sticks indicates that heat is achieved. Alternatively, judge the intensity by the blue, smoky haze over the pan, which appears when oil is extremely hot. Some ingredients, particularly seafoods, are first deep-fried quickly to seal the surface, before being finished in a stir-fried dish. This method is known as *peng* and produces a velvety texture in the food.

EXPLODE FRYING is a style of stir-frying used particularly in northern China. Done on extremely high heat with a generous amount (usually $1/2$–$3/4$ cup/4–6 fl oz/125–180 ml) of oil, the sliced or shredded marinated ingredients, together with their marinade, are added all at once to the pan which causes loud explosions of sound. An intense and quick-cooking method, it locks in flavors and maintains tenderness.

POACHING is also known as simmering, slow cooking or slow simmering and is a method of gently cooking ingredients in a clear liquid, lightly seasoned. It is applied to seafood and poultry to cook without toughening, or to foods that require lengthy cooking time to tenderize. This latter technique is known as *hui*. Usually done in a heavy pot such as the Chinese "sand pot," it can also be done in the oven in a casserole. The pot should be tightly closed and the heat kept low.

RED BRAISING is a traditional Chinese method also known as *hong-shao* or *men*, "red stewing" or "red cooking." The name comes from the red-brown color imparted to the food by the initial browning and from the soy sauce, seasonings and sugar used in the stock base. Red-braised foods are generally slow-cooked in a tightly sealed casserole with a minimum of liquid for tenderness and to allow time for seasonings to be fully absorbed into the food, giving a rich, salty-sweet taste. Whole cuts of meat and poultry are prepared in this way, often flavored with fragrant local spices such as Sichuan peppercorns and star anise.

ROASTING, or *kao*, is one of the world's oldest cooking methods. In China, roasting is carried out on racks over charcoal, wood or gas fires, in brick or clay ovens, or over open charcoal fires.

SHALLOW-FRYING, or *jian*, in the Chinese tradition, is often a secondary technique following steaming or poaching. Food is cooked in a thin film of oil, in a flat pan over medium heat.

SIMMER-STEW involves braising the food in its own juices, either plain or with piquant seasoning ingredients which usually include soy sauce, bean pastes and chilies. Cooking takes place either vigorously over high heat, or slowly over very low heat, in a tightly covered casserole. This method is known as *dun* or *wei*.

SOFT FRYING is a method of deep-frying carried out in warm rather than hot oil. The food is cooked gently, allowing subtle flavoring.

STEAMING is used extensively in Chinese cooking. The main methods include foods in baskets or on plates, placed on a rack in a wok or steamer, tightly covered and cooked over simmering water. *Dim sum* and whole seafoods and poultry respond well to this method. Steaming in closed containers such as china or clay pots gives a different result. This is applied to meat such as pork and beef, and to

poultry and game meats. They will have a minimum of liquid added, and often intense seasoning ingredients such as medicinal herbs, garlic, black beans, chili and ginger, the flavor of these saturating the foods during cooking.

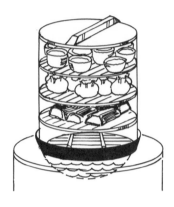

Traditional Chinese steamer over wok, inset into brick wood-burning cooker

STIR-FRYING is a simple and quick cooking method that produces tender-crisp food. Ingredients are shredded, diced or thinly sliced in uniform sizes. They are cooked over intense heat with a minimum of oil with a constant, brisk, stirring-tossing-mixing motion so that all surfaces of the food are given even application of heat, oil and seasonings. Meats are tender and moist, vegetables crisp and brightly colored.

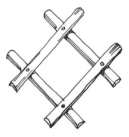

Chinese bamboo steamer rack

CHINA, CUTTING AND SLICING TECHNIQUES:

The shape of ingredients is as important to the overall appearance of a Chinese meal as the proper cooking of that ingredient. Food must be cut into bite-size pieces so that it will cook quickly and be easily handled with chopsticks. There are many different styles of cutting and slicing employed in the Chinese kitchen where the essential tools are no more than a sharp Chinese cleaver (sometimes two) and a cutting board.

CHOPPING cleavers can cut through quite heavy bones. Place food in the center of the board and hit down sharply with the blade of the cleaver, cutting right through. Place ingredient on the board, hold cleaver on the place to be cut, hit upper edge of the blade with the base of the hand or a wooden mallet. For heavier bones, hit down into the food, lift blade with food attached and strike against the board, repeating until severed. Herbs and seasoning such as garlic and ginger can be finely chopped by piling them in the center of the board and rapidly chopping straight down with short, sharp strokes. Regroup the ingredients as they spread over the board and continue chopping. This is also known as mincing.

CRUSHING: Seasonings such as garlic and ginger can be crushed by hitting them with the flat side of the cleaver. Crushing releases flavor while keeping the ingredient in one piece. Small items such as spices are crushed in a bowl using the end of the cleaver handle.

DIAGONAL SLICING: Hold the cleaver at a 45° angle to the board and cut the food at the same angle as the cleaver. Cut slightly toward you for most ingredients, but reverse the process when handling slippery ingredients to avoid accidents. Press knuckles of holding hand against blade of the cleaver to guide the thickness of slices.

HORIZONTAL SLICING is a useful technique for making thin slices of soft foods such as liver, or small slippery foods such as water chestnuts or abalone. Hold food firmly on the board with fingers, then with cleaver parallel to the board slice through in even thicknesses.

Like the cutting techniques, horizontal slicing can be done straight through or by pushing or pulling. The former applies to thick, fleshy vegetables, the latter to firm and fibrous foods.

MASHING soft food is done using the end of the cleaver handle.

MINCING: Place boneless ingredients, usually meat, in the center of the board and use two cleavers, one in each hand, to chop rapidly until the food is the required consistency. Several times during mincing, scrape food into a pile and turn over on the board.

PULLING CUT: For delicate ingredients such as bean curd, cut straight downward, then draw cleaver backward.

PUSHING CUT: For firm-textured foods, cut downward, then push cleaver forward.

ROCKING CUT: Use a cleaver with the blade rounded in front for best effect with this technique. Place food such as onion or pickled cabbage on the board and place cleaver at right angles on food, with the butt of the hand resting firmly on top of the blade. Push forward on the blade using the other hand to ensure it does not lift from the board. Rock blade backward and forward across the food until chopped to desired consistency.

ROLLING CUT: For long, cylindrical ingredients such as carrots and parsnips, rotate the vegetable a one-third turn after each cut. Cut obliquely into pieces of even size.

SAWING CUT: For fibrous foods and ingredients that may squash if a straight cut is used. Cut downward, while simultaneously sawing back and forth.

SCORING: For food such as squid and kidneys, the fibers can be tenderized and the meat made to look attractive by scoring the surface. Hold cleaver at the angle for diagonal slicing and make a series of close cuts across the surface, then turn food through 45° and repeat the scoring from this angle. This produces a diamond pattern and may also cause the food to roll up during cooking.

SHREDDING: Use straight cut or horizontal slicing to make thin, even slices. Keep ingredients stacked together and cut straight down, using push or pull technique as required, to cut into very fine shreds.

STICKS AND BLOCKS: Use straight cut to make thick slices. Stack slices together, turn over and cut again to make sticks of even size. Cut from opposite angle to make into even-size blocks.

STRAIGHT CUT: Used for slicing ingredients such as carrots. Holding cleaver in one hand, place food flat against cutting board. With fingers of the other hand, rest knuckles against the blade of the cleaver. Push cleaver straight down through food, feeding progressively under the blade.

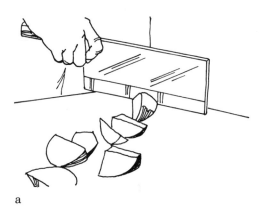

a

b

a. A rolling cut is used for firm vegetables
b. Chopping

CHINA, GARNISHES: are used as an attractive plate decoration in China. Carrots are cut into "peonies," five-petaled "plum blos-soms" and "roses." Sections of giant white radish are shredded to make "chrysanthemums." Onions are carved similarly into "chrysanthemums" or formed into "lotus flowers." Brass vegetable stamps cut slices of carrot, radish and cucumber into phoenixes and dragons, the auspicious symbol of the fish, birds, frogs, and other shapes. Artisans carve delicate, nearly transparent rose petals from radish, potato, and yam and dye them delicately with food coloring. Dramatic presentation is given to banquet platters by centerpieces of carved vegetables, carrots, radishes and cucumbers transformed into towering pagodas,

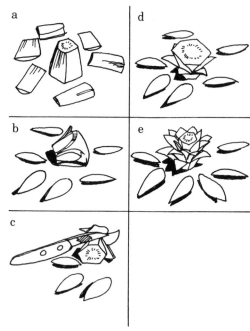

Five stages of carving a carrot "flower"
a. Pare sides to give five even sides,
    narrower at one end
b. Cut points from widest end towards
    narrow end from the edges of the five
    sides
c. Trim away from beneath first row of
    "petals"
d. Cut a second layer of "petals," trim
    away and repeat to the center
e. Gently bend "petals" outwards, chill
    finished flower in ice water

rampant dragons, soaring phoenixes.
See also: JAPAN, GARNISHES

CORIANDER leaves on their long slender stems are perhaps one of the most popular of the Chinese garnishes. They give a fresh, attractive appearance to any dish.
Also known as Chinese parsley; cilantro

CUCUMBER FANS AND FLOWERS are a classic garnish for stir-fries, steamed fish, omelettes and cold cuts. The cucumber is halved lengthways, then a diagonal section sliced thinly, without cutting right through at one edge. Every second strip is folded back and wedged between its two neighboring slices, to give a decorative shape. Store in cold water to firm up and retain its shape. Fans are made by cutting even thinner slices, then pressing gently on top so the "blades" fan out. Extensive use is also made of thin, overlapping slices of cucumber as an edging border to a plate.

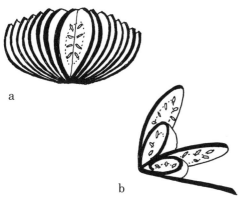

a
b

a. Cucumber fan
b. Cucumber garnish

SCALLIONS have several uses for garnishing. The green tops can be sliced diagonally to sprinkle over many types of Chinese dishes. The white end can be shredded 2 in (5 cm) at one or both ends and placed in ice water to curl. Both green and white can be shredded finely, crisped in ice water and scattered around or over dishes.
Also known as green onions; spring onions

EASTERN CHINA RECIPES

Appetizers
Shanghai Meat Dumplings (Pork)

Main Courses
Eels Braised in Brown Sauce with Chives
"Lion's Head" Meatballs
"Westlake" Fish

Accompaniments
Mushroom Platter with Hair Vegetable

Dessert
Red Bean and Glutinous Rice Pudding
(Azuki Bean)

NORTHERN CHINA RECIPES

Appetizers
Jellyfish Salad
Pork Ribs Crisp-fried with Pepper-Salt

Main Courses
Cloud Ear Fungus and Fish in Wine
Sauce
Drunken Chicken
Eight Treasure Chicken
Mongolian Hotpot
Mu Shu Pork
"Squirrel-cut" Fish in Sweet and Sour
Sauce

Accompaniments
Kale, Bamboo Shoots and Conpoy Crisp-
fried
Lotus Seeds and Quail Eggs in Clear
Sweet Soup
Scallion Pastries

Dessert
Bird's Nests in Sweet Soup

73

SOUTHERN CHINA RECIPES

Appetizers
Abalone in Oyster Sauce
Quail Double-boiled in Soup
Shark's Fin Soup with Crab Roe
Steamed Shrimp
Wontons in Clear Soup

Main Courses
Bean Sprouts Stir-fried with Shredded
Pork
Goat Casserole with Fermented Bean
Curd Sauce
Roast Pork Cantonese
Salt-baked Chicken
Steamed Whole Garoupa with Scallions

Accompaniments
Bitter Melon Stuffed with Pork
Broccoli with Crabmeat Sauce
Congee
Gai Larn with Oyster Sauce
Lotus Leaf Parcels
Water Spinach with Shrimp Sauce

Dessert
Almond Jello with Diced Fruit

SOUTHEAST COASTAL CHINA

RECIPES

Pickled Cabbage in Chicken Soup
with Ham
Taro-coated Crispy Duck

WESTERN CHINA RECIPES

Bean Curd Casserole
Camphor- and Tea-Smoked Duck
"Ma Po" Dofu
Sichuan Cabbage with Pork
Sichuan Dumplings in Hot Sauce

MENUS
(see recipes)

EASTERN-STYLE DINNER
Serves 6

Shanghai Meat Dumplings

"Westlake" Fish
"Lion's Head" Meatballs
Mushroom Platter with Hair Vegetables
White Rice or Boiled Noodles

Fresh Fruit

NORTHERN-STYLE DINNER
Serves 8

Jellyfish Salad
Pork Ribs Crisp-fried with Pepper-Salt

"Squirrel-cut" Fish in Sweet and Sour
Sauce
Eight Treasure Chicken
Kale, Bamboo Shoots and Conpoy Crisp-
fried
White Rice

Bird's Nests in Sweet Soup

SOUTHERN-STYLE BANQUET
Serves 10

Shark's Fin Soup with Crab Roe

Salt-baked Chicken
Abalone in Oyster Sauce
Lotus Leaf Parcels
Broccoli with Crabmeat Sauce
White Rice, Fried Rice or Noodles

Pastries
Fresh Fruit

SOUTHERN-STYLE FAMILY MEAL

Wontons in Clear Soup

Steamed Whole Garoupa with Scallions
Bean Sprouts Stir-fried with Shredded
Pork
Water Spinach with Shrimp Sauce
White Rice

Fresh Fruit

WESTERN-STYLE DINNER
Serves 8

Sichuan Cabbage with Pork

Bean Curd Casserole
Camphor- and Tea-Smoked Duck
"Ma Po" Dofu
White Rice

DIM SUM

Cha Siew Bow
Fun Gor
Siew Mai
Spring Rolls

CHINA POTS: see UTENSILS, STEAMERS

CHINA ROSE RADISH: see RADISH, GREEN ORIENTAL

CHINESE ALMOND: see APRICOT KERNEL

CHINESE AROMATIC PEPPER: see SICHUAN PEPPERCORNS

CHINESE BEAN SAUCE: see BEAN PASTES AND SAUCES

CHINESE BEEF MARINADE: (recipe) see BEEF

CHINESE BROCCOLI: see CABBAGE, CHINESE (GAI LARN)

CHINESE CABBAGE: see CABBAGE, CHINESE

CHINESE CELERY: see CELERY, CHINESE

CHINESE CHARD: see CABBAGE, CHINESE (BOK CHOY)

CHINESE CHEESE: see BEAN CURD BY-PRODUCTS (FERMENTED)

CHINESE DATE: see JUJUBE

CHINESE DOUGHNUT: see YOU TIAU CRULLERS

CHINESE GARNISHES: see CHINA, GARNISHES

CHINESE GELATIN: see AGAR AGAR

CHINESE GREEN CABBAGE: see CABBAGE, CHINESE (JIU LA CHOY)

CHINESE HOT BEAN PASTE: see BEAN PASTES AND SAUCES

CHINESE KALE: see CABBAGE, CHINESE (GAI LARN)

CHINESE MUSTARD CABBAGE: see CABBAGE, CHINESE

CHINESE OKRA: see LUFFA, ANGLED

CHINESE PARSLEY: see CORIANDER, FRESH

CHINESE PEPPERCORN: see SICHUAN PEPPERCORNS

CHINESE PICKLED MUSTARD CABBAGE: see CABBAGE, PICKLED

CHINESE RED DATE: see JUJUBE

CHINESE SPINACH: see AMARANTH

CHINESE SWEET PICKLES: see MELONS AND GOURDS

CHINESE WHITE CABBAGE: see CABBAGE, CHINESE (BOK CHOY)

CHINESE WINE: see WINE, CHINESE

CHINGDAUWAN: (*CHING-DAW-ONE*, Malaysia) see MUSHROOMS AND EDIBLE FUNGI

CH'ING TS'AI: (*CHING CHOY*, China) see CABBAGE, CHINESE (BOK CHOY)

CHIRONJU: (*CHI-RON-JOO*, India) see CHAROLI NUT

CHIVES, CHINESE: (*Allium tuberosum*) There are four types of chive sold at Asian produce markets: dark green known as Chinese or garlic chives (*gau choy*); a pale yellow, flat chive known as yellow chive or chive shoot (*gau wong*); a round-stemmed chive with a pointed flower bud on top (*gau choy fa*); and another of similar appearance (*gau choy sum*) with a strong flavor. Asian chives are readily available, and should be kept wrapped in damp paper in the refrigerator. They will remain fresh for only a few days.

Chinese chives

FLOWERING CHIVES: When the Chinese chive plant is allowed to mature, it forms stiff tubular stems each topped with a pointed flower bulb. They make an attractive garnish, but are also cooked in stir-fries and enjoyed as a vegetable. the lower ends of the stems may be tough and should be removed. The flowers can be eaten.
Also known as *gau choy chow sin, gau choy fa, gau choy sum, gau choy chow shan* (China)

GARLIC CHIVES have flatter dull-green leaves and have a pronounced garlic flavor because they belong to the garlic group of the onion family. Garlic chives are used in *dim sum* dumplings, soups and stir-fries, and may also be cooked by themselves as a vegetable although in this way the flavor is too strong to be widely enjoyed.
Also known as *gau choy* (China); *nira* (Japan); *ku cai* (Malaysia); *la he* (Vietnam); Chinese chives

YELLOW CHIVES are prized for their mild onion flavor. They are Chinese chives grown undercover without exposure to sunlight, so that they do not turn green. Used in soups, stir-fries and noodle dishes, they are usually cut into 2 in (5 cm) lengths but may also be chopped to use in fillings. Because they are a moist, limp plant, they will keep for only 1–2 days in the refrigerator.
Also known as *gau wong* (China); blanched Chinese chives
See also: ONION

CHOCOLATE RICE: (recipe) see RICE

CHOMPOO: (*CHOM-PHUU*, Thailand) see ROSE APPLE

CHOPPING TECHNIQUES: see CHINA, CUTTING AND SLICING TECHNIQUES

CHOPSTICKS: The utilitarian utensils that serve as eating, cooking and serving tools throughout China, Japan and Korea and in Chinese communities elsewhere in Asia. The earliest type of chopsticks were made from bamboo and were of a length determined by the notches in the bamboo stems, from which they were made. Today wood, plastic, silver and bronze are used. In Chinese Imperial times chopsticks were slender and held together at the handle-end with a fine chain. They were made from gold, silver or ivory; silver was preferred by the mandarin suspi-

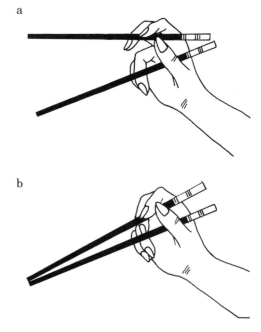

a. Hold one chopstick at base of thumb supporting with third and fourth fingers Hold the other like a pencil between tip of thumb and index finger
b. Bring tips together, using index finger to control the movement

cious of the intentions of his host, as they would discolor if they came into contact with poison. In Korea, a bride should have as part of her dowry, thin, square-shaped, silver chopsticks and spoons. In Japan, chopsticks for everyday and restaurant use come in disposable pairs that must be snapped apart. For more formal occasions Japanese chopsticks are carved from a lightweight wood, squared at the handle-end and tapered to a point at the other. They are decorated and lacquer-glazed.
Also known as *fai chee* (China); *hashi, waribashi* (disposable) (Japan)

COOKING CHOPSTICKS are like oversize eating chopsticks. Made of fine-grain pine wood or bamboo, they may be held together at the handle-end with a string. They range in length from 12–20 in (30–50 cm) and are used for stirring, beating and turning foods when shallow- or deep-frying. In Japan long metal chopsticks with wooden, hollow metal or twisted wire grips and fine-pointed ends are used for deep-frying. Small, pointed, wooden chopsticks are used for arranging very delicate foods.
Also known as *fai gee* (China)

CHOW CHOW PICKLES: see CUCUMBER
CHOY SUM: (*CHOY SUM*, China) see CABBAGE, CHINESE

CHRYSANTHEMUM: (Chrysanthemum family) It is impossible to imagine China or Japan without chrysanthemums. They bring joy throughout the year. Spring is planting time with hopes for bigger blossoms, longer petals, taller stems, thicker growth than the preceding year. Summer heat is combated by cooling herbal infusions of dried chrysanthemum flowers. Autumn sees the chrysanthemum in full-bloomed glory, banked high in shopping centers, in florists, on street corners, swathing hillsides and filling vases. In winter, chrysanthemum greens appear in the kitchen as a vegetable, while the petals are floated on snake meat soup. There are three kinds of chrysanthemum cultivated for the kitchen in Asia: the greens, eaten by the Japanese and Chinese, come from two different types and there is another grown for its edible petals. Additionally one or more types are cultivated

for their tiny flowers, which are dried to use as a tea. The Chinese chrysanthemum looks like a slightly furry, grayish-green bunch of Chinese cabbage with lobed, rounded stems, the leaf extending along the stem to the root. The Japanese version has more distinctly-lobed leaves. It has the tender texture of spinach and a subtle, spicy, "floral" taste. The leaves when young are tender enough to eat raw, but are usually lightly cooked or added to simmered dishes and hotpots in the final few minutes of cooking. They may turn bitter if over cooked. In Japan they are parboiled, then plunged into cold water to arrest cooking and retain their bright green color. They are then served as a salad with a vinegar dressing. Fresh chrysanthemums can be kept refrigerated for only a few days loosely wrapped in paper.
Also known as *tong ho* (China); *kiku, kikuna, shungiku* (Japan); edible chrysanthemum; garland chrysanthemum
See also: JAPAN, GARNISHES (KIKU)

Chrysanthemum greens

CHUB: see CARP
CHUK GAAI CHOY: (*JUK GAI CHOY*, China) see CABBAGE, CHINESE
CHUK SURN: (*JUK SURN*, China) see BAMBOO SHOOT
CHUN CHOW: (*CHAN CHAU*, Sri Lanka) see AGAR AGAR
CHUOI: (*CHOO-I*, Vietnam) see BANANA
CILI PADI: (*CHEE-LEE PA-DEE*, Malaysia) see CHILI

CINNAMON: (*Cinnamomum zeylanicum*)
The cinnamon tree is a small evergreen of the
Lauraceae family native to Sri Lanka. Cinnamon is an ancient sweet spice used around the
world and was one of the important trading
commodities between Europe and Sri Lanka
several centuries ago. The bark is peeled, rolled
into "quills" and sun-dried, while the residue,
broken quills or inferior cinnamon, is ground
to a fine powder. The bark of the cassia tree is
often substituted for cinnamon, being less expensive, but it lacks the subtlety of flavor.
Cinnamon is an essential ingredient in most
curry powders. Whole sticks (quills) are added
to rice dishes and curries. Ground cinnamon
should be bought in small quantities and kept
in a sealed spice jar as its intensity begins to
diminish after opening.

Also known as *thit-ja-bo-gauk* (Burma); *jou
kuei* (China); *dalchini, darchini* (India); *kayu
manis* (Indonesia, Malaysia); *seiron-nikkei*
(Japan); *kurundu* (Sri Lanka); *op cheuy*
(Thailand)

See also: CASSIA; MASALA

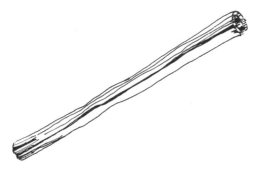

Cinnamon quills

CITRON: (*Citrus medica* var. *limetta*) This
globe-shaped, green to yellow citrus fruit has a
thick, aromatic skin that has a flavor unlike
that of any other type of citrus fruit. It is used
in many parts of Asia for flavoring foods and to
make candied peel. The tart flesh is a pale
yellow and is rarely used for cooking, although
occasionally the juice is added to a dish. In
Japan the citron, or *yuzu*, is the most commonly
used citrus fruit; its brightly colored rind is
carved into traditional shapes to add an attractive garnish to simmered dishes, soups
and sweet confections. The rind of bitter orange could be substituted.

Also known as *jeruk bodong, jeruk sekade*
(Indonesia); *yuzu* (Japan); *jeruk asem, jeruk
sekade* (Malaysia); *som saa* (Thailand)

See also: JAPAN, GARNISHES (YUZU)

Citron

CLAM: (*Circe scripta, Venus scripta, Paphia
undulata*) Of the many different clams eaten
in Southeast Asia, the ridged sand clam and
surf clam are considered to be the best tasting.
The sand clam, of which there are two main
types, has a rounded body ridged in a semicircular pattern from hinged edge to opening. It
inhabits beaches with surf and strong tidal
currents. The surf clam is found in deeper
water, is triangular-shape and has an intricate pattern of dark brown, zigzag markings
over the yellowish shell. They are boiled in
soup, steamed with egg custard or eaten cooked
or raw with spicy sauce.

Also known as sand clams: *moke-kaung*
(Burma); *him* (China); *kere* (Indonesia); *tepeh*
(Malaysia); *bigatan* (Philippines); soup clams:
dendang (Indonesia); *remis* (Malaysia); *hoy lai*
(Thailand)

CLARIFIED BUTTER: see GHEE

CLOUD EAR FUNGUS: (*Auricularia poly-trica, A. auriculajudae*) Edible wood fungi have been used in Chinese cooking since the sixth century. They are highly regarded for their medicinal properties which are thought to be prodigious, particularly for cleansing and purifying the blood. They are also enjoyed for their texture. The Chinese value cloud ear fungus for its subtle, delicate flavor and slightly crunchy "bite." This fungus is always sold in dried form and has the appearance of a miniature version of the curly seaweed the Japanese call *wakame*. It is known by several names: cloud ears for its resemblance to the clouds

---

CLOUD EAR FUNGUS AND FISH IN WINE SAUCE
Serves 4–6

1 lb (500 g) thick white fish fillets
1 egg white, beaten
2 tsps ginger wine
1/2 tsp salt
1 tbsp cornstarch (cornflour)
vegetable oil
1 scallion (spring/green onion), sliced
2 oz (60 g) cloud ear fungus, soaked
3/4 cup (6 fl oz/180 ml) fish stock
2 tbsps fermented red rice
sugar

Cut fish at an angle into thin slices and marinate with egg white, ginger wine, salt and cornstarch. Leave 20 minutes. Fry in shallow oil until lightly colored; drain. Heat 2 tbsps oil and stir-fry scallion briefly. Drain fungus; cut into small pieces and fry briefly. Add fish stock and fermented red rice; cook for 1 minute. Thicken with extra cornstarch mixed with cold water and sugar to taste. Add fish and heat through.

---

rendered with a paint brush in a Chinese painting; wood ears and tree fungus from its habitat of decayed wood; Judas or Jew's ear from its botanical name or perhaps other inspiration; and rat's ear as the Thai name translates. It expands up to five times its size when soaked, and must be trimmed of its hard central stems before using. Rinse thoroughly,

chop into usable sizes and add to semi-cooked dishes. It does not require long cooking. It is used in soups, stir-fries, vegetarian dishes (usually with bean curd), simmered and braised dishes and in stuffings for *dim sum*. It has little flavor of its own but readily absorbs seasonings. Like all Asian dried goods, moisture is its enemy, so store in a sealed container in a cool, dry place. A little goes a long way. Buy small cellophane packs of whole, larger, curly "cloud ears" or the finer, darker flakes, which need no washing before use.

Also known as *mu er, won yee* (China); *guchi, khum* (India); *kikurage* (Japan); *taingang daga* (Philippines); *hed hunu, het kanoo* (Thailand); black fungus; black tree fungus; Jew's ear; Judas ear; rat's ear; tree ears; wood ears; wood fungus

See also: MUSHROOMS AND EDIBLE FUNGI; WHITE FUNGUS; CLOUD EAR FUNGUS AND FISH IN WINE SAUCE (recipe)

CLOVAS DE COMER: (*CLO-BAS DE COH-MER*, Philippines) see CLOVES

CLOVES: (*Eugenia aromatica, E. caryophyllus*) The tall, evergreen clove tree is native to the Moluccas, the legendary Indonesian "Spice Islands," and grows extensively throughout Southeast Asia as well as in the West Indies. The clove spice is the flower bud which has been hand picked and sun-dried. Shaped like a small nail with a round tip, it is

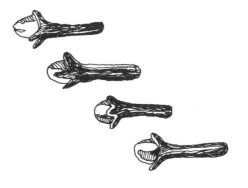

Cloves

used whole or in powdered form. It has a distinct and very strong flavor and aroma, so must be used sparingly. Powdered clove is an essential ingredient in *garam masala*, a mixed spice from India. Both whole and ground cloves are used in curries, rice, sauces and sweet dishes. The bulk of Indonesia's clove crop is ground and mixed with tobacco to make the distinctive *kretek* cigarette which has a mild anaesthetizing effect on the smoker.

Also known as *ley nyin bwint* (Burma); *ting hsiang* (China); *laung* (India); *cengkeh* (Indonesia); *bunga cingkeh* (Malaysia); *clovas de comer* (Philippines); *karabu nati* (Sri Lanka); *gram goo* (Thailand)

See also: MASALA

CLUSTER BEAN: see GWAAR KI PHALLI

CLUSTER BEAN, TWISTED: see PARKIA

COCONUT: (*Cocus nucifera*) One of Asia's most valuable commodities, the coconut palm, which grows prolifically throughout tropical Asia, makes an important contribution to many aspects of life. Its towering trunk and wide leaf fronds provide building materials for housing and boats; its sap is fermented into potent wine and its nuts have manifold uses in cooking as well as yielding oils for soap making and other commercial uses. The outer husk of the coconut makes the fibrous coir that is important to the rope industry.

To obtain the white meat of the nut from the coconut shell, it is first cracked open with a hammer or machete and then the meat is removed by prizing it away from the shell with a strong blade, or grating it on a coconut grater. The thin brown skin which is attached to the meat should be removed with a vegetable parer.

COCONUT CREAM: This is referred to throughout this book as thick coconut milk, and is the first thick extraction of coconut milk.

COCONUT LEAVES are used in Indonesia (and particularly in Bali where they have developed it into an art form) to weave standards and sculptures for table decoration and temple offerings that include elaborate food and flowers. They are also used for wrapping foods before cooking.

See also: RICE CAKES WRAPPED IN COCONUT LEAVES (recipe)

COCONUT MEAT: The firm white meat within the coconut is known as copra. It is high in oil, has a sweet, nutty taste and is one of the most versatile and important ingredients in the cuisine of all parts of tropical Asia. Ripe coconut meat is eaten as a snack, or is grated and dried to make desiccated, and shredded coconut. Undried grated coconut is added to sweet dishes, rice and curries to add thickness and a rich flavor. It is often toasted.

COCONUT MILK is made by passing coconut meat through a grater and then squeezing it to remove the milky fluid which, is thinned with water, leaving behind dry fiber pulp. It adds special creaminess to Indonesian and Malaysian curries, replaces dairy cream in Asian desserts, and makes cooling drinks to soothe the palate after hot spices. Coconut milk and the thicker first extraction, coconut cream, has a tendency to curdle during cooking. This can be avoided by the slow and continual stirring of the sauce using a wide, flat spoon in a lifting and pouring technique. Coconut milk-based curries are not completely cooked until a film of oil separates from the sauce. In Asian communities it is possible to buy freshly produced coconut milk, but it is more accessible in cans, of which there are a number of excellent brands on the market. Fresh or opened cans of coconut milk will keep for only a few hours at room temperature, or a maximum of 2 days in the refrigerator, so it should be frozen if storage is necessary. Coconut milk can be made by soaking desiccated coconut in hot water or milk until softened enough to squeeze in a piece of cloth to extract the milky fluid.

Also known as *minyak kelapa, kelapa muda santan* (Indonesia); *kelapa sentengah tua santen* (Malaysia); *gata* (Philippines); *nam katee* (Thailand); *nuoc cot dua* (Vietnam)

See also: EGGS IN COCONUT SAUCE (recipe); STEAMED STICKY RICE IN COCONUT MILK (recipe)

COCONUT SYRUP is a clear, viscous syrup extracted from the coconut palm as the first stage of the making of coconut wine. It is used

displays of desserts and in packing certain types of bottled and canned fruits.
See also: NATA

COCONUT VINEGAR is a mild vinegar made from coconut sap.
See also: VINEGAR

COCONUT BALLS
Yields 24

1 cup (120 g) glutinous (sticky) rice flour
3/4–1 cup (6–8 fl oz / 180–250 ml) thin coconut milk
1/2 tsp salt
24 small cubes palm sugar (or substitute brown sugar)
1 cup (3 oz / 85 g) desiccated coconut

Make a firm, moist dough of flour and coconut milk, adding salt. Form sugar into 24 small balls and press a piece of sugar into the center of each. Seal by pinching dough over filling. Cook in simmering salted water, 8 at a time, until they float. Lift out and coat with coconut. Serve cold.

COCONUT-COATED VEGETABLES
Serves 4–6

1 lb (500 g) mixed leafy green vegetables
2–4 fresh green chilies, seeded and shredded
2 1/2 tbsps oil
1/2 tsp turmeric
8 curry leaves
1 large onion, very thinly sliced
2/3 cup (2 oz / 60 g) grated fresh or desiccated coconut
salt
pepper
lemon juice

Wash, trim and shred vegetables. Place in covered saucepan and simmer for 3 minutes. Fry chilies in oil for 1 minute. Add turmeric, curry leaves and onion; fry 2–3 minutes. Add coconut and vegetables; season with salt, pepper and lemon juice. Heat gently, stirring continually.

COCONUT WATER is the slightly opaque liquid contained within a fresh coconut. It is a thirst-quenching drink on which newborn babies and children are nourished in many rural parts of tropical Asia, and is used in tropical resorts as the base for exotic cocktails. The water is not, as is often thought, the coconut milk used in cooking and curries. Coconut water is extracted from the grated meat.
Also known as *nuoc dua tuoi* (Vietnam)
See also: BEEF SIMMERED WITH LEMON GRASS (recipe)

COCONUT WINE, or toddy, is made by fermenting the sap of the coconut palm into wine–which in the Asian tropics takes only a few hours. A further process distills the sap into the fiery *arak*.
Also known as *arak* (Indonesia); *lamb anog* (Philippines)

COCONUT FISH CURRY
Serves 6

3 medium white pomfret (John Dory, sole or flounder)
2 cups (16 fl oz / 500 ml) thin coconut milk
1 tsp salt
1/3 cup sliced shallots
1/2 cup vegetable oil
1/4 cup minced red chilies
2 tsps minced ginger
1 tsp turmeric
1 1/2 tsps shrimp paste
1/2 cup (4 fl oz / 120 ml) tamarind water
2 tsps sugar
1 cup (8 fl oz / 250 ml) thick coconut milk
pepper

Cut fish crossways into 3/4 in (2 cm) slices. Place in a wide pan with thin coconut milk and salt. Cook gently until fish is tender and liquid well reduced. Separately fry shallots in oil until crisp. Add chilies; fry until oil separates then stir in minced ginger, turmeric and shrimp paste. Fry about 2 minutes. Add tamarind water and sugar and simmer 4–5 minutes. Add thick coconut milk and salt and pepper to taste. Pour over fish and heat again.

COCONUT LEAF CHICKEN PARCELS
Serves 4

1¹/₂ lbs (750 g) boned chicken pieces
2¹/₂ tsps minced garlic
2¹/₂ tsps black pepper
1 tbsp Oriental sesame oil
¹/₂ tsp salt
2 tsps fish sauce
12 coconut palm leaves
deep-frying oil

Cut the chicken into cubes and place in a dish with the garlic, pepper and sesame oil. Add salt and fish sauce, cover and marinate for 1 hour. Dip coconut leaves into boiling water, drain and wipe dry. Wrap a portion of the chicken in each leaf, making a triangular-shaped parcel. Deep-fry in hot oil for about 4 minutes, until chicken is cooked through.

COCONUT PUDDING
Serves 6–8

4 large eggs, beaten and strained
2¹/₂ cups (20 fl oz / 625 ml) coconut milk
¹/₂ tsp ground cardamom
¹/₄ tsp grated nutmeg
¹/₄ tsp ground mace
2 tsps rosewater
³/₄ cup (4 oz / 125 g) jaggery
fresh or desiccated coconut

Mix the eggs with coconut milk; stir in the spices and rosewater. Mix jaggery in enough hot water to dissolve it, then pour into the custard. Pour into a heatproof dish and stand in a baking pan half-filled with hot water. Bake at 300°F (150°C) for 1³/₄ hours, or until set. Sprinkle with fresh or desiccated coconut. Serve warm or cold.

KELAPA MUDA (Indonesia) is a young coconut, picked at about 10 months. It has soft, white, gelatinous, nutty, sweet flesh that is scraped from the shell to eat fresh or to use in desserts or drinks. The liquid (coconut water) within these coconuts is used as a refreshing beverage and is made into cocktails adding the scraped flesh, white rum and lime juice.
Also known as *nariyal* (India); *kelapa, kelapa sentengah tua* (Indonesia, Malaysia); *buko* (Philippines); *maprao* (Thailand); *dua nao* (freshly grated) (Vietnam)

PALM CABBAGE is the terminal bud of the coconut palm and is considered a delicacy in tropical Asia. Eaten as a vegetable, a whole tree may be cut down to obtain a cabbage that is cooked as any tender green vegetable.
See also: OILS AND FATS; UTENSILS, VARIOUS

COCONUT SAMBAL

³/₄ cup (2¹/₂ oz / 75 g) desiccated coconut
milk / water
2 tbsps minced onion
¹/₄ tsp chili powder
2 tsps lime juice
salt
³/₄–1 tsp paprika

Soften coconut with milk or water, then squeeze out liquid. Mix with remaining ingredients adding salt to taste and paprika.

INDONESIAN VEGETABLES IN COCONUT MILK
Serves 6

1 tsp minced garlic
¹/₂ tsp shrimp paste
2 tbsps vegetable oil
2 tsps ground coriander
1¹/₂ cups (12 fl oz / 375 g) thick coconut milk
¹/₂ tsp turmeric
1 tsp salt
2 cups (8 oz / 225 g) shredded cabbage
8 small new potatoes, halved

(cont'd)

(Indonesian Vegetables in Coconut Milk cont'd)

1 cup (4 oz / 125 g) green beans or long beans
1¹/₂ cups (12 oz / 350 g) sliced onion
1 red bell pepper (capsicum), sliced
¹/₂ cup (2 oz / 60 g) sliced water chestnuts
lemon juice or tamarind water

Fry garlic and shrimp paste in oil for 1 minute. Add coriander, coconut milk, turmeric and salt and bring to a boil. Add cabbage and potatoes; simmer 6–8 minutes. Add remaining vegetables. Cook 1 minute, then cover. Leave for 5 minutes before serving. Season to taste with lemon juice or tamarind water.

COLTSFOOT: A starchy vegetable related to a type of oriental rhubarb, it is grown and used in Japan. Coltsfoot has flat, rounded leaves, similar in appearance to lotus or water lily leaves, although smaller, on long thick stalks like rhubarb. Only the green stalks should be eaten. It is rarely available and is usually expensive in Western countries. The flavor is celery-like, making celery an acceptable substitute. To prepare coltsfoot, the stalks should be rinsed and dried, sprinkled with salt to draw out the bitter juices, then rinsed again after 10 minutes. Parboil, like rhubarb, stripping off the fibrous outer coating.
Also known as *fuki* (Japan); bog rhubarb; butterbur

Coltsfoot

CONGEE: (China) Rice gruel, the breakfast of millions, is eaten throughout China and in Chinese communities everywhere in the world. This bland-tasting soup of boiled rice and water is like a blank canvas on which a colorful array of ingredients are scattered to suit a whim: diced, grilled fish or liver, chopped chicken, roasted peanuts or sesame seeds, raw eggs, shredded scallions, fresh coriander, steamed shrimp and sliced and fried *crullers*. In Thailand *congee* is called *khao tom gung* and is flavored with *nam pla* (fish sauce). In northern China *congee* is replaced by a thick gruel made from millet.
Also known as *jook, juk* (China); *khao tom gung* (Thailand); rice gruel; rice soup
See also: RICE; YOU TIAU CRULLERS

CONGEE

3 cups (1¹/₄ lbs / 625 g) raw short-grain white rice, soaked for 4 hours
2 tsps salt
2 qts (2 l) water

Drain rice and place in large saucepan with water and salt. Bring to a boil, reduce heat and cook until rice is reduced to a starchy soup. Serve hot with sliced *you tiau crullers*, minced scallions, fresh coriander and a choice of stir-fried fish, sliced pork liver, diced chicken or steamed shrimp. Add light soy sauce and chili sauces to taste.

CONGER MAW: see FISH MAW

CONPOY: The amber-colored, dried discs known as *conpoy* come from a type of sea scallop. They are an almost prohibitively expensive ingredient usually coming suitably gift-boxed in packs of twelve. The flavor is distinctive enough that a little shredded, deep-fried *conpoy* sprinkled over a dish imparts a notable flavor. Because of their extreme cost, these dried scallops usually appear only in banquet menus when they may be slow-cooked until tender in a rich stock and dressed with a dribble of oyster sauce. One delightful northern Chinese dish combines crisp-fried kale or

Conpoy, sliced and dried

other green vegetables with dry-fried young bamboo shoots and fried, shredded *conpoy*. They also enrich soups and slow-simmered dishes. Dried *conpoy* can be kept for many months in an airtight container, but it rarely finds itself on a kitchen shelf for long. It must be soaked to soften and may then be steamed or added straight to a dish.

Also known as *gong yiu chee* (Cantonese); dried scallops

See also: KALE, BAMBOO SHOOTS AND CONPOY CRISP-FRIED (recipe)

KALE, BAMBOO SHOOTS AND CONPOY CRISP-FRIED
Serves 6

³/₄ *cup (6 oz / 180 g) canned whole bamboo shoots*
1 tbsp salt
1 tbsp plus 1 tsp yellow rice wine
1 tbsp plus 2 tsps sugar
12 pieces dried conpoy*, soaked*
1¹/₂ tsps finely shredded ginger
5 oz (150 g) fresh kale leaves, shredded
2 cups (16 fl oz / 500 ml) peanut oil
1 tsp salt

Marinate bamboo in 1 tbsp each of salt, wine and sugar for 20 minutes. Steam drained *conpoy* with ginger and 1 tsp wine for 15 minutes.

(cont'd)

(Kale, Bamboo Shoots and Conpoy Crisp-fried cont'd)

Break into shreds. Drain bamboo shoots. Heat oil in a wok and deep-fry bamboo shoots until browned on the surface. Remove. Fry kale for about 1 minute until crisp. Drain. Fry *conpoy* until crisp. Arrange kale on a plate with bamboo shoots on top. Sprinkle on 2 tsps sugar and 1 tsp salt. Toss lightly. Garnish with *conpoy*.

COOKING OILS AND FATS: see OILS AND FATS

COPRA: see COCONUT (MEAT)

CORIANDER: (*Coriandrum sativum*) A seed spice from the parsley family, this annual is grown extensively throughout the world. Three months after sowing, the plant is harvested and the seed stems tied in bunches and hung to dry. Ground coriander is one of the essential ingredients in curry powders, giving it a fresh, lemony-sweet flavor. In India, ground coriander is used in many curries and in the sweet aromatic spice mixture, *garam masala*. The whole, or cracked, dried seeds flavor vegetables, rice, chutneys and pickles. A mixture of ground coriander and cumin known in India as *dhansak masala* and in Indonesia as *ketumbar jinten* is used to season specific curry dishes. It is best to buy the seed spice whole and grind when needed, although ground coriander keeps

---

DHANIA-JIRA
Yields 1¹/₂ cups (12 oz / 375 g)

1 cup (8 oz / 250 g) coriander seeds
¹/₂ cup (4 oz / 125 g) cumin seeds

Dry-roast the spices in a pan over medium to low heat or in a warm oven until very aromatic. Grind to a fine powder, then cool and store in an airtight jar.

---

successfully for several months in a tightly sealed spice jar. To draw out the full flavor of coriander whole seed spices, they should be

first toasted in an oven, then finely ground.
Also known as *nan nan zee* (Burma); *dhania*
(India); *ketumbar* (Indonesia, Malaysia);
mellet pak chee (Thailand)
See also: CORIANDER, FRESH; DHANIA-JIRA
(recipe); DRY SPICED BEEF (recipe); MASALA

CORIANDER, FRESH: (*Coriandrum
sativum*) A herb also known by its Mexican
name *cilantro*, it is used extensively in Southeast Asian cooking, except in Japan where its
particular taste is not appreciated, and its use
as a garnish is replaced by their native *mitsuba*
(trefoil). The bright green, indented leaves
which are always grouped in threes on firm,
straight, narrow stalks, resemble parsley in
appearance, although flatter, but here the
similarity ends. The flavor of coriander is
fresh, strong, earthy and something of an
acquired taste. The Chinese use coriander
extensively as a garnish, and to a lesser extent

FRESH CORIANDER CHUTNEY

4 oz (125 g) fresh coriander (cilantro) leaves
1/3 cup (1/2 oz / 15 g) chopped scallions
(spring / green onions)
2 fresh green chilies, seeded and sliced
1 tsp minced ginger
1/4 tsp minced garlic
1 tsp garam masala
1 tsp salt
2 tsps sugar
1/3 cup (3 fl oz / 90 ml) lemon juice

Grind ingredients in mortar or food
processor, adding salt, sugar and lemon
juice. Work to a fairly smooth paste.

---

in cooking, usually in *dim sum* stuffings and
soups. The Indians add large amounts of
chopped coriander to certain curry sauces to
make them bright green. Of all Asian countries Thailand uses the coriander herb the
most, grinding the roots and stems for curry
pastes and sauces, using the leaves in salads
and as a garnish, the stems and whole sprigs
in soup. Coriander is easily grown from seed,
its growth cycle being only a few weeks. When
it flowers the plant becomes spindly, losing its

flavor and must be replanted. Most good
Asian stores keep fresh coriander on their
vegetable shelf. If the stems are cut, store in
its plastic bag in the refrigerator, otherwise
stand roots in water and cover loosely with
plastic.
Also known as *nan nan bin* (Burma); *yuen sai*
(China); *hara dhania* (India); *daun ketumbar*
(Indonesia, Malaysia); *koyendoro* (Japan);
phak hom pom (Laos); *wansuey* (Philippines);
pak chee (Thailand); Chinese parsley; cilantro
See also: CORIANDER; FRESH CORIANDER CHUT-
NEY (recipe)

Coriander leaves

CORN: (*Zea mays*) Sweet or Indian corn
(maize) is grown throughout India and to a
smaller extent in most parts of Southeast
Asia. The dried kernels of the *indentata* type of
corn are ground to a semi-fine flour used in
breadmaking and some desserts. The starch is
ground into a fine powder extensively used as
a thickener. The ripe grains and cobs of the
sweeter *saccharata* type are eaten as a vegetable. In China sweet corn is enjoyed in a thick
soup usually with chicken or crabmeat. In
Indonesia it is made into crisp-fried fritters to
serve as a snack. In Malaysia and Thailand it
appears, perhaps unexpectedly, in dessert
dishes, with diced yam and sago or tapioca.
Canned corn kernels or crushed corn are readily available.

MINIATURE CORN: (*Z. saccharata*) Small whole heads of corn are used as a vegetable in Chinese cooking. Rarely available fresh, they are sold in cans packed in water and require little cooking. Usually used in stir-fried dishes and combination vegetable dishes.
Also known as *sock mai jai* (China); *jagung* (Indonesia, Malaysia); baby corn
See also: FLOURS AND THICKENERS; SWEET CORN FRITTERS (recipe)

SWEET CORN FRITTERS
Yields 24

1 can (16 oz/500 g) corn kernels (sweet corn)
2 eggs
¹/₂ cup (2oz/60 g) all-purpose (plain) flour
¹/₃ cup (3 oz/90 g) tapioca or potato starch (flour)
¹/₂ cup (4 fl oz/125 ml) coconut milk
1¹/₂ tsps minced garlic
¹/₂ cup (1 oz/30 g) chopped scallions (spring/ green onions)
¹/₄ cup (2 oz/60 g) celery leaves
2 tsps ground coriander
1¹/₂ tsps salt
¹/₂ tsp pepper
¹/₂ tsp chili powder
vegetable oil
chili sauce

Lightly crush corn. Mix with eggs, flour, starch and coconut milk. Grind garlic, scallions, celery and coriander together. Stir into corn mixture with salt, pepper and chili powder. Deep- or shallow-fry spoonfuls of the mixture in vegetable oil. Drain and serve hot with chili sauce.

CORN OIL: see OILS AND FATS

CORNSTARCH: see FLOURS AND THICKENERS

COTTAGE CHEESE: see PANIR

COTTON BEAN CURD: see BEAN CURD (COTTON)

COTTONSEED OIL: see OILS AND FATS

CRAB: Crabs are plentiful and inexpensive in most Asian countries as they abound in the coastal rivers, mangrove swamps and lakes. Freshwater crabs are considered a great deli-cacy and are prized for their delicious sweet-flavored meat. The most delicate part of the crab is the rich, orange roe and the choicest meat is usually the tender claw meat.

Large-clawed crabs thrive in the mangrove swamps that fringe many parts of the Indonesian coast. By tradition, those of the Muslim faith do not eat certain shellfish and crustaceans, however visitors to Indonesia and non-Muslims can enjoy crab cooked in many ways.

Changi Beach, a near-city beachside suburb of Singapore, boasts rows of giant barn-like restaurants where chefs vie to produce the ultimate chili crab. Succulent, meaty mud crabs (*Scylla serrata*) from nearby mangrove swamps are cracked and tossed with ginger and chilies in giant-sized woks over roaring gas fires until the meat is tender and the accompanying sauce has a satisfying degree of searing hotness.

Live crabs can be killed before cooking by putting the point of a knife into the shell between the eyes. Hit the back of the knife with a hard, quick blow which kills the crab instantly. Put the crab into cold water. Cover pan and bring to a boil, simmer 5–20 minutes depending on the size or about 8 minutes per 1 lb (500 g) once the water is simmering.
Also known as *zuwai-gani* (Japan); blue swimmer crab, green crab, mud crab
See also: TOMALLEY *and recipes following*

CHILI CRAB
Serves 6–8

3–4 lbs (1.5–2 kgs) fresh crab
¹/₂ cup (4 fl oz/125 ml) peanut oil
6 fresh red chilies, seeded and sliced
2 tsps minced garlic
2 tsps minced ginger
1 tsp chili powder
1 tbsp sugar
¹/₂ cup (4 oz/120 g) minced scallions (spring/green onions)
¹/₂ cup (4 fl oz/125 ml) water
1¹/₂ tsps cornstarch (cornflour)

Cut away undershell of crabs and discard inedible parts. Rinse in cold

(cont'd)

(Chilli Crab cont'd)

water. Cut crabs and claws into large pieces. In a large wok heat peanut oil. Add crab and stir-fry for about 6 minutes; drain off excess oil. Add chilies, garlic and ginger. Stir-fry briefly. Add chili powder, sugar, scallions and the water mixed with the cornstarch. Stir until sauce thickens.

CRABMEAT AND BAMBOO SHOOT OMELETTE
Serves 4

4 large eggs, beaten
1 tbsp sago flour or cornstarch (cornflour)
1/3 cup (3 fl oz / 90 ml) water
1/2 cup (4 oz / 120 g) chopped scallions
(spring / green onions)
1/2 cup (4 oz / 120 g) shredded bamboo shoots
2 tbsps vegetable oil
3/4 cup (6 oz / 180 g) flaked, cooked crabmeat
salt
pepper
shredded chilies

Mix eggs and flour or cornstarch with water. Stir-fry scallions and bamboo shoots in oil for 2 minutes. Add crabmeat and heat through. Pour on eggs and add salt and pepper to taste. Cook until firm underneath then cut in halves and turn. Cook other side to golden and serve, garnished with shredded chilies.

SHANGHAI HAIRY CRAB: Small, square-bodied crabs from the waters of the northeastern China coast near the city of Shanghai. They have a covering of dark hair along their legs and the edge of the upper shell. The sweet meat is much prized, but it is the yellow yolk that is considered a real delicacy. To counteract the excessive richness of their meat, they are usually served with tea made by infusing sliced ginger in boiling water. They may also be seasoned and packed raw in wine, when they will be known as "drunken crabs."

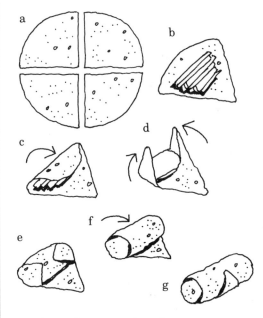

a. Cut each wrapper into four
b. Place filling towards wider end
c. Fold end over filling
d. Tuck in two sides
e-f. Roll
g. Completed cha gio

CRABMEAT AND CHICKEN ROLLS
Yields 36

8 oz (250 g) minced chicken breast
4 oz (125 g) flaked, cooked crabmeat
1/2 cup (4 oz / 120 g) minced scallions (spring / green onions)
1 cup (2 oz / 60 g) cooked rice vermicelli, chopped
1 carrot, grated
1 egg, beaten
salt
pepper
banh trang wrappers, each 6 in (36 x 15 cm) in diameter
3 tbsps light corn syrup or sugar syrup
1 cup basil leaves
1 cup fresh coriander (cilantro)
lettuce leaves
nuoc cham sauce

(cont'd)

(Crabmeat and Chicken Rolls cont'd)

Mix chicken, crabmeat, scallions, vermicelli, carrot and egg. Season with salt and pepper. Soften wrappers by dipping into cold water; drain well. Brush one side of each wrapper with sugar syrup. Place a portion of filling in the center and wrap. Deep-fry until crisp, golden and cooked through. To serve, wrap each roll in a lettuce leaf with sprigs of each of the herbs. Dip into *nuoc cham* sauce.

CRAB SAUCE

Yields 3 cups (24 fl oz / 750 ml)

12 oz (375 g) flaked, cooked crabmeat
1/2 cup (4 fl oz / 125 ml) thick coconut milk
1 cup (8 fl oz / 250 ml) thin coconut milk
1/4 cup (1/2 oz / 15 g) minced shallots
2–4 tbsps (1–2 oz / 30–60 g) minced chilies
salt
pepper
sugar
lime juice
fresh coriander (cilantro), chopped

Simmer first 5 ingredients slowly until thickened. Add salt, pepper, sugar and lime juice to taste. Garnish with fresh coriander. Serve hot or cold.

CURRIED CRAB

Serves 6

2 crabs, each 1 1/2 lbs (750 g)
2 1/2 tsps minced garlic
1 tbsp chopped greater galangal
2 or 3 red chilies, seeded and chopped
1 tsp shrimp paste
4 crushed candlenuts
1 tsp salt
1/2 tsp black pepper
1/4 tsp turmeric
3 tbsps vegetable or coconut oil

(cont'd)

(Curried Crab cont'd)

6 sliced shallots
2 stalks lemon grass, bruised
2 cups (16 fl oz / 500 ml) thin coconut milk
tamarind water
fresh coriander (cilantro)

Cut each crab into 6 pieces, removing the undershell and inedible parts. Crack shells and claws. Make a *rempah* by grinding garlic, *greater galangal,* chilies, shrimp paste and candlenuts with salt, pepper and turmeric. Fry in oil for 2 minutes. Add shallots, lemon grass, crab pieces and coconut milk. Bring to a boil; simmer for about 15 minutes, until the crab is cooked. Add tamarind water to taste and garnish with fresh coriander.

CREAM, INDIAN: see KHOYA; MALAI

CRUCIAN CARP: see CARP

CUAN: (*GWAN*, China) see CHINA, COOKING METHODS (BOILING)

CUCUMBER: (*Cucumis sativus*) From the Cucurbitaceae family, this annual, creeping plant bears pendulous fruits of all shapes and sizes which grow from the base of the flowers. The skin is generally green with a white, cool, juicy interior with many seeds. Introduced to England in 1573 from India where the plant is thought to have originated, it is widely cultivated throughout the world and extensively used in Asian cuisines. Many varieties are grown but can be divided into two main groups. Long cucumbers are 10–25 in (25–65 cm) in length, with smooth, deep-green skin. Ridged cucumbers have grooved, indented or knobbly, rough skin. The fruit is eaten raw in salads, lightly cooked in warm salads and vegetables dishes, and in curries. It is pickled with vinegar, salt, and sugar to accompany many dishes, being particularly good with cold or roasted meats. It is used extensively as a garnish, being sliced or carved into intricate or simple traditional shapes and designs. Cucumbers have a slightly bitter juice which can upset digestion. This may be removed by sprinkling the peeled or sliced fruit or rubbing the unpeeled fruit with salt, which will draw it off. When cutting cucumber, always start from the flower end as this also helps prevent bitterness.

JAPANESE CUCUMBERS are of the ridged variety and are small with a clear, slightly sweet flavor. Many are no more than 2 in (5 cm) long, and slightly knobbly on the surface. The skin is thin and the seeds small, both are usually eaten. Used extensively, sliced paper thin, as a garnish for *sushi* and *sashimi*.

CUCUMBER SAUCE
Yields 2¹/₂ cups (20 fl oz / 625 ml)

¹/₄ cup (2 oz / 60 g) sugar
¹/₂ cup (4 fl oz / 125 ml) white vinegar
¹/₄ cup (2 fl oz / 60 ml) boiling water
¹/₃ tsp salt
¹/₂ tsp finely chopped red chili
2 tbsps peanut butter
1 cup (8 oz / 250 g) cucumber, peeled, seeded and thinly sliced
2 tbsps chopped fresh coriander (cilantro)

Mix sugar, vinegar, boiling water and salt. Cool. Add chili and peanut butter. Place cucumber in a salad bowl, pour on the sauce, add coriander, toss and serve.

YELLOW CUCUMBER is a variety grown in China. It has a coarse, yellow-colored, rough skin and a melon-like taste. Generally used in soups, the skin, flesh and seeds are all used as they are thought to be cooling and beneficial to the body during summer. This cucumber, and the smaller tea melon–more like the Japanese cucumber in size), are peeled, cut into fine shreds, and preserved in honey—sometimes with ginger to flavor—to make a sweet preserve known as Chinese sweet pickles or *chow chow*. It is used in stir-fries, is added to sauces such as sweet and sour or ginger sauce, is scattered over steamed fish and stirred into certain types of spicy noodles. Cucumber is also pickled in soy sauce for use as a seasoning and condiment. This is sold in jars and cans

and can be stored in the refrigerator for many weeks after opening.

Also known as *cha gwa, tseng gwa, wong gwa* (China); *kakda, kheera* (India); *ketimun* (Indonesia); *kaga, kariha, kyuri, suyo* (Japan); *timun* (Malaysia); *taeng kan* (Thailand); tea melon

See also: CUCUMBER SAUCE (recipe); CHINA, GARNISHES; RAITA (recipe); SALAD OF WARM AND SPICY CUCUMBER (recipe); VEGETABLE SALAD (recipe); VINEGARED SEAWEED WITH CRAB AND CUCUMBER (recipe)

SALAD OF WARM AND SPICY CUCUMBER
Serves 4

1 large cucumber, peeled and seeded
salt
2¹/₂ tbsps Oriental sesame oil
2 tbsps minced scallions (spring / green onions)
2 tbsps light soy sauce
3–4 tsps sugar
¹/₂ tsp chili powder
1 tbsp ground toasted white sesame seeds

Slice cucumber; sprinkle lightly with salt. Leave 10 minutes; rinse and dry. Heat sesame oil in a skillet and fry cucumber with scallions until softened. Add soy sauce, sugar and chili powder. Mix. Serve warm or chilled, garnished with ground sesame seeds.

CUCUMBER TREE: see BELIMBING

CUMIN: (*Cuminum cyminum*) Mediterranean in origin, this member of the parsley (Umbelliferae) family yields a strongly flavored seed that is widely used as a spice, particularly in the Middle East, India and Malaysia. The dried seed is similar to caraway seed in appearance but with an entirely different flavor, being both pungent and aromatic. Caraway seeds with their licorice flavor cannot be substituted. The seed, both whole and powdered, is used extensively in curry-making and as an ingredient of *garam masala*. It is often teamed with ground coriander to give a pungent-lemony-aromatic spice mixture which is known as *dhania-jira* and can be used as a condiment or seasoning. Cumin seeds are used in chutneys and pickles and are sometimes added to *papadams*. In Thailand and Indonesia the name for cumin is synonymous with fennel seed, which is named "sweet cumin." Cumin seeds should be roasted in a dry pan or a very hot oven to release their full flavor before using whole, or grinding to a powder. The temperature should be high enough to make the seeds pop. There are two types of cumin in use.

BLACK CUMIN is a dark brown-black color and is more expensive than white cumin. It has a sweeter taste and is known in Malaysia as sweet cumin. It is used whole in *pillaus* and ground in *garam masala*. In India it is chewed as an anti-flatulent. "Black cumin" is another name for the small, dark-colored seed spice known as *nigella* or *kalonji*.
Also known as *kala jira*; *shah jira* (India); *jintan manis* (Indonesia, Malaysia); sweet cumin

SWEET CUMIN is another name for fennel seeds.

WHITE CUMIN is not white in color but a dull brown. It is used in curries, pickles and chutneys and is an ingredient of *garam masala*.
Also known as *ma chin* (China); *safed jira* (India); *jintan* (Indonesia); *kumin* (Japan); *jintan putih* (Malaysia); *suduru* (Sri Lanka); *yira* (Thailand)
See also: CURRY PASTES, POWDERS AND SAUCES; DHANIA-JIRA (recipe); DHANSAK (recipe); FENNEL; JIRA PANI (recipe); MASALA; NIGELLA

CUMIN WATER: see JIRA PANI

CUP LEAF: see DAUN MANGKOK

CURDS: see YOGURT

CURLY KALE: see CABBAGE, CHINESE (SEEN CHOY)

CURRY LEAF: (*Murraya koenigii*) Best associated with Sri Lankan cooking, these small, shiny, fragrant leaves are gathered from a shrub-like tree which grows in most Southeast Asian countries. The curry leaf plant grows easily in subtropical climates and can be propagated by transplanting runners which emerge from the soil around the parent tree. Used fresh or dried, the leaves are fried in oil to impart their flavor or are pulverized or powdered to add to marinades and omelettes. Bay or cassia leaves can be substituted. Both fresh and dried leaves can be found where Indian and Malaysian foods are sold.
Also known as *pyin daw thein* (Burma); *cariya patta, katnim, kitha neem* (India); *daun kari pla, karupillam* (Malaysia); *karapincha* (Sri Lanka); *bai karee* (Thailand)
See also: CASSIA; COCONUT COATED VEGETABLES (recipe)

CURRY PASTES, POWDERS AND SAUCES: A wide variety of different flavors can be obtained by using one of the many different types of curry pastes or powders readily available.
See also: CAMBODIAN SPICY PORK (recipe); KORMA OF MUTTON (recipe); KRUNG GAENG; MASALA; REMPAH; VINDALOO PASTE (recipe)

CURRY PASTES come in jars and are usually quite pungent in flavor. They cover a full range of different Indian curry styles, most of the brands on the market having a quite authentic taste and if used according to directions will give excellent results. Unopened curry paste can be kept without refrigeration indefinitely, but once opened should be refrigerated and used within two months to retain maximum flavor.

CURRY POWDERS come in many flavors and compositions. The Western-style powders are quite different from those used by Indian, Indonesian and Malaysian communities; although in the cuisines of certain of their neighbors, the less subtle, turmeric-dominated powders may be used. Generally cooks in Asia prefer to blend their own spices, but may also purchase reliable commercial blends, which range from the bland *korma* powder to the full-flavored *masalas* and hot *vindaloos*.

KORMA POWDER is an aromatic spice mixture used to season the Indian and Malaysian mild curries known as *korma*. The mix usually has white pepper instead of chili powder to give it its characteristic flavor.

PANCHPHORAN derives from the Hindi word *panch*, meaning five. It was popularized in the eastern coastal state of Bengal. *Panchphoran* is made up of five aromatic spices which are cumin, fennel and fenugreek, combined with the small black *nigella* or *kalonji* seeds and another small aromatic Indian spice known as *radhuni* for which black mustard seeds can be substituted. It is used in whole-seed spice form to impart flavor to oil before cooking. The spices are discarded or allowed to remain in the dish during cooking, depending on the strength of flavor required.

PANCHPHORAN

2 tbsps black mustard seeds
2 tbsps cumin seeds
1 tbsp nigella seeds (or use black cumin)
1½ tbsps fennel seeds
1 tbsp fenugreek seeds

Mix well and store in a spice jar.

SRI LANKAN CURRY POWDER is a richly roasted blend of curry spices which give the unique flavor to curries from Sri Lanka. Sold commercially, but usually best when freshly roasted and ground.

SRI LANKAN CURRY POWDER

½ cup coriander seeds
2 tbsps cumin seeds
1½ tsps fennel seeds
½ tsp fenugreek seeds
3 dried red chilies
3 whole cloves
3 green cardamom pods, peeled and seeds crushed
1 tbsp dried curry leaves
1 tbsp lightly toasted, finely ground rice (optional)

In a dry pan or oven, roast the coriander, cumin, fennel, fenugreek and chilies until very well colored. Stir constantly to prevent burning. Grind to a fine powder with remaining ingredients, add the ground rice at the end, if used. Cool and store in a spice jar.

CURRY PUFFS
Yields 30

2 tbsps oil or ghee
4 oz (120 g) minced beef or mutton
¾ cup (3 oz / 90 g) finely chopped onion
½ tsp minced garlic
1 tsp minced ginger
1 tbsp minced fresh coriander (cilantro)
1½ tbsps garam masala
½ tsp turmeric
¾ tsp salt
½ tsp pepper
2 medium potatoes, peeled, boiled and finely diced
½ cup (2 oz / 60 g) cooked peas
1 lb (500 g) prepared puff pastry
mint chutney

Heat the oil or ghee in a pan and sauté meat and onion until colored. Add garlic, ginger, coriander, *garam masala*, turmeric, salt and pepper. Cook, stirring on high heat, for 1½ minutes; turn and add potato and peas. Heat through for 3 minutes; cool. Roll out pastry until thin; cut into 30 rounds 3 in (8 cm) in diameter and place a spoonful of filling on each. Fold in halves and pinch edges together into a fluted pattern. Bake at 380°F (190°C) for 20–35 minutes, or deep-fry until golden. Serve with mint chutney.

GREEN CURRY PASTE

20 green prik khee noo chilies
1 lemon grass root, chopped
1 tbsp minced kaffir lime rind
2 tbsps chopped coriander root
2 tsps minced greater galangal
2 tsps minced garlic
2 tbsps minced shallots
1 tsp ground toasted coriander seeds
1 tsp ground toasted cumin seeds
½ tsp turmeric
1 tsp shrimp paste

In a food processor, grind chilies and lemon grass. Add remaining ingredients and grind to a paste adding a little water or vegetable oil if needed. Store for up to 10 days in the refrigerator.

ORANGE CURRY PASTE
Yields ¹/2 cup (4 oz / 125g)

*10 medium-size dried red chilies, soaked and
seeded
2 tbsps minced shallots
1 tsp shrimp paste, toasted
1 tsp salt
2 tsps white vinegar*

Grind chilies until well broken. Add
shallots and shrimp paste and grind
until smooth. Add salt and vinegar and
mix thoroughly. Can be refrigerated for
about 8 days.

RED CURRY PASTE
Yields ³/4 cup (6 fl oz / 180 ml)

*4–6 small dried red prik khee noo chilies,
seeded, soaked and chopped
2 tsps minced greater galangal
2 pieces kaffir lime rind, soaked and chopped
1 lemon grass root, chopped
2 tbsps minced garlic
¹/4 cup minced shallots
1 tsp shrimp paste
¹/4 cup minced coriander root*

Combine all ingredients and grind to a
smooth paste in a mortar or food
processor. Refrigerate for up
to 10 days.

CUTTLEFISH: (*Sepia pharaonis*) From the
family Sepiidae, the cuttlefish is like a very
small, flattened octopus or a large squid, having a thick brownish mantle and eight short
tentacles. It is fished in all Asian waters and is
used extensively as a food. Cuttlefish ink,
taken from the sac located where the head
joins the body, was used in the past to make
the color sepia. Its powdered bone or "cuttle" is
used medicinally, and in Burma was used by
goldsmiths to rub over finished objects as a
final soft polish. The flavor is bland and very
slightly fish-tasting; the texture marginally
more chewy than squid, although small cuttle-

fish can be very tender. They are used in stir-
fried dishes and very small ones may be deep-
fried whole. Sold fresh in most Asian fish
markets, they must be thoroughly rinsed before use and will keep fresh for only about two
days. Canned cuttlefish is packed in soy sauce
and can be added directly to a dish. Its texture
is disagreeably softened by the preserving
process.

CUTTLE FISH STRIPS: In Japan, strips of
dried cuttlefish sold in small packs, are used
for flavoring stocks and soups and are used in
some simmered dishes.
Also known as *kha-wel* (Burma); *maik yu, mak
mo, woo chak* (China); *biekutak* (Indonesia);
ika, mongo-ika (strips) (Japan); *sotong karang*
(Malaysia); *bagolan* (Philippines)
See also: SEAFOOD, DRIED; SQUID

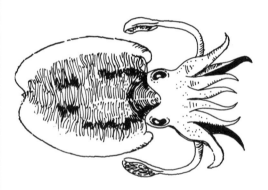

Cuttlefish

D

DAAI DAU NGA CHOY: (*DAI DOW NA CHOY,* China) see BEAN SPROUT (SOYBEAN)

DAAI GAAI CHOY: (*DAI GAI CHOY,* China) see CABBAGE, CHINESE

DAHI: (*DA-HEE,* India) see YOGURT

DAI CHOY GOH: (*DAI CHOY GO,* China) see AGAR AGAR

DAIKON: (*DAI-I-KON,* Japan) see RADISH, GIANT WHITE

DAIKON NIMONO: (*DAI-I-KON NEE-MOW-NOH,* Japan) see RADISH GIANT WHITE

DAIKON OROSHI: (*DAH-I-KON O-ROW-SHI,* Japan) see RADISH, GIANT WHITE

DAIKON SHREDS: (Japan) see RADISH, GIANT WHITE

DAIKON SPROUT: see RADISH, GIANT WHITE

DAING: (*DA-ING,* Philippines) see FISH, PRESERVED

DAI ZU: (*DAH-I ZOO,* Japan) see SOYBEAN

DAL: (*DAAL,* India) see LENTIL

DALCHINI: (*DAAL-CHEE-NEE,* India) see CINNAMON

DANG GUI: (*DONG GWAI,* China) (*Angelica sinensis*) Aromatic *dang gui,* with its slightly bitter, leguminous flavor, is an invaluable food medicinally. It is a relative of the sweeter tasting European herb *Angelica archangelica* known in ancient times as "root of the Holy Ghost." The root of the angelica plant, *dang gui* is cooked in soups to restore vitality and improve blood tone. Dried *dang gui* is sold in Chinese groceries and pharmacies and looks like tiny pieces of bleached driftwood. It is also sold sliced. It should be soaked to soften before using. A popular use of this herb is to simmer it in a clear chicken stock with a pâté of finely minced pigeon breast. This is cooked in a bamboo container made from a section of large bamboo, placed inside a steamer pan. Sliced, dried *dang gui* also forms part of Chinese tonic soup preparations.
Also known as *dong guei, pai chih, tang kuei* (China)
See also: MEDICINAL FOODS

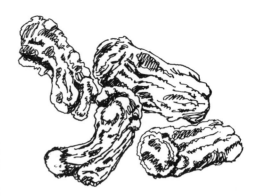

Dang gui

DARANG: (*DAH-RANG,* Philippines) see FISH, PRESERVED

DARK SOY SAUCE: see SOY SAUCE

DARN: (*DARN,* China) see EGG

DASHEEN: see TARO

DASHI: (*DAH-SHI,* Japan) *Dashi* is a distinctively flavored fish and seaweed stock which gives the authentic base flavor to many Japanese dishes. It is made by steeping *kombu,* a form of kelp (seaweed) in hot water, then adding *hana-katsuo* (shaved, dried bonito). Instant *dashi* is sold ready-to-use in powder, liquid and granule forms, in pre-measured sachets, bottles or small dispensers. There is also one packed in a teabag. It dissolves in warm water and a little goes a long way. Generally 1 tsp of instant *dashi* is used to flavor 3 cups (24 fl oz/750 ml) of water. *Hon dashi* granules require 1/4 tsp per 1 cup (250 ml) of boiling water. *Katsuo dashi,* the liquid concentrate, requires about 1/3 tsp per 1 cup of lukewarm water and *dashi-no-moto* instant powder requires 1 bag, sachet or tsp for 1 cup of boiling water. *Dashi* made by the traditional method comes in two grades. The first is known as *ichiban dashi* or primary *dashi,* and is the first infusion. The secondary infusion, known as *niban dashi,* is less intense in flavor and is suitable for braised and simmered dishes where a milder taste is needed.
See also: BONITO; CLEAR SOUP WITH KAMABOKO (recipe); SEAWEED

ICHIBAN DASHI
(primary *dashi*)

3 tbsps kombu *(kelp)*
3 tbsps hana-katsuo *(bonito shavings)*

Wipe *kombu* with a damp cloth to remove the surface mold and salt residues. Slash the surface on both sides with a sharp knife. Bring 5 cups (40 fl oz/1.25 l) water to a boil, add *kombu* and remove from heat. Let stand for 10 minutes, then remove *kombu*. Add another 1 cup (250 ml) of water and bring just to a boil, add *hana-katsuo*, remove from heat and strain.

NIBAN DASHI
(secondary *dashi*)

Boil the above *kombu* and *hana-katsuo* in a second lot of 5 cups (40 fl oz/1.25 l) water.Simmer for 15–20 minutes, then add an additional 2 tbsps *hana-katsuo*. Let stand for 1 minute; strain.

DASHI-NO-MOTO: (*DAH-SHI-NO-MO-TO*, Japan) see DASHI

DATE: (*Phoenix dactylifera*) This palm is an ancient tree, that has been cultivated in subtropical parts of the world since 3000 BC. It produces small, soft, black, fleshy fruit that is intensely sweet. In Asia, dates are grown in India and Sri Lanka where they are used in sweets and chutneys, and they were introduced in southern China in the late eighth century. Dates were originally known in China as Persian *jujubes* for their similarity to the fruit of the Chinese *jujube,* which is itself called a "red date." Chinese use dates in steamed sweet buns and pastries.
Also known as *hoan jo* (China); *chawara, khajur* (India)
See also: JUJUBE

DATE, CHINESE RED: see JUJUBE

DAU HU: (*DOW HOO*, Vietnam) see BEAN CURD

DAU HU CHIEN: (*DOW HOO CHEE-IAN*, Vietnam) see BEAN CURD (FRIED)

DAU HU CHUNG: (*DOW HOO CHEE-UNG*, Vietnam) see BEAN CURD

DAU HU KI: (*DOW HOO KEE*, Vietnam) see BEAN CURD (PRESSED)

DAUN KARI PLA: (*DA-WOON KAH-REE PLA*, Malaysia) see CURRY LEAF

DAUN KEMANGI: (*DA-WOON KEH-MA-NGEE*, Malaysia) see BASIL

DAUN KESOM: (*DA-WOON KAY-SOM*, Malaysia) see POLYGONUM

DAUN KETUMBAR: (*DA-WOON KEH-TOMB-BAR*, Indonesia, Malaysia) see CORIANDER, FRESH

DAUN KUNYIT: (*DA-WOON KOO-NYIT*, Malaysia) see TURMERIC

DAUN LIMAU PURUT: (*DA-WOON LEE-MAW POO-ROOT*, Malaysia) see KAFFIR LIME

DAUN MANGKOK: (*DA-WOON MUNG-COCK*, Indonesia) (*Polyscias scutellarium*) A shrub that grows in Indonesia with young leaves that are dark-green above and light-green on the underside and are aromatic when crushed or bruised. They are cut finely and mixed with grated coconut to cook as a green vegetable. In the Celebes and Sumatra they are cooked in a traditional dish with brains. The individual leaves are used as platters and containers for food, and it is probably for this reason that they are also known as cup leaf.
Also known as *godong mangkokan* (Indonesia); cup leaf
See also: LEAVES USED AS FOOD CONTAINERS, PLATES, WRAPPERS

DAUN PANDAN: (*DA-WOON PUN-DUN*, Malaysia) see PANDANUS LEAF

DAUN SALAM: (*DA-WOON SAH-LARM*, Indonesia, Malaysia) (*Eugenia polyantha*) This tree from the Myrtaceae family grows wild throughout Indonesia and has tough, aromatic leaves that are similar to bay leaves and used in the same way. Dried or fresh they add flavor to soups, meat dishes, sauces and fried rice (*nasi goreng*).
Also known as *manting* (Indonesia); *salam* (Malaysia)

DAUN SELASIH: (*DA-WOON SEH-LA-SEEH*, Malaysia) see BASIL

DAU PHONG RANG: (*DOW FONG RAN*, Vietnam) Roasted peanuts are frequently used in Vietnam as a garnish and to add extra flavor to sauces. To make, use shelled peanuts in their red skins.
See also: PEANUT

DAU PHONG RANG

8 oz (250 g) shelled, unskinned peanuts

Heat skillet or wok over high heat. Add peanuts and stir continually until skins turn deep brown-black. Remove from pan and spread on a cloth to cool. Rub with the cloth to loosen skins; shake in a colander to sift out skins. Cool and store in an airtight container.

DAYAP: (*DA-YAP*, Philippines) see LIMAU KESTURI

DEER: Various types of deer roam wild through the mountainous regions of Asia and for many centuries their meat—venison—has been put to culinary use. In central Sichuan province, surrounded by a towering mountain range, deer is one of the most commonly used meats. The slim, subtly flavored tendons taken from deer shanks are a delicacy in this region, just as the liver is in Laos. In India the deer-shooting season extends from October to March and during that time venison kebabs and curries appear on menus. In India venison meat is also made into a delicious pickle, *keran ka achar*. The meat is dark-colored, strong-tasting and distinctly flavored, complemented by strong seasonings.
Also known as *lurou* (China); *heran ka gosht* (India)

DEGI MIRICH: (*DE-GEE MIRCH*, India) see CHILI

DENDANG: (*DEN-DUNG*, Indonesia) see CLAM

DENGAKU
Serves 4

2 cakes cotton bean curd, drained
1 cup (8 fl oz / 250 ml) white miso
4 tbsps sake
4 tbsps mirin
2 tbsps sugar
1¹/₃ cups (11 fl oz / 340 ml) dashi
4 egg yolks
¹/₂ cup (4 fl oz / 125 ml) red miso
kinome leaves or parsley
2 tsps black sesame seeds
2 tsps shredded citron or lemon rind

Place bean curd on a dish, press a plate on top and add a weight. Leave 2 hours. Cut into ¹/₂ in (1 cm) thick slices and insert a flat bamboo skewer into each. Grill both sides to golden brown. Mix ³/₄ cup (6 fl oz/180 ml) white miso with half the *sake, mirin*, sugar and *dashi*. Beat in 2 egg yolks; heat mixture gently in a double-boiler until thick. Heat remaining ¹/₄ cup (2 fl oz/70 ml) white miso, the red miso and remaining *sake, mirin*, sugar, *dashi* and yolks and simmer in the same way until thick. Spread red *dengaku* topping thickly over one side of half the bean curd pieces. Spread the white topping over the remaining pieces of bean curd. Add sesame seeds or *kinome* leaves. Grill 1–2 minutes. Garnish with citron or lemon rind.

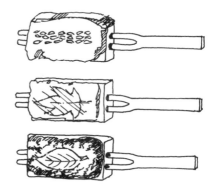

Dengaku on skewers

95

DESSERT-MAKING UTENSILS: see UTEN-
SILS, CAKE AND DESSERT MAKING
DEVIL'S TARO: see AMORPHOPHALUS KONJAC
DEVIL'S TONGUE: see AMORPHOPHALUS
KONJAC
DHANIA: (*DHA-NI-AA*, India) see CORIANDER

DHANSAK
Serves 10

1 onion, sliced
1/4 cup (2 oz / 60 g) ghee
2 tsps minced garlic
1 1/2 tsps minced ginger
6–8 dried red chilies, soaked and chopped
1 tbsp dhansak masala
2 green cardamom pods, peeled and seeds
crushed
2 cinnamon sticks
3/4 tsp peppercorns
1 1/2 tsps turmeric
1 1/4 lbs (625 g) lean lamb or mutton, diced
3 medium tomatoes, chopped
2 tsps salt
8 cups (2 qts / 2 l) water
1/2 cup (3 oz / 90 g) each yellow, green and red
lentils
4 oz (125 g) diced eggplant (aubergine)
4 oz (125 g) spinach leaves, rinsed
4 oz (125 g) diced pumpkin
1/2 cup (4 fl oz / 125 ml) tamarind water
1 tbsp palm sugar (or substitute brown sugar)
1 tbsp chopped fresh coriander (cilantro)
1 tbsp fried onion flakes

Fry onion in ghee until well browned;
add garlic, ginger and chilies; fry
briefly. Add *masala*, cardamom, cinnamon sticks, peppercorns and turmeric.
Add lamb and cook until meat is lightly
colored. Add tomatoes with salt and
water. Bring to a boil, cover and simmer
gently until the meat is half-cooked,
about 25 minutes. Add the lentils, diced
vegetables and spinach and cook until
tender. Add tamarind water and salt
and sugar to taste. Garnish with
coriander and onion flakes which have
been fried in oil until a rich brown.
Serve with *dhansak* brown rice, onion
kachumber and *dhansak* kebabs.

DHANSAK BROWN RICE
Serves 10

2 large onions, sliced
1/3 cup (3 oz / 90 g) ghee
1 1/2 tbsps palm sugar (or substitute brown
sugar)
2 1/2 cups (18 oz / 515 g) short-grain white rice
2 cinnamon sticks
5 whole cloves
1 1/2 tbsps salt
3 1/2 cups (28 fl oz / 800 ml) water

Fry onions in ghee to a deep, rich brown.
Add sugar and stir until melted. Add
rice and spices, salt and water. Bring to
a boil, then cook for 25 minutes on very
low heat until liquid is absorbed and rice
tender. Quickly stir rice 2–3 times
during cooking to distribute the onions
evenly.

DHANSAK KEBABS
Serves 10

1 lb (500 g) lean minced beef or lamb
1/2 cup (4 oz / 120 g) mashed potato
1 tsp chili paste
2 tbsps minced onion
1 tsp minced ginger
1/2 tsp minced garlic
1 egg, beaten
1 tsp turmeric
1/2 tsp ground cumin
1/2 tsp dhansak masala
1/2 tsp garam masala
salt
pepper
2 tbsps chopped fresh coriander (cilantro)
vegetable oil

Mix meat and potato with chili paste,
onion, ginger and garlic. Add egg,
turmeric, cumin, *dhansak masala* and
garam masala. Season with salt and
pepper and add coriander. Mix until
very smooth. Form into walnut-size
balls and fry gently until well-colored
and lightly crisp. Drain well before
serving.

DHANSAK MASALA: (*DHAN-SAK MA-SAA-LAA*, India) see MASALA

DHWEN-JANG: (*DWEN-JANG*, Korea) A thick, red-brown, salty bean sauce, similar to Chinese soybean paste and Japanese *akadashi*-miso or *hatcho*-miso, but with a particularly fine, rich flavor. It is used in many Korean dishes as a seasoning and can be purchased where Korean ingredients are sold. Like other bean pastes, it keeps indefinitely in a sealed jar. Substitute *akadashi*-miso.
Also known as Korean bean paste
See also: BEAN PASTES AND SAUCES; CHEEGAY OF FISH (recipe); MISO

DILIS: (*DEE-LEES*, Philippines) see BAGOONG; ANCHOVY

DILL: (*Anethum graveolens*) A feathery green, licorice-flavored herb, the leaves of which are used fresh and dried as a garnish and to flavor yogurt, soups, fish and egg dishes. In Sri Lanka it is an important ingredient in the Dutch dish called *Frikkadels*. It is a close relative of coriander and is used in Thai, Vietnamese and Laotian cooking. The Thais know it as Laotian coriander or *pak chee lao*. Fennel leaves have a similar, although less intense, flavor and can be substituted.

DILL SEED has a different flavor to the leaves and is more intense, slightly less like licorice. Dry-roasting the seed enhances the flavor. Dill has a natural affinity with fish and in India it is often added to fish curries. In Indonesia the herb *kenikir* is used like dill.
Also known as *anithi, sua, sua bhati* (India); *adas manis* (Indonesia); *phak si* (Laos); *enduru* (Sri Lanka); *pak chee lao* (Thailand);
See also: FRIKKADELS (recipe); MEATBALLS OF PORK WITH SALAD GREENS (recipe)

DIM SUM: see YUM CHA

DONG GUEI: (*DONG GWAI*, China) see DANG GUI

DO PIAAZA: (*DO PI-AA-JAA*, India) see INDIA, COOKING METHODS

DO PIAAZA
Serves 8

2 lbs (1 kg) onions, peeled
2½ tsps minced garlic
1½ tsps minced ginger
1 tsp paprika
3 tbsps chopped, fresh coriander (cilantro) leaves
2 tbsps ground coriander
2 tsps black cumin seeds
⅓ cup (3 fl oz / 90 ml) plain (natural) yogurt
1–2 tsps chili powder
⅓ cup (3 oz / 90 g) ghee
2 tbsps vegetable oil
3 lbs (1.5 kgs) lamb shoulder, cubed
8 green cardamom pods, peeled and seeds crushed
1 tsp garam masala

Finely slice half the onions and chop the rest. Grind chopped onions with garlic, ginger, paprika, coriander leaves, ground coriander, cumin seeds, yogurt and chili powder to a smooth paste. Heat ghee and vegetable oil in a large, heavy pan. Fry the sliced onions until evenly browned. Reserve. Fry cubed meat in batches until well colored. Fry the blended onion mixture over medium heat, stirring, until well cooked with oil separating. Return meat to pan; add cardamom, stir well, cover and cook on low heat until meat is tender and liquid almost absorbed. Add *garam masala* and reserved fried onions; leave on very low heat for a further 15 minutes.

DOSA: (*DO-SAA*, India) see BREAD, INDIAN; SOUTHERN INDIAN BREAKFAST BREAD (recipe)

DOUBAN LAJIANG: (*DAU-BARN LART-JEUNG*, China) see BROAD BEAN

DOUBJIANG: (*DAU-JEUNG*, China) see BROAD BEAN

DOUFOU KAN: (*DAU-FU GON*, China) see BEAN CURD, (GRILLED) (PRESSED)

DOU-FU: (*DAU-FU*, China) see BEAN CURD

DOUFU NAO: (*DAUFU NOU*, China) see BEAN CURD ("BRAINS")

DOUFU POK: (*DAUFU PORK*, China) see BEAN CURD, FRIED

DOW FOO: (*DAU FU*, China) see BEAN CURD

DRESSED FOODS: see AEMONO

DRIED ABALONE, PREPARATION OF: see ABALONE

DRIED AND SALTED FISH: see FISH, PRE-SERVED

DRIED BAMBOO SHOOTS AND CHICKEN NOODLES IN SOUP: (recipe) see BAMBOO SHOOT

DRIED SCALLOP: see CONPOY

DRIED TANGERINE/MANDARIN PEEL: see TANGERINE/MANDARIN

DRUMSTICK VEGETABLE: (India) (*Moringa pterygosperma*) This long, round, bean-like vegetable has a hard, deep-green skin, with regularly spaced, shallow indentations along its length. It grows on a tree and has the delicate taste and texture of marrow. The popular name may have come from the British in India, as in size and shape it resembles a wooden drumstick and no doubt could be used like one. It is cut into lengths and cooked in bunches like asparagus and can be curried. The root of the *moringa* (drumstick) tree can be grated to make a substitute for horseradish, so the tree may also be known as the horseradish tree.

Also known as *seeng* (India); *sai jar* (Indonesia); *buah keloh* (Malaysia); *nihura* (Nepal)

See also: DRUMSTICK VEGETABLE CURRY (recipe)

DRUMSTICK VEGETABLE CURRY

Serves 4

3 drumsticks, sliced
1/3 cup (3 oz / 90 g) chopped onion
1/2 tsp chopped garlic
1 tsp chopped ginger
2 green chilies, seeded and chopped
2 tbsps desiccated coconut
2 tbsps vegetable oil
1/4 tsp black mustard seeds
1/4 tsp asafoetida
1 cup (4 oz / 125 g) besan *flour*
1 1/2 tsps salt
1/2 tsp chili powder

(cont'd)

(Drumstick Vegetable Curry cont'd)

1/2 tsp turmeric
1 1/2 tsps tamarind concentrate
1/2 tsp garam masala
1 tsp ground cumin
fresh coriander (cilantro)

Boil drumsticks in lightly salted water until tender; drain. Grind onion, garlic, ginger, chilies and coconut to a paste. Heat oil and fry mustard seeds and *asafoetida* until seeds stop popping. Add *besan* flour and fry until very aromatic. Add 2 cups (16 fl oz/500 ml) water, the ground ingredients, salt, chili powder, turmeric and tamarind concentrate. Stir and bring a boil; add *garam masala*, cumin and the drumsticks and cook until thick. Garnish with coriander.

Drumstick vegetables

DRUNKEN CHICKEN: (recipe) see CHICKEN

DRY BEAN CURD: see BEAN CURD (PRESSED)

DRY ROASTING: see INDIA, COOKING METHODS

DRY SPICED BEEF: (recipe) see BEEF

DUA NAO: (*YOO-A NOW*, Vietnam) see COCONUT (KELAPA MUDA)

DUCK: The famed Beijing duck of northern China, with its lacquered red-gold skin and moist, sweet meat is one of the highlights of Chinese cuisine. The ducks are specially bred to grow plump in the breast with a layer of fat separating skin and meat. This fat melts during cooking so that the crisp, sweet skin can be lifted off, cut into bite-size pieces and served with soft, thin pancakes. Sichuan province has its unique Camphor- and Tea-Smoked Duck, while a favorite dish in Nanjing is pressed duck which has a distinctive gamey flavor. Elsewhere in Asia, duck finds its way into the curry pot, accepting the pungent spices of *vindaloo* and *rendang*.

Also known as *tianya* (Beijing duck), *ya* (duck) (China); *batakh* (India); *bebek* (Indonesia); *itik* (Mayalsia)

See also: BEIJING DUCK; CAMPHOR- AND TEA-SMOKED DUCK (recipe); EGG; OILS AND FATS (DUCK FAT); VINDALOO OF DUCK (recipe)

DUCK GIZZARDS may be used in slow-cooked dishes, where they are flavored with strong seasoning such as ginger, garlic and chilies. They are added to stocks and soups to improve the flavor.

Also known as *yazhen* (China)

DUCK HEARTS are considered a delicacy and are sometimes served at Chinese banquets. Spiced hearts tossed in the wok over very intense heat are favored in northern China.

Also known as *yaxin* (China)

DUCK LIVERS, being strongly flavored, are best used in soups and slow-cooked dishes. They are excellent in a curry with a coconut milk base.

Also known as *yagan* (China)

DUCK SKIN (*yapi*) is used separately, like chicken skin, for its crispy texture. This is the most prized part of the Beijing duck or other crisply-cooked ducks. Tongues (*yashe*), simmer-steamed until tender and served in a light sauce, are a banquet dish.

See also: BEIJING DUCK; VIETNAMESE-STYLE BEIJING DUCK (recipe)

DUCK WEBS: The skin that forms the duck paddle is considered a delicacy in China; the paddles are painstakingly deboned and softened by slow cooking. For family meals they are braised in a rich brown sauce with soy and caramelized sugar, but at banquets chefs perform the delicate operation of stuffing the fine webs with duck meat or shrimp mousse and poaching them in a well-flavored broth.

Also known as *ngup jern, yazhang* (China)

DUCK, DRIED: Chinese ducks, deboned leaving wing and drumstick bones in place, are seasoned with salt and spices, pressed flat and hung by the neck to dry. They are sold whole in Chinese delicatessens where pieces can be cut to order. Smaller cuts are sold in the markets in vacuum-sealed plastic. Dried duck adds an intense flavor to soup stock and stewed dishes and can also be steamed. Rinse before use, cut into cubes and add directly to the pot. It can be kept for several months in the refrigerator.

Also known as *lap ngup* (China); pressed duck

DUCK EGG: see EGG

DUCK EGG, SALTED: The Chinese method for preserving duck eggs is to pack them in tubs filled with a mixture of finely ground charcoal and brine. The egg changes consistency as the salt enters the shell by osmosis. The yolks become firm resembling dried apricots; the whites take on a salty flavor. In Chinese moon cakes, duck egg yolks are used in the filling. In Malaysia salted duck eggs sometimes accompany lavish curry meals. The black coating should be scraped off, and the egg thoroughly rinsed before cooking. They are placed in cold water and slowly brought to a boil and then simmered for 10 minutes. Unopened salted eggs can be kept for many months. Opened eggs or yolks can be refrigerated for several days. In Thailand, salted eggs are made by storing whole eggs in a strong brine. They are hard-cooked, then served with hors d'oeuvre, used as an ingredient in some curries and made into a spicy sauce to serve with rice and steamed fish.

Also known as *haam daan* (China); *telur asin* (Indonesia, Malaysia); *kai kem* (Thailand)

See also: SALTED EGGS (recipe); SALTED EGG SAUCE (recipe); THOUSAND-YEAR EGG

DUCK EGGS, SALTED

12 duck eggs, well washed
1 cup (7 oz / 220 g) coarse cooking salt
1 tbsp Sichuan peppercorns
1/2 cup (4 fl oz / 125 ml) yellow rice wine
7 cups (56 fl oz / 1.75 l) warm water

Place eggs in a large jar. Mix together the remaining ingredients, stirring to dissolve salt. Pour over eggs, cover and set aside in a cool place for 1 month.

Chinese preserved duck eggs

DUCK FAT: see OILS AND FATS
DUCK GIZZARD: see DUCK
DUM: *(DUM)* see INDIA, COOKING METHODS

DUMPLING WRAPPERS
Yields 24

2 cups (8 oz / 250 g) all-purpose (plain) flour
1 tsp baking powder
1 tsp salt
2 egg yolks
³⁄4 cup (6 fl oz / 180 ml) warm water

Combine the flour, baking powder and salt in a mixing bowl and mix well. Make a well in the center. Beat the egg yolks and water together and pour into the well, working in lightly with chopsticks. When well mixed, remove to a work surface and knead for 3–4 minutes. Cover with a damp cloth. To use, roll out thinly on a lightly floured surface. Cut into squares or circles and fill. Pinch the edges firmly together to seal. If necessary, brush edges with water or beaten egg before sealing.

DUN: *(DANG)* see CHINA, COOKING METHODS (SIMMER-STEW)

DUNG MEIN: *(DANG MIN,* China) see FLOURS AND THICKENERS (WHEAT STARCH)

DURIAN: *(Durio zibethinus)* This large, globe-shaped fruit has a hard, yellow-to-green and heavily spiked shell over a fleshy segmented interior of soft, sweet flesh. When ripe it has a strong, nauseating odor which makes it a difficult fruit to stock. It is, therefore, rarely available fresh. Even in Malaysia and Indonesia where it is grown, it reaches only selected fruit stands for its two annual seasons. Its flavor is intense and can best be described for its similarity to tropical fruit salad. Eating it fresh can be an acquired taste. It is used raw in ice cream, desserts and to make candy. It is sometimes fried, cooked in the skin over charcoal or steamed in the same way as breadfruit. A yellowing of the skin indicates the fruit is ripe.

Durian is sold in cans or bottles, packed in sugar syrup. Each segment of flesh has one or several large, black, shiny seeds which, in Indonesia, are roasted and eaten as snacks. The petals from durian flowers are eaten in the Batak provinces, while in the Moluccas islands the peel is used as fuel to smoke fish.

Also known as *ambetan, dooren* (Indonesia); *doorian* (Malaysia); *turian* ("king of fruit") (Thailand)
See also: BREADFRUIT

Durian

E

EDAMAME: (*E-DAH-MA-ME*, Japan) see SOYBEAN

EDIBLE CHRYSANTHEMUM: see CHRYSAN-
THEMUM

EEL: (*Anguilla anguilla*) Both fresh and saltwater eels are cooked in Asia. They are particularly popular in Japan and the northern-
coastal Chinese region of Shanghai. There
they are braised and served in a richly flavored
brown sauce, liberally sprinkled with white
pepper and chopped chives. Freshwater eels
are readily available from the inland waterways in China and are included in many
recipes.

ANAGO: (Japan) The sea eel has rich, oily
meat and is usually coated with a sweet soy
sauce, *sake* and sugar glaze and then grilled. It
makes a popular topping for *sushi* on hand-
rolled rice.

UNAGI (Japan) is the freshwater eel, slightly
less oily and with a sweet, soft-textured meat.
It is used in braised and simmered dishes.
Also known as *moon sin* (China); *malong*
(Malaysia); *igat*, *pindangga* (Philippines); *pla
lai*, *pla mangkor* (Thailand)
See also: SUSHI

EEN CHOY: (*YIN CHOY*, China) see AMARANTH

E-FU NOODLES: (*YI-FU*) see NOODLES

EGG: Poultry has been domesticated in China
since early times, with archeological findings
from tombs of the early Han period (206 BC–AD
220) including bamboo slips listing eggs as one
of the common foods of the period. Duck and
chicken eggs are the most commonly used,
with duck generally regarded as having a
superior flavor. But the eggs of quail, pigeon
and other game birds are also featured in
Chinese cuisine, as well as the food of other
parts of Asia. Most Asian cuisines feature
omelets in several variations, and a frequently
used garnish in Indonesian, Malaysian and
Thai cuisine is finely shredded egg that has
been cooked in a thin sheet in the wok. Egg
cooked in this way is used as the wrapper for
"egg rolls" which are known in Asia as *lumpia*,
poh pia or spring rolls. In Asia, particularly
China, preserved eggs have been used through
the ages.

QUAIL and **PIGEON EGGS** are enjoyed for
their delicate flavor and because their small
size makes them attractive in a dish. Whole
poached quail eggs are floated on soups and
when hard-cooked, are used in *dim sum*. In
Japan they are threaded onto skewers to cook
as *yakitori* or kebabs, or are broken raw over
finely grated mountain yam for a delicately
flavored dish. They are also used in Vietnam
and Thailand.
Also known as *darn*, *jidan* (chicken); *yadan*
(duck), *gedan* (pigeon), *amchundan* (quail)
(China); *ande* (India); *telur* (Indonesia, Malaysia); *tamago*, *uzura no tamago* (quail) (Japan); *kukhura ka phool* (chicken), *haas ko phool*
(duck) (Nepal); *kai* (Thailand)
See also: DUCK EGG, SALTED; LUMPIA WRAPPERS
(recipe); THOUSAND-YEAR EGGS *and recipes
following*

EGG CUSTARD STEAMED IN A TEACUP
Serves 4

1 tbsp plus 1 tsp mirin
1 tbsp plus 1 tsp light soy sauce
4 oz (120 g) chicken breast, diced
12 stalks mitsuba, *blanched*
4 medium eggs, beaten
2 cups (16 fl oz / 500 ml) dashi
¼ tsp salt
*4 medium shrimp (prawns), peeled and
deveined*
12–16 canned ginkgo nuts

Sprinkle 1 tsp *mirin* and 1 tsp soy
sauce over chicken. Divide *mitsuba*
into bunches of 3 stems. Mix eggs
with *dashi*, salt, and remaining 1
tbsp *mirin* and soy sauce. Strain into

(cont'd)

(Egg Custard Steamed in a Teacup cont'd)

4 cups. Add chicken, shrimp, *mitsuba* and ginkgo nuts. Cover and steam for 20 minutes, until set. (See JAPAN, GARNISHES (MITSUBA) for tying *mitsuba* leaves)

EGGS IN COCONUT SAUCE
Serves 4

3/4 cup (6 oz / 180 g) minced onion
1 1/2 tsps minced garlic
3 tbsps peanut oil
1 tsp turmeric
1 tsp ground laos
1/2 tsp mashed shrimp paste
1 tsp sambal ulek
4 candlenuts, crushed
1 stalk lemon grass, split
1 cup (8 fl oz / 250 ml) thick coconut milk
salt
pepper
lemon juice
basil leaves
4–6 hard-cooked eggs, peeled and
quartered

Fry onion and garlic in peanut oil until golden. Add turmeric, *laos*, shrimp paste, *sambal ulek*, candlenuts and lemon grass, frying briefly. Add coconut milk and simmer for 5 minutes. Season with salt, pepper, lemon juice and basil. Add eggs, warm through.

OMELETTE ROLL
Serves 4–6

7 large eggs
3/4 cup (6 fl oz / 180 ml) dashi
1 tbsp mirin
1 tbsp light soy sauce
1/2 tsp salt

Lightly beat eggs. Add *dashi*, *mirin*, soy sauce and salt. Strain, dividing between 2 bowls: Rub an omelette

(cont'd)

(Omelette Roll cont'd)

pan with an oiled cloth. Heat to moderately hot. Pour in 1/3 of one bowl of batter. Tilt so egg covers pan, then when underside is firm but has not begun to color, push the omelette toward the bottom of the pan, making it roll up. Pour another 1/3 batter into the pan; cook in the same way then wrap around first roll. Cook final 1/3 of the bowl of batter in this way, wrapping around the roll. Slide the egg roll into a bamboo mat and gently squeeze it into a rectangular shape. Remove and slice into 1/3 in (1 cm) pieces. Cook other bowl of batter. Serve warm with soy sauce and *daikon oroshi*, or use as a *sushi* topping.

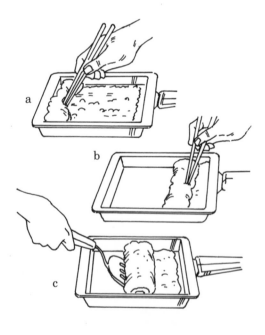

a. *Spreading omelette in pan*
b. *Rolling up*
c. *Removing cooked omelette roll from pan*

OMELETTE SHREDS

2–3 eggs; well beaten and strained

Heat a nonstick pan or well-seasoned wok. Pour in ⅓ of the egg. Slowly shake pan to spread egg thinly over bottom. Cook until just lightly colored underneath, then flip over and cook briefly on the other side. Spread to cool, roll up and cut crossways into very thin slices.

SALTED EGGS

¾ cup (6 oz / 180 g) salt
12 eggs

Pour salt into a pan; add eggs and water to cover. Boil for 2 minutes. Transfer eggs to sterilized jars; pour on water. Cover and leave for 1½ months. Hard-cook eggs before use.

SALTED EGG SAUCE

8 hard-cooked egg yolks, salted
1½ tsps minced garlic
1½–2 tsps minced red chili
⅓ tsp shrimp paste
½ tbsp palm sugar (or substitute brown sugar)
fish sauce
lime juice
2 tbsps minced scallions (spring / green onions)

Grind egg yolks to a paste with garlic, chili and shrimp paste. Dissolve palm sugar in a little water and add fish sauce and lime juice to taste and stir in scallions.

TEA EGGS (CHA YIP DARN)

10 chicken or duck eggs
10 cups (2½ qts / 2.5 l) water
1½ tsps salt
½ cup (1 oz / 30 g) black tea leaves
3 star anise
1 cinnamon stick

Place eggs in a large pot with the water. Bring to a boil and simmer for 10 minutes. Remove eggs from the water and lightly tap the shells until the surface is completely covered with fine cracks. Add salt, tea leaves, star anise and cinnamon to the cooking water. Bring back to a boil. Return the cracked eggs; simmer for 1 hour. Remove and let cool. Remove shells, cut eggs into quarters and serve as an hors d'oeuvre.

EGG NOODLES: see NOODLES

EGG NOODLES: (recipe) see NOODLES

EIGHT TREASURE CHICKEN: (recipe) see CHICKEN

EGGPLANT: (*Solanum melongena*) The eggplant (aubergine) is native to Asia, having been cultivated in China from 600 BC. Its original Chinese name, translated as "Malayan purple melon," indicates its origin in Peninsular Malaysia. The fruit is eaten as a vegetable and it varies in shape and size from a large globe to long, thin and cucumber-like. Color varies from white and green to golden and deepest purple. It has a pithy white interior with many small seeds. The raw fruit is bitter and is only very occasionally eaten in salads. Normally it is cooked by baking, frying, grilling or braising in a curry or sauce. When buying eggplants choose those with unwrinkled, firm and unmarked skin, with a hollow sound when tapped. They can be kept unwrapped in the refrigerator for several weeks.

BRINJAL and **BAIGAN** are the names given to the long and thin eggplants used by Indian cooks in curries and vegetarian cooking.

Brinjal, with its bland-tasting, porous flesh, readily accepts seasonings and spices, cooking into wonderful curries. It is also cooked in the Indian *bartha* style.

See also: EGGPLANT PUREE (recipe)

GLOBE EGGPLANT grows to 8 in (20 cm) in diameter and 15 in (38 cm) long, although at this stage it becomes woody and dry in texture. The skin is usually black-purple but also can be creamy-white tinged with green. It is sliced or diced for use, and if being fried, should be sprinkled with salt some time before use to draw out the bitter juices it contains. It is used extensively in Sichuan province in China and in Laos and Cambodia. Laotian cooks use raw eggplant pounded to a paste to flavor and thicken dishes.

HAIRY EGGPLANT (*ma uk*) is a Thai variety with orange skin covered with fine, dark hairs. Thinly sliced, it is used raw in salads or minced in sauces for its bitter-tart taste.

JAPANESE EGGPLANT tends to be smaller than those used as a vegetable elsewhere in Asia. Slender cylinders no more than 3 in (7 cm) long, or small, oval and pear-shaped, they are sliced and battered to cook as *tempura*, or are cooked by a combination of simmering in sauce and deep-frying. Small, whole eggplants shredded at the flower end and deep-fried are known in Japan as "tea whisk" eggplants for their resemblance to the small, curled and split bamboo whisks used to froth Japanese powdered green tea in the tea ceremony.

Also known as *nasu* (Japan)

See also: CHA NO YOU (TEA CEREMONY)

PEA EGGPLANT: (*Solanum torvum*) is a type used exclusively in Thailand. Growing in clusters, they look like pea-size, unripe tomatoes, usually dark green, but occasionally white. They have a tart flavor and are added whole to curries and unripe or raw to Thai chili sauces known as *nam prik*. Slightly larger than these is the golf-ball size white, yellow and green *makua yae* of Thailand and *terong enkol* of Indonesia.

Also known as *makua phuong* (pea eggplant) (Thailand)

See also: NAM PRIK

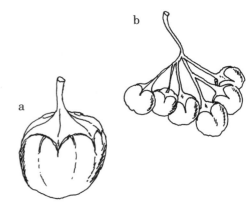

a. Thai makua yae *eggplant*
b. Thai pea eggplant

WHITE EGGPLANT, which is of a very light green color, is favored in China but is not used frequently, except in the central provinces.

Also known as *ai gwa* (China); *baigan, baingan, brinjal* (India); *terung* (Indonesia); *nasu* (Japan); *terong* (Malaysia); *talong* (Philippines); *makua* (Thailand); aubergine

See also: NAM PRIK (recipe)

EGGPLANT IN SAUCE
Serves 4

1 medium eggplant (aubergine)
deep-frying oil
1¼ cups (10 fl oz / 300 ml) dashi
¼ cup (2 fl oz / 60 ml) mirin
¼ cup (2 fl oz / 60 ml) light soy sauce
1 tbsp cornstarch (cornflour)
¼ cup hana-katsuo
¼ cup toasted nori seaweed, shredded
⅓ cup (1 oz / 30 g) chopped scallions (spring / green onions)

Quarter eggplant lengthways and deeply score the flesh with crosshatch slashes. Heat oil. Slide in eggplant and fry 6–7 minutes, until flesh is golden; drain. Bring *dashi*, *mirin* and soy sauce almost to a boil; reduce heat. Thicken with a paste of cornstarch in ¼ cup (2 fl oz/60 ml) cold water. Serve eggplant in a small dish with the sauce. Garnish with *hana-katsuo*, *nori* and scallions.

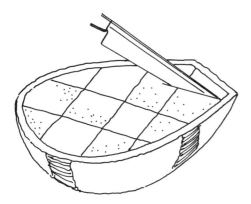

Crosshatch slashes in eggplant

EGGPLANT PUREE
Serves 4

1 large eggplant (aubergine)
1/2 cup (4 oz / 120 g) ghee
1 cup (4 oz / 125 g) chopped onion
1 1/2 cups (6 oz / 185 g) chopped tomatoes
1 tbsp chopped fresh coriander (cilantro) leaves
1 tsp ground coriander
1/2 tsp ground cumin
1/2 tsp chili powder
1/2 tsp turmeric
1 tsp salt
1 tsp fennel seeds

Bake or grill eggplant until the skin blackens and the flesh becomes soft. Peel under cold running water, then mash smoothly. In a medium pan, heat ghee and sauté the onion, tomatoes and coriander leaves. Add the ground coriander, chili powder, turmeric, salt and fennel seeds; cook for 2–3 minutes. Add the eggplant pulp and cook on a low heat for 5 minutes more, stirring constantly.

EGGPLANT SAMBAL

4 thin eggplants (aubergines)
1 cup (8 fl oz / 250 ml) vegetable oil
1/4 cup (2 oz / 60 g) minced onion
1 red chili, seeded and chopped
juice of 1 lime
3/4 tsp salt

(cont'd)

(Eggplant Sambal cont'd)

Wash the eggplant; dry and cut into small dice. Heat oil and fry the eggplant until browned. Remove and drain. Place in a dish with onion, chili, lime juice and salt. Mix well.

ELAICHI: (*ILAA-AI-CHEE*, India) see CARDAMOM

EMPING: (*REM-PING,* Indonesia) see KRUPUK; MELINJO

ENASAL: (*ENA-SAAL*, Sri Lanka) see CARDAMOM

ENDURU: (*E-NDU-RU*, Sri Lanka) see DILL

ENOKITAKE: (*E-NO-KEE-TA-KE*, Japan) see MUSHROOMS AND EDIBLE FUNGI

ENTOSENSAL: (*EN-TOS-SEN-SAL*, Philippines) see CAUL FAT

ESCABECHE: (*ES-KA-BET-CHE*, Philippines) see FISH, PRESERVED

ESTOFADO: (*ES-TOH-PAH-DOH*, Philippines) Deep-fried pieces of meat, usually tongue, chicken or pork are cooked in vinegar, salt, sugar, water and spices until tender. Fried potatoes and sweet bell peppers can also be added.
Also known as *humba* (Philippines)

ESTOFADO
Serves 6

2 lbs (1 kg) pork loin, rind on
1 tbsp minced garlic
1 cup (8 oz / 250 g) chopped onion
1 cup (8 fl oz / 250 ml) white vinegar
1/4 cup (2 fl oz / 60 ml) soy sauce
2 cubes fermented bean curd
1/2 cup (4 oz / 125 g) sugar
1/2 tsp black pepper
1 bay leaf

Combine pork, garlic, onion, vinegar and soy sauce with water to cover in a deep saucepan. Simmer until the skin of the pork is fork-tender. Mash bean curd and add to the pan with sugar, pepper and bay leaf. Cook until sauce is thick and the pork is cooked through. Slice and serve with the sauce.

F

FAGARA: (*FA-GAI-LART*, China) see SICHUAN PEPPERCORN

FAI CHEE: (*FAI JI*, China) see CHOPSTICKS

FAI GEE: (*FAI JI*, China) see CHOPSTICKS

FAT CHOY: (*FAT CHOY*, China) see SEAWEED (HAIR VEGETABLE)

FAVA: see BROAD BEAN

FENNEL: (*Foeniculum vulgare*) Originally from southern Europe and Southwest Asia this plant grows wild throughout the world. The licorice-flavored leaves, root and seeds are all used. The seeds are sweet with a strong anise fragrance. Ochre-green colored, they comprise about 10 lineal ridges compressed together. The seeds are used occasionally as a condiment with fish or in salad dishes. They are invaluable in pickling and are used whole or ground in curries, particularly with fish or shellfish. Fennel has been used medicinally in Asia for centuries particularly for stomach ailments. In India, fennel seeds are offered after a meal as a digestive aid and breath freshener. Indonesians chew wild fennel stems as a candy. The Thai, Indonesian and Malaysian names for fennel are the same as those used for cumin, and translate as sweet cumin. To add further confusion aniseed has similar names.
Also known as *samong-saba* (Burma); *moti sonf* (India); *adas*, *jintan manis* (Indonesia, Malaysia); *maduru* (Sri Lanka); *yira* (Thailand); sweet cumin
See also: CUMIN

FENUGREEK: (*Trigonella foenum-graecum*) Originally from the Mediterranean region, this annual herb from the pea family is cultivated in India. The fresh leaves are used as a vegetable and although bitter when raw, after cooking they become almost sweet.

DRIED FENUGREEK LEAVES are used to impart their distinct flavor and green color to some curries, but more often are ground and used in the marinade for *tandoori* foods.

FENUGREEK SEEDS are small, irregularly shaped and a yellow-brown color with a restrained maple syrup aroma. They have been used medicinally since ancient times and are also used as a spice. They must be roasted to enhance their flavor, care being taken not to overcook them as they can become bitter. Used whole or ground in pickles, chutneys and fish curries and added to some blends of curry powder when a pronounced flavor is required, such as *vindaloo*.
Also known as *methi ka saag* (leaves); *methi ka beej* (seeds) (India); *halba* (Malaysia); *uluhaal* (Sri Lanka)
See also: TANDOORI BAKED POMFRET (recipe)

FERMENTED BEAN CURD: see BEAN CURD BY-PRODUCTS

FERMENTED BEAN CURD CAKE: see BEAN CURD BY-PRODUCTS; TEMPE

FERMENTED BLACK BEAN: The original *shih* or darkened, salted soybeans of China. Dried soybeans are cooked, salted and fermented, causing them to turn almost black and soft. They are a popular seasoning in Western countries, and in China are used in

FERMENTED BLACK BEAN SAUCE

1$^{1}/_{2}$ tbsps fermented black beans
1 tsp minced garlic
2 tbsps light soy sauce
2 tsps yellow rice wine
1$^{1}/_{2}$ tsps sugar
2 tsps chopped red chilies
2 tbsps vegetable oil

Rinse the beans, dry thoroughly and chop finely. Mix with the other ingredients. Fry lightly in vegetable oil. Sprinkle over meat or fish before steaming, or make into a sauce by adding 1 cup (8 fl oz/250 ml) chicken stock or water with 1 tbsp cornstarch (cornflour). Boil briefly. Pour over cooked meat.

stir-fried, steamed or braised dishes, most often in combination with chilies and garlic. The soft beans are sold by weight in plastic packs. Transfer them to a jar and they will keep indefinitely without loss of flavor. They should be washed and dried before use and may be cooked whole, finely chopped or mashed. The garlic black bean flavor is popular.

To prepare garlic black bean seasoning, mash 1 tbsp beans with 1 tsp garlic and use to season up to 2 cups of food.

Also known as *dau see* (China); black beans; dried black beans; preserved black beans
See also: BEAN PASTES AND SAUCES; SOYBEAN

FERMENTED FISH: see FISH, PRESERVED; PADEK

FERMENTED RED RICE: A colorful flavoring with a yeasty, fermented taste, made by adding a red, edible, food-color solution, usually obtained from annatto seeds, to rice wine lees left after brewing rice wine. It is used in northern Chinese cooking, particularly with seafood, for its bright red color and the distinct, musky flavor it gives to a dish. It can be made at home by soaking cooked white rice in Chinese yellow wine (*shaohsing*) but a

---

FERMENTED RICE (WINE LEES)
Yields about 3 cups (1¹/₂ lbs / 750 g)

*3 lbs (1¹/₂ kgs) long-grain glutinous (sticky)
white rice
1¹/₂ tbsps all-purpose (plain) flour
2 wine balls / cubes*

Soak rice overnight, then steam for 15 minutes. Transfer to a glass or stainless-steel bowl. In a small jug mix flour with crumbled wine balls. Stir into the warm rice and make a depression in the center. Cover and place in a warm part of the kitchen for about 48 hours. A clear liquid should accumulate in the depression. Transfer the liquid and some of the rice into a sterilized jar; seal and store in the refrigerator. Discard remaining rice. Keeps for several weeks.

---

reasonable substitute is Japanese yellow miso paste. The rice is sold in bottles with liquid, or is dried and sold in small plastic bags. It will keep for many months.

Also known as *hong mei*, *hong zao* (China); *sake kasu* (Japan); red distillers' mash; red rice; wine lees
See also: FERMENTED RICE (WINE LEES) (recipe); WINE BALL/WINE CUBE; WINE LEES PASTE (recipe)

WINE LEES PASTE
Yields ¹/₃ cup (3 fl oz / 90 ml)

*2 tbsps yellow rice wine
1 tsp fermented bean curd
1 tbsp white miso paste
2¹/₂ tsps sugar*

Mix all of the ingredients to dissolve sugar, adding a little water to make the consistency of cream.

FERNTOP: (*Diplazium esculentum, Athyrium esculentum*) Many ferns of the Polypodiaceae family are eaten in Indonesia. The two types most commonly used are similar in appearance, with delicate, curling, green lace-like leaves. The very young leaves are eaten raw or steamed and used as an attractive garnish. They often appear in *gado gado*.

Also known as *daun pakis*, *sayur paku* (Indonesia); *daun paku* (Malaysia)
See also: GADO GADO (recipe)

FINLABONG: (*FIN-LAH-BONG*, Philippines) see BAMBOO SHOOT

FISH: Fish are a major food source throughout Asia, as well as being an important export commodity in many regions. Both fresh and saltwater fish are used extensively, with several types being particular favorites. Preserving fish by drying, salting and other forms of curing is also an important industry in many Asian countries.

Also known as *ca cum* (anchovy, long jawed), *trey andeg* (catfish), *trey lort* (goby), *trey pama* (greenback jewfish—saltwater fish which is also found in the lakes of Cambodia as well as far upstream in the Mekong) (Cambodia);

gui yu (crucian carp), hong yu (red snapper), huang yu (croaker), hung sam (golden/thread/ threadfin bream), li yu (carp), ngup yu (cuttlefish), paak cheong (white pomfret), quing yu (black carp), sha lan (red emperor), shek paan (garoupa), sinn (eel); tat sha (Macao sole), tsim tau sha (shark), tsing kaau (mackerel), you yu (squid) (China); begti (bekti), bhing (giant herring), bummaloe (Bombay duck), hilsa (Indian shad), katai (whitebait), naharm (mahaseer), pomplet (silver pomfret), rawas (Indian salmon), shingala (catfish), surai, surmai (seerfish), tambusa (red snapper) (India); bawal puteh, ikan bawal putih (white pomfret), beikutak, sotong karang (cuttlefish), cumi cumi, sotong (squid), ikan alu-alu, kacang-kacang, tenok (barracuda), ikan bawal hitam (black pomfret), ikan karau (similar to salmon), ikan kembong (similar to small bonito), ikan merah, ikan merah puchat, tambak merah (snapper/bream), ikan selar kuning (yellow mackerel), ikan senangin (small threadfin), ikan tenggiri, tenggiri batang (Spanish mackerel), ikan terubok (herring), ikan tongkol, madidahan (yellowfish tuna) (Indonesia, Malaysia); albagore, maguro (tuna), anago, unagi (eel), buri (yellowtail), hirame, karei (flounder), kamasu (saury pike), katsuo (bonito), kisu (sillago), masu (sea trout), saba, sawara (mackerel), tai (sea bream), shirano (whitebait), suzuki (sea bass) (Japan); alumahan (striped or rake-gilled mackerel), apahap (sea perch), banak (grey mullet), bangus (milkfish), bidbid (ten pounder or giant herring), burong dalag (mudfish), dilis (long-jawed anchovy), lapu lapu (spotted grouper), tamban (Indian sardine), tangigi (Spanish mackerel), tulingan (tuna, bonito) (Philippines); hoo pla chalarm (shark's fin), pla chalamet (pomfret), pla chalarm (shark), pla duk (cat fish), pla haeng (dried fish), pla i see (mackerel), pla kapong (sea bass), pla lai (eel), pla muek (squid), pla o (tuna), pla roo (fermented fish) (Thailand); ca be cam (golden trevally), ca bon (Oriental/Macao sole), ca bo uang (yellowfin tuna), ca chem (sea perch, giant), ca chim den (black pomfret), ca chim trang, ca chim mi (white pomfret), ca lap (hairin anchovy), ca muc (cuttlefish), con chom chom (sea urchin), sua (jellyfish) (Vietnam)

See also: ALBACORE; BANGUS; BOMBAY DUCK; BONITO; CARP; CLOUD EAR FUNGUS AND FISH IN WINE SAUCE (recipe); FISH PASTE; FISH, PRESERVED; GAROUPA; MEATBALL (illustration); POMFRET; REMPAH (FISH) *and recipes following*

BARBECUED FISH BALLS ON SKEWERS
Serves 6

2 lbs (1 kg) firm white fish
1 tbsp minced ginger
1/2 cup (4 oz / 120 g) minced scallions (spring / green onions)
2 tsps minced green chilies
2 tsps minced lemon grass
3 1/2 tsps salt
1 tsp white pepper
1 tsp aniseed
3/4 cup (6 fl oz / 180 ml) water
vegetable or Oriental sesame oil
lemon juice
fish sauce
1 large onion, thinly sliced
1 large carrot, thinly sliced
1 cucumber, thinly sliced
1/3 cup (3 fl oz / 90 ml) tamarind water or vinegar and sugar
chili sauce

Cut fish into chunks. Place fish in a food processor with ginger, scallions, green chilies and lemon grass and grind to a smooth paste. Add 2 tsps salt, the pepper, aniseed and water. Process until the mixture is smooth. Use wet or oiled hands to form into small balls, and drop into lightly salted water. Poach until fish balls float to the surface; remove and drain. Thread onto oiled bamboo skewers and brush with vegetable or sesame oil. Grill until the surface is colored. Sprinkle with lemon juice and fish sauce. Marinate onion, carrot and cucumber in a mixture of tamarind water, or vinegar and sugar; season with fish sauce and the remaining 1 1/2 tsps salt. Leave for 15 minutes; then drain. Serve with the grilled fish balls and chili sauce to taste.

FISH BALL CURRY
Serves 6

1 lb (500 g) chopped white fish
¹/₂ tsp salt
5 dried red chilies, soaked and seeded
1¹/₂ tsps minced garlic
*¹/₄ cup (2 oz / 60 g) minced shallots
or onion*
*1 tbsp minced coriander (cilantro) roots
on stems*
2 tsps minced ginger
1 minced lemon grass root
1 tsp shrimp paste
2 tbsps vegetable oil
2–3 tbsps fish sauce
basil leaves, chopped
minced red chilies
2 tbsps ground roasted rice

In a food processor, grind fish with salt and 3–4 tbsps water to a smooth paste. Form into small balls. Poach in boiling salted water until they float; remove and drain. Grind chilies, garlic, shallots, coriander, ginger, lemon grass and shrimp paste together until smooth. Fry in vegetable oil for 2 minutes. Add fish balls and 3 cups (24 fl oz/750 ml) water and bring to a boil. Simmer for 2–3 minutes. Season with fish sauce, basil and chilies to taste. Add ground rice and simmer for 15–20 minutes.

FISH BALL SOUP
Serves 6

*12 oz (350 g) skinless white fish,
cubed*
1 tbsp minced fresh coriander (cilantro)
*¹/₃ cup (3 oz / 90 g) scallions (spring / green
onions)*
1¹/₂ tsps salt
¹/₃ tsp pepper
6 cups (1¹/₂ qts / 1.5 l) fish stock
1 tbsp shredded ginger
8 oz (250 g) sliced mustard greens
shredded chilies

(cont'd)

(Fish Ball Soup cont'd)

Grind fish to paste with coriander, scallions, salt and pepper. Work to a smooth consistency, then form into small balls. Bring fish stock to a boil; add ginger, extra salt and pepper, and the mustard greens. Simmer for 2–3 minutes. Add fish balls and cook until they float to the surface. Garnish soup with shredded chilies.

FRIED FISH WITH GINGER SAUCE
Serves 4–6

*1¹/₂ lbs (750 g) whole red snapper or sea bass,
cleaned*
*1 cup (4 oz / 125 g) all-purpose (plain) flour or
2 tsps cornstarch (cornflour)*
1 tsp salt
1 tbsp vegetable oil
oil for deep-frying
1 recipe ginger sauce

Clean and dry fish. Make deep incisions in a crosshatch pattern on both sides. Mix flour with salt, oil, cornstarch and enough water to make a creamy batter. Heat oil for deep-frying. Coat fish with batter and deep-fry until well browned all over. Drain and serve with hot ginger sauce.

GRILLED FISH
Serves 6

*1 whole sea perch or sea bass about
2¹/₂ lbs (1.5 kgs), cleaned and boned*
2 scallions (spring / green onions)
8 slices greater galangal
salt
pepper
1 bunch spinach
1 bunch watercress
2 lettuces
*1 medium cucumber, unpeeled,
sliced*

(cont'd)

(Grilled Fish cont'd)

1¹/2 cups (3 oz / 90 g) fresh bean sprouts,
blanched
small quantity fresh herbs, such as dill, basil,
mint, fennel, coriander (cilantro)
1–2 fresh red chilies, seeded and shredded
¹/4 cup (2 fl oz / 60 ml) thin coconut milk
1 tbsp crushed, roasted peanuts
1 tsp minced fresh red chili
¹/2 tsp minced greater galangal
¹/2 tsp minced lemon grass
¹/4 cup (2 fl oz / 60 ml) fish sauce
2 tbsps lime juice
1–2 tsps sugar

Wash fish and pat dry. Place scallions
and *greater galangal* in cavity with
plenty of salt and pepper. Grill for about
7 minutes on each side, until done.
Wash leafy vegetables and arrange on
wide platter with cucumber, bean
sprouts, herbs and shredded chilies.
Take fish from grill; skin and place on
serving platter. Mix together coconut
milk, peanuts, minced chilies, *galangal*
and lemon grass with fish sauce, lime
juice and sugar. Serve as a dip.

REMPAH FISH
Serves 4–6

1 fresh red chili, seeded and minced
2 tsps shrimp paste
1 lb (500 g) white fish fillets, sliced
1 cup (4 oz / 125 g) minced onion
³/4 cup (6 fl oz / 180 ml) vegetable oil
¹/3 quantity Rempah *(For Fish)* see
recipe
4 kaffir lime leaves
2 cups (16 fl oz / 500 ml) water
1 tbsp coriander seeds
1 tsp cumin seeds
1 tsp fennel seeds
lime juice
1 tsp minced garlic, crisp fried
¹/2 cup (4 oz / 120 g) sliced scallions
(spring / green onions), crisp fried

(cont'd)

(Rempah Fish cont'd)

Grind chili and shrimp paste; rub over
sliced fish. Fry onion in ¹/4 cup (2 fl oz/
60 ml) vegetable oil for 3 minutes, add
rempah and lime leaves with the water.
Bring to a boil; add coriander, cumin
and fennel seeds and simmer for 6–8
minutes. Fry sliced fish in remaining ¹/2
cup (4 fl oz/120 ml) oil until surface is
colored. Add to the sauce and simmer
until tender. Add lime juice to taste.
Garnish with fried garlic and scallions.

SPICED WHITEBAIT
Serves 6

8 oz (250 g) whitebait or other fish fry
3 egg whites, beaten
1 tsp salt
1 tsp ground white sesame seeds, toasted
¹/2 tsp chili powder or chili flakes
deep-frying oil

Rinse and dry fish. Mix beaten egg
whites with salt, sesame seeds and chili
powder or flakes. Coat fish with seasoned egg batter and deep-fry in hot oil
until golden.

STEAMED FISH IN BANANA LEAF CUPS
Serves 6

1 lb (500 g) white fish fillets, diced
2 tbsps red curry paste
2 tbsps desiccated coconut
2 eggs, beaten
1 tbsp fish sauce
salt
pepper
6 rounds of banana leaf, each 6 in (15 cm) in
diameter
vegetable oil
1¹/4 cups (4 oz / 125 g) shredded cabbage
1 fresh red chili, seeded and shredded
1 cup (8 fl oz / 250 ml) thick coconut milk

(cont'd)

(Steamed Fish in Banana Leaf Cups cont'd)

Mix fish with curry paste, coconut, eggs, fish sauce, salt and pepper. Beat well. Blanch banana leaves; drain. Brush leaves with oil and use to line rice bowls or ramekins. Pour in fish and add cabbage and shredded chili. Pour on thick coconut milk. Steam for about 15 minutes until set. Serve hot.

"WESTLAKE" FISH
Serves 6

2–3 lbs (1–1.5 kgs) silver carp
2 tbsps yellow rice wine
2 tsps minced garlic
2 cups (8 oz / 250 g) cornstarch (cornflour), plus 1 tbsp extra
water
3 tbsps deep-frying vegetable oil
1 tbsp shredded ginger
3 tbsps shredded scallions (spring / green onions)
1 red chili, shredded
1 tbsp sugar
3 tbsps rice vinegar
1 tbsp dark soy sauce
1 cup (8 fl oz / 250 ml) fish stock or water
Oriental sesame oil
salt
pepper

Cut fish in halves, discarding backbone. Rub 1 tbsp wine and 1 tsp garlic over fish; leave for 20 minutes. Make a paste with 2 cups of cornstarch and cold water. Coat fish, then deep-fry for about 5 minutes, until surface is crisp. Drain.
In vegetable oil, stir-fry ginger, scallions, chili and remaining 1 tsp garlic; remove. Add sugar; cook until golden brown. Add vinegar, soy sauce, remaining 1²/₃ tbsps wine and the stock or water. Bring to a boil, then thicken with the 1 tbsp cornstarch, mixed with cold water. Boil. Season to taste with salt, pepper and sesame oil. Pour over fish.

FISH MAW: This is a bladder-like organ that works within a fish like a decompression chamber. It is usually the conger pike that supplies this unusual delicacy to the Chinese cookpot. The maw is dried, cleaned and then fried, which causes it to puff up into the cream-colored, bubbly mass we find at the markets. Fish maw has little flavor of its own, but absorbs seasonings and the flavor of other ingredients, so its value as a food is really more for its agreeable, spongy texture. Dried maw keeps indefinitely as long as it has no contact with moisture. Soak for about three hours before use, squeezing occasionally to remove air bubbles. Drain, squeeze out water, soak in vinegared hot water briefly to remove the last vestiges of fishy taste, then cut into strips. It does not have to be cooked for more than a few minutes.
Also known as *yu to* (China); conger maw; pike maw
See also: SEAFOOD, DRIED

FISH MAW PREPARATION: Place whole pieces of fish maw in warm water; weigh down to keep it below the surface for at least 6 hours. Drain and trim off any yellow membrane. Cut maw into small pieces. Heat a pan of water, and 1–2 tbsps white vinegar and the fish maw. Simmer gently for 2 minutes, then drain. Soak in cold water until ready to use.

FISH PASTE: Seasoning or flavoring a dish with a fermented fish paste is one of the oldest cooking techniques used in the world. It simultaneously adds depth to flavor while imparting a salt taste. Many different types of fish paste are made in Asia, particularly in Burma, Cambodia, Laos and the Philippines, and they vary markedly in quality and composition. Some are very thin with fragments of fish suspended in a cloudy liquid, others are thick and paste-like in consistency. Rice bran or flour is often added to the paste to thicken and vary flavors and textures. In Laos, the giant *pa boeuk* and other smaller types of fish caught from the Mekong River are preserved by salt or rice bran-fermenting to make *padek*. The Cambodian fish paste *prahok* is prepared from cleaned fish and yields both fish sauce and fish paste, the latter being the fish pulp residue left after the fish sauce has been strained off. The *bagoong* of the Philippines uses anchovies to achieve a very pungent, fermented fish paste known as *heko*, and there they also produce the widest range of other fermented fish products.

Also known as *ngapi* (Burma); *prahok* (Cambodia); *padek* (Laos); *bagoong, heko* (Philippines)

See also: BAGOONG; FISH, PRESERVED; FISH SAUCE

FISH, PRESERVED:
Preserved fish are a vital ingredient in Asian cooking and make a significant contribution to both nutrition and flavor. In each country, fish are preserved by a number of different techniques, for a multitude of uses. Drying, pickling and salting are the basic methods used and often the techniques differ little from those used in prehistoric times.

DAING: (Philippines) Salted and dried fish that can be of any type and size. They are cut, cleaned, salted and hung on racks or placed on bamboo trays to dry in the sun.

DARANG: (Philippines) Dried, smoked fish that have not been salted. The word translates as "exposed to warm heat." The fish develops a characteristic bloodred color.

DRIED AND SALTED FISH: Whole fish, ranging in size from the minuscule fry of anchovies to large bonito, are dried by the simple process of dehydration. Racks, lines and woven cane trays of fish drying in the strong sunlight is a sight one can readily equate with a visit to any tropical or subtropical Asian seaside village. The purpose of drying is threefold. Firstly, as the main means of storage when refrigeration is not an option—dried fish keeps indefinitely in dry conditions; secondly, to provide fish for inland areas; and thirdly, to intensify its flavor so that it may be used in cooking not just as an ingredient, but as a seasoning. Fish is dried in both salted and unsalted states, the former resulting in a strong, salty flavor which must be modified by soaking before use. The latter need only be rehydrated by soaking, or if a recipe calls for long, slow cooking it can be added dry. In India the most important dried fish is Bombay duck, served mostly as a side

dish. Throughout Southeast Asia and China, dried fish adds flavor to soups or is crisp-fried as a small dish to serve with main courses. Tiny anchovy or sardine fry, the *ikan bilis* or *ikan teri* of Malaysia and Indonesia, the *joetkal* of Korea and *niboshi* of Japan are used as flavoring, or fried as a snack food or side dish. In Japan the prime source of flavor in dishes requiring a sauce or stock is *katsuobushi* made by shaving blocks of rock-hard, dried bonito fish.

Also known as *chao pai* (China); *ikan bilis, ikan teri* (small fry), *ikan kering* (Indonesia, Malaysia); *katsuobushi, niboshi* (Japan); *joetkal* (Korea); *daing, tuyo* (Philippines); *pla chalard, pla chawn, pla ka-dee, pla kulao, pla salit, pla siew* (Thailand)

See also: IKAN BILIS CRISPLY FRIED (recipe)

ESCABECHE: (Philippines) This Spanish technique of curing fish is widely used in the Philippines. Sliced fish is fried then marinated in vinegar with garlic. In the Philippines it may also have peppers and ginger added to the marinade.

FERMENTED FISH: Equally important to Asian cooking are fermented fish, made more as a preliminary step toward producing strongly flavored sauces and seasonings, than as an ingredient, although in the Philippines, Laos and Cambodia fermented fish are made into many popular dishes. Obviously most countries have developed their own style of fermentation, but the general technique involves layering whole or filleted raw fish with salt in large pots that are then sealed and left for the contents to ferment. The Laotian *padek* is made with the gigantic *pa boeuk* or *trey reach* fish from the Mekong River, the Philippine *bagoong* uses tiny anchovies, while elsewhere all types of fish are pot-fermented. Sometimes the pot is placed over low heat to partially cook the fish, a technique used in the Philippines for *tinapa, pinaksiw* and *sinaeng*. The resultant, distinctly flavored, pungent liquid that accumulates in the pot is drawn off, filtered and becomes the sauce known variously as *nuoc mam, nam pla, nam pa*, or simply, fish sauce, and is used like soy sauce. The fish itself may be mashed and further processed into a pungent seasoning known in Burma as *ngapi*, in Cambodia as *prahok*, and in the Philippines as *bagoong*.

See also: ANCHOVY; BAGOONG; FISH PASTE; FISH SAUCE; PADEK

PAKSIW: (Philippines) A term applied to fish (or meat) pickled with vinegar and salt and sometimes also ginger and sugar. It is cut into large pieces, placed in a clay pot, the pickling ingredients added, brought to a boil and simmered until cooked. It keeps for several days and is served cold, usually with some of the pickling liquid.

PINAKSIW: (Philippines) A pickling technique for sardines. The fish are layered in large pots with banana leaves, salt and coconut vinegar, then simmered over a fire, preferably wood, for about 20 minutes.

TUYO: (Philippines) Salted and dried small fish, which are fried or grilled. Usually served with sliced tomatoes.

See also: BOMBAY DUCK; NOODLES FILIPINO (recipe)

FISH SAUCE: Fish sauce is a strongly flavored, pungent seasoning sauce used extensively in Southeast Asian countries such as Thailand, Vietnam, Cambodia and Burma. It is a clear liquid, ranging from amber to dark brown in color, is salty to taste and is used in much the same way as soy sauce. It is made by layering fish and salt into large jars or barrels and allowing the fish to ferment for three or more months before the accumulated liquid is siphoned off, filtered and bottled. High in B vitamins and protein, fish sauce is a valuable dietary asset. Cooks in the Thai capital of Bangkok are recorded as having used *nam pla,* a salty, thin sauce made from fermented fish, over 1000 years ago, and it has a similar history in the ancient city of Angkor Wat, Cambodia, and in Laos, Vietnam and Indonesia. The Vietnamese version, *nuoc mam,* is served as a condiment with most meals and is made into different dipping sauces by adding chilies, ground, roasted peanuts, sugar and other ingredients.

SQUID sauce is made in the same way using fermented squid. It is almost identical in taste, and is sometimes preferred.

Also known as *ngan pya ye* (Burma); *tuk trey* (Cambodia); *yu chiap, yu lu* (China); *kecap ikan, kecap petis* (Indonesia); *nam pa* (Laos); *patis* (Philippines); *nam pla, nam pla raa* (Thailand); *nuoc mam* (Vietnam)

See also: FISH PASTE; FISH, PRESERVED; HEKO; SHRIMP AND CRABMEAT BALLS IN NOODLE SOUP (recipe); SOY SAUCE

FISH, SQUIRREL-CUT: An attractive way to prepare fish for frying whole. Clean and scale fish; remove fillets or leave fish whole. With a sharp knife or Chinese cleaver score unfilleted fish to the bone (unfilleted fish are cut from meat side to skin) in a crosshatch pattern, using the knife at a slight angle so that the result looks something like a pine cone. Open the scores by running a finger lengthways against the direction of the cuts. Dust with cornstarch before cooking.

"SQUIRREL-CUT" FISH IN SWEET AND SOUR SAUCE
Serves 4–6

1 whole croaker / sea bass (2 lbs / 1 kg)
1 tbsp light soy sauce
1 tbsp yellow rice wine
1 tsp salt
1 tsp sugar
2 cups (8 oz / 230 g) cornstarch (cornflour)
water
deep-frying oil
1 tbsp shredded ginger
1 red chili, shredded
1/2 cup (4 oz / 125 g) shredded scallions (spring / green onions)
sweet and sour sauce

Rinse fish, leaving head on. Cut along both sides of the backbone; remove backbone, flatten fish and score in squirrel fashion. Mix soy, wine, salt and sugar. Set aside for 10 minutes. Make cornstarch into a paste with cold water; use to coat fish. Deep-fry until crisp and golden, about 8 minutes. Drain, garnish with the shredded ingredients. Pour on hot sweet and sour sauce immediately before serving.

113

FIVE-SPICE POWDER: This aromatic, Chinese spice powder with its unique flavor is used as a seasoning and condiment. It is made from an ancient formula using three spices native to the area: star anise, cassia bark and Sichuan peppercorns, with seeds of wild fennel and cloves from the nearby Moluccas (Spice Islands). The same combination of spices in whole form are added to braised and simmered dishes and may be tied in a small cheesecloth (muslin) bag for use in the same way as a *bouquet garni*, being retrieved before serving. Five-spice powder is added to heated salt to make spiced salt, a fragrant salty dip.
Also known as *heung neu fun, ng heung fun* (China); *gia vi pha lau, ngu vi huong* (Vietnam)
See also: ANISE, STAR; CASSIA; SICHUAN PEPPERCORNS

FIVE-SPICE POWDER
Yields about ¹/₄ cup (1 oz / 30 g)

40 Sichuan peppercorns
2 cinnamon sticks 2 in (5 cm) in length
1¹/₂ tsps fennel seeds
12 whole cloves
2 whole star anise

Place the spices in a mortar or spice grinder and grind to a fine powder. Transfer to a spice jar and keep tightly closed to preserve aroma. Can be stored for 2–3 months.

FIVE-SPICE SALT
Yields ¹/₄ cup (1 oz / 30 g)

¹/₄ cup (2 oz / 50 g) fine table salt
2 tsps Chinese five-spice powder

Heat a wok or pan over medium heat. Pour in salt and heat through, continually stirring, until well heated. Cool briefly before stirring in five-spice powder. When cool store in a spice jar. Use as a dip or condiment with roasted, grilled and fried meats. Spiced salt can be sprinkled over foods to season before deep-frying.

FIVE-SPICE SEASONING BAGS: Use the whole spices in recipe for five-spice powder to make two seasoning bags. Tie spices in a small square of clean cheesecloth (muslin). Use for convenience in braised and simmered dishes in the same way as a *bouquet garni*. Remove and discard before serving the dish.

FLAT CABBAGE: see CABBAGE, CHINESE (TAAI GOO CHOY)

FLAVORINGS: Various aromatic ingredients are used in Asian cooking to add their distinct flavor and fragrance to dishes of both sweet and savory nature. They are mostly obtained from leaves or flowers. Jasmine, known as *mali* in Thailand, is used extensively where a particular type of large, strongly aromatic jasmine blossom grows profusely. Rosewater, or *gulab*, is a favored aroma in Indian cooking and is sprinkled over desserts, curries and rice dishes. A flavoring ester, amyle essence, *nam nomao*, gives a banana-like taste and fragrance to certain Thai foods. Orange flower water is used in the same way as rosewater. The pungent flavoring and fragrance of two types of pandanus leaf make *kewra* and *toey* unique. Otherwise, citrus fruits in various forms as well as aromatic lemon grass, are important sources of flavor in Asian cooking.
See also: AMYLE ESSENCE (EXTRACT); KEWRA ESSENCE/EXTRACT; LEMON GRASS; MALI; PANDANUS LEAF; ROSEWATER (ESSENCE)

FLOURS AND THICKENERS: Flour made from different cereals, roots, pulses and plants, is used throughout Asia to make noodles, breads, batters, pastries, sweets and as a binder and thickener. Wheat flour breads are an important part of the Indian diet, in many places virtually replacing rice as the staple food. Rice flour is used widely, principally for noodles and pastry making, confectionery and as a thickener. Cornstarch is another popular thickener for sauces.

ARROWROOT STARCH: The roots or tubers of the arrowroot plant (*Maranta arundinacea*) are dried and ground to a fine, grayish-white powder that is easily digested so it is often made

into a gruel for invalids and infants. The starch is often used for baking, but mainly for sauces. Its thickening properties are greater than cornstarch, it has a neutral flavor and gives a better glaze. Arrowroot-thickened sauces should not be cooked long as the starch breaks down causing the sauce to separate.
Also known as *pang tao yai mom* (Thailand)

ATTA: (India) A finely milled whole wheat flour used extensively in the making of Indian unleavened breads, particularly *chapatis* and *parathas*. It is sold packaged or in bulk at Indian food stores, but can be substituted by any finely ground or stone-ground whole wheat flour. It should be stored in an airtight container and refrigerated in humid climates.
See also: BREAD, INDIAN

BESAN FLOUR (India) is made from ground chick-peas, and sometimes also from Bengal gram (peas) and yellow *dal* (peas/lentils). It has a leguminious aroma and taste and is used extensively in Indian vegetarian cooking for making batters, dough, pastry, dumplings and savory noodles. It is readily available where Indian foods are sold and should be stored in an airtight jar and preferably refrigerated in warm climates. When using in a dish ensure that it is well-cooked. Toasted *besan* is sometimes sprinkled over foods as a condiment.
Also known as gram flour

CORNSTARCH is one of the most commonly used thickeners in Asian cooking. Derived from Indian corn, it is a quick-dissolving starch that makes a transparent, viscous sauce. Like arrowroot, a cornstarch-thickened sauce will break down if it is excessively cooked. It is excellent for coating fried foods, produces lightly textured cakes and pastries and is used as a binder for ground meats and fillings.
Also known as *gandianfen* (China); *pang khao phod* (Thailand); cornflour

GLUTINOUS RICE FLOUR is a fine white flour made from ground glutinous (sticky) white rice. Popular particularly in China, but also in other parts of Southeast Asia and Japan, it is used to make a soft, slightly chewy dough for making a variety of sweets, buns and dumplings.
Also known as *tepong pulot* (Indonesia, Malaysia); *shiratamako* (Japan); *pang khao niew*

(Thailand); *bot nep* (Vietnam)
See also: MOCHI; GLUTINOUS RICE DOUGH, SWEET (recipe)

KATAKURI: (Japan) The roots of the dog tooth violet (*Erythronium dencanis*) are dried and ground into a starch that is used as a thickener, known as *katakuri-ko*. Potato starch also goes by the same name and is now generally used as a replacement for *katakuri-ko*, which is expensive.

KUZU: (Japan) A vine that grows wild in Japan and many parts of China and is related to jicama, or the yam bean of Southeast Asia. The root resembles a large, dryish sweet potato and was originally used as a vegetable in China. Today, however, it is used, albeit rarely, mainly for its pale gray starch which provides an excellent thickener for Japanese dishes, as it produces a translucent sauce. As a coating for fried foods, it gives an unequaled crisp surface.

Kuzu starch is sold in Japanese food stores and looks like a lumpy version of arrowroot. It readily dissolves in water and can be used in any recipe that requires cornstarch or arrowroot. Store in an airtight jar away from moisture and heat. *Kuzu* is usually expensive.
See also: YAM BEAN

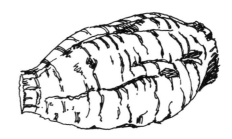

Kuzu

LOTUS ROOT STARCH has a similar appearance to water chestnut starch, being grayish in color and slightly granular. Used for making sweet dishes and soft-textured cakes, it is occasionally used as a thickener.

MAIDA FLOUR (India) is a fine, white flour used in India for breadmaking, especially for the soft-textured *naan*. All-purpose (plain) white flour can be substituted.

See also: BREAD, INDIAN; TANDOORI BAKED BREAD (recipe)

MUNG BEAN FLOUR resembles arrowroot in appearance and cooking properties. It is sold in three forms—in its natural color, or dyed pink or green—for use in making a variety of popular Southeast Asian sweets. Arrowroot or tapioca flour tinted with food coloring, or pandanus (*kewra*) essence can be substituted.

Also known as *hoen kwe*, *tepong hoen kwe* (Indonesia, Malaysia)

POTATO STARCH is used in some parts of Asia as a thickener and has a stronger binding power than cornstarch. In Japan potato starch now replaces the more expensive original form of *katakuri-ko*, which was made from the bulb of the dog tooth violet.

Also known as *katakuri-ko*; potato flour

RICE FLOUR is used widely throughout Asia. Made from finely milled white rice, it is used for noodle and pastry making, for sweets and confections and as a thickener in puddings. In Malaysia and Indonesia it is mixed with tapioca starch for making sweet dishes. Sold in attractive paper packs, it keeps well if stored away from moisture. Not to be confused with glutinous rice flour which may also be labeled sweet rice flour.

Also known as *joshinko* (Japan); *tepong beras* (Indonesia, Malaysia); *pang khao chao* (Thailand); *bot gao* (Vietnam)

SOY FLOUR is a low-starch flour made from soybeans that is used in bread- and cakemaking and in confectionery. It is used extensively in vegetarian preparations such as meat substitutes, as it gives an acceptable texture and taste and has a high protein content. *Kinako*, the Japanese flour made from soybeans, is used in confections and to make noodles. *Kinako* sweetened with sugar is sometimes sprinkled over steamed white rice. In China, a thick, nutty-tasting noodle is made from soy flour.

TAPIOCA STARCH: A farinaceous, fine, white powder extracted from the roots of the cassava (manioc) plant. Used for thickening, it produces a clear, fine-textured sauce that holds its consistency well, usually better than when arrowroot or cornstarch are used. It is sometimes added to rice flour or wheat starch to strengthen a dough.

Also known as *ling fun* (China); *pang mun* (Thailand)

See also: TAPIOCA

WATER CHESTNUT STARCH is a gray-colored starch made from ground, dried water chestnuts. It is considered one of the best starches for making crisp batter and coatings and gives a gloss to sauce when used as a thickener. In China and Thailand it is used to make sweet dishes such as thick, warm, sweet soups and soft-textured cakes.

WHEAT STARCH is a gluten-free starch which is the residue when protein is extracted from wheat to make gluten. A finely textured white powder, it is sold in small packs at Chinese food stores as *dung mein* flour. It is used as a thickener, but a dough of this particular flour is what makes the soft, opaque white wrappers that enclose various kinds of *dim sum*, such as *har gow* and *fun gor*. The wheat starch and boiling water dough is kneaded until smooth, then covered to allow the heat to soften the flour and make it more elastic. It is rolled out with a rolling pin, or "spread" with a blunt-edged cleaver, into thin discs. The soft pliability of the dough makes it easy to handle. For the tiny, shrimp-filled dumplings known as *har gow*, it is gathered around the filling into neat little half-moon shapes pleated on one side, while for *fun gor* it is simply folded over the filling.

Har gow dumplings made with wheat starch dough

A dough of this flour, sometimes strengthened with tapioca starch, is also used to make short, pin-shaped noodles known as "silver pin noodles," and as the pastry for molded cookies. **Also known as** *cheng mein, ngun jump fun* (China)
See also: FUN GOR (recipe); GLUTEN; NOODLES (SILVER PIN); WHEAT STARCH DOUGH (recipe)

FUN GOR
Yields 36

1 quantity Wheat Starch Dough (see recipe)
6 oz (180 g) coarsely minced lean pork
8 oz (250 g) shelled small shrimp (prawns)
1/3 cup (3 oz / 90 g) chopped bamboo shoots
2 tbsps chopped garlic chives
1 1/2 tbsps light soy sauce

Divide dough into walnut-size pieces and roll out on an oiled board; cut into rounds. Place pork and shrimp in a food processor. Grind to a paste; add remaining ingredients. Place a portion on each dough wrapper, fold over and pinch edges together. Place in an oiled steamer basket and steam for 12–15 minutes.

WHEAT STARCH DOUGH
Yields about 50 wrappers

1 cup (4 oz / 120 g) wheat starch
1/2 cup (2 oz / 60 g) tapioca starch (tapioca flour)
1/2 tsp salt
2 tsps vegetable oil
1 cup (8 fl oz / 250 ml) water

Mix starches, salt and oil in a metal bowl. Bring water to a brisk boil in a small saucepan; then pour quickly over the starch, stirring it in with a strong pair of chopsticks. Upturn the bowl over the dough for a few minutes, until partially cooled and the starch is thoroughly moistened. Then knead lightly to a smooth, soft dough. To roll out the dough, pull off walnut-size pieces and press into rounds with the fingers, or flatten with a cleaver or tortilla press.

FLOWERING CHIVES: see CHIVES, CHINESE
FLOWERING WHITE CABBAGE: see CABBAGE, CHINESE (CHOY SUM)
FOO BAN: (*FU BARN*, China) see CUTTLEFISH

FOOD COLORING:
Various natural food colorings are employed in Asian cooking. Red is the most predominant of these, as it is regarded as an auspicious color, particularly in Chinese communities. It is obtained in the Philippines from their native plants *angkak* and *grana*, but more commonly from annatto seeds, which are also used in other parts of Asia. Yellow colorings, derived from saffron and turmeric, are favored by the Indians. Blue is obtained, in Thailand, from the flower *anjan*. Green comes from spinach, which yields *ao-yose* in Japan, pandanus leaves, which are used in Malaysia and Indonesia, and some kinds of seaweed. When rich, deep brown colors are needed in a sauce, dark soy sauce, sweet soy sauce or a coloring made from caramelized sugar are used. *Tandoori* baked foods are colored a characteristic bright orange.
See also: ANJAN; ANNATTO SEED; CARAMEL COLORING; CRISP JELLO SWEETS (recipe); GRANA; JALEBI KA RANG; PANDANAS LEAF; SAFFRON; TANDOORI COLORING; TAPIOCA DESSERT (recipe); TURMERIC

FOO YU: (*FU YUE*, China) see BEAN CURD BY-PRODUCTS (FERMENTED)
FORNG TAO HU: (*FONG TAO HUU*, Thailand) see BEAN CURD BY-PRODUCTS (BEAN CURD STICKS)
FREEZE-DRIED BEAN CURD: see BEAN CURD
FRIED FISH WITH GINGER SAUCE: (recipe) see FISH
FRIED GARLIC FLAKES: (recipe) see GARLIC
FRIED NOODLES: (recipe) see NOODLES
FRIED NOODLES WITH MEAT AND VEGETABLES: (recipe) see NOODLES
FRIED ONION FLAKES: (recipe) see ONION
FRIED RICE: (recipe) see RICE
FRIED SAMBAL: (recipe) see SAMBAL
FRIKKADELS: (recipe) see BEEF
FU: (*WHO*, Japan) see GLUTEN

FUGATH: (*FOOGATH*, India) see INDIA, COOKING METHODS

FU JOOK PIN: (*FU JUK PIN*, China) see BEAN CURD BY-PRODUCTS (BEAN CURD STICKS)

FUKASA-ZUSHI: (*WHO-KOO-SAH ZOO-SHI*, Japan) see SUSHI

FUKI: (*WHO-KEE*, Japan) see COLTSFOOT

FUNGI: see MUSHROOMS AND EDIBLE FUNGI

FURI-JIO: (*WHO-REE-JEE-O*) see JAPAN, COOKING METHODS (SALTING)

FU-RU: (*FU-YUE*, China) see BEAN CURD BY-PRODUCTS (FERMENTED)

FUZZY MELON: see MELONS AND GOURDS

G

GADO GADO
Serves 6–8

1 small head lettuce, rinsed and separated
2 large boiled potatoes, sliced
1¹/₂ cups (6 oz / 185 g) sliced green beans or long beans, parboiled
1¹/₂ cups (2 oz / 60 g) fresh bean sprouts, blanched
1¹/₂ cups (4 oz / 125 g) shredded white or Napa cabbage, blanched
2–3 medium tomatoes, cut into wedges
1 medium onion, sliced
2–3 scallions (spring / green onions), cut into 1 in (25 cm) lengths
1 medium cucumber, sliced
2 slices pineapple, cubed
1 cup (1 oz / 30 g) fresh herbs, such as coriander (cilantro), basil, parsley
1–2 fresh, red chilies, seeded and shredded
2–4 hard-cooked eggs
omelette shreds
peanut sauce

Arrange lettuce on a platter with potato slices overlapped around the edge. Toss remaining vegetables and pineapple together until well mixed and pile into the center of the platter. Surround with herbs and chili shreds. Quarter the eggs and arrange on the salad; cover with omelette shreds. Chill. Pour on peanut sauce before serving.

GAI CHOY: (*GAI CHOY*, China) see CABBAGE, CHINESE

GAI LARN: (*GAI LARN*, China) see CABBAGE, CHINESE

GAI LARN WITH OYSTER SAUCE: (recipe) see CABBAGE, CHINESE

GAI TS'AI: (*GAI CHOY*, China) see CABBAGE, CHINESE

GAJAR: (*GAA-JUR*, India) see CARROT

GAJUS: (*GAH-YOOS*, Malaysia) see CASHEW NUT

GALANGAL, GREATER: (*Alpinia galanga*)
From the Zingiberaceae family, this rhizome
has white- to cream- colored flesh with distinct
pink shoots. It is now most commonly known
as *laos* (Thai or Siamese ginger) and grows
prolifically throughout Southeast Asia. In the
past it was well known in Europe under the
name *galingale* and had a reputation as an
aphrodisiac. It has a hot, peppery taste and is
not usually eaten alone but is merely used for
flavoring. It is used extensively in Thai cooking, being ground with chilies and other herbs
and spices to make the base seasoning mix of
green and red curries, added to soups and
steamed dishes, or ground to make a refreshing drink. In Indonesia *greater galangal* is
added to many dishes in preference to common
ginger. If it is unobtainable, use ginger and
double the amount. Both the open flower and
buds are eaten, sometimes battered and fried
and served with a hot chili sauce, or used as a
garnish. The young, undeveloped shoots are
steamed or otherwise cooked to eat as a vegetable. A starch extracted from the roots is
used medicinally, and throughout Southeast
Asia it is taken to alleviate symptoms of gas-
tric disorder, usually as a drink with lime
juice. In Thailand a refreshing, stomach-
soothing drink called *khing* is made from sliced
laos steeped in water and sweetened with
sugar. A similar drink known as *salabut* is
made in the Philippines from ginger.

Greater galangal

LAOS is powdered *greater galangal*, sold in
small bottles. It should be stored away from
moisture. It imparts a more intense and slightly
peppery flavor than the fresh root.

Also known as *pa de gaw gyi* (Burma); *romdeng*
(Cambodia); *lam keong* (China); *laos, lengkuas*
(Indonesia); *lenkuas* (Malaysia); *ka, kha*
(Thailand); galingale; Laos ginger; Siamese
ginger; Thai ginger

See also: GALANGAL, LESSER; GINGER; GRILLED
FISH (recipe); GULAI OF LAMB (recipe); LAOTIAN
CABBAGE SOUP (recipe); THAI GINGER AND
CHICKEN IN COCONUT SOUP (recipe); TURMERIC;
ZEDOARY

GALANGAL, LESSER: (*Kaempferia
pandurata, K. galanga*) This rhizome, related
to the ginger family, is rarely found in Western
countries and even in Asia is not well known.
It is thought to have originated in India. The
finger-like tubers, brown on the outside with a
yellow-orange juicy interior, grow in clumps.
Care should be taken when cutting the tubers
not to get the juice on clothes or hands as it
stains. In China *lesser galangal* is not cooked
but used medicinally. It is eaten in Thailand as
a vegetable, both raw and cooked, and is usually added to fish curries. In Indonesia it is
used like *greater galangal*, as a spice, its taste
being even hotter and stronger. Only very
occasionally can *lesser galangal* be found in
markets away from the East, but it is available
pickled in brine, which does not unduly spoil
the flavor or texture. It is sold in powdered
form under the name *kencur*.

Also known as *kencur* (Indonesia); *kunchor*
(Malaysia); *ingurupiyali* (Sri Lanka); *krachai*
(Thailand); pickled rhizome; preserved rhi-
zome

See also: GALANGAL, GREATER; GINGER; TUR-
MERIC; ZEDOARY

GALAPONG: (*GA-LAH-PONG*, Philippines) see
RICE DOUGH

GALINGALE: see GALANGAL, GREATER

GANDIANFEN: (*GUN-DIAN-FEN*, China) see
FLOURS AND THICKENERS (CORNSTARCH)

GAN MODOKI: (*GUN MOH-DOH-KEE*, Japan) see
BEAN CURD

GARAM MASALA: (*GARAM MA-SAA-LAA*, India)
see MASALA

GARHI YAKHNI: (*GAA-RHEE YAA-KH-NEE*, India) This is the Indian equivalent of a French *glacé de viande*, a concentrated meat bone stock with the consistency of partially set jelly. Its primary use is to add intense flavor to *biriyani* and *pullao* rice dishes. *Akni* is a less concentrated form of stock.

Also known as *yakni*
See also: RICE COOKED IN RICH MEAT BROTH (recipe)

GARI: (*GAH-REE*, Japan) see GINGER (PICKLED)

GARLAND CHRYSANTHEMUM: see
CHRYSANTHEMUM

GARLIC: (*Allium sativum*) A member of the lily family, this popular, pungent seasoning ingredient has many varieties ranging from compact white heads with small white cloves and an intense flavor, to larger heads with purple-tinted plump cloves, and the Chinese, round, bulb garlic that resembles a scallion (spring/green onion). It grows readily, and like onions, is important in the base seasoning of curries. In Thailand, Burma and Indonesia crisply fried, sliced garlic is a crunchy, tasty garnish. Chinese pickle their garlic in a sweet sauce and grow a bulbous type in Sichuan province. In Korea garlic is an essential ingredient in *kimchi* and is used extensively in cooking. The Japanese use garlic sparingly and are trying to cultivate an odorless variety. Medicinally, its capacity to reduce blood cholesterol is now being recognized in Western countries and it has been known in China for centuries that it decreases the incidence of bowel cancer.

Also known as *chyet-thon-phew* (Burma); *suen tau* (China); *lasun*, *vellay poondoo* (India); *bawang puteh* (Indonesia, Malaysia); *sudulunu* (Sri Lanka); *katiem*, *gratiem* (Thailand); *toi* (Vietnam)

BULB GARLIC: In China's Sichuan province, where garlic is an indispensable ingredient in the kitchen, they also have a round-headed, white garlic that resembles a small onion. Mild in flavor, it is usually added to braised dishes. Substitute garlic cloves or small white onions together with garlic.

Also known as ball garlic

PICKLED GARLIC: Whole garlic cloves, pickled in a sweet or tart vinegar, are enjoyed in China and Thailand as a side dish. Sold in cans or jars, they are readily available and keep well in the refrigerator. They can be served also with cold cuts or roast poultry and can be shredded to add to noodle dishes and sauces such as sweet and sour.

Also known as *kratiem dong* (Thailand)
See also: FRIED GARLIC FLAKES (recipe); GARLIC PORK (recipe); OYSTERS WITH GARLIC AND HERBS (recipe)

FRIED GARLIC FLAKES
Yields 1 cup

deep-frying oil
1¹/₂ cups (5 oz / 155 g) thinly sliced garlic

Heat oil and fry half the garlic to a deep golden brown; avoid burning. Drain on a rack covered with paper towels. Cook the remaining garlic. Store in an airtight jar for up to 1 month.

GARLIC SAUCE
Yields ²/₃ cup (6 fl oz / 180 ml)

2¹/₂ tbsps minced garlic
¹/₂ cup (3 ¹/₂ oz / 100 g) sugar
¹/₂ cup (4 fl oz / 125 ml) white vinegar
1–2 tsps chili paste
1 cup (8 fl oz / 250 ml) water
¹/₂ tsp salt

Combine all the ingredients in a nonaluminum pan and boil slowly until the mixture is reduced by one-half and is the consistency of heavy cream. Use immediately, or store for up to 2 months in the refrigerator.

GARLIC BLACK BEAN SEASONING: see
FERMENTED BLACK BEAN

GARLIC CHIVES: see CHIVES, CHINESE

GAROUPA: (*Pletctropomus leopardus*) Of the family Serranidae, which includes sea bass, coral cod and coral trout, this fish is favored by Chinese chefs and diners alike. There are many varieties of this large fish, but the red- and the blue-spotted varieties are most popular. Red garoupa has orange-red spots over a pink body. The blue has blue spots over a red body. They are available all year round and range 1–3 ft (30–100 cm) in length. In the Philippines it is one of the most prized fish.

STEAMED WHOLE GAROUPA WITH SCALLIONS
Serves 4–6

1–1¹/₂ lbs (500–750 g) whole fresh garoupa (grouper)
2 tsps vegetable oil
¹/₂ tsp sugar
1 tbsp yellow rice wine
2 tbsps light soy sauce
1 tbsp finely shredded ginger
2 dried black mushrooms, soaked and shredded
2 scallions (spring/green onions), shredded
fresh coriander (cilantro)

Slash fish on each side and place in an oiled dish. Sprinkle oil, sugar, wine and soy sauce over fish, then top with shredded ingredients. Place in a steamer, cover and steam over boiling water for about 20 minutes. Garnish with coriander.

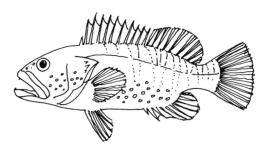

Garoupa

Also known as *kyauk-nga* (Burma); *sheh paan, tsut sing paan, wong paan* (China); *kerapu lodi* (India); *kerapu bara* (Malaysia); *pla karang, apu lapu* (Philippines); *pla karang, pla karang daeng jutfa* (Thailand); *ca mu cham* (Vietnam); grouper

GATA: (*GAH-TA*, Philippines) see COCONUT (MILK)

GAU CHOY: (*GAU CHOY*, China) see CHIVES, CHINESE (GARLIC)

GAU CHOY CHOW SHAN: (*GAU CHOY CHOW SHAN*, China) see CHIVES, CHINESE (FLOWERING)

GAU CHOY CHOW SIN: (*GAU CHOY CHOW SIN*, China) see CHIVES, CHINESE (FLOWERING)

GAU CHOY FA: (*GAU CHOY FA*, China) see CHIVES, CHINESE (FLOWERING)

GAU CHOY SUM: (*GAU CHOY SUM*, China) see CHIVES, CHINESE

GAU GEI CHOY: (*GAU GEI CHOY*, China) see BOXTHORN

GAU WONG: (*GAU WONG*, China) see CHIVES, CHINESE (YELLOW)

GEDAN: (*GAP-DAN*, China) see EGG

GEE JOOK: (*JI JUK*, China) see BEAN CURD BY-PRODUCTS (BEAN CURD STICKS)

GEN MAI RICE: (*GHEN MAI-I*) see RICE (NON-GLUTINOUS)

GHEE: Clarified butter is a yellow-colored, hard, pure butter obtained by boiling butter and straining off the sediment that separates from the pure butterfat. In India ghee is regarded as the purest food, being a product obtained from the sacred cow, so it is used in religious ceremonies and caste rituals. Although considerably more expensive than vegetable oil, it gives a rich, buttery taste to foods and is used for shallow-frying Indian bread and for deep-frying certain sweetmeats. Ghee is also preferred for the preliminary frying of ingredients when making certain curries and is stirred into rice dishes to enrich them. Because of its purity, ghee can be kept without refrigeration for many months. It is sold in cans and waxed tubs.
Also known as *ghi* (India); *ghiu* (Nepal); clarified butter

GHEE
Yields 1 cup (8 oz / 250 g)

1 lb (500 g) salted butter

Cut butter into cubes, place in a small pan and heat gently until butter has completely melted. Do not boil or stir. Leave to sit for 5 minutes, then skim foam from surface and carefully pour clarified butter from the layer of white sediment beneath.

GHI: (*GHEE*, India) see GHEE

GHIU: (*GHEE-YOO*, Nepal) see GHEE

GIA: (*YA*, Vietnam) see BEAN SPROUT

GIANT WHITE RADISH: see RADISH, GIANT WHITE

GIA VI PHA LAU: (*YA VEE FAR LOU*, Vietnam) see FIVE-SPICE POWDER

GINGER: (*Zingiber officinale*) Ginger is one of the most extensively used spices in Asian cooking. It comes from a family that encompasses both *lesser* and *greater galangal*, turmeric and zedoary. It is preferred in fresh or pickled form—only very rarely is ground or candied ginger called for in an Asian recipe. When young, the rhizomes are branching knobs with smooth, light cream to ocher skin and a light buff flesh that is juicy and not fibrous. As ginger ages, the skin darkens to a deeper buff color and the flesh dries, becoming more fibrous and intense in flavor. It is peeled before use and can be used in "knobs" of a single joint. It is sliced, chopped, shredded, grated or minced for use in stir-fries, soups, simmered, braised and steamed dishes, and as a garnish. Ginger, being more readily available, can be used in place of *greater galangal* in most recipes.
Also known as *gin*, *gyin sein* (Burma); *khnehey* (Cambodia); *jeung*, *sang keong* (China); *adrak*, *ingee* (India); *aliah*, *jahe* (Indonesia); *shoga* (Japan); *halia* (Malaysia); *luya* (Philippines); *inguru* (Sri Lanka); *khing* (Thailand); *gung* (Vietnam)
See also: FRIED FISH WITH GINGER SAUCE (recipe); GALANGAL, GREATER; GALANGAL, LESSER; JAPAN, GARNISHES; GINGER BUDS; GINGER JUICE (recipe); SWEET AND SOUR SAUCE (recipe); TURMERIC; ZEDOARY

CANDIED GINGER: Although it is made in China, it is not used frequently in Chinese cooking, being considered more a confection. It is used sparingly elsewhere in Asia, usually in desserts.

DRIED GINGER: Dried and finely ground ginger has little application in Asian cooking. It is occasionally used in cakes and is the main ingredient in an Indian sweet and sour sauce known as *sonth*; otherwise ginger in its various other forms is preferred.
Also known as *sonth* (India)

GINGER PRESERVE: Ginger preserved with vegetables, particularly cucumber, fruits and spices, is known as *subgum* in Thailand and is popularly known as *chow chow* or sweet pickles in China. It is used as a relish and in sweet and sour sauces.
Also known as *chow chow*, *sub gum geung* (China); *khing dong* (Thailand); sweet pickled vegetables

PICKLED GINGER: In China and Japan the whole, sliced or shredded, peeled root is preserved in brine, rice wine or rice vinegar. It naturally acquires a light pink color through chemical reaction, but may also be colored a garish deep pink by adding food coloring, when it becomes known as "red ginger." Thinly sliced pink ginger pickled in sweet vinegar is known in Japan as *beni shoga* and *gari*, and is a fre-

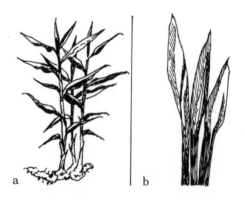

a. Ginger stalks with roots   b. Ginger shoots

quently used garnish. Red ginger is served as an accompaniment with certain Chinese dishes. In Japan *hajikami shoga* are used as a garnish. They are tiny pink shoots on long tender stalks. The base of the stalk has a pink blush of color, which earns them their name "blushing ginger." Harvested in spring they are pickled in vinegar and sold in bottles.

Also known as *beni shoga, gari, hajikami shoga* (Japan); red ginger; sweet pickled ginger

---

GINGER JUICE
Yields about 1 tbsp

3 tbsps minced peeled ginger

Place the ginger in a piece of thin, clean cloth such as muslin or cheesecloth. Squeeze tightly directly over the dish, or into a measuring cup. (Young ginger contains more juice than older ginger.)

GINGER SAUCE
Yields 1¹/₃ cups (14 fl oz / 430 ml)

4 dried black mushrooms, soaked and minced
2 tbsps minced scallions (spring / green onions)
2 tsps minced red chilies
1 tbsp light soy sauce
³/₄ cup (6 oz / 180 g) minced sweet pickled ginger
¹/₂ cup (4 fl oz / 125 ml) white vinegar
¹/₂ cup (3¹/₂ oz / 100 g) sugar
³/₄ cup (6 fl oz / 180 ml) water
1 tbsp cornstarch (cornflour)

Simmer first 5 ingredients with vinegar, sugar and water for 3 minutes. Thicken with cornstarch mixed with a little cold water. Refrigerate and use within 2 days.

GINGER WINE
Yields 1 cup (8 fl oz / 250 ml)

1 cup (8 fl oz / 250 ml) shaohsing rice wine
6 in (15 cm) piece peeled ginger, bruised

Place ginger in a jar with a non-metal lid, pour on the wine and cover. Leave for at least 2 weeks before using. Keeps for several months.

GINGER BUD: (*Phaeomeria sepciosa, Nicolaia atropurpurea*) Fragrant, pink, edible buds of several types of ginger plant, which grow profusely in Asian countries. In Indonesia, the slender, pink-tinged bud and its deeper pink stem is known as *honje* or "torch ginger." In Japan delicate pink *myoga* ginger is shredded as a garnish for *sashimi*, salads and soups, and in Malaysia the *bunga siantan* is rather larger and deeper in color. Only the tip and petals are used, finely sliced and eaten raw in salads and used as a garnish.

Also known as *honje, kecombrang* (Indonesia); *myoga* (Japan); *bunga kantan, bunga siantan* (Malaysia); pink ginger buds
See also: GINGER

Ginger buds

GINGER PRESERVE: see GINGER

GINKGO NUT: (*Ginkgo biloba*) Ginkgo nuts are hard-shelled, cream-colored nuts which are the kernels of the odiferous fruit of the beautiful maidenhair tree that has grown in China for millions of years. Ginkgos have a long history as a medicine for urinary malfunction and for cleansing the system. They are believed to bring good fortune so are often planted around Buddhist temples and are eaten at weddings. The shells are colored an auspicious bright red for such occasions. In China the slightly bitter-tasting ginkgo nut is used in stuffings, desserts and in clear, sweet soups. It can replace lotus seeds in "eight treasure" or "eight jeweled" dishes. Japanese and Koreans enjoy them as a snack, threaded onto pine needle skewers, grilled and sprinkled with salt. They add them to delicate, savory custards like *chawan mushi*. The hard shells must be cracked with a nutcracker and the soft, creamy-white nut soaked in hot water to loosen the skin. They turn an attractive shade of pale green, rather like a pistachio, when cooked. Unshelled nuts can be kept for many weeks; once shelled, however, they should be refrigerated and will keep for only a few days.

Also known as *bark gor* (China); *ginnan* (Japan); gingko

See also: EGG CUSTARD STEAMED IN A TEACUP (recipe); EIGHT TREASURE CHICKEN (recipe); SHINSULRO HOTPOT (recipe)

Ginkgo nuts

GINNAN: (*GUIN-NAN*, Japan) see GINKGO NUT

GINSENG: (*Panax ginseng*) A root vegetable resembling a yellowish radish and having a human shape with arms and legs, which in the past was seen to indicate that it was a panacea for ailments in every part of the human body. It is still widely regarded for its health-giving properties, which are thought to border on the magical, and is taken as a curative and rejuvenating tonic. Ginseng grown in Korea is believed to be the best, but those from Liaoning, Hopei, Manchuria and Shansi are also of fine quality. In China there are a number of popular recipes for cooking ginseng, usually in a soup. It is taken in Korea in the form of a tea for its stimulating, warming effect which has

an acquired taste—the flavor of ginseng is strongly vegetative. Ginseng, while expensive, is readily available from Chinese pharmacies and herbalists, and from some Asian food stores in various forms from dry slices and whole, pickled roots in jars, to granules for tea.

Also known as *jen-shen, yun sum* (China); *insahm* (Korea)

See also: MEDICINAL FOODS

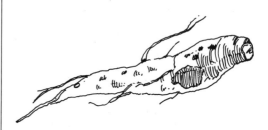

Ginseng

GLOBE EGGPLANT: see EGGPLANT

GLUTEN: Dried, spongy cakes of gluten dough used in Chinese and Japanese cuisines, particularly in vegetarian cooking. Gluten is made by extracting the gluten from wheat and making it into a dough with water. It is partially cooked, making a spongy soft mass which is used as a meat substitute in vegetarian dishes. It has very little taste, but absorbs the flavors of seasonings and the other ingredients cooked with it. Gluten is sold by the piece or in cellophane-wrapped packs in Chinese delicatessens or groceries. The fried type can be kept for many months in an airtight jar; softer gluten may be frozen, which will affect its structure but not spoil it. There are several types of Chinese gluten:

KAU FU resembles half-cooked bread dough and is spongy in texture and appearance. It is added to braised dishes.

KOHANA FU is the attractive "flower fu" found in instant noodles and soups. It can be purchased in packs to sprinkle directly over dishes and does not require cooking.

MATSUTAKE FU: A baked "fu" shaped like mushroom slices scented with aroma from *shiitake* mushrooms and frequently used in *sukiyaki*.

MEIN JIN PAU are golfball-size pieces of golden gluten which have been deep-fried, making them hollow and lightweight. They require little cooking and can be added to soups and hotpots.

NAMA FU is fresh gluten cake, rarely used in this form.

SU TANG is a long, thin roll of gluten dough that looks like an uncooked croissant. It can be sliced and cooked in vegetarian stir-fried and braised dishes. Japanese gluten differs from the Chinese product, being roasted to make it dry and feather-light.

Sliced su tang gluten

YAKI FU are larger cubes of *nama fu*, roasted to a toasted brown color.
Also known as *kau fu, mianjin, mein jin pau, su tang* (China); *kohana fu, nama fu, yaki fu* (Japan)
See also: FLOURS AND THICKENERS (WHEAT STARCH)

GLUTEN-FREE FLOUR: see FLOURS AND THICKENERS (WHEAT STARCH)

GLUTINOUS (STICKY) RICE: see RICE (GLUTINOUS)

GLUTINOUS RICE DOUGH, SWEET: (recipe) see RICE

GLUTINOUS RICE FLOUR: see FLOURS AND THICKENERS (GLUTINOUS)

GLUTINOUS RICE WITH MANGO: (recipe) see RICE

GOAT: Goat is eaten in India, Pakistan, Nepal and northern areas of China, being virtu-ally interchangeable with lamb in both name and use. It is preferred in many parts of India, although it is commonly thought that lamb is favored. A lean meat with a pronounced, slightly gamey flavor, it readily accepts strong curry seasonings and spices. Marinated goat meat is made into many different types of kebab.

In southern China goat is rarely used except in one notable case, believed to be of Hakka origin. Kid, the meat of young goat, is braised in a clay pot with turnips and flavored with "Chinese cheese" (fermented bean curd) and finely shredded lime leaves. Indian communities in Malaysia and Singapore occasionally use kid in their cooking.
Also known as *gosht* (India); *bokko ko masu* (Nepal)
See also: LAMB; GOAT CASSEROLE WITH FERMENTED BEAN CURD SAUCE (recipe)

GOAT CASSEROLE WITH FERMENTED BEAN CURD SAUCE
Serves 6

2 lbs (1 kg) lean kid or young lamb, cubed
2 tbsps vegetable oil
1 white turnip, peeled and cubed
8 slices fresh ginger
2 chopped scallions (spring/green onions)
6 cups (1½ qts/1.5 l) chicken stock
2 pieces dried orange peel, soaked
2 tbsps soybean paste
3 squares fermented bean curd, mashed
1 tsp salt
1 tsp sugar
black pepper
1 tbsp yellow rice wine
young lettuce
lemon leaves

Blanch meat in boiling water; drain. Heat oil and fry turnip with ginger and scallions for 1 minute; add meat and fry for 2 minutes. Add stock, orange peel, soybean paste, bean curd, salt, sugar, pepper to taste and wine. Cover and simmer for 1½ hours. Rinse lettuce, place in a serving dish and pour on the cooked meat with sauces. Serve with finely shredded lemon leaves and extra mashed fermented bean curd.

GOAT PEPPER: see CHILI

GOBO: (*GO-BOH*, Japan) see BURDOCK ROOT

GOCHUJANG: (*GO-CHOO-JANG*, Korea) A salty chili paste with a mild flavor. Any chili can be used instead, in particular *sambal ulek*, which has a similar salty flavor. Most Korean households make up bean pastes and sauces in the spring, just as they do *kimchi* in autumn. *Gochujang* is packed into stoneware jars to mature.
See also: CHILI PASTE; CHILI SAUCE; KOREAN BARBECUE SAUCE (recipe); SAMBAL ULEK; SILGOCHU

GODONG MANGKOKAN: (*GAW-DONG MUNG-COCK-KUN*, Indonesia) see DAUN MANGKOK

GOLDEN NEEDLE: see LILY BULB

GOLDEN PURSE: see BEAN CURD (FRIED POUCHES)

GOLDEN THREADS
Serves 6

10 egg yolks, beaten
3 cups (24 fl oz / 750 ml) sugar syrup

Strain egg yolks through a fine non-metal sieve. Pour strained yolks into a pastry bag fitted with a fine tip. Bring sugar syrup to a boil. Pipe about 2 tbsps egg onto the hot syrup to form a lacy pattern. When cooked, remove with a slotted spoon and roll loosely into a log shape. Cook remaining egg in this way, adding more water as needed to prevent syrup from thickening.

GOMA: (*GO-MA*, Japan) see SESAME SEED

GAMASIO/GOMASHIO: (*GO-MA-SHI-O*, Japan) see SESAME SEED

GONE: (*GON*, China) see BEAN CURD (GRILLED)

GONG YIU CHEE: (*GON YIU CHUE*, China) see CONPOY

GOOSE: Although goose is not used widely in Asia, the Chiu Chou Chinese, in the southern coastal province of Fukien, have a penchant for it. They roast or slow-simmer it in stock until it is supremely tender. It is served very finely sliced with a white vinegar dip to balance its excessive richness and fattiness. The liver is usually served separately.

GOROKA: (*GORAKA*, Sri Lanka) An orange-colored fruit native to Sri Lanka that is used to give a strong tart flavor to certain dishes, particularly fish. It is quartered and dried, which turns it almost black. *Belimbing*, *ma-dun* or tamarind are possible substitutes. In the southern Indian state of Kerala, smoke-blackened rind of *kodampoli* is used in the same way, while further north, a similar, although unsmoked, flavoring is known as *kokum*.
See also: BELIMBING; MA-DUN; TAMARIND

GOURDS: see MELONS AND GOURDS

GOURD STRIPS, DRIED: see KAMPYO

GRAINS: see FLOURS AND THICKENERS; RICE

GRAM: see CHICK-PEA; LENTIL (GREEN); MUNG BEAN

GRAM FLOUR: see FLOURS AND THICKENERS (BESAN)

GRAM GOO: (*KAAN PHIU*, Thailand) see CLOVES

GRANA: (*GRA-NAH*, Philippines) Red coloring used in salted eggs, resembling sand in appearance. Only a small amount is required. Other red food colorings extensively used in the Philippines are *ankak* and *annatto*.
See also: ANNATTO SEED; FOOD COLORINGS

GRASS CARP: see CARP

GRASS JELLY: see AGAR AGAR

GRATIEM: (*KRATHIEM*, Thailand) see GARLIC

GREATER GALANGAL: see GALANGAL, GREATER

GREEN CURRY PASTE: (recipe) see CURRY PASTES, POWDERS AND SAUCES

GREEN CURRY PASTE: see KRUNG GAENG

GREEN GRAM: see MUNG BEAN

GREEN LENTIL: see LENTIL

GREEN MUNG BEAN FLOUR: see FLOURS AND THICKENERS

GREEN PEPPERCORN: see PEPPERCORN

GREEN SHISO: see BEEFSTEAK PLANT

GREEN SHRIMP CURRY: (recipe) see SHRIMP

GRENADINE SYRUP/ESSENCE: see POME-GRANATE

GRILLED BEAN CURD: see BEAN CURD (GRILLED)

GRILLED FISH: (recipe) see FISH

GROUND NUT: see PEANUT

GROUND ROASTED CHILI: see CHILI, GROUND ROASTED

GROUND TOASTED (ROASTED) RICE: (recipe) see RICE

GROUPER: see GAROUPA

GUANABANO: (GUANA-BAN-NO, Philippines) see SOURSOP

GUAR BEAN: see GWAAR KI PHALLI

GUCHI: (GOO-CHEE, India) see CLOUD EAR FUNGUS

GUCHUL PAN: (GU-JEOL PAN, Korea) A dish known as "nine varieties" comprising tiny pancakes served with a tart, salty sauce with crushed sesame seeds, together with an array of at least eight different types of fillings including finely shredded omelette, vegetables such as carrot and giant white radish, and meat. It is usually served as an appetizer with drinks and is traditionally presented in a specially constructed lacquered or china tray containing interlocking bowls, boxes or compartments.

GUINITAAN: (GI-NA-TAN, Philippines) see PHILIPPINES, COOKING METHODS

GULAB: (GU-LAAB, India) see ROSEWATER (ESSENCE)

GULAB JAMONS
Serves 6

1²/₃ cups (6 oz / 185 g) powdered whole milk
2 tbsps ghee
1 cup (4 oz / 110 g) self-rising flour
1 tsp baking powder
¹/₃ tsp ground cardamom
deep-frying oil or ghee
1¹/₄ cups (9 oz / 250 g) sugar
1³/₄ cups (14 fl oz / 430 ml) water
1¹/₂ tsps rosewater

(cont'd)

(Gulab Jamons cont'd)

Pour the powdered milk into a mixing bowl. Lightly rub in softened ghee to make fine crumbs. Mix in flour, baking powder and cardamom with enough cold water to make a very stiff dough. Wrap in plastic wrap and set aside for 3–4 hours. Break up dough, and rub hard on a lightly floured board until it breaks into fine crumbs again. Moisten with water, then form into walnut-size balls. Heat the oil or ghee for deep-frying over medium heat. Fry milk balls gently until golden brown. Bring sugar and water to a boil; simmer for 10 minutes. Remove from heat. Transfer cooked *gulab jamons* to a glass serving dish. Sprinkle with rosewater. Pour on sugar syrup and leave for 30 minutes before serving.

GULAI: (GOO-LIE, Indonesia) see INDONESIA, COOKING METHODS

GULAI OF LAMB: (recipe) see LAMB

GULA JAWA: (GOO-LA JA-WA, Indonesia) see SUGAR

GULA MALACCA/MELAKA: (GOO-LA ME-LA-KA, Malaysia) see SUGAR

GULA MALACCA
Serves 6

1¹/₂ cups (12 oz / 350 g) sago, rinsed
1 pandanus leaf
6 cups (1¹/₂ qts / 1.5 l) water
1¹/₄ cups (10 oz / 300 g) crumbled palm sugar
(or substitute brown sugar)
1 cup (8 fl oz / 250 ml) hot water
2 cups (16 fl oz / 500 ml) thick coconut milk

Boil sago with pandanus leaf in water until tender. Drain; discard leaf. Melt sugar in a small pan with hot water; cook to a thick syrup. Cool. Pour sugar syrup and coconut milk over sago.

GULAMAN: (*GOO-LA-MAN*, Philippines) see AGAR AGAR

GUMBO: (*GUMBO*) see BHINDI

GUNG: (*GOO-UNG*, Vietnam) see GINGER

GUR: (*GURH*, India) see SUGAR

GWAAR KI PHALLI: (*GU-AAR KEE PHA-LEE*, India) Guar or cluster beans are an Indian vegetable used in vegetarian cooking and are very popular in the state of Rajasthan where they are eaten with *chapatis* and a hot chili chutney. A bushy perennial, it yields clusters of small, straight, hairy pods, very similar to soybeans, which to be eaten fresh must be picked when very young. The ripe seeds vary in color from white to black and are eaten as a starch. *Parkia*, the bean-like pod eaten as a vegetable in Indonesia, is another type of bean sometimes referred to as a "twisted cluster bean" but is not to be confused with *guar*. Green or French (haricot) beans can replace cluster beans in a recipe.
See also: PARKIA

GWAYTIO/KWAY TIO: (*KUAY-TIEW*, Thailand) see NOODLES (RICE RIBBON)

GYIN SEIN: (*GIN SANE*, Burma) see GINGER

H

HAAM DAAN: (*HARM DARN*, China) see DUCK EGG, SALTED

HAAS KO PHOOL: (*HAAS KOH FULL*, Nepal) see EGG

HAIGA-MAI: (*HAH-I-GAH-MAH-I*, Japan) see RICE (NON-GLUTINOUS)

HAIR VEGETABLE: see SEAWEED

HAIRY BASIL: see BASIL

HAIRY EGGPLANT: see EGGPLANT (HAIRY)

HAIRY GOURD: see MELONS AND GOURDS

HAJIKAMI SHOGA: (*HA-JI-KARMA SHOW-GA*) see JAPAN, GARNISHES

HAKUSAI: (*HAH-KOO-SAH-I*, Japan) see CABBAGE, CHINESE (NAPA)

HALBA: (*HAL-BA*, Malaysia) see FENUGREEK

HALDI: (*HAL-DEE*, India) see TURMERIC

HALIA: (*HA-LEE-YA*, Malaysia) see GINGER

HAM, CHINESE: see PORK, CURED

HAM, FRESH: see PORK

HANA HOJISO: (*HANA HO-ZEE-SO*, Japan) see BEEFSTEAK PLANT

HANA-KATSUO: (*HANA KAH-TZU-O*, Japan) see BONITO

HANOI BEEF SOUP: (recipe) see BEEF

HANPEN: (*HAN-PEN*, Japan) see KAMABOKO

HARA DHANIA: (*HA-RAA DHA-NI-AA*, India) see CORIANDER, FRESH

HARA MIRICH: (*HA-REE MIRCH*, India) see CHILI

HARE CHANNA: (*HA-RAA CHA-NAA*, India) see CHICK-PEA

HAR GEE: (*HAR JI*, China) see CAVIAR (SHRIMP EGGS)

HASHI: (*HAH-SHE*, Japan) see CHOPSTICKS

HA SHOGA: (*HAA-SHOW-GA*, Japan) see GINGER

HATCHO-MISO: (*HATCHOO MEE-SO*, Japan) see MISO

HEART OF PALM: see UBOD

HEART OF PALM ROLLS: (recipe) see UBOD

HEAVENLY GRASS: see AGAR AGAR

HED HUNU: (*HED HUU-NUU*, Thailand) see CLOUD EAR FUNGUS

HEIKO: (*HI-COE*, Malaysia) A smooth, thick, shrimp paste the color of molasses (treacle). Used in Thailand and Malaysia (especially in Nonya cooking) for its distinct flavor.
Also known as *kapi leaw* (Thailand)
See also: SHRIMP PASTE

HEKO: (*HEH-KOH*, Philippines) A condiment made by cooking *bagoong* and water (1:3 by volume) for half an hour and allowing it to stand. The resulting sediment is *heko*, a mildly flavored, salty seasoning ingredient used to give its unique of-the-sea flavor to certain Philippine dishes.
See also: BAGOONG; FISH PASTE; FISH, PRESERVED; FISH SAUCE

HET KANOO: (*HED HUU-NUU*, Thailand) see CLOUD EAR FUNGUS

HEUNG NEU FUN: (*HEUNG LIU FEN*, China) see FIVE-SPICE POWDER

HIJIKI: (*HEE-JEE-KEE*, Japan) see SEAWEED

HIM: (*HIEN*, China) see CLAM

HING: (*HEENG*, India) see ASAFOETIDA

HIYAMUGI: (*HEE-YAH-MOU-GUI*, Japan) see NOODLES (MISWA)

HIYU: (*HEE-YOU*, Japan) see AMARANTH

HOAN JO: (*HUNG JO*, China) see DATE

HOEN KWE: (*HOON KWAY*, Indonesia, Malaysia) see FLOURS AND THICKENERS (MUNG BEAN)

HOI SIN CHEUNG: (*HOI SIN JEONG*, China) see BEAN PASTES AND SAUCES

HOISIN SAUCE: (*HOI-SIN*) see BEAN PASTES AND SAUCES

HOKKIEN MEI: (*HOCK-KEY-YEN ME*, Malaysia) see NOODLES (EGG)

HON DASHI: (*HON DAH-SHI*, Japan) see DASHI

HONEY DEW: see MELONS AND GOURDS

HONG DOW: (*HUNG DAU*, China) see AZUKI BEAN

HONG KONG: More than 3000 restaurants in Hong Kong are proof positive of the importance of food to the Chinese people. Many of the larger, tourist-oriented restaurants have menus incorporating the best or, perhaps more to the point, the most popular dishes from the four major culinary styles of China, and these could be said to exemplify Hong Kong cuisine. But specialty restaurants also offer a wide spectrum of dishes from virtually every region of China, as well as foods of particular types, such as *dim sum*, game and exotica, Muslim, vegetarian, pigeon, seafood, snake, etc. The predominant cuisine in Hong Kong is Cantonese, from the adjacent province of Guangdong.
See also: CHINA

HONJE: (*HON-JEAH*, Indonesia) see GINGER BUD

HONG MEI: (*HUNG MAI*, China) see FERMENTED RED RICE

HONG SHAO: (*HUNG SIL*) see CHINA, COOKING METHODS (RED BRAISING)

HOPPER: see APPA

HORAPA: (*HORAPHAA*, Thailand) see BASIL

HORENZO: (*HOO-WREN-SOO*, Japan) see SPINACH

HORIZONTAL SLICING: see CHINA, CUTTING AND SLICING METHODS

HORSERADISH: see WASABI

HOT BEAN PASTE: see BEAN PASTES AND SAUCES (CHILI BEAN)

HOT BLACK BEAN SAUCE: see BEAN PASTES AND SAUCE

HOT DIEU MAU: (*HORT DUE MOW*, Vietnam) see ANNATTO SEED

HOT RED CURRIED BEEF COUNTRY-STYLE: (recipe) see BEEF

HOY LAI: (*HOY LAI*, Thailand) see CLAMS

HSIEN TS'AI: (*HIAN CHOY*, China) see AMARANTH

HTAMIN LETHOKE: (*TA-MIN LET-TOOK*, Burma) An interesting eating experience, which involves cooked long-grain rice, a variety of different noodles and a host of accompaniments. The name literally translates as "rice finger mixed." The cold components are arrayed on platters and are taken to the eater's bowl in the fingers, where they are "finger mixed" with the sauces and other spicy accompaniments, which may include fried and raw garlic and onions, roasted chick-pea powder, chili powder, fish sauce and tamarind.

HTAMIN LETHOKE
Serves 6–8

1¹/2 cups (12 oz / 350 g) long-grain white rice
2¹/4 cups (18 fl oz / 550 ml) water
2 oz (60 g) cellophane noodles, cooked and
drained
4 oz (120 g) fine egg noodles, cooked and
drained
2 large potatoes, cooked and sliced
2 cups (3 oz / 90 g) fresh bean sprouts,
blanched and drained
4 oz (120 g) rice vermicelli, cooked and
drained
omelette shreds
2 fresh red chilies; seeded, chopped and fried
10 medium onions, sliced and crisp-fried
20 garlic cloves, sliced and crisp-fried
1 cup (1 oz / 30 g) dried shrimp, ground to a
fine powder
1 cup (5 oz / 155 g) roasted chick-peas, ground
to a fine powder
2 tbsps chili powder
¹/2 cup (4 fl oz / 120 ml) fish sauce
³/4 cup (6 fl oz / 180 ml) tamarind sauce

Cook rice with water by the absorption
method. The noodles, potatoes and bean
sprouts are served cold, arranged in
separate groups on a tray. All of the
other ingredients are served in small
dishes as accompaniments.

HU CHIAO: (*WU JIL*, China) see SICHUAN
PEPPERCORN

HUNDRED-YEAR EGG: see THOUSAND-YEAR
EGG

HUNG: (*HUNG*, Vietnam) see VIETNAMESE MINT

HUNG ZAO: (*HUNG JO*, China) see JUJUBE

I

ICHIBAN DASHI: (*EE-CHEE-BAN DAH-SHI*, Japan) see DASHI

ICHIMI: (*EE-CHEE-MEE*, Japan) see SHICHIMI

IDDI APPA: (*EE-DEE AA-UP-PA*, Sri Lanka) see APPA

IDLIS: (*ID-LEE*, India), Small, fluffy breakfast
cakes made from a dough of ground rice and
urad dal which has been left to ferment overnight. *Idlis* are steamed in a special pan, which
has several smoothly rounded indentations to
shape the cakes. It is placed over a pan of hot
coals to steam-bake until the cakes are cooked
through, when they will feel springy to the
touch and dry on the surface. They are a
specialty of the southern Indian states where
they are eaten with coconut chutney. They are
equally delicious dipped into a nutty, spicy
mixture called *milagai podi* of toasted seeds
and spices. Garlic-flavored *idlis* are also much
enjoyed.
See also: BREAD, INDIAN; MILAGAI PODI

Steamed idlis

IGAT: (*IH-GAT*, Philippines) see EEL

IKA: (*EE-KAH*, Japan) see CUTTLEFISH

IKAN BILIS: (*E-KUN BE-LEASE*, Indonesia,
Malaysia) see ANCHOVY

IKAN KERING: (*E-KUN KEH-REENG*, Indonesia,
Malaysia) see FISH, PRESERVED (DRIED AND
SALTED)

IKAN TERI: (*E-KUN TEH-REE*, Indonesia) see
ANCHOVY

IKURA: (*EE-KOO-RA*, Japan) see CAVIAR

INAKA-MISO: (*EE-NAH-KAH-MEE-SO*, Japan) see
MISO

INDIA: It is hardly surprising that a country that stretches from the towering icy ranges of the Himalayas in the north to the warmth of tropical waters in the south, has a cuisine as complex, diverse and as dramatically distinct as its own landscape.

The food of the north languishes under the spell of the old Moghul courts, with intricately blended flavors, subtle spicing, esoteric garnishes and wonderfully fragrant aromas. Here, too, the clay *tandoor* is used for baking breads and roasting chicken, fish and meat kebabs. The southern Tamils, by contrast, favor fiery tastes, redolent of chili, garlic and pepper. Here the majority of the population follows a vegetarian regime. Sauces are often as thin as a soup, of incendiary heat, and are eaten with copious amounts of rice or steamed breads made from a fermented dough of rice and lentils. The food of the western coast is similar to that of Indonesia and Malaysia in its use of coconut, palm sugar, chili and herbs. Bengal, to the east, enjoys a cuisine dominated by the abundance of seafood in its bay, and adds a distinct pungency from mustard oil which, except in pickles, is little used in other states. Two other unique cuisines can be found on India's west coast. The state of Goa, formerly under Portuguese rule, has incorporated many of the culinary customs of its European colonizer. Its cuisine is an enticing blend of East and West. The Parsis brought with them to India a sense of their Middle Eastern homeland in a cuisine that favors lamb and beans with aromatic rather than hot seasonings.

Throughout India curries are usually the main part of the meal, with anything from one to ten being served together. Accompaniments vary from region to region. There is always rice or bread—leavened and *tandoor*-baked, unleavened and griddle-cooked, deep or shallow-fried. A meal is considered incomplete without an array of complementary side dishes. These typically include a creamy whipped yogurt *raita*, a salad in a vinegar dressing or marinade, chutney or pickles. *Dal*, a dish of lentils flavored to add contrast to the main dish and as a vegetable protein dietary supplement, is served with almost every meal, and is an indispensable facet in the diet where little meat is eaten.

As alcohol is prohibited in most Indian states, beverages include cooling fruit drinks and sherbets, spicy palate-stimulating iced drinks, tea flavored with spices, and a creamy, soothing whipped yogurt or buttermilk drink known as *lassi*.

There are many tasty appetizer-style foods in the Indian cuisine, and several types may be served at the beginning of a meal. The main dishes are usually served together, or in several batches if the menu is a large one, with rice and bread served throughout. Soups can be eaten at any time during the meal. Indians enjoy desserts and are particularly fond of the rich sweetmeats, *mithai*, which are made by specialist cooks. However, these are usually eaten as snacks during the day.

Eating is customarily done with the fingers. The thumb and first two fingers of the right hand are used to tear bread or ball rice, which is dipped into curry sauces or employed as an edible scoop.

INDIA, COOKING METHODS:

BHARTA: This describes a dish that has been cooked and puréed, and particularly those made with vegetables.
See also: EGGPLANT PUREE (recipe)

CHAMAK: A technique for searing the surface of food with hot ghee. It is applied mainly to cooked meats and vegetables and to *dal* and rice. Whole or crushed spices and garlic are added to flavor. When poured over *dal*, the result is similar to *baghar*.

CHARCOAL COOKING in small clay or cast-iron stoves or stone pits is used extensively in Indian cooking.
See also: UTENSILS (BARBECUES AND CHARCOAL COOKERS)

CHASNIDARH: A term applied to dishes with a sweet-sour flavor, achieved by steeping foods in *chasni* syrup. Sweet and tart fruits and vegetables, as well as *kewra* essence, are added to Indian sweet-sour dishes. This name is also given to a sweet rice dish.
See also: CHASNI; KEWRA ESSENCE

DO PIAAZA: Onions, finely chopped and allowed to cook to a purée, lend their texture and rich, sweet flavor to almost all Indian curries. *Do piaaza*, a popular cooking style in Hyderabad and other areas where onions are a major crop, uses onions as a main ingredient, usually with lamb, to delightful effect.
See also: DO PIAAZA (recipe); ONION

DRY ROASTING or **TOASTING** are descriptions applied to whole spices that are cooked in a pan or oven without oil or fat. It is done to intensify the flavor and to add a certain nutty overtone.

DUM: A delicate way to cook vegetables or meat to retain the natural shape, flavor and texture. The lid of the pot is sealed with a strip of dough and the whole foods are cooked gently, with heat above and below.

FUGATH: In this style of cooking, popularized in Maharashtra state, vegetables are fried with onions and *masala* (spices).
See also: PUMPKIN WITH ONION AND SPICES (recipe)

KOFTA: Balls, dumplings and rolls made of ground or mashed meat or vegetables. Koftas are usually grilled or fried and may be served dry or in a sauce, gravy or curry. They are often stuffed with spices, diced nuts or *panir* (cottage cheese).

KORMA: Mildly flavored curries, usually with a creamy sauce. Heat is provided by white pepper in preference to chili.
See also: KORMA OF MUTTON (recipe)

TANDOORI COOKING is oven roasting in a specially made clay oven.
See also: TANDOOR

TARKARI: Any dish containing vegetables fried in ghee and cooked gently in their own juices.

VINDALOO is the name given to a fiercely hot form of curry made on the east coast of India.
See also: VINDALOO

INDIA RECIPES

Appetizers
Kebabs of Ground Meat
Samoosas
Skewered Lamb
Tandoori Baked Pomfret
Tandoori Chicken Tikkas

Main Courses
Biriyani of Rice and Chicken
Buttermilk Curry
Chaat Murgh
Chick-peas Braised with Spices
Dhansak
Dhansak Kebabs
Do Piaaza
Drumstick Curry
Kashmiri Meatballs, in Rich Sauce
Korma of Mutton
Lamb with Creamed Spinach Sauce
Roghan Josh
Shrimp in Coconut Milk
Spiced Red Lentils
Sprouted Lentil Kichardi
Vindaloo of Duck
Xacutti Chicken
Yogurt Chicken

Accompaniments
Black-eyed Pea (Bean) Salad
Chapatis
Dal and Vegetable Sauce
Dhansak Brown Rice
Drumstick Curry
Eggplant Purée
Fresh Coriander Chutney
Fried Balloon Bread
Layered Buttered Bread
Mango Pickles
Masala Cabbage
Onion Kechumber

(cont'd)

(India Recipes cont'd)

Rice Cooked in Rich Meat Broth
Roasted Masala Potatoes
Southern Indian Breakfast Bread
Spinach Purée
Tandoori Baked Bread
Vegetables in Coconut Sauce

Desserts
Gulab Jamons
Jalebis
Kulfi
Muslim Rice Dessert
Parsi Semolina Dessert

MENUS
(See recipes)

SPECIAL OCCASION DINNER
Serves 8

Appetizers
Chaat Murgh
Samoosas

Main Courses
Roghan Josh
Tandoori Chicken Tikkas

Accompaniments
Eggplant Purée
Layered Buttered Bread or Naans
Mango Pickles
Rice Cooked in Rich Meat Broth
Roasted Masala Potatoes

Dessert
Jalebis

DINNER MENU
(Mildy Hot)
Serves 6

Main Courses
Lamb with Creamed Spinach
Spiced Red Lentils
Yogurt Chicken

Accompaniments
Chapatis
Rice

Dessert
Muslim Rice Dessert

VEGETARIAN DINNER
Serves 6–8

Main Course
Chick-peas Braised with Spices

Accompaniments
Black-eyed Pea (Bean) Salad
Fried Balloon Bread
Rice
Spinach Purée

Dessert
Parsi Semolina Dessert

INDIAN CURRY SPICES: see MASALA

INDONESIA: The cuisine of Indonesia has been shaped by many influences—Arab, Chinese, Dutch, Indian, Portuguese. Traders of spices exchanged cinnamon, cloves, nutmeg and pepper for European cooking ideas, Eastern religious philosophies—and the piquant chili pepper. Indeed, the use of spices is the most notable characteristic of Indonesian cooking, for the famed "Spice Islands" have their own vast plantations of fragrant, exotic spices. These, together with their other native produce—the creamy milk of coconuts, the brown syrupy sugar extracted from palmyra and coconut palms, and the pungency of chilies,

133

garlic, ginger and shallots–create dishes with a unique, complex flavor that is typically Indonesian.

Curried dishes dominate the cuisine, but in many dishes the rich color and flavor of soy sauce take the palate in an entirely different direction. Blending and balance are the keywords to this cuisine: the interesting, adventurous blending of spices, herbs and seasonings; the balance of elements—color, texture, taste. For each salty or sour taste there is a hint of added sweetness; for every spicy hot taste—and in Indonesian cuisine these can be searing—there is a cool and refreshing counterpoint such as the cubes of cucumber that accompany a hot satay sauce. Rich, buttery, nutty flavors come to sauces, not from dairy products or grains but from coconut milk, peanuts and candlenuts, ground to thicken and enrich. Rice is the staple, and is served in mountainous quantities with every meal. But there are interesting innovations involving noodles—particularly *laksa*, in which thin rice vermicelli is flooded with a highly spiced coconut sauce and a thicker, more intensely flavored sauce containing shredded meat, vegetables or seafood.

Table etiquette is informal. Food is served on the table in bowls or large platters and everyone helps him- or herself. Two wonderful traditions are the feasts known as *rijstaffel*, a banquet devised during the time of Dutch occupation, and its Indonesian equivalent, *selamatan*. Many courses of curries, meats, vegetable and egg dishes are served with soups, rice and myriad *sambals*. The food is placed on the table or is brought to the diners by a line of sarong-clad waiters, and a little is taken from each bowl. It is not unusual for the selection to run to more than 30 different dishes in one meal.

Drinks are usually refreshing rather than alcoholic, although in Indonesia there are several types of brewed and distilled wine based on coconut palm made in Indonesia.

INDONESIA, COOKING METHODS:

ASAM PEDAS literally means "sour hot." This is the term for fish or meat cooked in very hot, sour gravy.

GULAI is a dish where the ingredients are simmered in a large amount of liquid, which is either coconut milk or a sauce made tart and sour with tamarind or pineapple, and with *rempah* and spices. This is a distinctive style of curry-making that is usually slightly sweet from the addition of *gula jawa* (palm sugar).

PADANG is the term for very spicy and hot dishes from the island of Sumatra. It is a popular cooking style.

PANGGANG refers to food roasted over a fire, such as *ayam panggang* (roasted chicken). The food is usually seasoned with spices before roasting.

RENDANG is a coconut-milk-based curry, strongly flavored with spices and *rempah*. It is cooked until the liquid has been absorbed into the meat.

SAYURS are dishes cooked with vegetables. They are usually crisp-cooked and swimming in thin coconut milk sauce.

INDONESIA RECIPES

Appetizers
Chicken Livers in Spicy Sauce
Eggs in Coconut Sauce
Peanut Fritters
Rice Cakes Wrapped in Coconut Leaves
Satay Beef with Peanut Sauce
Satay Shrimp
Soup with Shrimp and Noodles
Sweet Corn Fritters

Main Courses
Bean Curd Sauté
Chicken in Creamy Spiced Sauce
Curried Crab
Gado Gado
Gulai of Lamb
Indonesian Vegetables in Coconut Milk
Nasi Goreng
Parkia and Shrimp Sambalan
Spiced Fish
Sweet Soy Sauce Pork

(cont'd)

ITO KONNYAKU

(Indonesia Recipes cont'd)

Accompaniments
Fried Noodles
Gado Gado
Indonesian Vegetables in Coconut Milk

Desserts
Banana Cakes
Coconut Balls

MENUS
(See recipes)

"RIJSTAFFEL" MENU
Serves 12

Appetizers
Eggs in Coconut Sauce
Satay Shrimp
Sweet Corn Fritters

Main Courses
Chicken in Creamy Spiced Sauce
Gulai of Lamb
Spiced Fish
Sweet Soy Sauce Pork

Accompaniments
Gado Gado
Indonesian Rice Vegetables in Coconut Milk

Dessert
Banana Cakes

FAMILY MEAL

Bean Curd Sauté
Nasi Goreng
Soup with Shrimp and Noodles

INDONESIAN SEASONING PASTE: see REMPAH

INDRING: (*EEN-DRING*, Indonesia) see BASIL (HAIRY)

INGEE: (*IN-GEE*, India) see GINGER

INGURU: (*I-NGU-RU*, Sri Lanka) see GINGER

INGURUPIYALI: (*I-NGU-RU-PIYA-LI*, Sri Lanka) see GALANGAL, LESSER

INIHAW: (*EE-NEE-HOW*, Philippines) see PHILIPPINES, COOKING METHODS

INSAHM: (*IN-SAM*, Korea) see GINSENG

INSAHM CHA: (*IN-SAM CHA*, Korea) Tea made with ginseng root. It has a distinctive earthy, medicinal taste and is highly regarded for its powerful rejuvenating properties.
See also: GINSENG

ITA-KAMABOKO: (*EE-TAH-KAH-MAH-BOW-KO*, Japan) see KAMABOKO

ITO-KEZURI-KATSUO: (*EE-TO KE-ZOO-REE KAH-TZU-O*, Japan) see BONITO

ITO KONNYAKU: (*EE-TO CON-NYA-KOO*, Japan) see AMORPHOPHALUS KONJAC

135

J

JA: (*JA*) see CHINA, COOKING METHODS (DEEP-FRYING)

JACKFRUIT: (*Artocarpus integrifolia*) A large tropical fruit with a yellow-green, thick, hard skin segmented into small, short spines. Its flesh resembles pineapple in appearance, although it is paler cream-yellow in color and less sweet and juicy. When green it is used as a vegetable in curries, salads and vegetable dishes; when ripe it develops an oversweet fragrance rather like durian and has a waxy texture and sweet, agreeable taste which goes well in fruit salads. The flowers and young leaf shoots are used in salads and as a vegetable. Jackfruit is sometimes available fresh in Asian vegetable markets and is sold in cans and jars.

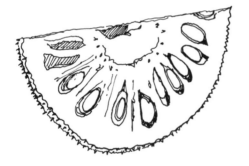

Cross section of jackfruit

JACKFRUIT STONES are the many large cream-colored stones in jackfruit which, particularly in India, Indonesia, Malaysia and Thailand, are cooked as a vegetable, roasted to eat as a snack and sliced into coconut milk to make a dessert.

Also known as *kathal, kathal ke beej* (India); *nangka* (Indonesia, Malaysia); *langka* (Philippines); *kanoon, kha-nun; med-kha-nun* (Thailand)

See also: JACKFRUIT IN CREAMY CURRY SAUCE (recipe); MOCK JACKFRUIT SEEDS (recipe)

JACKFRUIT IN CREAMY CURRY SAUCE
Serves 4–6

8 oz (250 g) lean beef or lamb, cubed
1 stalk lemon grass, halved lengthways
3 slices fresh ginger
$1/4$ cup (2 oz / 60 g) minced scallions (spring / green onions)
$1/2$ tsp minced garlic
2 tbsps minced red chilies
1 in (2.5 cm) piece fresh turmeric, minced
2 tsps shrimp paste
4 oz (125 g) unripe jackfruit, cubed
3 cups (24 fl oz / 75 ml) thick coconut milk
tamarind
salt
pepper

Boil meat, lemon grass and ginger in salted water to just cover for 10 minutes. Grind scallions, garlic, chilies, fresh turmeric and shrimp paste together; add to the meat. Simmer until tender. Add jackfruit and coconut milk and simmer until tender. Add tamarind and salt and pepper to taste. Heat through.

MOCK JACKFRUIT SEEDS
Serves 6

2 cups (1 lb / 500 g) mung beans, soaked overnight
1 cup (8 fl oz / 250 ml) thick coconut milk
$1^1/2$ cups ($10^1/2$ oz / 300 g) sugar
6 cups ($1^1/2$ qts / 1.5 l) sugar syrup
6 egg yolks, lightly beaten

Drain beans, pick off skins. Steam without liquid until tender. Mash to a smooth paste, adding coconut milk and sugar. Cook over very low heat, stirring, until very stiff. Cool, press into small oval shapes to resemble jackfruit seeds. Bring half of the syrup to a boil. Dip the "jackfruit seeds" into the egg yolks and cook in the syrup until they float. Serve hot or cold with the remaining sugar syrup.

JAGGERY: see SUGAR

JAGUNG: (*JAH-GOONG*, Indonesia, Malaysia) see CORN

JAHE: (*JAH-HEAH*, Indonesia) see GINGER

JALAPENO CHILIES: see CHILI

JALEBI KA RANG: (*JA-LAI-BEE KAR RANG*, India) Artificial yellow food coloring used in India to color foods—particularly sweet dishes,

JALEBIS
Serves 6

2½ cups (10 oz / 300 g) maida *flour*
1½ tsps baking powder
8 strands saffron, ground
2 tbsps boiling water
deep-frying oil or ghee
1½ cups (10½ oz / 300 g) sugar
1½ tsps rosewater

Sift flour and baking powder into a bowl. Add enough warm water to make a batter of pouring consistency. Infuse saffron in boiling water. Mash and strain yellow liquid into batter. Heat oil or ghee. Pipe batter through a small funnel into curled shapes, each about 2 in (5 cm) across, onto the oil. Cook on both sides until golden and crisp. Drain. Make a syrup by boiling the sugar with 1¼ cups (10 fl oz/300 ml) water for 8 minutes. Flavor with the rosewater. Pour over *jalebis* and set aside for 30 minutes before serving.

Jalebis

such as the crisp-fried curls of batter soaked in sugar syrup and known as *jalebis*. When affordable, saffron is preferred for its delicate flavor.
See also: SAFFRON

JAPAN: Japanese cooks revel in the artistry of their craft. The Japanese love of nature is a challenge to present each ingredient as a reminder of its origins: to bring nature to the table in the selection of garnishes; to create a myriad of flavors with a few simple seasonings; to create a harmony that makes eating a joy. The cook's thoughts will be as much on the layout of the food and its garnishes and the selection of the plate itself, as on the taste of the food. For these three facets combine with equal emphasis into the unique whole that is Japanese cooking.

In this country where *gohan* means both "boiled rice" and "a meal," a rice of tender-textured, short-grain type is the staple served with all meals and the bulk of the available farming land is layered into waving emerald paddies. Vegetables appear in the Japanese diet in moderation and are rarely eaten raw, being simmered or deep-fried, or "vinegared." Root vegetables are favored and include the pencil-slim burdock, carrots and the giant white *daikon* radish. Mushrooms are plentiful and of exquisite flavor. The tiny, knobbly Japanese cucumber is vinegar-dressed for salads and appears as a ubiquitous garnish, shredded into paper-thin "petals" and fanned onto platters of *sashimi* or *sushi*.

The regionality of Japanese cooking is not of great importance. The rarest and most unique of the regional dishes remain for the most part where they began, by virtue of the fact that freshness is a major criterion of Japanese cooking, and freshness is best obtained at the point of origin. There are not, as in China, dramatically different culinary styles in north, south, east and west. There is, rather, an overall style of eating, with each area boasting its own specialty dishes. And to miss, for instance, eating *wakasagi* (pond smelt) while in Tsuchiura on the Kasumigaura Lagoon, or *kaki*-miso (oysters cooked in miso) in Sendai, or *soba* from Araki-ya, the 300-year-old noodle shop in Izumo, would be to deny oneself some of the true culinary pleasures of this magical country.

The Japanese ritual at mealtimes is as stylized as the food itself. A formal banquet introduces the diner to all the major cooking techniques in one meal. It begins with a dainty *zensai* or hors d'oeuvre—a mere few bites exquisitely cooked and impeccably arranged. A soup follows, and then *sashimi,* one of the highlights. The meal proper comprises a grilled, simmered, steamed and crisp-fried dish, then an *aemono* or *sunomono* ("dressed" or "vinegared" dish), the rice, a miso-based soup and a dish of assorted *tsukemono* (pickles). Finally there are tea and fresh fruit. In cooler months a *nabemono* or "one-pot" dish may form the meal proper. Family meals are, of course, less grand but always include several different dishes. Soup is almost always served, as is a vinegared dish, and the choice of main dishes will range between simple *nimonos* and grills, or "one-pot" dishes. There is always a pickle with the rice at the end, and in rural areas this is still usually homemade.

Eating out in Japan presents an opportunity to experience the type of dishes rarely made at home. *Sushi* and *sashimi* which, while not difficult to make, require several different types of ultra-fresh seafood, tend to be classed as restaurant fare, as does *tempura* with its sophisticated light, crisp batter. *Teppan-yaki* is a relative newcomer to the Japanese food scene. In restaurants the diners sit at benches which are half eating area and half hotplate; the chef, on the other side, presides over the grilling of meat, seafood and vegetables with dramatic flourishes of the implements and entertaining patter. At home, over an electric griddle or skillet, it's an easy and informal way to entertain friends.

The choice of dishes for serving Japanese food is dictated as much by tradition as by the chef's sense of esthetics. Soup and rice are in small bowls, porcelain or lacquered wood, similar to those used in China, but with shallow lids. Simmered foods are in a similar, although larger, lidded bowl raised on a foot. Salad and certain vegetables come in a deep narrow dish; custards come in a straight-sided, lidded cup. Appetizers and vinegared foods can be served on flat, decoratively shaped dishes, often with a shallow lip. Noodles are eaten from a large deep bowl, or a flat closely woven basket. Rice is served from a wooden bowl with a paddle. Fried foods are served on similar baskets or flat platters. An assortment of small dishes accommodates dips and sauces. Tea is drunk from a squat, rounded cup without a handle, or from a taller version of this same shape, again without a handle. *Sake* is drunk from tiny porcelain cups, and the beverage is served in a narrow-necked flask. Several dishes are placed on the table at once, and it is not unusual for the entire meal to be served at once on a tray or low table.

JAPAN, COOKING METHODS:

AEMONO is a term that describes "dressed foods" or salads.

AGEMONO refers to deep-frying, which is done in a pan known as an *agemono-nabe* and shaped like a Chinese wok. For *tempura,* a semi-circular rack may be fitted to the inside rim of the pan for draining. Thick-handled, pointed metal chopsticks are used for retrieving.

AJI-SHIOYAKI is a technique in which ingredients (often seafoods) are thickly coated with coarse sea salt before grilling or broiling. The salt forms a crust on the surface of the food, but only marginally penetrates, so that the taste does not become too salty. It is similar to the

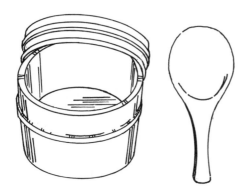

Japanese rice bowl and paddle

Chinese technique of salt-baking.
Also known as *shioyaki*

DENGAKU is skewered food, grilled and coated with a sweetened miso paste.

KARA-AGE indicates food with a dusting of flour, which is then deep-fried.

MUSHIMONO is the Japanese term for steaming and encompasses any dish cooked over simmering water or liquid.

NIMONO is a simmering technique, popular in Japan, in which cubed foods are gently cooked in seasoned liquid. It is applied to vegetables and some meats.

NITSUKE describes simmering in clear liquid or a thin sauce.

SAKA-MUSHI is the Japanese technique of steaming foods which have been marinated in *sake*, or steaming over water to which *sake* has been added.

SALTING: There are several terms that describe different techniques for salting prior to cooking.

Beta-jio refers to dredging food with salt before cooking it. Salt should be applied at least one hour before cooking and rinsed off.

Furi-jio is hand-sprinkled salt, used on fish and poultry.

Kami-jio is a technique exclusive to Japanese cooking. It is used when a light salting is needed on raw fish for *sushi* or *sashimi*. A work surface is sprinkled with salt, and the fish is placed on the salt between two pieces of paper, with more salt on top. It is allowed to stand for one hour to allow the salt to draw through the paper.

Su-age is designated as "naked" frying in which food is deep-fried at a moderate oil temperature without first being coated with, for example, flour or batter. It is usually used on items, such as small whole fish or eggplant, whose shape would be spoiled if they were coated.

Sunomono are "vinegared foods."

Tate-jio translates as "seawater salting" and involves soaking food in a mild brine solution to which *kombu* kelp has been added.

Teppan yaki is the method of cooking ingredients on a hotplate, which may be located directly on the serving table. It has been popularized in Western countries where the cooking is performed with elaborate ritual in front of diners. It also describes foods that are barbecued or grilled over charcoal.

Ingredients cooking on teppan yaki hotplate

Teriyaki is seafood or meat, skewered on thin bamboo or metal rods, marinated in soy sauce, sugar and either *sake* or *mirin*, which is brushed repeatedly over the food as it grills, to give a rich red-brown glaze.

Yakimono describes quick cooking over high heat, either on a grill or in a pan, to crisp the outside, leaving the inside of the food lightly cooked and tender.

Yakitori is a barbecue technique applied to chicken basted with soy sauce and usually skewered.

JAPAN, CUTTING AND SLICING TECHNIQUES:

BEVEL-EDGED cylinders are popular as a shape for vegetables such as carrots, giant white radish and turnip. The sides are cut straight and the edge at top and bottom is

pared off to make an attractive, neat edge.
See also: DAIKON NIMONO (recipe)

CLAPPER-CUT RECTANGLES are known as *hyoshigi-giri* after the wooden blocks used by nightwatchmen in times past. Vegetables such as radish and carrot are cut along the grain into sticks.

CUBE CUTTING is known as *sainomo-giri*, in which food is cut into 1/2 in (1 cm) cubes.

CUCUMBER FANS known in Japan as *senmen-giri*, are made by using a cross-cut piece of cucumber that is sliced from one side at narrow intervals, leaving the other side connected.

CUCUMBER PEAKS are cut from a 2 1/2 in (6 cm) length of cucumber by making a cut through the center without cutting through the top or bottom. A diagonal cut on each side connects the top of the cut with the bottom, so that when the pieces are divided each has an identical peaked shape.

a. Clapper-cut rectangles
b. Mincing
c. Slicing
d. Katsura-muki

HEXAGONAL CUTTING is applied to firm vegetables such as turnips, which are cut flat at each end, then hexagonally at the sides.

KATSURA-MUKI are tissue-thin slices of giant white radish cut into fine shreds.
See also: RADISH, GIANT WHITE

PLUM BLOSSOMS are made from slices of carrot or radish by cutting a five-sided section, rounding off the edges to give five rounded petals, then slicing. Known as *baika-giri*, they are used in vegetable dishes and as a garnish.

ROLLING WEDGE is a cut for pointed vegetables such as burdock, carrot or cucumber. The vegetable is rotated while being cut at a sharp angle to give uneven pieces.

JAPAN, GARNISHES: The beautiful garnishes that are used in Japan to decorate *sashimi* are collectively known as *tsuma* and include a number of leaves, sprouts, petals and stems. Other garnishes used in Japan are attractively cut citron rind, carved and sliced cucumber and radish, pine needles, bamboo, chrysanthemum and maple leaves, which reflect the season, and ginger shoots or sliced ginger.

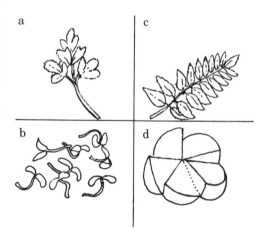

a. Bofu
b. Benitade
c. Kinome
d. Plum blossom carved from vegetables

BAKUDAI: A type of bean or pea used to garnish *sashimi* and vinegared salads in Japan. The pods are opened by steeping in tepid tea for about 20 minutes and then the seeds are removed and washed in cold water.

BENI SHOGA: Otherwise known as *gari*, thinly sliced or shredded ginger pickled in vinegar, of a pale to scarlet-pink color.

BENITADE: Minuscule, wine-red sprouts with short stems and two petals or leaves. They have a slightly tangy taste. Usually added to a dish in a clump.

BOFU: Slender red stems from young parsnips are used for their attractive appearance as a garnish, particularly on dishes such as *sushi* and *sashimi*. A pin is used to split the stems lengthways into quarters, which are curled in ice water.

CUCUMBER: Paper-thin slices of the tiny Japanese cucumber, *kyuri*, decorate *sushi* platters and salads. Very tiny cucumbers with their flowers still attached, known as *hanatsuki kyuri*, are a popular garnish, as are small whole cucumbers with one end pared to a point.
See also: JAPAN, CUTTING AND SLICING TECHNIQUES

HAJIKAMI SHOGA: Literally "blushing ginger," pink-colored ginger shoots that garnish grilled food.

KIKU: Chrysanthemum flowers or leaves decorate an assortment of dishes. White radish, pared into a chrysanthemum flower, is another commonly used garnish.
See also: CHINA, GARNISHES

KINOME: The delicate, bright-green sprigs of the fragrant prickly ash tree, which also provide the spice known as Sichuan pepper in China and *sansho* in Japan.

MITSUBA is a low-growing plant related to parsley and resembles the flat-leaf parsley used in Italian cooking. Each slender, deep-green stalk is crowned with three flat, serrated-edged leaves of a bright mid-green. It has a subtle flavor. Used chopped or whole as a garnish. Sometimes several stems are tied together in a knot.
Also known as Japanese parsley; trefoil

See also: EGG CUSTARD STEAMED IN A TEACUP (recipe)

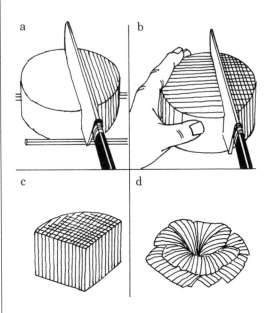

Slices of giant white radish carved into a "chrysanthemum"
a. Make deep downwards cuts close together
b. Turn and cut in opposite direction
c. Cut into quarters for smaller flowers
d. Gently fan out "petals" with fingers

Tied mitsuba stems
Group three stems together, carefully tie into a knot near the leaves, fan out leaves, trim stems to 2 in (5 cm)

PINE NEEDLES: Pairs of fresh pine needles are used as a garnish or as delicate skewers for certain grilled foods. They are also used in certain steaming and simmering methods to impart a subtle flavor to a dish.

YUZU: The golden yellow citron provides its rind as garnish, carved into traditional shapes to add to soups and custards. The most typical shape is achieved with a rectangle of rind into which three cuts are made, then the strips are lifted and crossed over.

JAPAN RECIPES

Appetizers
Beef Sashimi
Clear Soup with Kamaboko
Dengaku
Egg Custard Steamed in a Teacup
Omelette Roll
Miso Soup
Nori-maki Sushi
Sashimi with Lemon
Sashimi Platter
Sushi
Vinegared Seaweed with Crab and Cucumber

Main Courses
Buckwheat Noodles wth Chicken
Oysters in a Pot
Rice in a Lacquered Box with Beef and Onions
Sake-simmered Mackerel
Salt-broiled Shrimp
Scattered Rice
Sukiyaki
Tempura
Teriyaki
Tonkatsu
Yakitori
Udon Noodles in Broth

Accompaniments
Bean Curd Cubes Crisp-fried
Chilled Fine Noodles with Mushrooms
Daikon Nimono
Eggplant in Sauce

(cont'd)

(Japan Recipes cont'd)

Green Beans with Sesame-miso Dressing
Shiitake Mushrooms with Ponzu Sauce

Desserts
Sweet Red Bean Soup with Mochi
Sweet Potato Purée

MENUS
(See recipes)

DINNER MENU
Serves 6

Sashimi with Lemon

Egg Custard Steamed in a Teacup
Vinegared Seaweed with Crab and Cucumber
Yakitori
Salt-broiled Shrimp
Chilled Fine Noodles with Mushrooms
Eggplant in Sauce

Rice
Pickles
Miso Soup

Sweet Potato Purée

JAPANESE FAMILY MEAL

Clear Soup with Kamaboko

Tonkatsu
Daikon Nimono

JAPANESE APRICOT: see PLUMS

JAPANESE CUCUMBER: see CUCUMBER

JAPANESE EGGPLANT: see EGGPLANT, JAPANESE

JAPANESE GELATIN: see AGAR AGAR

JAPANESE PEAR: (*Pyrus pyrifolio* Nakai) There are several types of firm, white-fleshed pear grown in Japan and China. The shape can vary from a flattened globe to the traditional pear shape, with skin that is usually a dull greenish yellow. The texture is crunchy and occasionally slightly dry, the flavor semisweet. In China these pears are eaten raw as a fruit, often dipped in salted water to flavor them. In the past they were steamed or fried and served as a vegetable, often with game. During his travels through China in the Sung Dynasty (AD 960–1279), Marco Polo noted that large, soft, fragrant, white pears were eaten. They are now readily available in Western countries, and while they may be expensive, they make delightful eating.
Also known as *pei sooli, ta suan li* (China); *nijuseki* (Japan); Beijing (Peking) pear; nashi; pear apple; snowpear

JAPANESE PICKLES: see TSUKEMONO
JAPANESE RICE VINEGAR: see RICE VINEGAR
JASMINE ESSENCE/WATER: see FLAVORINGS
JAVANESE PARKIA: see PARKIA

JELLYFISH: (*Rhopilema esculenta*) The salted and sun-dried skin of the mantle of the marine jellyfish is a food much enjoyed by the Chinese. Although it has little taste, except for a slight sea flavor, it is liked for its crunchy texture, which Westerners have been known to liken to that of rubber bands. Jellyfish looks like a piece of creamish-yellow plastic and is sold by the whole piece or in small packs, precut into shreds. It needs to be soaked in lukewarm water for several hours but requires no further cooking. Excesses of temperature, either boiling or freezing, will toughen it to an inedible state. Jellyfish is usually finely shredded, marinated in vinegar or other acidulating ingredients and served as a salad, generally with seaweed or cucumber. The flavor of Oriental sesame oil transforms this unusual combination into a delightful, crunchy salad that is usually served at the beginning of a meal.
Also known as *hoi git* (Cantonese); *hai zhe* (China); *sua* (Vietnam)
See also: JELLYFISH SALAD (recipe)

Fresh jellyfish

JELLYFISH SALAD
Serves 6

4 oz (125 g) salted jellyfish, soaked
water
1 small cucumber, shredded
1/2 giant white radish, shredded
1 1/2 tsps light soy sauce
2 1/2 tsps rice vinegar
1 1/2 tsps finely chopped garlic
Oriental sesame oil
salt
pepper
sugar

Drain jellyfish. Cover with warm water and soak 20 minutes. Drain again and mix with cucumber and radish. Mix soy and vinegar with garlic adding sesame oil, salt, pepper and sugar to taste. Toss with salad; serve cold. Shredded cooked chicken can be added.

JEMUJU: (*JEH-MOO-JOO*, Malaysia) see CARAWAY SEED
JEN-SHEN: (*YAN SUM*, China) see GINSENG
JERN CHA: (*JEUNG CHA*, China) see CAMPHOR WOOD CHIPS
JEW'S EAR: see CLOUD EAR FUNGUS
JERUK ASEM: (*JEH-ROOK AH-SEM*, Malaysia) see CITRON
JERUK BODONG: (*JEH-ROOK BO-DONG*, Indonesia) see CITRON

JEUNG: (*GEUNG*, China) see GINGER

JIAN: (*JEUN*) see CHINA, COOKING METHODS (SHALLOW-FRYING)

JIANG: (*JEUNG*, China) see BEAN PASTES AND SAUCES

JICAMA: see YAM BEAN

JIDAN: (*GAI-DARN*, China) see EGG

JINTAN: (*JEAN-TUN*, Indonesia) see CUMIN (WHITE)

JINTAN MANIS: (*JEAN-TUN MAH-NIECE*, Indonesia, Malaysia) see ANISEED; CUMIN (BLACK); FENNEL

JINTAN PUTIH: (*JEAN-TUN POO-TEAH*, Malaysia) see CUMIN (WHITE)

JIRA PANI: (*JEE-RAA PAA-NEE*, India) A tart, strongly seasoned beverage served in the northern Indian state of Uttar Pradesh.
Also known as cumin water

JIRA PANI
Yields 6 cups

2 tbsps concentrated tamarind
2 tbsps sugar or jaggery
1 tsp salt
5^{1}/$_{2}$ cups (44 fl oz / 1.30 l) water
1 tbsp cumin seeds
pinch of asafoetida
pepper
1 tsp ground ginger
^{1}/$_{2}$ tsp chili powder
^{1}/$_{2}$ cup (1 oz / 30 g) chopped fresh mint leaves

Dissolve tamarind, sugar and salt in 1 cup (8 fl oz/250 ml) of the water. Toast cumin, *asafoetida*, pepper, ginger and chili powder in a dry pan; grind to a fine powder. Stir into the tamarind water. Add mint and the remaining 4^{1}/$_{2}$ cups water. Serve over ice cubes.

JIU LA CHOY: (*JUE LAR CHOY*, China) see CABBAGE, CHINESE

JOOK: (*JUK*, China) see CONGEE

JOSHINKO: (*JO-SHEE-NN-KO*, Japan) see FLOURS AND THICKENERS

JOU KUEI: (*JO KWAI*, China) see CINNAMON

JUDAS EAR: see CLOUD EAR FUNGUS

JUJUBE: (*Zizyphus jujuba*) The jujube is usually known as the Chinese red date. It has a firm, red, slightly wrinkled skin and tender, fibrous flesh similar to that of a black date. It is an ancient fruit that is known to have grown in China from prehistoric times. In northern China there are several edible types of jujube, including one with a very sour taste. A sweetish-flavored red jujube is the type most commonly found in the market; two popular types are *yu land* and *mushinghong*. It is called the "food of harmony" as it calms the nerves, combats insomnia and builds up the blood. It is, therefore, included in food for invalids and is added to many different types of soups, stews and sweet dishes. It is particularly good in soup with watercress. In traditional Chinese households, jujubes were cooked with millet or rice as a kind of sweet porridge or were dipped into sugar syrup or honey to make a glazed sweetmeat. Jujubes are also used to some extent in Korean cooking. Although they have grown in India for centuries they are rarely used there today.

Black dates, which the Chinese named "Persian jujubes," were introduced to China from Turkestan and are used to some extent as a filling in pastries and sweet buns.
Also known as *hung jo, hung zao* (China); Chinese date; Indian jujube; jujube nuts; red date
See also: DATE

JUK: (*JUK*, China) see CONGEE

JUNG-JONG: (*JEONG-JONG*, Korea) see WINE, ASIAN

K

KABULI CHANNA: (*KAA-BU-LEE CHA-NAA*, India) see CHICK-PEA

KACANG DJONG: (*KAH-CHUNG JONG*, Malaysia) see BEAN SPROUT

KACANG IJO: (*KAH-CHUNG E-JOE*, Malaysia) see BEAN SPROUT

KACANG METE: (*KAH-CHUNG MAW-TAY*, Indonesia) see CASHEW NUT

KACANG MONYET: (*KAH-CHUNG MAW-NYET*, Indonesia) see CASHEW NUT

KACANG PADI: (*KAH-CHUNG PA-DE*, Malaysia) see BEAN SPROUT

KADJU: (*KAA-JOO*, India) see CASHEW NUT

KAFFIR LIME: (*Citrys hystrix*) A type of lime grown in Southeast Asia. The fruit has a textured, knobbly, mid-green skin and is the size of a large lime. Although kaffir lime juice is used in cooking, it is the leaves that are the most important ingredient. Fresh or dried, they are used in soups, curries and as a condiment. Added, like bay leaves, to a gravy, sauce or soup, they slowly release flavor during cooking, and are particularly good with fish. In former times in Singapore the leaves were used when washing the hair to give it fragrance; in Thailand it was believed that this fragrance would ward off evil spirits. The juice is also used medicinally.

Powdered kaffir lime leaf is sold in small packs in Asian stores. It is convenient, although not a good substitute for the dried whole leaf, which is generally readily available and keeps well in a sealed spice jar.

Also known as *shauk-nu, shauk-waing* (Burma); *krauch soeuch* (Cambodia); *jeruk perut* (Indonesia); *daun limau purut* (Malaysia, Singapore); *bai makrut, makrut* (Thailand)
See also: GREEN SHRIMP CURRY (recipe); LIME

KAGA: (*KAH-GAH*, Japan) see CUCUMBER (JAPANESE)

KAI KEM: (*PHAI PHEM*, Thailand) see DUCK EGG, SALTED

KAI LAARN: (*GAI LARN*, China) see CABBAGE, CHINESE (GAI LARN)

KAJANG MERAH: (*KAH-CHUNG MEAH-RAH*, Indonesia) see BLACK-EYED PEA (BEAN)

KAJANG PANJANG: (*KAH-CHUNG PUN-JUNG*, Indonesia) see BLACK-EYED PEA (BEAN)

KAJU: (*KAA-JOO*, India) see CASHEW NUT

KAKDA: (*KAK-DAA*, India) see CUCUMBER (YELLOW)

KAKI: (*KAA-KEE*, Japan) see PERSIMMON

KALA JIRA: (*KA-LA JI-RA*, India) see CUMIN (BLACK)

KALAMANSI: (*KA-LA-MAN-SEE*, Philippines) Native lemon, with the appearance of a small, round lime with bright green skin and yellow flesh and juice. Used to add a sour flavor to some foods, such as the tart *sinigang*, its most popular use is as a refreshing drink or cocktail mixer. The juice is readily available canned and concentrated. The rind is candied to make a sweet–tart snack or garnishes for desserts and ice cream.
See also: LIME; NOODLES FILIPINO (recipe); SINIGANG

KALE: see CABBAGE, CHINESE (SEEN CHOY)
KALE, BAMBOO SHOOTS AND CONPOY CRISP-FRIED: (recipe) see CABBAGE, CHINESE

KALLAPPAMS: (*KA-LA-UP-UMS*, Sri Lanka) see APPA

KALONJI: (*KA-LON-JEE*, India) see NIGELLA

KAMABOKO: (*KAH-MAH-BOW-KO*, Japan) Firm, slightly rubbery-textured cakes of ground fish are a popular ingredient in Japanese cooking. They are added to soups, simmered dishes and noodles and are served as hors d'oeuvre. The name comes from an ancient word for the "cattail" reed. Fish is puréed, bound with a starch—usually *kuzu*, arrowroot or potato—formed into blocks and steamed. Sometimes food color—most often pink–red, but occasionally green, yellow or brown—is brushed over the top to give an attractive slice when cut. It is sold in vacuum-sealed packs that should be refrigerated and used within one week. To use, slice *kamaboko* and add in final stages of cooking, as it needs only to be heated.

CHIKUWA are fish cakes formed into a cylindrical shape around a bamboo sliver which remains after they have been steamed. This is the most ancient form of *kamaboko* and has a grilled surface.

HANPEN is a soft-textured fish cake, sold in squares or rounded shapes, which is usually eaten as a snack, dipped in soy sauce. It may also be deep-fried, grilled or poached.

ITA-KAMABOKO is *kamaboko*, shaped onto a small rectangle of wood, usually cypress, which in olden times imparted its flavor. Today, however, it is done only for aesthetic reasons. The fish cake is white and the surface may be colored or grilled to give it a brown tone and toasted flavor.

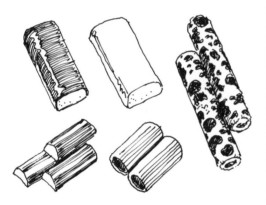

Various types of kamaboko

CLEAR SOUP WITH KAMABOKO
Serves 4

2¹/₂ *cups (20 fl oz / 625 ml)* dashi
¹/₂ *tsp salt*
1 tbsp tamari *soy sauce*
4 slices kamaboko
4 dried shiitake *mushrooms, steamed and halved*
1 tbsp sliced scallion (spring / green onion) tops
4 pieces yuzu *rind*

Heat *dashi* and pour into covered soup bowls. Divide remaining ingredients among the bowls and serve covered.

NATUTO is a fish cake in cylindrical shape which is marked with a swirling design picked out in red coloring. As a result, slices make a decorative garnish in soups.
Also known as fish cakes; fish paste; Japanese fish balls; Japanese fish sausage
See also: CLEAR SOUP WITH KAMABOKO (recipe); FLOURS AND THICKENERS (KUZU)

KAMIAS: (*CA-MI-YAS*, Philippines) see BELIMBING

KAMPYO: (*KAM-PYOO*, Japan) The flesh of the bottle gourd is shaved into thin sheets, cut into ribbon-like strips and dried. In Japan these dried gourd strips are used in rolled *sushi* as a filling, and function as edible ties for various little parcels of food. Sold in small packs, they should be washed and kneaded to soften, using tepid water and plenty of salt. They should be rinsed thoroughly and boiled until tender, but not too soft for effective use.
Also known as dried gourd strips
See also: MELONS AND GOURDS; SUSHI

KANGKONG: (*KUNG-KONG*, Indonesia, Malaysia) (*Ipomoea reptans, I. aquatica*) A green-leafed vegetable of the Convolvulaceae (sweet potato) family, this perennial creeping plant thrives in exceptionally damp to pond-like environments. It grows wild along the edges of waterways. It is also planted on the pond banks of fish farms so that the fish may feed on it. Its leaves have an appearance, texture and taste similar to spinach. There are two varieties in common use throughout Southeast Asia. One has pale green, triangular-shaped leaves and thick hollow stems; the other has deeper green leaves and narrower, hollow stems. In Thailand, yet another variety has a pink-red tinge to the stems. It is eaten raw in salads and cooked as a vegetable. Chinese and Malays enjoy it stir-fried with shrimp sauce and in Indonesia it is used in *gado gado*.
Also known as *kong syin tsai, ong choi* (China); *kangkong* (Philippines); *pak bung* (Thailand); *rau muong* (Vietnam); swamp cabbage; swamp spinach; water convolvulus; water spinach
See also: AMARANTH; SPINACH; WATER SPINACH WITH SHRIMP SAUCE (recipe)

Kangkong

WATER SPINACH WITH SHRIMP SAUCE
Serves 4–6

1/2 cup (4 oz / 125 ml) vegetable oil
1 shredded scallion (spring / green onion)
1 1/2 tsps minced garlic
1 lb (500 g) kangkong (water spinach)
2 tsps shrimp (prawn) sauce
salt
pepper
1/4 cup (2 fl oz / 60 ml) chicken stock
1/2 tsp cornstarch (cornflour)

Heat oil in a wok. Stir-fry scallion and garlic briefly. Add spinach and stir-fry for 1–2 minutes on medium heat. Add shrimp sauce and salt and pepper to taste. Pour on chicken stock mixed with cornstarch. Stir until thickened.

KANTEN: (*KAN-TEN*, Japan) see AGAR AGAR

KAO: (*HAU*) see CHINA, COOKING METHODS (ROASTING)

KAPI: (*KA-PI*, Thailand) see FISH PASTE

KARA-AGE: (*KAH-RAH-AH-GUE*) see JAPAN, COOKING METHODS

KARABU NATI: (*KA-RAA-BU NA-TI*, Sri Lanka) see CLOVES

KARAPINCHA: (*KA-RA-PIN-CHA*, Sri Lanka) see CURRY LEAF

KARE-KARE: (*KA-RE KA-RE*, Philippines) A meat and vegetable dish made with beef shank, oxtail or tripe thickened with chopped peanuts. It is traditionally served with sautéed *bagoong* made from small salted and fermented shrimp (*alamang*).
Also known as *kari kari* (Philippines)
See also: BAGOONG

KARE-KARE

4 lbs (2 kgs) beef shin
1 cup (8 oz / 250 g) lard, softened
2 tbsps annatto seeds
2 tbsps minced garlic
2 large onions, sliced
2 tbsps soy or fish sauce
2 cups (12 oz / 375 g) diced turnip
3 cups (1 lb / 500 g) sliced green beans
salt
black pepper
3/4 cup (4 oz / 125 g) peanuts, roasted
1/3 cup (2 oz / 60 g) rice, roasted

Ask the butcher to saw the shin bones into 1 1/2 in (4 cm) lengths. Drop into a large pot of boiling water, return to a boil and simmer for 5 minutes. Drain. In a large saucepan melt the lard and fry the *annatto* seeds until the fat is red. Strain off and discard the seeds, fry the garlic and onions in the colored lard to soften and color. Remove. Fry the meat, 4–5 pieces at a time, until evenly colored. Add water to cover and soy or fish sauce; bring to a boil. Cook for 1 3/4–2 hours over medium-low heat. Add onions and vegetables with salt and pepper and cook until almost tender. Grind peanuts and rice to a coarse powder. Add to the stew and cook until the sauce is thick. Check seasoning and serve hot.

KARIBU: (*KAH-REE-BOO*, Indonesia) see BUFFALO

KARIKA: (*KAH-REE-KAH*, Japan) see CUCUMBER

KARUPILLAM: (*KAH-ROO-PEEL-LUM*, Malaysia) see CURRY LEAF

KASHIA KEIHI: (*KAH-SHE-AH KEI-HEE*, Japan) see CASSIA

KASHMIRI CHILI: see CHILI

KASHMIRI MASALA: see MASALA

KASHMIRI MIRICH: (*KAASH-MEE-REE MIRCH*, India) see CHILI

KASHMIRI TEA
Serves 2

2 cups (16 fl oz / 500 ml) water
2 tsps green tea leaves
2 green cardamom pods, peeled and seeds
crushed
4 almonds, blanched and chopped
1 whole clove
1/2 in (1 cm) cinnamon stick

Boil water in a small kettle. Add tea leaves, cardamom, almonds, clove and cinnamon. Reheat.

KAS KAS: (*KUSH KUSH*, Malaysia) see POPPY SEED

KATAKURI: (*KAH-TAH-KOO-REE*, Japan) see FLOURS AND THICKENERS

KATI: (China) This traditional Chinese measurement weighs approximately 1¹/₄ lbs (625 g) and is still in use today in Chinese vegetable markets.

KATIEM: (*KA-THI-EM*, Thailand) see GARLIC

KATNIM: (*KAT-NEEM*, India) see CURRY LEAF

Thali with Indian meal in katoris

KATORI: (*KA-TO-REE*, India) These small bowls are often used to serve food in at Indian meals. They are usually arranged on a *thali* or *thal*, a brass tray or short-legged table. Several dishes, plus bread or rice, pickles or chutney, are served together and the meal is eaten directly from the *thali*. *Katoris* are also used for cooking individual items such as the steamed bread known as *idli*.
Also known as *kachora* (Nepal)

KATSUOBUSHI: (*KAH-TZU-O BOO-SHI*, Japan) see BONITO; FISH, PRESERVED (DRIED AND SALTED)

KATSUO-DASHI: (*KAH-TZU-O-DAH-SHI*, Japan) see DASHI

KATSUO-KEZURI-KI: (*KAH-TZU-O-KE-ZOO-REE-KEE*, Japan) see BONITO

KATSURA-MUKI: (*KAH-TZU-RAH-MOO-KEE*, Japan) see RADISH, GIANT WHITE

KAU FU: (*HAUFU*, China) see GLUTEN

KAYU MANIS: (*KA-YOU MAH-NIECE*, Indonesia, Malaysia) see CINNAMON

KEBAB: (India) People usually think of *kebabs* as cubes of meat shredded on skewers, often with other ingredients, and grilled over a charcoal barbecue. But the term actually encompasses any type of meat cooked on a barbecue or grill or in the oven, from a whole leg of lamb to narrow strips of meat or *koftas* (sausages) of ground meat. The criterion is that the meat be tenderized by marination—usually in an acidulating ingredient such as yogurt, vinegar or lemon juice—and cooked until the surface is lightly charred and crusty. The inside of the meat is uniformly tender and succulent. Lamb or mutton are the meats most commonly used in India. Finely grated unripe mango or papaya are effective as tenderizing agents and are combined with yogurt, garlic, ginger and spices to soften and flavor the meat so that it cooks quickly. A charcoal brazier or small charcoal stove covered with a wire grid, or the *tandoor* oven, are used for cooking *kebabs* in India.
See also: TANDOOR; UTENSILS (BARBECUES AND CHARCOAL BURNERS)

KEBABS OF GROUND MEAT
Serves 4

1¼ lbs (600 g) boneless lamb
1½ tsps minced ginger
1 tsp minced garlic
¼ tsp ground cloves
1 green cardamom pod, peeled and seeds
ground
½ tsp ground cumin
1 tsp ground coriander
1½ tbsps besan flour, toasted
2 tsps ground white poppy seeds
½ cup (4 fl oz / 125 ml) plain (natural) yogurt
1½ tsps salt
ghee, melted
onion rings
lime wedges

Chop lamb and grind to a smooth
paste in a food processor. Mix in remaining ingredients with yogurt
and salt. Knead until smooth. Press
the meat onto oiled metal skewers in
sausage shapes and roll across a
greased surface to smooth. Brush
with ghee; grill or barbecue until
done. The meat should be tender
and moist inside and the
surface crisp and fairly dark.
Serve with onion rings
and lime wedges.

KECAP ASIN: (*KET-CHUP A-SEEN*, Indonesia)
see SOY SAUCE, SWEET AND SALTY

KECAP CAIR: (*KET-CHUP CHA-EAR*, Malaysia)
see SOY SAUCE (LIGHT)

KECAP HITAM: (*KET-CHUP HE-TUM*, Indonesia) see SOY SAUCE, SWEET AND SALTY

KECAP IKAN: (*KET-CHUP I-KAN*, Indonesia)
see FISH SAUCE

KECAP MANIS: (*KET-CHUP MAH-NIECE*,
Indonesia) see SOY SAUCE, SWEET AND SALTY

KECAP PETIS: (*KET-CHUP PET-IS*, Indonesia)
see FISH SAUCE

KECOMBRANG: (*KEH-CHOM-BRUNG*, Indonesia) see GINGER BUD

KEDGEREE: (*KHI-CHE-RHEE*, India) An English adaptation of the Indian dish of cooked
rice known as *kichardi* or *khichhari* which was
a favorite in many parts of India. The Mogul
emperor, Aurangzeb, was known to be particularly fond of it, as were the Gujeratis, who
cooked an especially lavish version heavy with
spices, nuts and raisins. Kedgeree, in its English mode, is a moist dish of rice and fish, while
in India *bhuni khichhari* is quite dry. A
moister type, known as *gili khichhari,* is given
to children and invalids.
See also: SPROUTED LENTIL KICHARDI (recipe)

KEEM: (*GEEM*, Korea) see SEAWEED (NORI)

KELA: (*KE-LAA*, India) see BANANA

KELAPA MUDA: (*KEH-LA-PA MOO-DA*, Indonesia) see COCONUT

KELAPA SENTENGAH TUA: (*KEH-LA-PA SEH-
TEH-NGA TOO-WA*, Indonesia, Malaysia) see CO-
CONUT

KELEDEK: (*KEH-LEH-DECK*, Malaysia) see
SWEET POTATO

KEMANGI: (*KEH-MAN-GEE*, Indonesia) see
BASIL (SELASIH)

KEMIRI: (*KEH-ME-REE*, Indonesia) see
CANDLENUT

KENCUR: (*KEN-CHOOR*, Indonesia) see
GALANGAL, LESSER

KENIKIR: (*KEH-NEE-KEER*, Indonesia) see DILL

KEPILLAGA: (*KEH-PEEL-LAH-GAR*, Indonesia)
see CARDAMOM

KERAPU BARA: (*KEH-RAH-POO BAH-RAH*, Malaysia) see GAROUPA

KERAPU LODI: (*KERA-POO LODEE*, India) see
GAROUPA

KERE: (*KEH-RAY*, Indonesia) see CLAM

KESAR: (*KE-SAR*, India) see SAFFRON

KESONG PUTI: (*KE-SONG POO-TEE*, Philippines) A type of cottage cheese usually made in
the home from water buffalo (*karabao*) milk.
Also known as *quesong puti* (Philippines)
See also: PANIR

KETA CAVIAR: (*KETAH*, Japan) see CAVIAR
(IKURA)

KETIMUN: (*KEH-TEA-MOON*, Indonesia) see
CUCUMBER (YELLOW)

KETUMBAR: (*KEH-TOMB-BAR*, Indonesia, Malaysia) see CORIANDER

KEWRA ESSENCE/EXTRACT: (*Pandanus odoratissimus*) A flavoring essence used in Indian and Sri Lankan cooking, mostly in sweets, but also in rice dishes cooked for festive occasions. It came into vogue in the Punjab under Mogul rule and remains an appreciated taste in the state of Uttar Pradesh. Extracted from the blossoms of a variety of screw pine, it is stronger than its cousin *Pandanus amaryllifolius,* the leaves of which are used extensively in Malaysia and Indonesia to flavor curries, rice and sweet dishes.

It is sold in small bottles, usually with dropper tops or inserts and its fragrance and flavor are excessively strong. It should, therefore, be stored carefully and used with discretion.

Also known as *ruh kewra* (India); *kevada* (Nepal); *lamchiak* (Thailand)
See also: PANDANUS LEAF

KEZURI-BUSHI: (*KE-ZOO-REE-BOO-SHI*, Japan) see BONITO

KHA: (*KHAA*, Thailand) see GALANGAL, GREATER

KHAJUR: (*KHA-JOOR*, India) see DATE

KHA MIN: (*KHAA MIN*, Thailand) see TURMERIC

KHAMIR: (*KHA-MEER*, India) A natural yeast ferment made from flour and yogurt, used in India for leavening *naans* and various other soft breads.

Also known as bread yeast, *ibu roti* (Malaysia)
See also: BREAD, INDIAN

KHAMIR

3/4 *cup (3 oz / 90 g) maida flour*
2 tbsps plain (natural) yogurt, at room temperature
2 tsps sugar
2 tbsps warm water
1 tsp black peppercorns (optional)

Mix ingredients together; beat well. Leave in warm place overnight. Discard peppercorns before using. *Khamir* should be used within 24 hours.

KHANOM: (*KHAA-NOM*, Thailand) In Thailand sweet dishes are popular and are served throughout the day. The many liquid desserts, puddings and sweetmeats made in Thailand are known collectively by this name.
Also known as *kanom, kong wan*

KHANOM CHINE: (*KHAA-NOM JEEN*, Thailand) Although the name suggests that these Thai noodles are named after a type of Chinese noodle, they are in fact exclusively Thai. They are little bite-size bundles of cooked rice noodles that are sold fresh in the markets. They are usually served with curries and several hot sauces. They need not be cooked, but for hygienic reasons most Thai housewives choose to steam them before use.

KHAO CHAE: (*KAO CHE*, Thailand) see THAILAND; RICE (TREATED)

KHAO MAO: (*KAO-MAO*, Thailand) see RICE (TREATED)

KHAO PHOUNE: (*KA-OO POON*, Laos) A popular soup-noodle breakfast meal of rice vermicelli in a thick, creamy sauce of coconut milk with meat and/or fish, similar to the Indonesian *laksa* and the Burmese *mohinga*. The cooked vermicelli is placed in large bowls, topped with shredded banana flowers, bean sprouts, salad greens and herbs, then covered with hot coconut sauce flavored with chilies and ground peanuts.
See also: LAKSA; LAOTIAN TRADITIONAL NOODLE FISH (recipe); MOHINGA (recipe)

KHAO TOM GUNG: (*KHAO TOM KUNG*, Thailand) see CONGEE

KHA-WEL: (*KER-WER*, Burma) see CUTTLEFISH

KHEERA: (*KHEE-RA*, India) see CUCUMBER (YELLOW)

KHING: (*KING*, Thailand) see GINGER

KHING DONG: (*KING DONG*, Thailand) see GINGER (GINGER PRESERVE)

KHNEHEY: (*KA-NEY*, Cambodia) see GINGER

KHOYA: (*KO-YAA*, India) A thick, creamy substance produced by the reduction of milk until only the solids remain. It is compressed into cakes and sold commercially for use in

Indian fudge and other sweetmeats and to enrich sweet dishes. *Khoya* is also used to add a rich creaminess to savory dishes and curries, although for this purpose its counterpart, *malai,* is usually preferred. *Khoya* has a raw, milky taste and may require a quick fry in ghee before use. A granular form of *khoya* is made by adding lemon juice to the milk at the beginning of reduction.

Also known as *khoa* (India); *khuwa* (Nepal)
See also: KULFI (recipe); MALAI; PANIR

KHOYA
Yields 4 oz (125 g)

4 cups (1 qt / 1 l) fresh whole milk

Pour milk into a wide pan; bring to a boil. Simmer while slowly stirring, until the liquid reduces to a thick, dryish paste. It may take as long as 45 minutes. Press into a bowl, cover and refrigerate until needed.

KHUM: (*KHUM*, India) see CLOUD EAR FUNGUS

KIKU: (*KEE-KU*, Japan) see CHRYSANTHEMUM; JAPAN, GARNISHES

KIKUNA: (*KEE-KU-NA*, Japan) see CHRYSANTHEMUM

KIKURAGE: (*KEE-KU-RA-GUE*, Japan) see CLOUD EAR FUNGUS

KILAWIN: (*KEE-LA-WIN*, Philippines) see PHILIPPINES, COOKING METHODS

KIMCHI: (*GIM-CHEE*, Korea) A pungent, fermented pickle made from chopped Napa/Peking cabbage seasoned with salt, garlic and chilies. Adored by the Koreans, who rarely serve a meal without it, *kimchi* can be something of an acquired taste as it has a powerful flavor, a pervasive smell and is usually extremely chili-hot. *Kimchi* is made commercially and sold in small plastic tubs, but it is also still made in many Korean households using a favorite family recipe. It is packed into large pots and is stored underground to ferment and mature. It is retrieved throughout the year to provide much of the vegetable content of the Korean diet. *Kimchi* is usually served as a side dish but can also be used in cooking. A popular example is *kimchi jun,* which is sliced beef and *kimchi* fried in a thin egg batter.

Also known as Korean cabbage pickle
See also: CABBAGE, CHINESE (NAPA); CABBAGE, PICKLED

KIMCHI
Yields 2 lbs (1 kg)

2 lbs (1 kg) Napa cabbage
1 tbsp salt
2 tbsps chopped scallions (spring / green onions)
1 tbsp minced garlic
1 tbsp minced ginger
1/2 cup (4 fl oz / 125 ml) light soy sauce
1 1/2 tsps sugar
1/2 cup (4 fl oz / 125 ml) white vinegar
1 tbsp chili flakes
Oriental sesame oil

Chop the cabbage coarsely and place in a glass dish. Sprinkle with salt and let stand for 3–4 hours until wilted. Squeeze until the cabbage has softened, then drain off excess liquid and add all of the other ingredients, except the sesame oil. Transfer to sterilized jars, seal and leave in a cool place for at least 24 hours before using. It will keep for several weeks in the refrigerator. Sprinkle with sesame oil before use.

KINCHAY: (*KEEN-CHAY*, Philippines) see CELERY, CHINESE

KINILAW: (*KEE-NEE-LAU*) see PHILIPPINES, COOKING METHODS

KINOME: (*KEE-NO-ME*, Japan) see JAPAN, GARNISHES; SICHUAN PEPPERCORN

KINUGOSHI TOFU: (*KEE-NOO-GO-SHE TOH-WHO*, Japan) see BEAN CURD (SILK)

KIRIBOSHI DAIKON: (*KEE-REE-BOW-SHI DAH-EE-KON*, Japan) String-like strips of sun-dried giant white radish of a buff color. It is sold in cellophane-wrapped bundles. It is added to simmered dishes and broths for its flavor.
See also: RADISH, GIANT WHITE

KIRIN: (*KEE-REE-N*, Japan) see BEER, ASIAN

KICHIDI: (*KHI-CH-RHEE*, India) see KEDGEREE

KITHA NEEM: (*KEE-THA NEEM*, India) see CURRY LEAF

KLUAY: (*KLU-AY*, Thailand) see BANANA

KNIVES AND BOARDS: see UTENSILS, KNIVES AND BOARDS

KOBE STEAK: (*KOW-BE*) see BEEF

KOCHUJANG: (*GO-CHOO-JANG*, Korea) see BEAN PASTES AND SAUCES; CHILI PASTES, POWDERS AND SAUCES

KOFTA: (*KOF-TAA*, India) see INDIA, COOKING METHODS

KOHANA FU: (*KOW-HAH-NAH HU*, Japan) see GLUTEN

KOHLRABI: (*Brassica oleracea* L. var. *gongylodes* L.) This vegetable is not common in Asia except in the far north of China, India, Kashmir and Nepal. It has an unusual appearance, having a pale green or purple-tinged globe about the size of an orange, with firm stems branching from it evenly all over. It is similar to a turnip in taste and appearance, yet is closely related to the cabbage.
Also known as *gai laarn tau* (China); *ganth gobhi, knol-khol* (India)

Kohlrabi

KOI-KUCHI SHOYU: (*KOW-EE-KOO-CHEE SHOW-YOU*, Japan) see SOY SAUCE

KOMBU: (*COM-BU*, Japan) see SEAWEED

KONNYAKU: (*CON-NYA-KOO*, Japan) see AMORPHOPHALUS KONJAC

KOREA: Korean food is hearty and uncomplicated, robust in flavor and containing good natural ingredients. From the sea comes octopus, abalone and edible seaweed as well as *joet khal* (minuscule silvery fry that cook crisp and crunchy), crabs and crustaceans. Napa cabbage is grown in abundance. It is used as a fresh vegetable but, more importantly, it is made into *kimchi*, the potent chili-hot, salty, crunchy and pungent pickle that is served with every meal. *Kimchi* is also used extensively as an ingredient: it is added to soups and simmered dishes; chopped and added to fritters such as *bindae duk* made with ground mung beans, as well as to other fried foods. It is also used in stuffings and fillings for tiny pancakes such as *guchalpan*, with its nine different stuffing ingredients. The unique flavor of Korean food comes from a few simple seasonings: from soy sauce and bean pastes such as the potent *dhwen-jan*; from chili powder; from *silgochu* (dried chili shreds); and from sesame seeds, which are toasted and ground to a coarse powder. They are also added generously to marinades and dressings and are sprinkled with chopped scallions as garnish.

The Korean enjoys cook-at-the-table meals. What has become known as the Korean "barbecue" is cooked on a traditional domed hotplate—like the "Genghis Khan" griddle—or on a Mongolian barbecue plate in the center of the table over glowing charcoal or a gas flame. The Korean cooking term *kui* infers broiling or griddle cooking and encompasses the *bulgogi*—or barbecue of slivers of marinated chicken, beef or pork—and the *dwaeji* or *amsoh galbi kui* of marinated pork or beef short ribs. The barbecued meat is invariably accompanied by several small, mildly flavored or pickled side dishes, known as *namool* and the inevitable *kimchi*. In this country, where warming foods are a necessity through most of the year, *sinsulro*—a tabletop "steamboat" of bite-size fish balls, meat and vegetables, enhanced with toasted pine nuts and *ginkgo* nuts—is a traditional favorite. The richly-flavored broth is served at the end as a soup. Similar tastes are achieved in *cheegay* dishes, midway between a stew and a soup, and using seafoods or bean curd as their main ingredient. Soups, too, are popular. Many contain seaweed or bean sprouts; some are literally red-hot with chili powder.

Desserts are minimal and not dissimilar to those eaten in Japan, where *ginkgo* nuts, *azuki* beans, chestnuts and rice are the main ingredients. Pine needles are sometimes added to give an interesting regional flavor when small sweet dumplings are being steamed.

KOREA RECIPES

Appetizers
Scallion-Chili Beef Soup
Seaweed Soup

Main Courses
Bulgogi Barbecue
Cheegay of Fish
Shinsulro Hotpot

Accompaniments
Kimchi
Na Mool of Spinach
Radish Shreds
Salad of Warm and Spicy Cucumber
Seaweed Side Dish
Spiced Whitebait

MENU
(see recipes)

DINNER MENU
Serves 6–8

Seaweed Soup

Bulgogi Barbecue
Kimchi
Radish Shreds
Rice
Salad of Warm and Spicy Cucumber
Spiced Whitebait

KOREAN BEAN PASTE: see DHWEN-JANG

KOREAN CABBAGE: see CABBAGE, CHINESE (NAPA)

KOREAN CABBAGE PICKLES: see CABBAGE, PICKLE (KIMCHI)

KORMA OF MUTTON: (recipe) see LAMB

KORMA POWDER: see CURRY PASTES, POWDERS AND SAUCES

KOSHI-AN: (*KOW-SHE-AN-NN*, Japan) see AZUKI BEANS (AN)

KOYA TOFU: (*KOH-YAH TOH-WHO*, Japan) see BEAN CURD, FREEZE-DRIED

KOYENDORO: (*KOH-YAH-EN DO-RO*, Japan) see CORIANDER, FRESH

KRACHAI: (*KRACHAI*, Thailand) see GALANGAL, LESSER

KRAPOW: (*KRA-PAO*, Thailand) see BASIL (PURPLE)

KRAVEN: (*KRA-WAAN*, Thailand) see CARDAMOM

KRUNG GAENG: (*KROENG KAENG*, Thailand) This term describes the curry pastes used in Thai cooking. There are several distinct kinds, each with its particular flavor and color obtained by its blend of herbs and spices.

KRUNG GAENG KARE LEUNG is yellow curry paste, relatively mild in flavor, that uses fresh turmeric root for color.

KRUNG GAENG KEO WAN is green curry paste. Its extreme hotness results from the use of fresh green chilies to achieve the color. Usually made fresh, the paste can, however, be kept for up to a month in the refrigerator. For a milder flavor, use less chili than the recommended amount.

KRUNG GAENG PED DAENG is a red-colored curry paste that can be bought commercially. It is highly aromatic and of medium- to extreme-intensity, although not as hot as a standard green curry paste.

KRUNG GAENG SOM is an orange-colored curry paste that is usually used in a sour-flavored curried soup with shrimp, and also in other dishes with seafood.

NAM PRIK PAO, a type of strongly flavored curry paste made with roasted dried red chilies, is used in certain Thai dishes.

See also: GREEN CURRY PASTE (recipe); NAM PRIK PAO (recipe); ORANGE CURRY PASTE (recipe); RED CURRY PASTE (recipe)

KRUPUK: (*KE-ROO-POOK*, Indonesia) Hard, thin, dried wafers, processed in Indonesia and Malaysia, that are deep-fried to serve as a snack and to use as a garnish. They are usually made from shrimp (*krupuk udang*) or fish (*krupuk ikan*) and from tapioca starch and cassava chips (*singkong*) and *tempe* (*krupuk tempe*). A smaller variety, known as *emping,* with a strong, slightly bitter taste, is made from the *melinjo* nut (*emping melinjo*).

Also known as *emping, kerupuk* (Indonesia); cassava chips

See also: MELINJO

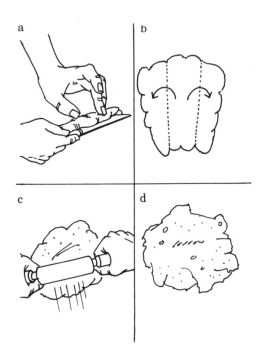

Making shrimp krupuk
a. Cut open shrimp and devein
b. Fold out flat
c. Roll very thin
d. Allow to dry

KRUPUK

peanut or vegetable oil
shrimp (prawn) crisps

Heat oil, until hot but not smoking, in a wok or deep pan. Cook 1–3 pieces at a time by placing in oil and pushing immediately below the surface. They should swell to at least twice their size, becoming crisp and light in color. Remove quickly from the oil to a rack covered with paper towels. Cooked *krupuk* can be stored in an airtight container for several weeks, but are usually best served at once.

KUBIS BUNGA: (*KOO-BEES BOO-NGA*, Indonesia, Malaysia) see CAULIFLOWER

KU CAI: (*KOO CAI*, Malaysia) see CHIVES, CHINESE (GARLIC)

KUEI: (*GWAI*, China) see CASSIA

KUI TEOW SEN LEK: (*KUAY TIEW SEN LEK*, Thailand) see NOODLES (RICE RIBBON)

KUI TEOW SEN YAI: (*KUAY TIEW SEN YAI*, Thailand) see NOODLES (RICE RIBBON)

KUKHURA KA PHOOL: (*KOO-KHOO-RAA KAAH-FULL*, Nepal) see EGG

KULCHAS: (*KUL-CHAA*, India) see BREAD, INDIAN

KULFI: (*KUL-FEE*, India) A rich, creamy ice cream made with full-cream milk and finely chopped almonds and pistachios, flavored with rose essence. It is frozen in little metal cones,

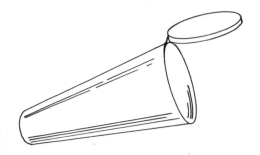

Kulfi mold with hinged lid

which give it a distinctive shape. *Kulfi* is easily made at home. It should be removed from the freezer a few minutes before serving to give it time to become soft enough to eat.

See also: CHATTI; PISTACHIO NUT; UTENSILS, CAKE AND DESSERT MAKING

KULFI
Serves 8

$4^1/2$ cups (1 qt / 1 l) milk
1 tbsp cornstarch (cornflour)
water
$^3/4$ cup ($5^1/2$ oz / 150 g) sugar
3 oz (90 g) khoya
2 tbsps pistachios, blanched and chopped
1 tbsp almonds, blanched and chopped
$1^1/2$ tsps rosewater

Boil milk until reduced by half. Mix cornstarch with cold water to a paste; stir into milk and simmer, stirring until the consistency of cream. Add sugar; stir to dissolve. Remove from heat; cool. Add *khoya*, nuts and rosewater. Pour mixture into conical *kulfi* molds or small metal dishes; cover with aluminum foil. Freeze for 3–4 hours. Remove from molds to serve.

KULITIS: (*KOO-LEE-TEES*, Philippines) see AMARANTH

KUMQUAT: (*Fortunella japonica*) Small, round or elongated orange-colored citrus fruits of which there are several common types grown in Asia. The *marumi* kumquat of Japan has a round shape and strong acid taste. The *nagami*, also of Japan, is oval in shape and acid in taste, and the *meiaw*, which grows both in China and Japan, is round and sweet and is the only one commonly eaten raw as a fruit.

The Chinese revere the kumquat, as they do the orange, for its fortuitous golden color. Small, potted kumquat trees bearing fruit are purchased for the family home, or given as gifts to friends at Chinese New Year to ensure good fortune for the year to come.

In former times in China, the skin or whole fruits of kumquat were steeped in honey and eaten as a confection, the best coming from Lingnan. Kumquats are used in making jams, jellies and preserves.

Also known as *marumi* (Japan); cumquat

KUNCHOI: (*KAN-CHOY*, China) see CELERY, CHINESE

KUNCHOR: (*COON-CHORE*, Malaysia) see GALANGAL, LESSER; ZEDOARY

KUNG YUE: (*GON YUE*, China) see ANCHOVY

KUNYIT: (*KOO-NYIT*, Malaysia) see TURMERIC

KUNYIT KERING: (*KOO-NYIT KEH-REENG*, Malaysia) see SAFFRON

KURI: (*KU-REE*, Japan) see CHESTNUT

KURIAMA-NI: (*KU-REE-AH-MAH-NEE*, Japan) see CHESTNUT (CANDIED)

KURUNDU: (*KU-RU-DHU*, Sri Lanka) see CINNAMON

KUS KUS: (*KHUS KHUS*, India) see POPPY SEED

KUWAI: (*KOO-WA-I*, Japan) see ARROWHEAD

KUZU: (*KU-ZOO*, Japan) see FLOURS AND THICKENERS

KWAY TIO: (*KWAY TEOW*, Malaysia) see NOODLES (RICE RIBBON)

KYAINTHEE: (*JAIN-TEE*, Burma) see CANDLENUT

KYAUK KYAW: (*CHAUK-JAU*, Burma) see AGAR AGAR

KYAUK-NGA: (*CHAUK-NGA*, Burma) see GAROUPA

KYURI: (*QUE-REE*, Japan) see CUCUMBER

LAAB

L

LAAB: (*LAAB*, Thailand) see THAILAND, COOK-ING METHODS; THAILAND

LABONG: (*LAH-BONG*, Philippines) see BAMBOO SHOOT

LADA: (*LAH-DA*, Malaysia) see CHILI

LADA HIJAU: (*LAH-DA HE-JAW*, Malaysia) see CHILI

LADA MERAH: (*LAH-DA MEAH-RAH*, Malaysia) see CHILI (RED)

LADLES: see UTENSILS, VARIOUS

LADY'S FINGERS: see BHINDI

LA HE: (*LA HAIR*, Vietnam) see CHIVES, CHI-NESE (GARLIC)

LAKSA: (*LUCK-SA*, Philippines) The Philippine word for "ten thousand" is *laksa*, and in culinary terms it refers to a dish containing various vegetables with shrimp, pork and *sotanghon*, a fine bean flour vermicelli. In Indonesia and Malaysia *laksa* is the name for a rice noodle dish with fish, shrimp or chicken in a creamy curry or tart tamarind sauce.

LAKSA WITH CHICKEN AND COCONUT MILK
Serves 8

3 large onions, 1 sliced, 2 minced
6 tbsps peanut oil
2 tsps minced garlic
2 tbsps minced chilies
6 candlenuts, ground
2 tbsps ground coriander
1½ tbsps ground cumin
1 tsp shrimp paste
2 qt (2 l) thin coconut milk
2 tsps salt
pepper
2 tbsps sugar
1 lb (500 g) chopped cooked chicken
2 cups (1 lb / 500 g) bean sprouts, blanched
2 cakes pressed bean curd, shredded
2 tbsps chopped scallions (spring / green onions)   *(cont'd)*

(Laksa with Chicken and Coconut Milk cont'd)

1 lb (500 g) cooked rice vermicelli
fresh coriander (cilantro)
shredded chili

Fry sliced onion in 3 tbsps of the peanut oil until deeply colored; remove. Fry chopped onion and garlic to golden. Add chilies, candlenuts, coriander, cumin and shrimp paste. Fry for 2 minutes. Add coconut milk and bring just to a boil. Simmer for 10 minutes. Season with salt, pepper and sugar. Stir-fry chicken in the remaining 3 tbsps oil. Add bean sprouts and stir-fry briefly; remove. Fry bean curd until golden. Add scallions and fry briefly. Divide vermicelli among 8 deep bowls. Add fried sliced onion to each, and add other ingredients. Cover with sauce. Garnish with scallions, coriander and chili.

LAL MIRICH: (*LAAL MIRCH*, India) see CHILI

LAMB: Lamb, the meat of young sheep, and mutton, from the older animal, are eaten extensively in Asia, particularly in India, Malaysia, Nepal and the northern Chinese regions. It is not enjoyed elsewhere in Asia, mainly because of its distinctive smell. In India, it is interchangeable with goat meat and is used there for many different dishes. In northern Kashmir, lamb and goat meat are the mainstays of the diet. Northern Chinese enjoy lamb as their most important meat. Here their chefs have acquired such skill in slicing the meat into paper-fine slices that 1 lb (500 g) of meat can serve a table for 12 people for their famed Mongolian barbecue in which meat and vegetables are flash-cooked on massive wood-fired, drum-shaped stoves. A specialty of the central Hunan province is braised lamb shanks in a richly seasoned brown sauce, an adaptation of a dish that was originally cooked with deer shanks.
Also known as *yangrou* (China); *gosht* (India); *kambing* (Indonesia, Malaysia); *bhedaa* (Nepal)
See also: DHANSAK (recipe); GOAT *and recipes following*

GULAI OF LAMB
Serves 6–8

1¹/₂ lbs (750 g) lean lamb, cubed
salt
white pepper
¹/₄ cup (2 fl oz / 60 ml) vegetable oil
1 onion, thinly sliced
1 cup (8 oz / 250 g) chopped onions
3 tbsps minced garlic
2 tbsps minced ginger
2 tsps turmeric
1¹/₂ tbsps greater galangal
1 tsp shrimp paste
2 tsps brown sugar
1–2 fresh red chilies, seeded and sliced
2 cups (16 fl oz / 500 ml) thin coconut milk
¹/₂ cup (4 fl oz / 125 ml) thick coconut milk
fresh coriander (cilantro) leaves
basil leaves

Dust lamb generously with salt and pepper. Heat oil in a large pan and fry the meat in several batches until evenly colored. Set aside. Fry the sliced onion in the oil until very well colored. Remove. Fry chopped onion and minced garlic and ginger for 3 minutes. Add turmeric, *greater galangal*, shrimp paste and sugar with salt and pepper to taste. Fry for 2 minutes, stirring. Add chilies and all of the coconut milk. Bring to a boil; simmer, stirring constantly, until oil rises to the surface of the sauce. Add the lamb and simmer gently for about 1¹/₂ hours. Add herbs with salt and pepper to taste.

KORMA OF MUTTON
Serves 4

1 large onion, thinly sliced
2 tbsps ghee
1¹/₂ lbs (750 g) boneless mutton, cubed
¹/₂ tsp chili powder
³/₄ tsp salt
1 heaped tsp ground coriander
6 garlic cloves, crushed
2 tsps minced ginger
1 cup (8 fl oz / 250 ml) plain (natural) yogurt
³/₄ cup (6 fl oz / 180 ml) water

(cont'd)

(Korma of Mutton cont'd)

Fry onions in ghee until lightly colored; remove half and fry the remaining half until dark. Remove and mash to a smooth paste. Brown mutton evenly; season with chili powder, salt, coriander, garlic and ginger. Stir on a high heat for 3 minutes. Add yogurt, a little at a time, stirring until the liquid evaporates. Add the fried and mashed onion with water. Cover and simmer gently for about 45 minutes, without lifting the lid.

LAMB WITH CREAMED SPINACH SAUCE
Serves 6

1¹/₂ lbs (600 g) lean lamb, cubed
1 fresh green chili, seeded and minced
1¹/₂ tsps minced garlic
1¹/₂ tsps minced ginger
2 tbsps ghee
1 tbsp white poppy seeds, ground
1¹/₂ tsps salt
2 tbsps plain (natural) yogurt
1 green cardamom, broken
1 cup (8 fl oz / 250 ml) water
1 lb (500 g) fresh spinach, rinsed and coarsely chopped
¹/₂ cup (4 fl oz / 125 ml) heavy cream
¹/₂ tsp nutmeg

Blanch lamb in boiling water; drain. Sauté chili, garlic and ginger in ghee for 2 minutes; add lamb and sauté to color. Add poppy seeds and salt. Fry lightly, then add yogurt and cardamom with water. Bring to a boil; reduce heat, cover tightly and cook gently until lamb is tender. Cook spinach separately without water in a tightly covered pan over low heat for about 7 minutes. Drain, then purée. Add to the lamb; simmer 2–3 minutes. Stir in cream and nutmeg; heat through.

MONGOLIAN HOTPOT
Serves 8

2 lbs (1 kg) lean lamb
4 cakes soft bean curd, cubed
1 lb (500 g) napa cabbage
1 lb (500 g) spinach, finely chopped
8 oz (250 g) bean thread vermicelli, soaked
and chopped
hot water or lamb stock
4–6 dried black mushrooms, soaked and
halved
fermented bean curd, mashed
fresh coriander (cilantro), chopped
scallions (spring/green onions), chopped
Oriental sesame oil
sesame paste
shrimp paste
soy sauce
yellow rice wine
red vinegar
sugar
chili oil

Cut lamb into paper-thin slices and
arrange on a platter. Place soft bean
curd, cabbage, spinach and vermicelli on
another platter. Fill a hotpot, fondue or
crockpot with hot water or stock. Add
mushrooms. Bring to a boil. Reduce
heat. Place the remaining ingredients in
small dishes on the table. Cook lamb
and vegetables by holding briefly in the
stock. Dip into sauce or sauces mixed
from the accompanying ingredients.
Serve the broth at the end with any
remaining vegetables, soft bean curd
and vermicelli.

ROGHAN JOSH
Serves 6

2¹/₂ lbs (1.25 kgs) mutton or lamb, cubed
2 tbsps ghee
1 tbsp salt
4 whole cloves
¹/₄ tsp asafoetida, *lightly toasted*
¹/₂ cup (4 fl oz/125 ml) plain (natural) yogurt
3 ³/₄ cups (30 fl oz/900 ml) water
¹/₂ tsp ground ginger
1 tbsp coriander seeds, toasted and ground
(cont'd)

(Roghan Josh cont'd)
1–2 tsps Kashmiri chili powder
¹/₂ tsp saffron strands
¹/₃ cup (3 fl oz/90 ml) milk, heated
1–2 tsps sugar
3 tbsps thick cream or malai
2 green cardamom pods; peeled and seeds
crushed
1–2 tbsps Kashmiri masala

Fry the meat in ghee, salt, cloves and the
asafoetida until well browned. Mix
yogurt with 1³/₄ cups (14 fl oz/400 ml)
water and add slowly to the pan, allowing each addition to dry up before adding
more. Cook on medium-high heat,
stirring continually. Sprinkle on the
ginger, ground coriander and chili
powder and stir on a high heat for 2
minutes. Pour in 2 cups (16 fl oz/500 ml)
water, bring to a boil, uncovered, and
cook on medium heat for 15 minutes.
Grind the saffron and steep in the hot
milk. Stir sugar into the saffron milk;
add cream and cardomom. Cover and
simmer until the meat is very tender
and the sauce thick, about 45 minutes.
Sprinkle on *masala*.

SKEWERED LAMB
Serves 4

2 tbsps lemon juice
¹/₂ cup (4 oz/125 ml) plain (natural) yogurt
2 tsps Kashmiri masala
1¹/₂ tsps salt
¹/₂ tsp pepper
1¹/₂ lbs (600 g) boneless lamb, cut into 1 in
(2.5 cm) cubes
2 medium onions, cut into squares
1 large bell pepper (green pepper/capsicum),
cut into cubes
ghee

Mix lemon juice, yogurt and
Kashmiri *masala* with salt and pepper.
Pour over meat and marinate overnight.
Thread onto oiled metal skewers,
alternating with onions and bell pepper.
Brush with ghee. Grill over charcoal
until meat is tender and the surface
flecked brown. Brush again with ghee
and serve immediately.

LAMBANOG: (*LAM-BA-NOG*, Philippines) see TUBA; WINE, ASIAN

LAM KEONG: (*LAM GEUNG*, China) see GALANGAL, GREATER

LAMPRIES: (*LUMP-RICE*, Sri Lanka) The name of this festive meal in Sri Lanka comes from the Dutch *lomprijst*. It is actually a dish that comprises several important Sri Lankan dishes wrapped together in banana leaf parcels and baked. The components are the Dutch-style meatballs known as *frikkadels*, ghee-flavored rice, a curry known as *lampries*, curry that is made with several different kinds of meat, thick coconut milk to moisten everything and hold it together, and spoonfuls of two or three different sambals for piquancy. Usually large quantities of *lampries* are made. Both the making and the eating of the dish are part of the fun.

See also: FRIKKADELS (recipe)

LAMUT: (*LAM-UD*, Thailand) see SAPODILLA

LAOS: Landlocked Laos has Vietnam to its east and is separated from Thailand, to the west, by the swirling brown waters of the Mekong River. The southernmost tip of China extends into its northern boundaries. Over the centuries this has been the point of entry to Laos for many of the ancient ethnic Chinese races who still remain in substantial numbers in these remote regions.

Laotian housewives have not allowed the scant variety of available produce to limit their creativity in the kitchen. From their backyards and the river banks herbs, such as local mint and basil, southernwood and dill, and indigenous leafy greens like *kangkong* are gathered to supplement cabbage, yams and bamboo shoots. (The latter are sliced and salted—the salt both preserving and adding flavor to this indispensable Asian ingredient.) Peppers, both hot and sweet, as well as ginger, garlic and *galangal*, add flavor to simmered and braised dishes of venison and buffalo meat.

One particular characteristic of Laotian food, which differentiates it from any other cuisine of this area, is a penchant for creamy purées that are scooped into salad leaves and rolled into cones to be eaten. Thorough pounding in a wooden mortar produces the desired effect, with herbs and spices added in the process. Eggplant and ground, roasted rice thicken and add richness to stewed dishes as well as to these soft creamy dishes. In a tradition borrowed from Thailand, toasted peanuts are also added.

The mighty Mekong River is home to the gigantic *pa boeuk* fish (or *trey reach*, as it is known in Cambodia), the enormous roe of which (often weighing more than 20 lbs/10 kgs) is made into a delicate, rose-gray-hued dip known as *som khay*, or Laotian caviar. If there is fish left over from a meal it is sometimes pickled with rice bran and salt to make *padek* which is later used as a seasoning or strongly-flavored ingredient in other dishes, or for *som pa*, another pungent ingredient of pounded fish and fermented rice. When pork is preserved in this way it is known as *som mu*. *Nam pa* is a salty, thin amber fish sauce of similar type to the Vietnamese *nuoc mam*. It is used in the same way as soy sauce, as both a seasoning and condiment.

Dried meat is enjoyed for its strong flavor, and a particular favorite is the dried skin of the Indian buffalo which is served crisp as a snack or made into a delicious well-spiced and herb-scented dish with *galangal*. Rice is the staple carbohydrate food, and it is grown like a wild grass on the hillsides. It is cooked by soaking then steaming in woven cane funnels. At meals rice is served in closely woven, lidded baskets and is rolled into small balls and eaten like bread.

Khao phoune is the local specialty dish, and equates with the Burmese *mohinga* with its milky coconut base, rice vermicelli and multifarious added ingredients, of which thinly sliced banana trunk heart and flowers are a feature. Flavors in general are mild, but salty *nam pa* and piquant *tieo* (chili paste) are always there to add bite.

Laotian cooking, and its preparation, are fastidious and often extremely time-consuming; fish and chicken are boned before use and ingredients are painstakingly ground to just the right consistency.

The following recipes and menu selection combine dishes from both Laos and Camdodia.
See also: CAMBODIA

LAOS AND CAMBODIA RECIPES

Appetizers
Laotian Cabbage Soup
Oysters with Garlic and Herbs
Sweet Tamarind and Chicken Soup

Main Courses
Barbecued Fish Balls on Skewers
Buffalo Meat Stew
Cambodian Spicy Pork
Grilled Fish
Laotian Tartare Steak
Laotian Traditional Noodle Dish

Accompaniments
Bamboo Shoot Salad

Dessert
Tapioca Dessert

MENU
(see recipes)

DINNER MENU
Serves 6–8

Oysters with Garlic and Herbs
Sweet Tamarind Chicken Soup

Barbecued Fish Balls on Skewers
Cambodian Spicy Pork
Bamboo Shoot Salad

Tapioca Dessert

LAOS: see GALANGAL, GREATER

LAOTIAN TARTARE STEAK: (recipe) see BEEF

LAOTIAN TRADITIONAL NOODLE DISH: (recipe) see NOODLES

LAP: (*LARP*, Laos) A finely ground, raw meat dish, *lap* is the Laos version of "steak tartare," but is made from buffalo meat or venison seasoned with chili and herbs. *Lap* is served, like so many dishes in this part of Asia, with lettuce and herbs which are wrapped into bite-size rolls.
See also: BUFFALO; LAOTIAN TARTARE STEAK (recipe)

LAP CHEONG: (*LARP CHEONG*, China) see PORK, CURED

LAP NGUP: (*LARP NGAP*, China) see DUCK, DRIED

LAPU LAPU: (*LA-POO LA-POO*, Philippines) see GAROUPA

LARD: see OILS AND FATS

LARD NET: see CAUL FAT

LASSI: (*LAS-SEE*, India) A palate-soothing, nutritious drink enjoyed throughout India, *lassi* can be made from buttermilk, or whipped yogurt, thinned with water. In the northern states of India it is flavored with salt, pepper and ground, toasted cumin seeds, or may be even be sweetened with sugar. Southern Indians, however, prefer a spicy mixture flavored with a paste of ground green chili, ginger, coriander leaves and garlic.
See also: BUTTERMILK; YOGURT

LASSI
Yields 3 cups (48 fl oz / 750 ml)

1/2 cup (4 fl oz / 125 ml) plain (natural) yogurt, well beaten
salt
1/4 tsp toasted cumin, ground
2 1/2 cups (20 fl oz / 625 ml) water

Mix yogurt and seasonings together, whisk in water.

> ## SOUTHERN INDIAN LASSI
> *Yields 3 cups (48 fl oz / 750 ml)*
>
> ¹/₂ *cup (4 fl oz / 125 ml) plain (natural) yogurt, well beaten*
> *1 green chili, ground to a paste*
> *1 tsp finely minced ginger*
> *1 tsp fresh coriander (cilantro), ground to a paste*
> ¹/₃ *tsp crushed garlic*
> *salt*
> 2¹/₂ *cup (20 fl oz / 625 ml) water*
>
> Mix yogurt with seasonings. Add salt to taste and whisk in water.

LASUN: (*LAH-SAN*, India) see GARLIC

LAT CHU JEUNG YAU: (*LART JIL JEUNG YAU*, China) see BEAN PASTES AND SAUCES (CHILI)

LATIK: (*LA-TICK*, Philippines) A brown curd-like substance, left after coconut milk is heated until oil separates. Latik is used for topping Philippine desserts or snack foods such as *biko*, and the popular *suman* and *maja blanca*.
See also: BIKO

LAT JIU: (*LART JIL*, China) see CHILI PASTES, POWDERS AND SAUCES

LAT JIU DIN: (*LART JIL DIM*, China) see CHILI PASTES, POWDERS AND SAUCES

LAT JIU JIANG: (*LART JIL JEUNG*, China) see CHILI PASTES, POWDERS AND SAUCES

LAT JIU KEUNG YAU: (*LART JIL JEUNG YAU*, China) see CHILI PASTES, POWDERS AND SAUCES

LAT YOU: (*LART YAU*, China) see CHILI OIL

LAUNG: (*LONG*, India) see CLOVES

LAYERED BUTTERED BREAD: (recipe) see BREAD, INDIAN

LEAVES USED AS FOOD CONTAINERS, PLATES, WRAPPERS: Various fresh and dried leaves are put to practical and economical use in Asia, and particularly in the southeastern countries, such as Indonesia and Malaysia. Leaves of bamboo, banana, cardamom, coconut, lotus, tapioca and turmeric, as well as the leaves of many types of native plants, are used to wrap foods before steaming, boiling or grilling, just as aluminum foil is used in the West. A square of banana leaf is satisfactory as a plate for a curry dinner and, twisted into a cone, it is a convenient take-out container. *Daun mangkok*, the Indonesian cup leaf, is well named for its capacity to hold food for steaming. Banana leaf sections or strips, as well as bamboo and coconut leaves, replace baking paper in cake- and sweet-making and are usually left on the food as a wrapper when it goes to market. In Japan, cherry leaves are used to some extent in cake-making. In Indonesia, and particularly the island of Bali, intricately woven decorations of dried or fresh coconut palm leaves are used extensively. In Thailand, and to a lesser extent in the Philippines, decorative use of young banana leaves is an integral part of the cuisine. As part of their training, apprentice cooks must master the classic table and dish decorations involving folded banana leaves.
See also: BAMBOO LEAF; BANANA; COCONUT; COCONUT LEAF CHICKEN PARCELS (recipe); DAUN MANGKOK; LOTUS; STEAMED FISH IN BANANA LEAF CUPS (recipe)

LECHON SARSA: (*LE-CHON SAR-SA*, Philippines) A thick, slightly sweet sauce made from ground pork liver with brown sugar, *biscocho*, vinegar, pounded garlic and other seasonings. It is traditionally served in the Philippines with spit-roasted pork.
See also: BISCOCHO; LIVER SAUCE (recipe); ROAST SUCKLING PIG, PHILIPPINE STYLE (recipe)

LEEKS, ASIAN: (*Allium ramosum*) Several types of small, slender leeks are grown in China and Japan. They look like scallions (spring/green onions), although they have thicker leaves, a mild flavor and very slight bitterness. The outer leaves are dark while the inner leaves are pale green to white in color. Usually only the white part of the onion is used in cooked dishes, although the green leaves may be used as a garnish.

NAGANEGI/NEGI is the Japanese leek, which is thinner than a common leek, but still larger than a scallion. It is the onion used most frequently in Japanese cooking and is a favorite of chefs in Osaka.

Also known as *dai suen, quingsuan* (China); *naganegi, negi* (Japan); *bawang bakung* (Malaysia)

See also: ONION

LEI YU: (*LEI YUE*, China) see CARP

LEMON: (*Citrus limon*) Throughout Asia, limes and other forms of citrus fruits are traditionally used in preference to lemon when a tart flavor is required. But a number of different types of native lemons are grown for culinary use in Asian countries. As well, acidic ingredients, such as tamarind and vinegar, are used when a sour taste is needed in a dish. So too are various tart native fruits: *belimbing*; the Philippine fruit *santol*; the Indonesian *kedongdong;* green mango and papaya (paw paw); and small eggplants such as *makua phuong*.

Also known as *neebu, nimbu* (India)

See also: BELIMBING; KALAMANSI; LIME; MANGO, GREEN

LEMON GRASS: (*Cymbopogon citratus*) A fragrant grass that grows profusely throughout the tropics, which is used medicinally and as a herb. It grows in clumps of long, tapering, pale green, serrated-edged leaves that emanate from tightly packed cream-white narrow bases. It is the base that is used to flavor curries, soups and simmered dishes in most parts of Southeast Asia, while the leaves are used in infusion as a cooling tea. Buddhist monks serve lemon grass tea in their temples, its quality as a relaxant fitting their calm existence. Named for its distinct lemon scent and flavor, lemon grass has been in use for centuries in Europe, where it is known as citronella. It acts as an effective insect repellent. Lemon grass is preferred in fresh form for cooking, and is now readily available in Asian vegetable markets and in many larger supermarkets. It can be kept, loosely wrapped, in the refrigerator for up to 10 days. The compact bulb end should be rinsed and dried, then finely sliced or chopped, or the whole piece may be bruised or slit open lengthways to release flavor and added to a dish for retrieval before serving. Lemon grass is a major flavoring ingredient in the curries of Indonesia, Malaysia and Thailand and is often used in combination with shrimp paste and turmeric to achieve a distinctive taste style.

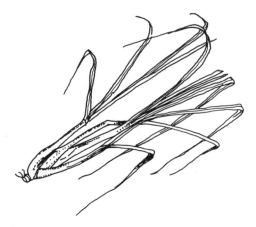

Lemon grass

BEEF SIMMERED WITH LEMON GRASS
Serves 6

2 lbs (1 kg) boneless beef shin, cubed
2 tbsps vegetable oil
1¹/₂ tsps minced garlic
2 stalks lemon grass, halved lengthways
2 tbsps fish sauce
salt
black pepper
sugar
2 cups (16 fl oz / 500 ml) water
1¹/₂ tsps curry powder
1 cup (8 fl oz / 250 ml) thin coconut milk or water from 1 fresh coconut

Fry meat in little oil until well cooked. Add garlic and fry briefly. Add lemon grass, fish sauce and salt, black pepper and sugar to taste. Add water, cover tightly, and simmer for 1¹/₂ hours. Add curry powder and thin coconut milk or coconut water and cook gently until tender.

DRIED LEMON GRASS: In its dried and shredded or powdered form it is commonly known as *sereh*. It lacks the distinct lemony flavor of the fresh herb and has an intense, peppery taste. It should be soaked in water before use.

Also known as *zabalin* (Burma); *bai mak nao* (Cambodia); *heung mao tso* (China); *sera* (India); *sereh* (Indonesia); *serai* (Malaysia); *takrai* (Thailand); *xa* (Vietnam); citronella

See also: BEEF SIMMERED WITH LEMON GRASS (recipe); CHICKEN WITH LEMON GRASS (recipe); REMPAH

CHICKEN WITH LEMON GRASS
Serves 4

2 lbs (1 kg) chicken, cubed
1 stalk lemon grass, finely chopped
1¹/2 tsps minced garlic
2 tbsps fish sauce
1 tbsp sugar
1¹/2 tbsps black pepper
2 tbsps vegetable oil
1 tbsp nuoc mau
roasted chili flakes

Marinate chicken for 30 minutes with lemon grass, garlic, fish sauce, sugar and pepper. Heat oil in a large pan and fry chicken until colored. Reduce heat, cover tightly and cook gently until chicken is tender. Add *nuoc mau* and chili flakes to taste. Heat through.

LENGKUAS: (*LENG-KWAS*, Indonesia) see GALANGAL, GREATER

LENKUAS: (*LENG-KWAS*, Malaysia) see GALANGAL, GREATER

LENTIL: (*Lens esculenta*) One of the world's oldest foods, and probably of Asian origin, lentils have been grown since early times in Asia, Greece, Egypt and Mesopotamia. Today lentils are used sparingly in the Chinese and Japanese cuisines, but are used extensively in other Asian countries, particularly by vegetarian Indians who regard them as a vital element of their diet. Lentils propagate easily and ripen just three months after sowing.

They are rich in protein and easily digested. In India, lentils are usually served in the form of *dal*, a side dish that accompanies almost every meal. *Dal* can change in taste and consistency to complement the menu, ranging from thick and mild to explosively hot and soup-like. Lentils may also be sprouted for cooking or used raw as a vegetable.

BLACK LENTIL: (*Phaseolus mungo*) The *urd* or *urad dal* originated in India. It has hairy pods which are eaten whole when young, and the black seeds, with distinct white hilum, are dried to use as a *dal*, either whole, split or split and polished. They are considered to have the best flavor and texture of the many types of lentils used in Indian cooking. Ground *urad dal* is used in vegetarian cooking to make pastries, dumplings and snacks. When polished, black lentils are known as *urad dal dhuli* (India); split, unskinned black lentils are called *urad dal chilke wali*. The whole seeds are *saabat urad* and require extensive cooking.

GREEN LENTIL: (*Phaseolus aureus*) The green lentil, or *gram*, is in fact the mung bean, which is used in India in its dried state to make *dal*. It is also used fresh and is cooked like peas. Elsewhere in Asia this bean is sprouted into bean sprouts. It is ground into flour or used whole for certain dessert dishes.

Also known as *moong ke dal* (split); *saabat moong* (whole beans) (India)

See also: BEAN SPROUT; MUNG BEAN

RED LENTIL: (*Lens esculenta*) These are the oldest of the lentil family, and are known to have been grown and eaten in China, India and Egypt well over 4000 years ago. Polished red lentils cook quickly without presoaking and are favored for their fine, distinctive taste. These are the lentils used for highly spiced, puréed types of *dal* and in soups.

Also known as *malka sabat* (split and skinned), *masoor dal* (whole, unpolished red lentils) (India)

See also: SPICED RED LENTILS (recipe)

RED MUNG BEANS are more popular than their green cousin in the Indian states of Gujarat and Rajasthan. Here they are cooked ripe as a vegetable, are dried to use as a *dal* or are sprouted.

YELLOW DAL (*Pisum sativum*) are large, round, yellow-colored peas, which are sold split and polished. A yellow cousin of the green garden pea, it is rarely cooked in its fresh state. These peas are used in Indian cooking to make *dal* in vegetarian cooking and soups. Yellow lentils should be soaked for about 1 hour before cooking. Dry-roasted and seasoned with sharp spices and chili, they are a popular nibble.

Also known as *harhardal, matar dal* (India); yellow lentils; yellow split peas
See also: BEAN PATTIES (recipe); DHANSAK (recipe)

BEAN PATTIES
Yields 12

1 cup (8 oz / 250 g) yellow lentils or mung beans
3 tbsps minced scallions (spring / green onions)
2 fresh red chilies, seeded and chopped
1 tsp minced garlic
1 tbsp chopped fresh coriander (cilantro)
$^1/_2$ tsp turmeric
$^1/_2$ tsp salt
6 cups (1$^1/_2$ qts / 1.5 l) vegetable oil

Soak the lentils or beans overnight; grind to a paste in a blender or food processor. Mix with onions, chilies, garlic, coriander, turmeric and salt. With oiled hands, roll mixture into small balls and flatten slightly. Deep-fry in the oil until golden brown.

SPROUTED LENTIL: These were commonly eaten in India in the past, but they are less popular today. Lentils sprout in just a few days if kept in warm, moist conditions and can be cooked like mung bean sprouts or used raw in salads.

Also known as *dal, gram*
See also: BEAN SPROUT; SPROUTED LENTIL KICHARDI (recipe)

DAL AND VEGETABLE SAUCE
Serves 4

$^3/_4$ cup (6 oz / 180 g) mung beans (moong ke dal)
1 medium carrot, diced
1 large potato, cubed
1 medium eggplant (aubergine), peeled and cubed
1 large green bell pepper (green pepper / capsicum), diced
$^1/_2$ cup (4 oz / 120 g) chopped onion
1 tsp toasted coriander seeds
1 tsp toasted white cumin seeds
2 green chilies, seeded and minced
2 tsps sambar masala
1 tbsp black mustard seeds
1 tsp turmeric
2 tbsps tamarind pulp
1$^1/_2$ tbsps desiccated coconut
1$^1/_2$ tsps salt
6 curry leaves or 2 bay leaves
chili powder or paste, to taste
3 cups (24 fl oz / 750 ml) water

Rinse and drain mung beans. Place all ingredients in a pan. Bring to a boil; simmer until tender. Serve with *dosa* (southern Indian breakfast bread).

SPICED RED LENTILS
Serves 6

2 cups (1 lb / 500 g) red lentils (masoor dal)
3$^1/_2$ cups (28 fl oz / 885 ml) water
1$^1/_2$ tsps salt
1 tsp turmeric
1 tsp chili powder
2 tsps ground coriander
1 tsp garam masala
1 tbsp lemon juice
1 medium onion, sliced
2–3 tbsps ghee
fresh coriander (cilantro)

Rinse lentils. Combine with water, salt, turmeric, chili powder, and ground coriander for about 45 minutes, until tender. Add *garam masala* and lemon juice. Make a *baghar* by frying onion in ghee until brown and crisp. Pour over the lentils and garnish with the fresh coriander.

SPROUTED LENTIL KICHARDI
Serves 4

1¼ cups (10 oz / 300 g) long-grain rice
⅓ cup (3 fl oz / 90 ml) vegetable oil
2 tsps minced garlic
1¾ cups (14 oz / 430 g) sprouted lentils
1 fresh red chili, seeded and chopped
½ cup (1½ oz / 40 g) grated fresh coconut
¼ cup (½ oz / 15 g) chopped fresh
coriander (cilantro)
2 tsps dhania-jira
½ tsp chili powder
¼ tsp turmeric
1 tsp sugar
1½ tsps salt
2 cups (16 fl oz / 500 ml) warm water

Thoroughly wash rice and drain in a colander. Heat oil and fry garlic for 30 seconds. Add the sprouted lentils, rice, chili, coconut, fresh coriander and *dhania-jira* with chili powder, turmeric, sugar and salt. Add water; cover and cook for about 20 minutes, until soft.

LESSER GALANGAL: see GALANGAL, LESSER

LETTUCE: (*Lactuca sativa*) Chinese, or Oriental, lettuce has a small head of long, flat loose leaves, similar to a cos (romaine). The edges may be jagged or smooth. It is used extensively in salads in Vietnam, Laos and Thailand. Chinese rarely eat lettuce raw, preferring to cook it by blanching in boiling water with a little oil added to prevent it turning brown. They serve it with an oyster sauce or crabmeat dressing, or make it into a soup with shreds of fish.

The Chinese name for lettuce is a homonym—*saang* meaning first or fresh, the sound of *choy* meaning either money or vegetable, depending on the tone. It is, then, the auspicious lettuce that is offered to the dragon or lion at Lunar New Year celebrations, and it is also served at special celebrations. *Saang choy bow* is a popular dish in which finely diced pigeon meat, stir-fried with spices and *lap cheong* (Chinese sausage), is wrapped into

tasty bite-size parcels in crisp lettuce leaves.
Also known as *saang choy* (China); *salad patta* (India); *sayur salat* (Malaysia); *pak kard hom* (Thailand)
See also: VEGETABLE PLATTER (recipe)

Chinese leaf lettuce

LEY NYIN BWINT: (*LAY NYIN PWINT*, Burma) see CLOVES

LIANG-BAN: (*LEUNG-BOON*) see CHINA, COOKING METHODS (BOILING)

LICORICE ROOT: (*Glycyrrhiza glabra*, *G.* spp.)

From the sixth century in China the strong-tasting licorice root has been cooked in tonic soups and braised dishes for its remarkable restorative powers. It is believed to counteract every sort of poison in vegetable preparations. Dried sliced licorice, looking like pieces of gray blotting paper, are sold at Chinese herbalists and pharmacies.
Also known as *kan ts'ao* (China)
See also: MEDICINAL FOODS

LIGHT SOY SAUCE: see SOY SAUCE

LILY BUD: (*Hemerocallis fulva*)

These are the slim, burnished-gold, unopened flower buds of a type of day lily known in China as *khim chiam*, and not the tiger lily after which they are named. About 2 in (5 cm) in length, they have a slightly furry texture and an earthy fragrance that appeals to Chinese vegetarians. As they are fragile, they should be knotted individually or in small clusters to prevent them falling apart during cooking. They are usually cooked in slow-simmered dishes and are sold in small packs, but should be transferred to a jar. They will keep for many months, as long as they are stored away from moisture.

Dried lily buds

LILY BULB: *(Lilium tigrinum)* These are the starchy bulbs from a type of lily that resembles a large garlic bulb with small, gray, flattened cloves. The whole bulb is sold fresh in Japan and Korea, where it is used sparingly as a vegetable, particularly in simmered dishes. It must be parboiled before use to remove bitterness. Petals or cloves of the bulb are dried for use in Chinese cooking, where they add their unique taste to braised and simmered dishes. Dried bulbs must be soaked to soften before cooking.
Also known as *"golden needles"*; *gum jum*, *shannai* (China); *gum kum* (India); *yuri-ne* (Japan); *kim cham* (Vietnam); tiger lily buds

LIMAU: *(LEE-MAU,* Malaysia) see LIME

LIMAU KESTURI: *(LEE-MAU KES-TOO-REE,* *Citrus microcapa)* This small lime is the size of a marble and is grown and used in the Philippines, Malaysia and Singapore to give a sour taste to dishes.
Also known as *dayap* (Philippines)

LIME: *(Citrus aurantifolia)* A shrub-like, heavily branched tree, that is one of the smallest of the citrus varieties. The fruit is a small, round citrus with a delicate flavor and fresh, tart taste. Limes are used in preference to lemons in most part of Asia for their tart juice that imparts a unique, fresh taste to sauces and soups, and is used as an acidulant and tenderizer. Fresh lime juice is the base of many sauces, particularly in Thailand and Vietnam, where it is mixed with fish sauce, garlic and ground peanuts. One of the most popular, refreshing beverages served in Asia is a soda squash of lime juice sweetened with sugar syrup. In India, the whole fruit is slit, filled with spices and made into a pungent pickle, while in other parts of Asia sliced lime is salted and dried, or preserved in soy sauce. In China, finely shredded lime leaves are served as an accompaniment to braised sharks' fins and certain other dishes to give a unique taste contrast. Kaffir lime leaves, from a related tree, are used in this way elsewhere in Asia. In the Philippines, the tiny yellow-fleshed kalamansi lime is extensively used.
Also known as *djeruk nipis* (Indonesia); *limau kesturi, limau nipis* (Malaysia); *apog, dayap*

LIME SAUCE
Yields ¹/₂ cup (4 fl oz / 125 ml)

4 fresh red chilies, seeded and minced
¹/₄ cup (2 fl oz / 60 ml) fresh lime juice
2¹/₂ tbsps fish sauce

Combine all ingredients in a small serving bowl. Can be refrigerated for 4–5 days.

SALTED LIMES

18 small limes
coarse salt

Wash fruit well, brushing skin; rinse. Cut a deep slit in each. Place 1 tsp salt in each lime. Pack in sterilized jars and seal. Place in a very low oven or in hot sunlight, 4 hours daily for 20 days. Store untouched for several months before use.

(small lime) (Philippines); *ma-nao* (Thailand)
See also: KAFFIR LIME; KALAMANSI; LIMAU KESTURI; LIME SAUCE (recipe); SALTED LIMES (recipe)

LIME PASTE: see LIME SOLUTION

LIME, PICKLED: Limes pickled in various ways are used as condiments, pickles and sweets in different parts of Asia. They are preserved in soy sauce with sugar, salt and vinegar. In China, sliced limes are salted and sun-dried, while in India whole limes are slit, filled with spices and pickled in oil.
See also: LIME

LIME SOLUTION: A finely ground powder of calcium hydroxide is used in a solution with water to add crispness to batter. It is also used with fruit for desserts and in certain forms of pickling. In Thailand a red-colored lime paste is used. One of the base ingredients in the chewing paste, *betel*, is lime paste.
Also known as *khanewala choona* (India); *kapor* (Malaysia); *apog* (Philippines); lime paste; *poon dang* (Thailand); red lime paste; slaked lime
See also: ALUM; AMORPHOPHALUS KONJAC; BEAR'S PAW

LING FUN: (*LING FEN*, China) see FLOURS AND THICKENERS (TAPIOCA STARCH)

"LION'S HEAD" MEAT BALLS: (recipe) see MEATBALL

LITCHI: (*LAI-JI, Nephelium litchi*) A sweet, delicately flavored fruit with a spiny red skin. It grows in bunches on an attractive tree which is native to southern China. The fruit has a crisp, sweet, opalescent white, juicy flesh that has the texture of firm jelly. The taste is deliciously sweet and unique. Each fruit contains a single large shiny black stone. During the T'ang Dynasty (AD 618–907) the Empress Yang kui-fei found this fruit irresistible and ordered them to be delivered to her household by a special "pony express." Litchis will grow in most subtropical climates, and so are now available in many major cities. Fresh litchis

can be kept in the refrigerator for several weeks, unpeeled. They are probably best known in canned form, and seem to retain a reasonable amount of their texture and flavor. They are served as a dessert in most Chinese restaurants in the West, although this is not a traditional Chinese practice. They are also occasionally added to Chinese stir-fried dishes and savory soups.
DRIED LITCHIS look like raisins and are sweet and chewy. Eaten as a confection, they are also added to desserts for their strong flavor. They keep well in an airtight container.
Also known as *lichi, li chih* (China); *leenchee* (Thailand); lychee

Litchi fruit

LIU: (*LIU*) see CHINA, COOKING METHODS (BOILING)

LIVER AND PORK BALLS: (recipe) see PORK

LIVER SAUCE: (recipe) see PORK

LI YU: (*LEI YUE*, China) see CARP

LOBAK: (*LOH-BUCK*, China, Malaysia, Indonesia) see RADISH, GIANT WHITE

LOBHIA/LOBIA: (*LO-BHI-AA*, India) see BLACK-EYED PEA (BEAN)

LOMBOK: (*LOM-BOK*, Indonesia) see CHILI, GROUND ROASTED

LON: (*LON*, Thailand) The name given to cooked sauces, which are usually made with coconut milk and served with roasted or fried fish and raw vegetables.
See also: CRAB SAUCE (recipe)

LONG BEAN: (*Vigna unguiculata, V. sesquipedalis*) This annual legume, which is native to Africa, is grown in most parts of Southeast Asia as the principal bean crop. It is of the same genus as the black-eyed pea (bean) and in India and northern China is grown to maturity for its yellow beans which are cooked as starch. In southern China, and in most other parts of Southeast Asia, the long, slender, young bean pod is preferred. It comes in two types: a pale green variety that has slightly fibrous flesh; and a deep green variety that has a firmer texture and is marginally more slender. They are brought to the market when young at about 15 in (38 cm) long, but if left on their branchy vines, they will grow to more than 3 ft (1 m). Because of their length they have to be grown on high trellises. Cantonese cooks favor long beans in a black bean sauce, stir-fried with meat or in an omelette. In Thailand and Burma it makes a cameo appearance in innumerable curries.

Also known as *baak dau gok* (light colored), *dau gok*, *tseng dau gok* (dark-colored) (China); *kacang panjang* (Malaysia); *paayap*, *sitaw* (Philippines); long-podded cow pea; snake bean; yard-long bean

See also: GADO GADO (recipe); VEGETABLES IN COCONUT SAUCE (recipe)

LONG-PODDED COWPEA: see LONG BEAN

LONTONG
Serves 4–6

2 cups (1 lb / 500 g) short-grain white rice
4 cups (1 qt / 1 l) boiling water
1 x 12 in (30 cm) square banana leaf

Wash and drain rice; place in a pan with boiling water. Cook until soft. Press into a greased square pan. Cover with banana leaf and wait until the rice is cold. Cut into cubes and serve with satay.

LOTUS: (*Nelumbo nuciferum*) The lotus's long, colorful history encompasses three cultures—Chinese, Indian and Egyptian. It symbolizes the peace and harmony that characterize Buddhism. In Indian art the full, rounded shape of the flower equates with womanly

curves as a symbol of purest beauty. Lotus blossoms and the majestic, floating leaves of the lotus plant appear in paintings, carvings and sculptures in ancient Egypt, even though the lotus now no longer grows there in its natural state.

The lotus has proved practical as well as beautiful, its seeds, stems, flowers and roots are all edible. With its series of bulbous rhizomes separated by narrow necks, the root resembles a string of hard brown sausages.

LOTUS CANDY are candied slices of lotus root and are traditionally offered to guests during the Chinese Lunar New Year season.

LOTUS FLOWERS are occasionally used in Chinese and Thai cooking. The petals are scattered over foods, or the open flower is used as a food container.

LOTUS LEAVES are dried and used to wrap "lotus parcels" of chopped chicken, pork or duck and "sticky" rice. These are steamed. As well as lightly browning the food, the leaf imparts its fragrance and an appealing flavor. Young fresh leaves can be shredded and cooked like spinach.

a   b

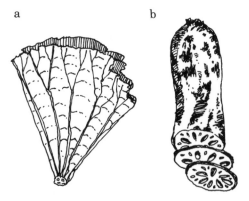

a. Folded dried lotus leaf
b. Whole and sliced lotus root

LOTUS ROOT, the tuberous rhizomes that grow in the mud beneath this water plant, are ochre-colored, with fibrous flesh and several lateral, round holes. A cross-sectional slice has a flower-like appearance, a fact not lost on the aesthetic Japanese chef. Lotus roots have a

crunchy texture and taste rather like arti-
chokes, and should be eaten while young. The
Japanese boil lotus root as *nimono*, and make
one of the most attractive snack dishes for the
bento (lunch box) by stuffing the holes with
mustard, deep-frying the root and then cutting
into slices. For special events Chinese cooks
may stuff lotus root with a mung bean purée or
braise it with pork. They add its distinctive
taste to vegetables, slow-cooked dishes and
soups. A classic example is dried squid or
octopus boiled with whole lotus roots and pork
shanks. In Thailand and some other parts of
Southeast Asia, where water-grown plants are
an important part of the diet, young lotus
stems are also eaten.

LOTUS LEAF PARCELS
Serves 8

1 lotus leaf, fresh or dried
boiling water
1³/₄ cups (13 oz / 400 g) glutinous (sticky)
white rice, soaked for 8 hours
2 lap cheong (Chinese) sausages, sliced
1 cup (4 oz / 125 g) diced boneless chicken
¹/₂ cup (2 oz / 60 g) diced roast duck / pork
¹/₄ cup (¹/₂ oz / 15 g) chopped straw mush-
rooms
2 tbsps soaked dried shrimp
1¹/₂ tbsps minced scallions (spring / green
onions)
¹/₂ tsp minced ginger
1³/₄ tsps salt
¹/₄ tsp black pepper
1 tbsp light soy sauce
2 tsps Oriental sesame oil

Soak lotus leaf in boiling water to
soften. Drain rice and mix with chicken,
pork, mushrooms, shrimp, scallions and
ginger. Season with the salt, pepper and
soy sauce. Add the sesame oil. Fold in
leaf and place on an oiled dish. Steam
for 30–40 minutes, until rice is tender.
Cut open top to serve.

LOTUS SEEDS have medicinal value as a restorative tonic, and as a food are boiled in
sweet or savory soups, added to stuffings, or
roasted and salted as a snack. The core, or

embryo, of the seed has a bitter taste and can
be slightly toxic, so it is removed by pushing
out with a thin skewer. Dried lotus seeds are
the choice of many cooks. They should be
rehydrated by soaking overnight. Lotus seeds
are featured in Chinese "eight treasure/eight
jeweled" dishes. A thick sweet paste made of
cooked, mashed and sugar-sweetened lotus
seeds is used as a filling in Chinese sweet buns
and pastries and in the "moon cakes" eaten
during the mid-autumn festival.

Both lotus root and lotus seeds are sold
either fresh or dried in Chinese markets. The
canned product is acceptable, although it lacks
the flavor and texture of the fresh. Store the
unused portion from an opened can in a container of fresh water in the refrigerator for up
to five days, changing the water daily. Dried
lotus leaves should be kept in a dry storage
area.

Also known as *leen ngau* (China); *nadru* (India);
renkon (Japan)
See also: BENTO; EIGHT TREASURE CHICKEN
(recipe); JAPAN, COOKING METHODS (NIMONO);
LOTUS LEAF PARCELS (recipe); LOTUS SEEDS AND
QUAIL EGGS IN CLEAR SWEET SOUP (recipe)

LOTUS SEEDS AND QUAIL EGGS IN CLEAR SWEET SOUP
Serves 8

4 oz (125 g) dried lotus seeds, soaked
water
1¹/₂ cups (12 oz / 350 g) crumbled rock
candy sugar
8 quail eggs

Drain lotus seeds. Place in a
saucepan with cold water to cover.
Add ¹/₂ cup of the sugar; bring to a boil,
stirring to dissolve. Simmer until seeds
soften, about 20 minutes. Drain and
remove core of seeds. Hard-cook the
quail eggs; cool and peel. Boil 6 cups
(1¹/₂ qts/1.5 l) water with remaining
1 cup sugar, stirring to dissolve.
Add lotus seeds and heat
thoroughly. Add eggs; simmer
2 minutes. Serve hot.

LOTUS ROOT STARCH: see FLOURS AND THICKENERS

LOTUS SEED PASTE: see LOTUS

LUANG PRABANG: (Laos) A hand woven basket, usually round in shape, with a close fitting lid, in which cooked rice is served at the table in Laos. The rice is compressed into small balls with the fingers and eaten like bread. In Laos, rice is grown on mountainsides rather than in paddy fields and is cooked by steaming in another conical shaped basket.

LUFFA, ANGLED: (*Luffa acutangula*) The fruit of an annual climber, native to India, which can grow up to 9 ft (2.75 m) in length. It has a dull green skin and ten lateral, sharply acute ribs, which give a star-shaped slice. The spongy, fibrous flesh has a bland, faintly bitter taste. Its similarity, in taste and texture, to okra have earned it the name "Chinese okra." It is used as a vegetable, particularly in China. Before cooking, the ribs must be trimmed with a vegetable parer to reduce the bitterness. Steaming, sautéing and braising are the usual cooking methods employed with this vegetable. The very large, overripe luffa provides a bitter juice that is used medicinally as a purgative. Choose firm, young luffa no more than 18 in (45 cm) in length and with unblemished skin. Can be stored in the refrigerator for at least 10 days.

Angled luffa

SPONGE GOURD is the smooth-skinned luffa (*L. cylindrica*). It is closely related to the angled luffa and resembles an overgrown version of the Indian drumstick vegetable. It is used in the same way as its cousin, but can also be dried and its fibrous pith used as a sponge—hence its name. The flowers, buds and young leaves of this variety can also be eaten.

Also known as *seui gwa* (smooth), *sze gwa* (angled) (China); *patola* (Philippines); *buab* (Thailand); bonnet gourd; Chinese okra; loofa; pleated squash; ridged gourd; ridged melon; strainer vine

See also: DRUMSTICK VEGETABLE; MELONS AND GOURDS

LUK KRAVEN: (*LUUK PRAWAAN*, Thailand) see CARDAMOM

LUK MANGLAK: (*LUUK MAENG-LAK*, Thailand) see BASIL (HAIRY)

LUMI: (*LOO-ME*, Malaysia) see BOMBAY DUCK

LUMPIA WRAPPERS
Yields 10–12

2 large eggs
2 tbsps oil or softened lard
1 cup (4 oz / 125 g) cornstarch (cornflour)
1 cup (4 oz / 125 g) all-purpose (plain) flour
1 tsp salt
2 cups (16 fl oz / 500 ml) water

Beat eggs with oil or lard. Add cornstarch, flour, salt and water; beat until smooth. Cook in an omelette or nonstick pan into thin crêpes.

LU SOY: (*LO SHUI*, China) see SOY SAUCE

LUT TZEE: (*LUT JI*, China) see CHESTNUT

LUYA: (*LUH-YAH*, Philippines) see GINGER

LYCHEE: see LITCHI

M

MACE: (*Myristica fragrans*) This aromatic spice is the net-like aril that encases the large oval-shaped spice, nutmeg. Crimson in its fresh state, mace turns ocher-red in color as it dries. It has a delicate, sweet flavor, similar to, but milder than, nutmeg and it is more expensive. It is sold as "blades" in chip form or ground to a slightly coarse powder. The whole ground mace is sometimes used in cooking, particularly in Indian rice dishes with other whole spices such as cinnamon, cloves and cardamom. Mace is used medicinally and is used in pickles and curry spices as well as in sweet dishes and pastries. Grated nutmeg can substitute.

Also known as *javitri* (India); *fuli* (unground mace), *sekar pala* (Indonesia); *kembang pala* (Malaysia); *wasa-vasi* (Sri Lanka); *dauk chand*, *dok chan* (Thailand)

Mace

MA CHIN: (*MA CHIN*, China) see CUMIN (WHITE)

MA-DUN: (*MA-DAN*, Thailand) (*Gardinia schomburghiana*) This juicy, sour fruit resembles the tiny, tart sour finger carambola. An obscure fruit, known also as carcinia, it is used in soups and curries for its tart taste and is made into pickles. Substitutes are *belimbing* and unripe gooseberry or plums.
See also: BELIMBING

MADURU: (*MAA-DU-RU*, Sri Lanka) see FENNEL

MAIDA FLOUR: (*MAI-DAA*, India) see FLOURS AND THICKENERS

MAIK YU: (*MAK YUE*, China) see CUTTLEFISH

MAIZE: see CORN

MAKAPUNO: (*MA-KA-POO-NOO*, Philippines) (*Cocos nucifera*) A mutant coconut full of soft, gelatinous meat that is sweetened and served as a dessert or used in ice cream. Bottled *makapuno* packed in coconut syrup is readily available where Philippine and Indonesian food products are sold. Once opened, it will keep for only 1–2 days in the refrigerator.
Also known as *kopyor* (Indonesia); freak coconut; sports coconut
See also: COCONUT

MA KHAM PEAK: (*MA-KHAM PICK*, Thailand) see TAMARIND

MAKI-ZUSHI: (*MAH-KEE-ZOO-SHI*, Japan) see SUSHI

MAKKI KI ROTI: (*MAK-KEE KEE RO-TEE*, India) see BREAD, INDIAN

MAK MO: (*MAK MO*, China) see CUTTLEFISH

MAKRUT/MA GRUT: (*MAK-RUUD*, Thailand) see KAFFIR LIME

MAKUA: (*MAK-HU-AA*, Thailand) see EGGPLANT

MAKUA PHUONG: (*MAK-HU-AA PHUONG*, Thailand) see EGGPLANT

MAKUA YAE: (*MAK-HU-AA A*, Thailand) see EGGPLANT

MALAGKIT: (*MA-LAG-KIT*, Philippines) see RICE

MALAYSIA, COOKING METHODS: see INDIA, COOKING METHODS; INDONESIA, COOKING METHODS

MALAI: (*MA-LAA-EE*, India) A rich milk product used in desserts and sweetmeats and in fillings for *kofta* (meat or vegetable balls). Milk is boiled in a wide pan until a skin forms on top. This is removed and the milk reboiled, skinned and reboiled until the liquid has reduced to a firm, dryish, creamy substance. It should be crumbled with the fingers into small granules before use. As it is a time-consuming process, it may be replaced in certain recipes by a very thick or clotted cream.

See also: KHOYA; ROGHAN JOSH (recipe)

MALAI
Yields 3 oz (90 g)

4 cups (1 qt / 1 l) fresh whole milk

Pour milk into a wide pan; bring to a boil. Reduce heat and simmer until a thick skin forms. Lift off skin and set aside. Reboil milk and repeat until all is made into *malai*. Rub between fingers to reduce to a crumbly paste. Keep cool until needed.

MALAYSIA: In Peninsular Malaysia, three nationalities—Malays, Chinese and Indians—live together in a unique blending of culture and tradition. The harmony of this liaison is reflected in a unified cuisine which takes elements from each. The Indians contributed the art of spice blending. Shredded chili, for example, will give extra bite to a mildly flavored southern Chinese-style dish; a curry may gain depth by the addition of soy sauce and pickles. Chutneys and Indian-style unleavened breads generally accompany a meal. As Indonesia is Malaysia's near neighbor, and as both countries share a similar topography and climate, it is not surprising that there are also many similarities between their cuisines: they both produce coconut, cassava, palm sugar and an array of fragrant cooking herbs.

Curries figure prominently in Malaysian cooking. They are coconut milk-based and yellow with turmeric. The grated fresh turmeric root is often used, spiked with chili, fragrant with lemon grass and *galangal*, and pungent with the compressed dark cakes of fermented shrimp paste (*blacan*). Here too, tamarind lends its palate-stimulating tartness to many dishes. Curries range from the mild Indian-style *kormas* to fiery dishes in the southern Indian and Indonesian traditions. Curry-making begins with a *rempah* (see entry), a blend of herbs, onions, garlic, ginger and spices, that dictates the final texture and flavor of the dish.

Serving and eating Malaysian food is a casual affair. Platters of food are served at a center table, usually several dishes at once, with tasty garnishes of shredded omelette and chili, crisply fried garlic and shallots, *sambals*, pickles and chutney, and there are usually chilies and soy sauce as well. Eating implements are dictated by the meal. A curry may be served on a section of banana leaf and is eaten with the fingers, Indian fashion. Chinese dishes call for chopsticks and a porcelain spoon, while other dishes require a fork and spoon. Refreshing dessert drinks based on iced coconut milk and sugar syrup and local coffee or Chinese tea served in tall glasses are the beverages best enjoyed in Malaysia.

One unique offshoot of Malaysian cuisine is Nonya cooking, which integrates Malay and Chinese elements.

See also: NONYA CUISINE

MALAYSIA RECIPES

Appetizers
Curry Puffs
Pancake Roll Malay-style
Rice Ribbon Noodles Stir-fried
Satay with Sweet Sauce

Main Courses
Coconut Fish Curry
Laksa with Chicken and Coconut Milk
Liver and Pork Balls
Rempah Fish
Rendang Chicken
Squid in Mild Curry Sauce
Tamarind Beef
Tamarind Chicken

Accompaniments
Hokkien Fried Noodles
Jackfruit in Creamy Curry Sauce
Pickled Vegetables
Roti Jala

(cont'd)

(Malaysia Recipes cont'd)

Desserts
Gula Melaka
Sweet Noodle Dessert

MENUS
(see recipes)

DINNER MENU
Serves 8

Pancake Roll Malay-style

Coconut Fish Curry
Tamarind Chicken

Hokkien Fried Noodles
Pickled Vegetables
Rice

BANQUET MENU
Serves 10

Curry Puffs
Satay with Sweet Sauce

Jackfruit in Creamy Curry Sauce
Liver and Pork Balls
Rempah Fish
Rendang Chicken
Roti Jala
Squid in Mild Curry Sauce

Sweet Noodle Dessert

FAMILY MEAL

Rice Ribbon Noodles Stir-fried

Rice
Tamarind Beef

Fresh Fruit

MALAYSIAN SEASONING PASTE: see REMPAH
MALDIVE FISH: see BOMBAY DUCK

MALI: (*MA-LI*, Thailand) (*Jasminum sambac*) Jasmine, both as fresh flowers and as a potent liquid essence, is used extensively in the Thai kitchen. A fragrant essence extracted from local jasmine flowers gives its rich, heady fragrance to dessert syrups, rice and other dishes, and is added to finger bowls for use after eating. It is sold in Asian food stores in small bottles as water or essence. The latter has an intensely strong fragrance and should be used with discretion. Unopened jasmine flower buds, picked the evening before they open, are strung into decorative strands for use as table decoration in Thailand, or used to scent drinking water, teas and desserts.
Also known as *dok mali, malee, yod nam mali* (jasmine oil) (Thailand); jasmine essence; jasmine water
See also: FLAVORINGS

MALONG: (*MAH-LONG*, Malaysia) see EEL

MALTOSE: A thick, treacle-like ingredient, made by fermenting germinated grains of barley. It is what is used to give Beijing (Peking) duck its lacquered appearance and is brushed over other types of roasted meats in northern China. It is usually diluted with water or vinegar and, when used to glaze foods, may have soy sauce and a red food coloring added. Maltose is sold in small plastic tubs where Chinese food products are available. It lasts indefinitely with or without refrigeration. Dark corn syrup, honey or treacle are all possible substitutes.
Also known as *mark yang tong, yi tong* (China); malt sugar
See also: VIETNAMESE-STYLE BEIJING DUCK (recipe)

MA-NAO: (*MA-NAO*, Thailand) see LIME
MANDARIN: see TANGERINE/MANDARIN
MANGLAK: (*MAENG-LAK*, Thailand) see BASIL

MANGO, GREEN: The flesh of unripe mango contains enzymes that are useful for the tenderizing of meats. Grated green (unripe) mango is used particularly in Thailand, India and Malaysia for this purpose, as well as to impart a pleasant tart flavor to vegetable and lentil dishes. Unripe papaya (pawpaw), pomegranate juice, tamarind, vinegar or tart citrus juices have a similar effect. Whole small green mangoes are pickled in oil with spices and chili to serve as an accompaniment to Indian meals. *Aamchur* is a tart seasoning powder made from dried green mango.
Also known as *hara aam* (India); *ma muang mun* (Thailand)
See also: AAMCHUR; MANGO PICKLES (recipe)

MANGO, GREEN, DRIED: see AAMCHUR

MANGO PICKLES
Yields 2¹/₄ lbs (1 kg)

2 lbs (1 kg) green mangoes
2 tsps salt
2 tsps turmeric
2 cups (16 fl oz / 500 ml) vegetable or mustard oil
1¹/₄ tbsps black mustard seeds
1 tsp asafoetida
2 tbsps chili powder

Wash unpeeled mangoes and cut into small pieces. Sprinkle thickly with the salt and turmeric and set aside for 6 hours. Heat the vegetable oil (or 1 cup each of vegetable and mustard oil) to smoking. Cook mustard seeds and *asafoetida* until the seeds stop popping. Cool and mix in chili powder. Squeeze mangoes to remove excess liquid. Place in sterilized jars and cover with the oil. Keep in a dark place for at least 6 days before use.

MANGOSTEEN: (*Garcinia mangostana*) A native of the Moluccas Islands, but now growing in Malaysia, this very slow-growing tree usually reaches only to a height of 45 ft (13.5 m) and does not mature until it is about 15 years old. Owing to its slow growth and the difficulties of propagation, it is not cultivated on a large scale. The fruit is a berry, brownish-purple in color with a tough external rind. The crisp-soft, white flesh is divided into segments, each containing small, oval seeds, although sometimes they can be seedless. It is one of the most attractive of the Asian fruits and is enjoyed for its delicate texture and sweet-sour flavor, which is slightly suggestive of molasses (treacle). It is sometimes cooked with rice, and is made into a dark, sweet, jelled confection, known in Malaysia as *dodol*.
Also known as *manggis* (Indonesia); *mangkut* (Thailand)

Mangosteen, whole and in cross section

MANG TRE: (*MAN TRAIR*, Vietnam) see BAMBOO SHOOT

MANTING: (*MUN-TEENG*, Indonesia) see DAUN SALAM

MAO-TAI: (*MAU-TOI*, China) see WINE, CHINESE

"MA-PO" DOFU: (recipe) see BEEF

MA PRAO: (*MA PRAO*, Thailand) see COCONUT

MASALA: (*MA-SAA-LAA*, India) The spice mixtures used in Indian cooking are known as *masalas*. There are many different types, blended to suit taste preferences, particular dishes and regional specialties. They are all highly aromatic, but can vary in intensity of flavor from mild to extremely hot. *Masalas* are made by grinding whole spices to a fine powder. This is done commercially, but many Indian cooks still prefer to blend at home to their own family recipe. Ground spices quickly lose their flavor and aroma, so it is preferable to grind small amounts of whole spices when needed. Several types of ground *masala* blends are available in Asian stores. They should be stored in tightly closed spice jars and, preferably, should be used within three months. Extra flavor can be added by "dry-roasting" the spices in a pan or oven before grinding. This gives the dish a darker color and a nutty, toasted flavor.

See also: CURRY PASTES AND POWDERS

CHAAT MASALA is a tart and salty spice mixture that gets its unique taste from *aamchur*, the sharp, lemony seasoning made from ground, dried, unripe mangoes. It is used to flavor the salad-like dishes known as *chaats* (the most popular ones are made with shredded cooked chicken and mixed fruit) and as a seasoning when a sharp, hot and tart flavor is required.

See also: CHAAT MURGH (recipe)

CHAAT MASALA

1 oz (30 g) coriander seeds
2 oz (60 g) cumin seeds
1 tbsp black peppercorns
1/2 oz (15 g) dried red chilies
1 oz (30 g) aamchur
1/3 cup (3–4 oz / 90–120 g) salt
1 tsp dried mint
1 tsp ground ginger

Dry-roast coriander and cumin seeds in a pan or hot oven, then grind to a fine powder with the remaining ingredients. Cool and store in a spice jar.

DHANSAK MASALA is a spice mixture used in the central-western states of India to flavor a traditional Parsi dish known as *dhansak*. This dish, which is served in Parsi homes every Sunday, is made up of several types of lentils cooked with diced lamb, *dhansak* spices, cardamom and cinnamon. It comprises four parts toasted and ground coriander to one part toasted and ground cumin. *Dhansak* is always accompanied by small grilled kebabs and a tart salad pickle known as *kachumber*.

See also: DHANSAK (recipe)

DHANSAK MASALA

1/2 cup (4 oz / 125 g) coriander seeds
1 1/4 tbsps cumin seeds

Toast the spices in a dry pan or hot oven until very aromatic, taking care they do not burn. Cool briefly, then grind to a fine powder. Cool and store in a spice jar.

GARAM MASALA is the best known of the Indian spice mixtures. It was popularized in northern India during the Moghul reign when sauces were highly aromatic, subtle in flavor and creamy-smooth in texture. *Garam masala* does not contain turmeric, the ingredient that gives Western-style curries and many of the curries in Indonesia, Malaysia and the southern states of India their characteristic yellow color. North Indian curries are usually brown or pale in color, yellow tones being acquired from saffron rather than the less subtly flavored turmeric, which grows and is used extensively in the south. *Garam masala* is also used as a condiment that is sprinkled over grilled, fried and roasted food and finished dishes.

GARAM MASALA

1/4 cup (2 oz / 60 g) coriander seeds
1/4 cup (2 oz / 60 g) black peppercorns
3 tbsps cumin seeds
20 green cardamom pods, peeled and seeds crushed
20 whole cloves
1 x 2 in (5 cm) cinnamon stick
2 tsps ground nutmeg
1/2 tsp ground mace

Dry-roast coriander, peppercorns and cumin seeds in a pan or hot oven until very aromatic, about 6 minutes. Grind all of the spices together in a spice grinder or mortar until reasonably fine, but not too powdery. Cool and store in a spice jar.

MASALA CABBAGE
Serves 4–6

2 tbsps ghee
3 cups (1¹/₂ lbs / 700 g) shredded cabbage
1 onion, thinly sliced
2 tsps minced garlic
¹/₂ tsp chili powder
1 tsp turmeric
1 tsp salt
1 tsp garam masala
lemon juice

Heat ghee and fry cabbage, onion and garlic to lightly color. Add chili powder, turmeric and salt. Stir-fry for a few minutes. Cover and simmer gently till tender. Uncover, raise heat and cook 2 minutes. Sprinkle with *garam masala* and lemon juice.

KASHMIRI MASALA relies on fragrant cardamom to give it characteristics that differ from its cousin, *garam masala*. It is used in the far north of India and in Kashmir, particularly to season dishes cooked by the baked-in-a-pot method known as "*dum.*" Kashmiri *masala* is best with chicken or lamb; it is considered too fragrant for most fish dishes. Like *garam masala*, it can be sprinkled over cooked food as a condiment.
See also: ROASTED MASALA POTATOES (recipe); ROGHAN JOSH (recipe)

KASHMIRI MASALA

30 green cardamom pods, peeled and seeds crushed
1 tbsp cumin seeds
1 tbsp black peppercorns
20 whole cloves
1 x 2 in (5 cm) cinnamon stick
¹/₄ tsp ground nutmeg
¹/₂ tsp ground mace

Grind all spices to a fine powder; store in a spice jar.

ROASTED MASALA POTATOES
Serves 4–6

1 lb (500 g) small potatoes
vegetable or mustard oil
¹/₈ tsp asafoetida
4 whole cloves
1¹/₂ tsps cumin seeds
¹/₂ cup (4 oz / 125 g) ghee
2 tsps ground coriander
1 fresh green chili, seeded and chopped
1 tsp minced ginger
1¹/₄ cups (10 fl oz / 300 ml) water
1¹/₂ tsps salt
2 tsps Kashmiri masala
1 tsp dried mint
chili powder

Peel potatoes, rinse and dry. Fry in the oil until lightly colored. Fry *asafoetida*, cloves and cumin seed in ghee until aromatic. Add coriander, chili and ginger and fry briefly. Add water, salt and potatoes and bring to a boil. Reduce heat, cover and cook very gently for 25 minutes, or bake on 350°F (180°C) for 30 minutes, until tender. Season with *masala* and mint, and add chili powder to taste.

SAMBAR MASALA is a tart spice mixture used in southern India to season a thin vegetable curry that is the traditional accompaniment to a large, thin, crisp pancake-like bread known as *dosa*. It is made of toasted ground lentils,

SAMBAR MASALA
(Mild)

2 tbsps urad dal (split black lentils)
1 tbsp coriander seeds
1 tbsp cumin seeds
2 tsps black peppercorns
1 tsp fenugreek seeds

Toast the lentils and spices in a pan or hot oven for about 6 minutes. Grind to a fine powder. Cool and store in a spice jar.

coriander, cumin, black peppercorns and fenugreek. Hotter varieties also contain dried chili, mustard seeds and curry leaves. It can be purchased from Indian food stores or homemade.
See also: BREAD, INDIAN; DAL AND VEGETABLE SAUCE (recipe)

SAMBAR MASALA
(Hot)

6 curry leaves
1 tsp fenugreek seeds
1½ tbsps coriander seeds
1 tsp black peppercorns
1 tsp brown mustard seeds
1½ tsps cumin seeds
8 dried chilies

Toast the spices; seed the chilies. Grind spices to a reasonably fine powder. Cool. Store in a spice jar.

XACUTTI MASALA is a specialty of the western coastal Indian state of Goa. Sweet spices with coconut, roasted until quite dark in color and then fried in ghee, give a particular toasted, nutty taste and a dark color to curries. Excellent with chicken, pork and whole shrimp in their shells.
Also known as *shakuti* (India)
See also: XACUTTI CHICKEN (recipe)

XACUTTI MASALA

1 cup (2 oz / 60 g) freshly grated or desiccated coconut
6 dried Kashmiri chilies
1 tbsp coriander seeds
½ tsp cumin seeds
½ tsp black peppercorns
½ tsp fenugreek seeds

In a dry pan or oven, roast the coconut and spices until quite dark in color, stirring slowly and continually. Cool and store in a spice jar.

MATCHA: (*MATCHAH*, Japan) see TEA

MATHA: (*MAT-THAA*, India) see BUTTERMILK

MATRIMONY VINE: see BOXTHORN

MATSUTAKE: (*MAH-TZU-TAH-KE*, Japan) see MUSHROOMS AND EDIBLE FUNGI

MATSUTAKE FU: (*MAH-TZU-TAH-KE WHO*, Japan) see GLUTEN

MA-UK: (*MA-EUK*, Thailand) see EGGPLANT (HAIRY)

MEAN SEE JIANG: (*MIN SEE CHING*, China) see BEAN PASTES AND SAUCES

MEATBALL: Bite-size balls of finely ground meat or fish are a common ingredient in the

a

b

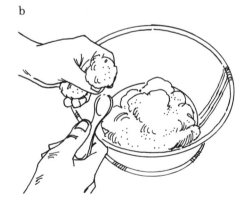

Making meatballs
a. Take a handful of the paste and squeeze a ball between forefinger and thumb
b. Use a spoon to scoop off the meat or fish balls

cuisines of China, Japan, Thailand and Vietnam. They are formed by a simple technique. Grind, process or pound the ingredients to a *very smooth* paste, then add volume and lightness by beating in as much ice water as possible. Scoop a handful of the paste and squeeze a portion out from between curled forefinger and thumb. Scrape the ball-shaped paste off with a spoon. It should be about the size of a walnut. Drop into boiling water or deep oil. Cook meatballs until they float to the surface. To store uncooked balls and retain their shape, drop into ice water.

"LION'S HEAD" MEATBALLS
Serves 6

1½ lbs (750 g) lean pork, coarsely
ground
2 tbsps chopped scallions (spring / green
onions)
2 tbsps chopped bamboo shoots
2 tsps chopped fresh ginger
1 tsp salt
⅓ tsp pepper
2 tsps yellow rice wine
1 tbsp light soy sauce
1 tbsp cornstarch (cornflour)
1 lb (750 g) napa cabbage, cut into
wide strips
¼ cup (2 fl oz / 60 ml) vegetable oil
2 tsps Oriental sesame oil
4 cups (1 qt / 1 l) hot chicken stock

In a food processor, chop pork with scallions, bamboo shoots and ginger to a smooth paste. Add salt, pepper, wine, soy and cornstarch. Mix well, then form into 6 large balls. Stir-fry cabbage in vegetable oil and sesame oil for 1 minute. Transfer half of the cabbage to a casserole; place meatballs on top, and cover with remaining cabbage. Pour in stock and add salt to taste. Cover and simmer gently or bake in a moderate oven for 1–1½ hours, until tender. Serve in the casserole.

MEATBALLS OF PORK WITH SALAD GREENS
Serves 6

1 lb (500 g) lean pork, finely ground
½ cup (4 oz / 120 g) minced scallions (spring /
green onions)
1 tsp minced garlic
1 tsp minced fresh ginger
2 small egg whites
salt
white pepper
water, salted
18 banh trang wrappers, each 6 in (15 cm) in
diameter
lettuce leaves
fresh coriander (cilantro)
dill
mint
basil
1 cup (8 oz / 250 g) rice vermicelli
1½ cups (12 oz / 350 g) fresh bean sprouts
1 small cucumber, cut into sticks
1 medium carrot, cut into sticks
¼ cup (2 oz / 60 g) giant white radish, cut
into sticks
Vietnamese peanut sauce

Mix pork, scallions, garlic and ginger with egg whites and salt and white pepper to taste. Knead until mixture is very smooth. Use oiled hands to form into small balls. Drop into a pot of salted water and simmer until they float to the surface. Remove with a slotted spoon. Cut a cross in the top of each. Grill until golden. Dip *banh trang* into water to soften; drain. To eat, line a *banh trang* wrapper with lettuce. Add meatballs, herbs, vermicelli and vegetables. Roll up. Dip into Vietnamese peanut sauce.

MEDICINAL FOODS: The Chinese are noted for their confidence in the beneficial effects of herbs and medicinal foods for the maintenance of health and the cure of various ills. Throughout their long history they have studied and documented the value and effect of hundreds of different herbs and continue to use many that were popularized centuries ago. Ordinary foods, too, are ascribed with health-giving qualities and are classified into *yin* and *yang*; cooling or warming. Most popular of the many herbs in use are *dang gui*, a pungent root used in soups; *gingseng*, the herb also revered by the Koreans; the date-like red jujube; licorice root; wolfberries and the seed of the boxthorn plant. Matrimony vine—which is cousin of the boxthorn—myrobalans and southernwood all have their medicinal uses, as does the Indian wood apple and the tart *belimbing*.

See also: BELIMBING; BOXTHORN; DANG GUI; GINSENG; JUJUBE; LICORICE ROOT; MELONS AND GOURDS (BITTER MELON); SOUTHERNWOOD; WOOD APPLE; YIN AND YANG

MEE: (*ME*, Malaysian) see NOODLES (EGG)

MEEHOON: (*ME-HOON*, Malaysia) see NOODLES RICE VERMICELLI

MEIN JIN PAU: (*MIN GUN PAU*, China) see GLUTEN

MEJISO: (*MEE-JEE-SOW*, Japan) see BEEFSTEAK PLANT

MEKONG WHISKY: see WINE, ASIAN

MELINJO: (*M'LEAN-JO*, Indonesia) (*Gnetum gnemon*) The elegant *melinjo* tree is cultivated in Indonesia for its fruit, which are small and red when fully matured. The fruit is peeled and cooked to soften. The kernel and the horny covering around it are beaten or rolled flat and dried in the sun. This dried chip is made into *emping*, a thin wafer that is fried to serve as a snack or used to garnish soups and salads. The young flowers and leaves are eaten, raw or steamed, as a vegetable, and the ripe red peel is fried in oil to make a side dish to serve with rice. The immature nuts are added to soup in Java.

Also known as *belinjo; blindjo* (Indonesia)
See also: KRUPUK

MELLET PAK CHEE: (*MALED PHAK CHEE*, Thailand) see CORIANDER

MELONS AND GOURDS: The Cucurbitaceae family is expansive, encompassing many varieties of cucumbers, gourds, marrows, melons, pumpkins and squashes, as well as sweet melons.

See also: LUFFA, ANGLED

SWEET MELONS (*Cucumis melo*) grow on annual trailing herbs that are thought to have originated in tropical Africa, but the cultivation of which has spread throughout the world. They belong to a large family that includes vegetable melons and gourds. Sweet melons are eaten raw as a fruit and are enjoyed at the end of many Asian meals in preference to a sweet dish. Certain types of sweet melons are also used in soups, pickles and preserves. The flesh comprises approximately 94 percent water and 4 percent sugar, making them refreshing and thirst-quenching. Cantaloupe, honeydew, musk and watermelons are the most common. In many Asian countries the seeds of watermelons—and also of pumpkins—are lightly salted and dry-roasted to serve as snacks. In Chinese communities these have particular importance during the festive season. They are sold in the shell, and there is a particular art in extracting the nut kernel without using the fingers.

Cantaloupes recognizable by their warty or scaly rind and with apricot-colored skin and flesh, are grown in Indonesia and other Southeast Asian countries.
Also called rockmelon

Honeydew melons have smooth, green skin and sugar-sweet flesh. They are much enjoyed as a dessert fruit.

Musk melons are the most prized of the family. Favored by the wealthy of India, in the past they were brought from Samarkand. Elsewhere in Asia only the Japanese regularly enjoy these expensive fruits, which are distinguished by their green to pink-yellow skin covered with a distinct network of buff-colored veins. They have a luscious fragrance and flavor.
Also known as netted melon; nutmeg melon

Watermelons (*Citrullus vulgaris*) are cultivated in warmer regions worldwide and have been eaten in Asian for many centuries. They came originally from tropical Africa. The large, round or ovoid fruit, with its speckled pale to deep-green skin, grows on a fast-growing climbing plant. In Thailand and China, the art of carving the outside of watermelon (and other melon) skins with floral and traditional designs for use as banquet table decorations is a highly developed skill. The hollowed, carved skin becomes a serving dish for fresh fruit or sweet soups. Like the skin of its white-fleshed cousin, the winter melon, watermelon skin is cut into slivers and pickled or candied. Uncut watermelon can be kept for several weeks but once cut, should be refrigerated and consumed within 2–3 days.

Also known as *sai gwa* (China); *semargka* (Indonesia, Malaysia)

See also: THAILAND, GARNISHES

VEGETABLE MELONS AND GOURDS come in many types, shapes and sizes and are characterized by their soft-crisp, bland to slightly bitter-tasting flesh, which ranges from white to green or golden orange. Most are elongated in shape with a central seed core and a firm, but not necessarily tough, skin.

Bitter melon (*Momordica charantia*) is the fruit of a tropical climber, which has a warty skin and grows to a maximum length of 8 in (20 cm). The skin is light to bright green when immature, which is when it should be eaten. Its firm, green, bitter flesh is something of an acquired taste. The fibrous seed core is usually cut away, leaving a thin ring of flesh. The ripe melons are usually orange-yellow in color, although there is a white variety which, however, is less enjoyed at this stage of maturity, when the texture is less agreeable and the flavor indistinct.

Bitter melon is highly regarded throughout Asia for its blood-purifying and system-cooling capabilities and is known to contain quinine. This makes it a valuable vegetable in tropical Asia, where malaria-carrying mosquitoes are a health hazard.

It is cultivated for eating in India and throughout China and southern Asia. The Chinese cook it by braising or steaming, and to a lesser extent by stir-frying. A dish of sliced bitter melon stuffed with ground spiced pork is a popular Chinese *dim sum* choice. It is usually combined with strong-tasting seasonings, such as garlic and chili or fermented black beans. In India and Sri Lanka it is curried and made into pickles, and in Indonesia it is used raw in salads. Steeping the sliced melon in salt water helps to reduce the bitterness. Its young tender shoots and leaves can be eaten like spinach.

When buying, choose the ones that feel firm to the touch and are a mid-green color. They can be stored in the vegetable compartment of the refrigerator for several weeks. Bitter melons can be bought sliced in cans, but the flavor is less appealing and the texture soft.

Also known as *foo gwa*, *mo gwa* (China); *karela* (India); *pare*, *peria* (Indonesia); *ampalaya* (Philippines); balsam pear; bitter cucumber; bitter gourd

See also: BITTER MELON STUFFED WITH PORK (recipe)

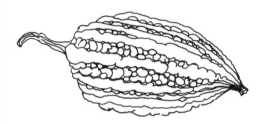

Bitter melon

Bottle gourd (*Lagenaria siceraria* Mol.), closely related to the hairy gourd, this is believed to have originated in Africa. These vegetables have grown in Asia for many centuries and are represented in ancient Chinese and Japanese art and noted in old documents as containers for water or herbs. Similar to summer squash in taste and texture, they have a fine-grained firm white flesh.

The name comes not from its shape, which resembles an old-style soft-drink bottle, but from the fact that for many centuries and in several different countries, the hardened, dried skin of this gourd was one of the only receptacles available for carrying liquids. To make bottles, the gourds must be harvested when absolutely ripe, the flesh scraped out and the shell dried over an open fire. The fresh gourds can, like winter melon, be hollowed and used for cooking and serving soup. It can be kept in the refrigerator for several weeks.

Also known as *woo lo gwa* (China); *labu air* (Malaysia); bottle squash; trumpet gourd
See also: KAMPYO

Chayote: (*Sechium edule*) is a vigorous, herbaceous, perennial vine that is extremely easy to grow. The Cantonese names for this vegetable suggest that it resembles the hands of the praying Buddha, and so it was cultivated by Buddhist monks and encouraged to grow near temples. The fruit is pear-shaped, 4–6 in (10–15 cm) long, with a light to deep green, slightly spiny skin and firm white flesh that exudes a sticky sap. Unlike other melons, it has a single hard central seed, which can be eaten when the melon is very young. The leaves, young shoots and large, fleshy roots are edible. In China, sliced chayote is cooked in soup with pork and is stir-fried with meat. It is an excellent substitute for winter melon.

Also known as *faat sau gwa, hop jeung gwa* (China); *labu siam; walu jepan* (Indonesia); *sayote* (Philippines); choko

Fuzzy melon (*Benincasa hispada*) is a small relative of the winter melon, and looks like a dumbbell-shaped zucchini, with blotchy green skin, covered with fuzzy white hairs. It is sometimes confused with the hairy gourd, a relative of the bottle gourd. It should be picked and eaten when young, when the melon has a delicately flavored pale green flesh. Peeled and seeded, it can be stir-fried, braised, boiled and made into soups. Like most melons this vegetable has the ability to absorb flavors. Sold at Chinese vegetable markets, these melons can be kept unwrapped in the refrigerator for up to 10 days.

Also known as *jit gwa, tseet gwa* (China); *timum balu* (Malaysia); Chinese vegetable marrow; hairy brinjal; hairy melon
See also: TWELVE PARTS SOUP (recipe)

Hairy gourd (*Lagenaria siceraria*) is light green in color and is a close cousin of the bottle gourd. It is baton-shaped and grows from 10–30 in (25–75 cm). One end is slightly thicker than the other and the gourd is sparsely covered with fine hairs. Do not confuse this melon with the delicately flavored fuzzy melon.
Also known as *po gwa* (China)

Snake gourd (*Trichosanthes anguina, T. cucumerina*) grows on an annual climber. The fruits are narrow and cylindrical and become slightly wider at the end. They can grow to 6 ft (2 m) in length. During growth, the base of the gourd may be weighted so that it will grow straight, and not curl into a spiral shape. It grows wild in many parts of Asia and is cultivated in India. Picked when immature, when they have a delicate, zucchini-like taste, snake gourds are sliced and boiled in the same way as other types of gourd or squash. The mid-green skin is thin and there is a narrow central core of seeds which must be discarded. Occasionally available in Asian food markets, they can be substituted in a recipe for zucchini or other types of Asian gourd.
Also known as *ketola ular* (Malaysia)

BITTER MELON STUFFED WITH PORK
Serves 6

4 fresh bitter melons, sliced and seeded
pinch of baking soda (bicarbonate of soda)
6 oz (180 g) minced lean pork
1 tsp salt
1½ tsps minced garlic
cornstarch (cornflour)
1 cup (8 fl oz / 250 ml) vegetable oil
2 tbsps fermented black beans, finely chopped
½ cup (4 oz / 125 ml) chicken stock
sugar
dark soy sauce

Place melon in a pan with water to cover and a pinch of baking soda. Boil for 2 minutes; drain and cool. Mix pork with salt and half the garlic. Press into the center of each melon ring. Coat lightly with cornstarch. Shallow-fry in the hot oil until golden and cooked through. Remove and pour off all but 2 tbsps oil. Fry remaining garlic and black beans; pour in chicken stock, add sugar and soy sauce to taste. Bring to a boil and thicken with a little cornstarch. Pour over dish and serve.

Winter melon (*Benincasa hispida*) is one of the largest vegetables grown. In maturity it resembles watermelon in appearance and shape but can grow as heavy as 100 lbs (45 kgs). The skin is mid-green, thin, hard and waxy—hence its common name, wax gourd. Winter melon is an ancient food of China and its most acclaimed application is as the soup *dong gwa jong*, or Winter Melon Pond, in which a rich broth is cooked and served in the skin. The skin has been elaborately carved with such auspicious motifs as the mythical dragon and phoenix.

Winter melon is sold as a sugared confection, especially during the Chinese New Year. A similar type of sweet, *petha*, was popularized in India at Agra, the city of the Taj Mahal. Strips of the melon are softened with lime solution, then boiled in sugar syrup until candied. *Petha* is eaten dry or with the syrup.

Winter melon, cubed or sliced, can be cooked by steaming, braising or simmering, or may be parboiled and stir-fried. Cubes, slit and stuffed, then steamed, are served as a Chinese *dim sum* dish. Medicinally, winter melon is cooling on the system. The melon is usually sold in pieces by weight and will keep, loosely wrapped, in the vegetable compartment of the refrigerator for up to six days. Uncut melons keep for many weeks.

Also known as *doan gwa*, *dong gwa* (China); *lauki*, *petha*, *sufed kaddu* (India); *togan* (Japan); *fak* (Thailand); wax gourd; white gourd; winter gourd
See also: CHINA, GARNISHES; LIME SOLUTION

Winter Squash (*Cucurbita maxima*) has many varieties, including banana squash, butternut, turban and pumpkin. All are relevant to Asian cooking. The varieties differ in size, shape and color, but all have a tough outer skin, orange flesh and a central seed cavity full of edible seeds. The fruit contains less water, more protein, fat, carbohydrates and vitamin A than summer squashes or marrows.

It is best eaten fully matured when the squash is tender, smooth, sweet and full of flavor. In China winter squash is not as popular as the white-fleshed summer melons, but in Japan it is used in many dishes, including *tempura*, and the hollowed whole small tur-

ban-shaped pumpkin is used as a receptacle for steamed custard. In India this squash is curried and added as a vegetable to many dishes; sliced, it is pickled and made into a chutney. The dried seeds are, like watermelon seeds, dry-roasted, salted and eaten like nuts.
Also known as *naam gwa* (China); *kadu* (India); *lapu merah* (Indonesia, Malaysia); *kabocha* (Japan); *farshi* (Nepal)
See also: SONGAYA (recipe); TEMPURA

MEN: (*MEN*) see CHINA, COOKING METHODS (RED BRAISING)

MERIENDA: (*ME-RIY-EN-DA*) see PHILIPPINES

METHI: (*MAI-THEE*, India) see FENUGREEK

METHI KA BEEJ: (*MAI-THEE KAA BEEJ*, India) see FENUGREEK

METHI KA SAAG: (*MAI-THEE KAA SAAG*, India) see FENUGREEK

MIANJIN: (*MIEN-GAN*, China) see GLUTEN

MIEN SEE: (*MIEN-SI*, China) see BEAN PASTES AND SAUCES

MIKAN: (*MEE-KAH-N*, Japan) see TANGERINE/MANDARIN

MIKI: (*MEE-KEE*, Philippines) see NOODLES (EGG)

MILAGIA PODI: (*MEE-LA-GI-A PO-DHI*, India) A spicy seasoning mixture used in southern India as a condiment over breads and different kinds of fried or steamed vegetarian snacks. It comprises toasted sesame and coriander seeds, red chili and split peas, such as *urad* or *channa dal*, coarsely ground together.
See also: IDLIS

MILK FISH: see BANGUS
MING DYNASTY EGG: see THOUSAND-YEAR EGG

MINT: (*Mentha arvensis*) A mildly pungent, green leaf herb many different types of which are grown and used around the world in cooking. In Asia several types of common and indigenous mints are used in the cuisines of Cambodia, Laos and Vietnam as an important part of the salad vegetables that are served with many dishes. In India dried mint is added to ground meats used to make *kebabs* and *koftas* (meat or vegetable patties) and the fresh, chopped herb is made into an aromatic, piquant chutney that is commonly served as a dip with fried snacks such as *samosas* and *pakoras*. The Thais use mint in their salads and green curry sauces, and as a garnish. A type of mint with purple-black stems and small, oval, deep green, dark-edged leaves is known as ginger mint and has a distinctive ginger aroma. Basil, caraway and coriander leaves, polygonum and other indigenous and introduced herbs are used with or in place of mint in Asian dishes. Sprouted caraway seeds produce a herb known as caraway mint; it is used often in Vietnam, where it is known as *rau la tia to*. Another plant, *rau ram*, known commonly as Vietnamese mint, is of the polygonum variety, with a strong flavor and long, tapering aromatic leaves.

Also known as *pak hom ho* (Cambodia); *pudina ki patti* (Indian); *daun pudina* (Malaysia); *meenchi* (Sri Lanka); *bai sa ra nai* (Thailand); *hung que*, *rau ram*, *rau thom*, *tia to* (Vietnam)
See also: CHICKEN SALAD WITH MINT LEAVES (recipe); MINT CHUTNEY (recipe); POLYGONUM; RAU LA TIA TO; VIETNAMESE MINT

MINT CHUTNEY
Yields 1/2 cup (4 fl oz / 125 ml)

1 cup (2 oz / 60 g) packed fresh mint leaves
1/4 cup (2 oz / 60 g) chopped scallions (spring / green onions)
1–3 fresh green chilies, seeded and chopped
2–3 tsps white vinegar
sugar
salt

Combine the mint, scallions, chilies and vinegar in a food processor, blender or mortar and grind until fairly smooth. Season to taste with sugar and salt.

MINYAK KELAPA: (*ME-NYAK KEH-LA-PA*, Indonesia) see COCONUT (MILK)

MIRIN: (*MEE-REEN*, Japan) see WINE, ASIAN

MISO: (*MEE-SOW*, Japan) A protein-rich, thick paste that is one of the most important ingredients used in Japanese cooking. A purée of soybeans and other ingredients, miso comes in several types, each with a distinctive flavor and color and therefore culinary application. Boiled soybeans are ground to a paste with wheat, barley or rice and injected with a yeast mold, then matured for anything from three to 30 months. As a general rule, the lighter the miso the milder and sweeter its flavor. Care should be taken that when adding miso to hot liquids it does not separate into granules that will not dissolve. It should be thinned with some of the liquid from the dish, then added when the liquid is not too hot. It is sold in tubs or plastic packs and will keep in the refrigerator for many months, although it will dry out if left uncovered.

MISO SOUP
Serves 6

6 in (15 cm) square kombu *seaweed*
5 cups (1 1/4 qts / 1.5 l) dashi
3 shiitake *mushrooms, soaked*
5 tbsps red miso
2 scallions (spring / green onions), shredded
4 oz (125 g) diced soft bean curd

Wipe *kombu* with a damp cloth.
Bring 4 cups (1 qt/1 l) *dashi* to a boil.
Simmer *kombu* and mushrooms gently until softened. Lift out and cut *kombu* into small squares; slice mushrooms.
Warm remaining 1 cup (8 fl oz/250 ml) *dashi* and add miso. Stir into the soup, add *kombu*, mushrooms, scallions and bean curd. Heat gently but do not boil.
Serve in covered bowls.

HATCHO-MISO is a strongly flavored, dark and salty miso. Granular, even lumpy, and rich in taste, it is made mainly of beans and is used in soups. A similar type is known as *aka*-miso or *akadashi*-miso, which equates with the Korean seasoning paste *dhwen-jang*.

INAKA-MISO or **SENDAI MISO** is red in color, rich in flavor and good for soups and braised stew-like dishes. Barley mold is used to make this type, and it can be either sweet or salty.
Also known as red miso

SHINSHU-MISO is yellow-colored, smooth and salty. It is the type most commonly available in the West and is suitable for most cooking. It is usually made with a rice-based mold.

SHIRO-MISO or "white miso" has an almost sweet taste. It is ideal for dressings and can also be used in soups.
See also: BEAN CURD; BEAN PASTES AND SAUCES; DENGAKU (recipe); DHWEN-JANG; MISO SOUP (recipe)

MISWA: (*MI-SWA*, Philippines) see NOODLES (RICE STICK)

MITHAI: (*MI-THAA-EE*, India) Sweetmeats served at the end of an Indian meal are known as *mithai*. Many are made from reduced milk or cream (*khoya*), combined with almonds and pistachio nuts. Particular favorites are *barfi*—fudge-like confections flavored with rose or kewra essence, filled with nuts and colored in rainbow hues with edible food dyes. *Mithai* are difficult to make and are usually purchased from vendors who have dedicated years to perfecting their own recipes.
Also known as *methai* (India)
See also: KHOYA

MITSUBA: (*MEE-TZU-BAH*, Japan) see JAPAN, GARNISHES

MOCHI: (*MO-CHEE*, Japan) A cake made from steamed glutinous rice, that is pounded to a paste in a large mortar. *Mochi* cakes are made for New Year festivals and come in various shapes but are usually round, like small buns. They are grilled and served with a soy sauce dip. Sweetened glutinous rice is made into dumplings, which are also known as *mochi*. A sweet form of *mochi* is wrapped in a cherry leaf and eaten in the cherry blossom season.
See also: RICE, GLUTINOUS; SWEET RED BEAN SOUP WITH MOCHI (recipe)

MOHINGHA: (*MONT-HIN-GAR*, Burma) The national dish of Burma. Like the popular Laotian dish *khao phoune*, *mohingha* combines fine egg noodles or rice vermicelli in a fish and coconut-milk sauce, with local vegetables and the tender heart of banana palms. *Mohingha* is available at virtually every street corner and marketplace, where itinerant vendors set up their portable fires to heat up noodles, sauce and the various essential components of this filling and delicious meal.
See also: BANANA; KHAO PHOUNE; NOODLES (RICE VERMICELLI)

MOHINGHA
Serves 8

1¹/₂ lbs (750 g) mackerel, cubed
water
2 stalks lemon grass, halved lengthways
¹/₃ cup (3 fl oz / 90 ml) fish sauce
³/₄ tsp turmeric
2–4 fresh red chilies
2 onions, chopped
vegetable oil
1¹/₂ tsps minced garlic
2 tsps minced ginger
2 tbsps rice flour
2 tbsps besan *flour*
2 cups (16 fl oz / 500 ml) thick coconut milk
8–9 in (20–22 cm) piece young banana tree heart; soaked, blanched and sliced
1¹/₄ lbs (625 g) rice vermicelli, soaked in boiling water

Place fish in a saucepan with water to cover. Add lemon grass, fish sauce, turmeric and chilies; simmer 15 minutes. Fry onions in a little oil until colored. Add garlic and ginger; fry briefly. Flake fish, add fried onion and flours with coconut milk. Boil 5 minutes. Add banana heart and vermicelli just before serving. Serve in a deep dish with the Mohingha Platter, adding its ingredients to the soup to taste.

MOHINGHA PLATTER

3–4 duck or hen eggs; hard-cooked and quartered
3 limes, cut into wedges
2–3 tbsps chopped fresh coriander (cilantro)
10–12 garlic cloves; sliced and fried
20 shallots or 5 small onions, sliced and fried
2–3 tbsps ground roasted chick-peas
1 cup (2 oz / 60 g) broken rice vermicelli, crisp-fried

(cont'd)

8–10 scallions (spring / green onions), chopped
1 recipe bean patties
*fresh chilies and fish sauce ***

Arrange all ingredients attractively on a
wide platter or several smaller plates.
Serve with *mohingha*.
* Seed chilies and grind to a paste
with a little peanut oil and fish
sauce to flavor.

MOMIJI-OROSHI

4 in (10 cm) length peeled giant white radish
3 thin red chilies

Push a chopstick lengthways
into the radish. Insert chilies into
the cavities. Finely grate. It can be
served wet, or the juice extracted by
twisting the purée in a piece of
cloth into which the liquid
is expelled.

MOH LOUNG YE BAW: (*MONT LONE YEAH BAW*, Burma) A Burmese dessert of small flour and coconut dumplings filled with *jaggery* sugar and floating in a coconut milk sauce. Its popular name is "teething cake." *Moh loung ye baw* is taken to relatives, neighbors and the poor in celebration of the arrival of a baby's first tooth.

MOKE-HAUNG: (*MOAK-KAUNG*, Burma) see CLAM

MOLDY BEAN CURD: see BEAN CURD BY-PRODUCTS

MOMEN TOFU: (*MOMEN TOH-WHO*, Japan) see BEAN CURD

MOMIJI-OROSHI: (*MO-MEE-JEE OWE-ROW-SHI*, Japan) A condiment served as a garnish with various Japanese dishes.
See also: RADISH, GIANT WHITE

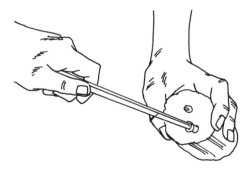

Momiji-oroshi
Push a chopstick into the radish piece

MONGO IKA: (*MOWN-GO EE-KAH*, Japan) see CUTTLEFISH

MONGOLIAN BARBECUE: see UTENSILS, HOTPLATES AND GRIDDLES

MONGOLIAN HOTPOT: (recipe) see LAMB

MONG YAU: (*MONG YAU*, China) see CAUL FAT

MONOSODIUM GLUTAMATE: The continued use of this crystalline, white powder in Asian cooking has caused considerable controversy. A natural salt, which was originally extracted from seaweed or wheat gluten, but more commonly from sugar beets or glucose, it is used to effectively enhance the natural flavors of food. However, it has been known to cause severe allergic reactions. It is used extensively in Japanese, Vietnamese, Thai and Chinese cooking, particularly in soups and dishes with a large amount of liquid that requires an intense flavor. It is readily available in shaker-packs or little cans.
Also known as *mei jing* (China); *aji no moto* (Japan); *servuk perasa* (Malaysia); *ve tsin* (Vietnam); M.S.G.; taste essence/powder

MOONG KE DAL: (*MOO-NG KEE DAAL*, India) see MUNG BEAN

MOON SIN: (*MUN SIN*, China) see EEL

MOTI SONF: (*MO-TEE SAUN-PH*, India) see FENNEL

MOUNTAIN YAM: see YAM

MOYASHI: (*MOW-YAH-SHI*, Japan) see BEAN SPROUT

MO YU: (*MOR YU*, China) see AMORPHOPHALUS KONJAC

M.S.G.: see MONOSODIUM GLUTAMATE

MU ER: (*MUK YI*, China) see CLOUD EAR FUNGUS

MUIK: (*MEE-YEOK*, Korea) see SEAWEED (KOMBU)

MULBERRY: (*Morus nigra*) The common black mulberry is the fruit of a deciduous tree that is native to western Asia. The tree was established in Europe in ancient times and mention of it dates back to early Greek and Roman times. The fruit is extremely perishable, so is rarely sold at markets. When ripe, its purple juice can leave an indelible stain. Its relative, the white mulberry (*Morus alba*), also grows on a tree that is native to Asia. It has pale green leaves that are used to feed the voracious silkworm from which come the renowned fine silks of Asia. White mulberries vary in shades of color from white, through pink, to purple. They are sweet, but lack the intense flavor of black mulberries.

Also known as *song tse* (China)

MULBERRY PAPER: A semi-absorbent white paper used as a wrapping during cooking. It is often tied over dishes that are simmer-steamed. It is not from the same tree as the paper mulberry, which has edible leaves. Oiled parchment (greaseproof) paper can be used instead.

MUNG BEAN: (*Phaseolus aureus*) A plant of the Leguminosae family whose small, round, green beans are extensively used in Asian cooking. We know them most commonly in their sprouted form as bean sprouts. However, dried mung beans are also ground into flour, which is used mainly for making desserts and, in the Sichuan province of China, a jelly similar to bean curd. They are candied as snacks or to be added to desserts. The dried green beans can be boiled as lentils or cracked to use in patties and fritters. Mung beans, cooked into a porridge with ginger, were once widely acclaimed in Asia as a remedy for *beriberi*. The young leaves and pods of the mung bean can be used as a vegetable. The clear, jelly-like vermicelli used in China, Vietnam and many other parts of Asia are made from mung bean flour.

Also known as *moong ke dal* (India); *kacang djong*, *kacang eedjo* (Indonesia); *kacang hijau* (Malaysia); *tau ngok* (Thailand); *dau xanh* (Vietnam); green gram

See also: BEAN JELLY; BEAN SPROUT; FLOURS AND THICKENERS; LENTIL; MOCK JACKFRUIT SEEDS (recipe); NOODLES (BEAN THREAD VERMICELLI)

MUNG BEAN FLOUR: see FLOURS AND THICKENERS

MUNG BEAN SPROUT: see BEAN SPROUT

MUSAMAN CURRY: (recipe) see BEEF

MUSHIMONO: (*MOO-SHI-MOW-NO*, Japan) see JAPAN, COOKING METHODS

MUSHROOMS AND EDIBLE FUNGI:

Throughout Asia mushrooms of many kinds, as well as many varieties of unusual, indigenous edible fungi, are grown. Perhaps the most popular, or at least the best known to the Western world, is the dried black mushroom of China.

BAMBOO FUNGUS (*Dictyophora phalloidea*) is a rare and exotic lacy fungal growth which proliferates in Sichuan and Yunnan, the central-eastern provinces of China. It grows on a certain type of bamboo, is buff to light cream in color and is shaped like a small lacy purse. It has a unique, musty, earthy taste and crunchy texture. Because it is extremely expensive, its use is limited to banquet dishes and fine vegetarian cuisine. It is unlikely to be found easily in Chinese markets.

The dried fungus should be soaked until tender, rinsed thoroughly and simmered briefly to tenderize and cook.

Also known as *goak sung*, *zhusun* (China); staghorn fungus

BLACK MUSHROOMS, CHINESE DRIED: (*Lentinus edodes*) Although commonly called black mushrooms, they are actually a pale buff to brown color. The best ones have a lighter color with plump caps. It was discovered long ago that their natural flavor intensifies on drying, so they are always marketed in dried form. Medicinally, dried mushrooms are thought to be beneficial to the respiratory system. Dried Chinese mushrooms can be very expensive. Sold in small packs, they should be transferred to an airtight container for storage and will keep indefinitely if not exposed to damp or strong light. They should be soaked for at least 25 minutes in tepid water, and the tough stems should be sliced off before use.

Their distinctive aroma and unique flavor lends itself to many culinary uses; they are added to Chinese dishes of all kinds and also served by themselves—often with a rich oyster sauce. To cook, they should be simmered gently in a light broth with soy sauce and rice wine. The liquid in which mushrooms are soaked or cooked can be added to sauces or braised dishes. The Japanese variety of dried black mushrooms is known as *shiitake*. This same type of mushroom, grown in northern China, is known as the winter mushroom, as it is harvested in the cooler months.

Also known as *donggu* (winter), *fa goo*, *xianggu* (China); *jamur hitam* (Indonesia); *shiitake* (Japan); *p'yogo* (Korea); *chingdauwan* (Malaysia); *hed hom*, *horm* (Thailand); *nam dong ca* (Vietnam); black forest mushroom; fragrant mushroom; oak mushroom; winter mushroom

CHAMPIGNONS are grown in many parts of Asia and are an important export product in both Taiwan and China. They can be used instead of straw mushrooms in most recipes.
Also known as button mushrooms

CLOUD EAR FUNGUS is the crinkly black fungus used in Chinese cooking and frequently in other Asian cuisines.
See also: CLOUD EAR FUNGUS

ENOKITAKE: (Japan) (*Flammulina velutipes*) Delicately flavored mushrooms with tiny white-gold caps on long slender stalks. They grow in clumps on the stumps of the *enoki* (Chinese hackberry) tree. No more than 5 in (8 cm) long, they are used in their small clumps, with the spongy root end trimmed, as an appealing garnish in Japanese soups and simmered dishes, and as an ingredient in *sunomono* and *aemono* dishes.

Enokitake are seasonal, and are brought to the markets in winter. They are sometimes available fresh from specialist Asian greengrocers, and will keep for up to one week in a perforated plastic bag in the refrigerator. They are more readily available packed in water in cans and plastic tubs. *Enokitake* mushrooms retain their crisp texture, but should be

drained and rinsed in ice water before use.
See also: AEMONO, SUNOMONO

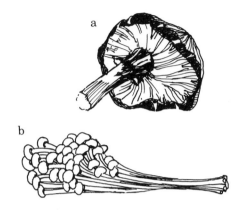

a. Shiitake b. Enokitake

KOUMOU: (China) (*Tricholoma gambosan*) Whitish, irregularly shaped mushrooms similar to an oyster mushroom, which grow in northern China and are used in the cuisine of Beijing.

MATSUTAKE: (Japan) (*Armillaria edodes*) These superbly flavored mushrooms are gathered from red pine woods in Japan during a short season in mid-autumn. They are now under limited cultivation, so are extremely expensive. They have dark brown, thick caps, slightly pointed in the center, and are usually picked before the cap has fully extended. The stems are thick and meaty.

Matsutake are not dried but used fresh and are usually cooked in a very simple way—grilled, baked in a closed container or aluminum wrap, or sautéed. They should be wiped with a damp cloth, the base of the stem trimmed and the cap cut into thick slices. Oyster mushrooms can be used as a substitute.
Also known as pine mushrooms

NAMEKO: (Japan) This unusual mushroom is deep amber in color, small to minuscule in size and has a pleasant, gelatinous texture. A fungus native to Japan, it is used in soups and one-pot dishes, and as a *sunomono*. Even in Japan these mushrooms are rarely available fresh, but are sold in cans and tubs in a light brine that does not unduly affect the flavor or tex-

ture. Drain and rinse thoroughly before use.
See also: SUNOMONO

OYSTER MUSHROOMS: (*Pleurotus ostreatus*)
These mushrooms, with their delicate, lop-sided appearance, and almost opalescent gray-beige caps, have become popular in Western countries. They have been cultivated in Asia, particularly northern China and Japan, for centuries and, like other Asian mushrooms, grow on decayed tree stumps. They have a subtle seafood flavor and the coloring of an oyster, and are used in stir-fried dishes. Their fragile beauty makes them a charming addition to clear soups.
Also known as *hou goo* (China); *jamur tiram*, *shimeji* (Indonesia, Malaysia); *hiratake* (Japan); abalone mushrooms; tree oyster mushrooms

---

CHILLED FINE NOODLES WITH MUSHROOMS
Serves 4

4 oz (120 g) somen *noodles*
4 dried shiitake *mushrooms, soaked and drained*
3 tbsps dark soy sauce
2 tbsps mirin
12 stalks mitsuba
1 recipe cold noodle sauce
1 tbsp grated fresh wasabi *or 2 tsps powdered* wasabi
2 tbsps finely chopped scallions (spring/green onions)

Boil noodles until tender; drain, rinse and cover with cold water. Combine mushrooms in 1 cup (8 fl oz/250 ml) cold water with soy sauce and *mirin*. Simmer for 15-20 minutes; drain and shred. Blanch *mitsuba*; discard leaves and chop stems. Serve noodles in mounds in glass dishes, adding 1/2 cup (4 fl oz/125 ml) ice water and ice cubes. Garnish with the shredded mushrooms and *mitsuba*. Serve the cold noodle sauce separately in small dishes as a dip. *Wasabi* and scallions are also served separately, to add as desired.

SHIITAKE: (Japan) (*Cortinellus shiitake*)
Closely related to the black mushroom of China, this black- to buff-colored mushroom is the most commonly used of the Japanese mushrooms, in both fresh and dried form. They are cultivated by introducing spores to the bark of a type of oak tree, *Pasania cuspidata*. This mushroom is also grown in China, where it is known as winter mushroom.

In general, the quality dictates the price, so the better ones will be quite costly. Although they are sold fresh by some Asian greengrocers, the dried type is readily available and, like black mushrooms, should be stored in an airtight container. Dried *shiitake* must be reconstituted in water before use, and the stems removed. A cross may be cut into the top of the cap, both for decorative purposes and to allow the mushrooms to cook through the thickest part. Fresh *shiitake* can be cooked like other fresh mushrooms. They will keep for 3–5 days in the refrigerator.
Also known as *donggu* (China); *hoshi-shiitake* (Japan); forest mushrooms; Japanese black mushrooms; winter mushrooms

STRAW MUSHROOMS: (*Volvariella volvacea*)
This cultivated fresh mushroom is globe-shaped and about the size of a quail's egg. The outer surface is buff in the young mushroom, becoming gray-black as it matures. A stemless mushroom, it retains its ovoid shape and, when cut in cross section, reveals an internal stem and cream-colored fine layers. Straw

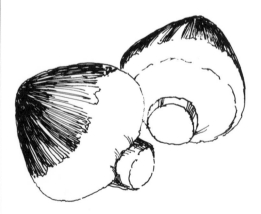

Straw mushrooms

mushrooms are grown on paddy-straw, left over from harvested wheat, and acquire a distinct, earthy, musty taste. Fresh straw

---

MUSHROOM PLATTER WITH HAIR VEGETABLE
Serves 4–6

6 dried black mushrooms
3 tsps yellow rice wine
4 tsps salt
1¹/₂ tsps sugar
8 lettuce leaves
water, boiling
4 tbsps oil
1¹/₂ cups (12 oz / 350 g) straw mushrooms
²/₃ cup (5 fl oz / 150 ml) chicken stock
3 tbsps cornstarch (cornflour)
2 tsps chicken fat
1¹/₂ cups (4 oz / 125 g) button mushrooms (champignons)
¹/₂ tsp pepper
¹/₂ cup (4 fl oz / 125 ml) heavy cream
1 tbsp oyster sauce
1 oz (30 g) hair vegetable, soaked

Remove black mushroom stems; place caps in a dish with 2 tsps rice wine, 1 tsp salt and the sugar. Steam for 25 minutes. Drain, reserving the steaming liquid. Blanch lettuce in boiling water with 1 tbsp of the oil and 1¹/₂ tsps salt for 45 minutes. Remove, drain well and arrange on a plate. Heat 2 of the tbsps of oil and stir-fry the straw mushrooms for 1 minute. Add the remaining 1 tsp rice wine, ¹/₂ tsp salt, ¹/₃ cup chicken stock and 1 tsp cornstarch. Simmer briefly. Add chicken fat and heat through. Stir-fry button mushrooms separately for 30 seconds; season with 1 tsp salt, pepper and add the cream mixed with 1 tsp cornstarch. Boil briefly. Stir-fry drained black mushrooms for 1 minute in 1 tbsp oil. Add ¹/₄ cup (2 fl oz/60 ml) of the reserved steaming liquid mixed with 1 tsp cornstarch until thickened. Add the oyster sauce. Wash and drain hair vegetable. Poach briefly in remaining ¹/₃ cup chicken stock; drain. Arrange mushrooms in separate groups and hair vegetables on top of lettuce.

mushrooms are sometimes available, but do not keep well, developing a gelatinous texture and rank taste. They are never dried, but are readily available, packed in water, in cans. Drain and rinse before use. Unused canned mushrooms can be refrigerated for several days.
Also known as *hmo* (Burma); *caogu, tso gwoo* (China); *jamur* (Indonesia, Malaysia); *hed fang* (Thailand); grass mushrooms; jelly mushrooms; paddy straw mushrooms

WHITE FUNGUS is a cream-white crinkly fungus used in sweet dishes and vegetarian cooking.
See also: WHITE FUNGUS (MAIN HEADING)

SHIITAKE MUSHROOMS WITH PONZU SAUCE
Serves 4

12 large fresh shiitake *mushrooms*
salt
2¹/₂ tbsps minced scallions (spring / green onions)
Ponzu Sauce

Cut each mushroom into several slices. Place each on a separate square of aluminum foil and salt lightly. Wrap loosely. Place foil parcels over hot charcoal or in a hot oven. Cook for about 6 minutes. Serve with minced scallions and *Ponzu* Sauce (see recipe).

MUSHROOM SOY: see SOY SAUCE (DARK)
MU SHU PORK: (*MOO-SHOO*, recipe) see PORK
MUSK MELON: see MELONS AND GOURDS
MUSLIM RICE DESSERT: (recipe) see RICE

MUSSEL: (*Perna viridis* Linnaeus) This shellfish of the Mytilidae family is the one most commonly eaten in Asia. It is vaguely triangular in shape and has a greenish-black shell. The flesh inside is an off-white or orange color and has a chewy texture and an interesting, full-bodied flavor. Thailand, Cambodia and the Philippines seem to make the most of

MUSSEL

mussels, while they are only occasionally enjoyed in other parts of Asia. The flesh can be removed from the shell and dried, and in Thailand is cooked by boiling and then coated with sugar and fried to eat as a snack. Mussels on the half-shell, covered with finely chopped fresh herbs and chili, and sometimes beaten egg, are steamed to make a memorable dish in Thailand. The mussels sold in the USA are of the black-shelled variety, which can be substituted for the Asian type in any recipe.
Also known as *kha-ya-nyo* (Burma); *chang hau* (China); *kupang* (Malaysia); *amahong, tahong* (Philippines); *hoy meng phu* (Thailand)
See also: SEAFOOD, DRIED

MUSTARD:
Mustard, made from the pale yellow seeds of the common mustard (*Sinaplis alba*) is only occasionally used in Asia. In Japan it is sometimes used in sauces and in an esoteric dish in which the holes of lotus roots (*rekon*) are filled with mustard, then coated with *tempura* batter and deep-fried. In Chinese restaurants a mild yellow mustard may be served as a dip with steamed *dim sum*, although chili sauce is usually preferred. Elsewhere in Asia black and brown mustard seeds are used in curries, spice mixtures and pickle preparations.
Also known as *karashi* (Japan)
See also: MUSTARD SEED

MUSTARD GREENS: see CABBAGE, CHINESE (CHUK GAII CHOY)

MUSTARD OIL: see OILS AND FATS

MUSTARD SEED:
Mustard, one of the world's oldest spices, has been used internationally for centuries. The black and red-brown mustard seeds used in Asian cooking differ from the yellow mustard seeds used to make the European style of mustard and mustard powder.

BLACK MUSTARD SEEDS (*Brassica nigra*) are used for their sharp, hot flavor in some curries and sauces, but are particularly associated with the making of Indian pickles, relishes and chutneys. The small, round, black seeds are picked by hand, and sun-dried. Mustard is usually sold in seed form as its

pungency quickly disperses after grinding.
Before using them in curries, toast mustard seeds in a dry pan or hot oven, until they begin to pop, to release the full flavor.
Also known as *rai* (India); *biji sawi* (Malaysia); *abba* (Sri Lanka)

BROWN MUSTARD SEEDS: (*Brassica juncea*) These round, red-brown seeds have a less pungent flavor than black mustard seeds. They are used for flavoring rice, *dal* and vegetable dishes, and are ground to season certain freshly made chutneys. The leaves of this plant are a commonly used vegetable in Asia.
Also known as *lal sarsu* (India)
See also: CABBAGE, CHINESE (CHUK GAII CHOY); CURRY PASTES, POWDERS AND SAUCES (PANCHPHORAN); MUSTARD, OILS AND FATS

MUTTON: see LAMB

MYOGA: (*MEWO-GAH*, Japan) see GINGER BUD

190

N

NAAN: (*NARN,* India) see BREAD, INDIAN

NA GANEGI: (*NAH-GAH-NE-GUI,* Japan) see LEEK, ASIAN

NAMA-AGE: (*NAH-MAH-AH-GUE,* Japan) see BEAN CURD, (FRIED)

NAMA FU: (*NAH-MAH WHO,* Japan) see GLUTEN

NAMA WUNI: (*NAH-MAH WU-NEE,* Japan) see CAVIAR

NAM CHA: (*NAM CHAA,* Thailand) see TEA

NAMEKO: (*NAH-ME-KOW,* Japan) see MUSH-ROOMS AND EDIBLE FUNGI

NAM JIM KRATIEM: (*NAM JIM KRATHIEM,* Thailand) A sweet-tart-flavored garlic sauce to serve with grilled or sliced cold meats.

NAM JIM KRATIEM
Yields ³/₄ cup (6 fl oz / 180 ml)

¹/₂ cup (4 fl oz / 125 ml) white vinegar
¹/₂ cup (4 oz / 100 g) sugar
1 tsp chopped red chili
1 tbsp chopped garlic
¹/₂ cup (4 fl oz / 125 ml) water
salt

Combine all of the ingredients except the salt in a small nonaluminum pan and bring to a boil. Cook slowly until reduced by half. Add salt to taste. Cool. Use at once, or store in a sealed jar in the refrigerator for several weeks.

NAM KATEE: (*NAM KATI,* Thailand) see COCONUT (MILK)

NAM NOMAO: (*NAM MANAO,* Thailand) see AMYLE ESSENCE

NA MOOL: (*NA MOOL,* Korea) A term describing cold-cooked side dishes, or marinated vegetables, that commonly accompany Korean meals. Ingredients frequently used in *na mools* are bean sprouts, radish and spinach.
See also: RADISH SHREDS (recipe)

NA MOOL OF SPINACH: (recipe) see SPINACH

NAM PA: (*NARM PAH,* Laos) see FISH SAUCE
NAM PLA: (*NAM PLAA,* Thailand) see FISH SAUCE

NAM PLA RAA: (*NAM PLAA RAA,* Thailand) An aromatic sauce made by boiling fermented fish (*pla roo*) with crushed lemon grass (*takrai*) and torn kaffir lime (*makrut*) leaves. It is strained and bottled for commercial sale.
See also: FISH SAUCE

NAM PRIK: (*NAM PHRIK,* Thailand) A hot Thai sauce that has been used as a dip since ancient times. Now made with chilies, it was probably first made with peppercorns, as chilies were not introduced to Asia until about the sixteenth century.
See also: EGGPLANT (PEA); NAM PRIK PAO; PRIK

NAM PRIK
Yields 1¹/₂ cups (12 fl oz / 375 ml)

2 tbsps dried shrimp
1¹/₂ tbsps chopped garlic
1¹/₂ tbsps chili flakes
¹/₂ cup (4 fl oz / 125 ml) fish sauce
¹/₂ cup (4 fl oz / 125 ml) lime juice
2–3 makua phuong *eggplants (aubergines)*

In a food processor or mortar grind shrimp, garlic and chili to a paste then slowly add fish sauce and lime juice to make a sauce. Chop *makua phuong* and stir in. Serve in small dishes as a dip. Keeps for several weeks in the refrigerator.

NAM PRIK PAO: (*NAM PHRIK PHAO,* Thailand) A hot chili sauce which traditionally accompanies rice, vegetables and salads.
Also known as roasted chili paste; roasted curry paste
See also: NAM PRIK; PRIK

NAM PRIK PAO
Yields ³/₄ cup (6 fl oz / 180 ml)

8–10 dried red chilies, seeded
1¹/₂ tbsps chopped garlic
3 tbsps chopped onions
1 tbsp dried shrimp paste

(cont'd)

(Nam Prik Pao cont'd)

1 tbsp vegetable oil
1 tbsp brown sugar
1 tsp tamarind concentrate
peanuts, roasted

Wrap chilies in a piece of aluminum foil and roast in a dry pan or oven 2–3 minutes on each side. Fry garlic, onions and shrimp paste in oil until well colored; add chili and fry briefly. Add sugar and tamarind; grind in food processor to a paste. Roasted peanuts can be added. Can be refrigerated for several weeks.

NAM SOM: (*NAM SOM*, Thailand) see VINEGAR

NAM SOM MAK KHAM: (*NAM SOM MAP HAAM*, Thailand) see TAMARIND

NAM TAN PEEP: (*NAM TAAN PEEB*, Thailand) see SUGAR (PALM)

NAN NAN ZEE: (*NAN NAN ZI*, Burma) see CORIANDER

NAN NAN BIN: (*NAN NAN BIN*, Burma) see CORIANDER, FRESH

NAPA CABBAGE: see CABBAGE, CHINESE

NARIYAL: (*NAA-RI-YAL*, India) see COCONUT (KELAPA MUDA)

NARM YU: (*NAM YUE*, China) see BEAN CURD BY-PRODUCTS (FERMENTED)

NASHI: (*NAH-SHEE*, Japan) see JAPANESE PEAR

NASI GORENG: (*NAR-SEE GOR--RENG*, Indonesia) *Nasi goreng*, or fried rice, is one of the best-known Indonesian rice dishes. An essential element of *rijstaffel*, it is also a popular everyday dish. Fried rice is served with shredded omelette, diced meat and chopped vegetables, flavored with spices.

NASI GORENG
Serves 6–8

¹/₄ cup (2 fl oz / 60 ml) vegetable oil
1 large onion, finely chopped
1¹/₂ tsps minced garlic
1 tsp minced ginger
³/₄ tsp turmeric
¹/₂–2 tsps chili paste

(cont'd)

(Nasi Goreng cont'd)

1 tsp shrimp paste
1 cup (8 oz / 250 g) diced cooked meat
1 cup (8 oz / 250 g) diced mixed vegetables
³/₄ cup (6 oz / 180 g) shredded Napa cabbage
1 cup (8 oz / 250 g) chopped bean sprouts
6–8 cups (1–2 lbs / 0.5–1 kg) cooked white rice
¹/₂ cup (4 fl oz / 125 ml) thick coconut milk
2 tbsps tamarind water
1 tbsp kecap manis or dark soy sauce
omelette shreds
fried onion flakes
fresh coriander (cilantro)

Heat oil in a large wok. Stir-fry onion and garlic for 1¹/₂ minutes. Add ginger, turmeric, chili and shrimp paste and stir-fry for 2–3 minutes. Add meat and vegetables; stir-fry 5 minutes. Add cabbage and bean sprouts; stir-fry a further 2–3 minutes. Add rice, season to taste, and stir-fry over high heat 1 minute. Add coconut milk, tamarind water and *kecap manis* or dark soy sauce. Shape the rice into a cone on a platter. Garnish with omelette shreds, fried onion flakes and coriander.

NASU: (*NAH-SUE*, Japan) see EGGPLANT (JAPANESE)

NATA: (*NA-TA*, Philippines) A thick, white translucent gelatinous layer, believed to be dextran. It grows on the surface of fruits, such as pineapple, coconut or sugar cane, that contain acid, sugar and nutrients in sufficient quantities to produce acid-forming bacteria. A pure culture is usually added to hasten fermentation.

After washing and boiling it is used in desserts as a flavoring. Common kinds are *nata de coco*, grown on coconut, and *nata de pina*, grown on pineapple. Both are obtainable in bottles from stores that stock Philippine or Indonesian products.
See also: COCONUT

NATTO: (*NAT-TO*, Japan) see SOYBEAN

NATUTO: (*NATU-TO*, Japan) see KAMABOKO

NAW MAI: (*NOR MAII*, Thailand) see BAMBOO SHOOT

NEGI: (*NE-GUI*, Japan) see LEEK, ASIAN

NEPAL: The food of the remote mountainous country of Nepal has many similarities to that of neighboring India. The meal centers around rice, known as *bhat*, and a thin dish of boiled lentils called, as it is in India, *dal*. Vegetables provide the base protein in this country, and are usually fried or stewed in a spicy sauce. Mustard oil, used in the same way as in India's north-eastern states, gives its unique, pungent flavor to many dishes. In general, tastes are bland. Flavor is highlighted by highly spiced *achars* (pickles) and many types of commercial and homemade chutneys. Beef is not eaten—in the Hindu tradition—but buffalo, goat and pork are included in the diet when affordable. Tibetan influence, with its own Chinese overtones, is also found in the cuisine, particularly in the form of noodles, of which the Nepalese are inordinately fond.
See also: INDIA

NEW MEXICAN CHILI: see CHILI

NGA CHOY: (*NGA CHOY*, China) see BEAN SPROUT

NGA-MAN-GYAUNG: (*NGA-MAAN-CHAUNG*, Burma) see ANCHOVY

NGAN PYA YE: (*NGAN PYAR YEAH*, Burma) see FISH SAUCE

NGAN PYA YE CHET: (*NGAN PYAR YEAH CHAT*, Burma) This is a strongly flavored sauce that is used as an accompaniment to Burmese dishes. It combines onion, lemon grass and garlic with *ngan pya ye* (fish sauce) and chili powder.
See also: FISH SAUCE

NGAPI: (*NGA-PIT*, Burma) see BURMA; FISH PASTE

NGAPI HTAUNG: (*NGA-PI TAUNG*, Burma) A pungently flavored sauce dip, combining *ngapi* (fermented shrimp paste) with onions, garlic and dried shrimp that have been ground to a fine paste.
See also: FISH, PRESERVED (FERMENTED); SHRIMP, DRIED

NGAPI HTAUNG

2 tbsps dried shrimp paste
2 medium onions, peeled
4 garlic cloves
2 tsps chili powder
2 tbsps dried ground shrimp
1 tsp salt
2 tbsps lemon juice

Wrap shrimp paste, onions and garlic in aluminum foil and broil until well colored; then grind to a paste with remaining ingredients.

NGA YUT THEE: (*NGA YOKE TEE*, Burma) see CHILI

NG HEUNG FUN: (*NG HEUNG FEN*, China) see FIVE-SPICE POWDER

NGUNN NGA CHOY: (*NGAN NGA CHOY*, China) see BEAN SPROUT (SILVER)

NGU VI HUONG: (*NGOO VEE HERN*, Vietnam) see FIVE-SPICE POWDER

NIBAN DASHI: (*NEE-BAHN DAH-SHI*, Japan) see DASHI

NIBOSHI: (*NEE-BOW-SHI*, Japan) see ANCHOVY; FISH, PRESERVED (DRIED AND SALTED)

NIGELLA (*NEEGELLA*, India) (*Nigella sativa*) Small black seeds from a type of wild onion originally grown in the northern Himalayan mountains and in Eastern Europe. They are used in pickles and to a lesser extent in curries and other dishes, particularly stuffed vegetables. Although they are known as "black cumin," they are not related to this spice and have a more aromatic and peppery fragrance and a complex taste. They are an essential ingredient in the spice mix known as *panchphoran*.
Also known as *kalonji, mungerela* (India); black cumin
See also: CUMIN; CURRY PASTES, POWDERS AND SAUCES; PANCHPHORAN

NIGER OIL: see OILS AND FATS

NIGIRI-ZUSHI: (*NEE-GUI-REE-ZOO-SHI*, Japan) see SUSHI

NIHAI-ZU: (*NEE-HAH-EE-ZOO*, Japan) see SUNOMONO

193

NIHURA: (*NEE-HOO-RAA*, Nepal) see DRUM-STICK VEGETABLE

NIMONO: (*NEE-MOW-NO*) see JAPAN, COOKING METHODS

NIRA: (*NEE-RAH*, Japan) see CHIVES, CHINESE (GARLIC CHIVES)

NITSUKE: (*NEE-TZU-KEE*) see JAPAN, COOKING METHODS

NON-GLUTINOUS FLOUR: see FLOURS AND THICKENERS (WHEAT STARCH)

NONYA CUISINE:

Nonya is the unique cooking style of the "Straits-born" Chinese-Malay families known as Peranakan. Descendants of the early Chinese who settled in Malacca, Penang and Singapore, the Nonya people created a cuisine which, while employing Chinese ingredients, took advantage of the local herbs and seasonings, such as the pungent *galangal* and turmeric roots, the aromatic *daun pandan* leaf of the pandanus plant, local limes, *polygonum*, torch ginger, tamarind and chili. *Rempah* is the basis for all good Nonya curried dishes and must be prepared with skill. Cooking is done in the Chinese-style wok known as a *kwali* and, as in most Asian cuisines, is served with rice.

Being lavish entertainers, the Peranankans often entertained far more guests than the size of their dining quarters allowed. A buffet table (*tok panjan*) offered plentiful food and guests were invited to the table in groups, so the meal often went on for many hours.

Lauk pering describes a Nonya dish of a sauceless kind, such as pork simmered with tamarind, *kuah putuh* a dish with a light-colored or white gravy, and *kuah pedas* a chili-hot, red-colored dish. There may be several types of each of these at a single large banquet, along with *sambals* and *achars* (pickles).
See also: SINGAPORE

NOODLE NEST:

Tasty edible nests are used to serve certain stir-fried Chinese dishes, particularly seafood or chicken with vegetables. These are made in a special Chinese double-layered "nest" frying basket. Dip the basket into the oil, then line the lower basket with a thin, even layer of noodles that have been softened in water and drained. Place the upper basket in position on top. Lower it into hot oil and fry until golden and crisp. Upturn onto a draining rack to drain before use. Store the noodle nest in an airtight container.

NOODLES:

An important mainstay in the Chinese diet, noodles are also used extensively in Vietnam where they are enjoyed in some form at every meal. The Japanese also relish noodle dishes, and their *shirataki*, buckwheat and tea-flavored noodles, are unlike anything eaten elsewhere in Asia. Noodles as a savory dish do not feature in the Indian cuisine, although Indians serve *sevian*—baked vermicelli in a creamy rosewater-flavored syrup—as a dessert and like to crunch crisp noodle-like nibbles. Rice flour noodles are more frequently used in Southeast Asia than those made with wheat flour, and rice "sticks" and fine strands of rice vermicelli form the basis of many dishes in Burma, Cambodia, Indonesia, Laos and Vietnam. In China both wheat and rice flour noodles have been consumed with equal enthusiasm for hundreds of generations. The range of noodle types is reasonably extensive, although Asians have never felt the need to produce as many varied shapes of pasta as the Italians have devised since Marco Polo introduced the noodle to his homeland.

All dried noodles should be kept in an airtight container where they can be stored for many months. They are usually cooked by boiling in salted water and should not be overcooked if the texture and consistency is not to be spoiled. Drain thoroughly before use. Fresh noodles can be refrigerated for several days in the plastic bag in which they were purchased. Rinse in boiling water and drain before cooking.

AGAR AGAR NOODLES are fine strips of *agar agar* gelatin, produced from seaweed. They are prepared by soaking in boiling water until just tender and are flavored with spicy ingredients such as bean paste, chili and garlic. They are served occasionally in China as a noodle dish but are more commonly used to bulk out cold appetizers such as shredded jellyfish or chicken. They are easily confused with the transparent vermicelli made from mung beans.

BEAN CURD NOODLES resemble slightly thick egg noodles of a cream-yellow to grayish color, but are actually strips of dried bean curd. Used in China as noodles, they have a pleasant, chewy texture and are of considerably higher nutritional value than standard egg noodles. Bean curd noodles are cooked gently in boiling salted water and are usually served "soft"— not fried after boiling—with shredded vegetables. A popular vegetarian food, bean curd noodles are also added to hotpots, simmered dishes and soups and are eaten cold as appetizers. They are sold, dried, in tangled bundles, but are sometimes available fresh from specialty stores.
Also known as soy noodles; soy vermicelli

BEAN CURD SKIN NOODLES are narrow strips of the firm skin which sets over bean curd as it gels. Used in vegetarian cooking, particularly in Chinese communities.

BEAN THREAD VERMICELLI is used throughout Asia in many ways. In appearance and feel it resembles strands of clear plastic and is commonly called "transparent" or "cellophane" vermicelli. It is made by extruding a paste of mung bean flour and water, which is then dried. Bean thread vermicelli is cooked as noodles and is used in soups, braised dishes and hotpots. In Sichuan and neighboring Tibet, it is softened in water, then stir-fried with shredded black wood fungus, chili and bean pastes to make a delicious vegetarian dish. In Indonesia, Malaysia and Singapore and, to a lesser extent, in other parts of Southeast Asia, the boiled noodles are added to sweet drinks and desserts, usually in combination with palm sugar syrup, coconut milk and diced vegetables such as yam or sweet potato, or sweet corn kernels. When dry they are so tough that they are almost impossible to cut, but when cooked they become slippery, soft and gelatinous. In appearance and characteristics they are similar to the Japanese *shirataki* noodles, for which, being more readily available, they can be substituted.
Also known as *fen si* (China); *su un* (Indonesia); *soo hoon* (Malaysia); *sotánghon* (Philippines); *woon sen* (Singapore, Thailand); cellophane noodles; jelly noodles; transparent vermicelli

E-FU NOODLES are flattish, yellow-colored egg and wheat flour noodles made in China. They are formed into loosely tangled bundles and are crisp-fried before sale. They need only a quick boil to soften them. Used in coastal China in braised dishes and soups, they are also served cold with shredded meat and a spicy sauce that may contain sesame paste. The noodles known in the Philippines as *pancit Canton* are of a similar type, made with duck eggs.

EGG NOODLES are made from a dough of wheat flour and egg in the same way as Italian pasta. The dough is flattened and then shredded or extruded through a pasta machine to form the required shape and thickness, which can vary from fine, round shreds to thick, square-shaped noodles. Most common are the thin, round strands that are sold dried in little tangled bundles, each of which is equivalent to one serving. Chinese egg noodles are sometimes flavored with shrimp to give them a flavor suited to seafood noodle dishes or soups.

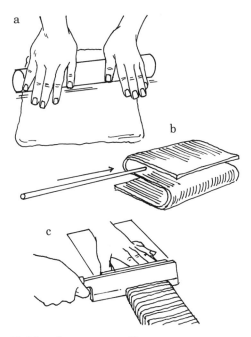

Making Japanese noodles
a. Rolling out dough
b. Folding before cutting into required shape
c. Cutting into narrow strips

Dried noodles should be cooked in simmering salted water until just tender; they use chopsticks to untangle them. Drain well and serve "soft" or fry in a very hot wok with a minimum of oil until the edges are crisp. They can also be fried to crisp, although it is not a common practice in Asia. Fresh egg noodles have a superlative flavor and texture and should be bought when available. They will keep in the refrigerator for up to three days. After an initial rinse in boiling water to remove the oil in which they have been coated, they require only a brief boiling.

Also known as *min*, *mien* (China); *mie*, *mee* (Indonesia); *tamago somen* (Japan); *hokkien mie* (Malaysia, Singapore); *miki* (Philippines); *ba mee*, *mee* (Thailand)

HIYAMUGI: (Japan) see WHEAT NOODLES

MISWA: (Philippines) These very fine white-colored wheat flour noodles are used in Philippine cooking. Sold in small bundles, they resemble skeins of yarn and should be cooked in simmering salted water until just tender before being added to soups or used in stir-fried dishes. It is important that they are not overcooked and are carefully handled to prevent breaking. They are similar to the Japanese *hiyamugi* noodles, which are traditionally served cold with a dipping sauce, or their very slightly thicker and better-known counterpart, *somen*.

RICE RIBBON NOODLES are the same as rice sticks, but are most often sold fresh. Made by steaming a thin dough of rice flour and water in wide flat tubs, the cooked dough, which has a firm, jelly-like texture, is brushed with oil, cut into strips and sold as fresh noodles. These are known as *kway tio*, *gway tio* or *hor fun* in Malaysia and Singapore and in Chinese communities throughout Asia. The ribbons, known as *kui teow sen yai* in Thailand, are usually about 1/3 in (1 cm) wide, although a narrower one, known as *kei teow sen lek*, is also popular in Thailand. The noodles should be rinsed in warm water, then quickly stir-fried and served with shredded meat and vegetables. Perhaps the most popular use of these noodles in the Chinese cuisine is in combination with strips of tender beef, florets of broccoli and "silver"

sprouts in an oyster sauce. They can be used with hotpots, being added at the end to the well-flavored broth in which the meats and vegetables have been simmered. The dough, cut into squares of approximately 8 in (20 cm), is filled with meat or shrimp and steamed to serve as the *dim sum* that is known as *cheong fun*. Dried *kway tio* noodles are also available, and require longer cooking. They are similar to *banh pho* noodles, which can be substituted.

RICE STICK NOODLES are short, flat noodles which are sold dry in bundles, in most parts of Asia. They are particularly popular in Vietnam where they are used in soups. They are classified by size, from narrow to as wide as 1/3 in (1 cm).

Bun are string-like in appearance, and very white when cooked, which is done by a very brief boiling in salted water. They are used in Vietnam in soup dishes, but also served cold with salad platters and added to spring rolls. The Japanese alimentary paste noodles known as *somen* or the Philippine *miswa* can be substituted, although these are made of wheat flour. They are not to be confused with rice vermicelli, which is slightly creamier in color.

Also known as thin rice stick noodles
See also: CHICKEN RICE NOODLES WITH PORK (recipe)

Banh Pho are white Vietnamese rice stick noodles of medium size, about 1/8 in (3 mm) wide. They are sold in flat packs. They cook in minutes in boiling water or soup and should not be overdone. They are used in Vietnamese soup-noodle dishes, particularly the popular Hanoi soup that goes by the common name of *pho*.

See also: HANOI BEEF SOUP (recipe)

RICE VERMICELLI is a type of fine, extruded, creamy-colored noodle, made from a dough of finely ground rice and water. They are sold in large bundles which are usually attractively wrapped in paper or cellophane and tied with red ribbon. Rice vermicelli cooks almost instantly, requiring only to be softened in very hot water, then drained thoroughly. When stir-frying, soften first and drain before use. To deep-fry, the dried noodles are added directly to the oil. They have a minimal flavor but as they readily absorb the taste of accompanying sauces or ingredients, they are suitable for use in both savory and sweet dishes. In India a popular dessert, known as *sevian*, uses either rice vermicelli or bean thread vermicelli. In Indonesia, too, these or bean thread vermicelli are the base of the tasty dish known as *laksa*, which has a rich coconut milk and curry sauce. A similar dish is known in Burma as *mohinga* and in Laos as *khao phoune*.

Rice vermicelli can be stir-fried and served as soft noodles. A particular favorite is the dish known as Singapore noodles, in which they are cooked with chili, shredded sweet pickled vegetables and curry powder. They are added to soups in the same way as rice stick noodles, and are used in desserts and sweet drinks. But perhaps their most distinctive use is as a garnish. When deep-fried quickly in hot oil (they burn easily so should not be left in the oil long enough to color) they expand to four or five times their dry size and become feather-light and delicately crisp. This white, light garnish appears beneath fried appetizers, surrounds stir-fried seafood and accompanies a number of fried and stir-fried Chinese dishes.
Also known as *mei fun*, *so fun* (China); *beehoon*, *bihoon*, *laksa*, *meehoon*, *mihoon* (Indonesia, Malaysia); *sen mee* (Singapore, Thailand); *banh hoi* (Vietnam)

SHANGHAI NOODLES are round, fresh egg noodles, thicker than spaghetti, which are indispensable in the north-coastal region of China around the city of Shanghai. Filling, sustaining and tasty, they are usually served in a well-flavored brown sauce made hot with a generous sprinkle of white pepper. They should be boiled until just tender in salted water and drained thoroughly before use. The thicker type of spaghetti can be used instead.

Another type of noodle, also called Shanghai noodles, are white wheat flour noodles that are similar to the Japanese alimentary paste noodles (*somen*).

SHIRATAKI NOODLES are exclusive to Japan, although they were made in China in early times and are an extrusion of a paste made from the root *Amorphophalus konjac*, known commonly in Japan as *konnyaku* or "devil's tongue." The name for the noodles translates as "white waterfall," as the noodles are as fine as a spray of water. A basic ingredient in *sukiyaki*, they can, however, be replaced by bean thread vermicelli, which are more readily available. The noodles are added directly to the dish and will soften on contact with the sauce. They have a pleasant crunchy texture, but little flavor of their own.

String-like strands of fine *shirataki* noodles are extruded into *ito konnyaku*. Fresh *shirataki* and *ito konnyaku* may be found in Oriental food stores in tubs of fresh water. They can be refrigerated for up to two weeks, if the water is changed daily.
Also known as snowed black bean curd

SILVER PIN NOODLES are not commercially manufactured, but are made at home or brought to market as a homemade product. From a dough of wheat starch, which turns almost transparent when boiling water is added, the noodles are made by rubbing small balls of the dough across an oiled board to form nail-shaped noodles about 2 in (5 cm) long. They are blanched in hot water, then stir-fried carefully in the same way as rice ribbon noodles.

SOBA: (Japan) Made from a mixture of buckwheat and wheat flours, *soba* are beige-colored noodles of medium thickness which are squared in shape. The dried noodles feel slightly soft and should be stored in an airtight container, where they will keep for many months. They are cooked in simmering water and are then usually cooled under running cold water and thoroughly drained. Fresh *soba* is sometimes available from specialty stores and should be cooked on the day of purchase. An interesting variety is created by the addition of powdered green *matcha* tea, and another less common type is colored and flavored with extract of beets.

Soba, served cold over a dish of ice with a soy-based dipping sauce, is a popular summer dish. But they are also served as a soup-noodle snack; they are reheated by being immersed in boiling water in a specially made, single-serve-size basket on a long bamboo handle.

SOMEN: (Japan) see WHEAT NOODLES

UDON: (Japan) A basic wheat flour and water noodle. They are usually made round, but can also be flat. In Japan they are usually served in soup-noodle or simmered dishes or are braised with a soy-based sauce.

WHEAT NOODLES are known in most parts of Asia as *mie* or *mein*. They differ from egg noodles in that they are whiter, owing to the absence of egg. The noodles are made of flour, salt and water, kneaded to a dough and then rolled and cut. They are usually sold dried, but may also be available fresh. Fine wheat noodles are known as *miswa* in the Philippines, *hiyamugi* or *somen* in Japan, *bamee* in Malaysia and may also be known as *ramen* or alimentary paste noodles.

BUCKWHEAT NOODLES WITH CHICKEN
Serves 4

8 oz (250 g) soba *noodles*
1 tsp ginger juice
6 oz (185 g) skinless, boneless chicken
1/2 cup (4 oz / 120 g) chopped scallions (spring / green onions)
1 1/2 tbsps vegetable oil
1 1/2 cups (13 fl oz / 400 ml) dashi
1 1/2 cups (4 fl oz / 125 ml) light soy sauce
1 tbsp mirin
1 tsp salt
2 tbsps shredded toasted nori *seaweed*
2 tbsps dried hana-katsuo
1 tbsp toasted white sesame seeds

Boil noodles in salted water until tender. Drain, rinse in hot water and drain again. Sprinkle ginger juice on chicken, then sauté with scallions in oil until it changes color. Heat *dashi* with soy sauce, *mirin* and salt. Add drained noodles and heat through. Divide among 4 bowls, top with chicken and onions and sprinkle on remaining ingredients.

CELLOPHANE NOODLE SOUP
Serves 6

1/2 cup (4 oz / 125 g) cellophane noodles
12 oz (350 g) chicken pieces
5 cups (40 fl oz / 1.25 l) water
1 tbsp fish sauce
1 tsp salt

(cont'd)

(Cellophane Noodle Soup cont'd)

6 dried black mushrooms, soaked
1 tbsp vegetable oil
1 cup (8 oz / 250 g) thinly sliced onions
1 tbsp sliced garlic
1/2 tsp ground black pepper
fresh coriander (cilantro) leaves
sliced scallions (spring / green onions)
chili powder or flakes
lemon wedges

Soak noodles in hot water, drain and cut into short lengths. Cook chicken until tender in water with fish sauce and salt. Cool to lukewarm; reserve chicken stock. Bone and chop chicken. Drain mushrooms, shred caps, simmer in reserved stock for 6 minutes. Heat oil in a boiler, sauté onions and garlic until slightly soft. Add to chicken broth with drained noodles. Bring to a boil, then simmer on low heat for 10 minutes. Add chicken and black pepper. Serve hot, garnished with coriander leaves and scallions with small bowls of chili powder or flakes and lemon wedges.

COLD NOODLE SAUCE

1 cup (8 fl oz / 250 ml) dashi
1/3 cup (3 fl oz / 90 ml) mirin
1/3 cup (3 oz / 90 ml) dark soy sauce
2 tbsps chopped dried shrimp

This sauce should be made in advance. Place all the ingredients in a saucepan; bring to a boil. Reduce heat and simmer for 6 minutes. Strain into a dish and cool quickly. Refrigerate.

EGG NOODLES
Yields 1 1/2 lbs (750 g) noodles

3 large eggs
3 cups (12 1/2 oz / 350 g) all-purpose (plain) flour
cornstarch (cornflour)

Beat water and eggs together in

(cont'd)

(Egg Noodles cont'd)

a bowl. Add 2 cups (8 oz/230 g) flour and mix well, then work in remaining 1 cup, kneading in bowl until mixture adheres. Turn onto board and knead for 10-15 minutes until smooth. Pass through pasta machine or roll out flat on floured board. Cut into noodles of desired size, dust with cornstarch and store in plastic wrap in the refrigator.

FRIED NOODLES
Serves 6–8

12 oz (375 g) thin egg noodles, cooked
3/4 cup (6 fl oz / 180 ml) peanut oil
4 oz (125 g) chopped boneless chicken breast
4 oz (125 g) chopped lean pork
1/2 cup (1 oz /30 g) chopped scallions (spring / green onions)
10 shallots, minced
2 tbsps minced garlic
2 tsps minced ginger
1–2 tsps sambal ulek
4 oz (125 g) chopped, shelled shrimp (prawns)
1 cup (4 oz /125 g) shredded Napa cabbage
2 tbsps light soy sauce
1 tsp sugar
1 1/4 tsps salt
1/2 tsp pepper
basil
fresh coriander (cilantro)
omelette shreds
fried onion flakes

Drain noodles, spread in wire strainer to cool and dry. Heat oil in a wok, fry noodles until crisp on the edges, turning twice; lift out and set aside. Stir-fry chicken and pork until color changes; remove. Fry scallions, shallots, garlic, ginger and *sambal ulek* until scallions are soft. Add shrimp and cabbage and toss with other ingredients, returning chicken and pork. Stir in soy sauce, sugar, salt and pepper and mix thoroughly. Return the noodles, toss lightly to reheat and mix. Garnish with herbs, omelette shreds and onion flakes fried to a rich brown.

FRIED NOODLES WITH MEAT AND VEGETABLES
Serves 6

8 oz (250 g) thin egg noodles
8 oz (250 g) shredded pork
8 oz (250 g) shredded chicken
vegetable oil
4 dried black mushrooms, soaked and shredded
12 shrimp (prawns), shelled and butterflied
1 1/2 cups (2 oz /60 g) fresh bean sprouts, blanched
1 cup (3 oz /90 g) sliced flowering white cabbage, parboiled
1/2 cup (2 oz /60 g) sliced chayote, parboiled
4 scallions (spring /green onions) cut into 1 1/2 in (4 cm) lengths
salt and pepper
1–2 tbsps light soy sauce
3/4 cup (6 fl oz /180 ml) chicken stock
1 tbsp cornstarch (cornflour)

Drop noodles into boiling water for 2 minutes; drain and spread out to dry. In a large wok, stir-fry pork and chicken in 2 tbsps oil until colored; remove. Add mushrooms and shrimp and stir-fry briefly; remove. Fry bean sprouts, cabbage and *chayote* with scallions for 2 minutes; remove. Pour 1/2 cup (4 fl oz/125 ml) oil into wok and heat to very hot. Pour off oil. Cook half the noodles until crisp; remove. Cook other half. Remove to a plate. Reheat meat and vegetables, adding salt and pepper to taste, soy sauce and stock mixed with cornstarch. Cook until sauce thickens, stir in mushrooms and shrimp. Pour over noodles.

HOKKIEN FRIED NOODLES
Serves 8

1 lb (500 g) fresh bacon, rind on
1 1/2 lbs (750 g) hokkien mie *noodles*
peanut oil
2 cups (1 lb /500 g) fresh bean sprouts
1 cup (8 oz /250 g) sliced choy sum
1 lb (500 g) shelled small raw shrimp (prawns)
(cont'd)

(Hokkien Fried Noodles cont'd)

2 cakes pressed bean curd, sliced
1 cup (8 oz / 250 g) scallions (spring / green
onions)
1–1¹/₂ tbsps chili bean paste
1–2 tsps minced garlic
dark soy sauce
salt and pepper
1¹/₂ cups (12 fl oz / 375 ml) chicken stock

Place bacon in a pan with water to cover. Bring to a boil and simmer for 30 minutes. Drain and cut into strips. Rinse noodles in boiling water; drain well. In a large wok heat ¹/₂ cup (4 fl oz/ 120 ml) peanut oil. Briefly stir-fry bean sprouts and *choy sum* and remove. Stir-fry shrimp and bacon and remove. Fry bean curd to golden in additional oil; remove. Reheat pan to very hot, adding more oil as needed. Fry noodles on one side without stirring, then turn over. Return cooked meat, bean curd, vegetables, and scallions and stir together. Push to the side of the pan and fry chili bean paste and garlic. Stir into noodles adding soy sauce and salt and pepper. Add stock, cover and simmer until absorbed into the noodles.

JAPANESE NOODLE BROTH

6 cups (1¹/₂ qts / 1.5 l) dashi
2 tbsps light soy sauce
1 tbsp mirin
2–3 tbsps dark soy sauce
1 tbsp sugar
1 tsp salt

Bring *dashi* to a boil; add all other ingredients. Simmer briefly. Reheat for use with noodles.

LAOTIAN TRADITIONAL NOODLE DISH
Serves 6–8

1 lb (500 g) fresh ham or picnic shoulder
1 large onion, quartered

(cont'd)

(Laotian Traditional Noodle Dish cont'd)

¹/₂ tsp minced garlic
water
1 lb (500 g) white fish
1 tbsp vegetable oil
1 tsp grated fresh ginger
1 tsp minced fresh red chili
8 cups (2 qt / 2 l) thin coconut milk
2 cups (7 oz / 220 g) roasted peanuts
salt
fish sauce
2 tsps tomato purée
1 lb (500 g) rice vermicelli
1 medium cucumber, sliced
1–2 banana flowers, sliced and blanched
1 unripe mango or papaya (pawpaw), peeled,
pitted and shredded
¹/₂ giant white radish, shredded
2¹/₂ cups (4 oz / 125 g) fresh bean sprouts
1¹/₄ cups (5 oz / 155 g) green or long beans,
crisp-fried
1 medium eggplant (aubergine), sliced and
crisp-fried
fresh mint
fennel
basil
dill
coriander (cilantro) leaves
scallions (spring / green onions)

Boil the the vermicelli in salted water and simmer until tender; drain. Cut the ham into cubes; place in a saucepan with the onion and garlic. Add water to cover. Bring to a boil, reduce the heat and simmer for about 1 hour. Remove meat, add the fish and simmer until very tender. Cut the meat and fish into small pieces; return to the broth, discarding the onion. Simmer again 5–6 minutes. Heat oil in another pan and fry ginger and chili for 2 minutes. Add the coconut milk and and bring to a boil. Simmer gently for 5 minutes, then add salt and fish sauce to taste and tomato purée. Pour over the meat and fish and add cooked vermicelli. Bring to a boil. Simmer together for 5 minutes. Serve the other ingredients and herbs separately, to be added to the soup to taste.

MEE SIAM
Serves 8

1¼ cups (10 oz / 300 g) rice vermicelli
(beehoon)
cold water
5 cakes pressed bean curd, shredded
¼ cup (2 fl oz / 60 ml) peanut oil
2½ cups (1¼ lbs / 625 g) cooked small
shrimp (prawns)
1 cup (8 oz / 250 g) minced scallions (spring /
green onions)
2 tbsps minced fresh red chili
1 tbsp shrimp paste
½ cup (4 oz / 120 g) salted yellow soybeans,
mashed
2 tbsps sugar
1 onion, sliced and fried to golden
3 cups (24 fl oz / 750 ml) thin coconut milk
1 tsp ground dried shrimp
3 cups (1½ lbs / 750 g) blanched bean sprouts
salt and pepper
chili powder
lime juice
1 hard-cooked egg, sliced
scallions (spring / green onions), shredded

Soak vermicelli in cold water. Fry
bean curd in oil until golden; remove.
Shell shrimp, and fry briefly; remove.
Grind scallions, chili and shrimp paste
together; fry in oil for 5 minutes. Add
soybeans with sugar and stir over
medium heat for 2–3 minutes. Add onion
and coconut milk and simmer 10 minutes.
Add drained vermicelli, ground dried
shrimp, bean sprouts, fried bean curd and
shrimp. Mix thoroughly and heat
through. Season with salt, pepper, chili
powder and lime juice. Garnish
with egg and scallions.

NOODLES FILIPINO
Serves 8–10

3 tsps minced garlic
6 tbsps lard or vegetable oil
½ cup (2 oz / 60 g) chopped onion
2 lbs (1 kg) whole shrimp (prawns)
15 cups (3¾ qts / 3.75 l) water
½ cup (½ oz / 15 g) annatto seeds

(cont'd)

(Noodles Filipino cont'd)
salt and black pepper
fish sauce
¾ cup (3 oz / 90 g) all-purpose (plain) flour
2 cups (4 oz / 125 g) rice vermicelli (bijon)
1 lb (500 g) boiled pork, cut into thin strips
½ cup (2 oz / 60 g) finely ground tinapa
½ cup (1 oz / 30 g) crisp sitsaron
hard-cooked eggs, sliced
scallions (spring / green onions), chopped
kalamansi juice

Sauté 1 tsp garlic in 3 tsps lard or
oil; add the onion and cook until soft.
Shell shrimp and boil shells in 6 cups of
the water.Pour 1 cup boiling water over
lightly crushed *annatto* seeds and strain
when colored. Add ¼ cup of the colored
water and the drained shrimp to the
onion; season with salt and pepper and
set aside. In another pan heat the remaining 3 tbsps lard or oil, the remaining
2 tsps garlic and strained liquid from
boiling shrimp shells. Boil 6 minutes,
strain. Add remaining colored water,
season with fish sauce and pepper.
Thicken this sauce by mixing flour into
1 cup water and stirring into sauce. Boil
8 cups of water in large saucepan, drop
in vermicelli and cook briefly; drain. Pour
noodles into a large serving dish, pour
on the thick sauce, the shrimp and sauce
and top with pork, *tinapa*, *sitsaron*,
eggs and scallions. Add *kalamansi*
juice to taste.

STIR-FRIED CELLOPHANE NOODLES
Serves 4–6

2 tbsps vegetable oil
2 tbsps Oriental sesame oil
8 oz (250 g) lean pork, shredded
1 tbsp finely chopped garlic
4 oz (125 g) Napa cabbage, shredded
1 celery rib, shredded
1 carrot, shredded
4 oz (125 g) cellophane noodles, soaked and
drained
2 tbsps fish sauce
1 tbsp sugar

(cont'd)

(Stir-fried Cellophane Noodles cont'd)

omelette shreds
3 tbsps chopped scallions (spring /
green onions)

Heat vegetable and sesame oils in a
wok or pan and stir-fry pork and
garlic for 3 minutes. Add cabbage, celery
and carrot and stir-fry until crisp-tender
for 3–5 minutes. Add noodles with fish
sauce and sugar; cook 1–2 minutes. Stir
in omelette shreds and scallions
before serving.

SWEET CRISP NOODLES
Serves 6

1/4 cup (2 fl oz / 60 ml) water
1 cup (7 oz / 200 g) sugar
1 cup (8 fl oz / 250 ml) white
vinegar
1 tsp salt
4 oz (125 g) soft bean curd,
thinly sliced
deep-frying oil
3 eggs, beaten and strained
4 oz (125 g) rice vermicelli, broken
4 oz (125 g) dried shrimp, soaked
and drained
2 fresh chilies, seeded and shredded
4 garlic chives, chopped

In a nonaluminum pan, boil
water, sugar, vinegar and salt together
for 6 minutes; reserve syrup. Fry bean
curd in 2 1/2 in (5 cm) oil until golden.
Reheat oil, pour egg in a thin stream
over surface to form a lacy film. When
golden, flip and cook other side; remove.
Deep-fry vermicelli until white and
crisp; drain. Deep-fry dried shrimp until
crisp; drain. In a clean wok or pan bring
half prepared syrup to a boil. Remove
from heat, add half the fried ingredients,
except egg; mix until sugar is absorbed.
Transfer to a plate. Repeat with other
half. Drape egg nets over noodles
and garnish with chilies
and garlic chives.

SWEET NOODLE DESSERT
Serves 8

3/4 cup (6 fl oz / 180 ml) ghee
3/4 cup (3 oz / 90 g) raw cashew nuts or
almonds
2/3 cup (4 oz / 125 g) golden raisins (sultanas)
5 oz (150 g) rice vermicelli, broken
4 cups (1 qt / 1 l) milk
3/4–1 cup (5–7 oz / 170–200 g) sugar
1/4 tsp ground cardamom
1 tbsp rosewater
1 cup (8 fl oz / 150 ml) heavy cream

Melt ghee, fry cashews or almonds
until golden; add raisins and fry briefly;
remove. Fry vermicelli until lightly
golden. Add milk, sugar and cardamom
and bring to a boil. Reduce heat and
simmer until the vermicelli is almost
tender, about 6 minutes. Add rosewater,
nuts and raisins and simmer briefly.
Stir in cream and heat gently until
vermicelli is tender. Serve warm.

UDON NOODLES IN STOCK
Serves 4

1 lb (500 g) dried udon noodles
3/4 cup (6 oz / 180 g) chopped scallions
(spring / green onions)
4–6 cups (1–1 1/2 qts / 1–1.5 l) noodle stock
shichimi

Boil *udon* until just tender. Rinse
in boiling water; drain. Place in a deep
bowls, sprinkle on scallions and pour
on the stock. Add *shichimi* to taste.

NOODLES, CRISP: Egg noodles can be fried
in advance and stored in an airtight container.
Rice noodles should be fried immediately before
use.

Soak egg noodles in cold water to soften.
Untangle bundles and drain in a colander. Set
aside to partially dry. Heat deep-frying oil, and
slide in noodles in small quantities. Turn once,
fry until crisp and golden. Rice noodles cook
within seconds and should be removed from oil
when well expanded, but still white.

NORI: (*NOW-REE*, Japan) see NORI NEST; SEA-WEED

NORI-MAKI: (*NOW-REE-MAH-KEE*, Japan) see SUSHI

NORI-MAKI SUSHI: (*NOW-REE-MAH-KEE ZOO-SHI*, Japan) see SUSHI (recipe)

NORI NEST: (*NOW-REE*, Japan)Use single or double sheet of *nori*, Japanese dried seaweed sheets, as spring roll wrappers to make a crisp "nest" for serving quick-fried vegetables or seafood in.

NUKA: (*NOUU-KA*, Japan) Rice bran is one of the most important ingredients used in Japan for pickling, either in dry form known as *nuka-zuke*, or in moist mash form as *nukamiso-zuke*. A wooden *tsukemono-ki*, or large crock, is filled with dry bran, or used for the preparation of mash. This mash is produced by mixing *nuka* with salt, beer and mustard and made into a paste with water. The vegetables, which are commonly giant white radish, Chinese cabbage, eggplant and cucumber, are salted, then pushed into the dry bran or bran mash to be left for at least 24 hours, and up to one month, to develop.
See also: TSUKEMONO

NUOC CHAM: (*NEE-UK CHAM*, Vietnam) The most important condiment on the Vietnamese table is *nuoc cham*, a tasty sauce that is sprinkled over soups and stir-fries, used as a dip for Vietnamese-style spring rolls, meat balls and grilled meats, or added to rice for extra flavor.

NUOC CHAM (1)

Yields 1/2 cup (4 fl oz / 120 ml)

2 dried red chilies, seeded
1 garlic clove
2 tbsps fish sauce (nuoc mam)
2–3 tbsps water
2 tsps sugar
1 1/2 tbsps lime juice

Grind chilies, garlic and sugar to a paste in a mortar or food processor. Add remaining ingredients and mix well. Serve freshly made for best flavor, although it can be kept for 1–3 days in the refrigerator.

NUOC CHAM (2)

Yields 1/2 cup (4 fl oz / 120 ml)

1 fresh red chili, seeded and shredded
2 tsps lime juice
1/4 cup fish sauce (nuoc mam)
1 tbsp crushed roasted peanuts
1 tbsp finely slivered carrot
water
sugar

Mix ingredients together with 1/4 cup (2 fl oz/60 ml) water and sugar to taste.

NUOC COT DUA: (*NEE-UK KORT YOO-A*, Vietnam) see COCONUT (MILK)

NUOC DUA TUOI: (*NEE-UK YOO-A TUOI*, Vietnam) see COCONUT (WATER)

NUOC MAM: (*NEE-UK MUM*, Vietnam) see FISH SAUCE

NUOC MAU: (*NEE-UK MAW*, Vietnam) A caramelized sugar used to add color and gloss to cooked dishes and food to be grilled.

NUOC MAU

Yields 1 cup (8 fl oz / 250 ml)

1/2 cup (3 1/2 oz / 100 g) sugar
3/4 cup (6 fl oz / 180 ml) water

Mix sugar and 1/4 cup water in a small pan. Bring to a boil and cook until it changes to a golden color. Reduce heat to low, simmer until brown and caramelized. Pour in 1/2 cup cold water, stirring until crystals dissolve. Store in the refrigerator.

NUTMEG: (*Myristica fragrans*) Nutmeg is the seed from an elegant low tree native to the Moluccas islands—the legendary "Spice Islands"—that proliferates in Indonesia and is grown as a crop and an ornamental. The beige-colored oval nut is encased in a hard husk surrounded by a web-like, orange-red, fibrous casing that is removed to be processed separately into mace. The nuts are treated by being placed to dry on frames above a smoking fire for six weeks. Nutmeg is a fragrant, sweet spice that enjoyed widespread popularity in Europe in the sixteenth century. In Asia it is an important ingredient in curries and spice mixtures and is used to flavor pastries, sweetmeats and puddings. The flavor is best from whole nuts that are grated when required.

Also known as *tau kau* (China); *jaiphal* (India); *pala* (Indonesia); *nikuzuku* (Japan); *buah pala* (Malaysia); *sadikka* (Sri Lanka); *look jun, luk chand* (Thailand)

See also: MACE; MASALA

OB CHOEY: (*OB CHEUY*, Thailand) see CASSIA

OBURO-EBI: (*O-BOO-ROW-EE-BEE*, Japan) see SHRIMP POWDER

OCTOPUS: Octopus is eaten in Japan and Korea, where it is usually prepared in a vinegar-based marinade. In Korea it is also stewed and served as a sustaining, soup-like dish.

OILS AND FATS: Many different types of oils and fats are used in Asian cooking. Edible oil, obtained by the pressing of seeds from oil-bearing plants, have been used in China for over 2,000 years, rapeseed oil being one of the earliest known. Highly flavored oils such as sesame and mustard are used to impart a distinctive taste. The oil extracted from coconuts and from various tropical palms have traditionally been mainstays in the cuisines of Southeast Asia. Vegetable oils from soybeans, sunflowers, maize, cotton and peanuts are all manufactured in Asia. Although they are blander, and do not bring their own taste to a dish, they allow high cooking temperatures without burning and help to achieve crisp textures when frying.

ANIMAL FATS are used in moderation in Asia. Butter, when used, is usually in the form of clarified butter or ghee, which is commonly used in India because it has religious significance. Rendered chicken, duck and pig fat (lard) are rich cooking fats which, in certain areas of China are the main fats used. However, they are employed infrequently elsewhere in Asia.

CHICKEN FAT is used in China as a highly flavored finish to many dishes, as well as for stir-frying. It is heated to a high temperature, then poured at a boil directly over a finished dish. The result is a glossy appearance and rich, toasty taste. Both chicken and duck fat can be rendered. To make renderered chicken fat, remove white fat from cavity of dressed

chicken. Place in a pan with ¹/₄ cup (2 fl oz/ 60 ml) water. Cook on moderate heat until the water has evaporated and fat has melted from the fat tissue. Pour off and store, covered, in the refrigerator.
Also known as *chi yu*, *gai yau*, *ji you* (China)
See also: CHINA, COOKING METHODS

COCONUT OIL is the rich, white, solid oil obtained from the endosperm of copra, the white meat of coconuts. Although called an oil, it is in fact a saturated fat as it solidifies at cool temperatures. It is a favorite cooking oil in southern India, Malaysia and Indonesia, where its wonderful, roasted nut aroma lingers around food stalls and kitchens. Although its use is gradually being phased out by the ready availability of other vegetable oils, most small villages in these regions still use their own presses to extract coconut oil from copra. Coconut oil burns easily, so should not be subjected to high temperatures. It adds a rich coconut taste to foods and a crisp shortness to pastries. It is sold in block form or in bottles. To prevent rancidity it needs to be refrigerated, but should be brought to room temperature before use.
Also known as *minyak kelapa* (Indonesia, Malaysia)
See also: COCONUT

CORN OIL is extracted from maize. A light, bland polyunsaturated and nonhydrogenated oil, it is suited to most kinds of cooking as it withstands high temperatures and does not impart a flavor. Safflower oil has similar properties.
Also known as maize oil

COTTON SEED OIL although strongly flavored, is little used as a cooking oil. Its main use is in the canning of certain foods. For cooking, it is usually blended with other bland oils.

DUCK FAT: Like chicken fat, melted duck fat is splashed over finished Chinese dishes to improve the flavor and glaze the surface. Being richer, it is usually a finish for vegetable dishes such as broad beans, asparagus or broccoli.
Also known as *ya you* (China)
See also: CHINESE COOKING TECHNIQUES

GHEE is clarified butter, obtained by heating butter to separate out the butter fat.
See also: GHEE

LARD, obtained from the melting of pork fat, is highly regarded as a cooking medium in China, particularly in the Sichuan province, and is used throughout Southeast Asia. It brings its rich flavor to many stir-fried dishes and pastries and may be used for shallow-frying. In the Philippines, lard is boiled with red *annatto* seeds to make a bright red cooking fat that imparts its delicate color and distinctive flavor.
Also known as *zhuyou* (China)
See also: ANNATTO SEED, ROAST SUCKLING PIG, PHILIPPINE STYLE (recipe)

MUSTARD OIL is a strong-tasting oil that has a distinctive aroma. Extracted from brown or black mustard seeds, it is used as the main cooking oil in the Bengal and Bihar states of India and to a much lesser extent in the southern Indian regions. It gives all dishes in which it is used a unique taste and fragrance, its pungency adding an intensity to oil-based Indian pickles. Mustard oil is too strong for general cooking and should always be blended with a blander oil for a better flavor. It contains vitamin D in sufficient quantities to be significant in a diet.
Also known as *sarson ka tel* (India)
See also: MUSTARD SEED; PICKLES, INDIAN

NIGER OIL is extracted from the long, thin black seeds of the plant *Guizotia abyssinica* which grows in India and Africa. A yellow, highly flavored oil, it may be blended with other oils for sale as a cooking oil and is used in Indian vegetarian dishes to give a nutty flavor.

PALM OIL obtained from the oil palm (*Elaeis guineensis*), is one of the world's most important edible oils, with the highest yield of any oil-bearing plant. It originated in tropical west Africa, but a smaller variety called *deli* now grows in Malaysia and Indonesia and, to a lesser extent, in other Southeast Asian countries. The oil is extracted from the large fruit bunch, which can contain up to 200 fruits— usually orange in color but ranging through brown to black. The kernel offers palm kernel oil which is used as a vegetable oil and in the making of margarine. Before it is refined, palm oil has a yellow-orange color, imparted by the pigment carotene.

PEANUT OIL is used throughout Asia. Some cooks prefer it in semi-refined form, when its nutty flavor and distinctive fragrance add to the taste of the dish. As peanuts contain up to 50 percent oil, the yield is high and the oil is generally inexpensive. More refined peanut oil is bland in taste and more akin to other vegetable oils, which can be substituted for it in recipes. The oil can withstand high temperatures without burning and can be reused without absorbing other food flavors.
Also known as *far sung yau, huashengyou* (China)
See also: PEANUT, KRUPUK (recipe)

PORK FAT, removed from beneath the skin, is frequently used in Chinese cooking, and in other Southeast Asian cuisines. Finely ground or diced, pork fat is added to meatballs to enrich the flavor and to give a moist, sticky consistency which holds the balls together. Most Chinese butchers are happy to sell pork fat separately, but it can be prepared at home using any cut of pork with a thick layer of fat. Remove fat, dice finely, or grind in a food grinder or processor.

RAPESEED OIL is one of the earliest forms of edible oil to be used in cooking, both in the Eastern and Western worlds. The oil is pressed from the black or red-brown seeds of the cabbage-like rape plant, and in its unrefined state has a distinctive, vegetable-like taste. Today rapeseed oil is mainly used in northern China, where it is widely grown for use as a vegetable.
See also: CABBAGE, CHINESE (RAPE)

SAFFLOWER OIL is extracted from the seeds of the plant *Carthamus tinctorius*, which grew mainly in India in earlier times, but which is no longer cultivated as an oil-producing plant in many parts of Asia or, indeed, the world. The bland-tasting oil is used in salads and stir-fries and is particularly suited to deep-frying.

SESAME CHILI OIL is made by frying red chilies in sesame oil until the oil turns bright red. Extremely hot and full of flavor, it is used mainly as a condiment but can also be used in moderation as a seasoning.
Also known as *lajiao xiangyou* (sesame chili); *xiangyou, zhimayou* (sesame) (China)

See also: CHILI OIL; OILS, FLAVORED; SESAME SEED

SESAME OIL is a strong tasting, aromatic and flavorful oil used for its distinct, nutty taste.
Also known as Oriental sesame oil

SOYBEAN OIL is obtained from soybeans. A bland-tasting edible oil, it is used extensively in Asia for cooking, for salad dressings and in making margarine.
See also: SOYBEAN

SUNFLOWER OIL is produced from the kernels of the brown-black pointed seeds within the large blossom heads of the sunflower *Helianthus annus*, a member of the daisy family. A bland-tasting oil, it is very pure and highly regarded as a cooking medium. It is ideal for stir-frying, as it can be heated to high temperatures without burning, and for deep-frying, as it does not impart its own taste to the food.

OILS, FLAVORED: Vegetable oils, flavored with strong spices, are used to add their distinctive taste to certain dishes. They are usually obtained by heating oil and adding the spices which are then allowed to macerate in the oil until cool. The most commonly used is chili oil, a clear, bright red condiment sold in small bottles at Chinese stores. Other flavored oils used in Chinese cooking are Sichuan pepper-oil, impregnated with the flavor of finely ground Sichuan peppercorns and known as *huajiaoyou* in China, and curry-flavored oil, which combines peanut oil with curry powder and is known as *yougali*. Sesame oil, heated with red chilies, produces *lajiao xiangyuo*. In India, ghee, made aromatic by the addition of seasonings, makes *baghar*, which is poured over finished dishes.
See also: BAGHAR; CHILI OIL; OILS AND FATS

OKARA: (*OWE-KU-RAH*, Japan) see BEAN CURD
OKRA: see BHINDI

OK-RONG: (*OK-RONG*, Thailand) A pale yellow mango that is considered the best dessert mango in Thailand and is used in a variety of popular sweet dishes.
See also: STICKY RICE WITH MANGO (recipe)

OLIVE SEED, CHINESE: (*Canarium album*) Flattish, layered, golden seeds with a texture and taste similar to pine nuts (which make an excellent substitute). They are the kernel of the small native Chinese kanari fruit, known as *kan lan*. The fruit itself is sour; in earlier times it was taken steeped in honey to sweeten the breath and to counter the effect of poisons in wine. As an ingredient, the seeds are most notably used as a garnish on a southern Chinese dish known as "fried milk."
Also known as *larm yum* (China)
See also: PINE NUT

Chinese olive seeds

OMUM: (*OMUM*, India) see AJWAIN
ONCOM: see TEMPE

ONION: (*Allium cepa*) Native to central Asia and with many varieties grown throughout the world, the onion is probably the most universally used vegetable and seasoning ingredient. In ancient China onions and their relatives were listed amongst the dietary taboos of the Buddhist religion. Scallions, garlic and various onions were a group of forbidden foods, the "five strong-odored foods" known as *wu hun*. Belonging to the Liliaceae family, onions are characterized by layered crisp flesh, usually white but in some types a red-purple. When raw they have a pungent odor and strong flavor, which becomes almost sweet when cooked. Onion is used extensively in most Asian cuisines. The Japanese, however, use it only sparingly. Although onion appears in many Chinese stir-fried dishes in Western cities, it is generally not used in this way in China. Their chefs

prefer the more subtle flavor and finer texture of scallions or native leeks. Yellow, brown and white-skinned onions, as well as a red-purple type similar to the Spanish onion, are all used. Onions are also used as a garnish in the form of fried onion flakes, which are frequently used by the Thais, Malays and Indonesians to decorate rice, noodle and meat dishes and salads.
Also known as *khtim baraing* (Cambodia); *congtou, yeung chung* (China); *bawang Bombay* (Indonesia); *pyaz* (India, Nepal); *bawang besar* (Malaysia); *hua hom* (Thailand); *hanh tay* (Vietnam)

PICKLED ONION is often served as a side dish, particularly in India where it accompanies deep-fried and *tandoor*-cooked foods or *kebabs*. It is prepared by a traditional pickling technique and sold in jars, but a homemade version is also enjoyed in India and in the countries of Southeast Asia, where it is marinated in vinegar with sugar and salt to serve with cold cuts, appetizers and fried or grilled foods.

PICKLED SHALLOTS: A type of small onion bulb resembling garlic, grown in China and Japan, and to a certain extent in Thailand. Not usually eaten raw, the bulbs are trimmed and pickled with vinegar and sugar and sold in jars or cans in their tart syrup to serve as a snack or side dish. They are also occasionally used in cooking. Peeled garlic cloves are pickled in the same way.
Also known as *tangyan suantou* (China); *rakkyo* (Japan)

RED ONIONS (*Allium cepa*) are small, red-skinned onions with a similar taste to shallots that are also used frequently in Asian cooking. In some countries they are preferred to shallots, as they are easier to use.

SCALLIONS: (*Allium fistulosum*) Extensively grown and used throughout Asia, and particularly in southern China, the scallion has deep green, hollow cylindrical leaves with elongated white ends which do not form a bulb. The flavor is milder than the onion and it cooks quickly, making it suitable for stir-fries and other quick-cooked dishes. Both the white part and green stems are used in cooking and the green stems are frequently used—diagonally sliced, shredded, curled and made into flowers—as a garnish. In Japan, before scallion is used it is rinsed, wrapped in a piece of fine cloth and squeezed to extract any bitter juices. In China it is usually added to a dish in the final stages of cooking so that it does not overcook, which can make it turn bitter.

Also known as *khtim slek* (Cambodia); *chung, cong, ts'ung* (China); *bawang daun, daun bawang* (Indonesia, Malaysia); *atasuki, wakegi* (Japan); *ton hom* (Thailand); Chinese onions; green onions; spring onions; Welsh onions

See also: SCALLION AND GINGER SAUCE (recipe); SCALLION-CHILI BEEF SOUP (recipe); SCALLION PASTRIES (recipe); STEAMED WHOLE GAROUPA WITH SCALLIONS (recipe)

SHALLOTS: (*Allium ascalonicum*) These red-skinned onions, which grow in clumps and resemble heads of garlic in shape, are used extensively in Southeast Asian cooking. They are pounded to a paste with lemon grass, garlic and chili to make *rempah*, the seasoning paste used in Malaysia and Indonesia for curry-making. Peeled and sliced, they can be eaten raw or fried to a golden crispness for use as a garnish over rice and other dishes. They are also used in *sambals*. These onions should not be confused with a small onion cultivated in the mountains of Kiangsi (China) and in Japan, which is pickled in a sweet-tart vinegar and sold as pickled shallots or pickled scallions.

Also known as *kyet-thun-ni* (Burma); *khtim kraham* (Cambodia); *chung tau, tangyan suantou (pickled), ts'ung tau* (China); *rakkyo* (pickled) (Japan); *bawang merah* (Indonesia, Malaysia); *horm lek* (Thailand); *khan kho* (Vietnam)

FRIED ONION FLAKES

Yields 1¹/4 cups (6 oz / 185 g)

2 cups (8 oz / 250 g) thinly sliced onions or shallots
deep-frying oil

Heat oil; add half of the sliced onions and fry over medium heat to a rich brown, avoiding burning. Remove and drain on a rack covered with paper towels. Cook remaining onions. When cool, store in airtight container for up to 1 month.

See also: CHIVES, CHINESE; DO PIAAZA (recipe); RICE IN A LACQUER BOX WITH BEEF AND ONIONS (recipe) *and recipes following*

ONION KACHUMBER

3 medium onions, thinly sliced
salt
2¹/2 tsps palm sugar (or substitute brown sugar)
2 tsps tamarind concentrate
3 tbsps water, boiling
³/4 cup (3 oz / 90 g) chopped tomato
1 tsp minced ginger
2 tbsps finely chopped fresh coriander (cilantro)
3–6 fresh green chilies, seeded and shredded

Sprinkle onions with salt and set aside for 1 hour. Drain. Mix sugar, tamarind and boiling water. Combine all ingredients and toss together thoroughly. Set aside for at least 15 minutes before serving.

ONION SAMBAL

Yields 2 cups (8 oz / 250 g)

2 large onions, thinly sliced
vegetable or coconut oil
1 cup (4 oz / 125 g) chopped onions
12 fresh red chilies, blanched
2 tsps chopped garlic
¹/4 cup (2 fl oz / 60 ml) thick coconut milk
1 tbsp palm sugar (or substitute brown sugar)
¹/2 tsp salt
1 tbsp lemon juice

Sauté sliced onions in 2 tbsps oil until well colored; set aside. Sauté chopped onions in more oil until softened. Grind chilies, garlic and coconut milk to a paste. Add to the pan with sliced onions and chopped onions, sugar, salt and lemon juice. Cook until oil appears on the surface. Can be kept in the refrigerator for 10 days or may be frozen.

SCALLION AND GINGER SAUCE
Yields ³/₄ cup (6 fl oz / 180 ml)

¹/₃ cup (3 fl oz / 90 ml) vegetable oil
2 tbsps peeled, minced ginger
3 tbsps minced scallions (spring / green
onions)
1¹/₂ tsps salt

Heat oil in a small pan over
medium heat. Add the ginger, scallions
and salt and warm through. Cool briefly.
Serve in small sauce dishes. This is the
usual accompaniment to Chinese
poached or steamed chicken and can
also be served with crisp-fried
poultry or game.

SCALLION-CHILI BEEF SOUP
Serves 6–8

8 cups (2 qts / 2 l) water
1 lb (500 g) braising beef
1¹/₂ tbsps chili powder
2¹/₂ tbsps Oriental sesame oil
12 scallions (spring / green onions),
shredded
2 tsps minced garlic
1 tbsp ground, toasted white sesame
seeds
1 tsp sugar
¹/₂ tsp white pepper
1¹/₂ tbsps dark soy sauce

Bring water to a boil, add
the meat, reduce heat and simmer
gently for 1¹/₂–2 hours. Mix the chili
powder with the sesame oil in a
saucepan and fry half the scallions
with the garlic for 2 minutes. Add the
sesame seeds, sugar, pepper and soy sauce
and fry for 2–3 minutes over medium
heat. Drain meat, reserving the stock.
Chop the meat finely and fry
in the seasonings for a few minutes.
Scrape the meat mixture
into the stock and bring to a boil;
simmer for 5–6 minutes.
Add remaining scallions.

SCALLION PASTRIES
Yields 6

2 cups (8 oz / 250 g) all-purpose (plain) flour
¹/₂ tsp sugar
¹/₂ tsp salt
2 tbsps vegetable oil
Oriental sesame oil
1 cup (2 oz / 60 g) chopped scallions (spring
/ green onions)
2 tbsps white sesame seeds

Sieve flour into a mixing bowl
with sugar and salt. Add vegetable oil.
Work in enough water to make a smooth,
soft dough. Knead lightly, divide into 6
portions. Roll out ¹/₄ in (¹/₂ cm) thick.
Spread sesame oil, scallions and salt
evenly over the top. Roll each piece of
dough into a tight roll, stretch out into a
rope, then shape into a coil. Sprinkle
lightly with flour and roll out ¹/₂ in
(1 cm) thick. Grease a wide, flat pan
with sesame or vegetable oil. Brush
top of each pastry with cold water; coat
with sesame seeds. Cook until the
underside is golden; turn and cook
other side, then return to first side
briefly. Remove when golden
and crisp.

Scallion pastries

SHALLOT SAMBAL

12 shallots, chopped or 3–4 Spanish onions,
sliced
1 tsp crushed garlic
¹/₂ cup (4 fl oz / 125 ml) white vinegar
1 tbsp sugar
¹/₂ tsp salt

(cont'd)

(Shallot Sambal cont'd)

Place shallots in a dish with the garlic. Pour on the vinegar and sprinkle on the sugar and salt. Marinate for at least 30 minutes before serving.

ONION SEED: see NIGELLA

OP CHEUY: (*OB CHEUY*, Thailand) see CINNA-MON

ORANGE CURRY PASTE: (recipe) see CURRY PASTES, POWDERS AND SAUCES

ORNAMENTAL CHILI: see CHILI

OSHI-ZUSHI: (*OWE-SHI ZOO-SHI*, Japan) see SUSHI

OSMANTHUS FLOWER: (China) Tiny, sweet-scented white flowers that grow profusely in the Kweilin region. They are used as a garnish in several forms—fresh, candied or preserved in a spirit with sugar. They are also used to make a fragrant liqueur.
See also: WINES, ASIAN

OTOSHI-BUTA: (*OWE-TOW-SHI-BOO-TA*, Japan) see UTENSILS, VARIOUS

OYSTER: (*Crassostrea* sp. *C. cucullata, C. pinctada maxima*) Three main types of oysters that are taken from Asian waters. The first is a very large oyster which is cultivated in Hong Kong and is found widely elsewhere. As it has a strong flavor and tougher flesh than can be enjoyed raw, it is the one that is cooked or dried. A percentage of the crop is also cooked to produce a concentrated flavoring liquid used commercially in the production of sauces and food products. The second, smaller type has a rectangular-shaped, blackish shell with a pink margin. Asians rarely eat raw oysters, as people do in the West with just a squeeze of lemon. Instead, in Thailand, Malaysia and Singapore, these tiny, tasty oysters are heaped into omelettes; in Japan they are simmered in a rich miso broth to make *kaki-no dote-nabe*, or simmered with miso and sake to make *kaki*-miso, a dish perfected in the bayside city of Shiogama. In Kampuchea, where oysters are plentiful, they are quick-cooked with chopped lemon grass, chili and herbs, then returned to the shell to be served. Pearl oysters are found in deep Asian waters and must be harvested by divers. The meat is delicious.

DRIED OYSTERS are produced in most coastal parts of Southeast Asia. They are sun-dried, usually without salting, and used to give a strong, of-the-sea flavor to braised dishes and soups. The Chinese revere them for their health-giving properties.

OYSTER SAUCE is a richly flavored, thick, brown sauce made from dried oysters. It has a salty taste, that tends to be less pronounced in more expensive brands, and a strong, briny flavor with overtones of caramel. It is an ancient seasoning. The original version, made on the south coast of China, was a thin salty sauce containing fragments of fermented, dried oyster. It is sold in bottles and, once opened, should be refrigerated to discourage mold growth. It is used to flavor and color braised and stir-fried dishes, and is an excellent accompaniment to Chinese stir-fried vegetables, being teamed with broccoli and various Chinese cabbages.
Also known as *kha mar* (Burma); *ho yo jeung, mau lai* (China); *ho see* (dried oysters) (China); *tiram* (Indonesia); *kaki* (Japan); *tiram batu* (Malaysia); *talaba* (Philippines); *hoy muk chan, hoy nangrom* (Thailand)
See also: OYSTERS IN CRISP BATTER (recipe); OYSTERS WITH GARLIC AND HERBS (recipe); SEAFOOD, DRIED; OYSTERS IN A POT (recipe)

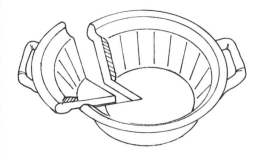

Cross section of Japanese casserole showing a thick layer of miso spread on sides

OYSTERS IN A POT
Serves 6

$1/2$ *cup (4 oz / 125 g) red miso*
$1/2$ *cup (4 oz / 125 g) white miso*
1 tbsp mirin
1 qt (1 l) dashi
8 in (20 cm) piece kombu *seaweed*
24–30 large oysters, opened
3 naganegi onions, sliced
3 stems chrysanthemum leaves; trimmed,
rinsed and dried
2 bunches enokitake mushrooms, washed
and trimmed
6 fresh shiitake *mushrooms, wiped*
$1/4$ *head Napa cabbage, coarsely*
shredded

Mix misos, *mirin* and $1/2$ cup
dashi to a paste and spread inside
a *donabe* (earthenware casserole).
Score the *kombu* with a sharp knife.
Place it in the casserole, gently adding the
remaining *dashi*. Bring the *dashi* just to
a boil on a portable cooker at the table.
Reduce heat. Add all the remaining
ingredients, and cook briefly. If
desired, the food can be dipped
into a beaten raw egg
before eating.

OYSTER SAUCE DIP
Yields 1 cup (8 fl oz / 250 ml)

1 tbsp light soy sauce
1 tbsp oyster sauce
$2/3$ *cup (6 fl oz / 180 ml) chicken stock*
2 tbsps minced scallions (spring /
green onions)
$1/2$ *tsp sugar*
1 tsp salt
1 tsp cornstarch (cornflour)

Mix all the ingredients in a small
pan, bring to a boil, then stir
until thickened.

OYSTERS WITH GARLIC AND HERBS
Serves 6

36 large fresh oysters, in the shell
2 tsps minced garlic
1 tsp minced fresh red chili
2 tsps minced greater galangal
2 tsps minced lemon grass
$1^1/2$ *tbsps vegetable oil*
$1/2$ *cup (4 fl oz / 125 ml) lime juice*
$1/2$ *cup (4 fl oz / 125 ml) fish sauce*
$1/2$ *tsp salt*
$1/2$ *tsp pepper*
1 tbsp sugar
2–3 tsps finely chopped Vietnamese mint

Open the oysters over a dish to
save their liquor. Remove top shells
and discard, loosen oysters. Place the
garlic, chili, *galangal* and lemon grass
in a small pan and fry gently for 2
minutes in the oil. Mix the lime juice
and fish sauce with the salt, pepper
and sugar. Add oyster liquid and cook
until hot. Poach oysters for 30
seconds. Return to their shells
with some of the sauce and
the fried ingredients.
Garnish with mint.

OYSTER MUSHROOM: see MUSHROOMS AND
EDIBLE FUNGI

OYSTER SAUCE: see OYSTERS

P

PAANI: (*PAA-NEE*, India) see WINE, ASIAN

PA CHIO: (*FA JIL*, China) see ANISEED

PADANG: (*PA-DANG*) see INDONESIA, COOKING METHODS

PA DE GAW GYI: (*PER DER GAW GHI*, Burma) see GALANGAL, GREATER

PADEK: (*PAH-DEK*, Laos) A fish product, often made at home, in which chunks of fish are preserved in brine and rice bran in large earthenware jars. The fish itself is eaten when fresh fish is scarce and added to dishes to give a strong, fish flavor. The pungent liquid that accumulates on the fish in the jars is drained off to be used as a salty seasoning in the same way as soy or fish sauce.
Also known as *prahok* (Cambodia)
See also: FISH, PRESERVED; FISH PASTE; FISH SAUCE; TREY REACH

PAI CHIH: (*BAK CHEK*, China) see DANG GUI

PAK CHAI: (*BAK CHOY*, China) see CABBAGE, CHINESE (BOK CHOY)

PAK CHEE: (*PHAK CHEE*, Thailand) see CORIANDER, FRESH

PAK CHEE LAO: (*PHAK CHEE LAO*, Thailand) see DILL

PAKISTAN: There is much that relates directly to Indian cooking in the Pakistani cuisine. Dishes are generally highly spiced or curried and served with a starch staple of rice or bread. Pakistan's close proximity to Afghanistan and the Middle Eastern states has also had an impact on the cuisine.
See also: INDIA

PAKORA: (*PA-KO-RAA*, India) Deep-fried snacks coated in a batter made with *besan* flour. Ingredients vary from grated or diced vegetables to whole, bite-size pieces of fresh vegetable, shrimp or fish, cooked rice or semolina, *panir* (cheese) or meat. They are crisp-fried and are usually served with a spicy flavored chutney.
Also known as *bhajias*
See also: FLOURS AND THICKENERS (BESAN)

PAKSIW: (*PAK-SIW*, Philippines) see FISH, PRESERVED; PHILIPPINES, COOKING METHODS

PALABOK: (*PA-LA-BOK*, Philippines) A Tagalog term that describes the many different ingredients used to garnish dishes in the Philippines. These may include flaked dried fish, pork cracklings, hard-cooked eggs, diced bean curd, scallions, dried shrimp.

PALAK: (*PAA-LAK*, India) see SPINACH

PALAYOK: (*PAH-LA-YOK*, Philippines) see CHATTI

PALM CABBAGE: see COCONUT

PALM HEART: see UBOD

PALM NUT: (*Borrasus flabellifer*) A sweet, gelatinous opaque sap is extracted from the hard, shiny nut of the palmyra palm that grows wild in parts of southern India, and in Sri Lanka and Burma, but which is cultivated elsewhere in Southeast Asia. The palm nut or palmyra fruit has a mildly nutty flavor, faintly suggestive of coconut, and is used in desserts in Indonesia and Thailand, usually being combined with coconut milk or syrup. It is sold fresh or in bottles packed in sugar syrup or in a syrup made from palm sap sugar, which is

Palm nut and kernel

obtained by tapping the sap of the palm. The fresh nut and the opened can or jar can be kept for a few days in the refrigerator. The sap is also used to make palm sugar, and is fermented to make *toddy*, a strong alcoholic beverage that is further distilled into the popular wine known as *arak*.

Also known as *siwalan* (Indonesia); *atap chee* (Malaysia, Singapore); *kaong* (Philippines); *luk taan* (Thailand); palmyra fruit

See also: PALMRYA FRUIT IN PALM SYRUP (recipe); SUGAR; WINE, ASIAN

PALMYRA FRUIT IN PALM SYRUP
Serves 4

*24 young palmyra fruit or 2 cups
(16 fl oz / 500 ml) bottled fruit
1 cup (6 oz / 185 g) palm sugar (or
substitute brown sugar)
1/2 cup (4 fl oz / 125 ml) thick
coconut milk
salt*

Peel palmyra fruit. Dissolve palm sugar in a small pan. Add the peeled fruit and cook over low flame until syrupy, about 1 hour. If using bottled fruit, drain and simmer in palm sugar for 10 minutes. Serve with thick coconut milk flavored with salt.

PALM OIL: see OILS AND FATS

PALM SUGAR: see SUGAR

PALMYRA FRUIT: see PALM NUT

PANCAKE FILLING

*2 cups (1 lb / 500 g) ground lamb or beef
2 tbsps oil or ghee
2 tsps garam masala
salt
black pepper
chili powder*

Sauté meat in oil or ghee until colored, add *garam masala* and season with salt and pepper and chili powder. Use for Pancake Roll Malay-style.

PANCAKE ROLL MALAY-STYLE
Yields 12

*3 cups (12 oz / 350 g) all-purpose
(plain) flour
2 tsps melted ghee
1 cup (8 fl oz / 250 ml) water
1 tsp salt
2 eggs, beaten
1 cup (8 oz / 250 g) sliced onion,
crisp-fried*

Sift flour into a bowl. Make a well in the center, add ghee, water and salt. Mix well with the fingers, then remove dough to an oiled surface and knead for 10 minutes. Divide into 12 equal pieces and roll into balls. Cover with plastic wrap. On a well-oiled surface, roll each ball of dough until it is as thin as strudel pastry. To cook, place the pancake on a well-oiled hot griddle, cook lightly on both sides. Spread egg over the center, add onion and filling and fold up into a rectangular parcel. Brown the surface.

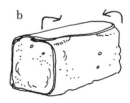

Pancake Roll Malay-style
a. Filling in center of dough
b. Formed pancake roll

PANCHPHORAN: (*PANCH-PHO-RAN*, India) see CURRY PASTES, POWDERS AND SAUCES

213

PANDANUS LEAF: (*Pandanus amary-llifolius*) The pungently aromatic screw pine of the Pandanaceae family, with its long, flat, tapering mid-green leaves, is used for both its color and unique fragrance in many Southeast Asian cuisines, and particularly in Indonesian and Malaysian cooking. Fresh or dried pandanus leaves are crushed and added to the dish during cooking or boiled to extract the green color, which is used mainly for coloring sweets. In Indonesia they are sometimes added to the liquid when making bean curd, to improve its taste. They are sold in dried form, which lacks intensity of flavor, and in frozen form, which gives acceptable results. An intensely strong essence known in Thailand as *toey* is sold in small dropper bottles and should be used with discretion. Vanilla essence can be substituted for pandanus in sweet dishes, but there is not a suitable substitute in other dishes. If not available it can be omitted. Another variety of screw pine (*Pandanus odoratissimus*) yields *kewra*, a flavoring essence used in India.
Also known as *daun pandan* (Indonesia, Malaysia); *rampe* (Sri Lanka); *bai toey* (Thailand); *lu dua* (Vietnam); screw pine
See also: FLAVORINGS; KEWRA ESSENCE/EXTRACT

Pandanus leaf

PANGGANG: (*PANG-GANG*, see INDONESIA, COOKING METHODS

PANG KHAO PHOD: (*PAENG KHAO BOD*, Thailand) see FLOURS AND THICKENERS (CORNSTARCH)

PANG KHAO CHAO: (*PAENG KHAO CHAO*, Thailand) see FLOURS AND THICKENERS (RICE FLOUR)

PANG KHAO NIEW: (*PAENG KHAO NIEW*, Thailand) see FLOURS AND THICKENERS (GLUTINOUS RICE FLOUR)

PANG MUN: (*PAENG MAN*, Thailand) see FLOURS AND THICKENERS (TAPIOCA STARCH)

PANG TAO YAI MOM: (*PANG TAO YUI MOM*, Thailand) see FLOURS AND THICKENERS (ARROWROOT)

PANIR: (*PA-NEER*, India) A type of firm cottage cheese with a texture like bean curd. It is made by acidulating fresh milk with yogurt or citrus juice, then leaving it to drip in a bag until the whey (buttermilk) has run off. It is then pressed into cakes. It is cut into cubes and used as an ingredient in vegetarian cooking and in stuffings.
Also known as *chenna*, *chhena* (India); cottage cheese

PANIR
Yields about 12 oz (375 g)

4 cups (1 qt / 1 l) fresh whole milk
1½–2 tbsps lemon juice
2 tbsps natural (plain) yogurt

Bring milk to a boil, stir in lemon juice and yogurt until milk curdles. Pour into a muslin bag or wrap in cheesecloth and hang for at least 3 hours until the liquid (whey) has drained off.

PANKO: (*PAN-KO*, Japan) A special type of large, dried, toasted bread crumb used in Japan for coating fried foods such as *tonkatsu* (breaded pork) and *kushi-age* (kebabs). Sold in cellophane or plastic bags, it is readily available. Normal bread crumbs can be substituted for it.
See also: TONKATSU (recipe)

PANSIT: (*PAN-SIT*, Philippines) A noodle dish that can be made in a variety of ways. Most commonly it is fried with garlic, onion, meat, shrimp and vegetables.
Also known as *pancit canton* (Philippines)
See also: NOODLES FILIPINO (recipe)

PAPADAM: (*PAA-PA-DUM*, India) Flat, dried wafers made from lentil, rice or potato flour, which are deep-fried until crisp and served as a snack. Certain types are highly spiced, with *ajwain*, pepper and dried chili flakes. They are eadily available in packs of 12–20 in several sizes. Uncooked they will keep indefinitely, but must be eaten soon after frying.
Also known as *papads*; *papadum*; *poppadom*

Papadams

PAPADS: (*PAA-PA-RH*, India) see PAPADAM

PAPRIKA: (*Capsicum tetragonum*) Sweet or bell peppers are dried and ground to a powder that is used as a seasoning, giving a mildly pungent flavor. As a seasoning paprika is used only infrequently in Asia. It is used mainly—in place of large quantities of chili—to impart a brilliant red color to curries, particularly in Sri Lanka.
See also: CHILI; PEPPER

PARATHA: (*PA-RAAN-THAA*, India) see BREAD, INDIAN

PARKIA: (*Parkia speciosa*) From the family Leguminosae, these medium-size trees have feathery fronds of leaves that resemble poinciana trees. They yield edible bright green, ridged seed pods about the size of broad beans—although flatter—with a peculiar smell and taste that have earned them the common name "stink bean." Parkia give a characteristic taste to many regional dishes from southern Thailand where the trees are cultivated. In Indonesia the pods are eaten as a vegetable and the seeds are eaten as a snack. They are sun-dried, peeled, and either fried in oil or steeped in water for 24 hours to soften. Medicinally, parkia is thought to purify the kidneys. Its name "twisted cluster bean" leads to some confusion with the Indian *gwaar ki phalli*, or guar bean, which is also called a "cluster bean."
Also known as *peteh*, *pete cina*, *sindootan* (Indonesia); *sa-taw* (Thailand); stink beans; twisted cluster beans
See also: PARKIA AND SHRIMP SAMBALAN (recipe)

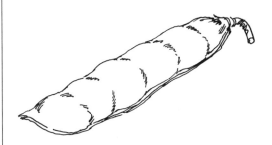

Parkia seed pod

PARKIA AND SHRIMP SAMBALAN
Serves 6

10 parkia beans, soaked
1 onion, chopped
1/2 tsp minced garlic
1/4 cup (2 fl oz / 60 ml) oil
1 tsp shrimp paste
1 tsp laos powder
1 tsp sugar
1–2 tsps sambal ulek
8 oz (250 g) shelled medium shrimp (prawns)
1 cup (8 fl oz / 250 ml) thin coconut milk
1 tbsp finely chopped lemon grass
salt
tamarind water or lemon juice
kaffir lime leaves, soaked

Drain and slice the parkia. Sauté onions and garlic in oil until colored. Add shrimp paste, *laos* powder, sugar and *sambal ulek*. Color well, add parkia and simmer for 5 minutes. Add shrimp, coconut milk, lemon grass, salt, tamarind water or lemon juice and lime leaves to taste. Simmer for 5–6 minutes.

PASTRY-MAKING UTENSILS: see UTENSILS
(BREAD AND PASTRY MAKING)

PATIS: (*PA-TEES*, Philippines) A clear, amber
sauce made from fish or shrimp, fermented
until a protein, hydrolysate, is formed. The
supernatant liquid, when drawn off, is called
patis and is similar to Thai *nam pla,* while the
pickled fish or shrimp residue is called *bagoong.*
The addition of limes refines its flavor.
See also: BAGOONG; FISH SAUCE

PATIS

2 cups (16 fl oz / 500 ml) liquid drained from
alamang bagoong *(pickled shrimp / prawn)*
2 limes, quartered

Pour liquid into a saucepan and add
limes. Boil for 5 minutes; transfer to a
sterilized jar and let stand for 1 day.
Siphon clear liquid from the top and
store separately.

PAU TS'AI: (*PAU CHOY*, China) see CABBAGE,
CHINESE (BOK CHOY)

PAZUN NGA-PI: (*PA-SOON NGA-PEAT*, Burma)
see BURMA

PEA EGGPLANT: see EGGPLANT (PEA)

PEA LEAF: (*Pisum sativum* L.) A vegetable
for special occasions. These tender leaves are
garden peas that have been prevented from
flowering or fruiting to encourage the growth
of their small, round, pea-green leaves. They
come to the market plucked from their stems,
in little clusters of two or three leaves. As a
vegetable they are stir-fried, usually with ginger, or may be served with another expensive
ingredient, crabmeat. Most commonly, however, pea leaves are cooked in a soup. Sometimes a pâté of fish or shrimp is stuffed between the leaves, and crabmeat and beaten
egg white are added to the broth to make a very
impressive banquet soup. Pea leaves stay fresh
for only a few days. They should be kept,
loosely wrapped in paper or plastic, in the
refrigerator.
Also known as *dau mil, dau miu* (China); pea
shoots

Pea leaf

PEANUT OIL: see OILS AND FATS

PEANUT: (*Arachis hypogaea*) A member of
the Leguminosae family, the peanut is an
annual with yellow flowers. When pollinated
the stalk elongates and pushes the flower
underground to complete the seed develop-
ment. The seed pod has a wrinkled surface and
usually contains two nuts or kernels, covered
with a beige-pink or red skin.

Peanuts contain up to 30 percent protein,
making them a valuable addition to a low-
protein diet. They are therefore used extensively in Asian vegetarian cooking. They also
supply an oil that is used widely throughout
Asia as a cooking medium. The Chinese in
particular enjoy the distinctive flavor of a
moderately refined peanut oil. Further refin-
ing can rid the oil of its noticeable nutty aroma,
making it suitable for most kinds of cooking
and for salad dressings.

India is the largest Asian producer of peanuts. Next is China, where peanuts are used
extensively in the central region as an ingredient in spicy dishes, are ground to make into a
sweet soup, or are boiled in brine to serve as an
accompaniment to cold cuts. In Cambodia,
Laos, Thailand and Vietnam peanuts play an
important role in the cuisine. Roasted and
crushed nuts are added to many of the dipping
sauces and salad dressings, and sprinkled
over finished dishes and added to sauces to
thicken and enrich them. A spicy peanut sauce
accompanies a number of Asian dishes, particularly the *satays* of Malaysia and Indonesia.
Also known as *far sang* (China); *moongphali*
(India); *kacang tanah* (Indonesia, Malaysia);
tooa lisong (Thailand); *dau phong* (Vietnam)
See also: DAU PHONG RANG; PEANUT FRITTERS

(recipe); PEANUT SAMBAL (recipe); SATAY BEEF WITH PEANUT SAUCE (recipe); VIETNAMESE PEANUT SAUCE (recipe)

PEANUT FRITTERS
Yields 18

3/4 cup (3 oz / 90 g) rice flour
2 tbsps cornstarch (cornflour)
1/4 cup (2 oz / 60 g) minced onion
1 tsp minced garlic
2 tsps ground coriander
1 1/2 tsps chili powder
2 1/2 tsps salt
warm water
1/4 cup (2 fl oz / 60 ml) boiling water
1 cup (5 oz / 155 g) crushed roasted peanuts
vegetable oil

Combine flour, onion, garlic, coriander, chili powder, salt and enough warm water to make a thick batter. Add the boiling water and let stand 15 minutes. Stir in peanuts. Heat 2 in (1 cm) oil in a pan and fry spoonfuls of the batter until crisp and golden. Drain and serve hot.

PEANUT SAMBAL
Yields 2 cups (500 g)

1 cup (5 oz / 155 g) roasted peanuts
3/4 cup (6 oz / 180 g) chopped onion
1 1/2 tbsps chopped garlic
2 1/2 tbsps chopped chilies or 1 1/2 tbsps sambal ulek
1/2 tsp shrimp paste
2–3 tsps minced kaffir lime rind
1 tbsp minced greater galangal
3 tbsps vegetable or coconut oil
1 1/2 tbsps palm sugar (or substitute brown sugar)
1/2 tsp salt
1/2 cup (4 fl oz / 125 ml) thick coconut milk
lime or lemon juice

Grind peanuts, onion, garlic, chilies, shrimp paste, lime rind and *galangal* to a paste. Sauté in the oil with sugar and salt for 3 minutes. Add the coconut milk and simmer gently until oil appears on surface. Add lime juice to taste. Can be stored in the refrigerator for several months.

PEANUT SAUCE
Yields 1 3/4 cups (14 fl oz / 430 ml)

2/3 cup (3 1/2 oz / 100 g) ground roasted unsalted peanuts
3 tbsps kecap manis
1 1/2 tbsps ground coriander
1/3 tsp turmeric
2 tsps chili sauce
1 tsp minced garlic
3/4 cup (6 fl oz / 180 ml) thin coconut milk
2–3 tsps palm sugar (or substitute brown sugar)
salt
lemon juice

Combine all of the ingredients in a small pan with sugar and simmer for 2–3 minutes. Cool. Add salt and lemon juice to taste.

VIETNAMESE PEANUT SAUCE
Yields 1 1/2 cups (12 fl oz / 400 ml)

1/3 cup (1 1/2 oz / 50 g) roasted peanuts
2 fresh red chilies, seeded and chopped
1 tsp minced garlic
1 tbsp finely chopped fresh mint
2 tbsps lime or lemon juice
1/4 cup (2 fl oz / 60 ml) fish sauce
1 cup (8 fl oz / 250 ml) thin coconut milk

Place all ingredients except fish sauce and coconut milk in a mortar or food processor and grind to a smooth paste. Stir in remaining ingredients.

PEANUT, ROASTED: see DAU PHONG RANG

PEA SHOOT/SPROUT: see PEA LEAF

PECHAY: (*PET-CHAY*, Philippines) see CABBAGE, CHINESE (NAPA)

PEPPER: (*Capsicum frutescens*) Sweet red and green bell peppers (red and green peppers/capsicums), the fruit of the capsicum plant, a member of the Solanaceae family, are used to a small extent in Asian cooking, although hot chilies are preferred and used generously in most countries. Introduced to Asia by Portuguese merchants, they are cultivated, particularly in China, India and Japan.

AO-TOGARASHI (Japan) are small green peppers, the size and shape of green chilies, but with a mild, sweet flavor. One type is the *shishi-to* or "lion pepper." They are served as side dishes, either skewered and grilled, deep-fried or simmered in soy sauce. The small red *togarashi* chili pepper is not used in this way, being too intensely hot to eat, but is powdered for use as a condiment.
Also known as *sun tsui* (China); *pahari mirich*, *simla mirich* (India); *piman, shishi-togarashi, shishi-to* (Japan); *prik yuah* (Thailand); bell pepper; capsicum; green pepper; red pepper
See also: CHILI

PEPPER, BELL: see PEPPER

PEPPERCORN: (*Piper nigrum*) The berries from a vine of the Piperaceae family provide both black and white peppercorns. Pepper grows extensively in Southeast Asia, notably in Sri Lanka, Indonesia and India. Until hot chili peppers were introduced to Asia, pepper provided the "heat" for all forms of Asian cooking. To obtain black peppercorns the unripe berries are picked, fermented and dried until they are hard and black. White pepper is made from the largest of the ripe berries, which are suspended in running water for several days. The berries swell, making removal of the outer skin easier; the pale colored inner seed is sun-dried, which turns it a pale beige color. Ground white pepper is most commonly used in Chinese cooking, while black pepper, ground or in whole berries, is used in curries and *garam masala*.

GREEN PEPPERCORNS, which are the unripe berries pickled in brine, are occasionally used in Asia, especially in Thailand.
Also known as *nga-youk-kuan* (Burma); *hu-chiao* (China); *gol mirich, kali mirich* (India); *merica hitam* (Indonesia); *kosho* (Japan); *phil noi* (Laos); *lada hitam* (Malaysia); *gammiris* (Sri Lanka); *prik thai* (Thailand)
See also: MASALA

PEPPER, HOT: see CHILI

PEPPER, SICHUAN: see SICHUAN PEPPER-CORN

PERILLA: see BEEFSTEAK PLANT

PERSIMMON: (*Diospyros kaki*) This species has many types, including the Japanese and Chinese persimmons, both of which have the size and appearance of a tomato, with smooth orange-red skin and soft, juicy, sweet flesh of the same hue. They are a popular dessert fruit and are also dried to be eaten as a confection. In ancient China, persimmons were eaten to relieve drunkenness.
Also known as *hong chee* (China); *kaki* (Japan)

PERUNKAYAN: (*PE-RUN-KAA-YAN*, Sri Lanka) see ASAFOETIDA

PETIS: (*P'TEASE*, Indonesia) see FISH SAUCE

PE TS'AI: (*BAK CHOY*, China) see CABBAGE, CHINESE (NAPA)

PHAI TONG: (*PHAI TONG*, Thailand) see BAMBOO SHOOT

PHAK HOM POM: (*PUK HOM POM*, Laos) see CORIANDER, FRESH

PHAK SI: (*PUK SEE*, Laos) see DILL

PHALAZEE: (*PAR-LA-ZI*, Burma) see CARDAMOM

PHEASANT: Pheasant is native to China. A most attractively feathered bird, it featured in Chinese imperial banquets in earlier times, where the bird was cooked and the long, rainbow-hued tail feathers used in the decoration of the dish. It is now eaten much less frequently.

PHEN: (*FEN*, Vietnam) see ALUM

PHILIPPINES: The cuisine of the colorful islands of the Philippines represents an adventurous fusion of many influences. The Spanish brought with them *tapas,* and translated it into the *merienda.* They brought recipes for *guisado, fritata* and *adobo* and introduced tasty *chorizo* sausages and *bacalao* (dried salt cod). The Chinese added soy sauce, their noodles, *wontons* and stir-fries. From the Pacific islanders they learned to cook with yams, taro and sweet potatoes. Their sweet snacks and puddings emulate those of Indonesia and Malaysia. From local sources came such popular Tagalog dishes as *kare-kare*, with its sauce rendered pink-red from *burong mustaza* (pickled mustard leaves) —in other dishes a traditional red color is obtained from *annatto* seeds. *Lechon* is the festive suckling pig, roasted crisp and tender with its rich sauce made from the liver; and *lumpia*, the local version of the Chinese spring roll or Malaysian *popiah*, is made from the delicately flavored *ubod* (heart of palm) which is wrapped in an egg crêpe.

Much of the Philippine cuisine centers around fish, for the bountiful blue oceans that lap the shores of these many islands, and the numerous rivers that are constantly replenished by tropical rains, offer fish in plenty. *Lapu lapu,* the spotted *garoupa* with its tender flesh; *bangus*, the milkfish that is considered to be amongst the best; *bidbid*, the tenpounder; *dilis* (anchovies); *apahap* (sea bass); and *malasugi* (swordfish)—all find their way into the pickling pot, or the *palayok* (the clay pot used for cooking many local dishes).

Tartness predominates in much of the cooking. Drinks are made refreshingly tangy with *kalamansi* (a type of local citrus) juice. Vinegar and tamarind give an edge to many dishes, and much of the fish is pickled in vinegar or brine, either to be served in that way or to be processed into the pungent seasoning pastes and sauces known as *bagoong, heko* and *patis*. Vegetables—and particularly mustard greens which, when cured, become known as *burong mustaza*—and also fish and meat, are cured into *buro*, by salting and soaking in rice washings.

Eating is an informal affair. Both at restaurants and at home food is often enjoyed buffet-style, amidst exotic tropical blooms and coconut or banana leaves—all for self-selection. There are *palayoks,* which contain several different dishes, over tabletop charcoal braziers, as well as salads and cold seafoods in giant clam shells.

The *merienda* is a custom of hospitality peculiar to the Philippines. Its origins are undoubtedly Spanish. *Tapas,* a selection of tasty, savory dishes of small size are served together on a platter, to be nibbled with drinks.

Merienda combines cakes and sweet dishes with savory snacks such as *ukoy*, little shrimp fritters, and *tapa,* a kind of beef jerky. A chocolate flavored "sticky" rice, known as *champorado*, is popular. A rich hot chocolate drink is also enjoyed. *Merienda* begins at about 4 p.m. and may be substantial enough to replace dinner.

PHILIPPINES, COOKING METHODS:

ADOBADO: A cooking method similar to *adobo*, in which pieces of meat and garlic are browned by pan-frying. A little broth and vinegar is added as a sauce before serving.

ADOBO: This is one of the many Spanish-inspired inclusions in the Filipino cuisine. *Adobo* dishes are crisply fried pieces of seafood, pork or chicken, with a pungent flavor of garlic and vinegar. *Adobo*-style cooking is often given a local touch by the introduction of thick coconut milk or by serving on skewers.

ASADO: A typical cooking style, combining Spanish and Chinese influences, in which meat is simmered in soy sauce with bay leaves, onions, tomato and peppercorns.

GUINATAAN: A method of simmering ingredients in coconut milk.
Also known as *ginitan*

GUISADO: A dish in which meat is first sautéed, and then braised or simmered until tender.

INIHAW: Describes grilling over a fire. Used for fish, poultry and skewered meats.

KILAWIN: A method of "cooking" fish by soaking in coconut vinegar, lime or *kalamansi* juice until it turns transparent. The fish is usually then mixed with coconut milk, onions, ginger and tomato. Known as *kinilaw* in the Visayan region, this is an extremely popular method of preparing fish there.

PAKSIW: A term applied to either meat or fish pickled with vinegar and salt, and sometimes also ginger and sugar. The meat is cut into large pieces, placed in a clay pot and the pickling ingredients added, brought to a boil and simmered until cooked. It keeps for several days and is served cold, sometimes with some of the pickling liquid.

PHILIPPINES RECIPES

Appetizers
Heart of Palm Rolls
Shrimp Patties
Tapa

Main Courses
Adobo Chicken
Estofado
Fish Stuffed with Vegetables
Kare-Kare
Roast Suckling Pig, Philippine Style
Sinigang

Accompaniments
Biko
Liver Sauce
Noodles Filipino

Dessert
Chocolate Rice

MENU
(see recipes)

DINNER MENU
Serves 8

Shrimp Patties
Heart of Palm Rolls

Estofado
Noodles Filipino

Chocolate Rice

PHOOL GOBHI: (*PHOOL GO-BHEE*, India) see CAULIFLOWER

PHULKAS: (*PHUL-KAA*, India) see BREAD, INDIAN

PICKLED BEAN CURD: see BEAN CURD BY-PRODUCTS (FERMENTED)

PICKLED CABBAGE: see CABBAGE, PICKLED

PICKLED CABBAGE IN CHICKEN SOUP WITH HAM: (recipe) see CABBAGE, PICKLED

PICKLED FISH: see FISH, PRESERVED; PADEK

PICKLED GARLIC: see GARLIC

PICKLED GINGER: see GINGER

PICKLED ONION: see ONIONS

PICKLED RHIZOME: see GALANGAL, LESSER

PICKLED SHALLOT: see ONION

PICKLED TURNIP: see TURNIP

PICKLED VEGETABLES

2 cups (1 lb/500 g) shredded cabbage
1 cucumber, cut into sticks
1 carrot, cut into sticks
1 tbsp salt
2–3 tbsps sugar
1 cup (8 fl oz/250 ml) white vinegar

Place vegetables in a dish. Add salt,
knead with the fingers, leave 1 hour.
Drain. Dissolve sugar in vinegar. Pour
over vegetables. Let stand 1 hour.
Drain to serve.

PICKLES, INDIAN: In India, pickles are known as *achar* and were originally devised as a means of preserving seasonal foods. At least one, and often several kinds of pickle are served with most Indian meals to stimulate the palate, aid digestion and to introduce complementary or contrasting flavors. The most popular Indian pickles are made from limes and mangoes, but many other ingredients, including game meats, fish, carrots, garlic, chilies and tomatoes, are also used. The base preservatives are oil, brine or vinegar, and chili, garlic, ginger, pepper and many different types of spices, both in whole seed form and powdered, add strong flavors. Pickles differ from chutneys and relishes, which are of a thick, jam-like consistency and are often freshly made.
See also: MANGO PICKLES (recipe)

P'IEN T'AO JEN: (*BIEN DAU YAN*, China) see APRICOT KERNEL

PIGEON: Pigeon is enjoyed throughout China and other parts of Asia. Pigeons are small birds, but their meat, particularly the breast, is tender and well flavored. There are more than forty types of pigeon used in cooking and a number of Chinese restaurants serve only pigeon dishes. The eggs are also eaten. *Sang choy bow* is a favored dish in which finely diced pigeon and Chinese sausage is wrapped in lettuce-leaf parcels. Another highly regarded Chinese dish that uses pigeon combines a finely textured pâté of pigeon breast cooked in a bamboo pot with sliced *dang gui* herb. A squab is a young pigeon, under a month old, especially bred for the table.

Also known as *ge* (China)
See also: DANG GUI

PIGEON EGG: see EGG

PIGEON PEA: (*Cajanus indicus, C. cajan*) A perennial shrub which produces pods of grayish yellow seeds the size of small peas. There are about 30 different types of pigeon pea, most of which are edible. The flattish, almost square pea resembles a yellow lentil or split pea and, when unpolished, it is surrounded by an orange-red skin. Used as a dried bean, either whole or split and polished, pigeon peas can replace chick-peas or yellow split peas in a recipe. They should be thoroughly rinsed before use and boiled in salted water until just tender.

Also known as *kacang goode* (Indonesia); *kacang eeris* (Malaysia); *bunga, kaldos, kaldios* (pod) (Philippines); gunga pea; red chick-pea; red gram
See also: CHICK-PEA; LENTIL

PIKE MAW: see FISH MAW

PIMAN: (*PEE-MAHN*, Japan) see PEPPER

PINAKSIW: (*PEE-NAK-SIW*, Philippines) see FISH, PRESERVED

PINDANGGA: (*PIN-DANG-GAH*, Philippines) see EEL

PINEAPPLE: (*Ananas comosus*) This plant is cultivated in most tropical countries for its delicious sweet-tart, juicy, fibrous fruit. The fruit, which grows on a thick stalk from the center of the long-leafed, spiky plant, is itself topped with a miniature version of the pineapple plant. This can be sliced off the tree and

returned to the soil to propagate the plant.

Pineapple is a versatile fruit that can be cooked or eaten raw. It is used in both sweet and savory dishes. In Southeast Asian countries it is common to find street hawkers selling peeled, sliced pineapple as snacks. Jackfruit, another common tropical Asian fruit, has similar, although drier, flesh and can be used in most savory recipes in place of pineapple.

Also known as *annanas* (India); *saparot, supparot* (Thailand)
See also: JACKFRUIT; SWEET TAMARIND AND CHICKEN SOUP (recipe)

PINE KERNEL: see PINE NUTS

PINE NEEDLE: Pine needles are used in Japan, Korea and northern China to add flavor to cooked or steamed foods, as elegant skewers for snack foods, and as a garnish. In Japan a delicately flavored soup, brewed in a small teapot known as a *dobin*, has pine needles pushed into the spout of the pot to impart their subtle flavor to the stock.

Also known as *chong gee* (China); pignolia; pine kernel
See also: JAPAN, GARNISHES; GINKGO; KIMCHI (recipe); OLIVE SEEDS

PINE NUT: (*Pinus* spp.) The pine nuts most often used in Asian cooking are grown in Korea where there are several important species. The Korean pine nut, *Pinus koraiensis*, has large, pointed, plump nuts which have the taste of pine sap when raw, but which when roasted develop a wonderful, nutty taste and crisp texture. Another type, *Pinus lambertiana*, comes from a long, thin, closely packed cone with more slender nuts. The *Pinus gerardiana*, grown in the Himalayas, also has nuts which are used in cooking, but to a lesser extent in that part of Asia.

Pine nuts are primarily a garnish; they are sprinkled over Chinese vegetarian dishes as well as the delightful "fried milk," which is a snowy mass of stir-fried milk with egg whites. In Korea they appear in candies, in desserts and are sometimes added to *kimchi* and meat dishes. Pine nuts are readily available in Asian or health food stores. A nut of similar size, although with a layered appearance and known as olive seeds, is used in Chinese cooking in the same way.

PINIPIG: (*PEE-NEE-PIG*, Philippines) see RICE (GLUTINOUS)

PINK GINGER BUD: see GINGER BUD

PIRURUTUNG: (*PEE-ROO-ROO-TONG*, Philippines) see RICE (NON-GLUTINOUS)

PISANG: (*PEA-SUNG*, Indonesia, Malaysia) see BANANA

PISANG KARI: (*PEA-SUNG-CAR-REE*, Malaysia) see BANANA

PISANG KEPOK: (*PEA-SUNG KEH-POCK*, Malaysia) see BANANA

PISANG PISANG: (*PEA-SUNG PEA-SUNG*, Malaysia) see BANGUS

PISANG RAJA: (*PEA-SUNG RAH-JA*, Indonesia) see BANANA

PISANG SUSU: (*PEH-SANG SUH-SO*, Philippines) see BANANA

PISI HUI LAL MIRICH: (*PI-SEE HUI LAAL MIRCH*, India) see CHILI POWDER

PISTACHIO NUT: (*Pistacia vera*) The small pistachio tree is native to the Middle East and central Asia. The kernels, inside their ovoid, buff-colored hard shells, are highly regarded for their superb flavor and bright green color. In Asia pistachio nuts are used mainly in India, where they are included in sweetmeats and used to garnish desserts.
Also known as *pista* (India)
See also: KULFI (recipe)

PLA BAI MAI: (*PLA BAI MAI*, Thailand) see ANCHOVY

PLA CHALARD: (*PLAA CHA-LAAD*, Thailand) see FISH, PRESERVED

PLA CHAWN: (*PLAA CHON*, Thailand) see FISH, PRESERVED

PLA NUA AWN: (*PLA NUA ON*, Thailand) see ANCHOVY

PLA KA-DEE: (*PLAA KA-DEE*, Thailand) see FISH, PRESERVED

PLA KARANG: (*PLA KAPONG*, Thailand) see GAROUPA

PLA KARANG DUENG JUTFA: (*PLAA KA-PONG DAENG JUT-FA*, Thailand) see GAROUPA

PLA KULAO: (*PLAA KU-LAO*, Thailand) see FISH, PRESERVED

PLA LAI: (*PLAA LAI*, Thailand) see EEL

PLA MANGKOR: (*PLAA MANG-KON*, Thailand) see EEL

PLANTAIN BANANA: see BANANA

PLA SIEW: (*PLAA SIL-IEU*, Thailand) see FISH, PRESERVED

PLEATED SQUASH: see LUFFA, ANGLED

PLUM: (*Prunus armeniaca, P. mume*) The native Chinese plum is actually a kind of apricot, red-gold in color, which has grown in China and Japan since ancient times. Myrobalans (*Prunus cerasifera*) are a smooth-skinned, dark red fruit that is closely related. They have been grown in Asia for many centuries; they are used medicinally, and are preserved and candied.

PLUM SAUCE: In China plums are used to make the sweet-tart condiment known as "plum" sauce, which goes under the name *timcheong* in Malaysia. It is used as a dip with fried meats and snacks and is sometimes served with Beijing (Peking) Duck.
Also known as red *tim cheong, sheung moy cheung* (China)

SALTED PLUMS are dried, heavily salted Chinese "plums" eaten as a confection, they have a sweet-sour taste that stimulates the palate and refreshes the breath. They were one of the earliest "candies" known to the Chinese. Steeped in Chinese yellow rice wine, they produce a sweet and aromatic liqueur.

UMEBOSHI: (Japan) In Japan plums, flavored and colored with red *shiso* (beefsteak plant) leaves, are pickled in salt. *Umeboshi* is served as a pickle at the end of a Japanese meal and is almost always served with Japanese breakfast as it is thought to be cleansing for the system. Puréed *umeboshi* is made into *bainiku*, which is added to some dips for its tart flavor. Sold in small jars and bottles, it keeps well, but should be refrigerated once opened.

UMESHU, a popular liqueur throughout Japan, is made from the unripe fruit of the *ume* apricot which comes to the markets in late May. The liqueur, which contains pure rice or potato spirits, is easy to make and is made in many Japanese homes. It is believed to soothe the stomach. It is also marketed commercially, usually under the name "plum liqueur."

PLUM LIQUEUR: see PLUM (UMESHU)
PLUM PICKLES: see TSUKEMONO
PLUM SAUCE: see PLUM

POLYGONUM: (*Polygonum* sp.) A herb with purple-tinged stems and deep green, long and slender leaves similar to spearmint, although smoother. The flavor is intense, akin to a concentrated mixture of basil and mint. It is used in fish and noodle dishes in Malaysia and is favored by Nonya cooks. It is called by its botanical name and often referred to, misleadingly, as Vietnamese mint, although it does also grow readily in Vietnam and is used there in salads.
Also known as *daum kesom* (Indonesia, Malaysia); *rau ram* (Vietnam)
See also: mint; Vietnamese mint

Polygonum

POMEGRANATE: (*Punica granatum*) The fruit of an ancient tree native to the Middle East. The globe-shaped fruit has a hard red skin which encloses many tiny pink-red sections, each with a small seed. Pomegranates have a unique, sweet flavor and delightfully crisp texture. The juice is made into a refresh-ing drink or concentrated into an essence or syrup which is sold as grenadine. In India, the seeds are scattered over desserts and are dried and ground for use as a seasoning when a tart flavor is required. They are also used as a meat tenderizer and in the making of chutneys. Choose large, firm, unwrinkled red pomegranates when buying. They can be refrigerated for several weeks. The fresh seeds can be frozen.

GRENADINE is a sweet-tart, red-colored syrup made from pomegranate juice. In India it is used to flavor milk drinks and desserts and may also be mixed with soda or lemonade to make an alcohol-free cocktail.
Also known as *anar, anardana* (dried seeds) (India); *daarim* (Nepal); *granada* (Philippines); Chinese apple

POMELO: (*Citrus grandis*) A large fruit of Chinese origin that resembles a grapefruit. It tapers slightly at the stem end and has thick, sweet, slightly rough-textured skin and dry, semisweet flesh. Like many other fruits, it is sometimes eaten in Southeast Asia with salt.
Also known as *suha* (Philippines); *som or* (Thailand)

POMFRET: (*Pampus argenteus*) There are two commonly used pomfrets in Asia. The white or silver pomfret from the Stromateidae family is silvery-colored and covered with tiny black spots. This is the species favored by the Chinese. The black or brown pomfret is squarer in shape with brown-gray coloration. It is fished more frequently in Indonesian and Philippine waters. It is slightly inferior in flavor to the white.

Pomfret is one of the most highly prized of the Asian fish. An upright flat fish with firm skin and very tiny scales, it has a squared or rounded body with distinctive fins. The face of the white pomfret has a downturned mouth which gives it a dog-like look; this has given rise to a popular Cantonese name which translates as "dog fish." One of the most popular Chinese ways of preparing pomfret is to smoke it over tea leaves, which turns it a rich brown. It is sliced and served with mayonnaise.
Also known as *nga-mote-phyu* (Burma); *paah cheong, trey pek chhieu* (China); *chhanna* (In-

dia); *bawal putih* (Indonesia); *bawal puteh* (Malaysia); *alumbeberas, duhay* (Philippines); *pla jara met khao* (Thailand); *ca chim trang* (Vietnam); white butter fish
See also: SPICED POMFRET (recipe)

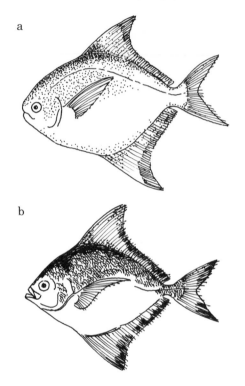

a. White pomfret   b. Black pomfret

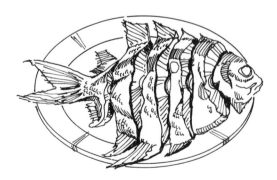

Chinese-style smoked pomfret

SPICED POMFRET
Serves 4–6

1¼ lbs (600 g) white pomfret
2 tsps minced garlic
1 tsp minced ginger
4 tbsps kecap manis
1 tbsp vegetable oil
1 tbsp sambal ulek
¼ cup (2 fl oz / 60 ml) fresh lime juice
salt
palm sugar (or substitute brown sugar)

Clean fish, rinse and dry and slash in several places on each side. Mix garlic, ginger and 2 tbsps *kecap manis* with oil. Brush over fish and marinate for 2 hours. Grill over a charcoal fire, brushing with extra marinade several times. Make a sauce of *sambal ulek,* lime juice and remaining 2 tbsps *kecap manis,* adding salt and sugar to taste. Serve as a dip with the sliced fish.

PONZU SAUCE: (*PON-ZOO*, Japan) A tangy, citrus juice-based sauce used as a dip with *sashimi,* as a dressing for *sunomono* dishes and with certain simmered dishes, usually containing seafood.
See also: BONITO; SASHIMI; SEAWEED; SUNOMONO

PONZU SAUCE
Yields 2 cups (16 fl oz / 500 ml)

1 cup (8 fl oz / 250 ml) lemon or citron juice
¼ cup (2 fl oz / 60 ml) rice vinegar
¼ cup (2 fl oz / 60 ml) mirin, boiled
2 in (5 cm) piece kombu kelp
¾ cup (6 fl oz / 180 ml) dark soy sauce
2 tbsps light soy sauce
¼ cup (2 fl oz / 60 ml) hana-katsuo (bonito flakes)

Mix all of the ingredients together. Let stand overnight, then strain through a fine nylon sieve or piece of cloth. Refrigerate.

PORK

POON DANG: (*PUNN DAENG*, Thailand) see LIME SOLUTION

POOTU: (*POO-TU*, India) A hot cereal made by steaming coarsely ground rice in a section of bamboo. Served on the southwest coast of India.

POPPADOM: (*PAA-PA-DUM*, India) see PAPADAMS

POPPY SEED: (*Papaver somniferum*)
Poppy seeds were used as early as 1500 BC by the Egyptians, who ground them for their oil. The tiny, round black or white seeds have a subtle, nutty flavor, and both black and white are used in Asian cooking. In India white seeds are ground to a paste and used to thicken and enrich curries, particularly in a strict vegetarian diet where even onions are taboo. They lend a nutty taste to both meat and vegetarian snacks, and to rice dishes. Black poppy seeds are preferred for garnishing, being sprinkled over breads, cakes and pastries in many Asian countries.
Also known as *ying-shu* (China); *khaskhas, kus kus* (India); *kas kas* (Malaysia)

PORK: The pig was domesticated by the
Chinese thousands of years ago and has become their most favored meat in all areas except the far north, where lamb predominates, and in the Muslim community. In all other Asian cuisines pork is included to a much smaller extent. Through the centuries, the Chinese devised their own style of pork cuts that differ slightly from those chosen by Western butchers.
See also: *recipes following*

FRESH BACON is the cut that the Chinese call "five flowered pork," after its five alternating layers of fat and meat. It is the pork belly cut and sold as fresh bacon on the rind. Because the interlayering of fat keeps the meat moist and tender, it is used for stir-fries as well as for a variety of other dishes.
See also: PORK, CURED

FRESH HAM, or pork butt, is the leg section, used frequently in Chinese cooking and in curry-making.
See also: PORK, CURED

HOCKS are enjoyed for their gelatinous skin, gristle, tendons and soft marrow. Fore hocks

have more meat than the rear ones. They require long cooking to tenderize and are usually strongly seasoned.

OFFAL AND OFFCUTS of pork are all used in some form in Chinese cooking. The blood is coagulated with a setting agent, then is used in soups, such as the strongly-flavored Sichuan sour and hot soup. Caul fat, the netlike web of fat that lines the stomach, is used to wrap food for frying. Ears, intestines, snouts and tails are crisped with lime solution, colored orange-red, and boiled until tender. Tripe is stewed with garlic, chili and bean pastes. Pork liver is enjoyed for its delicate texture. The Chinese prefer it barely cooked, adding it raw to bowls of hot *congee* or soup to cook in the hot liquid. When the Chinese cook kidneys, they invariably use pig kidneys, as they enjoy the particular taste and texture. The kidneys are usually sliced horizontally and scored in a crosshatch pattern to tenderize, which makes them curl up attractively when cooked.
See also: CAUL FAT

PORK RIBS: Lean spare ribs of pork, as well as rib and cutlet bones, covered with a $1/2$–1 in (1–2.5 cm) layer of fat meat, are used frequently in Chinese cooking and feature in other Asian cuisines. Spare ribs are marinated, usually with soy sauce, sugar, wine and Sichuan pepper or five spices, and are barbecued or grilled. The fatter ribs, known in Chinese as *pai gwat*, are slow-simmered with aromatic seasonings such as star anise, or red-cooked in soy sauce.
See also: PORK RIBS CRISP-FRIED WITH PEPPER-SALT (recipe)

PORK SHOULDER is used in curry-making and for many of the Chinese braised and slow-cooked dishes.

PORK TENDERLOIN is the most mildly flavored and tender of the cuts. The long thin strip of tenderloin or fillet is taken from inside the loin. It is excellent for quick-cooking, as in stir-fries and grills, and is used in China to make the red-colored roast pork strips known as *cha siew*.
See also: ROAST PORK CANTONESE (recipe); TERIYAKI (recipe)

SUCKLING PIGS are an important banquet dish in the cuisines of southern China and the

PORK

Philippines, and a temple offering on the island of Bali, although pork is not generally
eaten elsewhere in Indonesia. The young pig,
usually no larger than 30 lbs (14 kgs) in weight,
is roasted whole over charcoal until the meat is
tender and succulent and the skin is meltingly
crisp. Larger pigs can also be cooked in this
way. In the Philippines, roast suckling pig
(*baboy letsonin*) is served with a rich, thick
sauce, made with the livers and known as
lechon sarsa.

Also known as *babi guling* (roast pork) (Indonesia); *baboy letsonin* (Philippines)

See also: LIVER SAUCE (recipe); ROAST SUCKLING
PIG PHILIPPINE STYLE (recipe)

TENDONS from pork (and from beef and deer)
skins are enjoyed as a delicacy in China. When
cooked, the creamy white tendons become gelatinous and translucent and have a pleasing,
bland taste. When sold fresh or frozen, they
have usually been cleaned and parboiled to
soften, so require only gentle simmering in
stock flavored with soy and star anise. Dried
pork tendons require lengthy cooking to soften. Like honeycomb tripe and braised chickens' feet, braised tendon is an unusual, although popular, *dim sum* dish.

CAMBODIAN SPICY PORK
Serves 4

1¹/₂ lbs (750 g) lean pork, cubed
¹/₄ cup (1 oz / 30 g) mild curry powder or paste
2 tbsps fish sauce
¹/₂ cup (4 oz / 120 g) minced shallots
2 tbsps minced ginger
2 tsps minced garlic
¹/₃ cup (3 fl oz / 90 ml) vegetable oil
1 cassia stick
4 cassia leaves
1–2 tsps chili powder
4 cups (1 qt / 1 l) coconut milk
salt and pepper

Mix pork with curry powder
or paste, fish sauce, shallots, ginger
and garlic; set aside for 2 hours. Brown in
¹/₃ cup (3 oz / 180 ml) oil until well colored.
Add remaining ingredients with salt and
pepper to taste and simmer until tender
and the liquid well reduced.

CHA SIEW BOW
Yields 12

12 oz (350 g) Chinese roast pork, diced
4 dried black mushrooms, soaked and chopped
3 tbsps chopped scallions (spring / green
onions)
1 tbsp vegetable oil
1 tbsp hoisin sauce
1 tbsp oyster sauce
1 tbsp sugar
2 tsps cornstarch (cornflour)
2 tbsps cold water
bread dough

Stir-fry pork, mushrooms and
scallions briefly in the oil. Add sauces
and sugar. Thicken with cornstarch mixed
with the water. Cool. Make bread dough.
Roll dough into sausage shape. Cut into 12
pieces; roll each into a ball and flatten
with the fingers. Place filling in center.
Pinch dough up around filling, twisting
to close. Place each on a small square
of paper. Let rise for 15 minutes.
Set in a steamer basket and
steam for 15 minutes.

GARLIC PORK
Serves 4–6

10 oz (300 g) lean pork
1¹/₂ tbsps minced garlic
1 tbsp minced coriander (cilantro) roots or
stems
1 tsp minced ginger
1 tsp salt
1 tsp black pepper
1 tsp sugar
1¹/₂ tbsps light soy sauce
2 tbsps oil
1 tbsp chopped fresh coriander (cilantro)
leaves
1 tbsp chopped red chilies

Cut pork into narrow strips. Mix
garlic, coriander, ginger, salt, pepper,
sugar and soy sauce. Pour over pork, mix
well, refrigerate for 4–6 hours. Heat oil in a
frying pan, fry the pork over medium
heat until just done. Garnish with
chopped coriander and chilies.

LIVER AND PORK BALLS
Serves 4–6

4 oz (120 g) pork liver
1 sheet caul fat
1/2 cup (4 oz / 125 g) minced onion
3 tbsps oil
1 tbsp dark soy sauce
2 tbsps brown sugar
1 tbsp dry roasted, ground coriander seeds
1 tsp black rice vinegar
1 1/2 cups (12 oz / 375 g) ground lean pork
deep-frying oil
chili sauce

Boil pork liver in salted water until tender. Drain, cool in cold water. Grind to a coarse paste in food processor. Rinse caul fat and cut into 18 pieces. Fry onion in oil until well browned. Add soy sauce, sugar, coriander, vinegar and mix in ground liver. Cook until well mixed. Remove and cool. Mix with ground pork. Form into 18 meatballs, wrapping each in caul fat. Steam over simmering water for 10 minutes, then cool. Deep-fry quickly in hot oil and serve with hot chili sauce.

LIVER SAUCE
Yields 3 cups (24 fl oz / 750 ml)

2 pork livers
1 cup (8 fl oz / 250 ml) water
2 tbsps minced garlic
1/2 cup chopped onions
2 tbsps vegetable oil
3/4 cup (6 fl oz / 180 ml) white vinegar
1/2 cup biscocho or fresh bread crumbs
salt and black pepper
sugar

Cook livers under grill or in hot oven until well colored on the surface and lightly cooked through. Grind to a paste in food processor, adding water. Sauté garlic and onions in oil until golden. Add liver and vinegar and simmer 2–3 minutes. Add *biscocho* or crumbs, seasoning and sugar to taste. Cook until thick, stirring constantly. Serve with Roast Suckling Pig Philippine Style.

MU SHU PORK
Serves 6

8 oz (250 g) pork tenderloin, cut into small squares
1/2 tsp sugar
2 1/2 tbsps light soy sauce
2 tbsps yellow rice wine
2 tbsps cornstarch (cornflour)
3 tbsps vegetable oil
3 large eggs, beaten
3/4 cup (1 1/2 oz / 45 g) cloud ear fungus, soaked
6 small dried Chinese black mushrooms, soaked
2–3 fresh oyster mushrooms, sliced
1 1/2 oz (50 g) canned bamboo shoots, sliced
3 scallions (spring / green onions), sliced
3/4 tsp minced garlic
1 tbsp shredded ginger
1/2 cup (4 fl oz / 125 ml) chicken broth or water
1/2 tsp salt
1/2 tsp Oriental sesame oil

Marinate pork with sugar, 1/2 tsp of the soy, 1 tbsp of the wine and 1 tbsp of the cornstarch for 20 minutes. Heat 1 tbsp oil in wok and cook egg until almost firm. Remove and wipe out wok. Drain fungus and mushrooms and shred finely. Stir-fry pork in 2 tbsps oil until meat is white; remove. Stir-fry black mushrooms, oyster mushrooms, bamboo shoots, scallions, garlic and ginger for 3 minutes. Add 1 tbsp soy sauce and 1 tbsp wine. Mix 2 tsps cornstarch with the chicken broth. Stir into pan, adding salt and sesame oil. Stir in pork and egg. Heat and serve.

PORK CURRY IN BURMESE STYLE
Serves 6–8

3 lbs (1.5 kgs) fresh ham, cubed
1/2 cup (4 oz / 125 g) minced onion
12–15 garlic cloves, minced
2 tsps minced ginger
8 shallots, minced
2 tbsps white vinegar
3 tbsps peanut oil
1 tbsp Oriental sesame oil   *(cont'd)*

(Pork Curry in Burmese Style cont'd)

2 fresh red chilies, chopped
1 tsp turmeric
1 tsp shrimp paste
salt

Marinate ham with onion, garlic, ginger, shallots and vinegar for 2 hours. Fry the pork in 2 tbsps of the peanut and sesame oil for 5 minutes until lightly colored. Add water to cover generously, bring to a boil and simmer $1^{1}/_{2}$ hours. Heat the remaining 1 tbsp of peanut oil and fry the onion with chilies for 4 minutes. Add turmeric and shrimp paste and fry for 2–3 minutes, adding a little water. Add mixture to the pork with salt to taste and cook for 8–10 minutes, until tender.

PORK PARCELS
Yields 4

4 oz (125 g) ground, lean pork
$^{1}/_{2}$ tsp crushed garlic
$1^{1}/_{2}$ tbsps vegetable oil
1 tsp chopped green chili
2–3 tsps fish sauce
1 tsp sugar
salt
pepper
3 eggs, well beaten
4 sprigs fresh coriander
(cilantro)

Sauté pork and garlic in vegetable oil until the meat changes color. Add chili, fish sauce and sugar and cook gently until the pan is dry and the pork tender. Season to taste with salt and pepper and set aside. Rub the inner surface of an omelette pan or nonstick pan with oiled paper. Heat pan to moderate. Strain one-quarter of the eggs into a small funnel, holding a finger over the end. Release the egg into the pan in a very thin stream so that it forms a lacy net in the pan. Cook until firm and lightly

(cont'd)

(Pork Parcels cont'd)

colored underneath. Lift out. When all egg is done, fill each crêpe with the pork filling and a sprig of coriander. Roll and serve.

PORK RIBS, CRISP-FRIED WITH PEPPER-SALT
Serves 6

$1^{1}/_{2}$ lbs (750 g) lean pork ribs
2 tsps minced garlic
1 tbsp dark soy sauce
2 tbsps yellow rice wine
1 tsp black vinegar
$^{3}/_{4}$ tsp five-spice powder
$^{1}/_{2}$ tsp salt
1 tsp sugar
deep-frying oil
Pepper-Salt

Separate ribs and cut into 3 in (7.5 cm) lengths. Marinate with garlic, soy, wine, vinegar, five-spice powder, salt and sugar for 1–3 hours. Deep-fry ribs until crisp and well colored, about 4 minutes. Remove and drain. Serve with Pepper-Salt (see recipe).

ROAST PORK CANTONESE
Serves 6–8

2 lbs (1 kg) pork tenderloin
1 tbsp five-spice powder
2 tsps ground Sichuan peppercorns
$^{1}/_{4}$ cup (2 fl oz / 60 ml) dark soy sauce
1 tbsp Oriental sesame oil
red food coloring (annatto seeds)

Cut pork into 2 strips. Rub with five-spice powder and pepper. Mix soy, sesame oil and red coloring; brush over meat and leave overnight. Heat oven to 450°F (230°C). Suspend marinated meat on hooks from the oven racks and cook for 10 minutes. Reduce heat to 350°F (180°C) and cook 15–20 minutes. Brush occasionally with remaining marinade.

ROAST SUCKLING PIG PHILIPPINE STYLE
Serves 20

12–15 lbs (5.5–7 kgs) suckling pig
salt and black pepper
12 bay leaves
1¹/₂ lbs (675 g) melted lard
boiling water
1 recipe Liver Sauce

Sprinkle cavity of the pig generously with salt and pepper; place bay leaves inside and close opening with sturdy metal pins. Brush pig generously with melted lard, then pour on boiling water, allowing the oily liquid to run off into a metal drip tray or baking can. Rub with salt and pepper. Cover pig with greased paper and roast in a moderate oven at 380°F (195°C) about 4¹/₂ hours. Lift paper and baste frequently with pan juices during cooking. When almost done, remove paper and turn oven temperature up very high to crisp the skin. Suckling pig may be barbecued if preferred. Prepare as above and secure on a heavy metal rotisserie over a charcoal fire. Slowly turn over the coals until meat is done. It should be tender but still quite pink. Cooking time will depend on the heat of the fire and the size of the piglet, but it should be around 4 hours. Brush frequently with melted lard to prevent the skin becoming too dry. Slice suckling pig into thin pieces and serve with Liver Sauce (see recipe).

SHANGHAI MEAT DUMPLINGS
Yields 24

8 cabbage leaves, blanched
8 oz (250 g) lean pork, minced and ground
1 tbsp minced scallions (spring / green onions)
¹/₄ tsp minced garlic
1 tbsp light soy sauce
1 tbsp ginger juice
1 tbsp cornstarch (cornflour)

(cont'd)

(Shanghai Meat Dumplings cont'd)

2 tsps Oriental sesame oil
1 tsp sugar
¹/₄ tsp black pepper
1 quantity Dumpling Wrappers recipe
2 tbsps finely shredded chili
red rice vinegar

Chop half the cabbage very finely; place remainder in a large steamer basket. Mix pork, chopped cabbage, scallions and garlic, adding soy sauce, ginger juice, cornstarch, sesame oil, sugar and pepper. Roll dough into 24 wrappers. Place filling on the center of each, gather up edges and twist together to a point. Arrange in steamer on the leaves. Steam for about 18 minutes. Serve with dips of shredded chili in red vinegar.

Shanghai meat dumplings

SICHUAN DUMPLINGS IN HOT SAUCE
Serves 6–8

8 oz (250 g) pork tenderloin, ground
4 oz (120 g) pork fat, finely diced
¹/₂ cup (4 oz / 120 g) chopped garlic chives
1 egg white, beaten
1 tsp salt
1 tsp Oriental sesame oil
1 tbsp cornstarch (cornflour)

(cont'd)

PORK

(Sichuan Dumplings in Hot Sauce cont'd)

40 wonton *wrappers*
water
1 quantity Sichuan Hot Red Sauce recipe

Mix pork, fat, chives and egg white with salt, sesame oil and cornstarch. Place a spoonful in the center of each *wonton* wrapper, wet edges and pinch together to form triangular shapes. Pinch 2 outer edges together to form dumplings. Cook in a large pan of simmering water until they float, about 5 minutes. Serve in bowls with Sichuan Hot Red Sauce.

Sichuan dumplings in hot sauce

SWEET SOY SAUCE PORK
Serves 6

2 lbs (1 kg) lean pork, cut into 1¹/₂ in (4 cm) cubes
1 tsp salt
1 tsp black pepper
¹/₄ cup (2 fl oz / 60 ml) oil plus 2 tbsps
1 cup (8 oz / 250 g) chopped onion
2 tsps minced garlic

(cont'd)

(Sweet Soy Sauce Pork cont'd)

2 tsps minced fresh ginger
1–3 tsps minced fresh red chili
¹/₂ cup (4 fl oz / 125 ml) kecap manis
1 cup (8 fl oz / 250 ml) thin coconut milk

Season pork with salt and black pepper. Heat ¹/₄ cup oil in a large pan until very hot and fry the pork until evenly colored. In 2 tbsps, oil sauté onion, garlic, ginger and chili until softened. Add to the pork with the remaining ingredients. Bring to a boil, then simmer gently over low heat for about 1¹/₂ hours, until the meat is tender and the sauce well reduced.

PORK, CHINESE ROAST: Strips of pork tenderloin marinated in "roast pork spices"—a mixture of natural red food coloring (usually from *annatto* seeds), Chinese five-spice powder, sugar and soy sauce—are known as *cha siew* in Cantonese communities. The meat is cooked over a charcoal barbecue or hung in strips to cook in a charcoal-fired oven. The red-brown, glazed surface is quickly cooked so the inside remains pink and succulent. It is found hanging in the windows of Chinese delicatessens and is sold by the strip or by weight and you may request it sliced. *Cha siew* is the meat in the delicious, soft steamed white bun known as *cha siew bow*. It is used in other fillings and stuffings, is diced to enliven fried rice and noodle dishes and is sliced as a filling for *cheong fan*, a soft white steamed rice dough roll served in *dim sum* tea houses. It can also be used in stir-fries—an excellent quick dish that combines shredded peppers and *cha siew* with scallions stir-fried, then dipped in a bottled plum sauce.
Also known as *cha siew*; red pork; roast pork tenderloin
See also: CHA SIEW BOW (recipe); ROAST PORK SPICES; UTENSILS, BARBECUES AND CHARCOAL BURNER

PORK CRACKLING: see SITSARON

PORK, CURED: Drying meat is the oldest known form of food preservation and ancient Chinese records make frequent mention of meat drying on bamboo racks.

BACON: The belly cut (fresh bacon), known as "five flowered pork" for its alternating five layers of fat and meat, is cut into strips about 8 in (20 cm) long and 2 in (5 cm) wide, salted and then dry-smoked. It is sold in Chinese delicatessens or markets by the piece or packed in vacuum-sealed plastic, and can be kept for several months in the refrigerator. The Chinese use it in the same way as it is used in the Western kitchen, to add a depth of flavor to a dish. Cut it into cubes and put it into braised, simmered and steamed dishes, or add it, dried, to soups and stuffings. If it is not available, Chinese sausage (*lap cheong*) can be used instead.
Also known as *lap yoke* (China)

HAM, CHINESE: The superior quality of the cured ham from China's Yunnan province is known throughout China. *Chin hua,* the ham from Zhejiang, is also highly regarded. Salted and smoked, Chinese hams have a firm, very slightly dry texture, but a well-developed flavor. The blackened skin should be removed before use. Ham is usually a secondary ingredient in Chinese cooking, being added to soups, sauces and stocks for simmered and braised foods. It may also be finely diced to sprinkle over vegetable or other dishes as a flavorsome garnish. Smithfield and Westphalian ham or prosciutto can substitute. Outside China, Yunnan ham is sold in cans.
Also known as *chin hua, chin hwa* (China); Yunnan ham
See also: DOUBLE-BOILED QUAIL SOUP (recipe); PICKLED CABBAGE IN CHICKEN SOUP WITH HAM (recipe)

PORK FAT: see CAUL FAT; OILS AND FATS
PORK TONKATSU: (recipe) see TONKATSU

POTASSIUM NITRATE: A chemical used in preserving meat. In Asian cooking it is particularly associated with pork and is used in Chinese sausages.
Also known as Prague powder; saltpeter
See also: PORK, CURED

POTATO STARCH: see FLOURS AND THICKENERS

POWDERED KAFFIR LIME LEAF: see KAFFIR LIME

PRAHOK: (*PROR-HOK,* Cambodia) see FISH PASTE

PRESERVED BLACK BEANS: see FERMENTED BLACK BEANS

PRESERVED RHIZOME: see GALANGAL, LESSER

PRESSED BEAN CURD: see BEAN CURD (PRESSED)

PRESSED DUCK: see DUCK, DRIED

PRIK: (*PHRIK,* Thailand) This name refers to chili when it is used in Thai cooking. There are more than 10 varieties commonly in use.

PRIK CHEE FAR are cayenne peppers—finger-size red and green chilies, used mainly for making chili powder.

PRIK KHEE NOO translates as "rat droppings," because these very hot red or green chilies with their thin pods are thought to resemble them. They are used, fresh or dried, ground into flakes.
Also known as bird's eye chili

PRIK KHEE NOO KASET are serrano chilies, a variety originally from Mexico.

PRIK KHEE NOO LUANG are yellow-orange, explosively hot chilies.

PRIK KHEE NOO SUAN are very small, hot chilies.
Also known as bird's eye chili

PRIK LEUNG are mild, large yellow chilies.

PRIK NUN are chilies of medium strength, grown in Chiang Mai.

PRIK YUAK chilies are mid-size to large, light green to red chilies, which are used, usually stuffed and fried, as a vegetable for snacks and side dishes.
See also: CHILI

PRIK BOD: (*PHRIK BOD,* Thailand) see CHILI PASTES, POWDERS AND SAUCES

PULOT: (*POO-LOT,* Malaysia) see RICE (NON-GLUTINOUS)

PURIS: (*PURI*) see BREAD, INDIAN; FRIED BALLOON BREAD (recipe)

PURPLE BASIL: see BASIL; LUK MANGLAK

PUSO NO SAGING: (*POO-SO NO SAH-GING*, Indonesia) see BANANA

PYA YE: (*PYA-YEAH*, Burma) see BURMA

PYIN-DAW-THEIN: (*PYIN-DAW-THANE*, Burma) see CURRY LEAF

Q

QUAIL: Quail is an ancient Chinese Imperial banquet dish which is still enjoyed today, particularly as a small appetizer dish of crisply fried quail halves, taken with a dip of Chinese pepper-salt. Prized for their delicate flavor and small eggs, they are thought to lengthen life, so are usually included in banquets for special occasions.
Also known as *anchun* (China)

DOUBLE-BOILED QUAIL SOUP
Serves 4–6

4 quail, dressed and rinsed
8 oz (250 g) lean pork, diced
water
6 dried black mushrooms, soaked
1¹/₂ oz (45 g) Chinese ham, cut into strips
1 tsp shredded ginger
1 tbsp yellow rice wine
5 cups (1¹/₄ qts / 1.25 l) chicken stock

Halve quail and blanch with pork in boiling water for 2 minutes. Rinse in cold water, drain. Remove mushroom stems. Place ingredients, except liquids, in a Chinese steamer pot and add yellow rice wine and chicken stock. Steam 2¹/₂–3 hours.

QUAIL EGG: See EGG

QUE: (*K-WE*, Vietnam) see VIETNAMESE MINT

QUINCHOY: (*KAN-CHOY*, China) see CABBAGE, CHINESE (RAPE)

R

RADISH, GIANT WHITE: (*Raphanus sativus* spp.) An ancient vegetable that might have developed from the small red salad radish. It is an important vegetable in China and Japan and is grown throughout Asia. It is easy to find at an Asian market as it lives up to its name, being at least 8 in (20 cm) long and snowy white. But do not necessarily choose the larger ones, which can be fibrous. Instead, buy this mildly pungent vegetable when young, at around 9 in (23 cm) in length, when it will be agreeably crisp and crunchy.

The Japanese *daikon* is short, round and plump but has the same taste and texture. It can be peeled and thinly sliced for salads, added to simmered dishes, stir-fried, stuffed and steamed. Innovative Japanese chefs carve *daikon* into pot shapes, fill them with yellow miso and steam until sweet and tender. *Daikon* is also used to make the yellow pickle, *takuan*, and in Korea it is made into a type of *kimchi*. The Chinese grate the giant white radish for *lo baak gor*, a heavy pudding made with radish and rice flour, which is steamed and, when cooked, is sliced and fried. It is always eaten during Lunar New Year and served at *dim sum* restaurants. Thin sticks of radish with carrot and cucumber, lightly pickled with vinegar, sugar and salt, make a refreshing instant pickle, which is served as an appetizer in China. They are also laid under cold cuts. In certain recipes shredded *jicama* (yam bean) is used instead of white radish.

Also known as *mhon-la-u* (Burma); *moeum spey sar* (Cambodia); *loh baak* (China); *lobak* (Indonesia, Malaysia); *daikon* (Japan); *hua pak had* (Thailand); *cu cai tau* (Vietnam)
See also: DAIKON NIMONO (recipe); KIMCHI (recipe); MISO; RADISH, GREEN ORIENTAL; TSUKEMONO (TAKUAN); TURNIP

DAIKON OROSHI: (Japan) Finely grated, giant white radish is used in Japan as a marinade for tenderizing certain foods, particularly octopus, and to remove strong odors from fish such as mackerel. Grated, giant white radish is also used in a number of sauces, usually to accompany salad dishes such as *aemono* and *sunomono*, and is added to the sauce that accompanies crisp-fried dishes such as *tempura*.
See also: AEMONO; MOMIJI-OROSHI; SUNOMONO; TEMPURA (recipe)

DAIKON SHREDS: In Japan the apprentice *sushi* chef undergoes rigorous training in the art of preparing the garnishes that make *sushi* and *sashimi* a feast for the eye as well as the palate. One of the more difficult skills to acquire is the technique of *katsura-muki*, in which a piece of pared *daikon* (giant white radish) is shaved into one long continuous strip—a master chef can produce a strip of even thickness without nicks or tears of up to 4 ft (1.2 m) in length from one piece—which is then re-rolled and cut into hair-like strips. These are crisped in cold water and kept near the *sushi* preparation table for use as an edible garnish with a mild, hot-sweet taste and appetizing crunch.
See also: SASHIMI (recipe); SUSHI (recipe)

SALTED WHITE RADISH is sold in packs in most Chinese stores. It is in strips of a brownish color, specked with salt, and is used to add flavor to soups, braised dishes and vegetarian dishes.
Also known as *hua pak kad khem* (Thailand)

SPROUTED RADISH SEEDS yield slender white sprouts with green tops which resemble

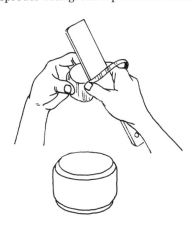

Bevelled edges of daikon pieces

miniature mung bean sprouts, but have an agreeable peppery hot taste. They are used as a salad ingredient and garnish, particularly in Japan.

Also known as *kaiware* (Japan); daikon sprouts; radish sprouts

---

DAIKON NIMONO
Serves 6

1 giant white radish
3 cups (24 fl oz / 750 ml) dashi
3 tbsps light soy sauce
1 tbsp mirin

Peel radish and cut into 1¹/₂ in (4 cm) pieces; bevel edges (see illustration). Boil in lightly salted water until tender; drain. In another pan bring *dashi*, soy sauce and *mirin* to a boil. Add radish, cover with *otoshi buta* (wooden drop lid) or paper and simmer gently for 25–30 minutes.

RADISH SHREDS
Serves 4–6

1 medium giant white radish
salt
2 fresh red chilies, seeded and shredded
water
¹/₂ cup (4 fl oz / 125 ml) Japanese rice vinegar
Oriental sesame oil
sugar

Peel and very finely shred the radish; place in a dish and sprinkle generously with salt. Knead with the fingers until the radish softens, then rinse in cold water and drain. Toss with the chili. Mix vinegar with salt, sesame oil and sugar to taste, pour over salad and let stand for 30 minutes before use.

RADISH, GREEN ORIENTAL: (*Raphanis sativus*) This radish is like its cousin, the Japanese *daikon* or giant white radish, but its skin and flesh are both pale green. It is a firm-fleshed root about 8 in (20 cm) in length and 2 in (5 cm) in diameter and is used in Chinese

and Japanese cooking, usually in soups and simmered dishes. "China Rose" radish is a variety with a large cylindrical bright red root. Choose radishes with a firm feel and unwrinkled skin. They can be stored for up to two weeks in the refrigerator.

Also known as *tseng loh baak* (China)
See also: RADISH, GIANT WHITE

RAMPE: (*RAMPE*, Sri Lanka) see PANDANUS LEAF

RAPE: see CABBAGE, CHINESE

RAPESEED OIL: see OILS AND FATS

RASAM: (*RA-SAM*, India) A fiery thin soup served in southern India. In the north, soups are milder in taste and are known as *shorba*.

RATHU MIRIS: (*RATH-U MI-RIS*, Sri Lanka) see CHILIES

RAT'S EAR: see CLOUD EAR FUNGUS

RAU LA TIA TO: (*ROW LA TEA TALL*, Vietnam) A spicy and pungent herb grown from caraway seeds. The round, green and purple leaves are used in salads. Mint can be substituted.

Also known as caraway mint
See also: CARAWAY SEED; MINT; VIETNAMESE MINT

RAU QUE: (*ROW K-WE*, Vietnam) see BASIL

RAU TUOM: (*ROW TOM*, Vietnam) see VIETNAMESE MINT

RAW FISH: see SASHIMI

REBURY: (*REH-BOO-REE*, Indonesia, Malaysia) see BAMBOO SHOOTS

RED BEAN: see AZUKI BEAN

RED BEAN AND GLUTINOUS RICE PUDDING: (recipe) see AZUKI BEAN

RED BEAN CURD: see BEAN CURD BY-PRODUCTS (RED BEAN CURD)

RED BEAN PASTE, SWEET: An important ingredient in Chinese and Japanese cooking, sweet red bean paste is made by boiling the red *azuki* bean and mashing it to a paste with lard or oil, then cooking until it is fairly dry and thick. In Japan red bean paste is made in two textures: the smooth purée is *koshi-an* and the chunky version, with the beans only partly crushed, is *tsubushi-an*. It is a filling for cakes and sweet buns, and is used in several desserts. Boiled and sweetened *azuki* beans, unmashed, are used in a sweet warm soup in China and served over ice cream or crushed ice in Japan.

Also known as *hong dow sar* (China); *an* (Japan)

See also: AZUKI BEAN; RED BEAN AND GLUTINOUS; RED BEAN PASTE, SWEET (recipe)

RED BEAN AND GLUTINOUS RICE PUDDING
Serves 6–8

2 cups (1 lb / 500 g) long-grain
glutinous (sticky) rice
1 1/4 cups (8 oz / 250 g) dried lotus seeds,
soaked and drained
1/2 tsp baking soda (bicarbonate of soda)
1 cup (8 oz / 250 g) crushed
rock candy sugar
1/4 cup (2 fl oz / 60 ml) melted lard
3/4 cup (6 fl oz / 180 ml) sweet
red bean paste
1 tbsp sugar

Pour rice into a pan of boiling water and simmer for 10 minutes. Drain, place in a cloth-lined dish and steam until cooked. Boil lotus seeds with baking soda in water to cover for 20 minutes; drain and remove central core of each seed. Steam with 1 tbsp rock candy sugar until tender. Grease a deep, round dish with lard; press in a layer of rice and make a well in the center. Put in lotus seeds and red bean paste and sprinkle remaining crushed rock sugar evenly. Add the melted lard and the sugar to the remaining rice and spread over pudding. Cover the top with wax paper secured firmly in place with string around the outside of the bowl. Put the bowl on a saucer in a saucepan of water, making sure the water only comes halfway up the bowl. Bring water to a boil and steam for 1 hour. Serve warm.

RED BEAN PASTE, SWEET
Yields 2 3/4 cups

2 cups (1 lb / 500 g) azuki *beans*
3/4 cup (6 oz / 180 g) sugar
3 tbsps lard

Rinse beans in 6 cups cold water, then boil in lightly salted water until tender. Drain thoroughly. Return to heat, adding lard and sugar. Mash to a smooth purée, removing from heat when the paste has warmed through. Do not overheat. Store in a covered non-metal container in the refrigerator for several weeks.

RED DATE: see JUJUBE

RED DISTILLER'S MASH: see FERMENTED RED RICE

RED GINGER: see GINGER (PICKLED)

RED GRAM: see PIGEON PEA

RED IN SNOW: see AMARANTH

RED LENTIL: see LENTIL

RED LIME PASTE: see LIME SOLUTION

RED MUNG BEAN: see LENTIL

RED ONION: see ONION

RED PEPPER: see CHILI

RED PORK: see PORK, CHINESE ROAST

RED RICE: see FERMENTED RED RICE

RED SHISO: see BEEFSTEAK PLANT

RED VINEGAR: see RICE VINEGAR

REMIS: (*REH-MEES*, Malaysia) see CLAM

REMPAH: (*R'M-PAH*, Indonesia, Malaysia) A variety of roots, herbs and spices which are pounded into a paste to make the base seasoning for Malaysian and Indonesian curried dishes. *Rempah* also seasons meat for satays and for dishes that require a combination of ground ingredients such as lemon grass, fresh or dried chilies, onions, garlic, candlenuts, fresh coriander, ginger or turmeric root and shrimp paste. It is sometimes fried in oil until very fragrant and well amalgamated before

other ingredients are added. Nonya households pride themselves on the quality of the *rempah* prepared in their kitchens, and girls are taught from a very young age to pound the ingredients to just the right consistency.
See also: CURRY PASTES AND POWDERS

REMPAH (CHICKEN OR PORK)
Yields 3 lbs (1.5 kgs)

1 stalk lemon grass, chopped
10 shallots, peeled and chopped
2 tsps ground coriander
1 tsp ground cumin
1 tsp turmeric
1/4 tsp cinnamon

Grind lemon grass and shallots to a paste, adding spices. Work until completely amalgamated. To store, add a little vegetable oil and keep refrigerated.

REMPAH (FISH)
Yields 3 lbs (1.5 kgs)

4 stalks lemon grass, chopped and ground
4 slices greater galangal, chopped and ground
12 candlenuts, chopped and ground
30 shallots, chopped and ground
2 garlic cloves, chopped and ground
8 chilies, chopped and ground
1/2 tsp sugar
1 tsp peppercorns
1 tsp turmeric
2–3 tsps salt

Combine all of the ingredients and grind to a smooth paste.

RENDANG: (*REN-DUNG*) see INDONESIA, COOKING METHODS

RENDANG CHICKEN: (recipe) see CHICKEN

RICE: (*Oryza sativa*) Although millet and sorghum predate rice in Chinese history, rice is thought to have grown wild in India since ancient times, and its cultivation has spread throughout Asia. It has become the staple grain of all cuisines throughout the area—although wheat is an important crop for bread flour and millet, in the form of a thick gruel, rice remains a staple in the northernmost areas of China as well as in Japan and Korea. There are two main types of rice that are eaten and ground into flour: most important is white rice, in both short and long grain; next is glutinous rice (sticky rice), the grains of which have a high gluten content which make it "sticky" when cooked. Throughout Asia rice is preferred in its polished white form; it is only occasionally cooked in its more nutritious, unpolished "brown" form. There are also several types of "colored" rice which are native to Asia. An important by-product of the rice polishing industry is the bran, which is used in the pickling industry. When fermented, rice provides delicately-flavored vinegars and rice wines such as the Japanese sake and Chinese *shaohsing*. Rice flour is used as a thickener as well as to coat foods. It is also made into dough for use as wrappers, and for noodles.

GLUTINOUS RICE: Long- and short-grain, and some types of dark-grain rice with a high gluten content, are used throughout Asia, particularly for desserts. When cooked, the rice compresses into a sticky mass, so this feature is emphasized in the dishes in which it is used. "Sticky" rice is wrapped in leaves with meats and seasonings and steamed or boiled, it is used in stuffings or is cooked as a rice dish for special occasions or to accompany specific dishes. It is ground into a flour that is made into a soft, spongy dough for sweet dumplings, cakes, pastries and wrappers.

Black rice grows in Indonesia and the Philippines. Its long, black grains resemble wild rice, and its nutty flavor enhances puddings and cakes. It is often combined with coconut milk and palm sugar. It has a high gluten content.

Mochi-gome (Japan) is a very small grain, high-gluten rice grown in Japan, with flattish, oval-shaped grains, similar in appearance to Italian rice. The grain is soaked and steamed, then ground into a flour used for making the dough for *mochi* cakes.
See also: MOCHI

Pinipig (Philippines) Toasted and flattened glutinous rice that is used in cakes and desserts. It can be gently fried in a dry pan until crisp and nutty, and used as a topping for ice cream and puddings.

Xoi nep (Vietnam) Cooked glutinous rice, often referred to as sweet rice, will sometimes accompany a Vietnamese meal in place of plain white rice. There are rules of etiquette as to when it should be served; it is acceptable with breakfast and dinner, but never with lunch.

GLUTINOUS RICE

rice
water

Use 1 part rice to 1 part water.
Soak rice in cold water for 8 hours. Drain and rinse. Place in a heavy pan with water, cover and bring quickly to a boil. Reduce heat to very low and cook gently for about 12 minutes. Remove from heat and let stand 10 minutes, covered.

NON-GLUTINOUS RICE:

Basmati rice prized throughout the world for its supreme flavor, is grown in India on the foothills of the Himalayas. It is used for prestige rice dishes such as *biriyanis* and *pillaus*, which are usually flavored and colored with the delicate saffron that also grows in that area. Another fine quality Indian rice comes from Dehra Dun in the northern state of Uttah Pradesh.

Bengali rice is a small-grain white rice with a superior flavor. It grows in the eastern Indian state of Bengal.

Brown rice is eaten to some extent in Japan, where it is known as *gen mai*.

Calrose rice has a higher starch content than most other kinds of white rice and is favored for its slight "stickiness" when cooked, which makes it easy to eat with chopsticks.

Haiga-mai rice (Japan) This literally translates as "rice germ" rice. The grains are incompletely polished, leaving the germ intact. *Haiga-mai* rice gives a nutty taste which is suggestive of brown rice and is more nutritious.

Laotian rice is often not paddy-grown, like rice elsewhere in Asia, but is grown dry on hillslopes. It is soaked before being steamed in a woven cane basket or cone over simmering water. Like bread, it is compressed into small balls before being eaten.
See also: LUANG PRABANG

Long-grain rice is a popular type of non-glutinous polished white rice with long slender grains. It is generally not used when the rice is to be eaten with chopsticks, but is suitable for all other rice dishes.

Pirurutung (Philippines) This dark, purple-colored rice is eaten in some parts of provincial Philippines, particularly in the area of Luzon.

Red rice has a dull, pale, red-colored grain and is grown in many parts of Asia, including China. It has a taste similar to brown rice, but is generally regarded as inferior and is not often used in cooking. It is not to be confused with the fermented red rice used in China as a seasoning.

Shinmai rice grows in Japan. It is the "new rice" harvested in autumn and has moist, tender, sweet grains that require less water when cooking.

Short-grain white rice is the most common rice variety grown in Asia. It is best cooked by the absorption method (see below). The cooked rice grains adhere together and facilitate the use of chopsticks.

Thai jasmine rice is a very aromatic rice with slender, long grains.
Also known as *htamin* (Burma); *faan* (China); *chawal* (India); *nasi* (Indonesia, Malaysia); *arroz* (Philippines); *kao* (Thailand); *gao* (Vietnam)

NON-GLUTINOUS RICE
(absorption method)

rice
water

Use 3 parts unwashed, unsoaked rice to 4 parts water. Cover and bring rapidly to a boil. Reduce heat to very low. Cook, tightly covered, for 15 minutes. Remove from heat and let stand 10 minutes, covered.

RICE

TREATED RICE:
Short- and long-grain white rice are treated in various ways for use in Asian cooking.

Khao chae (*kao chae*) is a particular method of serving rice in ice water, which is enjoyed as a special dish in Thailand.
See also: THAILAND, CUISINE

Kao mao (Thailand) is young rice, unhusked, flattened and roasted. It is used as a coating for fried foods and is particularly delicious on bananas. Flaked rice is also used in other Asian countries, particularly India.

Parboiled rice is made in India, particularly in the west coast state of Kerala, where it is cooked in a pan known as a *kozhul*. Parboiled and then dried, it develops a special taste and cooks quickly.

Thinh (Vietnam) is toasted, ground rice that is added to some dishes, particularly those made with ground pork, for its distinct aroma and texture. Short or long-grain rice is cooked in a heavy wok until the grains are a deep golden brown, then ground to a coarse powder. It should be stored in an airtight jar.
See also: GROUND TOASTED RICE (recipe)

WASHINGS: The water used to rinse uncooked rice is often added to dishes, particularly in the Philippines, for extra flavor and a slight starchiness.
Also known as *naw may* (China); *ketan* (Indonesia); *mochi-gome* (Japan); *pulot* (Malaysia); *malagkit* (Philippines); *kao nieo* (Thailand); *nep* (Vietnam); mochi rice; pearl rice; sticky rice; sweet rice
See also: BIKO (recipe); FERMENTED RED RICE; FERMENTED RICE (WINE LEES) (recipe); FLOURS AND THICKENERS; NOODLES *and recipes following*

CHOCOLATE RICE
Serves 6

1 cup (6 oz / 185 g) malagkit (*glutinous / sticky rice*)
3 tbsps cocoa or unsweetened powdered chocolate
5 cups (1¼ qts / 1.25 l) water
1 cup (7 oz / 250 g) sugar
½ cup (4 fl oz / 125 ml) milk

(cont'd)

(Chocolate Rice cont'd)

Wash glutinous rice and drain. Add cocoa or chocolate and water. Bring to a boil, stirring constantly, and cook until softened. Add sugar and milk. Stir and cook for 2 minutes more.

FRIED RICE
Serves 6

3 tbsps vegetable oil
12 oz (350 g) small shelled shrimp (prawns)
1 Chinese sausage (lap cheong) steamed, sliced
1 cup (8 oz / 250 g) cooked green peas
½ cup (4 oz / 125 g) chopped bamboo shoots
½ cup (4 oz / 125 g) chopped carrots, parboiled
2 eggs, beaten
6 cups (3 lbs / 1.5 kgs) cooked short-grain white rice
½ cup (2 oz / 60 g) chopped scallions (spring / green onions)
dark soy sauce
salt
pepper
1 tsp Oriental sesame oil
chili sauce

Heat vegetable oil in a large wok. Stir-fry shrimp, sausage, peas, bamboo shoots and carrots for 2 minutes; remove. Drain oil, wipe out pan and pour in beaten eggs, cook until just firm; finely chop. Stir-fry rice, scallions and all cooked ingredients over high heat, seasoning to taste with soy sauce, salt and pepper. Add sesame oil and chili sauce to taste.

GLUTINOUS RICE DOUGH, SWEET
Yields 20

3 cups (12 oz / 360 g) glutinous rice flour
½ cup (4 oz / 125 g) sugar
1 cup (8 fl oz / 250 ml) water

Mix ingredients together with water and knead to a smooth dough. Roll into a sausage shape and cut

(cont'd)

(Glutinous Rice Dough, Sweet cont'd)

into 20 pieces. To shape,
flatten with heel of hand on a lightly
oiled board. Fill, pinch edges together and
deep-fry.Used to wrap sweet or savory
fillings for a variety of *dim sum* and other
Asian snack foods. When deep-fried,
the surface becomes crisp and golden
brown, the inside soft and
pleasantly chewy.

GLUTINOUS RICE WITH MANGO
Serves 6

*1 cup (6 oz / 185 g) short-grain glutinous
(sticky) rice
1 cup (8 fl oz / 250 ml) thick coconut milk
2 tbsps sugar syrup
1/2 tsp salt
3 fresh mangoes, peeled and sliced*

Soak rice overnight. Cook in
a steamer without liquid for 15
minutes. Transfer to a mold, press
in firmly. Mix coconut milk, sugar syrup
and salt. Pour half over rice, then chill for
several hours. Slice the rice cake, serve
with a fan of sliced mango and
the remaining sauce.

GROUND TOASTED (ROASTED) RICE
Yields 1 1/2 cups (12 oz / 350 g)

1 cup (6 oz / 185 g) uncooked white rice

Place rice in a dry wok or
skillet and cook over medium heat,
stirring frequently, to a deep golden
color. Take care it does not burn. Grind
to a fine powder in a heavy-duty mortar or
blender. Cool and store in an airtight jar.
Keeps for several months. Rice can
also be cooked in a moderate
oven, stirring frequently.

MUSLIM RICE DESSERT
Serves 8

*2 tbsps raisins
water
1 tsp ground saffron
3/4 cup (6 fl oz / 180 ml) heated milk
2 1/2 cups (15 oz / 470 g) basmati rice
melted ghee
4 green cardamom pods,
peeled and seeds
crushed
1 small cinnamon stick
2 whole cloves
1 cup (8 oz / 250 g) superfine
(caster) sugar
1 tbsp lemon juice
blanched almonds*

Soak raisins in hot water for 10
minutes. Stir saffron into 1/4 cup
(2 fl oz/60 ml) hot milk. Bring rice to
a boil with 5 cups (1 1/4 qts/1.25 l) water.
Reduce heat and simmer gently until
the rice is half cooked, approximately 10
minutes. Drain. Heat ghee in a large
pan. Add drained rice, spices, the remaining 1/2 cup (4 fl oz/125 ml) milk and sugar.
Simmer gently, covered, until the rice is
tender. Drain the raisins, add to the rice
with lemon juice and the saffron-colored
milk. Mix and cook 5 minutes, then
remove from heat. Garnish
with almonds.

RICE CAKES, CRISP

*1 cup (6 oz / 185 g) short-grain white rice
1/2 cup (4 fl oz / 125 ml) water*

Boil rice with water until
tender and dry. Press into an oiled
jelly-roll pan (oven tray). Place in a
very low oven overnight, until compressed
into a dry cake. Break into pieces.
Store in an airtight
container.

RICE CAKES WRAPPED IN COCONUT LEAVES
Yields 24

2¹/2 cups (15 oz/470 g) short-grain glutinous (sticky) white rice
water
1¹/2 cups (12 fl oz/375 ml) thin coconut milk
1¹/2 tsps minced garlic
³/4 tsp mashed shrimp paste
6 curry leaves
2 tbsps oil
2 cups (1 lb/500 g) ground pork or chicken
1 tbsp ground coriander
1¹/2 tsps ground cumin
¹/2 tsp salt
¹/2 tsp turmeric
lemon juice
bamboo/banana leaves

Boil rice with 2 cups (16 fl oz/500 ml) water for 12 minutes. Turn heat down to low and cook 15 minutes. Stir in heated coconut milk and cook until absorbed. Cool. Sauté garlic, shrimp paste and curry leaves in oil until fragrant. Add meat and cook until colored. Add spices, salt and turmeric and moisten with water. Sauté 3–4 minutes. Flavor with lemon juice to taste. Cut banana leaves into 6 in (15 cm) squares, or rinse and dry bamboo leaves. Spread a layer of rice in center, top with meat filling, cover with rice and roll up. Grill on barbecue 8–10 minutes and serve hot.

RICE COOKED IN RICH MEAT BROTH
Serves 6–8

1 lb (500 g) lamb shank
6 cups (1¹/2 qts/1.5 l) water
1 onion, quartered
3 bay leaves
salt
1 tsp black peppercorns
ghee
1¹/2 cups (12 oz/375 g) sliced onions
1¹/2 tsps minced garlic

(cont'd)

(Rice Cooked in Rich Meat Broth cont'd)

2¹/2 cups (15 oz/470 g) long-grain rice
4 green cardomom pods, peeled and seeds crushed
1 tsp ground cumin
1 tsp garam masala
6 whole cloves
1 cinnamon stick
¹/2 tsp chili powder
¹/2 cup (4 fl oz/125 ml) plain (natural) yogurt

Boil lamb in water with quartered onions, bay leaves, 2 tsps salt and black peppercorns for 1¹/2 hours, uncovered. Drain, reduce broth to about 2¹/2 cups (20 fl oz/625 ml). Pull meat from bones and cut into small dice. Heat ghee in a heavy saucepan and fry sliced onions until deeply colored. Add garlic and rice and stir on the ghee to coat each grain. Then add cardamoms, cumin, *garam masala*, cloves, cinnamon stick, chili powder and yogurt. Add broth and diced meat. Bring to a boil. Add salt to taste, cover and cook over low heat about 20 minutes, until rice is dry and fluffy. Stir to distribute meat evenly.

RICE GRUEL WITH SHRIMP
Serves 6–8

2 cups (12 oz/375 g) long-grain white rice
12 cups (3 qts/3 l) water
2 lbs (1 kg) whole shrimp (prawns), steamed
8 eggs
2 Chinese sausages (lap cheong), steamed and sliced
³/4 cup (4 oz/120 g) crushed roasted peanuts
fish sauce
salt
white pepper
chili sauce

Boil rice with water until reduced to a thick soup, about 1¹/4 hours. Place several shrimp in each bowl and cover with rice gruel. Add a raw egg to each bowl, then add the other ingredients to taste.

RICE IN A LACQUERED BOX WITH BEEF AND ONIONS
Serves 4

3–4 tbsps vegetable oil
2 medium onions, thinly sliced
8 oz (250 g) beef, very thinly sliced
1/3 cup (3 fl oz / 90 ml) dark soy sauce
1/4 cup (2 fl oz / 60 ml) mirin
1 cup (8 fl oz / 250 ml) water
2 tsps ginger juice
6–8 cups (3–4 lbs / 1.5–2 kgs) hot cooked rice

In a large frying pan or wok heat oil and stir-fry onions until soft and lightly colored. Remove. Fry beef until it changes color. Mix soy and *mirin* with water and add to pan. Return onions and simmer gently for 1 minute; add ginger juice. Fill individual lacquered boxes with hot rice, cover with beef and onions and add remaining sauce.

SCATTERED RICE
Serves 4–6

1/2 quantity Sushi-Meshi (vinegared rice)recipe
8 oz (250 g) raw tuna, white fish fillets or smoked salmon, thinly sliced
1 sheet nori seaweed, toasted and shredded
1 tbsp white sesame seeds, toasted

Prepare rice and spread in a lacquered box or flat dish. Cut fish into squares, arrange over rice and scatter on *nori* and sesame seeds.

SPICED GROUND RICE

1 1/2 cups (8 oz / 250 g) long-grain white rice
1 1/2 tbsps Sichuan peppercorns
2 star anise

Place ingredients in a wok or pan and cook, stirring slowly, over medium heat until the rice is golden. Cool, then grind to a coarse powder. If preferred, the peppercorns and star anise can be ground first and added to the rice when grinding. Store in an airtight container for several months.

STEAMED STICKY RICE IN COCONUT MILK
Serves 6

1 1/2 cups (9 oz / 280 g) short-grain glutinous (sticky) white rice
6 1/2 cups (1 1/2 qts / 1.5 l) thin coconut milk
salt
2 x 8 in (20 cm) squares of banana leaf
water
vegetable oil
3/4 cup (6 oz / 180 g) crumbled palm sugar (or substitute brown sugar)
1 1/2 cups (12 fl oz / 375 ml) thick coconut milk

Thoroughly rinse and drain rice. Bring to a boil with thin coconut milk and salt in a heavy pan, then simmer until cooked to a thick paste. Blanch banana leaves in boiling water. Drain. Place one piece of leaf in an oiled 8 in (20 cm) baking pan and spread on rice. Cover with the other piece of oiled leaf. Place the pan on a rack in a steamer and steam until the rice is firm. Lift out, cool, then chill thoroughly. Boil palm sugar with an equal amount of water for 3–4 minutes. Cool. Remove banana leaf, cut rice into diamond-shaped pieces and serve in dessert dishes, covered with palm sugar and thick coconut milk.

THAI FRIED RICE
Serves 6–8

1/2 cup (4 fl oz / 125 ml) vegetable oil
1 1/2 cups (6 oz / 185 g) chopped onions
2 garlic cloves, minced
8 oz (250 g) fresh bacon, diced
4 eggs, beaten
5 cups (2 1/2 lbs / 1.25 kgs) cooked rice
1 bell pepper (capsicum / green pepper), seeded and shredded
1 1/2 cups (2 oz / 60 g) bean sprouts
1 cup (2 oz / 60 g) chopped scallions (spring / green onions)
8 oz (250 g) cooked shrimp (prawns) or crabmeat
1–2 tbsps fish sauce
chili sauce

(cont'd)

(Thai Fried Rice cont'd)
lime wedges
fresh coriander (cilantro)

Heat vegetable oil and fry onions and garlic for 5 minutes. Remove. Stir-fry bacon until browned. Cook eggs until firm; chop up, remove. Toss rice over high heat for 2 minutes, adding extra oil if needed. Add bell pepper, bean sprouts, scallions and shrimp, toss over high heat until cooked. Add 1–2 tbsps fish sauce, and chili sauce to taste. Garnish with lime and coriander.

RICE BIRD: A type of tiny sparrow that feeds in rice paddies. They are cooked whole after being marinated in sweetened soy sauce tinted with orange food coloring.

RICE CAKES: see MOCHI

RICE DOUGH: Throughout Asia, rice dough is used in the preparation of a variety of fresh and dried noodles, as well as in wrappers and doughs for dumplings and other snacks. It is also an important element in many different types of sweet snacks and puddings. It is made by mixing rice flour or finely ground rice to a dough with cold or boiling water, the latter producing a semi-transparent dough that is used for dumpling wrappers. A rice dough batter, steamed in layers in a cloth-lined box or basket, is used in China to make the rice rolls known as *cheong fun*. This is also cut into strips to make the fresh rice ribbon noodles known as *hor fun* or *kway teow*. Glutinous rice flour or ground glutinous rice is made into a dough that is used extensively throughout Asia, except in India. It has a more elastic consistency than dough made with ordinary rice. It is used to make wrappers, cakes and dumplings.

GALAPONG (Philippines) is a dough made from ground rice and water that has been left standing overnight and partially fermented. It is used in the making of sweet snacks such as the popular *bibingka*.
Also known as *kepong beras boh* (Indonesia)
See also: MOCHI; SAPIN SAPIN

RICE FLOUR: see FLOURS AND THICKENERS
RICE GRUEL: see CONGEE
RICE NOODLES: see RICE DOUGH

RICE PAPER: An edible paper, erroneously named "rice paper," that is produced from the pith of a tree, *Aralia papyifera*, the seeds of which are considered a delicacy in China. This paper is used for candies and as a wrapper during cooking.
Also known as *mei gee*, *t'ung ts'ao* (China)

RICE PAPER WRAPPER: see BANH TRANG (Vietnam)
RICE RIBBONS: see NOODLES
RICE SHOOT: see WILD RICE SHOOT
RICE SOUP: see CONGEE
RICE STICKS: see NOODLES

RICE VINEGAR: The vinegars used in Asian cooking are usually made from fermented rice and grains such as wheat, millet and sorghum. Vinegar is one of the oldest seasonings used in Asia and is named in documents from the twelfth century BC as *liu*. Asian vinegars are sold in bottles with shaker tops for easy dispensing into the wok or sauce dish. As a condiment they accompany dumplings, soups and snack foods and as a seasoning ingredient they give an extra piquancy to many different dishes. There are several main types.

BLACK VINEGAR is a dark, mild, almost sweet vinegar with an appealing depth of flavor that can be emulated by balsamic vinegar. Black vinegar is usually made from glutinous rice or sorghum, from which it derives its distinctive taste. The better black vinegars can have an impressive complexity of flavors and aromas, ranging from smoky to wine-yeasty. In central China and some parts of the north, black vinegar is added to almost every dish.

JAPANESE RICE VINEGAR is a clear liquid, mild in flavor and strength. Sold in small bottles, usually simply labeled "rice vinegar," it is used in dressings for *sunomono* and *aemono*. Cider or white wine vinegars can be substituted, but Japanese vinegar is readily available in large supermarkets.

RED VINEGAR is a clear, pale red liquid that was originally made in breweries in northern coastal Chinese provinces. It has a delicate, tart, slightly salty taste and is best used as a condiment with steamed dumplings and "pot sticker" dumplings. Shark's fin soup would be incomplete without a sprinkle of red vinegar.

SWEET VINEGAR is a brown-black, slightly thick rice vinegar that resembles dark soy sauce. Processed with sugar and the native spices cassia and star anise, it has an aromatic, caramel aroma. Sweet vinegar has a specific culinary function quite unlike that of its cousins; as it lacks the sourness of other vinegars it is added in large quantities to braised dishes, particularly pork. Its most important use is in a dish—known as "a gift from the stock,"—of pork knuckles, whole young ginger root and hard-cooked eggs. This is made after the birth of a Cantonese baby for the new mother to share with relatives and friends. As well as being a celebratory food, it is good for the mother, as it strengthens her body after confinement.

Black and sweet rice vinegars can be kept for many months without refrigeration after opening, but Japanese and red vinegar tend to lose their aroma quickly, so are best purchased in small bottles.

Also known as *mike cho* (Cantonese); *su* (Japan); *cuka* (Malaysia); *nam som* (Thailand)
See also: SHANGHAI MEAT DUMPLINGS (recipe); VINEGAR; "WESTLAKE" FISH (recipe)

RICE VERMICELLI: see NOODLES

RICE WASHINGS: see RICE (WASHINGS)

RICE WINE: see WINE, ASIAN (SAKE)

RICE WRAPPER: see RICE DOUGH

RIDGED GOURD: see LUFFA, ANGLED

ROASTED CURRY PASTE: see NAM PRIK PAO

ROAST PORK CANTONESE: (recipe) see PORK

ROAST PORK SPICES: A commercially prepared seasoning mix combining sugar, salt, dried soy sauce, *annatto* seeds, Sichuan peppercorns and five-spice powder. It is rubbed over pork tenderloin or suckling pig before roasting, to give a unique flavor and red-brown color.

Also known as *cha siew jeung* (China); *bot xa xiu* (Vietnam)
See also: ANNATTO SEEDS; FIVE-SPICE POWDER; SICHUAN PEPPERCORNS

ROCK CARP: see CARP

ROCK CANDY SUGAR: see SUGAR

ROLLED BEAN CURD: see BEAN CURD BY-PRODUCTS (BEAN CURD STICKS)

ROMDENG: (*ROUM-DENG*, Cambodia) see GALANGAL, GREATER

ROOMALI ROTI: (*ROO-MAA-LEE RO-TEE*, India) see BREAD, INDIAN

ROSE APPLE: (*Syzygium malaccensis*) The rose apple is an attractive fruit with a rose-pink, waxy skin and is about the size and shape of a small pear. Similar to an apple in taste, it has more seeds, a sweet juice and either a crisp or woolly texture. From the genus *Eugenia* and belonging to the myrtle family, it grows as a shrub-like tree in tropical countries; the fruit grows in clusters on the trees. There are three types of rose apple grown and used in Thailand, Sri Lanka, Malaysia and Indonesia.

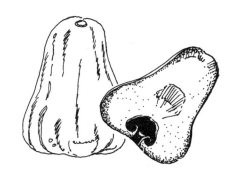

Rose apple whole and in cross-section

PINK ROSE APPLE: The pink variety is named *chompoo* (meaning "pink") in Thailand. The skin may be striped. It is eaten raw in salads and desserts.

WATER APPLE: The water apple or watery rose apple (*Eugenia aqua*) is eaten as a fruit and in Indonesia is made into a syrup called *roejak.* It is smaller, a deeper pink and has more juice than the rose apple.

The other type is larger than a rose apple. It may be greenish in color, and of a coarser texture and slightly tart taste.

Also known as *jambu ayer* (Malaysia, Indonesia); *atis* (Philippines); *chompoo* (Thailand); water apple; watery rose apple

ROSEWATER (ESSENCE): Rosewater is a light pink aromatic liquid with the aroma and flavor of roses. Rose essence is a more concentrated distillation of this same liquid. Roses are an ancient plant that grew wild in India, China and some other parts of Asia and, like most other native plants, were incorporated into the cuisine. The petals are used in salads, such as the delightful Thai *yum* (salad), made of yellow rose petals, and as a vegetable and garnish. They are also candied in desserts and are made into a thick, sweet jam. An essential ingredient in *lokum* (Turkish delight), they also flavor Indian sweetmeats of similar kind. Rose essence or rosewater gives a sweet fragrance to curries and rice dishes, being sprinkled over the finished dish. It is used to flavor milk drinks, desserts and cakes, and in finger bowls.

Also known as *gulab* (India); *ayer mawar* (Malaysia); *dok gulab* (Thailand)

See also: FLAVORINGS; GULAB JAMONS (recipe); JALEBIS (recipe); KULFI (recipe)

ROTI: (*RO-TEE*, India) see BREAD, INDIAN

ROTI JALA: (*RO-TEE JA-LA*, recipe) see BREAD, INDIAN

S

SAAG: (*SAAG*, India) see AMARANTH

SABA: (*SAH-BA*, Philippines) see BANANA

SAFED JIRA: (*SA-FAID JEE-RAA*, India) see CUMIN (WHITE)

SAFFLOWER OIL: see OILS AND FATS

SAFFRON: (*Crocus sativus*) This fragrant, exotic yellow spice is said to have been cultivated originally in Cilicia, in the southernmost part of Turkey. But now Kashmir is the most important producer of saffron—the word *kasmiraja* means saffron and may have been the inspiration for the name Kashmir. The world's most expensive spice, it is obtained from the crocus flower, each blossom of which grows just three stigmas. It takes more than a quarter of a million stigmas to make just 1 lb (500 g) of saffron. These fine golden strands are carefully handpicked and dried, then packed whole or ground to its characteristic fine orange powder.

Because of its enormous expense, saffron powder is often adulterated with the less costly Mexican saffron, *Carthamus tinctorious,* or the yellow-colored spice, turmeric, and may be sold in this form as "Indian saffron." To avoid using an adulterated powder, it is perhaps best to use the dark orange thread-like stigmas that are sold in small packs. They should be kept dry and away from strong light. Powdered saffron can also lack the subtle taste and fragrance of genuine saffron or may lose some of its delicate fragrance during grinding.

In Asia, saffron is used mainly in northern India, where it makes its unique contribution to rice dishes, coloring the grains a rich gold. It is made into an infusion that is sprinkled over finished dishes, and is used to decorate meats and breads baked in the *tandoor,* and to color and flavor desserts and sweetmeats. Its other important role in Indian life is as *tillak,* the red paste made from ground saffron that is used to mark the forehead as a gesture of blessing and good fortune. Indian brides may paint their whole palms with designs in saffron paste.

To use whole saffron, pound a small pinch of the stigmas in a small mortar, then steep in a little warm to boiling water or milk. This releases the delicate flavor, subtle aroma and deep yellow color. Powdered saffron can be added directly to a dish during cooking. Powdered or fresh turmeric, which is much less expensive, is used in Indonesia, Malaysia, Burma and other parts of Southeast Asia for its yellow color. Its flavor is decidedly pungent and tends to predominate over other seasonings.

Also known as *kesar*; *zafraan* (India); *safuran* (Japan); *kesari* (Nepal); *kunyit kering* (Malaysia); *kashubha* (Philippines)
See also: BIRIYANI OF RICE AND CHICKEN (recipe); TURMERIC

SAGING: (*SAH-GING*, Philippines) see BANANA

SAGO: (*Metroxylon sagu*) The tree from which sago is produced grows wild in low-lying freshwater swamps in Southeast Asia. Valued for the starch that builds up in the pith of the trunk, the tree trunk is split open, the pith scooped out and rasped or ground to a coarse, dryish paste. It is moistened to release a milky fluid containing the starch, which is dried into sago starch. Pearl sago is produced by pushing a moist paste through a forming sieve; the resulting "pearls" are dried. They are used in making desserts. In many parts of Southeast Asia sago palm fronds are used for thatching and the fruit, which has an astringent taste, is considered a delicacy.

Also known as *subadana* (India); *ambooloong booloo* (Indonesia); *pohon sagoo, rombeea* (Malaysia)
See also: GULA MELAKA (recipe)

SAI DAU NGA CHOY: (*SAI DAU NGA CHOY*, China) see BEAN SPROUTS (MUNG BEAN)

SAI JAR: (*SIE JAR*, Indonesia) see DRUMSTICK VEGETABLE

SAKA-MUSHI: (*SAH-KAH-MU-SHI*, Japan) see JAPAN, COOKING METHODS

SAKE: (*SAKE*, Japan) see WINE, ASIAN

SAKE KASU: (*SA-KE KAH-SUE*, Japan) see FERMENTED RED RICE

SAKIZUKE: (*SAH-KEE-ZOO-KE*, Japan) see AEMONO

SALAD OF WARM AND SPICY CUCUMBER: (recipe) see CUCUMBER

SALAK: (*SA-LUCK*, Indonesia, Malaysia) (*Salacca edulis*) This densely tufted palm is low, erect and virtually stemless. It grows readily in tropical climates and is cultivated for its unique small fruits, which have an agreeably firm, starchy and crunchy flesh, the texture of a potato and a sharp, slightly sweet flavor. The almost triangular fruit is covered with a red-brown, coarse, snakeskin-like peel. *Salak* is occasionally available in Asian vegetable markets and will keep for at least a week in the refrigerator. Crisp pear, Japanese pear or apples can be substituted in most dishes.

Also known as *salacca*; snakefruit; snakeskin fruit

SALAM: (*SAH-LARM*, Malaysia) see DAUN SALAM

SALIM: (*SA-LIM*, Thailand) A sweet dessert dish of thin tapioca noodles in a creamy coconut milk and palm sugar syrup. These noodles may also be chopped and served as a cooling drink in tall glasses with palm sugar syrup, coconut milk and crushed ice.

Also known as *saleem* (Thailand)
See also: UTENSILS (CAKE AND DESSERT MAKING)

SALMON CAVIAR: (Japan) see CAVIAR (IKURA)
SALMON ROE: (Japan) see CAVIAR (IKURA)

SALT: One of the oldest food seasonings, salt has at times played an important political role in China and India, where natural salt deposits provided a vital trade commodity. *Sanchal* is a blackish, richly flavored salt that is used particularly in the Indian state of Rajasthan. It gives a lift to the tart, spicy *chaat* salads of northern India. In the Chinese province of Sichuan immense salt deposits have been mined for centuries. Again this is a blackish salt of incomparable flavor.

Also known as *haam* (China); *kala namak*

245

(India); *garam* (Indonesia); *buro* (Philippines); *gluea* (Thailand)
See also: CABBAGE, PICKLED; FISH, PRESERVED; JAPANESE COOKING METHODS (SALTING); SALTED EGGS (recipe); SALTED EGG SAUCE (recipe)

SALT-BAKED CHICKEN: (recipe) see CHICKEN

SALT BROILED SHRIMP: (recipe) see SHRIMP

SALTED BAMBOO SHOOTS: see BAMBOO SHOOT

SALTED CABBAGE: see CABBAGE, PICKLED

SALTED EGGS: (recipe) see EGG

SALTED EGG SAUCE: (recipe) see EGG

SALTED FISH: see FISH, PRESERVED

SALTED LIMES: (recipe) see LIME

SALTING: see JAPAN, COOKING METHODS

SALTPETER: see POTASSIUM NITRATE

SAMBAL: (*SUM-BAHL*, Indonesia, Malaysia) Many appetizing side dishes and condiments are served with Malaysian and Indonesian meals to complement the flavors, to add taste highlights or to aid digestion. They are known collectively as *sambals*. Some *sambals* are cooked; others are made of uncooked ingredients. Some are mildly flavored, but in the main they are very spicy and hot. Dried, desiccated or ground chili is a principal ingredient and it combines with many different kinds of ingredients to achieve a diverse range of flavors. In Indonesia, certain spicy cooked dishes are also known as *sambals*. Bottled chutney and pickles, crisp-fried sliced onion, shredded omelette, fried *krupuk* and *ikan bilis* and toasted coconut are typical accompaniments that are all loosely categorized as *sambals*. Several different types of sambal are usually served with a meal.
Also known as *achar*, *chatui* (India); *sambal*, *sambola* (Sri Lanka)
See also: CHILI SAMBAL (recipe); COCONUT SAMBAL (recipe); EGGPLANT SAMBAL (recipe); FRIED GARLIC FLAKE (recipe); FRIED ONION FLAKES (recipe); FRIED SAMBAL (recipe); IKAN BILIS CRISPLY FRIED (recipe); KRUPUK (recipe); MINT CHUTNEY (recipe); PEANUT SAMBAL (recipe); OMELETTE SHREDS (recipe); ONION SAMBAL (recipe); SALTED LIMES (recipe); SHAL-LOT SAMBAL (recipe); SHRIMP PASTE SAMBAL (recipe); SQUID SAMBAL (recipe)

FRIED SAMBAL
Yields 2 cups (1 lb/500 g)

1/3 cup (3 oz/90 g) chopped red onion
2 tsps chopped garlic
4 tsps sambal ulek
1 tsp shrimp paste
1 tbsp chopped greater galangal
1/2 tsp salt
2 tsps lemon juice
2 tbsps vegetable or coconut oil
1 1/2 cups (12 oz/350 g) chopped tomatoes
1/4 cup (2 fl oz/60 ml) thin coconut milk
1/4 cup (2 fl oz/60 ml) thick coconut milk
tamarind water

Grind onion, garlic, *sambal ulek*, shrimp paste, *greater galangal* with salt and lemon juice. Sauté in the oil for 2 minutes. Add tomatoes, mix well for 2–3 minutes, add both coconut milks and heat through. Season to taste with tamarind water.

SAMBAR MASALA: (*SAAM-BHAR MA-SAA-LAA*, India) see MASALA

SAMBOL: (*SAM-BAL*, Sri Lanka) see SAMBAL

SAMBOLA: (*SAM-BO-LA*, Sri Lanka) see SAMBAL

SAMLA MCHOU BANLE (*SAM-LOR MA-CHOU BON-LAE*, Cambodia) see CAMBODIA, CUISINE

SAMONG SABA: (*SIR-MONG SIR-BAR*, Burma) see FENNEL

SAMOOSA: (*SA-MO-SAA*, India) Deep-fried triangular pastries filled with spiced potatoes or meat that are a popular snack throughout India. The "patties" of Sri Lanka and "curry puffs" of Malaysia are variations on the original recipe, which came from the Middle East and featured fruit, nuts and lamb as the filling. Creamy mint or tart tamarind chutneys usually accompany *samoosas*.
See also: CURRY PUFFS (recipe); MINT CHUTNEY (recipe)

Samoosas

SAMOOSAS
Yields 30

2 cups (8 oz / 250 g) maida flour
3 tsps garam masala
salt
1 tsp turmeric
1/2 tsp pepper
1 1/2 tsps chili powder
2 tbsps vegetable oil
water
8 oz (250 g) lean beef or lamb, ground
1 tbsp ghee or oil
3/4 cup (6 oz / 180 g) minced onion
1 tsp minced garlic
2 tsps minced fresh ginger
lemon juice
1–2 tbsps chopped fresh coriander (cilantro)
3/4 cup (6 oz / 180 g) cooked peas
deep-frying oil
mint chutney

Sift flour and 1 tsp *garam masala* into a bowl. Add 1 tsp salt, 1/2 tsp each turmeric, pepper and chili powder, vegetable oil and enough water to make a stiff dough. Knead until smooth. Wrap and set aside for 20 minutes. Sauté meat in ghee or oil until colored. Add onion, garlic and ginger; fry for 2 minutes. Add 2 tsps *garam masala*,

(cont'd)

(Samoosas cont'd)

1/2 tsp turmeric and 1 tsp chili powder. Stir, flavor with lemon juice and salt to taste and add coriander and peas. Cool. Roll dough thinly, cut into 15 x 5 in (12 cm) rounds and cut each in half. Place filling in the center and fold over; pinch edges together to make a triangular pastry. Deep-fry until golden. Serve hot with mint chutney.

SANBAI-ZU: (*SAN-BAI-ZOO*, Japan) see SUNOMONO

SANCHAL: (*SAN-CHAL*, India) see SALT

SANG KEONG: (*SANG-GEUNG*, China) see GINGER

SANSHO: (*SAN-SHOW*, Japan) see SHICHIMI; SICHUAN PEPPERCORN

SANTAN: (*SUN-TARN*, Indonesia) see COCONUT (MILK)

SANTEN: (*SUN-TERN*, Malaysia) see COCONUT (MILK)

SAPIN-SAPIN: (*SAH-PIN SAH-PIN*, Philippines) Steamed layered rice dessert made from *galapong*, or finely ground rice flour with coconut milk and sugar. The layers may be colored with *ubi* (yam) or other natural food colors.
See also: YAM

SAPODILLA: (*Manilkara achras sapota*) This native of Central America, which now grows throughout tropical Asia, is a large tree growing up to 60 ft (18 m) high. Its fruit has a potato-like appearance with rough buff-colored skin. The flesh is green when unripe, turning yellow to orange-red when ready to eat. It has black, shiny seeds in the center which should be removed before eating. The fruit has a grainy texture similar to guava. The sapodilla tree is the source of chicle, which is collected as a milky sap from incisions in the bark of the tree. The sap, or latex, coagulates when heated and is processed into chewing gum. Sapodilla fruit are occasionally available in Asian fruit and vegetable markets and can be kept for many weeks under refrigeration.

Also known as *chiku* (Indonesia); *sapote* (Philippines); *lamood*, *lamut* (Thailand)

SARANG BURUNG: (*SAR-RUNG BOO-ROONG*, Malaysia) see BIRD'S NEST

SASHIMI: (*SAH-SHEE-MEE*, Japan) Serving raw fish is a vital element of the classic Japanese cuisine, and has achieved the status of an art form. The preparation of the fish, selection of platter and garnish are the work of highly skilled, laboriously trained chefs who specialize in the field. When it is the main feature of a meal, *sashimi* is served at the beginning, but small dishes of *sashimi* may also be eaten midway through a meal. Freshness is mandatory for fish served as *sashimi*; for preference, it should only be fish in season. Sliced raw fish prepared in this way is also used as a topping for *sushi*. *Hon-maguro*, the fat-bellied yellowtail, which many consider makes the finest *sashimi*, is at its best in mid-winter. *Sawara* (mackerel), *shirauo* (whitebait) and *tai* (sea bream) are all popular, as are albacore, turbot and salmon. Different fish require different cutting techniques, dictated by their taste and texture, the size of their fillets and their color and appearance. *Sashimi* is arranged decoratively, accompanied by a dipping sauce and also *wasabi*, a hot horseradish-like paste.

Raw beef, surface-cooked by rolling across a hotplate, and chicken breast dipped into boiling water so that the surface is lightly cooked, are also served as *sashimi*. They are sliced paper-thin and accompanied by a sauce based on soy with lime or lemon juice. Both of these dishes are usually accompanied by onion rings that have been blanched in boiling water and lightly marinated in vinegar.

See also: SUSHI; WASABI

ALTO-ZUKURI is known as the thread cut and produces narrow slivers of fish from thin fillets. They are usually served in little mounds on the platter.

a. Sashimi with lemon
b. Slicing fish for sashimi
c. Arranging sliced sashimi

BEEF SASHIMI
Serves 4

1 lb (500 g) lean beef fillet (sirloin or tender loin)
½ large cucumber
shiso *leaves*
2 tsps wasabi
2 tsps water or sake
4 tbsps daikon oroshi
4 tbsps finely chopped scallions (spring / green onions)
1 tbsp minced fresh ginger
ponzu *sauce*
salt

Sear the surface of the beef on a lightly oiled hotplate. Cool in cold water and drain. Cut across the grain into thin slices. Form several slices together into 4 rosettes. Place on a small plate and garnish with decoratively cut cucumber and a *shiso* leaf. Mix *wasabi* to a paste with water or *sake*. Serve the remaining ingredients separately, to be mixed to taste.

HIRA-ZUKURI is an all-round cut, used for larger fillets. The meat is cut into a rectangular block, then into slices or sticks that can then be cut into cubes. Tosa soy sauce, a strongly flavored dip, usually accompanies fish cut in this style.

SASHIMI
Serves 4

12–14 oz (350–400 g) fresh raw fish *
giant white radish shreds
bofu *stems or cucumber shreds*
ice water
tosa *soy sauce*
wasabi

Choose fish that is absolutely fresh, preferably still live. Cut in the desired way and arrange on a large platter. Chill radish, split *bofu* stems or cucumber shreds in ice water, drain and pile on the platter. Serve with *tosa* soy sauce and *wasabi*.

* Different types of fish require different cutting methods. For tuna and other large thick fillets of fish use the *kaku-zukuri* cut to make cubes of approximately 1/2 in (1 cm) square. For fish such as snapper or sea bass skin fillets and cut crossways into slices by the *hira-zukuri* method. *Usu-zukuri* indicates very angular thin slices, suitable for fish of the firm-fleshed, flattish kind such as sea bream or flounder. For tiny fish such as whiting, *ito-zukuri* produces narrow strips about 2 in (5 cm) long by 1/8 in (30 mm) square.

USU-ZUKURI, the technique of diagonally cutting thin slices, is appropriate for firm fish fillets. *Daikon-oroshi* and a *ponzu* sauce can accompany these.

SASHIMI BEEF SAUCE
Yields 1/3 cup (3 fl oz / 90 ml)

1 tbsp mirin
1/4 cup (2 fl oz / 60 ml) citron juice
1 tbsp light soy sauce
1 tsp rice vinegar

Pour *mirin* into a pan and bring to a boil. Add juice and soysauce. Mix well, then add vinegar. Cool and refrigerate.

SASHIMI WITH LEMON
Serves 4–6

1 lb (500 g) yellowtail or sea bream
2 lemons, halved and sliced
shiso *or* mitsuba *leaves*
wasabi
soy sauce

Cut off the thin tail end of the fillet. Place fish, skin side up, on a board and cut crossways into thin slices. Arrange alternate slices of fish and lemon on small plates. Garnish with *shiso* or *mitsuba* leaves. Serve with *wasabi* and soy sauce.

SASHIMI SAUCE: *(SAH-SHEE-MEE)* see TOSA SOY SAUCE

SATAY: (*SA-TAY*, Indonesia, Malaysia) Skewers of seasoned meat, poultry or seafood that are grilled over a charcoal fire and served with a dipping sauce. In Malaysia the sauce is spiced coconut milk with ground peanuts; in Indonesia sauces based on *kecap manis* (sweet soy sauce) are generally preferred. On the Indonesian island of Bali, the favored *satay* is made from tender turtle meat. *Satay* is also served in Thailand, where the peanut-based sauce is creamy and richly spiced. Variations on this theme are found in menus throughout Asia.
See also: PEANUT SAUCE (recipe); SOY SAUCE (SWEET AND SALTY)

SATAY BEEF WITH PEANUT SAUCE
Serves 4–6

1¼ lbs (600 g) beef tenderloin
2 tbsps minced onion
1 tsp minced garlic
1 tsp minced fresh ginger
2 tbsps kecap manis
1½ tsps minced lemon grass
2 tsps ground coriander
1 tsp chili powder
1 tbsp palm sugar (or substitute brown sugar)
2 tbsps peanut oil
½ tsp salt
bamboo skewers, presoaked
1 large cucumber, cut into cubes
1 quantity Peanut Sauce Recipe

Cut beef into ¾ in (2 cm) cubes and place in a dish. Mix onion, garlic, ginger, *kecap manis*, lemon grass and coriander with chili powder, sugar, peanut oil and salt. Pour over meat and stir well; marinate 4–6 hours. Thread meat onto skewers and grill over charcoal until just cooked. Serve with cucumber and Peanut Sauce.

SATAY SHRIMP
Serves 6

2½ cups (1¼ lbs / 600 g) shelled raw shrimp (prawns)
1 tsp minced garlic
1 tsp laos powder
1 tsp sambal ulek
½ tsp mashed shrimp paste
5 candlenuts, crushed
1 cup (8 fl oz / 250 ml) thick coconut milk
2 tbsps kecap manis
1 tbsp palm sugar (or substitute brown sugar)
1 tbsp vegetable oil
bamboo skewers, oiled
lemon juice
onion flakes, fried

(cont'd)

(Satay Shrimp cont'd)

Place shrimp in a glass dish. Mix garlic, *laos* powder, *sambal ulek*, shrimp paste, candlenuts, coconut milk and *kecap manis* with sugar and oil. Pour over and marinate 3–4 hours. Thread onto skewers and grill over a charcoal fire. Bring remaining marinade to a boil, add lemon juice to taste. Cool. Serve *satay* with the sauce and fried onion flakes.

SATAY WITH SWEET SAUCE
Serves 4

1 lb (500 g) rump steak
bamboo skewers, presoaked
1½ tsps minced garlic
2 tbsps kecap manis
2 tbsps lime juice or 3 tbsps tamarind water
sugar

Cut meat into thin slices across the grain, then into narrow strips. Thread onto presoaked bamboo skewers. Mix garlic and *kecap manis* with lime juice or tamarind water and sugar to taste. Brush *satays* thickly with sauce, and marinate 4–6 hours. Grill over charcoal. Serve with extra *kecap manis*.

SAUCES: see BARBECUE SAUCE; BEAN PASTES AND SAUCES; CHILI PASTES, POWDERS AND SAUCES; FISH SAUCE; OYSTER; PLUM; SHRIMP SAUCE; SOY SAUCE; SOY SAUCE (SWEET AND SALTY)

SAUSAGE, CHINESE: These thin, linked sausages, about 6 in (15 cm) long, are made from a spicy mixture of diced and ground pork and pork fat. Sun- or air-dried, they become quite hard and should be steamed to soften before use. Chinese sausages are used, usually sliced, in *dim sum* dishes, and lend their distinctive taste to "sticky" rice dishes, soups and slow-simmered dishes. A particularly tasty combination of these flavors is found in *sang choy bow*, in which diced pigeon breast and Chinese sausage are combined in a lettuce-leaf wrapper. Sliced sausage is often served—along with sliced pork liver—as an accompaniment to *congee*. Chinese sausages are sold in packs of 8–10 in Chinese delicatessens and can be refrigerated for many months. In cooler climates they can be stored for many weeks without refrigeration.

DUCK AND LIVER sausages are strong-tasting, red-brown sausages of similar shape to Chinese sausages. Made from diced duck liver and ground duck with pork fat, they are too rich in flavor for some dishes.

Also known as *lap cheong* (China); *chorizo Canton* (Philippines); *lap xuong* (Vietnam)
See also: CONGEE; CHICKEN RICE NOODLES WITH PORK (recipe); LOTUS LEAF PARCELS (recipe); RICE GRUEL WITH SHRIMP (recipe)

SAYUR: (*SA-YOUR*) see INDONESIA, COOKING METHODS

SAYUR PAKU: (*SAH-YOUR PAH-KOO*, Indonesia) see FERNTOP

SCALLION: see ONION

SCALLOPS, DRIED: see CONPOY

SCATTERED RICE: (recipe) see RICE

SCORING: see CHINA, CUTTING AND SLICING TECHNIQUES

SCREW PINE: see KEWRA ESSENCE; PANDANUS LEAF

SEA CUCUMBER: see SEA SLUG

SEAFOOD, DRIED: The Chinese have been drying seafood for thousands of years. Dried fish is an important staple food, but other dried seafoods are more of a delicacy and usually expensive.
See also: ABALONE; BOMBAY DUCK; CONPOY, CUTTLEFISH; FISH, FERMENTED (SALTED AND DRIED FISH); FISH MAW; JELLYFISH; MUSSEL; OYSTER; SEA SLUG; SHRIMP, DRIED; SQUID

SEA SLUG: (*Holothuroidea*) This marine gastropod without a shell is considered by the Chinese as a gastronomic delicacy with special qualities. It was known as *hai-shu* ("sea rat") in the fifth century but today is more likely to be called *hai-shen* ("ginseng of the sea") for its aphrodisiac properties. Because of the harvesting of these prized sea creatures over the centuries many fishing areas close to Asia have been depleted and it is not unusual for a Chinese fisherman to travel as far as the Pacific Islands in search of this strange, slug-like fish. The flavor of sea slug is of-the-sea, and the texture, which takes some getting used to, is firm and gelatinous. The French name *bêche de mer* lends a touch of romance, but sea cucumber, its other common name, is more explicit, for it looks like a flat, spiny, gray-black cucumber. Fresh sea slug is rarely available in the stores. The dried product appears to lose none of its sparse flavor and the texture is not spoiled, so this is the form in which it appears in most Chinese markets. With luck you will find it already presoaked. It dries rock-hard, so must be soaked for several days before cooking. In the pan it readily absorbs the flavor of the ingredients and is usually cooked with strong seasonings like garlic, chili and bean sauces.
Also known as *hai shen* (China); *bêche de mer* (France); sea cucumber; sea rat
See also: SEAFOOD, DRIED

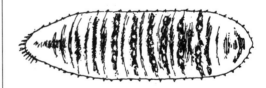

Sea slug

SEA URCHIN: (*Asthenosoma gracile, Diadema setosum*) A small, round, edible sea creature about the size of an apple, covered with many long, sharp, poisonous spines. The tiny ovaries (ripe egg sacs) contained in the lower half of the shell are what is eaten. They have a distinct, of-the-sea flavor which to many is an acquired taste. In Japan, bottled sea urchin is available. It is mixed with soy sauce and served with *sashimi* or as a topping for *sushi*, and is mixed with egg yolk and brushed onto grilled seafood and chicken. Its rich taste and bright orange-red color make it an attractive garnish on vinegared seafood salads.

Also known as *sin gaun, ye-khu* (Burma); *daam* (China); *uni* (Japan); *con chom chom* (Vietnam)

See also: CAVIAR

Sea urchin

SEAWEED: Seaweed of many types is harvested off the coasts of Asia, and is an important part of the diet in the northern regions. There are several types of major importance.

HAIR VEGETABLE: (*Gracilaria verrucosa*) This black algae is aptly named as it dries in fine strands like hair. It is generally regarded as a seaweed, but is in fact an alga. The bulk of the crop that is used throughout the world is gathered from the southern coast of China, but it grows on inland water as well and is found in the mountainous central west of China. Its Chinese name, *fa ts'ai* or *fat choy*, is a synonym of the Chinese New Year greeting *kung sei fa ts'ai* (wish you prosperity) and so is an intrinsic part of the main Lunar New Year feast, when it is braised with fresh bacon. In northern and central western China, it is added to soups, is steamed as a vegetable with a light sauce and is used as a decoration on stylized banquet dishes—the fine strands trace designs on serving platters to represent the fur of pandas, the feathers of the mythical phoenix or the bark and branches of trees. This ingredient can usually be found, in small packs, in Chinese pharmacies and markets. Expect it to be expensive.

Also known as *fat choy* or *fa ts'ai* (China); black moss; hair seaweed; hair-like vegetable

See also: CHENGTU VEGETARIAN PLATTER (recipe); MUSHROOM PLATTER WITH HAIR VEGETABLE (recipe)

HIJIKI: (Japan) (*Cystophyllum fusiforme*) are short, black, branch-like sticks of seaweed and are usually sold in dried form and resemble a coarse type of tea. They must be soaked before being used and will expand to at least three times their dried size. They are used as a garnish in vegetable, seafood and chicken dishes, and as an appetizer in salads. *Hijiki* has an interesting, almost nutty taste and texture. Sold in small cellophane packs, it will keep for many months in dry conditions. Transfer to an airtight jar once opened.

KOMBU (Japan) (*Laminaria japonica*), giant sea kelp, along with dried *bonito*, is one of the most important of the Japanese ingredients, for it gives its flavor to *dashi*, the stock used as a base for most savory dishes. *Kombu* is gathered mainly off the northern island of Hokkaido. It is deep olive-green and has a strong "of-the-sea" flavor and fragrance. It is cut into pieces—usually about 12 in (30 cm) long—and dried and folded before being sold in cellophane packs. It develops a sprinkling of white salty mold over the surface, which should be removed by wiping with a damp cloth before use. To release its full flavor, soak *kombu* until softened, then score the surface with the point of a knife. It can be used at least twice before its flavor diminishes.

Kombu is also marketed as *oboru kombu* and *tororo kombu*, which are shaved from the surface of a soaked *kombu* leaf. The former is shaved across, the latter lengthways, then cut into fine shreds. They both have a particularly distinctive flavor. *Shiraita kombu* is what remains of this operation and is a fine, ocher-colored sheet used as a wrapper.

Also known as *muik* (Korea); sea kelp; tangle kelp

See also: BONITO; DASHI; SEAWEED SOUP (recipe)

LATO (Philippines) is a seaweed with grape-like clusters of tiny balls. It is highly appreciated in the Visayan region of the Philippines.

NORI (Japan) (*Pophyra tenera, P. umbilicalis*) is a type of marine alga, harvested from the surface of the waters off Japan, Korea and northern China. Certain types of this alga are used to make *agar agar*, and also as a gelatin and for medical use. It is dried and compressed into paper-thin flat sheets, and ranges in color from deep purple to bright, deep green. It has a subtle flavor. Its principal use in Japan is as a wrapper for *sushi*; it is folded around rice and fillings, with the aid of the bamboo mat known as a *maki-su* or *sudare*. *Nori* is also shredded and added to soups, and can be formed into "nests" by deep-frying.

It comes in squares of two sizes, packed in cellophane, or in discs—the latter are usually of Chinese origin. It must be kept absolutely dry by being stored in an airtight container. It also comes, conveniently shredded, in shaker bottles for use as a condiment for Japanese dishes such as noodles, soups and rice. *Nori* should be crisped by holding over a flame or placing in a very hot oven for a few minutes before use.

Also known as *tsu ts'ai* (China); *ao nori* (shreds) (Japan); *keem* (Korea); *gamat* (Philippines); green laver; purple laver; sea laver

See also: NORI-MAKI SUSHI (recipe); SEAWEED SIDE DISH (recipe); SUSHI

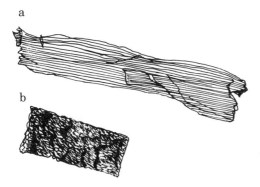

a. Kombu   b. Nori

WAKAME (Japan) (*Undaria pinnatifida*) is a deep green to brown, curly-leafed type of seaweed that belongs to the brown algae family, many different types of which are eaten in Asia. The green type is used as a vegetable in

northern China, Korea and Japan, being simmered in soups and stews and used in salads with a vinegar dressing. It is sold dried in small packs and should be kept very dry in storage. Soak in cold water until softened before use. The brown type, known as *arame* in Japan, is of a less delicate flavor; it is usually minced and added to dishes or served with rice. This seaweed, which is black-brown and crinkly in its dry state, bears a strong resemblance to wood ear fungus.

Also known as curly algae; curly seaweed; lobe leaf seaweed

See also: VINEGARED SEAWEED WITH CRAB AND CUCUMBER (recipe)

SEAWEED SIDE DISH
Serves 8

6 sheets dried keem *(sea laver)*
Oriental sesame oil
salt

Brush sheets on one side with sesame oil, sprinkle with salt. Suspend over gas flame or place under hot grill for a few seconds, until they turn bright green. Cut into small squares.

SEAWEED SOUP
Serves 6

4 oz (120 g) dried wakame *seaweed*
water
6 cups (1½ qts / 1.5 l) fish or beef broth
1 cup (8 oz / 250 g) chopped scallions (spring / green onions)
salt and white pepper
6 oz (180 g) lean beef, shredded
1 tsp minced garlic
1 tbsp Oriental sesame oil
soy sauce
1 tbsp ground toasted white sesame seeds

Soak seaweed in water for at least 30 minutes; drain and cut into strips. Bring broth to a boil with scallions, salt and pepper to taste. Fry beef and garlic in sesame oil. Add to broth. Add seaweed, soy sauce to taste and heat through. Sprinkle on sesame seeds.

SEAWEED GELATIN: see AGAR AGAR

SEAWEED JELLY: see AGAR AGAR

SECOND BAMBOO: see BEAN CURD BY-PRODUCTS (BEAN CURD STICKS)

SEE BYAN: (*SI PY-AN*, Burma) A term to describe a stage in curry-making in which the cooking oil and oils from the ingredients begin to float to the surface of the curry. Curries are judged not to have the right flavor until, by slow cooking to evaporate the water, this stage is reached.

SEEN CHOY: (*SIN CHOY*, China) see CABBAGE, CHINESE

SEENG: (*SEENG*, India) see DRUMSTICK VEGETABLE

SEIRON-NIKKEI: (*SE-II-RON-NICK-EI*, Japan) see CINNAMON

SELASIH: (*SE-LA-SEEH*, Indonesia) A variety of basil that grows wild in Indonesia. It has a very mild flavor and is considered inferior to the commonly used basil known as *daun kemangi*.
See also: BASIL

SEMOLINA: A product derived from hard or durum wheat during milling, when the larger particles of the endosperm can be removed and dried into a fine, granular substance. It is used to make sweet and savory dishes in both vegetarian and non-vegetarian cooking in India. It is also used by Indian populations in other countries, particularly Malaysia. It is used in a delicious cake in Burma.
Also known as *rava, ravo, soojo, suji* (India)
See also: PARSI SEMOLINA DESSERT (recipe)

PARSI SEMOLINA DESSERT
Serves 4

3 tbsps ghee
1/3 cup (1 1/2 oz / 45 g) fine semolina
1/4 cup (2 oz / 60 g) sugar
3 cups (24 fl oz / 750 ml) milk
2 tbsps raisins, soaked
1/3 tsp ground cardamom
15 almonds, blanched and slivered

(cont'd)

(Parsi Semolina Dessert cont'd)

10 whole almonds
varaq
nutmeg, grated

Heat ghee and fry semolina to golden. Add sugar and milk and stir over heat until thickened. Add raisins, cardamom and slivered almonds; cook briefly. Pour into a serving dish, decorate with whole almonds wrapped in *varaq*, and grated nutmeg.

SEMOLINA CAKE
Serves 8–12

1 1/4 cups (5 oz / 150 g) fine semolina
4 cups (1 qt / 1 l) thin coconut milk
1 cup (8 oz / 250 g) crumbled palm sugar (or substitute brown sugar)
1/3 tsp ground cardamom
1 cup (8 oz / 250 g) softened butter
3 large eggs, separated
1/2 tsp salt
extra butter
toasted sesame seeds

Toast semolina in a dry pan to a golden color. Add coconut milk and sugar, bring to a boil and simmer, stirring, until very thick. Add butter and beat over heat until smooth. Stir in egg yolks, salt and cardomom. Beat egg whites to firm peaks. Fold into mixture. Spread batter evenly in a buttered cake pan. Bake at 350°F (180°C) for 1 1/4 –1 1/2 hours. Spread with a little more butter and sprinkle on sesame seeds before serving.

SENDAI MISO: (*SEN-DAI MEE-SOW*, Japan) see MISO

SEN MEE: (*SEN MEE*, Malaysia, Thailand) see NOODLES (RICE VERMICELLI)

SERAI: (*SE-RYE*, Malaysia) see LEMON GRASS

SEREH: (*SE-REAH*, Indonesia) see LEMON GRASS

SERRANO CHILI: see CHILI

SESAME CHILI OIL: see OILS AND FATS

SESAME OIL: see SESAME SEED; OILS AND FATS
SESAME PASTE: see SESAME SEED

SESAME SAUCE/EXOTIC TASTING SAUCE

To accompany cold cooked noodles, or as a dressing for chicken and celery salad.

2 tbsps light soy sauce
2 tbsps cold water
2 tsps Oriental sesame oil
2 tsps brown rice vinegar
2 tbsps sesame paste
1/3 tsp minced garlic
1 tsp minced ginger
2 tsps minced scallions (spring/
green onions)
1 tsp sugar

Mix liquid ingredients
together, stirring until smooth.
Add remaining ingredients
and stir well.

Variation: Add extra 2 tsps
minced scallions and 1/2 –1 tsp
chili oil to make sauce known as
"exotic tasting," which is usually
served with shredded
poached chicken.

SESAME SEED: (*Sesamum indicum*) An annual herb of the Pedaliaceae family which grows extensively in Asia, particularly in Burma, China and India. Sesame plants yield many small, oval, edible seeds, two kinds of which are used in Asian cooking. They have an agreeable, nutty flavor and high oil content.
Also known as *hu ma* (foreign hemp) (China); *til* (India); *wijen* (Indonesia); *muki goma* (tan hulled) (Japan); *bijan* (Malaysia); *thala* (Sri Lanka); *nga dee la* (Thailand)
See also: GREEN BEANS WITH SESAME MISO DRESSING (recipe); SALAD OF WARM AND SPICY CUCUMBER (recipe); SESAME SAUCE/EXOTIC TASTING SAUCE (recipe)

BLACK SESAME SEEDS are used in Japan and China usually as a garnish, but also in desserts and puddings. One Chinese favorite is a hot sweet soup of ground black sesame seeds. They have a more pungent and slightly more bitter taste than the white seeds. The Japanese seasoning *gomasio* or *goma shio* comprises black sesame seeds mixed with salt.
Also known as *hak chih mah* (China); *kuro goma* (Japan)

SESAME OIL is a dark-colored, thick, aromatic oil made from crushed white sesame seeds. It is used extensively in northern China, Japan and Korea to add flavor to stir-fried and sautéed foods and as a seasoning. It has a rich, nutty flavor. It is not used by itself for deep-frying because the flavor is too strong and it has a low burning point. When deep-frying such foods as Japanese *tempura*, about 1 part sesame oil is used with 10 parts vegetable oil. It is occasionally sprinkled over cooked dishes as a condiment, and is frequently added to marinades.
Also known as *ma yau, tee ma yau* (China); *til ka tel* (India); *goma abura* (Japan)

SESAME PASTE is a thick, dryish paste made from toasted white sesame seeds. It differs from the Middle Eastern sesame paste, *tahini*, which is made from untoasted seeds and is a pale yellow color with a creamier texture. Sesame paste is used in Sichuan province in China as the sauce for various cold dishes, including noodles and chicken, and gives a pleasing nutty taste to marinades. It may be used in Japanese and Korean recipes that call for ground sesame seeds. Sesame paste keep indefinitely in the refrigerator, although it separates into firm dry solids—with the oil on top—and must be mixed well before use.
Also known as *cho kanjang* (Korea); sesame butter, sesame seed paste, tahini

WHITE SESAME SEEDS are used whole as a garnish in most parts of Asia. They are crushed for use in sauces and coatings, particularly in Japan and Korea; they are an important element in the sauce that accompanies the Korean barbecue. Ground white sesame seeds produce a nutty, thick paste—most commonly known by its Middle Eastern name, *tahini*—which in China is used in sauces. White sesame seeds should be toasted by cooking over low heat—in a dry pan or in the oven until golden—to release their rich flavor and improve their aroma.

Also known as *chih mah jee mah* (China); *goma shiro goma* (white unhulled) (Japan)

SHA CHA JIANG: (*SA CHA JE-ONG*, China) see BEAN PASTES AND SAUCES

SHAH JAHAN: (*SHAAH JA-HAAN*, India) Grandson of Akbar, the greatest sovereign of the Moghul Empire in India, Shah Jahan reigned during the golden age of Indian Saracenic architecture, best exemplified by the Taj Mahal. During this time, encouraged by the gourmet tastes of Shah Jahan, the culinary skills of the Moghuls attained splendid heights of achievement, setting precedents for the grand style of banquet cooking favored by the upper strata of society in northern India. A number of dishes still retain the name Shah Jahan, particularly one sumptuous *pillau* (rice) dish flavored with cardamom and garnished with cream, *varaq* and almonds.
See also: VARAQ

SCALLION: see ONION

SCALLION, PICKLED: see ONION

SHAH JEERA: (*SHAAH JE-RAA*, India) see CARAWAY SEED

SHAH JIRA: (*SHAAH JE-RAA*, India) see CUMIN (BLACK)

SHA JEN: (*SA JEN*, China) see CARDAMOM

SHANGHAI HAIRY CRAB: see CRAB

SHANGHAI MEAT DUMPLINGS: (recipe) see PORK

SHAOHSING YELLOW RICE WINE: (*SHIU-HING*) see WINE, CHINESE

SHARK'S FIN: Shark meat has been eaten in Asia for over 2000 years, but it is the strand-like cartilage from the shark's fin that is most appreciated. It is one of the most expensive ingredients in China and it is served—as a soup, or braised in a rick stock—as the feature dish at the beginning of a meal. Marco Polo was one of the first Europeans to enjoy the unique flavor and texture of shark's fin and to marvel at the possibilities that the Chinese claim it has for enhancing health and virility.

Shark's fin is sold whole, in which form it requires lengthy preparation to clean and soften it; in chips, which also require some advance work; or, most expensively, in cleaned strands. It is always cooked in a rich broth of poultry bones and pork shanks, supplemented, in its "superior" version, by dried oysters and *conpoy* (scallops). Shark's fin soup—usually done with chicken meat—has a rich, creamy flavor and fine texture, but it is braised sharks' fins that give a true indication of why this is one of the most highly regarded Chinese ingredients. Whole cleaned fins are also slow-cooked in "superior" stock until completely tender, then served with no embellishments, save perhaps a little dish of crisp pretzels and red rice vinegar. It is a sensational combination of flavor and texture. Shark's fin "needles" find their way into fillings for *dim sum* as well, but the effect is rather wasted. Rogue ingredients, such as cooked bean thread vermicelli and thin, handmade "silver pin" noodles often masquerade as shark's fin. Shark's fin soup is available in cans and is a reasonable alternative to a lower grade type of shark's fin dish.
Also known as *yu chee* (China); *hoo pla chalarm* (Thailand)
See also: RICE VINEGAR; SEAFOOD, DRIED; SHARK'S FIN SOUP WITH CRAB ROE (recipe); NOODLES (SILVER PIN); SUPERIOR BROTH (recipe)

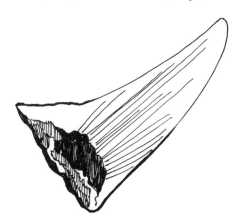

Whole shark's fin

SHARK'S FIN/SHARK'S SKIN PREPARATION: Dried shark's fin and shark's skin have to be pre-softened before cooking. Place whole or broken shark's fin or pieces of shark's skin in a large saucepan and cover generously with cold water. Bring very slowly to a boil, then simmer uncovered for 1¾ hours. Remove from heat and set aside until almost cool, then rinse in cold water and place in a dish with cold water to cover. Cover dish and refrigerate overnight. Bring to a boil again and simmer 1 hour. Drain, rinse and cool in cold water. Repeat this process if necessary. Pick out any fragments of skin from fins. Cut shark's skin into small squares. Prepared fins and skin can be refrigerated for several days before use.

SHARK'S FIN SOUP WITH CRAB ROE
Serves 4

5 oz (150 g) shark's fin, diced
5 cups (1¼ qt / 1.25 l) Superior Broth (see recipe)
3 oz (90 g) Chinese ham, sliced
2 tbsps minced scallions (spring / green onions)
1 tbsp finely shredded ginger
3 oz (90 g) shredded bamboo shoots
2 tbsps cornstarch (cornflour)
cold water
3 oz (90 g) crab roe, or tomalley

Prepare shark's fin according to directions. Heat Superior Broth, add ham, scallions, ginger and bamboo shoots and simmer for 20 minutes. Add cornstarch mixed with cold water to thicken. Simmer briefly; add crab roe or tomalley.

SHARK'S SKIN: Dried shark's skin is another of China's unusual seafood ingredients and is enjoyed for its unique soft-chewy texture and fishy taste. Sold in sheets, it should be softened before use by placing in cold water, bringing to a boil and simmering for about 2 hours. Drain and repeat. When softened, rinse in cold water and cut into small squares. It can be kept for up to three days in cold water in this condition, or frozen for later use. It is used, like other dried seafoods, to give flavor to dishes. Sturgeon skin is eaten in the same way.
Also known as *yu pei* (China)
See also: SEAFOOD, DRIED; SHARK'S FIN (PREPARATION)

SHEH PAAN: (*SEK BARN*, China) see GAROUPA
SHEINGHO: (*SHANE-CO*, Burma) see ASAFOETIDA

SHICHIMI: (*SHI-CHEE-MEE*, Japan) An all-round condiment used in Japan to add an extra touch of flavor to many types of dishes and particularly noodles. The name means "seven spices," and the mixture includes red chili flakes (*togarashi*), sansho (Sichuan peppercorns), white sesame feeds, flaked *nori*, flaked dried mandarin peel, black hemp seeds and white poppy seeds. It is sold in shaker containers and should be kept in a dry, dark cupboard as moisture and exposure to air can diminish its flavor. Look for the shaker with its ingredients in separate compartments as they keep better this way and can be added to taste. Two other popular condiments are:

ICHIMI: Finely flaked dried red chilies, which is also known as *togarashi*.

SANSHO: Ground prickly ash berries, which are known in China as Sichuan peppercorns.
Also known as *shichimi togarashi*, seven-spice powder
See also: CHILI; YAKITORI (recipe)

SHIH: (*SI*, China) see BEAN PASTES AND SAUCES
SHIITAKE: (*SHEE-EE-TAH-KE*, Japan) see MUSHROOMS AND EDIBLE FUNGI
SHIITAKE MUSHROOMS WITH PONZU SAUCE: (recipe) see MUSHROOMS AND EDIBLE FUNGI
SHINSHU-MISO: (*SHIN-SHOO-MEE-SOW*, Japan) see MISO

SHINSULRO HOTPOT
Serves 6–8

8 oz (250 g) calf's liver, thinly sliced
salt
pepper
Oriental sesame oil
4 oz (120 g) lean beef, sliced
4 oz (120 g) lean pork, ground
light soy sauce
1 egg, beaten

(cont'd)

(Shinsulro Hotpot cont'd)

8 cups (2 qts / 2 l) rich beef broth
8 oz (250 g) boiled tripe
1 small carrot, peeled and sliced
6 dried black mushrooms, soaked
3 oz (90 g) canned sliced bamboo shoots
12–18 canned ginkgo *nuts*
pine nuts, toasted
silgochu or chili flakes
scallions (spring / green onions), chopped
vinegar soy sauce

Season liver with salt
and pepper. Fry in 1 tbsp sesame oil
until evenly colored. Cut beef into narrow
strips, sprinkle with pepper and sesame
oil. Season pork with salt, pepper, soy
sauce and sesame oil. Add egg, form into
small meatballs and fry in sesame oil until
brown. Bring broth to a boil in a tabletop
hotpot; add tripe, carrot, mushrooms,
bamboo shoots and *ginkgo* nuts
and simmer 15 minutes. Sprinkle on
pine nuts, *silgochu* or chili flakes and
scallions. Season to taste with
soy sauce. Serve with a dip of
vinegar soy sauce.

SHIOYAKI/AJI-SHIOYAKI: (*SHI-O-YAH-KEE*),
see JAPAN, COOKING METHODS

SHIRATAKI: (*SHI-RAH-TAH-KEE*, Japan) see
NOODLES (SHIRATAKI)

SHIRATAMA KO: (*SHI-RAH-TAH-MAH KO*, Japan) see FLOURS AND THICKENERS (GLUTINOUS RICE)

SHISHI-TO PEPPER: (*SHI-SHI-TOW*) see PEPPER

SHISO: (*SHEE-SOW*, Japan) see BEEFSTEAK PLANT

SHOGA: (*SHOW-GA*, Japan) see GINGER

SHRIMP: Shrimp (prawns) are used extensively in Asian cooking. Small shrimp are important as a flavoring ingredient. They are made into *bagoong* in the Philippines, are dried, ground and processed into various types of pungent shrimp pastes for use in Indonesian, Malaysian, Chinese and Thai cooking, and are also peeled and dried.

Also known as *har* (China); *jinga* (India); *udang* (Indonesia, Malaysia); *ebi* (Japan); *alamang* (small shrimp), *camaroon* (large shrimp) (Philippines); *gung foi, gung narng* (Thailand); *tom bac gan, tom su* (Vietnam); prawns

See also: BAGOONG; SHRIMP, DRIED; SHRIMP PASTE *and recipes following*

BUTTERFLY-CUT: Cut along center back, cutting as deeply as possible without cutting all the way through. Leave final section and tail in place. Discard dark vein and press shrimp flat.

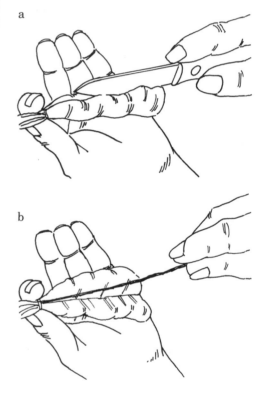

Butterfly cut shrimp
a. Cut along back   b. Remove dark vein

DEVEINING: Peel shrimp. Hold head and tail together so back is arched upwards. Insert the point of a wooden pick or skewer into center back; then lift point, bringing up vein. Gently ease out and discard. Rinse and dry shrimp. To whiten and remove fish smell, rinse in a mixture of cold water, salt and cornstarch.

GREEN SHRIMP CURRY

Serves 4–6

1 lb (500 g) medium shrimp (prawns), shelled
1 cup (8 fl oz / 250 ml) thick coconut milk
1 recipe Green Curry Paste
2–3 tsps fish sauce
2 cups (16 fl oz / 500 ml) thin coconut milk
2 tbsps finely shredded lesser galangal
3 kaffir lime leaves, soaked
2 fresh red chilies, seeded
salt
palm sugar (or substitute brown sugar)
black pepper
1/2 cup (1/2 oz / 15 g) basil leaves, shredded

Devein, rinse and drain shrimp.
Simmer thick coconut milk until oil
separates, add green curry paste and
cook for 5–6 minutes, stirring. Add fish
sauce, thin coconut milk, *lesser galangal*,
lime leaves and chilies. Bring almost to
a boil, then simmer for 5 minutes. Add
salt, sugar and pepper to taste. Add
shrimp and basil, cook until
tender, about 5 minutes.

SALT-BROILED SHRIMP

Serves 4

12 large unshelled shrimp (prawns)
1/2 cup (4 oz / 120 g) coarse salt
lemon

Chop off shrimp head, just
before eyes, then carefully cut deeply
through head and shell along back
and press open (butterfly cut). Devein.
Skewer sideways using 3 skewers. Roll
shrimp in salt. Place shell down over
a charcoal barbecue and grill for 2
minutes. Turn and grill other side;
turn again and finish cooking.
Serve with lemon wedges.

a
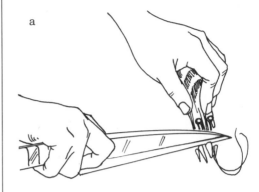

b

Salt-broiled shrimp
a. Cutting front tips of shrimp
b. Skewering shrimp on skewers

SHRIMP AND CRABMEAT BALLS
IN NOODLE SOUP

Serves 6

8 oz (250 g) bun noodles
8 oz (250 g) raw shrimp (prawns), shelled
1 1/2 cups (12 oz / 350 g) finely ground pork
1 tsp minced garlic
1/4 cup (2 oz / 60 g) minced scallions
(spring / green onions)
salt
pepper
8 oz (250 g) flaked, cooked crabmeat
fish sauce

(cont'd)

(Shrimp and Crabmeat Balls in Noodle Soup cont'd)

fish stock, chicken broth or water, lightly salted
fresh coriander (cilantro)

Boil noodles until tender;
drain. Grind shrimp, pork, garlic
and scallions to a smooth paste; add salt
and pepper to taste. Add crabmeat and 2
tsps fish sauce. Use wet hands to form
into small balls. Bring fish stock,
chicken broth or salted water to a boil.
Add 1½ tbsps fish sauce and cook
seafood balls until they float to the
surface. Serve over noodles, garnished
with fresh coriander and extra
minced scallions.

SHRIMP AND NOODLE SOUP
Serves 6–8

8 oz (250 g) thin rice vermicelli
water, salted
4–8 fresh red chilies, seeded and sliced
4 tbsps peanut oil
4–5 cups (1–1¼ qts / 1–1.25 l) chicken or fish
stock
1½ lbs (750 g) small shrimp (prawns),
unshelled
salt
pepper
tamarind water
2 tbsps palm sugar (or substitute brown sugar)
2 medium onions, sliced
1½ tsps minced garlic
2 cups (1 lb / 500 g) bean sprouts, blanched
⅓ cup (2 oz / 60 g) roasted peanuts

Boil vermicelli briefly in
salted water; drain. Fry chilies
in 2 tbsps peanut oil, until crisp.
Crush. Bring chicken or fish stock to
a boil. Add shrimp and simmer for 2
minutes. Drain and shell, reserving broth.
Season broth with salt, pepper, tamarind
water and sugar. Fry onions and garlic
in 2 tbsps peanut oil until golden and
beginning to crisp. Divide vermicelli
among 6–8 bowls, adding shrimp,
bean sprouts, chili, onion, garlic
and peanuts. Pour on stock.

SHRIMP CAKES
Yields 18

1½ lbs (750 g) shrimp (prawns), shelled
1 egg white
4 oz (120 g) coarsely ground pork fat
½ cup (1 oz / 30 g) minced scallions (spring /
green onions)
2 tbsps fish sauce
salt
pepper
sugar
vegetable oil
lettuce leaves
fresh herbs
1 cup (4 oz / 125 g) cooked rice vermicelli,
chopped
nuoc cham or chili sauce

Process shrimp, egg white,
pork fat, scallions and fish sauce
to a smooth paste in a food processor,
adding salt, pepper and a pinch of sugar.
Using oiled hands, form into small flat
cakes 1 in (2.5 cm) in diameter. Fry in oil
until golden. Serve wrapped in lettuce
leaves with fresh herbs and
vermicelli. Dip into *nuoc cham*
or chili sauce.

SHRIMP IN COCONUT MILK
Serves 4

1½ cups (12 oz / 350g) sliced onions
¾ tsp minced garlic
1 tsp minced ginger
1½ tbsps ghee or oil
2 fresh red or green chilies, seeded and slit
1 tsp turmeric
8 curry leaves
2 cups (16 fl oz / 500 ml) thin coconut milk
1 tsp salt
1½ lbs (750 g) large raw shrimp (prawns)
lemon juice

Shell and devein shrimp if
preferred, but they retain more
flavor if left in the shell. Fry onions,

(cont'd)

(Shrimp in Coconut Milk cont'd)
garlic and ginger in ghee or
oil until onions soften. Add chilies,
turmeric and curry leaves and fry for 1
minute longer. Add coconut milk and salt
and stir constantly as it comes almost
to a boil. Simmer uncovered for 10
minutes, then add shrimp and cook
10–15 minutes. Add lemon
juice to taste.

SHRIMP PATTIES
Serves 6

*10 oz (315 g) minced cooked shelled shrimp
(prawns)
1¼ cups (5 oz / 150 g) all-purpose (plain) flour
1¾ tsps baking powder
1 tsp salt
½ tsp pepper
water
1 tsp minced garlic
⅓ cup (3 oz / 90 g) minced scallions (spring /
green onions)
2 eggs
deep-frying oil*

Place shrimp in a mixing
bowl. Add flour, baking powder,
salt and pepper, with enough water to
make a batter of pouring consistency.
Beat in garlic, scallions and eggs. Cover
and set aside for 30 minutes. Heat deep-
frying oil. Drop small spoonfuls of
batter into the oil to cook until
patties rise to the surface and
turn golden brown. Remove
and drain. Serve hot.

STEAMED SHRIMP
Serves 4–6

*2 lbs (1 kg) large shrimp (prawns), in the shell
water
soy-chili dip*

Cut shrimp through
shells along center back and
remove vein. Rinse. Arrange on a plate
and set on a rack in a steamer. Steam
over rapidly boiling water for
5–7 minutes. Serve immediately
with soy-chili dip.

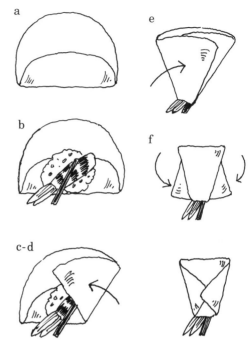

Triangular Rolls with Whole Shrimp
a. Fold in end of pastry
b. Position shrimp on top, tail outwards
c..-d. Fold in sides
e. Fold base over
f. Wrap sides over

TRIANGULAR ROLLS WITH WHOLE SHRIMP
Serves 6

*4 oz (125 g) shrimp meat (prawns), shelled
4 oz (125 g) coarsely minced pork
salt
white pepper
fish sauce
½ tsp minced garlic
1 tbsp vegetable oil
12 x 6 in (15 cm) banh trang wrappers
12 whole cooked shrimp (prawns), peeled
12 garlic chives, halved
nuoc cham sauce*

(cont'd)

(Triangular Rolls with Whole Shrimp cont'd)

Use a cleaver to flatten raw shrimp into a paste; add pork and mix well, seasoning with salt, white pepper, and fish sauce. Fry garlic in oil until golden; add mixture and cook briefly. Dip *banh trang* into water to soften; drain. Place a cooked shrimp and 2 pieces of garlic chive across each wrapper. Add a portion of the filling. Roll up and serve with *nuoc cham* sauce.

SHRIMP, DRIED: A ubiquitous seasoning and flavoring ingredient throughout Southeast Asia. Small peeled shrimp, dehydrated by sun- or air-drying, are added to soups, broths and stuffings—their flavor in a parcel of "lotus rice" is a good example of how they can enhance a dish. A few dried shrimp in a slow-cooked dish intensifies the taste of the whole dish. Add them also to stir-fries, noodles and salads. They should be softened before use, either by steaming or soaking in warm water or wine. The liquid can be used in the dish, depending on how much flavor you want. They are at their best when orange-pink in color; brownness suggests age and whiteness indicates they are beginning to mildew, which will give them a bitter flavor. Dried shrimp are sold in small packs and should be transferred to an airtight container to prevent deterioration. These little morsels, crisp-fried and tossed with salt and chili, are a tasty snack for the strong-hearted.
Also known as *ha mei* (China); *udang kering* (Indonesia, Malaysia); *kung haeng* (Thailand); shrimp floss
See also: LOTUS LEAF PARCELS (recipe); SEAFOOD, DRIED

SHRIMP CHIPS: see KRUPUK

SHRIMP EGG: see CAVIAR

SHRIMP FLOSS: see SHRIMP POWDER

SHRIMP PASTE: Shrimp paste is made by pulverizing salted, decomposed shrimp. The paste is dried and compressed into rectangular slabs, known commonly by the Malaysian name *blachan*, which turn a chocolate color and acquire an unmistakable, pungent smell. Another kind, which is softer, slightly less firm and dry in texture and a mushroom-pink color, is compressed into oval or square blocks. It is one of the more important seasoning ingredients in Burmese, Malay and Indonesian cooking and is also used in Thailand and Vietnam. In the Philippines, *alamang*, tiny shrimp, no more than ½ in (1 cm) long, are used to make a fermented shrimp seasoning known as *bagoong* and a thin salty sauce called *patis*.

Shrimp paste should be stored carefully so that its pervasive and rather repugnant odor does not impregnate other foods. The best method is to leave it in the paper in which it was originally wrapped and store in a vacuum-sealed jar. It can be cut into cubes and stored in a jar of oil, from which it may conveniently be added straight to a dish without handling. It should preferably be fried or roasted before use; this changes its naturally acrid flavor and turns it into a rich, aromatic seasoning. It can be roasted, without smell or fuss in small cubes, wrapped in aluminum foil and placed in a hot oven or dry pan.
Also known as *pazon ng api* (Burma); *terasi* (Indonesia, Malaysia); *blachan kapi* (Thailand); *mam tom* (Vietnam)
See also: BAGOONG; NASI GORENG (recipe); HEIKO; SHRIMP SAUCE; TAMARIND BEEF (recipe)

SHRIMP PASTE SAMBAL

5–6 red chilies, coarsely chopped
1 tbsp shrimp paste
½ tsp sugar
½ tsp salt

Grind chili, with seeds, and shrimp paste to a smooth paste, without breaking the chili seeds any more than necessary. Add sugar and salt and mix in well. Refrigerate no more than 2–3 days.

SHRIMP POWDER: This is made by grinding dried shrimp to a powdery fluff and is sold in bottles in Southeast Asian markets. But you

will get a much better flavor by grinding dried shrimp in a food processor or mortar. In Thailand, shrimp powder is as commonly used as salt and pepper. It is bettered only by shrimp powder with chili. This clever combination of flavors is sprinkled over salads, vegetables, noodles and rice dishes to give the unique taste of Thailand. It is an important ingredient in the Burmese condiment mix known as *balachuang*.
Also known as *oboro ebi* (Japan)
See also: BALACHUANG (recipe)

SHRIMP ROE: see CAVIAR

SHRIMP SAUCE: A moister, saltier version of shrimp paste is favored by the Chinese and Vietnamese and is known as shrimp sauce. It is made by a similar process to that used for shrimp paste. However it is not sun-dried, but is packed in its thick, moist state directly into jars. It has a light pink color when very fresh; it turns a grayish shade and acquires a less pleasant, more pungent flavor as it matures. It is also used in Thailand and Burma and is particularly good in stir-fried dishes and in sauces. It can be used as a condiment. There is also a shrimp sauce used in Nonya cooking. It is very dark, like molasses in color and is called *kapi leaw*, or *heiko* in Malay.
Also known as *hom ha* (China); *patis* (Indonesia) *bagoong* (Philippines); *nuoc mam* (Vietnam)
See also: WATER SPINACH WITH SHRIMP SAUCE (recipe)

SHUI DIAN FEN: (*SHUI HIAN FEN*, China) A paste of cornstarch dissolved in water that is used as a thickener in almost every Chinese dish that has a sauce, particularly stir-fries. *Shui dian fen* is mixed to the right consistency and kept near the wok to be added directly to a dish to thicken the sauce or to bind the liquids that have accumulated in the wok. It gives a glossy, smooth and translucent sauce. Other starches, such as arrowroot, *kuzu*, mung bean, tapioca, and water chestnut, are also used. The normal solution is one part cornstarch to two parts cold water and the solution must always be stirred immediately before using, as it separates.

Also known as cornstarch (cornflour) solution; cornstarch (cornflour) thickener
See also: FLOURS AND THICKENERS

SHUI DOUFU: (*SHUI DAU-FU*, China) see BEAN CURD (SILK)
SHUNGIKU: (*SHEWN-GHEE-KOO*, Japan) see CHRYSANTHEMUM
SIAMESE GINGER: see GALANGAL; GINGER
SICHUAN CABBAGE WITH PORK: (recipe) see CABBAGE (PICKLED)
SICHUAN CHILI SAUCE: see CHILI PASTES, POWDERS AND SAUCES
SICHUAN DUMPLINGS IN HOT SAUCE: (recipe) see PORK
SICHUAN HOT BEAN PASTE: see BEAN PASTES AND SAUCES (CHILI)

SICHUAN HOT RED SAUCE
Yields 1¼ cups (10 fl oz / 300 ml)

To accompany steamed pork dumplings or wontons, or to serve over boiled noodles when a very hot sauce is preferred.

2 tbsps Oriental sesame oil
1 tbsp chili oil
2 tbsps sesame paste
1½ tbsps dark soy sauce
water or vegetable oil
1 tbsp minced garlic
1 tbsp minced scallions (spring / green onions)
1 tsp ground Sichuan peppercorns
2 tsps sugar

Mix sesame and chili oil, sesame paste and soy sauce together thoroughly, adding a little water or vegetable oil, if needed, to make a smooth sauce, the consistency of cream. Stir in the remaining ingredients, stirring to dissolve sugar. Refrigerate 5–6 days.

SICHUAN PEPPERCORN: (*Xanthoxylum piperitum*) This is not actually a peppercorn, but the aromatic, small, red-brown seeds from the deciduous prickly ash tree known as *fagara*. It is an ancient spice in China, particularly in the central-western province of Sichuan—hence its popular name. The prickly ash pepper was known as *chiao*, and when black pepper was introduced into China it was given the name *hu chiao*. In Japan, dried prickly ash seeds are ground to a powder for use as a condiment, which is known as *sansho*. *Sansho* is mixed into several spice combinations, particularly *shichimi*. The delicate young leaf fronds from the prickly ash tree are used as a garnish in Japan, where they are known as *kinome*. They have a peppery, lemon-like flavor and pleasing aroma and when used in a dish, or as a condiment, impart a subtle flavor without the pungence of peppercorns.

The whole peppercorns can be kept for several years without loss of flavor if stored in a tightly sealed jar away from light, heat and moisture, but they quickly lose aroma and flavor when ground. Mixed into fine salt, which has been heated, they become pepper-salt, a fragrant, salty dip served in China with grilled and fried foods, and used in marinades.

Also known as *faa jiu, hu chiao* (China); *sansho* (Japan); *timur* (Nepal); brown peppercorns; Chinese aromatic pepper; xanthoxylum

See also: JAPAN, GARNISHES (KINOME); PEPPER-SALT (recipe); SHICHIMI; SICHUAN HOT RED SAUCE (recipe)

SICHUAN PICKLED MUSTARD CABBAGE: see CABBAGE, PICKLED

SIEN TS'AI: (*HIAN CHOY*, China) see CABBAGE, CHINESE (SEEN CHOY)

Fresh Sichuan peppercorns (Japanese sansho) with leaves (kinome)

PEPPER-SALT
Yields ¼ cup (2 oz / 60 g)

1½ tbsps Sichuan peppercorns
4 tbsps (¼ cup) table salt

Heat peppercorns in a dry pan over medium heat for 3 minutes, shaking pan gently to color them evenly. Grind to a fine powder in spice grinder. Return to pan, add salt and heat together, stirring and turning with spatula, until fragrant and well mixed. Cool and pour into a spice jar. Keeps for several months.

SIEW MAI
Yields 36

12 oz (350 g) ground lean pork
8 oz (250 g) shelled small shrimp (prawns)
¼ cup (2 oz / 60 g) chopped water chestnuts
4 dried black mushrooms, soaked and chopped
2 tbsps minced scallions
(spring / green onions)
½ tsp minced fresh ginger
½ tsp salt
¾ tsp sugar
1 tbsp soy sauce
36 wonton wrappers
1 tbsp finely chopped carrot

Place ingredients, except wrappers and carrot, in a food processor; grind to a paste. Cut corners from wrappers to make rounded shapes. Curl the forefinger of left hand to meet the thumb. Place wrapper over fingers, add a large tsp filling, press down between finger and thumb, forcing wrapper up sides of the filling in a cup shape (the top of the filling will remain exposed). Flatten base, sprinkle chopped carrot over filling. Place dumplings in an oiled steamer basket. Place on a rack in the steamer. Cover and steam for 12 minutes.

SILGOCHU: (*SIL-GO-CHOO*, Korea) Fine threads of dried red chili which in many Korean dishes are used instead of chili powder or fresh chili, either of which can be used as a substitute.
See also: GOCHUJANG; SHINSULRO HOTPOT (recipe)

SILING LABYO: (*SI-LING LA-BUH-YO*, Philippines) see CHILI, GROUND ROASTED

SILK BEAN CURD: see BEAN CURD (SILK)

SILVER BEAN SPROUT: see BEAN SPROUT

SILVER CARP: see CARP

SILVER FUNGUS: see WHITE FUNGUS

SILVER LEAF: see VARAQ

SILVER PIN NOODLES: see WHEAT STARCH DOUGH (recipe); NOODLES; FLOURS AND THICKENERS (WHEAT STARCH)

SILVER SPROUT: see BEAN SPROUT

SINAENG: (*SEE-NA-ING*, Philippines) see FISH, PRESERVED (FERMENTED)

SINGAPORE: Singapore is the island republic lying off the southern tip of Peninsular Malaysia and, with an area of about 260 square miles (675 sq km), is the smallest of the Asian countries. Its multiracial, multicultural population has wrought interesting effects upon its cuisine, mixing Chinese, Malay and Indian ingredients, cooking methods and preparation techniques.

The Chinese food in Singapore is typical of the southern Cantonese and Hokkien style, with bland flavors, thin clear sauces and much use of chicken, seafood and vegetables. But the addition of chilies, shrimp paste and tamarind gives it a local touch.

Malay cooking relates closely to the food of its near neighbor, Indonesia, with hot curried dishes, satays and coconut-flavored rice; while the Indian influence is evident in hot, aromatic spiced curries of the southern Indian Tamil style, tasty snacks such as curry puffs and *murtabah*—a kind of gigantic pancake filled with curried meat and onions.

Of course there are also local specialties. The most notable is undoubtedly Singapore Chili Crab—chunks of succulent crab tossed in a wok with chilies and ginger. It is a hands-on

feast not to be missed on a visit to the city. Also essential is a sample of Nonya cooking, a unique cuisine that has resulted from the intermarriage of Chinese settlers and local Malays. While resident Chinese enjoy their meals in the traditional manner, with chopsticks and bowl, a typical Malay meal, consisting of rice, several curries and a hot *sambal*, may be eaten with the fingers from makeshift plates made from cut pieces of banana leaf.

A bonus in this city-state, where so many religions are practised and cultural events celebrated, are the many festive meals that feature the finest dishes from a very diverse cuisine.
See also: NONYA CUISINE

SINGAPORE RECIPES

Appetizers
Fish Ball Soup

Main Courses
Chili Crab
Crabmeat and Bamboo Shoot Omelette
Crisp-fried Chicken
Singapore Steamboat

Accompaniments
Fried Noodles with Meat and Vegetables
Fried Rice
Mee Siam

Dessert
Fresh Fruit

MENU
(see recipes)

DINNER MENU
Serves 8

Fish Ball Soup

Chili Crab
Crisp Fried Chicken
Fried Noodles with Meat and Vegetables
Rice

Fresh Fruit

Singapore steamboat arrangement

SINGAPORE STEAMBOAT
Serves 8

1 lb (500 g) ground lean pork
2 tbsps minced bamboo shoots
2 tsps minced scallions (spring / green onions)
1³/4 tsps salt
1/2 tsp pepper
6 oz (180 g) beef tenderloin (fillet steak)
6 oz (180 g) boneless, skinless chicken breasts
6 oz (180 g) white fish fillet
2 tsps ginger juice
10 cups (2¹/2 qts / 2.5 l) chicken broth
10 slices fresh ginger
12 oz (350 g) cleaned squid, sliced
6 large shelled raw shrimp (prawns)
3–4 cups (1¹/2 –2 lbs / 750 g–1 kg) shredded
Napa *cabbage*
soy sauce
chili soy sauce
soy chili dip
eggs, beaten
scallions (spring / green onions), chopped

Grind pork to a smooth paste. Add bamboo shoots, minced scallions, ³/4 tsp salt and ¹/4 tsp pepper. With oiled hands, form into small balls. Thinly slice beef and chicken. Grind fish to a paste and season with ginger juice, 1 tsp

(cont'd)

(Singapore Steamboat cont'd)

salt and ¹/4 tsp pepper. Form into small balls. Arrange meat and seafood on serving platter. Bring broth to a boil in a steamboat on the tabletop. Add ginger. Cook meatballs, squid, shrimp and cabbage to taste by suspending in the steamboat, and dip into sauces before eating. Beaten raw egg can be served as a separate dip. Serve broth at the end, flavored with chopped scallions and soy sauce.

SINGHARA: (*SIN-GAA-RHAA*, India) see WATER CALTROP

SINIGANG: (*SEE-NEE-GANG*, Philippines) A soup-like meat or fish dish with vegetables, cooked in a tart liquid made sour with fruits such as the Philippine *santol*, green or ripe guavas, tamarind and young tamarind flowers, *belimbing* and *kalamansi*.
See also: BELIMBING; KALAMANSI

SINIGANG
Serves 8

1¹/2 lbs (750 g) braising beef
8 oz (250 g) lean pork
2 tbsps tamarind pulp
2 kalamansi *limes, or lemons*
2 medium unripe tomatoes
6 cups (1¹/2 qts / 1.5 l) rice washings
2 cups (1 lb / 500 g) shredded cabbage
2 tbsps fish sauce or light soy sauce
black pepper and salt

Cut the beef and pork into 1 in (2.5 cm) cubes. Place the tamarind, *kalamansi* limes or lemons with the tomatoes and the rice washings (water used to rinse uncooked rice) in a large nonaluminum pan and bring to a boil. Simmer for 10 minutes, stirring to dissolve the tamarind. Strain out the tamarind seeds. Add the meat, cover and simmer for about 1¹/4 hours, until tender. Add the cabbage, soy or fish sauce, pepper and salt to taste and simmer again briefly. Remove citrus pieces.

SIRACHA: (*SRI-RA-CHAA*, Thailand) see CHILI PASTES, POWDERS AND SAUCES

SIRSAK: (*SEAR-SUCK*, Malaysia) see SOURSOP

SITSARON: (*SIT-SA-RON*, Philippines) A crisp, dry snack made from pork skin, and also from the large and small intestines of pigs. Another kind of *sitsaron* has a little fat and meat.
Also known as *chitcharon*
See also: NOODLES FILIPINO (recipe)

SITSARON

large pork cuts
water
lard

Remove pork skin from pork cuts. Boil pork skin until soft, drain and cut into small squares or fine strips. Place in a dish, cover with lard and refrigerate for 1 week. Drain and drip on a rack for 3–4 hours. Deep-fry in hot lard until crisp.

SKEWERED LAMB: (recipe) see LAMB

SLAB SUGAR: see SUGAR

SLAKED LIME: see LIME SOLUTION

SNAKE BEAN: see LONG BEAN

SNAKE GOURD: see MELONS AND GOURDS

SNAKESKIN FRUIT: see SALAK

SNOWED BLACK BEAN CURD: see NOODLES (SHIRATAKE)

SNOW FUNGUS: see WHITE FUNGUS

SNOW PEA: (*Pisum sativum*, var. *macrocarpum*) Although snow peas seem typically Chinese in Western countries, they are in fact little used in Asia. The Chinese prefer the many other types of beans and peas they grow. Why they are called snow peas is hard to say because they do not appear to relish life in sub-zero temperatures. Another name, sugar peas, is more accurately descriptive because these tender pods are as sweet as sugar when young, which is when they should be eaten. Their Cantonese name is a corruption of Holland (*hoh laan*), and this may explain their origins.

They look similar to green garden peas, except that they are flatter. Snow peas develop a large, fleshy shell long before their peas develop. When they are fully developed, it is necessary to remove the string that runs along the top before cooking. Otherwise they are eaten as they are—either raw, steamed or quickly stir-fried. Long cooking does nothing for this delicate vegetable.

In India, a similar flat bean known as *papdi* is enjoyed.
Also known as *hoh laan dau* (China); *papdi* (India); *saya endo* (Japan); *sitsaro* (Philippines); Chinese pea; mangetout; sugar peas

SOBA: (*SO-BAH*, Japan) see NOODLES (SOBA)

SOCK MAI JAI: (*SUK MAI JAI*, China) see CORN

SOMEN: (*SOW-MEN*, Japan) see NOODLES (WHEAT)

SOM KHAY: (*SOM KAY*, Laos) A delicacy in Laos, this dish is made from the creamy, gray-pink roe of the *pa boeuk*, a fish caught in the Mekong River.
See also: TREY REACH

SOM SAA: (*SOM SAA*, Thailand) see CITRON

SONF: (*SONF*, India) see ANISEED

SONGAYA: (*SANG-KHA-YAA*, Thailand) A traditional Thai dessert consisting of egg custard baked inside the shell of a young coconut.

SONGAYA
Serves 4

1 cup (8 oz / 250 g) palm sugar (or substitute brown sugar)
¼ cup (2 fl oz / 60 ml) jasmine or orange flower water
1½ cups (12 fl oz / 375 ml) thick coconut milk
4 eggs, beaten
4 green young coconuts or small turban squash

Dissolve sugar in jasmine or orange flower water, then stir into the coconut milk. Add eggs. Cut tops off the coconuts or squash. Clean, rinse and drain. Strain custard into coconuts or squash. Set each in a small dish and steam until well cooked, about 25 minutes.

SONTH: (*SOUNTH*, India) see GINGER (DRIED)

SOO HOON: (*SOO HOON*, Malaysia) see NOODLES (BEAN THREAD VERMICELLI)

SOOJO: (*SOO-GEE*, Malaysia, India) see SEMOLINA

SORAMAME: (*SAW-RAH-MAH-ME*, Japan) see BROAD BEAN

SOS CIHI: (*SOS CHEE-HE*, Malaysia) see CHILI PASTES, POWDERS AND SAUCES

SOS PRIK: (*SOS PRIK*, Thailand) see CHILI PASTES, POWDERS AND SAUCES

SOTANGHON: (*SAW-TON-HUN*, Philippines) see NOODLES (BEAN THREAD VERMICELLI)

SOTONG KARANG: (*SAW-TONG KAH-RUNG*, Malaysia) see CUTTLEFISH

SOUR FINGER CARAMBOLA: see BELIMBING; STAR FRUIT

SOURSOP: (*Annona mircicata*) A small tree cultivated for its large ellipsoid or irregularly ovoid green fruits, that have soft spines on the skin. The fruit, which can weigh up to 3 lbs (1.5 kgs) is eaten fresh and has a creamy, sweet flavor similar to that of *durian* and its relative, the custard apple. The flesh separates into segments containing large black seeds. These should not be eaten as they contain a toxic substance. Soursop juice is a popular beverage throughout Southeast Asia and is available canned or bottled. This fruit does not travel well and is rarely available fresh in areas where it is not grown. Canned segments can be used in desserts or for ice cream-making.
Also known as *durian belanda*, *guanabana*; *nangka blanda*, *nangka sabrang* (Indonesia); *sirsak* (Malaysia); *guanbano* (Philippines); prickly custard apple
See also: DURIAN

SOUTHERNWOOD: The fibrous root of a perennial plant that grows wild in central Asia. It is used medicinally for many types of ailments. It has a pleasant taste and agreeable aroma and is used in Cambodia and Laos as a herb.
See also: MEDICINAL FOODS

SOW CABBAGE: see CABBAGE, CHINESE (JIU LE CHOY)

SOYBEAN: (*Glycine max*) An annual of the Leguminosae family, the small, bushy soybean plant bears clusters of hairy seed pods attached directly to the stem, each containing 2–3 seeds which may be green, yellow or black. The plant is native to China and has been used extensively in Chinese cuisine since recorded history began more than 4000 years ago. It is referred to in old Chinese documents as one of the "five ancient grains." Its high protein content—greater than that of red meat—has made it one of the most valuable foods in the world today, its versatility is legendary. The fresh and dried beans are eaten as a vegetable. It is boiled, puréed, diluted, sweetened and strained to make a drink which has become a worldwide substitute for milk. Liquefied with water, it is jelled to make bean curd, one of the world's most nutritious, nonanimal protein sources. Bean curd is further processed to make edible food wrappers for both vegetarian and non-vegetarian snacks. Processed soybeans are a prime source of TVP (textured vegetable protein), a meat substitute. The beans are sprouted to make soybean sprouts, fermented to make *tempe*, are salted and fermented to make a number of seasonings, including the classic soy sauce. It is pickled to make a pungent cheese and the oil extracted for cooking and other uses.

BLACK SOYBEANS are slightly smaller than the yellow variety. They are native to China, but are now grown in Japan and Korea. The dried seeds are oval in shape, with a smooth shiny black skin that may have a dusty appearance. They should be rinsed and are cooked by boiling in lightly salted water. They are usually served as a salad. In Japan the mashed beans are made into *natto*, which is used as a salad dressing. Sweetened puréed black soybeans are used as a filling for buns and pastries.

FRESH SOYBEANS are eaten in rural Asia, and are enjoyed as a vegetable in Japan and China. The whole, young pods are boiled and served with a dressing.

YELLOW SOYBEANS, dried yellow beans, are smooth, hard and of a rounded-oval shape that expands to a larger, distinctly oval shape when boiled. They are not eaten extensively in this form, the flavor being less appealing than that of other available beans, but they may be roasted and salted to be served as a snack. More commonly they are made into the many forms of bean curd used throughout Asia. As they are hard, they need to be soaked for several hours before being cooked for at least 3 hours. Pressure-cooking shortens cooking time to about 10 minutes. They are sold in cans, packed in lightly salted water, and should be rinsed before use.

Also known as *quingdou* (fresh) (China); *kacang kedele* (Indonesia); *daizu* (dried) *edamame* (fresh), *yuba* (soybean milk skin) (Japan); *bhatmas* (Nepal); *utaw* (Philippines)
See also: BEAN CURD; BEAN CURD BY-PRODUCTS; OILS AND FATS; SOYBEAN MILK

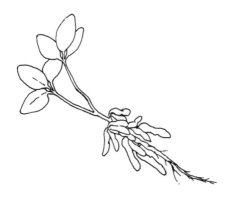

Soybean plant with pods

SOYBEAN CHEESE: see BEAN CURD BY-PROD-UCTS (FERMENTED)

SOYBEAN CONDIMENT: see BEAN PASTES AND SAUCES

SOYBEAN MILK: This milky beverage, made from yellow soybeans, replaces cow's milk in the diet of many Asians. The beans are soaked for about 10 hours, puréed with twice the quantity of boiling water, then strained and squeezed to extract the milky liquid. It is brought to a boil and simmered for 7 to 8 minutes, then sweetened to taste. Soybean milk, being highly nutritious, bacteria-free and easily digestible, is suitable for invalid and infant diets.

Also known as *tau cheing, tau ni* (China)
See also: SOYBEAN

SOYBEAN MILK
Yields 20 cups

1 lb (500 g) dried yellow soybeans
3 cups (24 fl oz / 750 ml) sugar
(or to taste)
water

Rinse soybeans thoroughly, then place in a large pan and add 6 cups (1½ qts/1.5 l) water. Soak for 8 hours in warm conditions, and about 12 hours in cold weather. The beans will expand to at least twice their original size. Drain, add 10 cups (2½ qts/2.5 l) water and grind in a food processor or blender until smooth, about 10 minutes. Line a colander with fine clean cheesecloth, place over a pan and pour in the liquid. Add another 10–12 cups (2½ –3 qts/2.5–3 l) cold water and allow to drip through. Squeeze cloth and discard dry pulp. Bring the liquid to a boil, reduce heat and stir in sugar. Simmer for 10 minutes, then strain into sterilized containers. Cool and refrigerate for up to 1 week.

SOYBEAN NOODLE: see NOODLES (BEAN CURD)

SOYBEAN OIL: see FATS AND OILS

SOYBEAN PASTE: see BEAN PASTES AND SAUCES

SOYBEAN SPROUT: see BEAN SPROUT

SOY FLOUR: see FLOURS AND THICKENERS

SOY SAUCE: An ancient seasoning, first used in China more than 3000 years ago. Known in its original form as *shih*, it was a thin salty liquid in which floated fragments of fermented soybeans. Its use has been documented throughout Chinese history and the process by which it is made has differed little over the years. It comes to our kitchens now in a more refined form, being strained to remove all traces of bean solids. Soy sauce is made from fermented soybeans mixed with a roasted grain—usually wheat, but sometimes barley or rice. It is injected with a yeast mold, *Aspergillus oryzae.* After the ferment begins it is salted and a *lactobacillus* starter and yeast are added for further fermentation. It is left in vats for many months, then filtered. The Japanese adopted the idea only about four centuries after it was first used in China. They experimented with their own techniques, and arrived at a product that was slightly sweeter and more refined than the Chinese types.

Soy sauce is to Chinese and Japanese cooking what the pungent, salty fish sauce known as *nam pla* or *nuoc mam* is to Thailand and Vietnam respectively. It imparts a slight saltiness and adds depth to the flavor of a dish without masking the essential flavors of the main ingredients. Chinese and Japanese soy sauces come in two main types, with several other variations now being manufactured. Soy sauce is now manufactured throughout Southeast Asia. Countries like Indonesia and Malaysia may differentiate between their own light and dark versions of soy sauce and the true Chinese soy sauce.

There is yet another important form of soy sauce manufacture—that of the thick, dark sweet and salty sauces used in Indonesian, Malaysian and Nonya cooking, and in south-coastal China. Synthetically or chemically hydrolized soy sauces are now being manufactured. They are inexpensive, but tend to have a metallic taste.

See also: SOY SAUCE, SWEET AND SALTY

DARK SOY SAUCE is dark and slightly thick, with a full-bodied flavor. It is used when a deep color is needed. Generally dark soy has less salt than the lighter types. The Chinese mushroom soy has an excellent flavor from the addition of mushroom flavorings taken from Chinese straw mushrooms. The Japanese *tamari* is a similarly made, thick, dark sauce with an intense soy flavor and aroma.
Also known as *jang yau see yau* (China); *koi-kuchi shoyu, tamari* (Japan); *kecap pekat* (Malaysia); mushroom soy

LIGHT SOY SAUCE is thinner, saltier and lighter in flavor. It is used as a condiment and in cooking where its light color will not spoil the colors of the ingredients, particularly seafoods. Like dark soy, it can be kept for many months without refrigeration.
Also known as *sang chau, see yau* (China); *shoyu, usu-kuchi shoyu* (Japan); *kecap cair* (Malaysia); *toyo* (Philippines); *nam siew* (Thailand); *xi dau* (Vietnam); thin soy sauce

LU SOY (China) is a "master sauce" based on soy sauce with sugar, ginger and five-spice. It is used for simmering poultry and other meats to give a rich flavor and to color the food a deep brown.
Also known as *lu shui* (China)

SOY CHILI DIP

To accompany steamed or poached fresh shrimp (prawns) or crab

3 tbsps light soy sauce
1 tbsp vegetable oil
1 green chili, sliced

Mix soy sauce and oil in a small dish. Seed chili if a milder taste is preferred. Stir chili into the sauce and serve in small dishes.

SOY SAUCE, SWEET AND SALTY:

KECAP ASIN (Indonesia) is a thick, salty, dark soy-based sauce used in Indonesian cooking to impart a strong color and flavor. Its sweet counterpart is *kecap manis.* It is similar to, but thicker than, several dark soy sauces used in Chinese cooking.

KECAP HITAM (Malaysia) is a sweet, dark soy sauce used in Malaysia. It is used in the same way as *kecap manis* is Indonesia. The flavor may be slightly less spicy.
Also known as *kicup kitam*

KECAP MANIS (Indonesia) is a dark, thick, aromatic sweet sauce used in Indonesia as a seasoning and condiment, particularly with *satay.* It is similar to, although finer in flavor than, Chinese sweet soy sauce.
Also known as *kecap bentang manis* (Indonesia); sweet soy sauce

SWEET SOY SAUCE (China) is a dark, sweet sauce combining soy sauce, sugar and malt sugar. Its distinctive malt-like taste goes well as a dip for fried snacks, poultry and seafood. Sweet soy sauce appears frequently on the table in homes and restaurants in the Fukien province on east-coastal China.

See also: CRABMEAT BALLS IN SWEETENED SOY SAUCE (recipe); MALTOSE; TARO-COATED CRISPY DUCK (recipe)

TIM CHEONG (Malaysia) is a thick, sweet, black soy sauce, similar to that used in China. In Malaysia it accompanies *poh pia*. It differs in flavor from the sweet Indonesian sauce known as *kecap manis*, being more akin to *kecap hitam*. It must not be mistaken for another sauce, also known as *timcheong*, which is red in color and made from preserved fruit, usually sour plums, and known commonly as "Chinese plum sauce."

SOY VERMICELLI: see NOODLES (BEAN CURD)
SPICED GROUND RICE: (recipe) see RICE
SPICED RED LENTILS: (recipe) see LENTIL
SPICED WHITEBAIT: (recipe) see FISH

NA MOOL OF SPINACH
Serves 4–6

1 lb (500 g) fresh young spinach
salt
2 tbsps shredded scallions (spring/green onions)
2 tsps minced garlic
2 tbsps Oriental sesame oil
1/2 –1 1/2 tsps chili flakes
1 tbsp ground toasted white sesame seeds or pine nuts

Rinse spinach and separate leaves. Place in a small pan, cover and steam gently for 4 minutes. Squeeze out excess liquid. Sprinkle on salt to taste. Lightly sauté scallions and garlic in the sesame oil. Add chili flakes and sesame seeds or pine nuts. Cook briefly, then add the spinach and stir to mix. Serve warm or cool. Swiss chard (silverbeet) may be used as a substitute for spinach.

SPINACH: (*Spinacea oleracea*) Several different types of spinach and spinach-like vegetables are cultivated in Asia. In India and China *amaranth* has been grown for many centuries, and throughout Southeast Asia *kangkong* or water spinach is a popular vegetable. Both have a similar taste and appearance to spinach. In Japan, *horenzo*, with its delicate, small, spear shaped and relatively flat leaves, is the local variety of spinach. The stems are a pink-red color, the flavor mild and sweet. It is very similar to Chinese spinach, and a cabbage-like Chinese vegetable known as "red in snow"—a delicate vegetable that is used in both fresh and salted forms.

Also known as *palak* (India); *talim num* (Philippines)
See also: AMARANTH; KANGKONG

SPINACH PUREE
Serves 4

1 lb (500 g) fresh spinach, washed and shredded
1 turnip, peeled and shredded
1 cup (8 fl oz / 250 ml) water
1 tsp salt
1 1/2 tbsps ghee
1/2 cup (4 oz / 120 g) finely chopped onion
1 tsp minced ginger
1/2 tsp paprika or chili powder

Boil spinach and turnip in a covered pan with water and salt until tender. Remove from heat; mash. Heat ghee and sauté onion, ginger and paprika or chili powder for 2 minutes. Add the mashed vegetables and stir-fry until excess moisture evaporates. Swiss chard (silverbeet) may be used as a substitute for spinach.

SPINELESS AMARANTH: see AMARANTH
SPONGE GOURD: see LUFFA, ANGLED
SPRING BAMBOO SHOOT: see BAMBOO SHOOT
SPRING ONION: see ONION

SPRING ROLL: Crisply fried spring rolls, packed with finely shredded fillings of meat, mushrooms, bean sprouts and bamboo shoots, epitomize the taste of China to the Westerner. The fillings are many and varied according to taste. Wrappers also vary from thin egg-based crêpes and wafer-thin rice flour rounds to the commercially prepared frozen square wrappers that are now readily available and simple to use. Suitable accompaniments are light soy sauce, chili sauce and ketchup for dipping. Traditionally, these tasty treats were prepared as a spring festival snack and were filled with the freshest of bamboo shoots.

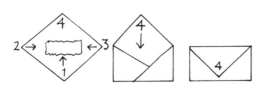

Wrapping spring rolls

SPRING ROLLS
Yields 12

12 x 8 in (20 cm) spring roll or egg roll
wrappers
2 dried black mushrooms, soaked
1½ tbsps vegetable oil
6 oz (180 g) lean pork or chicken, shredded
1 oz (30 g) pork fat, shredded
¼ cup (2 oz/60g) shredded bamboo shoots
1 cup (8 oz/250 g) chopped bean sprouts
2 scallions (spring/green onions), shredded
salt
white pepper
1½ tbsps light soy sauce
1 tsp sugar
2 tsps cornstarch (cornflour)
2 tbsps cold water
deep-frying oil
1 quantity Sweet and Sour Sauce recipe

Leave wrappers under a clean damp cloth until needed. Drain mushrooms and shred caps. Heat vegetable

(cont'd)

(Spring Rolls cont'd)

oil in a wok and stir-fry pork or chicken and pork fat for 1 minute. Then add the vegetables and stir-fry briefly. Add salt, pepper, soy sauce and sugar and stir together for 30 seconds over high heat. Mix cornstarch with cold water, pour in and stir briefly. Then spread on a plate to cool. Wrap spring rolls, moistening edge with water to adhere. Deep-fry until crisp and golden. Drain and serve with Sweet and Sour Sauce.

SPRING ROLL SKIN NEST: Chinese stir-fried dishes can be attractively served in crisp baskets made from spring roll wrappers.

Dip a Chinese "nest" frying basket into oil. Remove and line lower basket with one or two sheets of spring roll wrapper. Cover with upper basket and lower into hot oil. Fry until crisp and golden. Drain and carefully transfer to serving plate. Use immediately.

SPRING ROLL SKINS/WRAPPERS
Yields about 50

6 cups (1½ lbs/1.5 kgs) all-purpose (plain)
flour
1½ tsps salt
3 cups (24 fl oz/750 ml) water

Sift flour and salt into a mixing bowl. Gradually work in water to make a soft and sticky dough. Smooth top and cover with a thin layer of cold water to prevent surface drying. Set aside for 1 hour. Rub a flat iron griddle with an oiled cloth, then polish with dry cloth. Use medium heat to prepare griddle. Knead dough 3 minutes, working dough from outside to center. Mark a 6 in (15 cm) circle in center of griddle with an oiled cloth. Rub a handful of dough across hot surface so a thin layer adheres to pan. Cook on one side, removing when edges curl. Cool, stack and wrap to refrigerate or freeze.

SPROUTED LENTIL: see BEAN SPROUT; LENTIL

SPROUTS, MUNG BEAN: see BEAN SPROUT; LENTIL

SPROUTS, SOYBEAN: see BEAN SPROUT; SOYBEAN

SQUAB: see PIGEON

SQUID: (*Loligo edulis* Hoyle) This cephalopod from the family Loliginidae has a boneless, tubular, white-fleshed body and a head with eight short and two long tentacles. It has a transparent internal backbone or "quill." Most squid caught for food measure no more than about 10 in (25 cm) long; they are most tender when they are only about 2 in (5 cm) long. Squid can grow up to an impressive 60 ft (18 m) in overall length, at which stage they would probably still be edible because squid, even when smaller and more tender, is a meat known for its firm texture.

The Chinese name *chin sui yau yu* translates as "shallow water soft fish," which quite explicitly describes this boneless, shallow-water inhabitant. Squid is bland-flavored meat that is enjoyed more for its texture (and its low price) than for its taste. It is cooked in most parts of Asia. The Chinese and Japanese use a crosshatch scoring technique to tenderize and decorate squid. This causes it to roll up when cooked into attractive little spiky shapes, like miniature pine cones.

It is excellent in stir-fried dishes and curries. Stuffed squid features on menus in Korea, the Philippines and in most of the Indo-Chinese countries. Fresh squid is readily available but does not keep well. It must be cleaned by removing the "bone," eyes, "beak," ink sac and skin, and the body tube and tentacles should be thoroughly washed. It can be kept for no more than two days in the refrigerator.

DRIED SQUID is made in most countries where squid is fished. In Chinese cuisine it is used as an ingredient in soups and stewed dishes, but is more popular as a chewy snack which has become known as "Chinese chewing gum." The dried squid is rolled between spike rollers to flatten and tenderize it, then it is quickly roasted over charcoal to give a pungent, toast-like, taste. Strips of roasted squid are sold outside movie houses in Hong Kong for patrons to munch during the show.

Before cooking, dried squid must be soaked for up to 24 hours and the purple membrane removed.

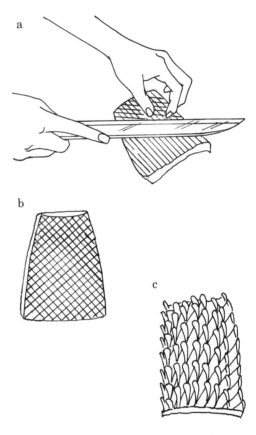

a. *Open squid and lie flat, score closely in one direction*
b. *Score in opposite direction*
c. *Cooked squid curls standing up*

Also known as *ba-wel* (Burma); *muk bampound* (Cambodia); *hin sui, tor yau yu, yau yu* (China); *cumi-cumi, sotong* (Indonesia); *ika* (Japan); *sotong* (Malaysia); *pusit calmar* (Philippines); *muk kluay* (Thailand)
See also: CUTTLEFISH; SQUID IN MILD CURRY SAUCE (recipe)

SQUID IN MILD CURRY SAUCE
Serves 4–6

1¼ lbs (600 g) squid, cleaned and rinsed
½ cup (2 oz / 60 g) chopped onion
1½ tsps minced garlic
8 dried chilies, soaked and seeded
2 tbsps ground coriander
2½ tsps ground cumin
½ cup (1½ oz / 45 g) desiccated coconut
⅓ tsp turmeric
1 tsp shrimp paste
3 tbsps coconut or peanut oil
6 slices fresh young ginger
1 stalk lemon grass, halved lengthways
3 lime leaves
2 cups (8 fl oz / 500 ml) thick coconut milk
salt and pepper

Cut squid into squares and score (see illustration on previous page). Grind onion, garlic and chilies to a paste, adding spices, coconut, turmeric and shrimp paste. Heat coconut or peanut oil in a pan and fry the seasoning paste for 3 minutes. Add ginger, lemon grass, lime leaves and coconut milk. Bring almost to a boil, then stir over low heat for 3–4 minutes. Add squid, salt and pepper and simmer just 5 minutes.

SQUID SAMBAL

8 oz (250 g) fresh squid, cleaned and rinsed
5 dried chilies, soaked
½ cup (4 oz / 120 g) chopped onion
1 tsp minced garlic
½ tsp shrimp paste
½ tsp salt
3 tbsps vegetable oil
¼ cup (2 fl oz / 60 ml) tamarind water
12–20 red bird's-eye chilies
2–3 tsps palm sugar (or substitute brown sugar)

Remove squid tentacles and chop finely. Cut squid bodies into rings. Grind chilies, onion, garlic, shrimp paste and salt into a paste. Heat oil and fry blended mixture over medium heat, stirring constantly until color changes to a dark red. Add squid, tamarind water, bird's-eye chilies and sugar, and sauté 4–5 minutes.

"SQUIRREL-CUT" FISH IN SWEET AND SOUR SAUCE: (recipe) see FISH, SQUIRREL-CUT

SRI LANKA: The "resplendent isle" has a cuisine as exotic and multifaceted as her history which has seen, over six or seven centuries, the arrival and departure of Indians, Dutch, Malays, Portuguese and English. Each nationality has left its imprint on the cooking of this tropical island.

Kari is the axis of the Sri Lankan foods, and her curries, as in the southern Indian tradition, are invariably intensely hot. "Red" curries, as the name implies, are brightly stained from dried chilies—as many as 40 in a single dish is not unheard of. "White" curries are less intense in their seasoning and made creamy with coconut milk. Most typical however, are glorious brown-tinged curries which use the toasted, aromatic Sri Lankan style of *masala* spices. The whole spices are roasted until black before being ground to achieve this particularly concentrated flavor.

Rice is served with most meals, but there are several types of bread that are important to the diet of the Sri Lankans. *Roti* is an unleavened flat bread made from wheat flour, but with a nutty taste imparted by grated coconut. *Appas* are wafer-thin crêpes made from a naturally fermented rice dough. Cooked in a *cheena chatti*, which resembles a tiny Chinese wok, they curl at the edges, making a natural bowl shape into which an egg may be broken for a tasty breakfast dish. Steamed tube-shaped *pittu*, made from coconut and flour, are also enjoyed with a meal; the bland taste, with its subtle hint of coconut, contrasts perfectly with the pronounced curry flavors.

From the Dutch came wondrous, rich yeasty cakes in the *breudher* style, and the tiny *frikkadel* meatballs, which have been integrated into *lampries*—named from the Dutch word *lomprijst*. The festive dish is of heroic proportions; it combines several curries, hot *sambolas*, rice cooked with ghee and a spoonful of thick coconut milk wrapped in oven-baked banana leaf parcels. Spicy *sam-bolas* are an intrinsic part of the meal; a housewife would be considered negligent if she did not offer at least one freshly made spicy little side dish with a typical meal of rice, bread, several curries, a soup and a vegetable dish.

SRI LANKA RECIPES

Appetizers
Frikkadels

Main Courses
Cashew Curry
Chicken Curry

Accompaniments
Appa / Bittara Appa
Coconut-coated Vegetables
Sri Lankan-style Flat Breads

Dessert
Coconut Pudding

MENU
(see recipes)

DINNER MENU
Serves 6–8

Frikkadels

Cashew Curry
Coconut-coated Vegetables
Rice
Sri Lankan-style Flat Breads

Coconut Pudding

SRI LANKAN CURRY POWDER: see CURRY PASTES, POWDERS AND SAUCES

STAR ANISE: see ANISE, STAR

STAR FRUIT: (*Averrhoa carambola*) A sweet, yellow fruit native to India. About 5 in (12 cm) in length, it has a thin, waxy skin and its body comprises five deep lateral ridges so that, when cut in cross section, it gives the star-shaped slices that have earned it the popular name "star fruit." It grows throughout Southeast Asia and is used as a fruit, making an attractive addition to fruit salads. Its texture is crisp and the juice is sweet-tart. The sliced fruit may be candied and eaten as a confection. The unripe fruit is bright green with a firm, crisp texture and tart taste, and is sometimes added to dishes that require an acid taste. Its close relative, the *belimbing*, is also used in this way.

Also known as *belimbing*, *belimbing manis* (Indonesia); *balimbing* (Philippines); *ma dun* (Thailand); star fruit

See also: BELIMBING

Star fruit

STEAMBOAT: Tabletop cooking is a popular communal activity in most parts of Asia. Elaborate "steamboats"—known as *ta pin* in Singapore, *yuek shih huo kwo* in Canton, and *chnang phleung* in Cambodia—are used to cook meat, seafood, noodles and vegetables at the table. In Mongolia and Korea a similar dish is known more commonly as a "hotpot." The pan is a circular "moat" around a chimney; it is heated over a charcoal fire. The moat is filled with hot broth and the ingredients are held by means of chopsticks or wire mesh baskets to be cooked in the liquid. They are dipped into sauces, and sometimes raw egg, before eating. Noodles and vegetables are served with the broth as a soup.

See also: SHINSULRO HOTPOT (recipe); SINGA-PORE STEAMBOAT (recipe); UTENSILS (HOT-PLATES AND GRIDDLES)

STEAMED FISH IN BANANA LEAF CUPS: (recipe) see FISH

STEAMED STICKY RICE IN COCONUT MILK: (recipe) see RICE

STEAMED SHRIMP: (recipe) see SHRIMP

STEAMED WHOLE GAROUPA WITH SCAL-LIONS: (recipe) see FISH

STINK BEAN: see PARKIA

STIR-FRIED CELLOPHANE NOODLES: (recipe) see NOODLES

STRAW MUSHROOM: see MUSHROOMS AND EDIBLE FUNGI

STRING HOPPERS: see APPA

STURGEON SKIN: see SHARK'S SKIN

SU: (*SUE*, Japan) see RICE VINEGAR

SUA: (*SU-AA*, India) see DILL

SUA BHATI: (*SU-AA BHAA-TEE*, India) see DILL

SU-AGE: (*SUE-AH-GUE*, Japan) see JAPAN, COOKING METHODS

SUAN: (*SU-EN*, China) see CHINA, COOKING METHODS (BOILING)

SUB GUM GEUNG: (*SUP GUM GEUNG*, China) see GINGER (GINGER PRESERVE)

SUCKLING PIG: see PORK

SUDURU: (*SUU-DU-RU*, Sri Lanka) see CUMIN (WHITE)

SUDULUNU: (*SU-DU-LUU-NU*, Sri Lanka) see GARLIC

SUEN TAU: (*SU-EN TAU*, China) see GARLIC

SUGAR: There are three main sources of sugar in Asia. Sugar cane, sugar palms and coconut palms are all cultivated extensively for sweet sap that is made into a variety of different types of sugar.

Cane sugar is made into two main types of sugar for use in Chinese cooking.

BROWN SLAB SUGAR is layered, semi-refined sugar, compressed into flat slabs and cut into 6 in (15 cm) fingers. They are usually of two tones of brown and look like a type of caramel candy. Sold in small packs, they can also sometimes be bought in bulk from large crocks in Chinese markets. Slab sugar has the flavor of a good brown sugar and can be used in any recipe as a substitute for brown sugar.

Also known as *chandagar* (Burma); *bin tong, pin tong* (China); *chini* (India); *gula* (white) *gula merah* (brown) (Indonesia, Malaysia); *asukal* (Philippines); *nam tan, nam tan sai* (Thailand); *nuoc mau* (brown)(Vietnam); brown candy sugar; lump sugar; rock sugar; yellow rock

JAGGERY, named from the Hindi word *jagri*, is the dark semi-refined sugar used in Indian cooking. It is formed into blocks and has a crumbly texture. *Jaggery* is usually made from sugar cane but can be made from palm sugar as well. Because of its unrefined state, it contains iron and minerals and so is more beneficial to the diet than refined sugar. Its flavor, however, is strong and may overpower subtler ingredients. In recipes a full-flavored brown sugar can be substituted for *jaggery*.

Also known as *gur* (India)

PALM SUGAR is obtained from two sources: palmyra palms, and the sugar palm (*Arenga saccharifera, Arenga pinnata*) which grows wild throughout Malaysia and Indonesia. The immature male tree is beaten over a three-day period to stimulate the sap; a cutting is made in the trunk and a bamboo pipe inserted to allow the juice to flow. The sap is drained morning and evening over a four- to-six month period. The raw palm juice is enjoyed, like the juice of sugar cane, as a drink. If cooked for a short while, it forms threads that are also used in drinks.

To make sugar the sap is boiled in large kettles over an open fire until it becomes a dark thick syrup. It is poured into bamboo- or coconut-shell molds, where it dries into cakes. In some instances it is smoked, turning it dark brown, almost black, in color and giving it a very strong aroma and taste.

Palm sugar is a thick, crumbly, richly flavored brown-colored sugar. In Malaysia it is called *gula melaka*, and is named after the coastal state of Malacca (Melaka) where its manufacture is a prime industry. In Indonesia, it is named after the island of Java, being called *gula jawa*. Making palm sugar is a home industry in most *kampongs* (villages) in Indonesia. The palm sugar made in Vietnam is lighter in both color and flavor.

Palm sugar is sold in Asian food stores and will keep for many months if stored in dry conditions. Any full-flavored brown sugar can be substituted.

Also known as *tanyet* (Burma); *gur*, *jaggery* (India); *gula jawa* (Indonesia); *gula malacca*, *gula melaka* (Malaysia); *panitsa*, *panucha*, (Philippines); *nam tan peep* (Thailand) *duong cuc vang* (Vietnam); coconut sugar, Java sugar
See also: CARAMEL COLORING; PALM NUT

ROCK CANDY is semi-refined sugar, pale honey color and looks like lumps of discolored crystal. It is essential for the right quality of sauce in Chinese "red cooking" and helps to make sauces and glazes translucent. It is readily available from Chinese food stores and will keep indefinitely. It should be crushed before using, although it can be added in a lump to slow-cooked dishes. It is ideal for use in sugar syrup as it produces a clear syrup.

CARAMELIZED SUGAR
Yields ½ cup (4 oz / 120 g)

½ cup (4 oz / 120 g) sugar
¾ cup (6 fl oz / 180 ml) water
1 tsp lemon juice

Put the sugar and half the water into a dry frying pan over high heat. When the sugar starts to brown, stir constantly until it turns dark brown. Add remaining water and stir on high heat for 5 minutes. Add lemon juice. Cool and store.

SUGAR CANE SHRIMP BALLS
Serves 6

6 x 6 in (15 cm) pieces sugar cane
1¼ lbs (600 g) shelled shrimp (prawns)
1½ tbsps fish sauce
salt
white pepper
2 egg whites
(cont'd)

(Sugar Cane Shrimp Balls cont'd)
1–2 tbsps ice water
vegetable oil
2–3 tbsps minced scallions (spring / green onions)
nuoc cham

Use a strong sharp knife to peel the sugar cane. Purée shrimp in a food processor or blender with fish sauce, salt, white pepper and egg whites. Add ice water to increase the volume of the paste and improve its texture. Using wet hands, mold the shrimp paste around the center section of each cane stick, leaving the ends exposed. Brush lightly with vegetable oil and roll in the scallions. Grill until the shrimp ball feels firm. Serve hot with *nuoc cham*.

SUGAR PEA: see SNOW PEA
SUJU: (*SO-JU*, Korea) see WINES, ASIAN
SUJI: (*SOO-GEE*, India) see SEMOLINA
SUKA: (*SU-KA*, Philippines) see VINEGAR

SUKIYAKI
Serves 6

2 lbs (1 kg) beef sirloin (rump steak), well marbled
8 oz (250 g) shirataki *noodles*
2 cakes yakidofu (grilled bean curd)
12 small pieces fu (gluten)
6 scallions (spring / green onions), cut into 2 in (5 cm) lengths
12 small fresh shiitake *mushrooms*
12 stems mitsuba
2 oz (60 g) beef suet
½ cup (4 fl oz / 120 ml) sukiyaki *sauce*
1 egg, beaten

Cut beef into paper-thin slices and arrange in an overlapping design on a wide platter. Parboil *shirataki* noodles to soften. Drain. Cube bean curd. Soak gluten to soften. Drain. Arrange scallions, mushrooms and *mitsuba* on platter with beef. On the table heat a *sukiyaki* pan or electric skillet. Melt suet over medium heat; add *sukiyaki* sauce. Cook the ingredients gently, adding enough sauce to cover bottom of pan. Serve with beaten egg as a dip.

SUMAN: (*SU-MAN*, Philippines) A native delicacy made from glutinous rice—sometimes with coconut milk added and wrapped in young coconut or banana leaves and boiled. Some are brownish in color and have a particular gummy texture because they have been treated with lye. *Suman* is also made from cassava root, corn or arrowroot. It is usually served with grated coconut and sugar.

SUNFLOWER OIL: see OILS AND FATS

SUNOMONO: (*SUE-NO-MOW-NO*, Japan) The term translates as "vinegared foods" and encompasses a variety of salad-like dishes with a vinegar dressing. Seafood, chicken, vegetables and exotic ingredients such as seaweed are served in this way, usually in small quantities, as a highlight in the meal. There are many different classic dressings for *sunomono* dishes, chosen to complement the main ingredient of the salad. The base of the dressing is known as *sanbai-zu* or "three flavors" vinegar, or *nihai-zu* or "two flavors" vinegar. These are mixed with other ingredients such as egg yolk, ginger, sesame seeds and citron.
Also known as "vinegared foods"
See also: AEMONO; PONZU SAUCE

NIHAI-ZU
Yields 1 cup (8 fl oz / 250 ml)

1/3 cup (3 fl oz / 90 ml) rice vinegar
1 1/2 tbsps soy sauce
1/2 cup (4 fl oz / 125 ml) dashi

Mix together and refrigerate.

SANBAI-ZU
Yields 1 cup (8 fl oz / 250 ml)

1/3 cup (3 fl oz / 90 ml) rice vinegar
1 1/2 tbsps soy sauce
1/2 cup (4 fl oz / 125 ml) dashi
1 tbsp mirin

Mix in a small saucepan,
bring to a boil, remove from heat,
cool and refrigerate.

SUPERIOR BROTH
Yields 4–5 cups (1–1 1/4 qts / 1–1.25 l)

Use when cooking shark's fin and whenever a strong-flavored broth is required for Chinese recipes

1 quantity Chicken Stock recipe
1 pork knuckle (hock) or ham bone
2–3 sets duck or chicken giblets
1–2 whole chicken or duck thighs

Make the Chicken Stock, adding the extra ingredients; simmer very gently for at least 1 3/4 hours. Strain and cool; skim fat. Store in refrigerator and use within 5 days.

SUSHI: (*SUE-SHI*, Japan) *Sushi* came into existence by accident, when it was discovered that the vinegar-impregnated rice on which a type of salted carp was stored developed a delicious taste. From this beginning, it developed into one of the most popular food trends in Japan, with some specialist restaurants selling nothing but these delectable morsels of rice and topping, laced with a smear of fiery *wasabi*. *Sushi* are essentially little formed ovals or rolls made of rice that has been flavored with rice vinegar, sugar and salt. The toppings, or fillings, for *sushi* are varieties of seafood, usually raw; layered sweet omelette; and shredded vegetables such as cucumber and *kampyo* (gourd shavings). Many are surrounded by a wrapping of the thin, crisp, bright green *nori* seaweed. *Sushi* falls into several basic categories.

MAKI-ZUSHI is a type of rolled *sushi*, with toasted *nori* seaweed sheets as the wrapper. The seaweed is placed on the bamboo mat known as *maki-su* or *sudare* and covered with the vinegared rice. Then a line of shredded fillings is placed across the center and the rice, with its seaweed wrapper, is rolled to encase the filling. It is pressed into a roll, and cut across into pieces about 1 1/4 in (3 cm) long. This type of *sushi* was first made in a Japanese gambling house; the gamblers wanted a snack that did not stick to the fingers as "hand-rolled" *sushi* tended to do.
Also known as *nori-maki*

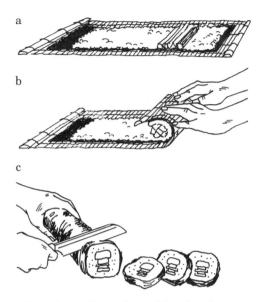

a. Ingredients for maki-zushi on bamboo mat
b. Forming the roll
c. Slicing the sushi

NIGIRI-ZUSHI is "hand-formed" *sushi* in which the rice is formed into an oval shape by being manipulated in the palm of the left hand. The first two fingers of the right hand do the shaping. This is the most common form of *sushi*—and usually the most expensive, although this depends on the type of toppings placed on the rice. The rice cake is smeared with a thin *wasabi* paste for extra flavor, then a thin sliver of raw fish or other toppings is pressed in place.

OSHI-ZUSHI is pressed into a wooden box mold, covered with topping, then unmolded and cut into squares. It is simple to do and is therefore less highly regarded than other forms of *sushi*.

There are a number of other types of dishes based on *sushi* rice. One is simply a plate of rice "scattered" with the type of toppings generally used on *sushi*—strips of raw fish, shredded *nori*, sesame seeds, sliced omelette, marinated broiled eel— and served, usually in an attractive lacquered box. This is known as *chirashi-zushi*, which translates as "scattered rice." *Fukasa-zushi* is the name for a fine silk scarf, and is *sushi* rice packed in a delicate crêpe;

and *inari-zushi* is *sushi* rice packed into a fried bean curd skin "pouch" made from *aburage*. A popular Americanized version of "hand-rolled" *sushi* is the California roll, in which a cone of *nori* is filled with *sushi* rice, slivers of crabmeat and fresh avocado. *Sushi* are dipped into soy sauce before eating. The vinegared rice is known as *sushi-meshi*.

See also: BEAN CURD; KAMPYO; SASHIMI; SEAWEED

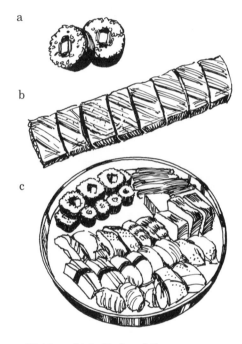

a. Maki-zushi (rolled sushi)
b. Oshi-zushi (pressed sushi)
c. Sushi moriawasi (mixed sushi platter)

NORI-MAKI SUSHI
Yields 12 pieces

4 cups (1 lb / 500 g) Sushi Meshi (vinegared rice)
6 dried shiitake mushrooms, soaked
2 cups (16 fl oz / 500 ml) dashi
¼ cup (2 fl oz / 60 ml) light soy sauce
3 tbsps sugar
1 tbsp mirin
2 oz (60 g) kampyo, soaked

(cont'd)

(Nori-maki Sushi cont'd)

¼ *cup (2 fl oz / 60 ml) dark soy sauce*
2 sheets nori *seaweed*
1 Japanese small cucumber, shredded
beni shoga *(vinegared sugar)*
wasabi
soy sauce

Prepare *Sushi Meshi*
(see recipe). Simmer mushrooms
in ½ cup (4 fl oz/ 125 ml) of the *dashi,*
the light soy sauce, 1 tbsp sugar and the
mirin for 10 minutes. Drain, remove
stems, shred caps. Soften the *kampyo* by
simmering in the remaining 1½ cups (12
fl oz/375 ml) *dashi,* the dark soy sauce
and the remaining 2 tbsps sugar for 20
minutes. Drain. Spread *nori,* shiny side
down, on a bamboo mat. Cover with rice,
pressing down firmly. Arrange mushrooms, *kampyo* and cucumber along
the center and roll rice and *nori* around
them. Squeeze gently. Remove bamboo mat and cut the rolls into 1½ in
(4 cm) pieces. Serve with a garnish
of *beni shoga* and dips of *wasabi*
mixed with soy sauce.

SUSHI
Serves 8–10

1 quantity Sushi Meshi *(vinegared rice) recipe*
*2 lbs (1 kg) assorted fresh seafood ***
1 quantity Omelette Roll recipe
1½ tbsps wasabi
water or sake
1 tbsp rice vinegar
2 cups (16 fl oz / 500 ml) water
beni shoga *(vinegared ginger)*
1 cup (8 fl oz / 250 ml) light soy sauce

Prepare *Sushi Meshi* (see recipe).
Prepare selected toppings and cut to fit
sushi rolls. Make *wasabi* into a paste with
water or sake. Mix vinegar with water;
use to wet hands. Pick up golfball-size
portions of rice and work into oval wads.
Spread with *wasabi.* Press on prepared
raw fish toppings, or slices of Omelette
Roll (see recipe). Arrange *sushi* on
a platter with *beni shoga.*
Serve soy sauce as a dip. *(cont'd)*

(Sushi cont'd)

* Use any of the raw fish
suggested for *sashimi.* Cut into
thin 2½ x 1½ in (6 cm x 2.5 cm) slices.
Other suggested toppings are: rectangles
of scored squid; cooked shelled shrimp;
salmon or flying fish caviar; slices
of braised or simmered eel;
raw clams.

Sushi Meshi
Stir the rice and fan to cool

SUSHI MESHI
Yields about 7 cups (3½ lbs / 1.75 kgs)

3 cups (1½ lbs / 750 g) short-grain rice
3½ cups (28 fl oz / 885 ml) water
3 in (8 cm) square kombu
¼ *cup (2 oz / 60 g) sugar*
1 tbsp salt
¼ *cup (2 fl oz / 60 ml) rice vinegar*

Thoroughly rinse and drain rice;
place in a heavy pan with the water.
Wipe *kombu* and add to the pan. Cover,
bring to a boil. Reduce heat and simmer
until rice is tender and liquid absorbed.
Remove from heat, cover with a towel and
let stand for 12 minutes. Dissolve sugar
and salt in the vinegar. While rice is
still hot, transfer to a wide tub. Add
the vinegar mixture by sprinkling

(cont'd)

(Sushi Meshi cont'd)

it lightly over the surface, while simultaneously tossing it with a large spoon. Fan the rice so that it cools fairly quickly. Cover with a damp cloth. *Sushi Meshi* should not be made long before use, as the vinegar causes a ferment to begin and it can turn sour. Do not refrigerate or the rice will dry out, making it difficult to form the *sushi*.

SUSHI MESHI: (*SUE-SHI ME-SHI*) (recipe) see SUSHI

SU TANG: (*SO TIU*, China) see GLUTEN

SUYO: (*SUE-YO*, Japan) see CUCUMBER, JAPANESE

SWAMP CABBAGE/SPINACH: see KANGKONG

SWATOW MUSTARD CABBAGE: see CABBAGE, CHINESE (DAAI GAAI CHOY)

SWEET AND SOUR SAUCE

1 tbsp shredded chow chow *pickles*
1 tbsp shredded ginger
1/2 cup (4 fl oz / 125 ml) tomato ketchup
3/4 cup (6 fl oz / 180 ml) white vinegar
1 tsp salt
3/4 cup (6 oz / 180 g) sugar
red food coloring
1 1/4 tbsps cornstarch (cornflour)
1 cup (8 fl oz / 250 ml) water

Mix ingredients:
simmer for 3–4 minutes.

SWEET BASIL SEED: see BASIL

SWEET BEAN PASTE/SAUCE: see BEAN PASTES AND SAUCES

SWEET CHILI SAUCE: see CHILI SAUCE

SWEET CORN: see CORN

SWEET CORN FRITTERS: (recipe) see CORN

SWEET CUMIN: see CUMIN; FENNEL

SWEET MELONS: see MELONS AND GOURDS

SWEET NOODLE DESSERT: (recipe) see NOODLES

SWEET PICKLED GINGER: see GINGER (PICKLED GINGER)

SWEET PICKLED VEGETABLES: see GINGER (GINGER PRESERVE)

SWEET POTATO: (*Ipomoea batatas*) originated in South America. This plant, with its edible tubers, grows throughout the tropics. The outer skin varies from white, through red, to purple, and the flesh is gray-white to gold. Nutritionally, the sweet potato is an important carbohydrate food with a small amount of protein and some sugar. In Asian cooking sweet potatoes are generally used less than taro and yams.

Also known as *faan sue* (China); *shakarkandi* (India); *ubi jalar, ubi manis* (Indonesia); *satsuma-imo* (Japan); *keledek* (Malaysia); *camotes* (Philippines)

See also: TARO; YAM; YAM BEAN

SWEET RED BEAN PASTE: see RED BEAN PASTE, SWEET

SWEET RED BEAN SOUP WITH MOCHI: (recipe) see AZUKI BEAN

SWEET RICE FLOUR/SWEET RICE POWDER: see FLOURS AND THICKENERS; RICE (GLUTINOUS)

SWEET SOY SAUCE: see SOY SAUCES, SWEET AND SALTY

SWEET SOY SAUCE PORK: (recipe) see PORK

SWEET TAMARIND AND CHICKEN SOUP: (recipe) see TAMARIND

SWEET VINEGAR: see RICE VINEGAR

T

TAAI GOO CHOY: (*DAI GOO CHOY*, China) see CABBAGE, CHINESE

TAENG KAN: (*TAENG KHAAN*, Thailand) see CUCUMBER (YELLOW)

TAHINI: see SESAME SEED (PASTE)

TAHO: (*TA-HO*, Philippines) see BEAN CURD ("BRAINS") (SILK)

TAHOE: (*TAH-HOO*, Indonesia, Malaysia) see BEAN CURD BY-PRODUCTS (FERMENTED)

TAHU: (*TA-HOO*, Malaysia) see BEAN CURD BY-PRODUCTS (FERMENTED)

TA HUA: (*TA-HU-A*, Malaysia) see BEAN CURD

TAHURE: (*TAH-KUH-RE*, Philippines) see BEAN CURD

TAINGANG DAGA: (*TAY-NGANG DAH-GA*, Philippines) see CLOUD EAR FUNGUS

TAIWAN: The cooking of Taiwan has many similarities to that of the adjacent mainland region of which the principal regional cuisine is Chiu Chou or Fukien. However, local specialties and the influence brought by its immigrants from many parts of China have resulted in a unique cuisine that is an amalgam of many styles.
See also: CHINA

TAKENOKO: (*TAH-KE-NOH-KO*, Japan) see BAMBOO SHOOT

TAKUAN: (*TAH-KOO-AHNN*, Japan) see TSUKEMONO

TALONG: (*TAH-LONG*, Philippines) see EGGPLANT

TAMAGO: (*TAH-MAH-GO*, Japan) see EGG

TAMARI: (*TAH-MAH-REE*, Japan) see SOY SAUCE

TAMARIND: (*Tamarindus indica*) A large tree of the Leguminosae family, the tamarind is believed to have originated in central Africa, but has grown for so long in India it is thought to be a native. The tree produces flat, bean-like pods similar to broad beans, which are green when young, but ripen to a brittle dark brown. Introduced to Indonesia and Malaysia by Indian migrants, tamarind has become an essential ingredient in the cooking of these countries, and they in turn introduced it to other parts of Asia. The flesh within the pods is fibrous, is extremely sour when unripe and full of hard brown seeds. Ripened, the flesh turns brown and softens but is still tart to the taste. In processing, the pods are opened and dried in the sun, the flesh and shiny black seeds are extracted and mixed with salt to form soft pliant blocks and are sold in this way. Further processing removes fibers and seeds and the pulp is kneaded into balls or flat cakes (*asam kawak*) that gradually turn a dark brown color. From this stage tamarind can be refined further to make a concentrated, smooth, thick, dark brown sauce that is so fine in flavor, it can be used as a dip. Tamarind gives its unique, sweet-tart flavor to sauces and braised dishes; is added to curries to sharpen the flavor and to marinades as a tenderizer and flavoring; and in India is made into a refreshing drink known as *imli panni*. The seeds rolled in sugar were the only sweet Indonesian children knew until the Western world intervened. They are also enjoyed in the Philippines. Tamarind chutney, from India, is delicious as a dip for deep-fried snacks. Medicinally, tamarind is taken to cool and cleanse the system, being particularly beneficial to the liver and kidneys.

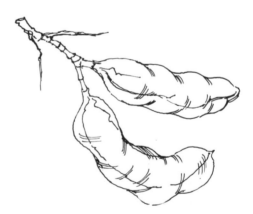

Tamarind pods

ASAM GELUGOR (Malaysia) is a flavoring of dried slices of tamarind, used extensively in Malaysian and Nonya cooking. It is also known as *asam jawa*.

Also known as *ma-gyi-thi* (Burma); *ampil khui*, *ampil tum* (unripe) (Cambodia); *asam koh* (China); *imli* (India); *asam jawa* (Indonesia, Malaysia); *sampalok* (Philippines); *ma kham*, *ma kham peak*, *nam som mak kham* (water) (Thailand); *me* (Vietnam); concentrated/instant tamarind; tamarind concentrate; tamarind pods; tamarind pulp
See also: SWEET TAMARIND AND CHICKEN SOUP (recipe); TAMARIND BEEF (recipe); TAMARIND CHICKEN (recipe); TAMARIND WATER (recipe)

SWEET TAMARIND AND CHICKEN SOUP
Serves 6

1 lb (500 g) skinless, boneless chicken, cubed
vegetable oil
1/2 cup (4 oz / 120 g) chopped shallots
1 tbsp minced ginger
1 cup (8 oz / 250 g) chopped tomatoes
salt and pepper
7 cups (1 3/4 qts / 1.75 l) chicken broth
1 cup (8 oz / 250 g) chopped pineapple
1 tbsp tamarind concentrate
sugar
fresh herbs

Sauté chicken in oil until lightly colored. Add shallots and ginger and sauté 3–4 minutes. Add tomatoes, cook briefly, then add salt and pepper to taste and chicken broth. Bring to a boil and simmer about 25 minutes, until chicken is tender. Add pineapple, tamarind and sugar to taste; simmer briefly. Add fresh herbs such as mint or coriander.

TAMARIND BEEF
Serves 4–6

1 1/4 lbs (620 g) beef chuck, round or shank
6 dried chilies, soaked
1/2 cup (4 oz / 120 g) chopped shallots
1 tbsp minced ginger
4 candlenuts
1 tsp shrimp paste
1/2 tsp turmeric
1/2 cup (4 fl oz / 125 ml) vegetable oil
1 1/2 tbsps tamarind concentrate
3 cups (24 fl oz / 750 ml) water
salt, sugar and pepper

(cont'd)

(Tamarind Beef cont'd)

Cut beef into 1 in (2.5 cm) cubes. Grind drained chilies to a paste with shallots, ginger, candlenuts, shrimp paste and turmeric. Heat oil and fry ground paste for 2–3 minutes; add beef and cook until evenly browned. Add tamarind concentrate with water, and salt, sugar and white pepper to taste. Bring to a boil, reduce the heat and simmer for about 1 1/2 hours until the beef is tender and gravy reduced.

TAMARIND CHICKEN
Serves 4–6

1 x 3 lb (1.5 kg) fresh chicken
3/4 cup (6 fl oz / 180 g) tamarind pulp
2 cups (16 fl oz / 500 ml) boiling water
3/4 cup (6 oz / 180 g) sugar (white or brown)
1/4 cup (2 fl oz / 60 ml) dark soy sauce
1 1/2 tsps minced garlic
1 cup (4 oz / 120 g) minced shallots
2 tbsps toasted coriander seeds
salt and pepper

Rinse chicken; drain. Mix tamarind with boiling water, mash, then strain tamarind water into a dish. Add sugar, soy sauce, garlic and shallots. Place whole chicken in the marinade, turn several times, then cover and leave for 6–8 hours, or overnight. Grind coriander, add to the chicken, transfer to a pot and simmer until tender, about 40 minutes. Season with salt and pepper to taste.

TAMARIND WATER

1 1/2 tbsps tamarind pulp (containing seeds)
1/4 cup (2 fl oz / 60 ml) warm water

Soak the pulp in the water for 5 minutes, squeeze the seeds and fiber with fingers to extract as much juice and flavor as possible. Strain and use. If using tamarind pulp with all seeds extracted use 1 scant tbsp per 1/4 cup (60 ml) water.

(cont'd)

(Tamarind Water cont'd)

(Instant or concentrated tamarind requires 1 tsp to give the same flavor as the above.)

TANDOOR: (*TAN-DOOR*, India) A barrel-shaped, mud or clay oven, used for roasting meats and baking bread. It is heated to a high heat by burning charcoal in the lower part of the oven. Food is placed in the oven through the narrow mouth at the top and is suspended in the oven on thick metal skewers, which are usually square or hexagonal to prevent them rolling in the oven. *Tandoors* have no temperature controls and require a degree of skill for perfect results. The fierce heat seals the outer surface of the food, ensuring the meat is quickly cooked and moist on the inside. Whole or portions of fish and chicken cook superbly in the *tandoor*, as do skewered *kebabs* of cubed or ground meat. Food is usually dyed a charac-teristic bright orange before cooking in the *tandoor*. *Naans*, the baked leaved bread that is the accepted accompaniment to these meats, is *tandoor*-baked by adhering to the inner oven wall. *Tandoor* ovens are usually situated outdoors as their intense heat and smoke cause discomfort in the kitchen. Modern Indian restaurants now often house their *tandoor* ovens in a ventilated, temperature controlled, glass-enclosed kitchen, offering diners a view of the cooking procedure. Small, unglazed clay *tandoor* ovens are available for domestic use.
See also: KEBABS; NAAN; TANDOORI BAKED POMFRET (recipe); TANDOORI CHICKEN TIKKAS (recipe); TANDOORI COLORING; UTENSILS, BARBECUES AND CHARCOAL BURNERS; UTENSILS, VARIOUS

TANDOORI BAKED BREAD
Serves 6

3 cups (12 oz / 370 g) maida *flour*
1³/₄ tsps *baking powder*
1¹/₂ tsps *superfine (caster) sugar*
³/₄ tsp *salt*
³/₄ cup (6 fl oz / 180 ml) *plain (natural) yogurt*
1 tbsp *vegetable oil*
1 egg, *lightly beaten*

Blend flour in a mixing bowl or food processor with baking powder, sugar and salt. Add the yogurt, oil and egg. Mix thoroughly to make a smooth, soft dough. Knead lightly for about 5 minutes. Wrap dough in plastic wrap; set aside in a warm place for at least 3¹/₂ hours. Divide into six pieces and use wet hands to stretch and pull each piece into a triangular shape. Wet one side of each bread, stick onto the inside wall of the *tandoori* oven and cook until done, or place on a preheated baking sheet and bake at 400°F (200°C) until puffed and browned on the surface. Remove and wrap in a cloth until ready to serve.

TANDOORI BAKED POMFRET
Serves 4

1¹/₂ lbs (450 g) pomfret (John Dory, sole or flounder)
1¹/₂ tsps *cumin seeds*
¹/₄ tsp *fennel*¹/₄
¹/₄ tsp ajwain
1–2 green chilies, *seeded and chopped*
2 tsps *minced garlic*
2 tsps *minced ginger*
2 tbsps *minced onion*
1 tsp *salt*
1 tsp *chili powder*
1 tbsp *lemon juice*
3 tbsps *plain (natural) yogurt*
vegetable oil
black pepper
¹/₂ tsp *ground dried fenugreek leaves*
onion rings

Clean the fish, clip fins and make several deep slashes diagonally across each side. Grind the spices, chilies, garlic, ginger and onion together with salt, chili powder, lemon juice and yogurt. Spread over the fish inside and out and leave for 4 hours to absorb the flavors. Cook the fish on a charcoal barbecue or under a moderate broiler (grill) until done, about 6 minutes on each side. Baste with a little oil during cooking to prevent the fish from drying out. Sprinkle on the pepper, dried fenugreek and lemon juice and return to the heat briefly. Serve with onion rings.

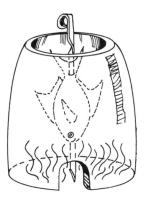

Tandoor oven showing fish suspended on skewer over fire

(Tandoori Chicken Tikkas cont'd)

cook in a *tandoor* oven or place on a rack in a roasting pan and bake for 30 minutes in a preheated oven at 350°F (180°C). Remove, brush with more ghee, sprinkle on cumin, fenugreek leaves and more lemon juice. Return to the oven and bake until brown. Serve with lemon wedges and onion rings marinated in vinegar.

TANDOORI COLORING: A nontoxic food coloring powder used to give the desired orange-red color to foods cooked in the *tandoor* oven. Obtainable from Indian food stores and also sometimes from Chinese food stores. The powder is mixed into marinades so that it penetrates the food prior to cooking.
See also: FOOD COLORINGS

TANGERINE/MANDARIN: (*Citrus reticulata*) The fruit of a citrus tree native to China and Laos. The trees are smaller than orange trees. Tangerines are one variety of mandarin, and there are several others including one known as *satsuma*. The fruit has thin, loose skin ranging from deep orange to red in color. It is easy to peel and the juicy, sweet and sometimes slightly tart flesh is flavorsome and aromatic. *Rangpur* lime is closely related to tangerine and is often used as a root stock for budding other kinds of citrus fruits. Generally eaten raw as a fruit, mandarin segments canned in a light syrup are used in desserts. In Japan, the mandarin, or *mikan* is hollowed out and filled with an orange-flavored jelly to serve as a dessert, and also used a dish for seafood salads.

DRIED TANGERINE PEEL: Dried peel of tangerines and mandarins has been used medicinally in China for centuries. It is also a commonly used seasoning in China and Vietnam, being added to simmered and braised dishes and occasionally to stir-fries. It is sold in Asian food stores, but can be substituted by lemon leaves or fresh orange peel. It should be stored

TANDOORI CHICKEN TIKKAS
Serves 6

6 whole chicken thighs
1 small onion, minced
1 tbsp minced garlic
1 tbsp minced ginger
2 tsps ground coriander
1 tsp ground cumin
3/4 tsp aamchur
1 tsp salt
1/2 tsp chili powder
1 tbsp lemon juice
2 tbsps plain (natural) yogurt
tandoori food coloring
melted ghee
1/2 tsp toasted cumin seeds
1/4 tsp dried fenugreek leaves, powdered
lemon wedges
onion rings

Skin the chicken thighs and cut each in half. Make deep slits across. Grind onion, garlic, ginger, coriander, cumin and *aamchur* with salt, chili powder, lemon juice, yogurt and *tandoori* coloring. Spread over the chicken, cover with plastic wrap, refrigerate to marinate overnight. Brush chicken with melted ghee, thread onto thick skewers and

(cont'd)

in an airtight jar and will keep for months.
Also known as *chen pi* (dried peel) *juzi* (China); *mikan* (Japan); *khiew wan* (Thailand)

TANG KUEI: (*DONG GWAI*, China) see DANG GUI

TAO CO: (*TAW CHO*, Indonesia) see BEAN PASTES AND SAUCES (BEAN SAUCE)

TAPA: (*TAH-PA*, Philippines) A snack of thinly sliced, dried salted meat which may be cured or uncured. It derives from the Spanish tradition of *tapas*, small snack dishes served with drinks, which are often eaten instead of a formal meal. In the Philippines it is served at the *Merienda*, their equivalent of the *tapa* snack meal.
See also: PHILIPPINES

TAPA: (recipe) see BEEF

TAPIOCA: (*Manihot utilissima*) A native shrub originally from America that is now grown throughout tropical Asia. There are sweet and bitter varieties, the bitter type being toxic to man and livestock if eaten raw. The crop can be left unattended in the ground for two years without any deterioration of the tubers. The leaves are pounded and cooked as a vegetable, and are used as a wrapper for steamed, grilled and baked foods. The root is sliced, shredded and rinsed to remove excess starch and dried for preservation and ease of transport and storage. In Southeast Asia, particularly Indonesia, Malaysia and southern China, tapioca pearls and chips are used in puddings, cookies and confectionery and in Indonesia thin tapioca chips are fried as *krupuk*. The dried tuber is also ground to a flour that is used extensively as a thickener and makes an excellent, crisp batter.
Also known as *ketala puhun*, *poheon* (Indonesia); *dang noi*, *man sum palung*, *pearks sakhoo* (Thailand); cassava
See also: FLOURS AND THICKENERS; KRUPUK; LEAVES USED AS FOOD CONTAINERS, PLATES, WRAPPERS; TAPIOCA DESSERT (recipe)

TAPIOCA STARCH: see FLOURS AND THICKENERS

TARAKO: (*TAH-RAH-KOW*, Japan) see CAVIAR

TARKARI: (*TAR-KA-REE*) see INDIA, COOKING METHODS

TAPIOCA DESSERT
Serves 6–8

1½ cups (7½ oz / 235 g) rice flour
1½ cups (13 fl oz / 300 ml) ice water
green and red food coloring
6 cups (1½ qts / 1.5 l) water
1¼ cups (7 oz / 220 g) tapioca
1 cup (8 oz / 250 g) sugar
½ tsp salt
2½ cups (20 fl oz / 625 ml) thick coconut milk

Mix rice flour with enough ice water and green coloring to make a thick, bright green batter. Into a large saucepan of lightly salted boiling water press the batter through the holes in a perforated ladle or skimmer so that it drops into the water in little pellets. Cook for 2–3 minutes, until they rise to surface; transfer to ice water. Boil tapioca in 6 cups water with red coloring to give a bright pink color. Cook about 30 minutes, until tender. Mix sugar with 1 cup cold water. Bring to a boil then simmer for 15 minutes to make a syrup. Cool. Add salt to coconut milk. Divide portions of rice flour "beans," tapioca, syrup and coconut milk into serving dishes, top with shaved ice.

TARO: (*Colocasia esculenta*) A large tuber vegetable that grows wild in most tropical countries beneath a plant with thick, purple-green stems and large triangular leaves. It is one of the most important staple foods throughout the Pacific Islands but is not used extensively in Asia, except in the southern part of the Philippines. The skin of the tuber is light brown and rough in appearance. The flesh is gray-cream to mauve in color, often interspersed with thin, pink-red veins and is similar in flavor to sweet potato or yam. It is thickly peeled, and the cubed flesh is boiled or steamed until tender to use as a vegetable. It is also used in desserts and puddings, a popular Chinese dessert being a thick, hot, heavily sweetened soup made from taro. A Chinese *dim sum* called *wu kwok* uses mashed taro around a meat filling. When deep-fried the surface becomes lace-like and crisp. Taro starch

is a grayish-colored flour made by grinding chips of dried taro. It is used as a thickener, and it is in this form that it is usually used for desserts. Sweet potato or yams can substitute.
Also known as *woo tau* (China); *talas* (Indonesia); *gabi* (Philippines); *puak* (Thailand); *khoai mon* (Vietnam); dasheen
See also: FLOURS AND THICKENERS; SWEET POTATO; TARO-COATED CRISPY DUCK (recipe); YAM;; YAM BEAN

TARO-COATED CRISPY DUCK
Serves 6

½ duck about 2lbs (1 kg) rinsed and dried
dark soy sauce
deep-frying oil
1½ star anise, broken
1 tbsp minced scallion (spring/green onion)
2 tbsp minced ginger
1 tsp Sichuan peppercorns
1 lb (500 g) taro, peeled and cubed
1 tbsp dried shrimp, soaked and chopped
2 tbsps chopped Chinese sausage (lap cheong)
½ tsp salt, ¼ tsp pepper
⅓ cup (3 fl oz/90 ml) boiling water
⅔ cup (3 oz/45 g) cornstarch (cornflour)
¼ cup (2 oz/60 g) lard, softened
sweet soy sauce or oyster sauce dip

Set duck, skin side up, on a plate; rub with dark soy sauce; let stand for 15 minutes. Deep-fry in hot oil until surface is crisp and deep golden in color. Drain; set, skin side down, on plate. Arrange star anise, scallion, ginger and peppercorns on duck. Steam over boiling water for 1½ hours. Steam or boil taro in salted water until tender; drain. Mash to very smooth; mix in dried shrimp, sausage, salt and pepper. Pour hot water over cornstarch. Mix quickly, then knead to a soft dough. Add to taro with softened lard and work to a smooth paste. Carefully remove bones from duck, retaining drumstick and wing bones. Sprinkle additional cornstarch over duck, spread taro mixture evenly over cavity side, coat thickly all over with extra cornstarch. Return to hot oil and deep-fry until golden and crisp. Slice. Serve with sweet soy sauce or oyster sauce dip.

TARO STARCH: see FLOURS AND THICKENERS

TASALA: (*TAH-SHA-LAA*, Nepal) see CHATTI

TATE-JIO: (*TAH-TE-JEE-OW*) see JAPAN, COOKING METHODS

TAUCHEO: (*TAW-CHEO*, Malaysia, Singapore) see BEAN PASTES AND SAUCES (BEAN SAUCE)

TAUGE: (*TAW-GAY*, Indonesia) see BEAN SPROUT

TAUHU KAO: (*TAO-JIEW KHAO*, Thailand) see BEAN CURD

TAUHU KUNING: (*TAW-WHO KOO-NING*, Indonesia, Malaysia) see BEAN CURD (PRESSED)

TAUHU LEONG: (*TAO-HUU LEONG*, Thailand) see BEAN CURD (PRESSED)

TAUHU TOD: (*TAO-HUU TOD*, Thailand) see BEAN CURD (FRIED)

TAUKWA: (*TAW-KWAH*, Indonesia, Malaysia) see BEAN CURD (PRESSED)

TAUN GAWK: (*THUA HOK*, Thailand) see BEAN SPROUT

TAU SA: (*TAW SAH*, Malaysia) see BEAN PASTES AND SAUCES (BEAN SAUCE)

TAUSI: (*TAW-SI*, Philippines) see BEAN CURD BY-PRODUCTS (FERMENTED)

TAWA: (*TA-VAA*, India) see UTENSILS, HOTPLATES AND GRIDDLES

TAWAS: (*TA-WAS*, Philippines) see ALUM

TEA: (*Camellia sinensis*) The discovery of tea as a beverage goes back over 5000 years in Chinese history. It is probably the single most documented food in the world with the first treatise on tea, the *Cha Ch'ing*, being written in the eighth century by the Chinese master Lu Yu. Over the centuries, tea has been planted in most parts of the world, but the prized growing areas remain in India (Assam and Darjeeling), in Sri Lanka (Dimbula), and in various parts of the vast country of China. Each area produces a distinct flavor and this is further enhanced by the method used of picking, rolling, fermenting and drying. The Chinese drink their tea without milk or sugar and enjoy several distinctly different types. Green tea, sometimes flavored with jasmine flowers, is the most widely used, with *bo lai* or *pu erh* a black tea favored in the south. *Oolong*, some of the best of which is grown in Fukien province, is a smooth, fruity, slightly spicy tea, while *lapsang souchong* is a strongly flavored black tea with a smoky aroma and taste from the addition of smoked leaves and stalks. A classic known as *gunpowder* has grayish leaves shaped like small pellets and is one of the earliest Chinese specialty teas still marketed worldwide. *Tit kwan yin* is an intensely flavored tea that is preferred by the Chinese of Chiu Chow and is served in minuscule porcelain cups that hold less than a single mouthful. Indian and Sri Lankan teas are of the black variety and are served English style with milk and sugar, or may be brewed with milk, sweeteners and aromatic spices to make *masala cha*. In Kashmir, green tea is brewed with almonds and spices added, which turn it an attractive pink color. A Russian-style samovar is used in most Kashmiri households. Japanese teas differ noticeably from Chinese. *Bancha* is the everyday drink, and has a slightly toasted taste achieved by smoking or roasting the leaves with some of the stem. *Genmaicha* is *bancha* with the addition of roasted and popped grains of rice giving it a refreshing mealy taste. *Sencha* is a better grade of green tea served on special occasions. *Gyokuro*, which translates as "jewel dew" is one of the highest grades of tea used in Japan and has a very delicate taste and fragrance. *Matcha* and *hiki-cha* are powdered teas which are used for brewing in the Japanese tea ceremony known as *cha no yu*. The tea is beaten into the hot water with a small bamboo whisk, making an unusual frothy texture. Throughout Indonesia, Malaysia, Thailand and the other Southeast Asian countries, tea drinking is not of major importance, although Chinese green tea may be served in a glass with a meal at a restaurant.

TEA CEREMONY: see CHA NO YU

TEA EGGS: (recipe) see EGG

TEA MELON: see CUCUMBER (YELLOW)

TEISHOKU SAKURA DENBU: (*TE-I-SHOW-KOO SAH-KOO-RAH DEN-BOO*, Japan) A bright, pink crystalline substance made from ground, dried cod fish, sugar and food coloring. It has a sweet, very slightly fishy taste and is used as a garnish, particularly on appetizer dishes.

TELUR: (*TE-LURE*, Indonesia, Malaysia) see EGG

TELUR ASIN: (*TE-LURE A-SEEN*, Indonesia, Malaysia) see DUCK EGGS, SALTED

TEMPE: (*TAME-PAY*, Indonesia, Malaysia) Fermented soybean cake, made from boiled soybeans, pressed into cakes and allowed to ferment. It develops a fine, downy white coating similar to that on camembert cheese, a nutty, yeasty flavor and a soft chewy texture. Tempe is used extensively in vegetarian diets and in Asia is stir-fried or used as meat in curries. Firm white bean curd can be substituted.

ONCOM (Indonesia) is a fermented paste made from the residue of soybeans that have been used to make bean curd, and sometimes also from peanuts. It is similar to *tempe*, although finer textured, and is usually eaten fried.

Also known as fermented bean curd cake; tempeh

See also: BEAN CURD

TEMPURA: (*TEM-POO-RAH*, Japan) *Tempura* is not native to Japan, being introduced by Portuguese and Spanish traders in the sixteenth century. Japanese chefs perfected the feather-light, crisp batter that makes *tempura* so special, and added the delicate dipping sauce of soy with grated giant white radish. Perfect *tempura* requires having all the ele-

Samovar used for serving tea in Kashmir

ments just right, so it tends to be more a restaurant dish than one made for family meals at home. The batter should be mixed at the very last moment, using ice water. The ingredients should be thoroughly dry and dredged lightly with flour, the oil just the right temperature—340°F (170°C). Equipment consists of a deep pan of oil, a draining rack, a fine mesh scoop for retrieving fried items and floating batter crumbs, and there should be fine-pointed metal cooking chopsticks, plus dishes for the batter, flour and ingredients close at hand. The ingredients cooked as *tempura* are firm vegetables such as sliced pumpkin or sweet potato, lotus root, onion, green beans, sliced fish, peeled large shrimp, whitebait, sliced squid, bell peppers, mushrooms, little bundles of noodles, *mitsuba* and *shiso* leaves. The batter is made of egg yolks beaten with ice water and sifted all-purpose flour. The dipping sauce is composed of *dashi*, *mirin* and soy sauce, with finely grated *daikon* (giant white radish) and ginger added at the table. The food should be quickly cooked until very lightly golden, drained and served at once plates or baskets lined with folded paper.

See also: BEEFSTEAK PLANT; MITSUBA; RADISH, GIANT WHITE

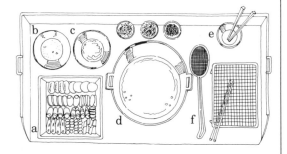

Placement of utensils for tempura
a. *Raw ingredients*
b. *Batter*
c. *water*
d. *Deep-frying oil*
e. *Chopsticks*
f. *Strainer*

TEMPURA
Serves 4

4 shiitake *mushrooms, soaked*
5 in (12 cm) piece lotus root or carrot
1 sweet potato
1 medium onion
1 bell pepper (green pepper / capsicum)
12 stalks mitsuba
tempura batter
deep-frying oil
1/2 cup (4 fl oz / 120 ml) Oriental
sesame oil
4 large shrimp (prawns), shelled and
deveined
2 squid; cleaned, squared and scored
8 small whitefish fillets
flour
tempura sauce

Remove mushroom stems. Cut a cross in cap. Cut lotus or carrot and sweet potato into rounds. Peel onion, cut in halves, slice thickly and secure each slice with a wooden pick. Quarter bell pepper, discarding seeds and stem. Tie *mitsuba* stalks together into a knot. Make half of the batter. Heat deep-frying oil, adding sesame oil. Coat the seafood and vegetables lightly with flour, dip into batter and gently fry, a few at a time, to light gold. Drain and serve on paper-lined plates with tempura sauce.

TEMPURA BATTER

2 egg yolks
2 cups (16 fl oz / 50 ml) ice water
2 cups (8 oz / 250 g) all-purpose (plain)
flour, sifted

Beat egg yolks into ice water. Pour over sifted flour and stir in very lightly. The batter should remain lumpy, with evidence of unmixed flour on the edges of the bowl. Use quickly, and preferably mix in two lots rather than all at once, for it to be at its best.

TEMPURA DIPPING SAUCE

1 cup (8 fl oz / 250 ml) dashi
¼ cup (2 fl oz / 60 ml) mirin
⅓ cup (3 fl oz / 90 ml) light soy sauce
1 cup (8 fl oz / 250 ml) daikon oroshi
2–3 tsps minced ginger

Mix *dashi, mirin* and soy
sauce in a bowl. Serve *daikon oroshi*
and ginger separately.

TEPEH: (*TEH-PAY*, Malaysia) see CLAM

TEPPAN YAKI: (*TEP-PAN YAH-KEE*) see JAPAN, COOKING METHODS

TEPONG BERAS: (*TE-PONG BEH-RUS*, Malaysia) see FLOURS AND THICKENERS (RICE FLOUR)

TEPONG HOEN KWE: (*TEH-PONG HOON KWAY*, Indonesia, Malaysia) see FLOURS AND THICKENERS (MUNG BEAN FLOUR)

TEPONG PULOT: (*TEH-PONG POO-LOT*, Indonesia, Malaysia) see FLOURS AND THICKENERS (GLUTINOUS RICE)

TERASI: (*TEH-RAH-SEE*, Indonesia) see SHRIMP PASTE

TERIYAKI

Serves 4

12 oz (350 g) pork tenderloin fillet
vegetable oil
1¼ cups (10 fl oz / 300 ml) teriyaki sauce
sansho pepper
radish "chrysanthemum"

Cut the pork at a sharp
diagonal into thick escalopes.
Beat gently between 2 pieces of plastic
to spread into larger pieces. Sauté in a
little vegetable oil until browned on both
sides. Remove. Bring *teriyaki* sauce to a
boil, return meat and cook gently until
sauce is reduced to a glaze. Sprinkle on
pepper and garnish each serve with
a radish "chrysanthemum."
(See illustration, JAPAN, GARNISHES.)

TERIYAKI SAUCE

Yields 1½ cups (13 fl oz / 400 ml)

This sauce adds a glossy glaze
to teriyaki dishes.

½ cup (4 fl oz / 125 ml) sake
½ cup (4 fl oz / 125 ml) mirin
½ cup (4 fl oz / 125 ml) dark soy sauce
1¼ tbsps sugar

Mix all of the ingredients in
a small saucepan. Bring to a boil and
cook long enough for sugar to dissolve.
Cool and refrigerate.

TERONG: (*TEH-RONG*, Malaysia) see EGGPLANT

TERUNG: (*TEH-ROONG*, Indonesia) see EGGPLANT

THAI CHILI: see CHILI; PRIK

THAI FRIED RICE: (recipe) see RICE

THAI GARNISHES: see THAILAND, GARNISHES

THAI GINGER: see GALANGAL, GREATER

THAI GINGER AND CHICKEN IN COCONUT SOUP: (recipe) see CHICKEN

THAI HOT SAUCE: see NAM PRIK; NAM PRIK PHAO

THAILAND: The tantalizing tastes of Thai food made a welcome entry into the Western world in the last decade. A gamut of flavors, colors and textures mingle together in Thai dishes—sharp, clear chili heat; sweet, buttery sauces redolent of ginger and coconut, tangy lime, tamarind and myriad other tart tastes; crisp-fried ingredients contrast with soft and chewy ones; fragrances sweet and dominant. Thai cooking is a dichotomy of local and Chinese, for many of its population are of Chinese extraction. Therefore, we find a typical menu comprises stir-fried meat and vegetable dishes and soft-fried noodles in classic southern Chinese mode, together with fiery Thai curries, fishy-fragrant and herbaceous salads and sauces. What we also find on menus, and in the stands and baskets of street vendors, is the plethora of delicate little sweet snacks that the Thais love to eat between meals. Water chestnuts in chilled salt water threaded on skewers, crisp *agar agar* jellies brightly-hued and made fragrant with *mali* (jasmine) and *toey* (pandanus), little bundles of egg thread fried in oil and soaked in sugar syrup. Much that is eaten in Thailand is subjected to an over-enthusiastic injection of chili heat, for here some of the hottest chilies in the world are grown and used with almost dangerous abandon in curries, soups, sauces and in the tiny side dishes like *kai pad bai kaprow* in which minuscule cubes of chicken are wok-tossed with fresh basil leaves, a splash of *nam pla* (fish sauce) and a handful of *prik khee noo suan* (bird's eye chilies). Salads, going under the title *yam* or *yum*, are an important feature of Thai cooking and incorporate many ingredients in a dressing based on fish sauce and lime juice, with crushed, toasted peanuts and dried shrimp a frequent addition. *Laab* dishes are also enjoyed. Part stir-fry, part salad, they are composed of chopped meat very lightly cooked, with onions and mountains of fresh herbs, particularly mint, basil and fresh coriander, the three most prominent herbs used in Thai food. Sour tastes are favored and are achieved by adding tiny tart eggplants, lime juice and rind, tamarind, *belimbing* and unripe mango, papaya and other fruits. Much of the preparation of classic Thai dishes is involved and tedious, as the best of Thai cooking evolved through the court kitchens and is therefore elaborate. But there are also simple everyday dishes that are equally enjoyable, such as the popular rice gruel dish *khao tom*. Similar to Chinese *juk* or congee, it is a bowl of plain white rice boiled in water until thick and soup-like. To this can be added ingredients of your choice from boiled shrimp or chicken to slivers of liver or *lap cheong* (Chinese sausage), raw egg, chilies, scallions, roasted peanuts and of course the inevitable *nam pla* and chili paste. A more refined use of rice is found in the *khao chae* tradition, where icy grains of cooked white rice are served with a selection of delectable nibbles such as grilled meats, seafood balls, stuffed chilies, pickled vegetables and so on. It is an elegant court tradition begun by the ladies of the palace in the days of King Chulalongkorn, as a cooling midday repast to ward off midsummer blues.

THAILAND, COOKING METHODS:

BING (PING) means to bake, roast or toast and is applied to foods cooked in the oven, over charcoal or by other dry cooking means.

DOM (TOM) is to boil or simmer in water. Foods cooked by a simple boiling or simmering technique.

DOON is the Thai word for steaming, and in this country steaming is not a frequently used technique. Achieved in the same way as in China, in woven cane baskets or perforated metal containers over a wok or pan of simmering water.

GAENG, KAENG OR KENG describe liquids, as in a curry or soup and this word is applied to most curried dishes.

LAAB is a cooked salad, usually meat with onions and herbs.

LON is a word that implies boiling until soft and tender or jellylike. It also describes a type of cooked sauce.

YAM (YUM) is any salad dish; they may comprise vegetables, or shredded meats, vegetables and fruit.

THAILAND, GARNISHES: Chilies, scallions and fresh coriander are frequently used to decorate Thai dishes. Also, artistically cut and folded pieces of banana leaf are a classic decoration on plate or table, as are tropical blossoms such as frangipani, hibiscus, jasmine and lotus. Crisply-fried flakes of onion, shallots and garlic, plus roasted peanuts and crisp-fried, dried shrimp are also favored.

CARVED MELON AND GOURD SKINS make interesting containers for cooked dishes, fruit and dips. Use a fine, pointed knife to shape floral patterns in the skin, remove the top in a scalloped or serrated pattern, scoop out the seeds and rinse in cold water.

EGG THREAD NETS: These delicate lacy crêpes are used not only in recipes for wrapping foods, but also to drape over cooked dishes as a garnish. Beaten, strained egg should be trailed over moderately hot oil by dipping one hand into the mixture and allowing it to run in fine streams from the fingertips. Cover the surface of the oil, allow it to cook until firm enough to remove on a wide spatula, then drain and cool.

THAILAND RECIPES

Appetizers
Coconut Leaf Chicken Parcels
Dry Spiced Beef
Garlic Pork
Pork Parcels
Sour and Hot Shrimp Soup
Sweet Crisp Noodles
Thai Ginger and Chicken in Coconut Soup
Warm Ground Beef Salad

Main Courses
Barbecued Chicken
Fish Ball Curry
Fried Fish with Ginger Sauce
Green Shrimp Curry
Hot Red Curried Beef Country-style
Musaman Curry
Steamed Fish in Banana Leaf Cups

Accompaniments
Rice Gruel with Shrimp
Stir-fried Cellophane Noodles
Thai Fried Rice
Winged Bean Salad

Desserts
Crisp Jello Sweets
Golden Threads
Mock Jackfruit Seeds
Palmyra Fruit in Palm Syrup
Songaya
Sticky Rice with Mango

MENUS
(see recipes)

BANQUET MENU
Serves 12

Sweet Crisp Noodles

Pork Parcels
Warm Ground Beef Salad
Fried Fish with Ginger Sauce

(cont'd)

(Thailand Menus cont'd)

Hot Red Curried Beef Country-Style

Winged Bean Salad
Rice

Golden Threads
Crisp Jello Sweets

DINNER MENU
Serves 6–8

Garlic Pork
Thai Ginger and Chicken in Coconut Soup

Fish Ball Curry
Musaman Curry
Thai Fried Rice
Winged Bean Salad
Rice

Sticky Rice with Mangoes

THAI SALADS: see YUM

THAI SPRING ROLLS: (recipe) see SPRING ROLL

THALI: (*THA-LEE*, India) see KATORI

THICKENERS: see FLOURS AND THICKENERS

THINH: (*THINK*, Vietnam) see RICE (NON-GLUTINOUS)

THIT-JA-BO-GAUK: (*THIT-JA-BOE-KAUT*, Burma) see CINNAMON

THOUSAND-YEAR EGG: The Chinese devised several methods of preserving eggs many centuries ago. Eggs preserved by this method are known variously as thousand-year-old eggs and hundred-year-old eggs, but in fact the preservation time is more likely to be about 100 days. Duck or chicken eggs (duck have a better flavor and texture in the finished product) are coated thickly in a mixture of lime, ash, salt and tea leaves or rice husk and packed into large, earthenware tubs. The chemicals osmose through the porous shells, preserving and flavoring the eggs. Thousand-year eggs have a grayish-green colored yolk with transparent, very pale amber whites. They should be rinsed thoroughly, the coating scraped away and the eggs peeled. They are usually served as an appetizer, cut into wedges with accompanying, thinly sliced, pickled ginger. Thousand-year eggs can be kept for several months in the refrigerator.

Also known as *pay darn* (China); ancient eggs; century eggs; hundred-year eggs; Ming dynasty eggs;
See also: DUCK EGG, SALTED

TIENTSIN: (*TIN-JUN*, China) CABBAGE, see CABBAGE, CHINESE (NAPA)

TIENTSIN RED BEAN: see AZUKI BEAN

TIFFIN: (*TIFIN*, India) Lunch or mid-morning snack. In the cities of India there is a brisk trade in deliveries of *tiffin* to homes and offices, which is carried out on ingeniously constructed, wheeled frames, some 6 ft (2 m) or more wide. Upwards of 50 tiered aluminum or enameled tiffin containers may be balanced on one frame, the runner rapidly transporting the lightweight but unwieldy vehicle through heavy traffic to bring food hot to the customers' doors. The tiered containers hold separate dishes of rice or bread, curry and dal.

TIGER LILY BUD: see LILY BUD

TIM CHEONG: (*TEAM CHEONG*) see SOY SAUCE, SWEET AND SALTY; PLUM

TIM MEAN JIANG: (*TIM MEIN JEUNG*, China) see BEAN PASTES AND SAUCES

TIMUN: (*TEA-MOON*, Malaysia) see CUCUMBER (YELLOW)

TINAPA: (*TEE-NA-PA*, Philippines) see FISH, PRESERVED (FERMENTED)

TING HSIANG: (*TIN HEUNG*, China) see CLOVES

TOBIKO: (*TOW-BEE-KOW*, Japan) see CAVIAR

TODDY: (*TO-DEE*, India) see WINE, ASIAN

TOEY: (*TO-EY*, Thailand) see FLAVORINGS; PANDANUS LEAF

TOFU: (*TOH-WHO*, Japan) see BEAN CURD

TOGARASHI CHILI: (*TOW-GAH-RAH-SHI*, Japan) see CHILI POWDER

TOGUE: (*TOW-GE*, Philippines) see BEAN SPROUT

TOI: (*TAOI*, Vietnam) see GARLIC

TOKWA: (*TOC-WA*, Philippines) see BEAN CURD (PRESSED)

TOLEE MOLEE: (*TOH-LI MO-LI*, Burma) A collective name describing the condiments that are served with a Burmese meal. This usually includes at least one of the pungent fish or shrimp-pasted sauces.
See also: BALACHUANG; NGAN PYA YE CHET; NGAPI HTAUNG

TOMALLEY: The rich, yellow, fatty "yolk" of crabs' eggs is highly prized by the Chinese and is used in shark's fin dishes and occasionally as a dressing for vegetables. In North America, tomalley refers to the fat or liver of the lobster.
Also known as *aligi* (Philippines); crab yolk
See also: CRAB

TONG HO: (*TONG HO*, China) see CHRYSANTHEMUM

TON HOM: (*TON HOM*, Thailand) see ONION

TONKATSU SAUCE: (*TON-KAH-TZU*, Japan) A dipping sauce rather like a standard barbecue sauce that accompanies the crumbed pork dish known as *tonkatsu*. It is available commercially, in tubes or tubs, but can also be homemade.

TONKATSU
Serves 6

10 oz (300 g) pork tenderloin fillet
salt and pepper
2 eggs, beaten
2 cups (8 oz / 250 g) panko *crumbs*
deep-frying oil
lettuce
lemon wedges
tonkatsu *sauce*

Cut pork into 6 thin slices and season with salt and pepper. Dip into beaten egg and coat thickly with crumbs. Deep-fry in hot oil until golden. Cut each slice crossways into strips. Place on finely shredded lettuce, garnish with lemon wedges and serve with *tonkatsu* sauce.

TONKATSU SAUCE

ketchup
dark soy sauce
sake *or* mirin
Worcestershire sauce
mustard

Mix all of the ingredients to taste.
Cover and refrigerate.

TORCH GINGER: see GINGER BUD

TOSA SOY SAUCE: (*TO-SA*, Japan) The classic *sashimi* accompaniment, this sauce has a distinct flavor of bonito from the addition of *hana-katsuo*, the finely desiccated, dried bonito.
See also: BONITO; SASHIMI

TOSA SOY SAUCE

Yields 1½ cups (13 fl oz / 400 ml)

1 tbsp sake
¼ cup (2 fl oz / 60 ml) mirin
3 in (7.5 cm) piece kombu *kelp*
¼ cup (2 fl oz / 60 ml) light soy sauce
1 cup (8 fl oz / 250 ml) dark soy sauce
¼ cup (2 fl oz / 60 ml) hana-katsuo

Bring *sake* and *mirin* to
a boil; remove from heat and cool.
Wipe kelp, score surface. Mix remaining
ingredients. Let stand overnight;
strain and refrigerate.

TREE EAR: see CLOUD EAR FUNGUS

TREFOIL: see JAPAN, GARNISHES

TREMELLA: see WHITE FUNGUS

TREY REACH: (*TAREY REECH*, Cambodia) This giant, freshwater fish that inhabits the fast flowing, muddy waters of the Mekong River, grows up to 6 ft (2 m) in length. In Laos this prized fish is known as *pa boeuk* and

folklore dictates that it be fished for only a few days during the third month of the Laotian calendar in the area of the Ang caves. It is fished more extensively in Cambodia. It has a large roe weighing more than 20 lbs (10 kgs), which in Laos is used, to make *som khay*, a type of caviar dish. The fish is eaten fresh, but because of its immense size, is mostly cut into pieces and fermented in pots to make *padek* (fermented fish) and its by-products *nam padek* and *nam pa*, or *tuk trey* and *prahok* as they are known in Cambodia.
Also known as *pa boeuk* (Laos)
See also: FISH, FERMENTED; FISH PASTE; FISH SAUCE

TRIANGULAR ROLLS WITH WHOLE SHRIMP: (recipe); see SHRIMP

TSEE GOO: (*TSE GOO*, China) see ARROWHEAD

TSENG GWA: (*CHENG GWA*, China) see CUCUMBER (YELLOW)

TSUBUSHI-AN: (*TZU-BOO-SHI-AH-NN*, Japan) see AZUKI BEAN (AN)

TSUKEMONO: (*TZU-KE-MOW-NO*, Japan) The collective name for the pickles that accompany almost every Japanese meal. Pickles are made by four main techniques, two involving *nuka* a rice bran in the form of a dry bean or mash, the others being salt or vinegar pickling, *shio-zuki* and *su-zuke*. Many households in rural Japan still produce their own *tsukemono*, but nowadays it is readily available, either as whole pieces or presliced, in supermarkets, packed in small tubs with liquid, or in plastic vacuum packs. Pickles are traditionally served at the end of a meal, with rice, in a small dish. They function as digestives and palate cleansers. Two of the most important pickles are:

TAKUAN, a yellow-colored, firm and crunchy pickle of medium saltiness, made from *daikon*, the giant white or icicle radish. It is pickled in dry rice bran after being hung to dry for 2–3 weeks. *Takuan* takes several months to mature, but once made keeps for many months.

UMEBOSHI is actually made from a kind of apricot, although it is commonly thought to be a plum. The salty pickle, popular throughout Japan, is made with underripe fruit, yellow in color, which acquire their characteristic red color from the red of *shiso*, the leaves of the beefsteak plant. Prepared by the *shio-zuke* method.

See also: BEEFSTEAK PLANT; NUKA; PLUM; RADISH, GIANT WHITE

TSUKI DASHI: (*TZU-KEE DAH-SHI*, Japan) see AEMONO

TSUT SING PAAN: (*CHAT SING BARN*, China) see GAROUPA

TUBA: (*TU-BA*, Philippines) A milky sap obtained by tapping young, flowering coconut palms. It is distilled to make the alcoholic drink *lambanog*.

See also: COCONUT; WINE, ASIAN

TUK TREY: (*TIK TREY*, Cambodia) see CAMBODIA; FISH SAUCE

TULSI: (*TUL-SEE*, India) see BASIL (HAIRY)

TUMPAENG: (*TOM-PEEANG*, Cambodia) see BAMBOO SHOOT

TUONG: (*T-URN*, Vietnam) A strong tasting, fermented sauce made in Vietnam. It is not readily obtainable in Western countries so is usually substituted with fish or squid sauce. *Tuong*, sweetened with sugar and mixed with crushed ginger and chili, is known as *nuoc cham tuong gung* and is served in Vietnam with roasted meats.

Also known as Vietnamese soy sauce
See also: FISH SAUCE

TUONG OT: (*TURN URT*, Vietnam) see BEAN PASTES AND SAUCES

TURBAN SQUASH: see MELONS AND GOURDS (WINTER)

TURMERIC: (*Curcuma domestica, C. longa*) A plant of the Zingiberaceae family that encompasses ginger and *galangal*. It grows as the rhizome of a tropical plant native to Southeast Asia with deep green, strong, pointed leaves on thick stems that produce clusters of pink-white flowers. The rhizome itself has papery, buff-colored skin and is knobbly in the way of a ginger root. It has a bright orange-yellow flesh with a characteristic strong, somewhat earthy smell and slightly bitter

taste. It grows freely throughout tropical Asia and is used extensively for its distinct taste. Turmeric is responsible for the bright yellow color we associate with curries and is an ingredient of curry powders. It has a tendency to overpower other flavors and so is omitted from the Indian spice mixture *garam masala*. In Indonesia and Malaysia, its most common partners are shrimp paste, lemon grass and chili, which combine to give a typical flavor to many dishes. Burmese cooks add turmeric freely to many dishes, particularly vegetables. It is rarely used in China, Japan or Korea. Fresh turmeric should be peeled and minced or grated in the same way as ginger. It is now available at many better Asian greengrocers and can be kept in the refrigerator for several weeks. The dried ground spice should be stored in a tightly capped spice jar and used with discretion in curries, pickles and chutneys, rice and vegetable dishes. It is an effective substitute for saffron, though inferior in flavor, for coloring rice dishes. It has a pleasant, slightly tangy, peppery taste. Both flowers and young leaves of turmeric are used as a vegetable, usually cooked by boiling, and the leaves are sometimes added to sauces for their flavor, or used for wrapping foods to be charcoal grilled or steamed. Medicinally, turmeric is taken internally and applied externally as an antiseptic.

WHITE TURMERIC (*Curcuma zedoaria*), commonly known as zedoary, is a another type

Fresh turmeric root

of turmeric grown in Asia which has white flesh and is used, particularly in Thailand, as a vegetable.

Also known as *sa-nwin* (Burma); *romiet* (Cambodia); *wong keung* (China); *haldi* (India); *kunyit* (Indonesia); *kunyit basah* (Malaysia); *dilaw* (Philippines); *kha min* (yellow), *kha min khao* (white) (Thailand)

See also: BURMESE CHICKEN (recipe); ZEDOARY

TURNIP: (*Brassica rapa* L.) Turnips have been eaten since prehistoric times. A member of the cabbage family, the young tops can be cooked as a vegetable, but it is the bulb that is usually eaten. Throughout Asia turnip roots are used as a vegetable, particularly in braised and simmered dishes. The Chinese habit of calling the giant white radish a Chinese turnip is misguided as the flavors of the two are quite different. In Japan, an attractive garnish known as *kiku kabu* is made by carving turnip to resemble a chrysanthemum blossom.

PICKLED TURNIP is used in China and Japan, where turnips are cubed and cured in a salty brine, sometimes also with soy sauce. They develop a strong, spicy taste and have a moist, chewy texture and a strong odor.

Also known as *choy pin*, *chung choy* (China); *salgam* (India, Nepal); *kabu* (Japan)

See also: RADISH, GIANT WHITE

TURTLE: (Green turtle, *Chelonia mydas* Linnaeus) Both sea and land turtles are eaten in various parts of Asia. In Indonesia, the green turtle is prized for its tender meat which is cooked as *satay*. Its eggs, which are also eaten, are like a ping-pong ball in size and shape and have a soft, parchment-like skin. When boiled, the albumen remains liquid.

Land or soft shell turtles are eaten throughout China, but are particularly enjoyed in Sichuan province where they are braised with bulb garlic or steamed with ham and mushrooms. The soft shell is parboiled and then steamed in a pot sealed with mulberry paper until tender.

TURTLE PREPARATION: Place live turtle on a board upside down. Remove head, then hold over a dish to drain blood. Drop turtle into a large pan of boiling water to cook for 3 min-

utes. Remove and scrape off skin. Cut body away from the shell, then cut open along the underside and remove stomach. Rinse thoroughly, cut meat into strips and place in cold water. Bring to a boil and simmer for 5 minutes. Drain and keep under cold water until ready to use.

Also known as *pyin tha-leik* (Burma); *hoy kwai* (China); *penyu* (Indonesia, Malaysia); *tao tanu* (Thailand); *con vich* (Vietnam); green turtle

See also: GARLIC; MULBERRY (PAPER)

TUYO: (*TU-YO*, Philippines) see FISH, PRESERVED

TWELVE PARTS SOUP
Serves 6

1 cup (4 oz / 125 g) sliced onion
2 tsps minced garlic
2 tbsps vegetable oil
2 tbsps Oriental sesame oil
8 oz (250 g) chicken, thinly sliced
8 oz (250 g) pork liver, thinly sliced
1½ tbsps dark soy sauce
¼ cup (2 oz / 60 g) each shredded
Napa cabbage, green beans, celery,
fuzzy melon, flowering white cabbage
3 dried black mushrooms, soaked and shredded
3 tbsps cloud ear fungus, soaked
5 cups (1¼ qts / 1.25 l) chicken broth
2 eggs, beaten
½ cup (2 oz / 125 g) chopped scallions
(spring / green onions)
salt and pepper

Fry onion and garlic in vegetable oil and sesame oil until golden; remove. Fry chicken and pork liver until colored. Add soy sauce, the shredded vegetables and shredded mushrooms and fungus. Cook, covered, for about 5 minutes. Add stock or water and bring to a boil. Pour in eggs in a thin stream. Add scallions, season with salt and pepper.

TWISTED CLUSTER BEAN: see PARKIA

U

UBOD: (*OO-BOD*, Philippines) This creamy-white, fibrous pith is the central core of the coconut palm (heart of palm), although a similar product can be obtained from other palms of the Palmaceae family, which includes date, sago and cabbage palms. It is known in Europe as *coeur de palmier* and is eaten raw, cut into slices for salads or cooked like asparagus. In the Philippines it is the main ingredient of *lumpia ubod*, a type of egg roll. *Ubod* is sold in cans, sliced and packed in water.
Also known as *pondah* (Indonesia); *palmetto* (Philippines); *coeur de palmier*; heart of palm; palm heart
See also: HEART OF PALM ROLLS (recipe); LUMPIA WRAPPERS (recipe)

HEART OF PALM ROLLS
Yields 10

2 lbs (1 kg) ubod (heart of palm), shredded
1 tsp minced garlic
³/4 cup (3 oz / 90 g) chopped onion
2 tbsps lard
¹/4 cup (2 fl oz / 60 ml) fish sauce
1 lb (500 g) small shrimp (prawns), shelled and sliced
1 lb (500 g) boiled pork, cut into narrow strips
1 lb (500 g) cooked crabmeat, flaked
salt and pepper
lumpia wrappers
lettuce leaves
hot sauce

Boil heart of palm for 5 minutes; drain. Sauté garlic and onion in lard until softened. Add fish sauce and shrimp and sauté for 3 minutes. Add the pork and crab and heat through; season with salt and pepper. Add heart of palm and cook for 3–4 minutes. Line each *lumpia* wrapper with a lettuce leaf and fill generously. Roll up and serve with hot sauce.

UDON: (*OO-DON*, Japan) see NOODLES

UKOY: (*OO-KOY*, Philippines) A fritter of ground rice or flour, diced scallion and small peeled shrimp. Fried and served as a snack with vinegar and minced garlic.
See also: SHRIMP PATTIES (recipe)

ULUHAAL: (*U-LU-HAAL*, Sri Lanka) see FENUGREEK

UME: (*U-ME*, Japan) see PLUM

UMEBOSHI: (*U-ME-BOW-SHEE*, Japan) see TSUKEMONO

UMESHU: (*U-ME-SHOO*, Japan) see PLUM

UNAGI: (*U-NA-GUI*, Japan) see EEL

USU-AGE: (*U-SU-AH-GE*, Japan) see BEAN CURD (FRIED PURSES)

UTENSILS, BAMBOO:

BAMBOO MATS are used in Japan to make *sushi* and for squeezing moisture from foods. These mats are usually 10 in (25 cm) square and are made from thin strips of bamboo woven with strong cotton. A piece of cloth or heavy plastic could be used instead.
Also known as *maki-su*, *sudare* (Japan)

BAMBOO WOK BRUSHES are made of stiff strands of split bamboo bound tightly together at one end to form a brush. They come in several gauges, from fine, almost hair-like, to coarse, with strands almost the thickness of matchsticks. They are used with running cold or hot water to clean a wok after use as they do not damage the carefully "cured" surface.

BAMBOO WOK MATS are open-weave strips of narrow bamboo or cane shaped into octagons. They are used inside woks or steamers to prevent the food from sticking, and can double as a trivet (pot stand).

CHASEN: (Japan) A whisk of finely split bamboo used for mixing the powdered tea used in the Japanese tea ceremony.

UTENSILS, BARBECUES AND CHARCOAL BURNERS:

CHARCOAL BURNERS: The burners used in many parts of Southeast Asia are made of unfired clay, buckle-shaped with a flaring top that usually has notches designed to stabilize the wok or cookpot on top. Charcoal cooking is also done in open trays ranging from the tiny rectangular *satay* cooker measuring no more than 15 in (30 cm) long and 4 in (10 cm) wide, to vast, open, charcoal-burning pits over which whole pigs or ducks are slowly turned.

Also known as *angethi chane, sigri* (India)

HIBACHI (Japan) variously shaped cast-iron barbecues comprising a receptacle for charcoal topped by a slatted iron grid on which the food is cooked.

KANA-AMI (Japan) the wire mesh grid used over a charcoal fire when grilling.

TANDOOR (India) the cone-shaped clay oven in which meat and bread are baked.

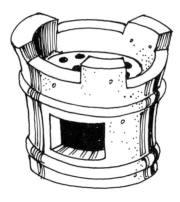

Chinese charcoal cooker

UTENSILS, BREAD AND PASTRY MAKING:

BOARDS: In India small, round boards, often with an attractive carved edge, are used for rolling out dough for breads such as *puris* and *chapatis*, using the short roller known as a *belan*. Known as *chaklas,* some have a recessed reverse side in which dough can be kneaded.

CHEENA CHATTI: (Sri Lanka) A wok-like pan used for cooking bread, particularly *appas*.

DOUGH ROLLERS: In China a long narrow roller is used for rolling out noodle dough and dough for dumpling wrappers. In India the dough roller is known as *belan* and may be a short, thin, wooden roller without handles, or

have a short, carved handle at each end. It is used with a board known as a *chakla*, see above.

ROTI JALA CUP: (Malaysia) A tin cup with four funnel spouts each with a fine hole in the base. The cup dispenses batter onto an oiled hotplate to form the lacy pancake known as *roti jala*. A similar piece of equipment can be used to make the Sri Lankan lacy bread, "string hoppers."

TANDOOR and **TAWA:** (India) The clay oven used for baking leavened breads, and metal cooking plate used for cooking unleavened Indian breads.

UTENSILS, CAKE AND DESSERT MAKING:

FOI TONG CONE: (Thailand) A brass-coated, cup-size pot with a conical, open base that is used for pouring thin threads of beaten egg into hot syrup to make the popular Thai dessert *foi tong*, known as "golden threads." It can also be used when making other Thai recipes requiring fine, lacy sheets of fried beaten egg in which foods are delicately wrapped.

JELLY MOLDS: In the Philippines, Thailand, Indonesia and Malaysia, bite-size jellied desserts are made by setting flavored and colored sweetened water or coconut milk with agar agar gelatin. The tiny metal molds used resemble chocolate molds and come in an assortment of shapes, sizes and designs.

KULFI MOLDS: (India) Small, conical, metal molds used when making *kulfi*, a rich ice cream.

NAGASHI-BAKO: (Japan) A small, square pan used as a mold when jelling ingredients for a dessert.

SALIM MAKER: (Thailand) These decorated, bronzed cans have a perforated base and an internal plunger that forces dough through the perforations to extrude like slim noodles.

SHELL MOLDS: Metal molds comprising a shaped base on a long handle are used to make wafer-thin, crisp cases to be filled with spicy ingredients and served as *hors d'oeuvre* in Malaysia and Thailand. The molds are heated in deep oil, dipped in batter and quickly deep-fried.

Also known as *pee tee* (Thailand)

UTENSILS, DEEP-FRYING:

DEEP-FRYING POTS: In Japan they have specially designed, thick cast-iron or brass pots with two handles for deep-frying, particularly for *tempura*. In China, deep-frying is done in the wok.

Also known as *agemono-nane, agemono no dogu* (Japan)

JHANNAA: (India) A long-handled spoon with perforated bowl used for forming batter into droplets over hot oil or boiling liquid.

KARAHI: (India) A heavy iron or brass pan used in India for deep-frying. It looks somewhat like a Chinese wok, but is deeper and has a thick, looped metal handle at each side. A flat-bottomed pan similar to a paella pan is also known in some areas of India as a *karahi*.

Also known as *kadhai, kurhai* (India, Nepal)

"NEST" FRYING BASKETS are wire, bowl-shaped double baskets used in the deep-fryer to shape ingredients such as finely shredded potato or taro, precooked noodles, thin pastry or seaweed sheets into nest-like shapes.

NET LADLES/OIL SKIMMERS are scoops made with fine wire mesh and used to collect food or for skimming unwanted batter from oil.

Also known as *ami-shakushi* (Japan)

OIL DRAINERS are shallow pans fitted with a rack specially designed to quickly drain away the maximum amount of oil from foods.

Also known as *abura-kiri* (Japan)

PERFORATED METAL SCOOP: A large, convex, metal scoop, perforated with round holes, that is used for retrieving food from the wok when deep-frying. It can double as a colander or drainer.

Also known as *gong jao lei* (China)

WIRE MESH SCOOP: A scoop made from twisted brass or aluminum wire shaped to fit the wok and attached to a long, flat bamboo handle. It is used to manipulate food in boiling water or oil.

Also known as *jao lei* (China); wire strainer

UTENSILS, GRINDING:

BATU GILING (Indonesia) is the granite slab and roller used in Malaysia and Indonesia to grind large amounts of spices, or "wet" seasonings such as ginger, fresh turmeric root, onion, chilies and garlic.

Also known as *batu lesong* (Indonesia, Malaysia)

CHOBEK (TJOBEK) and **PERGULAKAN** are the Indonesian clay mortar and pestle.

IMAMDUSTA and **DAANTI** are the Indian names for their clay or enamel mortar and pestles used for grinding grain and spices. For harder ingredients a brass or cast-iron set is more effective. These are known as *khalia* and *musaria*.

KHAL is the name for the stone mortar used in Nepal.

SURIBASHI and **SURIKOGI** are the Japanese pottery bowl and wooden pestle. The inside is given a rough surface by combing or adding a coarse, sandy compound to the glaze to help the grinding.

ULEKAN (Indonesia) is a small, deep, stone bowl with a stone pestle made from granite or volcanic rock.

UTENSILS, HOTPLATES AND GRIDDLES:

BULGOGI (Korea) is a circular and slightly conical metal hotplate shaped to fit over a tabletop heat source.

MONGOLIAN BARBECUE: (China) A large, round, flat metal plate over a roaring fire is

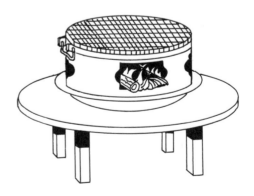

Mongolian barbecue

used in Mongolia and northern China for the fast-cooking of tissue-thin sliced lamb or beef and shredded vegetables. The hot surface is sprinkled with oil and the cook works with long chopsticks and a spatula, moving the food over the hotplate for just a few seconds to sear the surface, leaving it tender and juicy inside.

TAWA: (India) In India this very slightly concave, circular iron disc is used to cook several types of unleavened breads.

TEPPAN: (Japan) This tabletop griddle is used in specialty restaurants where the food is cooked in front of the diners.

UTENSILS, KNIVES AND BOARDS:

CHOPPING BLOCK: (China) The best kind of Chinese chopping block is a cross-cut from the soapwood tree (*Sapindus saponario*) that is soft enough not to damage the sharp blade of the cleaver.
Also known as *jump baarn* (China)

CLEAVERS: A Chinese kitchen would be incomplete without its versatile cleaver, that all-purpose cutting tool that can cut meat into slices so thin you can see through them. It can be used to dispatch a live chicken, chop through a bone, peel a pear and has quite a history of settling scores with enemies. Cleavers come in various weights and sizes. The wooden-handled, lightweight, narrow-bladed cleaver is used to pare and slice fruit and vegetables: the standard, broader-bladed cleaver, about 10 in (25 cm) long and 4 in (10 cm) wide, of medium to light weight is used for general purpose preparation such as slicing, dicing and chopping: the heavy blade is designed to cut clean through bones, and for use in pounding, mincing and puréeing meat and seafood. The end of the cleaver handle is used with a rice bowl as a convenient mortar and pestle for small grinding tasks in the Chinese kitchen. Most Chinese cooks don't believe in an excess of kitchen equipment and use the rough base of a "sand pot" to hone the edge of their cleaver.

DEBA-BOCHO: (Japan) A type of cleaver used in Japan for cutting chicken and fish.

MANAITA: (Japan) Rectangular chopping board used in Japan.

UTENSILS, POTS AND PANS:

CURRY POTS: Terracotta pots with curving bases and narrow, lipped necks are used in many parts of Asia, particularly India, Indonesia and Malaysia, for cooking curries. Similar pots are also used for cooking soups and braised dishes in the Philippines.
Also known as *chatty* (India); *belangah, blangah* (Malaysia); *palayok* (Philippines); *chatti* (Sri Lanka)

DEGCHI: (India) This useful cooking pot is like a heavy saucepan without a handle, and is usually made of brass, tinned on the interior. Its flat, thick base and straight sides are designed for cooking over charcoal or a wood fire.
Also known as *bhagoni, dechi, patila* (India); *dechi* (Nepal)

EARTHENWARE and **CLAY CASSEROLES** of various types are used throughout Asia for slow cooking, braising and soup-making. The Chinese type are known as "sand pots;" the Japanese *donabe* is made of a special clay that holds heat well. This type of pot can be used on a direct flame without damage, but must be heated slowly.

HOROKU: (Japan) A large, earthenware plate with a fitted lid that is used in the oven for baking. A casserole or covered baking dish can be used.

Traditional Thai clay cooking pot

OMELETTE PANS of a rectangular shape are used in Japan for cooking rolled omelette.

They are very suitable for cooking egg roll wrappers and crêpes.

Also known as *makiyakinabe, tamago-yakiki* (Japan)

SAND POTS are Chinese cooking pots made from a light, sandy, porous clay usually unglazed on the outer surface with the inner either glazed or unglazed, depending on their intended use. "Sand pots" may look and feel fragile but can be used directly over the heat source. A barrel-shaped "sand pot" is used for simmering soups.

Also known as *sar bo* (China)

SHIOGAME: (Japan) A heavy, earthenware platter that is heavily coated with coarse salt and used for broiling chicken and seafood.

SUKIYAKINABE: (Japan) The shallow, cast-iron pan used for cooking *sukiyaki*.

Sukiyakinabe

UTENSILS, STEAMERS:

BAMBOO STEAMERS: In Indonesia and Malaysia a type of steamer made from a length of large bamboo is used for cooking *putu bamboo*, a rice dough dessert served with bananas. In China a length of large bamboo, cut so that the closed section is near the base with the hollow opening above, is used as a steamer. One dish cooked in this type of steamer is the rejuvenating dish of steamed pâté of pigeon meat with the medicinal root *dang gui*. In Thailand bamboo steamers are filled with rice and morsels of fish or meats.

BASKETS: One of several types of steamer used by Chinese cooks. Made of woven strips of split bamboo, they have slatted bases to allow for steam circulation and closely woven bamboo lids. These steamers fit inside a wok. Bamboo steamers are useful for many types of food including *dim sum*, bread, buns and some sweet

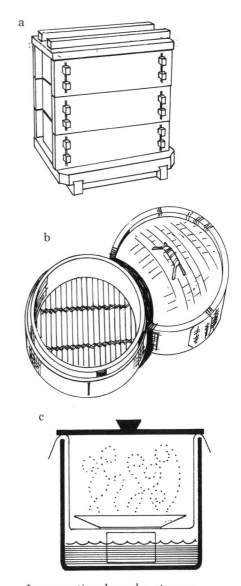

a. Japanese tiered wooden steamer
b. Chinese bamboo steamer basket
c. Improvised steamer showing plate on stand within a large cooking pot

dishes. In Japan steamers similar to the Chinese bamboo ones are used for some dishes.
Also known as *jing lung* (China)

CHAWAN: (Japan) A straight-sided porcelain or earthenware teacup in which foods, usually a savory egg custard, are steamed.

CHINA POTS of unglazed white china, with straight sides and tight-fitting lids have various uses in the Chinese kitchen. As steamers they are ideal for soups known as "double boiled" which are simmered once, then sealed and simmer-steamed. Some of these pots have a secondary flat lid that fits inside the rounded outer lid for better sealing.
Also known as *duun jung* (China)

DOBIN: (Japan) A small teapot with a shallow cup is the lid that is used in Japanese cooking for a clear soup with seafood. Pine needles are inserted into the spout to impart their flavor into the soup.

METAL STEAMERS/STEAMING POTS of beaten tin, formed stainless-steel or aluminum are less esthetically pleasing but more functional than bamboo steaming baskets. Some are simply a single-layered container, others are self-contained with a solid base for the water, beneath two or three layers of inter-fitting, perforated pans. In Japan, a square metal steamer is used for certain dishes.
Also known as *mushi-ki*, *seiro* (Japan)

MUSHI-KI: (Japan) Wooden steamers with bamboo latticework bases, used in tiers over a pot of simmering water.

RICE STEAMERS are used in most parts of Asia. In most countries rice is cooked by the absorption method and is known as steamed rice. It is done in a large, heavy saucepan or electric rice cooker. In Laos rice is cooked in a conical basket known as a *luang prabang*, over a pot of simmering water to steam slowly until cooked through. In Japan a heavy saucepan of copper or aluminum known as a *kama*, is used for rice cooking.
Also known as *fan kua* (China)

UTENSILS, VARIOUS:

COCONUT GRATER: A round-headed grater, with several serrated, metal blades that is used in Malaysia and other Southeast Asian countries to remove the meat from a fresh coconut. The traditional Thai coconut grater has a small, semicircular piece of metal fitted to a low, rectangular stool of carved wood.
Also known as *parut* (Indonesia, Malaysia)

GINGER GRATER: (Japan) A flat metal plate about 7 in (17 cm) in length and 3/4 in (1 cm) wide with raised spines running across it and one sharpened edge. It is used to grate fresh ginger root.
Also known as *oroshigame* (Japan)

LADLES: Shallow metal ladles are utilitarian in the Asian kitchen, where they are used for measuring, adding ingredients to a pan, stirring and serving.

SCISSORS: Short-bladed, handmade scissors are used in the Chinese kitchen in various facets of food preparation.

SIEVE/SIFTER: The Asian form of sifter or sieve is made on a bamboo form with fine copper wire mesh in the base.

SKEWERS of different lengths and thicknesses made of iron, steel, wood or bamboo are used throughout Asia. In Japan metal or bamboo skewers are used for grilled meats and seafoods. Throughout Indonesia, Malaysia, Thailand and Vietnam, thin, sharply pointed, bamboo skewers are used for *satay* and various types of grilled meatballs. To avoid burning, the skewers should be soaked in cold water for at least 15 minutes before use. Metal skewers as thick as a finger and as long as an arm are used in the *tandoor* oven when cooking meats, and a hooked metal skewer is used to remove baked breads from the oven.
Also known as *gushi*, *kushi*, *kana-gushi* (metal skewers) (Japan)

VEGETABLE STAMPS: Chinese cooks love to decorate dishes with sliced vegetables, usually carrot and turnip, cut into traditional shapes such as fish, dragons, phoenix and plum blossoms. While these can be done by hand by skilled cooks, generally they are made with a vegetable stamp shaped out of brass, covered metal or aluminum.

WOODEN DROP LID: (Japan) This is a wooden lid smaller than the pot, allowing it to be

placed directly on food that is being simmered or boiled. It prevents delicate foods from tumbling and breaking up.
Also known as *otoshi-buta* (Japan)

UTENSILS, WOK AND ACCESSORIES:
This wide pan, with its smoothly curved base and sides, is now known throughout the Western world and has been in use in the Chinese kitchen for of centuries. It is the perfect pan for stir-frying. Deep-frying is effectively and safely done in the wok, because the surface is wide and there is less risk that bubbling oil will spill over. For steaming *dim sum*, vegetables, fish and chicken, slat-bottomed bamboo baskets are placed in towering stacks in the wok. There are different kinds of woks. The Indonesian *wajan* is deeper with straighter sides, while the Vietnamese *chao* is smaller and shallower. The *dare-oh* of Burma is a rounded, deep pan similar to a wok; it is made of brass or cast iron and has a looped handle on either side. In Japan the *chuka nabe* or *shina-nabe* is used as a frying pan and its shape is very similar to that of a wok. A single-handled, flat-bottomed wok is now manufactured for use on electric cooktops, with reasonably good results.
Also known as *kuali*, *kwali* (Malaysia, Singapore); *carajay* (Philippines)

WOK LIDS are large domes with a handle on top, designed to fit just inside the lip of the wok. They are used when the wok is being used as a steamer, and to cook certain sautéed foods.

WOK SPATULA is the essential tool to use with a wok. It is a square-shaped, wide, flat spatula with its working edge shaped to fit the curve of the wok. Two can be used together to lift large foods such as fish or chicken from the wok.
Also known as *charn* (China)

UZURA NO IAMAGO: *(UZU-RA NO TAH-MAH-GO*, Japan) (Quail) see EGG

V

VARAQ: (*VARAK*, India) Tissue-thin, beaten silver which is sold in small, delicate sheets. It is used as a lavish decoration on dessert and rice dishes, and also to cover whole nuts, particularly almonds, being used as a garnish. More extravagantly, beaten pure gold is used on very special occasions in the same way. It is sold by the sheet, each interlayered with tissue paper, at specialty Indian stores, and price is generally dictated by current metal values. It should be handled gently, preferably transported to the dish on its protective sheet as it can easily tear or cling to the fingers.
Also known as *chandi ka barakh*, *chandi ka warq*, *warq* (India); *sone ka warq* (gold leaf) (India); silver foil/leaf

VEGETABLE MELONS AND GOURDS: see MELONS AND GOURDS

VEGETABLE SALAD
Serves 4–6

3 large cucumbers, peeled and seeded
¼ cup (2 fl oz / 60 ml) white vinegar
1 tsp salt
1½ cups (12 oz / 350 g) thinly sliced onion
2 tsps minced garlic
3 tbsps Oriental sesame oil
1 tsp turmeric
sugar
1½ tbsps toasted white sesame seeds

Very thinly slice cucumber and place in a pan with the vinegar, salt and water to cover. Bring to a boil, then drain thoroughly. Fry onion and garlic in sesame oil until golden and softened; add turmeric with cucumber and toss in the oil to heat through, add additional vinegar and sugar to taste. Sprinkle on sesame seeds. Serve cool.

303

VEGETABLE PLATTER: In Cambodia, Laos, Thailand and Vietnam a platter of raw vegetables and herbs is served with most meals. They are eaten as a side dish or wrapped in *banh trang* or *banh uot* wrappers with crisply fried rolls, grilled meats and meatballs to make crisp, fresh-tasting rolls which are eaten with the fingers.

A basic vegetable platter may contain: fresh herbs such as basil, fresh coriander, caraway mint, dill, mint, Vietnamese mint, polygonum; lettuce of several kinds; cucumber, cut into strips; carrot, cut into strips; scallions, cut into shreds; cooked thin rice sticks or transparent vermicelli. Arrange rinsed, prepared and

---

VEGETABLES IN COCONUT SAUCE
Serves 6

1 medium eggplant (aubergine), cubed
salt
2 unripe bananas, peeled and sliced
1 cup (4 oz / 125 g) sliced green or long beans
1 carrot, sliced
1 onion, sliced
1 green bell pepper (green pepper / capsicum),
cut into squares
sweet potato, cubed
1 tsp ground cumin
1/2 tsp turmeric
1 cup (8 fl oz / 250 ml) water
3/4 cup (1 1/2 oz / 45 g) grated fresh coconut
1 cup (4 oz / 125 g) chopped tomato
1/2 cup (4 fl oz / 125 ml) plain (natural) yogurt
sugar
lemon juice
2 green chilies, seeded and sliced
3 curry leaves
coconut or vegetable oil

Sprinkle eggplant with salt, leave 10 minutes, then rinse and dry. Place fruit and vegetables in a saucepan with cumin, turmeric, water and 1 tsp salt. Cover and simmer over medium heat until almost cooked. Add coconut, tomato and yogurt and simmer until the vegetables are almost tender. Season with sugar and lemon juice. Fry chilies and curry leaves in oil, stir into the vegetables and serve.

---

chilled vegetables and herbs on a wide platter or in a basket, with noodles piled at the side.
Also known as *dai rau song* (Vietnam)
See also: BANH TRANG, BANH UOT

VELLAY POONDOO: (*VEL-EE POON-DOO*, India) see GARLIC

VENISON: see MEAT, DEER

VIETNAM: Brought to world attention by the Vietnam war, the previously little-known subtropical country of Vietnam with its long and glorious coastline enjoys an elegant, though simple, cuisine. A period of French occupation brought skills in bread-making and French cooking techniques to an already refined cooking style. The range of dishes is not immense and is influenced by its northern neighbor China in its use of stir-frying, steaming and simmering methods to achieve natural flavors. Together with its western neighbor Thailand it has acquired a love of fresh herbs and green vegetables, an abundance of which are consumed with every meal. Eating sandwich-style, with cooked meats, herbs, soft vermicelli and slivers of pickled vegetable rolled in lettuce leaves then encased in the soft rice crêpes known as *banh trang,* is one of the most popular meals in Vietnam. The other is a simple, filling bowl of soup noodles of which their range is prodigious. Rice noodles from thin to thick, from narrow to wide and flat are dropped into large, deep bowls of steaming stock flavored with ginger or aniseed, floating with slivers, chunks or meatballs of pork, chicken, beef, fish or shrimp. A dusting of white pepper, a dash of chili paste or a splash of lime juice or potent, salty *nuoc mam* (fish sauce) complete the seasoning. Chopsticks and porcelain spoons, in the Chinese manner, are the order on the Vietnamese table, although certain foods are eaten with the fingers. Rice is the staple, but frequently comes to the table in noodle form. An impressive banquet tradition enjoyed at relatively few venues in this country is the special occasion meal known as "seven styles of beef" in which beef—or perhaps venison or buffalo—is cooked into seven quite different dishes and presented in a select sequence, each to enhance the other. Tabletop cooking, usually grilling, is enjoyed, and is done on small portable hot plates over glowing charcoal. They are invariably accompanied by *goi* (salad ingredients) and by a sauce dip similar to that served in Indonesia and Thailand with *satay*, based on ground roasted peanuts, or with a *nuoc mam* (fish sauce) based sauce combining chili and lime juice.

VIETNAM RECIPES

Appetizers
Beef Balls
Beef and Noodles in Rich Broth
Crabmeat and Chicken Rolls
Dried Bamboo Shoots and Chicken Noodles in Soup
Hanoi Beef Soup
Shrimp Cakes
Shrimp and Crabmeat Balls in Noodle Soup
Sugar Cane Shrimp Balls
Triangular Rolls with Whole Shrimp

Main Courses
Beef Fondue with Vinegar
Beef Simmered with Lemon Grass
Chicken with Lemon Grass
Chicken Rice Noodles with Pork
Meatballs of Pork with Salad Greens
Vietnamese-style Beijing Duck

Accompaniments
Chicken Salad with Mint Leaves
Nuoc Cham
Nuoc Mau

Dessert
Steamed Sticky Rice in Coconut Cream

MENU
(see recipes)

DINNER MENU
Serves 6–8

Crabmeat and Chicken Rolls
Shrimp Cakes

Meatballs of Pork with Salad Greens
Beef Simmered with Lemon Grass
Chicken Salad with Mint Leaves

Steamed Sticky Rice in Coconut Cream

VIETNAMESE CHILI FISH SAUCE: see NUOC CHAM

VIETNAMESE MINT: There are many different types of mint used in Vietnamese cooking, some of which are indigenous, others introduced from Europe. The most commonly used ones are known there as *que*, *rau tuom*, and *hung*. Many of these types are easily grown from seeds that can be purchased where Vietnamese foods are sold, or propagated by placing fresh mint stems in water until they grow roots. Common garden mints, polygonum, basil and other fresh herbs such as dill and coriander can be used in Vietnamese dishes. A fragrant herb *rau la tia to*, which is the leaves of the caraway seed plant, is also used.
See also: CORIANDER, FRESH; CHICKEN SALAD WITH MINT LEAVES (recipe); MINT; POLYGONUM; RAU LA TIA TO; VEGETABLE PLATTER

VIETNAMESE PEANUT SAUCE: (recipe) see PEANUT; PEANUT SAUCE (recipe)

VIETNAMESE SPRING ROLL WRAPPER: see BANH TRANG

VIETNAMESE SOY SAUCE: see TUONG

VIETNAMESE-STYLE BEIJING DUCK: (recipe) see BEIJING DUCK

VINDALOO OF DUCK
Serves 6–8

5 lbs (2 kgs) duck
2 cups (1 lb / 500 g) chopped onions
1 tbsp minced garlic
1/4 cup (2 oz / 60 g) ghee
3 green chilies, seeded and chopped
3 1/2–4 tbsps Vindaloo Paste (see recipe)
water
salt

Rinse duck and cut into serving pieces. Fry onions and garlic in ghee for 5 minutes. Add chilies and Vindaloo Paste and cook over medium heat for 4 minutes. Add duck, turn in the spices to coat evenly, sprinkle on a little water and cook, turning occasionally, until well colored. Add water to cover duck, cover pan and simmer until the duck is very tender and the sauce reduced. Season with salt.

VINDALOO: (*VIN-DAA--LOO*, India) This is an intensely hot Indian dish seasoned with a combination of ground roasted spices and chilies acidulated with vinegar and/or tamarind. Vindaloos, a specialty of central and western coastal India, have a very strong flavor best made with rich, strong-tasting meats such as pork, duck and game. Vindaloo seasoning paste can be purchased commercially or can be made at home and kept in the refrigerator. This potent curry develops a rounded balance of flavors if cooked several days before serving.

VINDALOO PASTE is a hot, tart spice paste used to flavor vindaloo-style curries (see recipe).

VINDALOO PASTE

5–12 dried red chilies
1¹/₂ tbsps coriander seeds
2 tsps cumin seeds
1 tsp fenugreek seeds
¹/₂ tsp black mustard seeds
¹/₂ tsp black peppercorns
³/₄ tsp turmeric
1¹/₂ tsps salt
3 tbsps white vinegar
1 tsp tamarind concentrate mixed with
2 tbsps cold water

Roast the chilies, coriander, cumin, fenugreek, mustard seeds and peppercorns in a dry pan or oven until well-colored, stirring frequently. Remove from pan, add the remaining ingredients and mix with the following:

1 large onion, minced
8 garlic cloves, minced
2 tsps minced ginger

To make a smooth vindaloo paste, process the mixture in a food processor or blender. Store for 1–2 weeks in the refrigerator, or omit the onions, garlic and ginger and store the spice mixture for many weeks.

VINEGAR: Distilled vinegar is used to a small extent in Asia. In China, Thailand and Vietnam it is used in sweet and sour dishes and also in marinades. In India it gives acidity to tangy Vindaloo Sauce and is used for pickles. It has a sharp flavor and is appreciated in the Philippines in many dishes, of which *estofado* and *adobo* are most well known. In Japan and China vinegar is made from rice. *Suka,* the Philippine "native vinegar," is made from coconut sap and is less acidic and more perfumed than vinegar.

Also known as *sirka* (India); *cuka* (Malaysia); *nam som* (Thailand)

See also: ADOBO CHICKEN (recipe); BEEF FONDUE WITH VINEGAR (recipe); RICE VINEGAR **and recipes following**

VINEGAR AND GARLIC SAUCE

To serve with sliced roast pork or goose:

2 tbsps red rice vinegar or distilled white vinegar
1 tbsp minced garlic

Mix together and serve in small sauce dishes.

VINEGAR AND GINGER SAUCE

Makes ¹/₄ cup (2 fl oz / 60 ml)

Traditionally served with steamed dumplings or pot stickers, and with some Chinese chicken and seafood dishes:

3 tbsps red rice vinegar
1 tbsp finely shredded ginger

Mix together and serve in small sauce dishes.

VINEGARED SEAWEED WITH CRAB AND CUCUMBER

Serves 6

4 Japanese cucumbers or 1 acid-free cucumber
salt
1 cup (8 oz / 250 g) dried wakame seaweed, soaked
Sunomono *Sauce* (sanbaizu) *(see recipe)*
8 oz (250 g) crabmeat

(cont'd)

Very thinly slice unpeeled cucumber, spread on a board and sprinkle lightly with salt. Let stand for 15 minutes to soften. Drain *wakame*, blanch in boiling water, drain and chop. Pour half the sauce over the salted cucumber; stir. Assemble cucumber, seaweed and crabmeat in a glass dish, pour on remaining sauce.

VINEGAR, CHINESE/JAPANESE: see RICE VINEGAR

VINEGARED FOODS: see SUNOMONO

WAH-BHO-HMYIT: (*WA-BOE-HMYIT*, Burma) see BAMBOO SHOOT

WAKAME: (*WA-KAH-ME*, Japan) see SEAWEED

WALNUT: (*Juglans regia*) The Chinese or cathay walnut is native to mountainous regions of Asia between Kashmir and western China. Though not used extensively in Asian cooking, walnuts are cooked in salt, dry roasted or coated with toffee to serve as a snack, particularly in the northern and central Chinese provinces. The young green nuts can be eaten raw or pickled in vinegar with spices. **Also known as** *hetaoren* (China); *arhrot* (India)

WARIBASHI: (*WAH-REE-BAH-SHI*, Japan) see CHOPSTICKS

WARI SHIO: (*WAH-REE SHI-O*, Japan) A mixture of salt, cornstarch and *aji no moto* (monosodium glutamate) used as a seasoned coating for fried foods.

WARISHITA: (*WA-REE-SHI-TA*, Japan) A mixture of *dashi* stock, soy sauce and *mirin* used to cook *sukiyaki*. The amount of each ingredient can be varied to personal taste, using this basic formula.

WARISHITA (SUKIYAKI SAUCE)

2 cups (16 fl oz / 500 ml) dashi
1/2 cup (4 fl oz / 125 ml) mirin
3/4 cup (6 fl oz / 180 ml) dark soy sauce

Mix the ingredients in a jug and present with the *sukiyaki* platter.

WARM MINCED BEEF SALAD: (salad) see BEEF

WARQ: (*VARAK*, India) see VARAQ

WASABI: (*WA-SAH-BEE*, Japan) (*Wasabia japonica*) This plant, native to Japan, and known otherwise as the mountain hollyhock, has edible roots that yield one of the strongest known spices. The gnarled, brown, green-skinned root, covered with tiny eyes, has bright green flesh that is grated and used fresh, or is dried and ground to a fine, pale green powder—in which form it is usually available in the West. It has the searing quality of mustard, but beneath the fire, a refreshing, cleansing taste that heightens the senses and gives a lift to bland foods. Neither *sushi* nor *sashimi* would have quite the same impact without a dab of *wasabi*. In the former, it is smeared over the rice ball before the topping is added; it accompanies the latter in the form of a little peak of paste—sometimes esthetically shaped into a leaf design—which is stirred into the dipping sauce. *Wasabi* in powdered form is sold in small, attractively painted cans; in paste form it comes in tubes or small tubs. Unopened it keeps indefinitely in dry conditions; once opened its flavor will disperse after some months. Keep refrigerated. It is sometimes known as Japanese horseradish.
Also known as *namida* (tears) (Japan)
See also: SASHIMI, SUSHI

Wasabi root

WASABI PREPARATION: In a small cup mix powdered *wasabi* with enough luke-warm water or sake to make a slightly dry paste. Turn the cup over and leave 5–6 minutes until the *wasabi* softens. Then pinch it into a little triangular shape and place on the

dish. It can be formed into a leaf or other shape, using a knife or small mold.

WATER APPLE: see ROSE APPLE

WATER CALTROP: (*Trapis bicornis*) This two-horned nut has shiny black skin, crisp, white flesh and a flavor similar to that of its less bizarre-looking cousin, the water chestnut. The caltrop has been eaten for over 4000 years, and in China was listed as one of the "five ancient grains." The Singhara nut (*T. bispinosa*), a similar two-horned nut, is still eaten in Kashmir and a four-horned variety (*T. natans*), otherwise known as Jesuit's nut, was one of the earliest foods eaten in Europe. Water caltrops only rarely appear in the markets, but when they are available they can be kept in the refrigerator for several weeks. The skin must be removed with a thick sharp knife or by cracking it with a nutcracker. The nuts must be boiled for at least one hour to destroy a parasitic bacterium that is harmful to the digestive system. The Chinese like to eat water caltrops during the mid-autumn moon festival.
Also known as *ling gok* (China); *singhara* (India)
See also: WATER CHESTNUT

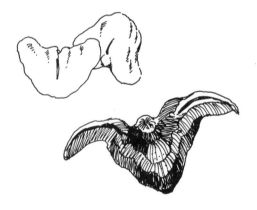

Walter caltrops

WATER CHESTNUT: (*Eleocharis dulcis*) This mahogany-colored nut resembles the chestnut, but has papery, buff-colored layers attached to the skin that come to a tufted point in the center. It is now available fresh in many Chinese food markets and if it is not peeled will keep for at least two weeks in the refrigerator. It has a semisweet, crisp flesh, rather like a jicama or raw potato, and can be eaten raw as a fruit, added to desserts or cooked as a vegetable. In Asia it is peeled, threaded onto short bamboo skewers and soaked in salt water. It retains its crisp texture when cooked, which gives an interesting dimension to stuffings, fillings for *dim sum* and soups. Although it is popular as a vegetable in Western countries, the Chinese do not appreciate it in vegetable dishes. Water chestnuts are used extensively in Thailand and other parts of Southeast Asia in sweet desserts and drinks, usually combined with coconut milk and palm sugar. Canned water chestnuts, whole or sliced, are sold in all Asian food stores. Once opened, they should be transferred to a container of clean water; they will keep for at least a week if the water is changed daily. Another vegetable sometimes known as water chestnut is the two-horned water caltrop.

Also known as *ma taai* (China); *pani singhara* (India); *apulid* (Philippines); *haew* (Thailand); Chinese water chestnut

See also: WATER CALTROPS; WATER CHESTNUTS IN COCONUT MILK (recipe)

WATER CHESTNUTS IN COCONUT MILK
Serves 6

2 cups (16 fl oz / 500 ml) thin coconut milk
3/4 cup (6 fl oz / 180 ml) ice water
1/3 cup (3 fl oz / 90 ml) sugar syrup, cooled
salt
1½ cups (12 oz / 350 g) sliced water chestnuts, rinsed
crushed ice

In a large pitcher mix coconut milk with ice water, sugar syrup and a large pinch of salt. Add water chestnuts and crushed ice. Serve in tall glasses.

WATER CHESTNUT STARCH: see FLOURS AND THICKENERS

WATER CONVOLVULUS: see KANGKONG

WATERCRESS: (*Nasturtium officinale*) Introduced to Asia by the British, watercress is now cultivated to a limited extent in southern China and in other countries. The Chinese like to boil it in a soup with pork and *jujube* (red dates). It is used in salads in Thailand, Laos and Vietnam and occasionally as a garnish in Japan.

Also known as *sai yeung choy* (China); *chamsur* (India, Nepal)
See also: JUJUBE

WATERMELON: see MELONS AND GOURDS

WATER SPINACH: see KANGKONG

WAX GOURD: see MELONS AND GOURDS (WINTER MELON)

WEI: (*WAY*) see CHINA, COOKING METHODS (SIMMER-STEW)

WELLAYAPPAM: (*VE-LA-YA-PAM*, Sri Lanka) see APPA

WELSH ONION: see ONION

WHEAT GLUTEN: see GLUTEN

WHITEBAIT: see ANCHOVY

WHITE CUMIN: see CUMIN

WHITE FUNGUS: (*Tremella fuciformis*) A silvery white, crinkly edible fungus closely related to the black fungus known in China as "cloud ear" or wood fungus. It is sold in dried form, when it is a pale golden color and resembles a ball of natural sponge. Enjoyed by the Chinese—particularly women, who believe that eating it will improve their complexion—it appears on their menus in sweet soups and in vegetarian dishes. Better-quality white fungus is sold in impressive cellophane gift boxes. Otherwise it is sold in bulk. It should be stored in an airtight container and will keep indefinitely. White fungus must be soaked to rehydrate it before use, and the root section may need to be snipped away. It has little taste of its own but readily accepts the flavors of accompanying ingredients. The texture is agreeably crunchy, rather like birds' nests. Its other name, "snow fungus," is a misnomer; this is actually a gland taken from a type of frog, which is used medicinally.

Also known as *seet gnee, yiner* (China); *shiro*

kikurage (Japan); silver fungus; snow fungus; tremella
See also: MUSHROOMS AND EDIBLE FUNGI

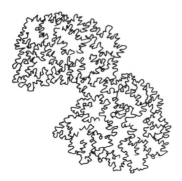

Dried white fungus

WHITE MUSTARD CABBAGE: see CABBAGE, CHINESE (BOK CHOY)

WHITE SESAME SEED: see SESAME SEED

WHITE TURMERIC: see ZEDOARY

WHOLEMEAL FLOUR: see FLOURS AND THICKENERS (ATTA)

WILD BOAR: This is eaten in some parts of Southeast Asia, India and central China for its strongly flavored meat.
See also: PORK, CURED

WILD RICE SHOOT: (*Zizania aquatica* L.) The edible young shoots of a grain crop known in the West as wild rice. It is grown from Japan, through central China, to the Indo-Chinese countries and northern India. The shoots come to the market as a spear-shaped vegetable, about 10 in (25 cm) long. They

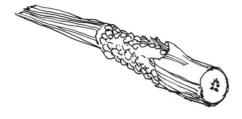

Wild rice shoot

resemble young sugar cane or underdeveloped ears of corn. They can be steamed, boiled or baked, or sliced and stir-fried.
Also known as *gaau sun* (China)

WINE, ASIAN: Throughout Asia many different types of alcoholic drink are consumed. Beer accounts for the bulk of drinks sold, but various types of brewed and distilled strong drinks are also made using locally available ingredients. In China there are fermented and distilled grain wines and grape wine; the Japanese have sake. In the Philippines, Malaysia and Indonesia the sap of a coconut palm is tapped to make *arak* and *lambanog*. In Bali the light pink *brem* is favored. Inhabitants of the lands along the banks of the Mekong have named their potent drink after that mighty river. India has a tradition of prohibition, except the state of Goa, which until recent times was under the jurisdiction of Portugal and manufactured various types of alcoholic drink.
See also: WINE, CHINESE

ARAK is a strong-tasting wine made from fermented rice or palm sap. It tastes like a coarse sake, but is higher in alcohol. It is the wine drunk by villagers of Southeast Asia in areas where rice or palms grow. This is not to be confused with the *arak* of the Middle East, which is anise-flavored.

BASI is a popular alcoholic beverage in the Philippines. Fermented from sugar cane, it is drunk extensively in sugar-growing regions of the country.

BREM BALI is a sweet-tasting rice wine made from fermented, boiled glutinous rice in a process similar to that which produces sake. It is sold in Bali and other parts of Indonesia, usually in small bottles. It has a light pink color.

JUNG-JONG is a potent, clear, brewed beverage, made in Korea from fermented rice by a technique similar to that used in sake-making. It is moderately low in alcohol and has a taste similar to sake.

LAMBANOG is a by-product of the coconut industry; an alcoholic drink distilled from *tuba*.
See also: TUBA

MEKONG WHISKY is a strong, raw-tasting spirit, made by the whisky-distilling method. It is the main locally made spirit drunk in the Indo-Chinese countries and Thailand. As brown as the turbulent waters of the Mekong itself, it is not a drink for the faint-hearted.

MIRIN is a sweetened golden wine, made as a cooking ingredient and not a beverage. *Mirin* is used to glaze broiled foods, to enhance the flavor of basting sauces such as those used on *yakitori* and *teriyaki*. It leaves an agreeable residual sweetness. The alcohol is usually burnt off by boiling before use, leaving just the intense sweet flavor. *Mirin* is not classed as an alcoholic drink, so is usually stocked with food products and is readily available. It keeps well, but in warm, humid conditions it is best to store it in the refrigerator after opening, to avoid the proliferation of a yeast mold on the surface. A well-flavored sweet sherry, or Chinese *shaohsing* yellow rice wine, can be substituted, with a little extra sugar to balance the flavor. A *mirin* with added salt and corn syrup, to stabilize the viscosity, is marketed under the name *aji-mirin*.

Also known as *aji-mirin*, *hon mirin* (Japan); Japanese sherry; sweet sake

SAKE is both the name for Japan's most popular alcoholic beverage and the word that refers to all Japanese alcoholic drinks. Its origins go back to prehistoric times but legend has it that sake was discovered by a Shinto shrine maiden, who found that cooked rice that had been chewed for some time developed a sweet, yeasty taste. The original formula for sake specified that chewed rice be used to begin the fermentation, and this method is still practiced at some specialty breweries in Japan. The yeast mold *Aspergillus oryzae*, introduced into steamed rice, has the same effect and begins the fermentation process. Lactic acid is added to prevent contamination, then the milky fermentation is filtered to produce the crystal-clear finished product. The entire process takes about 45 days. Connoisseurs advise that sake be drunk immediately, but it is usually at least three months old before it reaches the marketplace. It should, however, be drunk within a year of manufacture; once the bottle is open it begins to lose its flavor.

Tradition dictates that sake be drunk warm, poured from small, narrow-necked porcelain or glazed earthenware bottles into tiny porcelain cups. But it is also a delightful summer drink served over ice with a twist of lemon. Japanese cooks use sake extensively in cooking. In sauces, combined with soy sauce and sugar, it gives a rich flavor and makes a deep brown, shiny glaze on foods. It is usual to burn off the alcohol by bringing the sake to a boil before cooking with it in this way. Added to, or replacing, water when steaming or simmering, sake imparts its unique flavor and acts as a tenderizer.

Also known as Japanese rice wine
See also: SAKE-SIMMERED MACKEREL (recipe)

SUJU is a strong alcoholic drink distilled in Korea from grain or potatoes.

TODDY is an alcoholic beverage made in India from sap tapped from coconut or other palms. It is also used to begin the ferment of the dough for *appa* breads, and is reduced to a sweet, luscious nectar known as *paani*.
See also: APPA; COCONUT

SAKE-SIMMERED MACKEREL

1 lb (500 g) mackerel fillets
water
2/3 cup (5 fl oz / 150 ml) sake
1/2 cup (4 fl oz / 125 ml) mirin
1 cup (8 fl oz / 250 ml) dashi
1 x 4 in (10 cm) square of kombu seaweed
2 cakes soft bean curd
beni shoga
sugar
dark soy sauce

Blanch fish in boiling water for 30 seconds. Drain, dip into cold water; drain again. Heat sake to almost boiling; add *mirin* and *dashi*. Add *kombu* and fish and bring to a simmer. Reduce heat, cover with a drop lid (*otoshi-buta*); cook 20 minutes over very low heat. Remove fish, cut into slices. Simmer bean curd in the liquid for 2 minutes. Arrange bean curd and fish on plates and garnish with *beni shoga*. Serve with a sauce of sugar and soy sauce to taste.

WINE BALL/WINE CUBE (China) A type

of compressed brewer's yeast used in wine-making. They resemble small ping pong balls and can be purchased, usually in packs of two, from Chinese herbalists.

See also: FERMENTED RED RICE; FERMENTED RICE (WINE LEES) (recipe)

Wine balls

WINE, CHINESE: The Chinese have been

brewing alcoholic drinks for more than 4000 years. In that time every imaginable leaf, herb, blossom or spice—plus a variety of more esoteric additives such as whole eagles, fish and snakes—have been experimented with as a flavoring for alcoholic drinks, or as a base for medicinal wines.

The oldest form of brewing was based on a grain fermentation and used sorghum, millet and rice. But grape wines have been made since the seventh century. Today Chinese wines range from grape wines and mild brews of rice-based wines—many flavored with fruits and flowers such as lychee or rose—through to strong distilled spirits.

Also known as *chiew*; *chiu*; *jiu*

KWEILIN GUI HUA JIU (Cassia Blossom Wine) is an aromatic Chinese wine similar in taste to light, fragrant vermouth.

MAO TAI is an extremely potent distilled spirit made in China from sorghum. Often over 150 percent proof, this clear spirit is served as a toasting beverage at Chinese banquets. It achieved notoriety during President Nixon's China visit.

Also known as *bai-ga'r*, *gaoliang*, *mou tai* (China)

NANKING FENG GANG JIU ("sealed jug" wine) is an aromatic wine made from rice that has a flavor not unlike a German dessert wine.

SHAOHSING YELLOW RICE WINE is an amber rice wine from China's Shaohsing (Shaoxing) province that has been made for more than 2000 years. Glutinous rice, millet and a yeast mold are mixed with local waters and the resultant smooth-tasting wine is aged for between 10 and 100 years. It is now bottled like grape wines, but was originally stored in glazed pottery jars decorated with flower designs. From there it derived the name *hua daio*, which translates as "flower carving." In Sichuan province, and many other parts of China, Shaohsing wine may be known as "girl's or daughter's wine," because at the birth of a daughter families may store jars of the wine to be drunk at her wedding. Traditionally the wine is drunk warm in small cups or glasses. It may be flavored with preserved plums or slices of fresh lemon.

Shaohsing rice wine is one of the important ingredients in Chinese cooking. It is sprinkled into stir-fried dishes, and imparts a rich caramel-wine flavor. It is splashed onto the sides of the heated wok so that the alcohol burns off before the wine reaches the food. It is added liberally to simmered and stewed dishes and used as a marinade in "drunken" dishes.

Also known as *fen chiew*; *huang chiu*; *hua daio*; *hua tiao* (China); red girl wine; rice wine; yellow wine

WINE LEES: see FERMENTED RED RICE

WINGED BEAN: (*Psophocarpus tetro-

gonolobus*) This native plant of southern Europe grows freely in Southeast Asia and its unusual pods are enjoyed for their delicate flavor, which is very slightly suggestive of asparagus. Bright green in color, the short, square-shaped beans have a decorative frill along each side from which the name "winged bean" originates. It may also be called "asparagus bean" or "asparagus pea" and has sometimes been confused with the asparagus bean of South America which produces a black-eyed pea (bean) that is used dried.

Winged beans should be bought when

young, not longer than 2¹/2 in (6 cm) and can be stored in a perforated plastic bag in the refrigerator for up to a week. Cook by steaming, parboiling or stir-frying. In Thailand the raw beans are blanched, marinated in vinegar or lime juice and served as a salad.

Also known as *kecipir* (Indonesia); *goa*, *sigarilya* (Philippines); *tua poo* (Thailand); asparagus bean; asparagus pea

See also: WINGED BEAN SALAD (recipe)

Winged bean

WINGED BEAN SALAD
Serves 4–6

12 oz (350 g) winged beans, thinly sliced
boiling water
ice water
8 oz (250 g) peeled shrimp (prawns),
steamed
4 oz (120 g) diced pork or bacon, fried crisp
1 tbsp sliced garlic, fried crisp
1 tbsp chopped scallions (spring/green
onions), fried crisp
1 tbsp sliced dried chili, fried crisp
1¹/2 tbsps nam prik
lime juice
sugar
thick coconut milk
salt
pepper
¹/4 cup (1¹/2 oz/40 g) crushed
roasted peanuts
2 tbsps toasted desiccated coconut

Blanch winged beans in boiling water, then plunge into ice water to make beans green and crisp. Mix with shrimp, pork, garlic, scallions and chili. Mix *nam prik* with lime juice, sugar and coconut milk to taste. Add salt and pepper and pour over salad. Garnish with peanuts and coconut.

WINTER BAMBOO SHOOT: see BAMBOO SHOOT

WINTER MELON: see MELONS AND GOURDS

WINTER SQUASH: see MELONS AND GOURDS

WOK: see UTENSILS, WOK AND ACCESORIES

WOLFBERRY: see BOXTHORN

WONG BOK: (*WONG BAK*, China) see CABBAGE, CHINESE (NAPA)

WONG GWA: (*WONG GWA*, China) see CUCUMBER (YELLOW)

WONG NGA BAAK: (*WONG NGA BAK*, China) see CABBAGE, CHINESE (NAPA)

WONGPAAN: (*WONG BARN*, China) see GAROUPA

WONTONS IN CLEAR SOUP
Serves 6

4 oz (120 g) ground pork
2 oz (60 g) raw shelled shrimp (prawns)
1 tbsp finely ground pork fat
¹/4 cup (2 oz/60 g) water chestnuts or bamboo
shoots
2 tsps minced scallions (spring/green onions)
1 tsp salt and 1 tsp pepper
1 tsp sugar
18 wonton wrappers
lightly salted water
4 cups (1 qt/1 l) chicken stock
1 tbsp sliced scallions (spring/green onions)

Mix pork, shrimp, pork fat, water chestnuts or bamboo shoots and minced scallions with the salt, pepper and sugar. To form wontons, place filling on center of each wrapper, moisten edges and fold diagonally to form a triangle. Press edges together, then pinch two points together to make a circular shape and fold tail outwards. Poach in lightly salted water until they float. Serve in hot chicken stock with sliced scallions.

WONTON SKINS/WRAPPERS
Yields about 85

1 quantity Egg Noodles
cornstarch (cornflour)

Prepare dough, using recipe for Egg Noodles. Roll out as thinly

(cont'd)

(Wonton Skins / Wrappers cont'd)

as possible—the dough should be almost transparent—and cut into 3 in (8 cm) squares. Dust with cornstarch, stack together and wrap in plastic. Refrigerate or freeze.

WON YEE: (*WAN YI*, China) see CLOUD EAR FUNGUS

WOO CHAK: (*WOO CHAK*, China) see CUTTLE-FISH

WOOD APPLE: Indigenous to India, Nepal and Sri Lanka, wood apples are an edible fruit about the size of oranges. They are eaten raw or made into jellies and sherbets. They are considered good for the stomach; the ripe or unripe fruit contains a drug called *Belae fructus* which is used in the treatment of dysentery. The mashed fruit, sweetened with sugar and thinned with water, is enjoyed in Nepal as a sherbet. Wood apples are rarely sold fresh away from their native habitat, but are available canned.
Also known as *bel* (Nepal); aegletree; elephant apple

WOOD EAR: see CLOUD EAR FUNGUS

WOOD FUNGUS: see CLOUD EAR FUNGUS

WOON SEN: (*WOON SEN*, Indonesia, Malaysia) see NOODLES (BEAN THREAD VERMICELLI)

X Y Z

XACUTTI CHICKEN: (recipe) see CHICKEN

XANTHOXYLUM: see SICHUAN PEPPERCORN

XIU: (*SIL*, China) see CHINA, COOKING METHODS (BOILING)

YADAN: (*NGAP-DARN*, China) see EGG

YAIR CHOY FAR: (*YER CHOY FA*, China) see CAULIFLOWER

YAKHNI: (*YAKHNEE*, India) see GARHI YAKHNI

YAKI DOFU: (*YAH-KEE DOH-WHO*, Japan) see BEAN CURD (GRILLED)

YAKI FU: (*YAH-KEE WHO*, Japan) see GLUTEN

YAKIMONO: (*YAH-KEE-MOW-NO*) see JAPAN, COOKING METHODS (SALTING)

YAKI MYOBAN: (*YAH-KEE MYOW-BAN*, Japan) see ALUM

YAKITORI
Serves 4

8 oz (250 g) chicken livers, halved
2 lbs (1 kg) chicken thighs, boned
8 togarashi *peppers*
5 naganegi *onions*
bamboo skewers
Yakitori *Sauce (see recipe)*
sansho *pepper*/shichimi, soaked

Rinse and dry livers. Cut chicken into 1 in (2.5 cm) cubes. Quarter peppers. Cut onions crossways into 1 in (2.5 cm) lengths. Thread ingredients alternately on soaked skewers. Grill over hot coals, turning frequently, until done, brushing 2–3 times with *Yakitori* Sauce during cooking. Sprinkle on *sansho* or *shichimi*.

Taro, which is drier, and sweet potato, which has a softer, sweeter flesh, can be substituted. Yam bean, or *jicama*, known commonly in Southeast Asia as *bangkwang*, is a quite different vegetable with a sweet, crisp flesh.

MOUNTAIN YAM, "mountain yam" (the Japanese name translates as "long potato"), is another type of yam harvested in Japan. It has a gluey texture, similar to taro. It is finely grated and added to foods as a binder. It is considered an excellent digestive.

Also known as *shan yao* (China); *ko-imo, sato imo* (field yam); *arbi, ghuiyan* (India, Nepal); *arvi, banda, colcasia* (Indonesia); *yama no imo* (mountain yam) (Japan); *keladi* (Malaysia); *ube, ubi* (Philippines)

See also: SWEET POTATO, TARO; YAM BEAN

YAM BEAN: (*Pachyrhizus erosus*) From the family Leguminosae, this edible, turnip-shaped tuber is known more widely as *jicama* and, through most of Southeast Asia, as *bangkwang*. It has a white, crisp, starchy flesh. Peeled and sliced, or shredded, it can be eaten raw and is an important ingredient in salads and a type of uncooked spring roll known in Malaysia as *poh pia*. It can also be boiled, baked, steamed or stir-fried. If unobtainable, giant white radish can be substituted in many recipes.

Also known as *bangkwang* (Malaysia); *jicama, saa got* (China)

See also: FLOURS AND THICKENERS (KUZU); RADISH, GIANT WHITE; YAM

Yam bean

YAKITORI SAUCE
Yields 3 cups (24 fl oz / 750 ml)

1 cup (8 fl oz / 250 ml) sake
2/3 cup (5 fl oz / 150 ml) mirin
2/3 cup (5 oz / 150 g) crushed rock sugar
1 1/2 cups (12 fl oz / 375 ml) dark soy sauce
1/2 cup (4 fl oz / 125 ml) light soy sauce

Mix ingredients in a non-aluminum saucepan and bring to a boil. Reduce heat and simmer for 15–20 minutes. Cool and refrigerate.

Yakitori on skewers

YAM: (*Dioscorea opposita, D. japonica, D. esculenta*) Yam is the common name of the cultivated species of the genus *Dioscorea*, which has been a staple food since prehistoric times. The edible root of a fast-growing climbing plant, it ranges in shape and size from small and round to extremely large, elongated and irregular. The flesh ranges through gray-white, yellow, gold and orange-red to purple. The vegetable has a high starch content and a bland flavor. The texture is floury and slightly dry. Yams must be thickly peeled, to remove the bitter sap that is located immediately beneath the skin. Yam is used as a vegetable, mainly to add substance to a dish, and may be boiled, braised, simmered or steamed. In Japan it is battered and deep-fried as a *tempura* vegetable. In some regions the leaves and stems are still eaten as a vegetable. Diced yam is a common ingredient in coconut milk desserts in Malaysia and Indonesia.

315

YAN WO: (*YIN WOR*, China) see BIRD'S NEST

YAO DOU: (*YIU GWOH*, China) see CASHEW NUT

YAO HORN: (*YAO HORN*, Cambodia) A fondue in which thinly sliced beef, chicken and seafood are poached at the table in a charcoal-heated brass chafing dish and dipped in raw egg and a peanut sauce before being eaten. Another type of Cambodian tabletop-cooked dish is known as *chnang phleung*.
See also: STEAMBOATS (MONGOLIAN HOTPOT)

YARD-LONG BEAN: see LONG BEAN

YAY-KYIN-NGAR: (*YEAH-GEE-NGAR*, Burma) see ANCHOVY

YEAST, CHINESE BREWER'S: see WINE BALL/ WINE CUBE

YEAST, INDIAN: see KHAMIR

YELLOW BEAN SAUCE: see BEAN PASTES AND SAUCES (BEAN)

YELLOW CHICK-PEA: see CHICK-PEA

YELLOW CHILI: see CHILI

YELLOW CHIVES: see CHIVES, CHINESE

YELLOW CUCUMBER: see CUCUMBER

YELLOW RICE WINE: see WINES, CHINESE

YELLOW ROCK SUGAR: see SUGAR (BROWN SLAB)

YELLOW SOYBEAN: see SOYBEAN

YIN AND YANG: The interaction of opposites. According to Chinese philosophy, a balance of these elements is vital to nutrition and results in good health. Throughout their history the Chinese have eaten certain foods at particular times, or in times of illness, to balance the *yin-yang* elements.

Yin foods are cooling, neutralizing, moisturizing. Mildly flavored, tender foods—such as white fungus and jellyfish, watery fruits and vegetables—are classified as *yin*. *Yang* represents strong forces and heat. Spices, chilies, onions, ginger, as well as meats like lamb and beef, come into this category.

YIN WOR: (*YIN WOR*, China) see BIRD'S NEST

YIRA: (*YIRAA*, Thailand) see FENNEL; CUMIN (WHITE)

YIU GOR: (*YIU GWOH*, China) see CASHEW NUT

YOD NAM MALI: (*YOD NAM MALI*, Thailand) see MALI

YOGURT: Unflavored yogurt is used extensively in Indian cooking. Yogurt, or curd as it is called in India, is used to tenderize kebabs and whole roasts before they are cooked over charcoal or in a *tandoor*. It gives a creamy texture and rich flavor to sauces and curries, and is highly regarded for its carminative effect on the stomach. The side dish known as *raita*, made of yogurt flavored with spices, herbs, chopped fruit or vegetables, is served with most Indian meals to lessen the effect of hot chili and spices on sensitive stomachs and palates. Yogurt is also whipped and diluted to make the refreshing drink *lassi*. It is used to a much lesser extent in the cuisines of other Asian countries.
Also known as *dahi* (India); *dhai* (Nepal); *curds*
See also: LASSI; RAITA (recipe); TANDOORI CHICKEN TIKKAS (recipe)

RAITA
Yields 3 cups (24 fl oz / 750 ml)

1¹/2 cups (12 fl oz / 375 ml) plain (natural) yogurt
1 medium cucumber, peeled and grated
1 tbsp finely chopped fresh mint leaves
salt
sugar
black pepper

Beat the yogurt until smooth. Drain off excess liquid from cucumber. Mix cucumber into yogurt with mint, adding salt, sugar and black pepper to taste

---

YOGURT CHICKEN
Serves 4–6

3 lbs (1.5 kgs) chicken, skinned and rinsed
1 fresh green chili, chopped
2 tsps minced ginger
1¹/2 tsps minced garlic
1 cup (8 fl oz / 250 ml) plain (natural) yogurt

(cont'd)

(Yogurt Chicken cont'd)

1 tsp salt
1/3 cup (3 oz / 90 g) ghee
3/4 cup (6 fl oz / 180 ml) water
2–3 tbsps chopped fresh coriander (cilantro)
heavy cream

Cut chicken into 2 in (5 cm) pieces. Prick all over with a sharp skewer. Grind the chili, ginger and garlic to a paste. Mix into yogurt with salt. Rub over chicken and set aside for several hours to allow the spicy yogurt mixture to flavor the chicken. Brush the excess marinade from the chicken and reserve. Heat ghee and fry the chicken to color evenly. Add reserved marinade and water. Cover and cook gently until tender, turning occasionally. Stir in chopped fresh coriander and cream before serving.

YOU TIAU CRULLERS: (*YAU JA*, China) Long, doughnut-like, deep-fried pastries that are sliced and served with *congee* and other soup dishes, or eaten hot as a snack in many parts of China. A glass of soybean milk is the usual accompaniment to this snack.
Also known as *yau jaar gai* (China); *yau char koay* (Malaysia, Singapore)
See also: CONGEE

YUBA: (*YOU-BAH*, Japan) see BEAN CURD BY-PRODUCTS (BEAN CURD STICKS)

YU CHIAP: (*YUE JAP*, China) see FISH SAUCE

YU CHOY: (*YAU CHOY*, China) see CABBAGE, CHINESE (RAPE)

YU CHOY SIN: (*YOU CHOY SUM*, China) see CABBAGE, CHINESE (RAPE)

YUEN SAI: (*YUEN SAI*, China) see CORIANDER, FRESH

YU LU: (*YUE LO*, China) see FISH SAUCE

YUM: (Thailand) The Thai word for a salad or composed dish. The Thais traditionally serve a salad with every main meal, gathering leaves, herbs and fruits from their gardens and markets, as well as uncultivated shrubs and trees growing near their residences. These are as-sembled with cooked meats, fish or shellfish and tossed with thin, spicy dressings. Garnishes for *yum* dishes include crushed roasted peanuts, fried red chili flakes, crisp-fried slices of onion or garlic, herbs such as mint, basil and coriander, powdered dried shrimp and dried, unsweetened desiccated coconut.
See also: GREEN PAPAYA SALAD (recipe); ROAST PORK SALAD (recipe)

YUM CHA: (*YUM CHAR*, China) The tradition of serving small snacks with tea began in China during the Sung Dynasty, which began in AD 960 and continued almost until the thirteenth century. This was a period of the greatest flowering of art in China's history and a time when the science of food was investigated to its fullest extent, with chefs experimenting with every available ingredient and cooking method. Tea drinking was already well established at this time, and special "tea houses" were constructed where men could gather to relax, discuss business or partake of other pleasures. Cooks at these establishments produced delectable, bite-size snacks to serve with the tiny porcelain cups of tea, and these became known as *dim sum*. The words loosely translate as "dot hearts" or heart warmers, and from this time until the later, opulent, Ming Dynasty (AD 1368–1614) the range of these tasty little snacks grew to encompass over 100 varieties. *Yum cha*, or "taking tea," continues to be enjoyed by Chinese all around the world.

YUN SUM: (*YAN SUM*, China) see GINSENG

YU TO: (*YUE TO*, China) see FISH MAW

YU TS'AI: (*YAU CHOY*, China) see CABBAGE, CHINESE (RAPE)

YUZU: (*YOU-ZOO*, Japan) see CITRON; GARNISHES, JAPANESE

ZEDOARY: (*Curcuma zedoaria*) A plant of the Zingiberaceae (ginger/turmeric) family, the tuberous roots of which have a peculiar smell when bruised or cut. It has mid-green leaves that bunch up from the bulb and a layered straight stem. Only the heart of the young shoots, and sometimes the flowers, are eaten, raw or cooked, as a vegetable. It has a

peppery taste. It is closely related to turmeric and is known as white turmeric. It is also sometimes known, erroneously, as *kunchor* (Malaysia) or *kencur* (Indonesia); this is in fact the *kencur or Kaempferia galanga* , a rhizome, also of the ginger family, and known as *lesser galangal*.
Also known as *temu putih* (Indonesia, Malaysia); *kha min khao* (Thailand); *kencur*, kunchor; white turmeric; zedoary

See also: GALANGAL, LESSER; GINGER; TURMERIC

ZENZAI: (*ZEN-ZAH-I*, Japan) see AEMONO

ZONI: (*ZOE-NEE*, Japan) A soup served during Japanese New Year festivities. It consists of *mochi* rice cakes, *kamaboko*, chicken and vegetable in a *dashi* broth garnished with *yuzu* peel.
See also: CITRON; DASHI; GARNISHES, JAPANESE; KAMABOKO; MOCHI; YUZU

RECIPE INDEX

RECIPE INDEX